An Exploration of Unification Theology and the Christian Tradition

An Exploration of Unification Theology and the Christian Tradition

Theodore Shimmyo

HJI Press

Published in the United States of America by
HJI Press

HJI Press is the academic imprint of
HJ International Graduate School for Peace and Public Leadership
481 8th Avenue, Suite 1223
New York, NY 10001, USA
www.hji.edu

Library of Congress Cataloging-in-Publication Data
Shimmyo, Theodore, 1944–

An Exploration of Unification Theology and the Christian Tradition /
Theodore Shimmyo
pages cm
includes bibliographical references and index.
ISBN: 978-1-968692-00-1 (paperback)
ISBN: 978-1-968692-01-8 (ebook)

1. Religion, 2. Theology I. Title
Library of Congress Control Numbers: 2025947100

Design by Sun-Ae Rodriguez

A Publication of HJI Press

Dedicated to all the great Christian pioneers of theology to whom I am indebted for their legacy of wisdom.

Contents

Contents in Detail

Foreword

As we launch HJI Press, as an imprint of the HJ International Graduate School for Peace and Public Leadership, we are proud to publish Professor Theodore Shimmyo's *An Exploration of Unification Theology and the Christian Tradition*. He offers a well-researched and insightful exploration of many of the core theological issues that are at the center of both the Unificationist and the Christian traditions. More significantly, he, even as he points to the distinctiveness of Unification theology, addresses these matters in a way that underscores the common ground that both Unificationism and Christianity share. In many respects this is a volume that represents a dialogical encounter that seeks to build a base of understanding, if not consensus.

As a newer religious movement, if not denomination, Unificationism may be understood as a recent theological voice in the tradition that dates back to the coming of Jesus, the early church, the New Testament, and all that followed over the past two millennia. This is a crowded and often a cacophonous theological terrain. The family tree of Christianity speaks volumes. And yet, patterns and some dominant clusters of consensus have arisen with this grand and impactful tradition. Indeed, the theological development within the Christian tradition remains in many ways an ongoing intra-Christian dialogue, including voices that are not as welcome as others may be. Theology is a vastly complex discipline, impacted powerfully by historicity, context, culture, and other disciplines, most especially philosophy.

Shimmyo, as a Unificationist, and a former president of HJI, continues a tradition of encounter, dialogue, and theological reflection that has been a core feature of our institution. From the time of its inception, engagement with Christian scholars has been a central pillar of the educational program. In particular, he follows in the footsteps of one of the preeminent theologians of Unificationism, Professor Young Oon Kim, who taught at HJI from the late 1970s and well into the 1980s. Her works, including *Unification Theology* and *Unification Theology and Christian Thought*, were very significant efforts to illustrate the ways in which Unification theology, despite its unique features and innovative teachings, was neither alien nor irrelevant to the Christian tradition. Shimmyo's volume underscores this point.

From the Unificationist perspective the relationship with Christianity is extremely important. Indeed, despite decades of misunderstanding and to some extent the aversion that many within the larger "mainstream" Christian family have maintained toward Unificationism, dating back to the 1950s and 1960s in Korea, Unificationists still seek to be understood, respected, and welcomed as a partner in a broader ecumenical dialogue. Shimmyo's volume opens up that possibility, and serves as a very significant resource for Christian-Unificationist dialogue. Even where his arguments depart from mainstream Christian thought—on matters such as the doctrine of the Trinity, Jesus' mission, the status of Sun Myung Moon and Hak Ja Han, and the nature of God—he argues straightforwardly and forcefully.

His twelve chapters cover many of the most challenging theological topics that are of profound importance to believers. While he may be bold, he is no polemicist. I believe that readers who are interested in the teachings of new religious movements, the history of thought of the Unification tradition, and the traditional doctrines that Christian theologians have wrestled with, and continue to wrestle with, will find this volume rewarding and illuminating.

Founded in 1975 as Unification Theological Seminary by Rev. Sung Myung Moon and Dr. Hak Ja Han, HJI is now entering its 50th year of operations at the time of this publication. We will graduate our 50th class in May of 2027. Publishing has been a central part of the HJI tradition, dating back to the earliest years of our institution. We are pleased to publish this volume under our new imprint, HJI Press.

Thomas G. Walsh, Ph.D.
President
HJ International Graduate School
for Peace and Public Leadership

Preface

The Unification Church movement started drawing much attention in America and the world, especially after Rev. and Mrs. Sun Myung Moon, its founders, came to America from Korea in December 1971 to directly start their ministry there. While they had some success in reaching out to truth-seeking young people and peace-loving leaders in America in the 1970s and 1980s, their theology, in spite of its deep Christian origin based on the Bible, may have quite largely been misconceived by Christian theologians, clergy and laymen.[1]

This book intends to address that troublesome situation, so that the Unification Church movement and traditional Christian churches may be able to enhance their mutual understanding to work together for the will of God.

This is a collection of twelve articles on Unification theology dealing with various theological topics, selected from those which I published in the *Journal of Unification Studies* over the years. They are updated and edited for this publication, and they are also topically arranged according to the order of systematic theology, beginning with biblical hermeneutics and ending with eschatology.

In 1984, I obtained a Ph.D. in Christian theology from Drew University. In the following year, I started teaching at my alma mater, Unification Theological Seminary (UTS), in New York (now HJ International Graduate School for Peace and Public Leadership, abbreviated as HJI, since July 2023). I also served as UTS President from 1994 to 2000 and still teach there as an adjunct faculty member. I have taught not only "Unification Theology" but also standard theological courses such as "Systematic Theology," "God and Creation," "Theology of St. Augustine," "Trinity and Christology," "Theology of Grace," "Modern Theology," "Process Theology," "Radical Theologies" and "Apologetics in the 21st Century."

---

[1] In 1977, the Commission on Faith and Order of the National Council of the Churches of Christ in the USA (NCC) released a critique of the theology of the Unification Church, saying that it is "un-Christian."

By teaching both Unification theology and Christian theology for many years, I came to recognize that the two are closely related to each other and, in many ways, similar. Unification theology may be regarded as another school of Christian theology. The fundamental reason is that the Bible, including both testaments, is the common source for both of them. In fact, while Unification theology is a project to explain and express the Unification Church movement's "Divine Principle"[2] in the context of traditional Christian theology, this Divine Principle is none other than Rev. Moon's interpretation of the Bible as a Christian. It is the truth of God, as understood by him from the Bible. It was expressed or published somewhat differently as three different books at different times in the history of the Unification movement.[3]

There is, however, a considerable point of difference between Unification theology and Christian theology. The Divine Principle, which is the theological basis of Unification theology, is a unique interpretation of the Bible. Its uniqueness derives from a theological conceptuality of complete unity, if not pantheistic unity, between God and the world, whereas Christian theology traditionally teaches that the infinite God and the finite world of creation are so distinct that there can be no complete unity between them. This book will show that Unification theology with its conceptuality of a complete God-world unity addresses difficult theological issues (typically termed "mysteries of faith") that have arisen in Christian theology due to its conception of a gap between God and the world. This book covers twelve selected, critically difficult issues of Christian theology, one in each of its twelve chapters.

Some may wonder why someone like me who is from Japan, a non-Christian country, has been quite seriously involved in biblical and theological studies for many years. Let me, therefore, offer a brief autobiographical sketch.

I was a high school student in my country of Japan, when I received a copy of the New Testament from The Gideons International. In reading it, I began with the Gospel of Matthew, and I was profoundly moved by Jesus'

---

[2] The "Divine Principle" is an English rendition for the original Korean term 원리 ("Principle") or 통일원리 ("Unification Principle"), although the Korean term actually contains no word for "divine." The Divine Principle does not refer to any particular book but rather to the truth of God, as understood by Rev. Moon from the Bible.

[3] In 1952, the Divine Principle was hand-written by Rev. Moon himself as 원리원본 ("Original Text of the Principle"). In 1957, it was written and published by Hyo Won Eu, then-president of the Unification Church of Korea, as *원리해설* ("Explanation of the Principle"). In 1966, it was written and published again by Hyo Won Eu as *원리강론* ("Exposition of the Principle"). This last publication has two different English translations: *Divine Principle* (New York: HSA-UWC, 1973); and *Exposition of the Divine Principle* (New York: H.S.A.-U.W.C., 1996). We will use the 1996 translation for the present book.

Sermon on the Mount. I decided that he would be my teacher guiding me through this basically difficult, selfish world. As I wanted to appreciate and taste the profound person of Jesus on my own, I kept praying about him even without being affiliated with any organized Christian denomination.

When I was a student at the University of Tokyo, studying physics and nuclear engineering and hoping to make this world better through my area of expertise, I came across Jesus' Sermon on the Mount again. It happened so dramatically that it changed my life entirely. I was intensely reading Leo Tolstoy's *Resurrection*, and found in its final pages that Dmitri Ivanovich Nekhlyudov, the main character who was aware of evil in humans and in society, was determined to stand up to help to make this world better based on Jesus' Sermon on the Mount. The passages quoted from the Bible resounded vividly in my heart, giving me the courage to stand up like Nekhlyudov. It was around that time in 1966 that I was led to join the Unification Church. I realized immediately that this group, founded by Rev. Moon, was working to make the dream of Jesus' Sermon on the Mount a reality on earth rather than adhering to an apocalyptic hope.

I was continually engaged in Unification Church activities, but about three years after joining, I became something of an independent thinker, prayerfully asking God for answers to various theological questions I had in finding similarities and dissimilarities between the Divine Principle and Christian theology. In comparing the two, I worked quite hard on my own to familiarize myself with the thoughts of Christian theologians such as St. Paul, St. Augustine, St. Francis of Assisi, Martin Luther and John Wesley. My main concern was: How can we truly experience God, so that we may thereby be able to actually transform this world?

With that mindset, I came to America as a Unification Church missionary in 1973. After two years of missionary work in New York City, I enrolled in Unification Theological Seminary, at its founding in 1975. Since then, my work in comparing the Divine Principle and Christian theology has continued to the present.

My theological approach has always been primarily internal, in that I have looked to tackle theological issues through my quiet prayers to God rather than by being swayed by popular yet rather opinionated ideas that are generally available. It is with that approach that this particular book has been produced.

At this juncture, I want to appreciate my longtime UTS/HJI colleagues Dr. Andrew Wilson and Dr. Michael Mickler for their constant encouragement for me over the years to write on Unification theology. When my original article manuscripts were to be published in the *Journal of Unification Studies*, they kindly suggested useful points of improvement. Additionally, I want to express my heartfelt appreciation for the warm encouragement of Dr. Thomas G. Walsh, current HJI President, and Dr. Thomas J. Ward, former HJI President, for the publication of this book. I also want to acknowledge that Dr. Michael Mickler and Ms. Louise Perlowitz graciously read the whole manuscript prior to publication.

I also want to indicate my sincere thanks to Rev. and Mrs. Moon who introduced the Divine Principle in their lives of devotion to build the kingdom of God on earth as well as in heaven. My sincere thanks go especially to Mrs. Moon, who as the "only begotten Daughter"[4] tirelessly continues her active life of the same devotion for kingdom-building even after the passing away of her husband in 2012.

At this point, I also want to show my genuine thanks to many dedicated Christian predecessors who developed their precious theologies before us. I have been much indebted to their theologies in my own theological development.

Finally, my special appreciation goes to my wife, Sumie, who has always been supportive of me, staying by my side, in my long journey of research and education as a theologian.

Theodore Shimmyo
Manassas Park, VA
September 2025

---

[4] The Unification Church movement teaches that if Jesus' mission as the "only begotten Son" (Jn. 3:16, King James Version) is to restore the original position of unfallen Adam, there should also be a woman who can be called the "only begotten Daughter" and whose mission is to restore the original position of unfallen Eve.

Introduction

The Task of Unification Theology

§1. Unification Theology and Christian Theology

Unification theology is a theological expression of the Unification Church movement's "Divine Principle,"[1] and is usually presented in relationship to Christian theology. The Divine Principle, as will be explained in detail in Chapter 1, is the Rev. Sun Myung Moon's new interpretation of the Bible as a Christian. Needless to say, Christian theology, too, has historically arisen from interpreting the Bible. Having the Bible as the most important common source, therefore, both Unification theology and Christian theology are closely related, even though they originally come from two different parts of the world: Korea, which is a Far Eastern country, and European Christendom, in which traditional Christian theology emerged and flourished.

Although originating from two different geographical and cultural backgrounds, Unification theology and Christian theology are of service to each other. Unification theology benefits from Christian theology, in that it is helped by the latter to increase its self-clarification and self-understanding. For example, the important Unification notion of the "dual characteristics of God," which may initially sound terminologically unfamiliar to Christian theology, can be found to be the same as the "image of God" (Gen. 1:27), as understood especially in the relational views of the divine image by Karl Barth (1886–1968)

[1] As mentioned in n. 2 in the Preface, the "Divine Principle" is an English rendition for the original Korean term 원리 ("Principle") or 통일원리 ("Unification Principle"), although the Korean term actually contains no word for "divine." It does not refer to any particular book but rather to the truth of God, as understood by Rev. Moon from the Bible.

and Emil Brunner (1889–1966).[2]

Christian theology, in turn, can benefit from Unification theology. As many are aware, Christian theology contains quite difficult theological issues that have been regarded as "mysteries of faith" for centuries. The reason for this is that Christian theology has traditionally been based on the idea that there is a very large gulf between the infinite God and the finite world of creation. But these theological issues in Christianity can perhaps be addressed quite well by Unification theology, which theologically secures a real unity between God and creation based on the insights of Rev. Moon's Divine Principle.

To draw an example, Christology in the Christian tradition has long been faced with the difficult issue of not being able to truly unite the divine and human natures of Christ within his person, due to its recognition of an unfillable gulf between God, to whom Christ's nature of divinity belongs, and the created world, to which his nature of humanity belongs. This issue is honestly confessed by Christian theologians such as the American evangelical Millard J. Erickson (1932–), as he says: "the relationship between these two natures in the one person, Jesus… is one of the most difficult of all theological problems" because of the gap between God and the world.[3] But Unification theology, which has a unique theological conceptuality of a real unity between God and the created world, can help to address it.

This may sound a little too ambitious, but the purpose of the present book is to show how Unification theology can help to address such difficult theological issues in Christianity.

§2. Reason for Unification Theology

When it is stated that Christian theology can benefit from Unification theology in the above sense, many within the tradition of Christian theology might wonder whether that statement is acceptable. Hasn't the great tradition of Christian theology already been established historically by ecumenical councils such as the Councils of Nicea (325) and Chalcedon (451) and also by prominent theologians such as St. Gregory of Nazianzus (c. 329–390), St. Augustine (354–430), St. Thomas Aquinas (1225–1274), Martin Luther (1483–

[2] Regarding the relational views of the divine image by Barth and Brunner, Millard J. Erickson has an excellent explanation in his *Christian Theology*, vol. 2 (Grand Rapids, MI: Baker Book House, 1984), pp. 502-8.

[3] Millard J. Erickson, *Introducing Christian Doctrine*, 3rd ed., ed. L. Arnold Hustad (Grand Rapids, MI: Baker Academic, 2015), p. 260.

1546), John Wesley (1703–1791) and Karl Barth (1886–1968), to name a few? Haven't these theologians already spoken of God and his eternal truth fully and authoritatively? The answer to these questions, however, should be in the negative. The reason is that even authoritative, traditional Christian theology has at least the following three unavoidable, interrelated features that allow for the emergence of new theologies such as Unification theology.

First, traditional Christian theology, no matter how authoritative and orthodox it may be, is not God himself nor his eternal truth itself but rather a series of human endeavors to express God or his eternal truth. This point is evident from the received definition of "theology" (*theologia* in Greek) as our human "word" (*logos*), talk, account or expression of "God" (*theos*) as its content. Thus any theology, including authoritative Christian theology, is far from infinite, absolute and eternal. Only God or his truth, as the content of theology, is infinite, absolute and eternal. If this point is truly acknowledged, perhaps traditional Christian theology would be open-minded enough to hear what Unification theology communicates as another serious endeavor to express God or his eternal truth.

Second, Christian theology itself has much diversity, because it is a long series of human endeavors to express God or his eternal truth. Different theologians at different times and in different places and cultures within the Christian tradition have articulated diverse theological positions. Look at the differences among Eastern Orthodox, Roman Catholic, Lutheran, Calvinistic, Anglican, Methodist and other theologies. Also look at the theological variety of different individual theologians even within each and every one of these theological traditions. Moreover, there also exists a widespread, great tension between conservative and liberal theologies. All theological expressions, of course, have the same God as their subject, and in this sense the unity of theology can be recognized. But the diversity of theology is unquestionable from the differences of theological expressions, given the above definition of theology. This principle of diversity in unity would naturally allow Unification theology to participate.

Third, every theological expression is unique because it is a theology developed by a particular theologian or a particular group of theologians at a particular time and in a particular place or culture. For example, Augustine developed a uniquely insightful, biblically based theology of the transmission of original sin sparked by the Pelagian controversy at the beginning of the fifth century. Another example is John Wesley's unique insight into the idea of sanctification at a time when human corruption was a new issue in Christendom following Martin Luther's doctrine of justification. The uniqueness of each and every theology is to be appreciated. If so, one might also be able to appreciate the unique contribution Unification theology would offer, especially based on its notion of God's parental "Heart" (*shimjeong* in Korean), which is defined as his "emotional impulse to seek joy through love."[4] It was revealed to Rev. and Mrs. Moon as an essential part of the Divine Principle.[5]

To explain God's Heart a little further here, it is his "irrepressible... impulse of love,"[6] because of which he, in and after creating the world, not only unconditionally and sacrificially loves his objects of love but also fervently seeks to love the beauty they are expected to reciprocally return to him as his joy. It may very well resemble Jürgen Moltmann's (1926–2024) idea of "God's longing for 'his Other' and for that Other's free response to the divine love."[7] It may also be quite similar to the Old Testament notion of God's *chesed* (translated usually as "steadfast love," "loving-kindness" or "mercy"), as will be discussed in detail in Chapter 3.

§3. Unification Theology in Essence

According to Unification theology, if God's Heart is poured into the realm of creation, two kinds of unity are encouraged to be completely realized: 1) vertical unity between God and his created world; and 2) horizontal unity between a subject partner and object partner centered on God in the world. These two kinds of unity, if completely realized, will show their beauty of unity and give "joy to God."[8] But if they fail to be realized in spite of God's Heart, God will suffer due to the absence of their beauty of unity, i.e., due to the presence of their hideous disunity in the world. Thus the Old Testament states: "The Lord saw that the wickedness of man was great in the earth... [and] was

---

[4] *New Essentials of Unification Thought: Head-Wing Thought* (Tokyo: Kogensha, 2006), p. 23. Henceforth abbreviated as NEUT.

[5] Rev. Moon's numerous speeches, often dealing with the Heart of God directly or indirectly, were published, and the present book will reference some of them. Additionally, Mrs. Hak Ja Han Moon's words have also been published. See, for example, *True Mother Hak Ja Han Moon: An Anthology* (Seoul, Korea: Sung Hwa Publishing, Inc., 2018), which is a four-volume anthology; and *Mother of Peace: A Memoir by Hak Ja Han Moon* (Washington, DC: Washington Times Global Media Group, 2020).

[6] NEUT, p. 24.

[7] Jürgen Moltmann, *The Trinity and the Kingdom: The Doctrine of God*, trans. Margaret Kohl (Minneapolis: Fortress Press, 1993), p. 106.

[8] *Exposition of the Divine Principle* (New York: H.S.A.-U.W.C., 1996), pp. 33-36. Henceforth abbreviated as EDP.

sorry that he had made man on the earth, and it grieved him to his heart" (Gen. 6:5-6).[9]

The realization of these two kinds of unity reminds us of the importance of Jesus' two greatest commandments of love, to connect vertically with God and also horizontally with one's neighbor (Mt. 22:37-40; Mk. 12:29-31). According to the Divine Principle, vertical unity between God and the world and horizontal unity between a subject partner and object partner in the world are completely realized on the basis of what it refers to as the "four position foundation,"[10] which involves the unity of four stakeholders: 1) God, 2) subject partner, 3) object partner, and 4) both partners' unity centered on God in the world. It indeed marks "the realization of God's purpose of creation."[11] When two human beings, especially a man and woman, are a subject partner and object partner in the seamless four position foundation under the guidance of God's Heart, they, while being discrete from each other and also from God as well, can responsibly reach their complete unity with each other and also with God, being able to even acquire "a divine nature."[12] This echoes the Eastern Orthodox idea of "deification" (*theosis*), according to which human beings are made divine through the incarnation of the divine Logos.

The realization of the seamless four position foundation is made possible by what the Divine Principle refers to as "dual characteristics." No detailed explanation will be made here in the Introduction, but there are two kinds of dual characteristics: 1) those of "masculinity" and "femininity"; and 2) those of "internal nature" and "external form."[13] The dual characteristics of the latter kind are understood to be roughly similar to the duality of "form" and "matter" in Aristotelian philosophy. The dual characteristics of both kinds can universally be found in the whole of reality encompassing God and the created world. God has dual characteristics within himself, and the world also has dual characteristics at all different levels of creation. As will be shown in detail in Chapter 4, this makes possible the complete unity, centered on Heart, between God and the world and also between a subject partner and object partner in the world, while God, subject partner and object partner are discrete from one another.

This theological perspective of complete unity in the whole of reality may hardly be found in traditional Christian theology, which has stressed the

---

[9] The suffering of God will be discussed in detail in Chapter 6 in the present book.
[10] EDP, p. 25.
[11] Ibid.
[12] EDP, pp. 34, 164.
[13] EDP, pp. 15-19.

transcendence of God from the world far more than his immanence in it. It is, of course, very important to acknowledge the transcendence of God, as traditional Christianity does, for God as the ultimate source of direction for the world should never be confused with the world itself. In this respect, traditional Christianity deserves much appreciation. At the same time, the time should eventually come when the will of God is completely realized in the world, such that he completely resides with us, realizing his complete unity with the world, i.e., his real immanence in the world.

Traditional Christian overemphasis on the transcendence of God can be explained in part because Christian theology developed under the considerable influence of Platonism and Aristotelianism in ancient Greek philosophy. Platonic dualism already holds that there is a sharp distinction between the real, eternal and transcendent realm of ideas and this transitory world that only participates in it. Aristotelian philosophy holds that God, as a perfectly actualized deity, is "pure form" without any "matter," having no dual characteristics of "form" and "matter," while the world, which is never perfectly actualized, has these dual characteristics. It thus sees an unfillable difference between God and the world, and it has undoubtedly influenced Christian theology. Therefore, while in Unification theology the *universal* notion of dual characteristics helps to unify God and the world, in Christian theology the *non-universal* notion of dual characteristics of form and matter, which only applies to the finite world and not to God, rather separates God and the world and also, as will be seen in Chapter 4, separates a subject partner and object partner in the world as well.

From the above, it can be understood that Unification theology with its conceptuality of a complete unity between God and the world of creation, and also between a subject partner and object partner in the world, would be instrumental in helping to address various difficult theological issues in traditional Christianity that have arisen due to its lack of this kind of conceptuality.

In actuality, however, Unification theology is not alone in theologically trying to unify God and creation. As will be explained in Chapter 11, "Providential History of Modern Thought," there have been a number of important modern theologians who have tried to unify God and the world more or less similarly to Unification theology. They have therefore been forerunners of Unification theology. This point must not be overlooked. As will be seen, the forerunners of Unification theology in this regard include Friedrich Schleiermacher (1768–1834), Georg W. F. Hegel (1770–1831), the later Karl Barth, Reinhold Niebuhr (1892–1971), H. Richard Niebuhr (1894–

1962), Paul Tillich, Bernard Ramm (1916–1992), Karl Rahner (1904–1984) and Jürgen Moltmann. Needless to say, these theologians have also been interested in unifying a subject partner and object partner in the world as well in their own ways.

§4. Addressing Issues in Christian Theology

The present book will show how Unification theology, with its above-mentioned theological conceptuality of a complete unity primarily between God and the world and derivatively between a subject partner and object partner in the world, can help to address many difficult theological issues in Christianity that have emerged due to its lack of that kind of conceptuality. Throughout the book, which will take the form of systematic theology, the notion of the "four position foundation," among others, will be used as a significant theological idea to address twelve of the most seriously difficult issues of Christian theology: biblical hermeneutics, faith and reason, the nature of God's love, the God-world relationship, the Trinity, the suffering of God, the fall, theodicy, Christology, the atonement, the significance of modern theology, and eschatology. The book addresses each of them in a separate chapter.

Chapter 1, "Approaching the Bible," deals with the issue of interpreting the Bible. Unification theology does not leave biblical interpretation entirely to the interpreter nor to a literal reading of the biblical text. It rather borrows the well-known notion of "hermeneutical circle" to develop a "four position foundation" model of God-centered reciprocity between the interpreter as the subject and the text as the object to reach their "fusion," that is, an interpretation. Rev. Moon's unique interpretation of the Bible, which constitutes the Divine Principle, is also based on this model, which is considered to involve "rising to a higher universality" in interpretation, to use the words of Hans-Georg Gadamer (1900–2002).[14]

Chapter 2, "Faith and Reason," addresses how faith and reason are related to each other. There have historically been competing views ranging from that of complete separation between the two (Tertullian) to that of their basic unity. Unification theology shows how a complete unity between the two is possible based on insights of the Divine Principle into human growth and also complete

[14] Hans-Georg Gadamer, *Truth and Method*, 2nd rev. ed., trans. Joel Weinsheimer and Donald G. Marshall (New York: Crossroad Publishing Corporation, 1991), p. 305.

unity between God and the world. It holds that faith and reason, which respectively perceive God's "internal truth" and the world's "external truth," are to be completely united, as God and the world are eventually perceived to be completely united in the course of human growth.

Chapter 3, "God's Heart: Two Aspects of Love," addresses the issue of a basic conflict, considered to exist in Christian theology, between God's sacrificial and unconditional love (*agape*), on the one hand, and human beings' acquisitive and appreciative love (*eros*), on the other. Unification theology shows that God's loving "Heart," just like God's *chesed* in the Old Testament (translated usually as "steadfast love" or "loving-kindness"), is so comprehensive as to contain within itself the above-mentioned two kinds of love without any contradiction. Our human love, too, can contain within itself both kinds of love in resemblance to God's loving Heart.

Chapter 4, "God and the World," addresses the issue of an unfillable distance, perceived in Christian theology, between God and the world. This issue arises because Christian theology, in effect, holds, under the influence of Aristotelianism, that while the finite world has the dual characteristics of "form" and "matter," the infinite God as "pure form" with no "matter" has no such dual characteristics. Unification theology, by contrast, establishes a complete unity of reciprocity between God and the world, as it holds that they both have dual characteristics in common centered on God's Heart. This makes God a fully personal God who is very close to us.

Chapter 5, "The Trinity," treats the still unsolved mystery of Christian trinitarianism, the teaching of one God with three persons, each being God. One God or three Gods? This mystery emerged primarily because Tertullian (c. 155–c. 240) initiated the rather obscure idea that the three persons are not "separate" but only "distinct" within the one substance of God. Unification theology maintains both the real oneness and discrete threeness of the Trinity without any contradiction, by accommodating two distinguishable types of the Trinity in a comprehensive system: the inner Trinity of real oneness within God and the completely economic, outer Trinity of discrete threeness in the whole of reality encompassing God and creation.

Chapter 6, "The Suffering of God," handles the issue of whether or not God suffers. Christianity has decided that God, who is omnipotent and perfect, cannot suffer. For Unification theology, however, God's omnipotence does not mean his sovereign power, nor does his perfection mean his changelessness. Rather, they respectively mean the irrepressibility of God's deep, loving Heart and the perfect unity of his own dual characteristics. With these new definitions, which show a real closeness between God and the world, Unification theology holds that the omnipotent and perfect God suffers in response to the wickedness of the world. This well explains the Old Testament's descriptions of God's suffering.

Chapter 7, "The Fall," deals with the fall of Adam and Eve. Many Christians today unfortunately deny original sin, i.e., the lineal impact of the fall of Adam and Eve upon their offspring, by saying, under the influence of the Enlightenment and Darwinism, that each and every *individual* human being already has an innate animal nature to sin from the beginning. Ironically, this problem can perhaps be attributed to the traditionally individualist Augustinian doctrine of the fall that holds that Adam, Eve and the archangel severally fell through *individual* "free will" of each. To address this problem, Unification theology offers a sexual, relational interpretation of the fall, affirming the lineal transmission of original sin.

Chapter 8, "The Problem of Evil," deals with theodicy. *Simple* theodicies only solve a certain logical contradiction, and *aesthetic* theodicies, well received in Christianity, justify evil by harmonizing it with a greater purpose of God. These two types of theodicies are thus incapable of removing evil from the world. Unification theology, however, proposes a *practical* theodicy that removes evil through the Christ-like practice of bearing the pain of the victims of evil out of love, in order to build God's earthly kingdom. It is based on the idea that Christ and his followers undo what Adam did at his fall. There are some Christian *practical* theodicies, but they usually problematically deny the historicity of Adam and Eve's fall as the origin of evil.

Chapter 9, "Christology," addresses the difficult issue of how the divine and human nature of Christ are united in his person—an issue which even the Council of Chalcedon (451) could not address well. Unification Christology addresses this issue based on its conceptuality of a complete unity between God, to whom Christ's divine nature belongs, and the created world, to which his human nature belongs. It can also put an end to the conflict between high and low Christology.

Chapter 10, "The Atonement," addresses the issue of Christianity having no officially agreed-upon doctrine of the atonement. The ransom theory was divided into the satisfaction and moral influence theories in the eleventh century. Unification theology borrows the idea of John Macquarrie (1919–2007) that the ransom theory can reunify the two other theories to bring God and us together in a comprehensive scheme. Unification theology, after reunifying them through the ransom theory, lifts them up all to a substantial level where the atonement occurs both spiritually and physically, and suggests a very new perspective on the crucifixion.

Chapter 11, "Providential History of Modern Thought," addresses why the modern period of Christian history after the Middle Ages went through at least three stages of theological disintegration and reintegration between Cain-type and Abel-type theologies until the beginning of the twentieth century. This was a preparation for the Second Coming. Theologians such as Paul Tillich and Reinhold Niebuhr recognized these three stages, giving useful information on Cain-type and Abel-type theologies and their reintegrations, although they could hardly explain why these phenomena occurred.

Chapter 12, "Eschatology," addresses whether or not we, in individual eschatology, can spiritually grow after physical death, and whether the end of the world, in cosmic eschatology, is apocalyptic or non-apocalyptic. Christianity traditionally holds that there is no spiritual growth after death (so that hell is eternal), and that the world will be destroyed apocalyptically to be divided into heaven and hell for eternity. Given the genuine love of God, Unification theology explores a possibility of spiritual growth in the other world, and proposes a new cosmic eschatology which mediates between apocalyptic and non-apocalyptic eschatology, appreciating the role of human responsibility as well.

Prior to the present book, a good number of books and articles on Unification theology have been published. Young Oon Kim (1914–1989), who came to America as the first Unification missionary from Korea in 1959 and taught at Unification Theological Seminary from 1975 to 1988, wrote several Unification theology texts as the first serious pioneer of Unification theology in relationship to Christian theology.[15] Many other scholars, whether Unificationists or Christians, published conference proceedings, collections of papers, and journal articles that also related Unification theology to Christian theology.[16]

---

[15] Her books include: *Divine Principle and Its Application*, 7th ed. (Washington, DC: The Holy Spirit Association for the Unification of World Christianity, 1969); *Unification Theology and Christian Thought* (New York: Golden Gate Publishing, 1975; rev. ed., 1976); and *Unification Theology* (New York: The Holy Spirit Association for the Unification of World Christianity, 1980; rev. ed., 1987).

[16] They include: Darrol Bryant and Susan Hodges, eds., *Exploring Unification Theology* (New York: Rose of Sharon Press, 1978); Darrol Bryant and Herbert W. Richardson, eds., *A Time for Consideration: A Scholarly Appraisal of the Unification Church* (New York: Edwin Mellen Press, 1978); Richard Quebedeaux and Rodney Sawatsky, eds., *Evangelical-Unification Dialogue* (New York: Rose of Sharon Press, 1979); Darrol Bryant, ed., *Proceedings of the Virgin Islands' Seminar on Unification Theology* (New York: Rose of Sharon Press, 1980); Darrol Bryant and Durwood Foster, eds., *Hermeneutics and Unification Theology* (New York: Rose of Sharon Press, 1980); Herbert Richardson, ed., *Ten Theologians Respond to the Unification Church* (New York: Rose of Sharon Press, 1981); Constantine N. Tsirpanlis, ed., *Orthodox-Unification Dialogue* (New York: Rose of Sharon Press, 1981); Sebastian A. Matczak, *Unificationism: A New Philosophy and Worldview* (Jamaica, NY: Learned Publications, 1982); Henry O. Thompson, ed., *Unity In Diversity: Essays in Religion by Members of*

The present book, while being indebted to all the above publications for their useful suggestions and insights, tries to go beyond the level of a comparison of Unification theology and Christian theology. It rather tries to focus on identifying various difficult theological issues in Christianity and address them. If these theological issues in Christianity have historically created a lot of different theological interpretations, dividing Christianity into many competing groups and denominations, then addressing these issues successfully may help to bring unity in Christianity. *Exposition of the Divine Principle* therefore states that the Divine Principle is "to elucidate many difficult issues in Christianity" such as "the relationship between God, Jesus and human beings," "the Holy Trinity," "the extent of redemption by the cross," and "why… Jesus [must] come again," so that it, using "plain language that everyone can understand," may be able to "bring about Christian unity."[17]

As mentioned earlier, Unification theology and Christian theology benefit from each other. It is hoped that increasingly deeper dialogue will take place between the two for their mutual theological benefits and also for their increased cooperation of working together to build a peaceful world as one family under God that undoubtedly involves Christian unity.

---

the Faculty of the Unification Theological Seminary (New York: Rose of Sharon Press, 1984); Anthony J. Guerra, ed., *Unification Theology in Comparative Perspectives* (Barrytown, NY: Unification Theological Seminary, 1988); Theodore T. Shimmyo and David A. Carlson, eds. *Explorations in Unificationism* (New York: HSA-UWC, 1997); and a great number of articles on Unification theology by Theodore Shimmyo and others in *Journal of Unification Studies.*

[17] EDP, pp. 10-11.

Chapter 1

Approaching the Bible

Many Christians suspect that the Unification movement erroneously elevates the authority of its doctrine, the Divine Principle, above that of the Bible. But the present writer believes that the Divine Principle, no matter how unique and special it may be construed to be, is no more than the interpretation of the Bible by Sun Myung Moon (1920–2012), founder of the Unification movement. For him, the Bible is the main source of the Divine Principle.

Section 1 of the present chapter will show that Rev. Moon in his approach to the Bible acknowledges its real authority, and that his understanding of the authority of the Bible is no different from that in much of the Christian tradition, although it does differ from the fundamentalist doctrine of biblical inerrancy. His understanding, as in much of the Christian tradition, is that the Bible is authoritative because its content is the eternal truth of God, even while its verbal expression may be temporal and finite. This makes it legitimate, therefore, to interpret the Bible in searching for the eternal truth of God behind its verbal expression.

Section 2 will discuss how Moon interpreted the Bible in search of the truth contained in it, and how he came up with several fundamental points of the Divine Principle as a result. It will be shown that an underlying key idea in the Divine Principle is God's parental heart of love for human beings as his true children.

Section 3 will discuss the dynamics of the "hermeneutical circle" between the interpreter and the biblical text, and argue that Moon's interpretation, like any other genuine interpretation, emerged from the framework of this hermeneutical circle. The uniqueness of his biblical interpretation, the Divine

Principle, may be dealt with based on this hermeneutical framework, which is understood to represent a universal ontological structure.

§1. The Authority of the Bible

According to Sun Myung Moon, "The Bible is… not the truth itself, but rather a textbook of the truth."[1] He, of course, believes that the truth in the Bible is God's truth which is "unique, eternal, immutable and absolute," but he does not equate the Bible with God's truth itself. He instead considers the Bible to be a historical, temporal "expression" of the eternal truth, which was trying to teach and enlighten people at the time when it was written with a "depth," "extent" and "method" suitable to them.[2] Moon, therefore, does not accept the verbal inerrancy of the Bible adhered to by fundamentalists and many enthusiastic evangelicals: "Consequently, we must never regard such textbooks as absolute in every detail."[3]

1. Sun Myung Moon

This does not mean that Rev. Moon denies the authority of the Bible. On the contrary, he believes the Bible to be entirely authoritative in that it contains God's absolute truth as its "content," although its "expression," which is the Bible itself as "a textbook of the truth," may not be absolute. This distinction made by Moon between content and expression in the Bible is no different than the distinction between the two sides of "theology" in its traditional definition as "a word about God" (*theologia*): God (*theos*) is the absolute and eternal content of theology, on the one hand, and word (*logos*) is its relative and temporal expression, on the other. Accordingly, Moon entirely agrees with the long-established Christian tradition that the Bible *is* theological. To ignore the distinction between content and expression, confusing them as if expression were content itself, would mean to elevate something relative and temporal to the level of God; it would be idolatry.[4] Moon, who makes the distinction, does not idolize the Bible.

Rev. Moon's conviction that the Bible is authoritative because it contains God's absolute truth as its content was the reason why he seriously studied the

---

[1] *Exposition of the Divine Principle* (New York: H.S.A.-U.W.C., 1996), p. 105. Cf. pp. 7, 104. Henceforth abbreviated as EDP.

[2] EDP, p. 7. Cf. p. 104.

[3] EDP, p. 7.

[4] Paul Tillich has an excellent discussion of this issue in relationship to the definition of theology in his *Systematic Theology*, vol. I (Chicago: The University of Chicago Press, 1951), pp. 3-6.

Bible, especially when he was younger, in order to find God's truth behind its verbal expression: "I would read the same passages in three languages [i.e., Korean, Japanese and English] again and again. Each time I read a passage, I would underline verses and make notes in the margins until the pages of my Bibles became stained with black ink and difficult to read."[5] For him, although the verbal expression especially of "important parts" of the Bible may be in "symbols and parables," which are "open to various interpretations," giving rise to "numerous disagreements among believers," nevertheless finding God's truth in the Bible can eventually "elucidate" them to eliminate disagreements within Christianity, thus enabling "God's providence, which comes through the unification of Christianity… to reach its goal."[6] It was with the authority of the Bible in this sense of God's truth being found behind the biblical expression that Rev. Moon spoke to audiences on biblical topics during his 21-city speaking tour in America from October 1973 to January 1974: "I am telling you many unusual things, and you may ask by what authority I am speaking. It is the authority of the Bible, and with the authority of revelation. Let us read the Bible together, and see word by word how John the Baptist acted."[7]

2. The Reformation

Moon's distinction between content and expression in the Bible resembles the distinction of the Reformation between the gospel as the "material principle" and the Bible as the "formal principle," with the latter as the source expressing the former which is the content.[8] According to the Reformers, the gospel in the Bible as the content (the material principle) is the doctrine of justification by faith alone, and it is divine, eternal and infallible, while the Bible with respect to its role as the source (the formal principle) is human, historical and even fallible. For Martin Luther (1483–1546), biblical books such as James, Jude, Hebrews and Revelation were questionable and even fallible because they do not express the gospel satisfactorily; James, for example, was for him "an

[5] Sun Myung Moon, *As a Peace-Loving Global Citizen* (Washington, DC: Washington Times Foundation, 2010), p. 67.

[6] EDP, p. 105.

[7] Sun Myung Moon, "The Future of Christianity," *God's Will and the World* (New York: HSA-UWC, 1985), p. 214.

[8] Oswald Bayer reports that this distinction was first proposed by August Twesten in Germany in 1826; see his *Martin Luther's Theology: A Contemporary Interpretation*, trans. Thomas H. Trapp (Grand Rapids, MI: William B. Eerdmans Publishing Co., 2008), p. 69, n. 3. In 1845, the church historian Philip Schaff mentioned this distinction in his *The Principle of Protestantism as Related to the Present State of the Church*, trans. John W. Nevin (Chambersburg, PA: Publication Office of the German Reformed Church, 1845), pp. 54-94.

epistle full of straw."[9] Luther contended that the textual expression of the Bible written under God's inspiration can contain human limitation and error, although he did not exclude these questionable books from the biblical canon.

John Calvin (1509–1564), originally trained as a rhetorician, also was quick to observe that while God's message for salvation was expressed in the Bible under divine inspiration, the biblical writers themselves as imperfect humans made technical errors such as misquotations (e.g., Rom. 3:4 misquoting Ps. 51:4; and Heb. 10:5-9 misquoting Ps. 40:6-8) and factual discrepancies (e.g., Acts 7:14-16 being discrepant with Deut. 10:22 and Gen. 23:7-20 regarding the number of Jacob's kinfolks and the location of their burial; and Heb. 11:21 inconsistent with Gen. 48:2 about how Jacob, just prior to his death, blessed Joseph's children, whether over the head of his staff or in bed).[10]

Karl Barth (1886–1968), the main figure of neo-Reformation theology in the twentieth century, similarly maintained that because of divine grace the infallible Word of God is expressed by the fallible words of the biblical writers: "The truth of the miracle [is] that here fallible men speak the Word of God in fallible human words."[11]

For Reformers such as Luther and Calvin, and neo-Reformers such as Barth, therefore, the authority of the Bible lies in the material principle and not necessarily in the formal principle. They saw, as did Rev. Moon, that it lies in God's absolute truth as the content of the Bible and not in its verbal expression. Oswald Bayer, a major contemporary German Lutheran theologian, states regarding Luther's understanding of this point: "The authority of Scripture is not formal but is highly material and is content driven."[12]

3. Biblical Inerrancy

But the Reformation tradition had the doctrine of *sola scriptura* which holds that the Bible as the formal principle is the *only* authoritative *source* of the whole Christian doctrine. Because of that, the formal principle itself was treated quite

---

[9] Martin Luther, "Preface to the New Testament, 1522," in *Martin Luther: Selections from His Writings*, ed. John Dillenberger (Garden City, NY: Doubleday & Company, 1961), p. 19.

[10] Regarding Heb. 10:5-9 misquoting Ps. 40:6-8, Calvin says: "in quoting these words the Apostles were not so scrupulous, provided they perverted not Scripture to their own purpose. We must always have a regard to the end for which they quoted passages… but as to words and other things, which bear not on the subject in hand, they use great freedom"; see his *Commentaries on the Epistle of Paul the Apostle to the Hebrews*, trans. John Owen (Grand Rapids, MI: Wm. B. Eerdmans Publishing Co., 1948), pp. 227-28. Concerning Heb. 11:21's discrepancy with Gen. 48:2, Calvin again says: "the Apostles were not so scrupulous in this respect, as not to accommodate themselves to the unlearned, who had as yet need of milk"; ibid., p. 291.

[11] Karl Barth, *Church Dogmatics*, I/2 (Edinburgh: T&T Clark, 1956), p. 529.

[12] Bayer, *Martin Luther's Theology*, p. 69.

frequently as if it were the real locus of the authority of the Bible, from which even the material principle derives. As reported by many scholars,[13] this problematic overemphasis upon the formal principle was made by the following three schools of theology in the history of Christianity after the Reformation: 1) Protestant scholasticism in Europe in the late sixteenth and seventeenth centuries, of which the Reformed theologian Francis Turretin (1623–1687) was a well-known representative; 2) the Princeton Theology in America in the nineteenth and early twentieth centuries, which followed in the footsteps of Protestant scholasticism and whose main figures were the Presbyterian theologians Archibald Alexander (1772–851), Charles Hodge (1797–1878), Archibald Alexander Hodge (1823–1886) and Benjamin Breckinridge Warfield (1851–1921); and 3) fundamentalism and the enthusiastic segment of evangelicalism in America in the twentieth century, which started from the Princeton Theology but which eventually became widely nondenominational and revivalistic, drawing believers from other Protestant denominations.

This problematic identification of the formal principle as the real locus of the authority of the Bible occurred as a reaction to the rise of the historical-critical study of the Bible, and it yielded the peculiar doctrine of "inerrancy" based on a theory of "verbal plenary inspiration." According to this doctrine, God inspired the biblical writers in such a thorough manner that the inspiration was not only in the concepts or ideas in the Bible but extended also to the very words themselves (verbal) and to all parts of the Bible (plenary): "All scripture is inspired by God" (2 Tim. 3:16). The resultant doctrine of inerrancy holds that as long as every word in the entire Bible is inspired by God, the whole verbal expression of the Bible, at least in its original autographs, is absolute and eternal, being inerrant; therefore it is entirely free from error not only in matters of faith and morals but also in matters of history, science and geology.

Many of the proponents of this doctrine, of course, are aware of the existence of apparent errors in the text, but they do not call them errors but "phenomena" of the Bible, by which they mean accurate descriptions of how things appeared to the eyes of the biblical writers. They hold that any present

---

[13] Paul Tillich discusses about this problem in Protestant scholasticism and American fundamentalism in his *A History of Christian Thought: From Its Judaic and Hellenistic Origins to Existentialism* (New York: Simon and Schuster, 1968), pp. 280-83, 308-11; also in his *Systematic Theology*, vol. I, pp. 3-6. Oswald Bayer touches upon the same problem in fundamentalism in his *Martin Luther's Theology*, pp. 74, 82-83. Jack B. Rogers and Donald K. McKim substantially deal with the problem in both Protestant scholasticism and the Princeton Theology in their *The Authority and Interpretation of the Bible: An Historical Approach* (New York: Harper & Row, Publishers, 1979), pp. 147-99, 265-379.

difficulties in comprehending the "phenomena" can be solved in the future once sufficient information is made available.[14] However, according to the moderate evangelical Dewey M. Beegle (1919–1995), who is critical of inerrancy, "this series of suspended judgments indicates that the totality of biblical evidence does not prove the doctrine of inerrancy to be a fact. It is still a theory that must be accepted by faith."[15] In other words, biblical inerrancy is just an *a priori* deduced doctrine; hence there is no guarantee at all that all the "phenomena" will be explained in the end. Nonetheless, proponents of this doctrine give an absolute status to what is not necessarily absolute, thus being quite idolatrous, dogmatic and even militant. They also strongly but mistakenly believe that Luther and Calvin, too, adhered to biblical inerrancy.[16]

4. Evangelicals Addressing the Problem of Inerrancy

In order to address the problem of inerrancy within the Lutheran Church–Missouri Synod, a number of people within that highly confessional Lutheran denomination, centering on the faculty of Concordia Seminary in St. Louis, tried in the 1960s and 1970s to restore the priority of the material principle (the gospel) over the formal principle (the Bible):

> Any tendency to make the doctrine of the inspiration or the inerrancy of the Scriptures a prior truth which guarantees the truth of the Gospel or gives support to our faith is sectarian. The Gospel gives the Scriptures their normative character, not vice versa.[17]

But their efforts were severely criticized by the denominational leadership for regarding the gospel as the criterion of biblical interpretation in such a way as to give "considerable latitude" in the "non-literal, non-historical way" of interpreting the Bible so long as it does not harm the gospel, with the result that "for example, the fall of Adam and Eve or the world flooded need not be accepted as factual so long as the doctrinal lesson of sin and grace is preserved

---

[14] Everett F. Harrison, "The Phenomena of Scripture," in *Revelation and the Bible: Contemporary Evangelical Thought*, ed. Carl F. H. Henry (Grand Rapids, MI: Baker Book House, 1958), pp. 237-50.

[15] Dewey M. Beegle, *Scripture, Tradition, and Infallibility* (Ann Arbor, MI: Pryor Pettengill, Publisher, 1979), p. 196.

[16] For example, John Warwick Montgomery, *In Defense of Martin Luther* (Milwaukee, WI: Northwestern Publishing House, 1970), pp. 40-84; and John D. Woodbridge, *Biblical Authority: A Critique of the Rogers/McKim Proposal* (Grand Rapids, MI: Zondervan Publishing Co., 1982).

[17] Faculty of Concordia Seminary, *Faithful to Our Calling, Faithful to Our Lord*, part 1: *A Witness to Our Faith: A Joint Statement and Discussion of Issues* (St. Louis, MO: Faculty of Concordia Seminary, 1973), p. 21.

in the interpretation."[18] Such criticism directed at them may not have been entirely legitimate, but they were pejoratively called "Gospel reductionists,"[19] and they lost the battle and left the denomination for mainline Lutheranism.

Outside the Lutheran Church–Missouri Synod, moderate evangelicals such as G. C. Berkouwer (1903–1996), Dewey M. Beegle, Donald G. Bloesch (1928–2010), Jack B. Rogers (1934–2016), Donald K. McKim (1950–) and Peter Enns (1961–) have also addressed the problem of the doctrine of biblical inerrancy and made efforts to restore the priority of the material principle over the formal principle. Berkouwer, a noted Dutch Reformed theologian, points out the mistake of post-Reformation Protestant scholasticism in treating the Bible itself (the formal principle) *a priori* as if it were the divine message (the material principle). He maintains that "The trustworthiness of the Word does not subject itself to an *a priori* testing, but can only be understood in the all-pervasive power of the Word itself as the sword of the Spirit."[20] Bloesch distinguishes between God's revelation as the "content" of the Bible, on the one hand, and the human words of the Bible as its "form," on the other: "these words [of the Bible] are related to revelation as form to content";[21] and he means to talk about the priority of content over form when he says: "The Bible is imperfect in its form but not mistaken in its intent [of giving God's revelation]."[22] Enns argues that the Bible is authoritative as it was written under the inspiration of God to convey his message, but that verbal expressions of the biblical writers are imperfect, presenting at least three issues which challenge the doctrine of inerrancy. They are: 1) that the expression of the Old Testament contains legendary material from Ancient Near East traditions, which did not necessarily come from God; 2) that the Old Testament contains parts which are contradictory to one another; and 3) that the New Testament writers quote the Old Testament passages largely out of context.[23] Given the

---

[18] J. O. A. Preus, "Report of the Synodical President to the Lutheran Church–Missouri Synod, 1972," in *A Seminary in Crisis: The Inside Story of the Preus Fact Finding Committee*, ed. Paul A. Zimmerman (St. Louis, MO: Concordia Publishing House, 2007), p. 234.

[19] The name "Gospel reductionists" is a shortened form of "Law/Gospel reductionists," which was first used by John Warwick Montgomery in his two conference papers in 1966 criticizing them. They are published in his *Crisis in Lutheran Theology: The Validity and Relevance of Historic Lutheranism vs. Its Contemporary Rivals*, vol. I (Grand Rapids, MI: Baker Book House, 1967), pp. 81-123.

[20] G. C. Berkouwer, *Holy Scripture*, trans. Jack B. Rogers (Grand Rapids, MI: William B. Eerdmans Publishing Co., 1975), pp. 32-34.

[21] Donald D. Bloesch, *Holy Scripture: Revelation, Inspiration and Interpretation* (Downers Grove, IL: InterVarsity Press, 1994), p. 173.

[22] Ibid., p. 115.

[23] Peter Enns, *Inspiration and Incarnation: Evangelicals and the Problem of the Old Testament* (Grand Rapids, MI: Baker Academic, 2005).

reputation especially of Berkouwer and Bloesch, the approach of this moderate group of evangelicals has a good following without too much trouble, although in 2008 Enns was suspended from his faculty position at Westminster Theological Seminary due to his 2005 publication of *Inspiration and Incarnation: Evangelicals and the Problem of the Old Testament*, which explicitly stated his position.

Still another way of addressing the problem of the doctrine of inerrancy has been suggested by evangelicals such as George Eldon Ladd (1911–1982), David Hubbard (1928–1996), Daniel Fuller (1925–2023) and Stephen T. Davis (1940–). They maintain that while the Bible, written under God's inspiration, is infallible and inerrant in matters of faith and conduct, it is fallible in matters of history, science and geology.[24] Thus most of them propose to replace the term "biblical inerrancy" with "biblical infallibility" in the sense of infallibility only in matters of faith and conduct. Their position is sometimes called "partial inerrancy." It is very similar to the Second Vatican Council's *Dei Verbum*, the Dogmatic Constitution on Divine Revelation promulgated in 1965, which states that the Bible is "without error" in matters "for the sake of salvation."[25]

This alternative position of "biblical infallibility" among evangelicals does not attempt to restore the priority of the material principle over the formal principle, as with the Lutheran "Gospel reductionists" and the moderate evangelicals mentioned above. Rather, it makes a distinction only within the formal principle, between matters of faith and conduct, on the one hand, and matters of history, science and geology, on the other, asserting the primacy of the former over the latter. Strictly speaking, this distinction is not the same as the distinction between the material and formal principles of the Reformation where the former is the infallible content of the Bible while the latter is its fallible expression. But this interesting, alternative development is another indication that the doctrine of inerrancy is not desirable.

5. Relevance to Rev. Moon's Approach

The present section has dealt, in some detail, with the Reformation's distinction of the two principles and the problem of biblical inerrancy derived from a misunderstanding of the proper relationship of the two. This is relevant to Rev. Moon's approach to the Bible for three reasons. First, his

---

[24] George Eldon Ladd, *The New Testament and Criticism* (Grand Rapids, MI: Wm. B. Eerdmans Publishing Co., 1967). David Hubbard, "The Irrelevancy of Inerrancy," in *Biblical Authority*, ed. Jack Rogers (Waco, TX: Word Books, 1977), pp. 151-81. Daniel Fuller, "The Nature of Biblical Inerrancy," *Journal of the American Scientific Affiliation* 24 (June 1972): 47-51. Stephen T. Davis, *The Debate about the Bible: Inerrancy versus Infallibility* (Philadelphia: Westminster Press, 1977).

[25] Pope Paul VI, "Dogmatic Constitution on Divine Revelation *Dei Verbum*." http://www.cin.org/v2revel.html.

understanding of the Bible as a historical textbook expressing God's eternal truth as its content is in accordance with the basic thesis of the Reformers, neo-Reformers such as Barth, and moderate evangelicals such as Berkouwer, that the Bible as the formal principle is the source historically expressing the material principle which is the eternal content. Second, for Moon as well as for Luther, Calvin, Barth and Berkouwer, the authority of the Bible lies in the content of the Bible or the material principle rather than in the verbal expression of the Bible or the formal principle—although whether or not Moon and the others agree on what the content of the Bible or the material principle is exactly may be a different matter to be handled later. Third, if fundamentalists and enthusiastic evangelicals fault Moon for not adhering to the doctrine of inerrancy, they should also fault Luther and Calvin, their respected theological forefathers, for the same reason.

It is beyond the scope of the present section to survey patristic and Catholic theologians before the Reformation. But it can readily be observed that many of the patristic and Catholic theologians had the common idea that God stooped down to "accommodate" his absolute message to the relative level of human words in the Bible, resembling the Incarnation of God in the humanity of Christ.[26] This idea shows that they understood the distinction between divine content and human expression in the Bible, believing the human biblical expression to be truly human in a non-docetic way.[27] It also echoed the traditionally received definition of theology as a human word about God. These theologians before the Reformation did not stick to *sola scriptura* but included in the formal principle things other than the Bible, such as sacred tradition, papacy, *magisterium* and reason;[28] and perhaps that is the reason why

---

[26] Rogers and McKim in *The Authority and Interpretation of the Bible* report that theologians such as Clement of Alexandria, Origen, John Chrysostom and Augustine as well as Luther and Calvin clearly had the idea of God's accommodation of his message to the imperfect human level in the Bible.

[27] It is interesting that many of those evangelicals who do not want to accept the doctrine of biblical inerrancy join liberals in criticizing it for being "docetic," although they do not also forget to criticize liberals for having an "ebionitic" view of the Bible. See, for example, Donald G. Bloesch, *Essentials of Evangelical Theology*, vol. 1: *God, Authority, and Salvation* (San Francisco: Harper & Row, Publishers, 1978), p. 52. By the way, "docetism," derived from the Greek verb *dokeo* (which means "to seem or appear"), refers to a heresy during the first centuries of the Christian era that taught that the humanity and suffering of Jesus are apparent rather than real, i.e., that Jesus has no human nature at all. By contrast, "ebionism," derived from the Hebrew noun *ebyonim* (which means "the poor"), refers to a Jewish Christian sect's teaching that held not only that poverty is a blessing but also that Jesus is just an ordinary man with special gifts of righteousness and wisdom but without any divinity.

[28] The Lutheran scholar F. E. Mayor applies the material and formal principles to various Christian denominations of America to facilitate a comparative study in his *The Religious Bodies of*

the possibility of them developing a doctrine of biblical inerrancy was not as great as in the Protestant tradition.

From the above, it can be said that Moon's understanding of the authority of the Bible is no different from that in much of the Christian tradition.

§2. Interpreting the Bible

1. Studying the Bible Seriously

According to Berkouwer, who denies the doctrine of biblical inerrancy, the relative and "time-related" character of biblical language is not a discouragement at all but an encouragement for us to study the inspired Bible in search of the divine message:

> The problem of time-relatedness is not a shadow or a threat to the confession concerning Scripture; it exhorts us to caution and patience and to intensive Bible study. More and more the church has seen this not as a frightening complication of faith but as a task implied in God's Word, coming in the form of the temporal words of men… In contrast to [the doctrine of inerrancy], one must be reminded that all this Scripture research of analysis and gradation, of "history of the period" and literary genre, of searching for the goal and for the Word within the many words, is and must be related to the mystery of the God-breathed Scripture.[29]

In much the same way, Rev. Moon, not accepting biblical inerrancy, holds that it is important to study the Bible seriously in search of God's truth behind its verbal expression. Talking about his own experience with the Bible, he states: "Once I started seriously questioning a certain passage in the Bible, I would endeavor even for three years to solve the mystery of it";[30] also, "When I began to think seriously about something in the Bible, I used to devote myself to find the answer for one year, two years, or three years."[31]

Sun Myung Moon was born and raised in a country that was unjustly and tragically colonized by Japan. He witnessed much misery in his people and

---

America (St. Louis, MO: Concordia Publishing House, 1961), where he observes that non-Lutheran denominations add things other than the Bible to the formal principle.

[29] Berkouwer, *Holy Scripture*, p. 193.

[30] Sun Myung Moon, *Blessing and Ideal Family*, part 2 (Washington, DC: Family Federation for World Peace and Unification, 1998), p. 312.

[31] Sun Myung Moon, *The Way for Students* (Washington, DC: Family Federation for World Peace and Unification, 1998), p. 133.

society. As a teenage Christian, he started raising fundamental questions of human life and the universe such as:

> Who am I? Where did I come from? What is the purpose of life? What happens to people when they die? Is there a world of the eternal soul? Does God really exist? Is God really all-powerful? If He is, why does He just stand by and watch the sorrows of the world? If God created this world, did He also create the suffering that is in the world? What will bring an end to Korea's tragic occupation by Japan? What is the meaning of the suffering of the Korean people? Why do human beings hate each other, fight, and start wars?[32]

The night before Easter in 1935 (when he was 15 years of age), he was on a mountain praying all night and asking God in tears for answers to these questions. Early that Easter morning, after spending the entire night in prayer, he had a mystical encounter with Jesus, in which Jesus challenged him to take up the mission to fulfill God's will.[33]

During the next decade, he seriously studied the Bible to find God's truth, by which to answer the above fundamental questions toward the fulfillment of God's will. He especially devoted himself to connect to the circumstances of figures such as Adam, Noah, Abraham, Moses and Jesus in biblical history to discover the underlying truth. "Biblical history," according to Moon, "is not just written literature but the actual background behind the birth of the Unification Church."[34]

His years of prayers in search of God's truth behind the Bible were being gradually answered, but at one point he was led to realize a key idea: "The relationship between God and mankind is that of a father and his children, and God is deeply saddened to see their suffering."[35] When he came to this realization, he burst into tears and cried continuously. According to him, his eyes were now finally opened to the true love of God. This breakthrough helped him to resolve "all the secrets of the universe": "Suddenly, it was as if someone had turned on a movie projector. Everything that had happened since the time humankind broke God's commandment played out clearly before my eyes."[36]

This revelatory experience of Moon may resemble, among other things, Luther's "tower experience" at the Black Cloister in Wittenberg, where the

---

[32] Sun Myung Moon, *As a Peace-Loving Global Citizen*, p. 49.
[33] Ibid., pp. 49-50.
[34] Sun Myung Moon, "Leaders Conference, April 8, 1989," speech delivered. http://www.tparents.org/moon-talks/sunmyungmoon89/SM890408.htm.
[35] Moon, *As a Peace-Loving Global Citizen*, p. 76.
[36] Ibid., pp. 76-77.

Reformer struggled with, and meditated about, what he thought to be the difficult and even fearful biblical notion of the "righteousness of God" (Rom. 1:17), but finally reached a breakthrough by understanding the gospel to mean that the loving mercy of God makes the sinner righteous, bringing justification by faith alone.[37] Moon and Luther realized basically the same thing from the Bible: the love of God—although their understandings of what that really means naturally diverged, given their considerably different providential times, backgrounds and characters.

After his breakthrough experience, Rev. Moon came to realize the following fundamental points, which, according to him, would have remained as "secrets of the universe." These points may sound quite novel from the viewpoint of traditional Christianity, but they issued from his interpretation of the Bible, even as they may have reflected his unique religious consciousness.

2. Revealed Secrets of the Universe: the Divine Principle

The first fundamental point he came to realize is that God's parental love for humanity as his children is such that he wanted them to completely resemble him as his objects of love when he created them in his image. He wanted to see the reflection of his own character from his objects of love so as to receive and feel "joy" in loving them. This joy in love was God's purpose of creation.[38] This understanding of the purpose of creation is very rarely seen elsewhere in the Christian theological tradition, wherein God is posited to be already so perfect and completely blissful by himself that, even if he is understood to be a God of love in some sense, he is in want of nothing, in want of no object of love in order to experience joy. Since God does not need anything outside of himself to satisfy him, he could have chosen not to create the world at all, and this leaves the conventional theological viewpoint at a loss to explain the reason why God created the world in the first place. In the words of the evangelical theologian Millard J. Erickson, "He freely chose to create for reasons not known to us."[39]

Second, the parent-children relationship between God and human beings is such that God wanted them to be his "true children"[40] not just conceptually but substantially through his own "lineage" of love.[41] This lineage was to be

---

[37] Luther describes his "tower experience" in his "Preface to the Complete Edition of Luther's Latin Writings, 1545," in *Martin Luther: Selections from His Writings*, ed. John Dillenberger, pp. 10-12.

[38] EDP, p. 33.

[39] Millard J. Erickson, *Introducing Christian Doctrine*, 3rd ed., ed. L. Arnold Hustad (Grand Rapids, MI: Baker Academic, 2015), p. 125.

[40] EDP, pp. 285, 349.

[41] The notion of the "lineage" of God through Adam and Eve is referred to in EDP, pp. 60, 68.

established in the God-centered conjugal love between Adam and Eve as their first human ancestors. This task of Adam and Eve to create a God-centered ideal family to "multiply" (Gen. 1:28) true children in God's lineage was an important part of the purpose of creation because the intimate relationship of unity between Adam and Eve was to completely reflect the image of God, which is understood to be both male and female (Gen. 1:27), so that God might receive and feel joy from that reflection. Moon's understanding of created human beings as true children in God's lineage, although it may not mean to be pantheistic, is quite unthinkable in the Christian tradition, because the latter sees a fundamental gulf between the infinite realm of God and the finite realm of creation.[42] The New Testament only talks about the level of God's "adopted" children which can be reached through redemption (Rom. 8:23; Gal. 4:5); but according to Rev. Moon, while that level is closer to God than that of "servants" in the Old Testament Age (Lev. 25:55), which in turn is closer to God than that of "servant of servants" in the period prior to the Old Testament Age (Gen. 9:25), the final level of redemption which needs to be reached eventually is that of "children of God's direct lineage."[43]

Third, the fall of Adam and Eve means that they failed to create a family of God's direct lineage. Instead, they defiled it through their sexual misconduct centering on Archangel Lucifer, symbolized by a serpent. Lucifer first seduced Eve sexually and became Satan, and then Eve, under the influence of Satan, seduced Adam sexually. Thus all the descendants of Adam and Eve became what Jesus called a "brood of vipers" (Mt. 3:7; 12:34; 23:33), i.e., sinful children in the "lineage of Satan."[44] This sexual interpretation by Moon is again very rarely seen in the Christian tradition, in which the fall is believed to be a non-sexual event where the act of eating of the fruit of the tree of knowledge of good and evil in disobedience to God's commandment literally took place. (Many liberal Christians also deny the sexual interpretation, because they do not believe in the historicity of Adam or the historicity of the fall anyway.) St. Augustine (354–430) popularized the traditional, non-sexual interpretation, although he did also develop a theory of the transmission of original sin through procreational sex of concupiscense, which would be more compatible

---

[42] The Reformed tradition, for example, established the axiom of *Finitum non capax infiniti* ("The finite cannot contain the infinite") regarding the relationship between the infinite divinity and finite humanity of Christ. The Lutherans and other Christians, while not necessarily accepting this Reformed axiom regarding the two natures of Christ, still undoubtedly see a fundamental gulf between God and finite creatures.

[43] EDP, p. 284.

[44] EDP, p. 68.

with Rev. Moon's sexual interpretation than with his own non-sexual interpretation of the fall.[45]

Fourth, God suffered when he saw Adam and Eve fall and fail to achieve the purpose of creation. God has also been suffering by seeing his fallen children suffer from all kinds of problems throughout history. God's suffering occurs when his children, as his objects of love, fail to reflect the divine character. This idea is not familiar in the Christian tradition, in which God is normally understood to be impassible (incapable of suffering) and immutable (incapable of change) as a perfect God in his untroubled bliss. But Moon's idea of God's suffering undoubtedly came from his serious reading of biblical history in which God's grief and agony are evident, as is indicated in passages such as Gen. 6:6, according to which God, looking at much evil in fallen human beings, was "grieved" by it and "sorry" that he had created them.[46]

Fifth, out of his love for his children, God when he created them endowed them with creativity. He wanted them to inherit his creativity and, thus, to resemble him. He wanted them to use their God-given creativity in order to "participate in God's great work of creation."[47] This creativity is really a God-given freedom, the "freedom of the original mind," which "cannot exist outside of the Principle," which "is accompanied by the responsibility laid out in the Principle," and which "pursues accomplishments that bring joy to God."[48] This God-given freedom always chooses good and not evil, and thus it could not have been the cause of the fall of Adam and Eve. Rather, the reason their fall took place was because their freedom of the original mind was "overwhelmed" by "the stronger power of unprincipled love" when they were tempted by Lucifer.[49] Rev. Moon's understanding of freedom is very different from the Christian notion of "free will" or "free choice of the will" (*liberum arbitrium*), because while the former, resembling God's own freedom, always

---

45 For Augustine's non-sexual interpretation of the fall of Adam and Eve merely as their disobedient act of eating the fruit, see, for example, his *City of God*, ed. Vernon J. Bourke (Garden City, NY: Image Books, 1958), Book XIV, Chap. 13: "Our first parents… could commit the sin of eating the forbidden fruit" (p. 309). Thus a common misconception about Augustine, that he may have developed a sexual interpretation of the fall, needs to be avoided. For his doctrine of the sexual transmission of original sin through procreational sex, however, see his "Marriage and Concupiscence," in *A Select Library of the Nicene and Post Nicene-Fathers of the Christian Church*, ed. Philip Schaff, vol. V: *Saint Augustine: Anti-Pelagian Writings* (Grand Rapids, MI: Wm. B. Eerdmans Publishing Co., 1971), pp. 258-308.

46 EDP, pp. 82, 154, 155. God's suffering will be discussed in detail in Chapter 6 in the present book.

47 EDP, p. 43.

48 EDP, pp. 74-75.

49 EDP, p. 75.

chooses good, the latter, being able to choose good or evil, allows for the possibility of sinning. The so-called "free will defense" based on the latter in the Christian tradition is fairly easily subjected to the critique from atheists such as Antony Flew (1923–2010) and J. L. Mackie (1917–1981)[50] that this kind of human free will, which includes the possibility of sinning, cannot defend an omnipotent God from being ultimately responsible for evil in the world. Moon's interpretation, by contrast, may be able to defend God well, when he asserts that the God-given freedom of humans always chooses good, and that whether or not that freedom is used is up to humans and not to up to God: "If God were to interfere with human actions during their growing period, it would be tantamount to ignoring the human portion of responsibility [coming from their God-given freedom]."[51]

Sixth, given his true parental love for human beings, God could never abandon them even after their fall; he needs to have them all back as his children. God has "an intense craving to be with them and dwell within them."[52] This unbreakable love of God is the deepest reason why it can be said that God is "the absolute Being, unique, eternal and unchanging," that God's will to restore his lost children is thus "absolute, unique and unchanging," and also that his "predestination" of his will is "absolute."[53] Therefore, even though fallen humans may repeatedly sin, God absolutely continues to carry on his providence of restoration until its fulfillment: "I have spoken, and I will bring it to pass; I have purposed, and I will do it" (Isa. 46:11). Rev. Moon's frequent reference to God's "omnipotence"[54] derives from this kind of absoluteness which is rooted in God's irrepressible longing and craving for his children. Nevertheless, this definition of God's omnipotence is novel to the Christian tradition, in which divine omnipotence has usually been understood to mean that God—who is already so perfect and so completely blissful by himself that he does not need to have any craving for his creatures—is not affected by them at all, while he acts upon them, even to the point that he predestines some for salvation and others to damnation.

Seventh, because Jesus came as the second Adam (Rom. 5:18-19; 1 Cor. 15:45), he was what Adam was supposed to be from the viewpoint of God's

---

[50] Antony Flew, "Divine Omnipotence and Human Freedom," in *New Essays in Philosophical Theology, ed.* Anthony Flew and Alasdair MacIntyre (New York: Macmillan Co., 1955); J. L. Mackie, "Evil and Omnipotence," *Mind* 64: 254 (April 1955): 200-212.

[51] EDP, p. 77.

[52] Sun Myung Moon, "God's Day 1984," sermon delivered at World Mission Center, New York, NY, January 1, 1984. http://www.unification.net/1984/840101a.html.

[53] EDP, p. 155.

[54] EDP, pp. 42, 76, 81.

love in his purpose of creation. In other words, Jesus was the beloved Son of God, who, as what Adam was supposed to be, completely resembled God and completely reflected God's own character, so that God might be able to receive and feel joy in loving him. This perspective on Jesus may not sound very familiar in the Christian tradition, but it actually accommodates the full divinity of Jesus as well as his full humanity. It is neither a "low" Christology of the Antiochian type, which fails to recognize his full divinity, nor a "high" Christology of the Alexandrian type, which in turn fails to appreciate his full humanity. It is rather a Christology based on an ontology of unity between God and the world brought forth by Rev. Moon's understanding of the purpose of creation from the Bible. And it will be able to reconcile the above two opposing types of Christology, which in Christian history have not been satisfactorily reconciled with each other.[55] In addition to the person of Christ, the work of Christ is an important component of Christology, and according to Moon, what Jesus was supposed to do can be understood from what Adam was supposed to do to realize God's purpose of creation.[56]

Eighth, understanding human conflict through the lens of the story of Cain and Abel, Moon believes that the love of God for his children is such that he wants both Cain and Abel (or Cain-type and Abel-type children) to come back to him together. God wants all his children to come back. It is not God's desire that Abel only be saved and Cain not. But Cain and Abel can both be reconciled with God only if they reconcile with each other instead of hating or killing each other: "For if you forgive men their trespasses, your heavenly Father also will forgive you" (Mt. 6:14). According to Moon, the reconciliation of Cain and Abel constitutes the "foundation for the Messiah" and their eventual reconciliation with God.[57] Moon had an unusual character of love and compassion, especially for the unprivileged, even during his childhood: "After seeing a freezing beggar pass by [in winter], I couldn't eat or sleep that night... I asked my mother and father to take that beggar into our room and to feed him well."[58] Undoubtedly, this helped him to understand from the Bible the

---

[55] Although the Council of Chalcedon (451) is officially considered to have reconciled the two types of Christology by asserting that Christ is fully divine and fully human, and that these two natures are united "without confusion, without change, without division, without separation," nevertheless it is also usually observed that this negative expression of Chalcedon does not positively explain anything about the union of the two natures of Christ. Chapter 9 in the present book has a more detailed discussion.

[56] See Chapter 10 in the present book for a detailed discussion of this.

[57] EDP, pp. 195-97.

[58] Sun Myung Moon, "Sun Myung Moon's Life In His Own Words, Part 2: Childhood." http://www.tparents.org/Moon-Books/SunMyungMoon-Life/SunMyungMoon-Life-02.htm.

importance of compassion and love between Cain and Abel for the salvation of both. Also, for him this universal salvation is undeniable from Jesus' parables of the lost sheep (Lk. 14:4-7), the lost coin (15: 8-10) and the prodigal son (15:11-32).

The above fundamental points revealed to Moon constituted the Divine Principle, and we can assume that all other points in the Divine Principle were derived from them. This Divine Principle has quite an enormously ambitious task, which is "to elucidate many difficult issues in Christianity" such as "the relationship between God, Jesus and human beings," "the Holy Trinity," "the extent of redemption by the cross," the return of Jesus and the meaning of the phenomena prophesied in the Bible to happen in the last days, so that it may "bring about Christian unity" to build the kingdom of God.[59]

Rev. Moon's interpretation of the Bible is unique, given his own unique character, background and life experience, while his understanding of the authority of the Bible, as was seen in the preceding section, is very similar to that of the Christian tradition. This means that any interpretation of the Bible is subjective as well as objective, depending on what kind of person interprets the Bible. Although this subjective side in the interpretation of the Bible is unacceptable to fundamentalists and very conservative evangelicals who adhere to the doctrine of biblical inerrancy, we cannot deny the fact that any interpretation of the Bible involves serious give and take between the interpreter (the subject of interpretation) and the biblical text (the object of interpretation). There is no denying the subjective side of interpretation. Even among evangelicals, there has been an increasing awareness of a universal ontology of relationship which should apply also to the relationship between the interpreter and the Bible. The British evangelical Anthony C. Thiselton (1937–2023), for example, argues in his *The Two Horizons*, following the hermeneutics of Hans-Georg Gadamer (1900–2002), that the relationship of the horizons of both the interpreter and the Bible lets the biblical text "speak more clearly in its own right."[60]

§3. The Hermeneutical Circle

The word "hermeneutics," which refers to the theory of interpretation, is derived from the Greek verb *hermeneuein*, which has three slightly different

---

[59] EDP, pp. 10-11.

[60] Anthony T. Thiselton, *The Two Horizons: New Testament Hermeneutics and Philosophical Description* (Grand Rapids, MI: William B. Eerdmans Publishing Co., 1980), p. 445.

meanings: 1) to express aloud in words; 2) to explain; and 3) to translate. It can be associated with the messenger-god Hermes, whose task is to transmute something beyond our understanding into an understandable form.

The importance of the role of the interpreting subject as well as that of the interpreted object in hermeneutics was first recognized by the twentieth-century scholars Rudolf Bultmann (1884–1976), Gerhard Ebeling (1912–2001) and Hans-Georg Gadamer. This is usually explained in terms of the "hermeneutical circle." Gadamer refers to the hermeneutical circle as the "fusion of horizons"[61] of interpreter and text, in which the two continually converse with each other to have their horizons "gradually expanded,"[62] so that a deeper interpretation of the text may be reached. As Gadamer himself admits, this is quite similar to the Platonic dialectic of question and answer through which what is true emerges: "When a question arises [from the interpreter], it breaks open the being of the object, as it were."[63]

What is important here is Gadamer's understanding of horizon. A horizon is "the range of vision that includes everything that can be seen from a particular vantage point."[64] It is constituted by one's disposition, background, existential experience, cultural, linguistic and literary knowledge, etc. Thus it is not fixed or perfect, but finite, narrow and tentative, and it gets "gradually expanded," transformed and reconstituted when it encounters another horizon. This is the case with both the horizon of the present interpreter and the horizon of the text from the past. The finite horizon of the interpreter, rightly understood, stops him from being dogmatic, and the finite character of the text naturally precludes the fundamentalist doctrine of inerrancy. According to Gadamer, the text, in spite of its finite horizon, carries with it "an infinity of meaning"[65] or "an infinity of what is not said."[66] This would mean that the Bible, for example, contains behind its finite expression the infinity of what is not said about God's truth. This gives impetus to interpretation.

If the interpreter dogmatically thinks as if his horizon were fixed or perfect, he is without "the knowledge of not knowing" (Socrates' famous notion of learned ignorance), and he "engages in dialogue only to prove himself right and not to gain insight."[67] Hence he is not able to ask right questions to

---

[61] Hans-Georg Gadamer, *Truth and Method*, 2nd rev. ed., trans. Joel Weinsheimer and Donald G. Marshall (New York: Crossroad Publishing Corporation, 1991), p. 306.
[62] Ibid., p. 302.
[63] Ibid., p. 362.
[64] Ibid., p. 302
[65] Ibid., p. 458.
[66] Ibid., p. 469.
[67] Ibid., pp. 362-63.

break open the being of the object: "the continual failure of the interlocutor shows that people who think they know better cannot even ask the right questions."[68] Dialogue in this case is inauthentic. This kind of interpreter has no horizon and is not able to understand the text: "A person who has no horizon does not see far enough and hence overvalues what is nearest to him."[69] He simply imposes his perspective upon the text and distorts it.

By contrast, if the interpreter believes his horizon to be finite and imperfect, he is humble enough to have "the knowledge of not knowing." He knows that he does not know. Being anxious to know, he is therefore able to ask right questions to know. This involves authentic dialogue between the interpreter and the text, leading the interpreter to come closer to the truth behind the text. A profound paradox here is that a finite horizon leads us to see through the text: "'to have a horizon' means not being limited to what is nearby but being able to see beyond it."[70] And this dialogue "always involves rising to a higher universality that overcomes not only our own particularity but also that of the other."[71] The reason for the paradox is that if the interpreter humbly acknowledges the finitude of his horizon, then it grows and expands to be transformed and reoriented, so he may be able to realize "an infinity of meaning" behind the written text.

When Sun Myung Moon interpreted the Bible, he apparently went through this kind of hermeneutical circle. His horizon was characterized by his fervent desire to know and realize God's ideal on the earth, his prior understanding of the Bible, his upbringing in the Korean culture of filial piety, his first-hand experience of injustice and suffering in Korea under Japanese colonialism, his disposition of righteousness, his virtue of humility, his spirit of love, compassion and sacrifice for the underprivileged, etc.[72] Yet his horizon was still finite.

What is evident is that Moon had "the knowledge of not knowing." He therefore raised many serious questions of human life and the universe.[73] This means that he never believed his horizon to be fixed or perfect. His humility in this regard helped his horizon to be continuously enlarged in his encounter with the Bible, so that his interpretation might reach "a higher universality" beyond his own particularity and that of the Bible. This is how he eventually

---

[68] Ibid., p. 363.

[69] Ibid., p. 302.

[70] Ibid.

[71] Ibid., p. 305.

[72] To understand his horizon, see his autobiographical sketch of the formative years of his life in Chapter 1 and at least the first half of Chapter 2 of his *As a Peace-Loving Global Citizen*, pp. 2-77.

[73] See those questions in Section 2 above, n. 32.

came up with the Divine Principle as his interpretation of the Bible. Although some of the fundamental points of the Divine Principle he came up with, as were mentioned in the preceding section, are quite unique, uncommon and sometimes unimaginable from the viewpoint of the Christian theological tradition, nevertheless it must be clearly noted that he, like other theologians, went through the hermeneutical circle stipulated by insightful scholars such as Gadamer.

Unificationists, being still committed to this idea of the hermeneutical circle, would add that the reason why Rev. Moon was able to advance these quite unique, uncommon or unimaginable points largely new to the Christian theological tradition was because he was a man with a messianic mission—or so he confessed. Therefore he was able to approach the Bible through his unusual level of humility, love and sacrifice, and this transformed and enlarged his horizon to the utmost extent.[74]

At this juncture, the notion of the hermeneutical circle should be explained from the viewpoint of the Divine Principle. It can easily be shown that any interpretation through the hermeneutical circle always involves three elements: 1) an interpreter, 2) a text, and 3) their interaction, which results in that interpretation.[75] This actually resembles the Divine Principle notion of the "four position foundation"[76] in which a subject and object have their give and take action centered on God. The only apparent difference is that unlike the hermeneutical circle, the four position foundation in the Divine Principle has God explicitly at the center of the give and take action, thus involving not just three elements but four: 1) God, 2) a subject, 3) an object, and 4) their interaction centering on God.

This God-centered four position foundation, according to the Divine Principle, is "the fundamental foundation for all beings to receive God's governance and be provided with all the powers necessary for life."[77] When applied to biblical hermeneutics, the four position foundation must be the foundation for both the interpreter and the biblical text. First, it is the foundation for the interpreter because the interpreter is already related to God as a human being created in the "image of God" (Gen. 1:27). Second, it is also the foundation for the biblical text because God's absolute and eternal truth

---

[74] Theodore Shimmyo, "Kaishakugaku [Hermeneutics]," *Famiri* [Family, a Church magazine in Japan], December 1991, pp. 70-78.

[75] David Tracy, too, refers to "three basic steps" for interpretation. See his "Theological Method," in *Christian Theology: An Introduction to Its Traditions and Tasks*, rev. and enl. ed., ed. Peter C. Hodgson and Robert H. King (Philadelphia: Fortress Press, 1985), pp. 38-41.

[76] EDP, p. 25.

[77] EDP, p. 31.

lies behind the biblical text as "an infinity of meaning" or "an infinity of what is not said." What happens, therefore, is that God's truth lying behind the biblical text is revealed to the interpreter in dialogue with the text.[78] This way the apparent difference between the hermeneutical circle and the four position foundation disappears. This would result in the hermeneutical circle having four elements like the four position foundation, although hermeneuticians such as Gadamer do not explicitly mention about God as the center of the hermeneutical circle.

Another striking similarity between the hermeneutical circle and the four position foundation is that both require humility for there to be genuine interaction between interpreter and text, between subject and object. In the hermeneutical circle, the interpreter is supposed to be aware of his finite horizon, thus raising the right questions to break open the being of the text in order to reach a deeper interpretation. In much the same way, according to the Divine Principle, the four position foundation centering on God can only be formed properly when a subject and object are humble enough to "form a common base" for "interaction" called "give and take action." [79] The implication in the term, "give and take action," is that the subject gives first and does not take first, always willing to be selfless.

It is interesting to note that just as the hermeneutical circle "points to a universal ontological structure, namely to the basic nature of everything toward which understanding can be directed,"[80] the four position foundation is "a metaphysical principle" which is "absolutely general and universal, applying to everything that exists whatsoever."[81]

Conclusion

Sun Myung Moon understands the Bible to be authoritative in that while its expression may be finite and limited, it still contains God's truth which is

---

[78] This point was made also by Whitney T. Shiner, another Unificationist. See his "A Unificationist View of Scripture," in *Explorations in Unificationism*, ed. Theodore T. Shimmyo and David A. Carlson (New York: HSA-UWC, 1997): "Thus if the reader forms a four position foundation with scripture, God can participate in his or her reading of scripture in such a way as to communicate to him or her in that reading" (p. 11).

[79] EDP, p. 22.

[80] Gadamer, *Truth and Method*, p. 474.

[81] Herbert W. Richardson, "A Lecture to Students at the Unification Theological Seminary in Barrytown, New York," in *A Time for Consideration: A Scholarly Appraisal of the Unification Church*, ed. M. Darrol Bryant and Herbert W. Richardson (New York: Edwin Mellen Press, 1978), p. 302.

"unique, eternal, immutable and absolute." His understanding of the authority of the Bible is the same as that in much of the Christian tradition and does not agree with the fundamentalist doctrine of biblical inerrancy.

Hence, when seeking God's eternal truth in the Bible, it is important to interpret it taking into account what lies behind its textual expression. In fact, Rev. Moon seriously read the Bible repeatedly in search of the truth which could answer the many fundamental questions he had about human life and the universe. Even though the result of that search, the Divine Principle, has points that may be quite unique or even unimaginable from the traditional Christian point of view, it is still the product of a genuine effort at biblical interpretation. Moreover, one should bear in mind that the key idea that underlies the entirety of the Divine Principle is entirely biblical, namely, God's infinite parental heart of love for humankind as his true children.

Moon's interpretation of the Bible, no matter how unique or special, emerged from the basic framework of the hermeneutical circle, just like the interpretation of any other theologian. He started within his finite horizon to rise to a higher universality like any other genuine theologian. We can credit his unusual level of humility, love and sacrifice as a man with a messianic calling for enlarging his horizon in a special way to reach the infinity of meaning behind the horizon of the biblical text.

Chapter 2

Faith and Reason

In the Christian tradition, faith and reason are often juxtaposed as two different ways of cognizing the truth of God. They differ from each other at least in the following four senses. First, faith as a way of cognition is normally a gift of God's grace granted in the course of our redemption or restoration, while reason is usually regarded as an intellectual ability built into our human nature. Second, faith, based on our confidence in God, freely receives the truth of God as directly revealed to us ("special revelation"), while reason intellectually cognizes the truth of God as manifested in the created world ("general revelation"). Third, faith and reason, after cognizing the truth of God respectively as "special" and "general revelation," generate "revealed" and "natural theology," respectively. Fourth, faith involves all dimensions of the human person (including love, obedience, etc.) as it receives the truth of God, while reason usually involves our intellectual faculty.[1]

The problem, however, is that there has been no authoritatively definitive description of the relationship between faith and reason in the Christian tradition. Different theologies have had different views of the matter, depending on how they have dealt with the question of to what degree humans are fallen and/or saved. Theologies that regard humans as still predominantly fallen have discussed the primacy of faith over reason, emphasizing a tension between the two. By contrast, theologies that have a more optimistic view of

[1] For the meanings of "special revelation" (and "revealed theology" therefrom) and "general revelation" (and "natural theology" therefrom) in relationship to faith and reason, see, for example, Millard J. Erickson, *Introducing Christian Doctrine*, 3rd ed., ed. L. Arnold Hustad (Grand Rapids, MI: Baker Academic, 2015), pp. 25-48.

human nature have laid more trust in reason and tended to see some kind of connection between reason and faith. The issue of the relationship between faith and reason, therefore, remains unsolved.

How would the Divine Principle address this issue? According to the Divine Principle, the Old and New Testament Ages are over. Humankind has entered the "Completed Testament Age," in which "humanity's spirituality [i.e., faith] and intellect [i.e., reason] are to develop through the completion stage" for "the fulfillment of the providence of restoration" after the Second Coming of Christ.[2] In 2001, the Unification movement proclaimed, as a development of the Completed Testament Age, the age of "Cheon Il Guk," which in Korean means the kingdom in which "every dimension of the pair relationship [including faith and reason] is united as one."[3] Hence the Divine Principle would naturally see the complete unity of faith and reason in the end.

Therefore the Divine Principle—referring to faith and reason respectively as "spirituality" and "intellect," or as "spiritual cognition" and "physical cognition," or as "the spiritual and physical dimensions of cognition"—maintains that both "resonate together," so that we can "thoroughly comprehend God and the universe." It—further referring to special and general revelation respectively as the "experience of divine inspiration" and "the knowledge of truth"—holds that the two "become fully harmonious" with each other:

> The experience of divine inspiration [i.e., special revelation] gained through spiritual cognition [i.e., faith] and the knowledge of truth [i.e., general revelation] obtained through physical cognition [i.e., reason] should become fully harmonized and awaken the spirituality [i.e., faith] and intellect [i.e., reason] together. It is only when the spiritual and physical dimensions of cognition [i.e., faith and reason] resonate together that we can thoroughly comprehend God and the universe.[4]

The story does not end with this, however, as the Divine Principle has a unique notion of the "growing period," a temporal process of physical and spiritual growth, which would have existed in the ideal world of creation without the fall of Adam, and which also has turned out to exist in the fallen

[2] *Exposition of the Divine Principle* (New York: H.S.A.-U.W.C., 1996), p. 184. Henceforth abbreviated as EDP.

[3] Sun Myung Moon states: "What is the meaning of Cheon Il Guk? Two persons become one. Up and down, left and right, front and back. Every dimension of the pair relationship is united as one. That is the Kingdom of God on earth"; see his "What Is Cheon Il Guk?", speech delivered at Cheongpyeong Lake, Korea, January 31, 2003. https://www.tparents.org/Moon-Talks/SunMyungMoon03/SM030131e.htm.

[4] EDP, p. 104.

world as a process of restoration from fallenness to full maturity.[5] This growing period is inclusive enough to be able to map out and appreciate all the conflicting historical views on faith and reason in a comprehensive scheme and effectively solve the conflicts among them.

There will be two sections in this chapter. Section 1 will review at least four conflicting views of the relationship between faith and reason, which are well known in the history of Christian theology; and it will show how the Divine Principle's comprehensive view based on its notion of the growing period helps to solve the problem of the conflicts among them.

Section 2 will examine the view of St. Thomas Aquinas (1225-1274) on the relationship of revealed theology (formed from special revelation in faith) and natural theology (created from general revelation in reason). We will see that his view, in spite of its attempt to come up with some unity between the two, still has a tension between them. It will be shown that the Divine Principle can offer a solution to the problem of the tension between revealed and natural theology in Thomas' view. We cannot avoid referencing Thomas' view as our context because of its great influence on the subsequent generations ever since it emerged within the Catholic Church of the thirteenth century.

§1. The Relationship between Faith and Reason

1. Four Conflicting Views in Christianity

There have been at least four different, conflicting views on the relationship between faith and reason in the history of Christianity: 1) faith without reason; 2) faith as a basis of reason; 3) faith and reason independent from, yet related and not opposed to, each other; and 4) faith and reason completely harmonious.[6]

The first view, maintaining that like oil and water, faith and reason are entirely separate from each other, upholds faith and criticizes reason from the

---

[5] The growing period in the unfallen ideal world is explained in EDP, pp. 41-43 in the Principle of Creation. The growing period to be restored after the fall of Adam is touched upon in EDP, pp. 294-99 in the Principle of Restoration.

[6] This classification of four different views is a more or less commonly accepted one. See, for example, Jerry H. Gill, "Reason," in *The Westminster Dictionary of Christian Theology* (Philadelphia: Westminster Press, 1983), ed. Alan Richardson and John Bowden, p. 486; Gordon H. Clark, *Religion, Reason and Revelation* (Nutley, NJ: Craig Press, 1961), pp. 28-110; John A. Hutchison, *Faith, Reason, and Existence: An Introduction to Contemporary Philosophy of Religion* (New York: Oxford University Press, 1956), pp. 97-99; and Ed. L. Miller, *God and Reason: A Historical Approach to Philosophical Theology* (New York: Macmillan Publishing Co., 1972), pp. 117-36.

standpoint of faithful Christian commitment. Its representatives include Tertullian (d. 155–d. 240), Martin Luther (1483–1546) and Immanuel Kant (1724–1804). It is a well-known fact that Tertullian abhorred reason in philosophy. Thus he said: "What indeed has Athens to do with Jerusalem? What concord is there between the Academy and the Church?"[7] This position is well represented by his famous dictum: *credo quia absurdum* ("I believe because it is absurd").[8] Luther, who is famous for his idea that fallen human beings are justified "by faith alone" (*sola fide*) and not by good works, maintained that reason, which is part of completely corrupt human nature, is "the Devil's greatest whore."[9] Kant, in his *Critique of Pure Reason*, stated: "I have therefore found it necessary to deny *knowledge*, in order to make room for *faith*."[10]

The second view appreciates reason a bit, but it does so only in so far as it regards faith as a basis of reason. That is to say, reason functions properly only when it is grounded in faith. Its adherents include St. Augustine (354–430), St. Anselm of Canterbury (c. 1033–1109) and Karl Barth (1886–1968). Their dictum is: *credo ut intelligam* ("I believe so that I may understand"). Augustine, while appreciating the role of reason to a certain degree as a former Neoplatonist, adhered to the priority of faith over reason: "Unless we first believe the great and divine thing that we desire to understand, the prophet has said in vain, 'Unless you believe, you shall not understand' [(Isa. 7:9)]"[11] Anselm held that while his ontological proof for God's existence uses reason, the work of reason in this case is supported by faith.[12] Barth, in spite of his initial rejection of natural theology in favor of special revelation, later came to inherit Anselm's position on the relationship of faith and reason, when he

---

[7] Tertullian, "The Prescription Against Heretics," in Alexander Roberts, James Donaldson, and A. Cleveland Coxe, eds., *The Ante-Nicene Fathers: The Writings of the Fathers Down to A.D. 325*, American ed., vol. III: *Latic Christianity: Its Founder, Tertullian* (Grand Rapids, MI: Wm. B. Eerdmans Publishing Co., 1973), p. 246.

[8] Tertullian's actual statement was: *Credibile est, quia ineptum est* ("It is by all means to be believed, because it is absurd"). See his "On the Flesh of Christ," in Roberts, Donaldson, and Coxe, eds., *The Ante-Nicene Fathers*, vol. III, p. 525.

[9] Martin Luther, *Martin Luthers Werke: Kritische Gesamtausgabe* (Weimar: Herman Boehlaus Nachfolger, 1914), 51:126.

[10] Immanuel Kant, *Critique of Pure Reason*, trans. Norman Kemp Smith (New York: St. Martin's Press, 1965), p. 29. Preface to second edition. Italics from the book.

[11] Saint Augustine, *On Free Choice of the Will*, trans. Anna Benjamin and L. H. Hackstaff (Indianapolis: Bobbs-Merrill Company, Inc., 1976), Book Two, II, p. 39.

[12] Anselm's ontological proof for God's existence can be seen in his *Proslogion* (which means "Discourses"). Its original title was *Fides Quaerens Intellectum* ("Faith Seeking Understanding"), which has the same meaning as *credo ut intelligam* ("I believe so that I may understand").

published *Anselm: Fides Quaerens Intellectum* ("Faith Seeking Understanding") in 1931.[13]

The third view was held by St. Thomas Aquinas. He acknowledged the independence of reason from faith, maintaining that reason (even of Gentiles) without faith can naturally demonstrate God's existence and his attributes from the created world, while faith receives and cognizes God's supernatural revelation on mysteries beyond reason such as the Trinity, the incarnation and the atonement. Hence a "twofold truth" of God: "the twofold truth of divine things… One kind of divine truth the investigation of the reason is competent to reach, whereas the other surpasses every effort of the reason."[14] Here reason is naturally inferior to faith. According to Thomas, however, reason and faith, in spite of their independence from each other and the former's inferiority to the latter, are related to each other without contradiction: "the natural reason cannot be contrary to the truth of faith."[15] They are related in the following senses: 1) that reason is a preparation for faith which in turn presupposes reason; 2) that reason may contain error but can be corrected by faith; 3) that reason can serve and defend faith by providing a scientific form.[16]

The final, fourth view is shared by rationalists such as Baruch Spinoza (1632–1677) and Gottfried Wilhelm Leibniz (1646–1716) and the nineteenth-century German philosopher Georg Wilhelm Friedrich Hegel (1770–1831). They all highly regarded the power of reason, and proposed the complete unity of faith and reason based on their conviction that reason can understand all the content of faith. In the words of Hegel, "The substance of the Christian religion, the highest developmental stage of any and all religion, coincides completely with the substance of true philosophy."[17] According to this view, reason can cover the role of faith, so that we can even do without faith.[18]

2. *Faith and Reason in the Divine Principle*

How would the Divine Principle appraise the above four historical views? As was seen earlier, it teaches that faith and reason are to "resonate together" in

---

[13] Karl Barth, *Anselm: Fides Quaerens Intellectum: Anselm's Proof of the Existence of God in the Context of His Theological Scheme*, trans. I. W. Robertson (London: SCM Press, 1960).

[14] Thomas Aquinas, *Summa Contra Gentiles*, I, 9, 1. https://isidore.co/aquinas/english/ContraGentiles1.htm#9.

[15] Ibid. I, 9, 2. https://isidore.co/aquinas/english/ContraGentiles1.htm#9.

[16] Daniel Kennedy, "St. Thomas Aquinas." https://www.newadvent.org/cathen/14663b.htm.

[17] Georg Wilhelm Friedrich Hegel, *Lectures on the Philosophy of Religion*, vol. 3, ed. E. B. Speirs and J. Burdon Sanderson (New York: Humanities Press, 1974), p. 148.

[18] French atheistic rationalists such as Denis Diderot and Jean-Baptiste le Rond d'Alembert in the eighteenth century went so far as to entirely neglect faith in favor of reason. But this atheistic rationalism is out of our consideration here.

complete unity.[19] Would it, then, wholeheartedly agree with the fourth view above of completely harmonizing faith and reason, i.e., the view of Leibniz, Spinoza and Hegel? That does not seem to be the case. The reason is that the Divine Principle, because of its notion of the "growing period," can comprehensively include and map out all the four views, as was also mentioned earlier.

Echoing the dictum of the first historical view ("I believe because it is absurd"), the Divine Principle praises Noah as "the first father of faith" who built an ark on the top of a mountain in absolute obedience to God's direction,[20] although what he did would be considered "crazy" or "absurd" from a normal perspective.[21] Also the Unification movement, especially since the 1990s, has quite frequently been stressing the importance of the three-term dictum of "absolute faith, absolute love and absolute obedience,"[22] coined by Sun Myung Moon (1920–2012), in resemblance to the first view.

The dictum of the second view ("I believe so that I may understand") can also be seen in the Unification movement. For example, Rev. Moon says:

> If you are confronted with something that you cannot rationalize with your common sense, what will you do? It is very necessary that you train yourself to be [faithfully] ready for such eventuality. Always be ready to accept and do any task. Sometimes you will not be able to see the logic even though you attempt to apply the Divine Principle, but then as you pursue the task you will see the logical explanation.[23]

Even the third view, i.e., the Thomistic view—which teaches that reason, while being independent from faith, can become a preparation for faith—can be found in the Divine Principle, which states that reason can lead to faith:

> Without first understanding, beliefs do not take hold. For example, it is in order to understand the truth and thereby solidify our beliefs that we study holy scriptures. Likewise, it was to help the people understand that he was the Messiah, and thereby lead them to believe in him, that Jesus performed miracles. Understanding is the starting point for knowledge… Even internal truth demands logical and convincing explanations. Indeed, throughout the long course of

---

[19] EDP, p. 104.

[20] EDP, p. 199.

[21] Sun Myung Moon, "I Shall Follow with Gratitude and Obedience," sermon delivered at Belvedere, Tarrytown, NY, January 25, 1987. http://www.tparents.org/Moon-Talks/sunmyungmoon87/870125.htm.

[22] See the whole section of "Through absolute faith, absolute love and absolute obedience" of Sun Myung Moon, *Cheon Seong Gyeong: Selections from the Speeches of True Parents* (Seoul, Korea: Sunghwa Publishing Co., 2006), pp. 2517-27.

[23] *The Way of Tradition*, vol. II (New York: HSA-UWC, 1980), pp. 115-16.

> history, religions have been moving toward the point when their teachings could be elucidated scientifically. [24]

Hence the first three views as well as the fourth view that faith and reason are completely harmonious seem to be found in the Unification movement. If so, isn't the Unification view very unclear? What is really the Unification view?

Let us draw our conclusion here. The Divine Principle clearly teaches the *eschatological* unity of faith and reason.

If humans perfect God's purpose of creation and completely unite with him, their reason (intellect) will be a part of their original character of creation and will perfectly "respond to" God's perfect intellect,[25] so that the judgment of that reason will not be erroneous at all. In this case, cognition by reason and cognition by faith on the part of humans would completely coincide. Nay, it might be better to say that reason would be equivalent to faith in this situation. As was seen earlier, therefore, the Divine Principle says that what is cognized by faith and what is cognized by reason "become fully harmonized," as faith and reason "resonate together."

But it is not easy to reach this state of complete unity. Humans have been separated far from God due to their fall. In order for them to reach the state of completion, therefore, they should go through the "growing period," by making "indemnity conditions."[26] The fall began when Adam and Eve, the first human ancestors, abandoned God. So, in order for us humans to reach the state of completion, we must keep our faith, even though we might be abandoned by God and face tests and absurdities beyond reason. It is the indemnity course. From this point of view, we can understand the relevance of Tertullian's dictum: "I believe because it is absurd." But, as fallen humans gradually remove their fallen nature and grow spiritually through the growing period, their reason gradually becomes closer to the original character of creation. Therefore it is also natural that the second and third views emerged to show an increasing appreciation of reason. Finally, there emerged the fourth view, which saw the harmony and unity of faith and reason. Thus we can appreciate and map out all the historical views in the Divine Principle's notion of the growing period.

The Divine Principle clearly teaches the unity of faith and reason. Yet it cannot wholeheartedly agree with the fourth view, since the fourth view only talks about an ideal state of unity of faith and reason, perhaps forgetting the

---

[24] EDP, p. 6.
[25] EDP, p. 37.
[26] EDP, pp. 177-79.

need for making indemnity conditions in the course of the growing period. How difficult it is for fallen humans to acquire the divine reason that was their original birthright! In order to acquire it, unspeakable faith has been needed until today. If we forget about this point and praise reason uncritically in a quest for the unity of faith and reason, we might fall into Enlightenment-type humanism. In this regard, the Japanese Episcopal theologian Enkichi Kan (1895–1972) correctly warns in his article "Revelation and Reason" that this mistake, coming from Hellenism, distorts religion in the name of the unity of faith and reason.[27]

But, after all indemnity conditions are made in the course of the growing period, eventually the time of the genuine unity of faith and reason, and of revealed and natural theology, should come. When Hans Küng (1928–2021) talks about the unity of faith and reason in the "postmodern paradigm" in his *Theology for the Third Millennium: An Ecumenical View*, he most likely means this kind of unity, because he has considerable appreciation for the importance of faith being antecedent to this unity.[28]

§2. Revealed and Natural Theology

Revealed and natural theology in Christianity are formed respectively from special and general revelation, which are two different ways of God's truth being revealed. Special revelation is the truth of God revealed directly to us, and it is received by our faith. By contrast, general revelation is the truth of God revealed indirectly to us through the created world, and it is cognized from the created world by our reason.

1. Thomas Aquinas' View

Thomas Aquinas drew a clear distinction between revealed and natural theology. According to him, all the truth of God belongs to either of the two levels of upper and lower structures of reality: God and creation, or grace (the

---

[27] Enkichi Kan, "Keiji to Risei [Revelation and Reason]," in *Kyokai Kyogigaku Koza* [Course on Church Dogmatics], vol. 2, ed. Toshio Sato and Toshikazu Takao (Tokyo: Nihon Kirisuto Kyodan Publications, 1972), pp. 6-12.

[28] Hans Küng, *Theology for the Third Millennium: An Ecumenical View*, trans. Peter Heinegg (New York: Doubleday, 1988). He sees this importance of faith in Karl Barth's "theology of crisis" antecedent to the unity of faith and reason in the postmodern paradigm, when he appreciates Barth as the main challenger to the modern, rationalist synthesis of faith and reason. See pp. 188-91, 202-3, 271-75.

supernatural) and nature. Hence there is what he called the "twofold truth of divine things,"[29] giving rise to the distinction of revealed and natural theology.

The truth of God belonging to the realm of grace (the supernatural) is directly revealed by God to us and received by our faith, and it constitutes revealed theology. Topics of revealed theology include the Trinity, the incarnation and the atonement. They are not received by reason but by faith, as they go beyond the limits of rational judgment. Beyond reason, the Trinity is a mystery that contains a numerical contradiction: While the Father, the Son and the Holy Spirit are each God, there is only one God. The incarnation of God, too, is a mystery containing a contradiction when it maintains that Christ is both God and man at the same time.

By contrast, the truth of God belonging to the realm of nature, which is a created manifestation of God, does not need to be directly revealed by God to us but can be understood by our reason alone, and it constitutes natural theology. Topics of natural theology include God's existence and his attributes, which are understood by reason alone, without faith, as they can be demonstrated from the lower structure of reality. This demonstration from the lower structure by reason is possible because creatures' relationship with God is neither "equivocal" nor "univocal" but "analogical" in that they have a "proportional" resemblance to God as their cause. [30] Although "the resemblance of creatures to God is [thus] an imperfect one,"[31] nevertheless Thomas was still able to present his celebrated "five ways" to prove God's existence from the lower structure of reality.[32]

According to Thomas, natural theology is acceptable to all humans, including non-Christians, while revealed theology is unique to Christianity because of its authoritatively redemptive character centering on God. Natural theology is inferior to revealed theology for two reasons: 1) because the former only deals with "[created] things underneath reason," whereas the latter "leads to heights the reason cannot climb"; and 2) because the "certitude" of the former comes from "the natural light of human reason which can make mistakes," whereas that of the latter "is held in the light of divine knowledge which cannot falter."[33]

---

[29] Aquinas, *Summa Contra Gentiles*, I, 9, 1. https://isidore.co/aquinas/english/ContraGentiles1.htm#9.

[30] Thomas Aquinas, *Summa Theologiae*, Vol. I, part 1, ed. Thomas Gilby (Garden City, NY: Image Books, 1969), I, q. 13, a. 5, pp. 205-9.

[31] Ibid., p. 209.

[32] Ibid., I, q. 2, a. 3, pp. 67-70.

[33] Ibid., I, q. 1, a. 5, p. 48.

Despite this clear distinction between natural and revealed theology and the inferiority of the former to the latter, however, they do not contradict each other. According to Thomas, natural theology functions as a preparation for us to eventually understand revealed theology, because a part of natural theology is already authoritatively contained in revealed theology. So once natural theology encounters revealed theology, it is augmented by the latter to become more certain: "Grace does not scrap nature but brings it to perfection."[34] At the same time, revealed theology can "borrow from" natural theology "not from any lack or insufficiency within itself," but "for the greater [rational] clarification of the things it conveys."[35] In this sense, natural theology is the "maidservant" or "handmaid" of revealed theology.[36] In any case, their relationship is not distant or contradictory, but deeply connected.

In the modern era, David Hume (1711–1776) and Immanuel Kant critiqued Thomas' proofs for God's existence in natural theology. Hume was skeptical about the notion of causality involved in Thomas' proofs, and Kant found flaws in the efficacy of pure reason. In the twentieth century, natural theology was initially critiqued severely by Karl Barth. According to Barth, natural theology is wrong because it constructs concepts of God from fallen human perspectives and idolizes them, instead of reaching a true understanding of God through faith. In his later years, however, Barth had a bit more appreciation of natural theology and stood for Anselm's position of "faith seeking understanding," although he did not go so far as to agree with Thomas.

2. The Divine Principle View

The Divine Principle "cannot be discovered through an exhaustive investigation of scriptures or scholarly texts; nor can it be invented by any human intellect" but "must appear as a revelation from God."[37] In this sense, the Divine Principle is a revealed theology. On the other hand, its Principle of Creation asserts that the characteristics of the invisible God can be known "by observing the universe which He created," referring to Rom. 1:20 as a biblical ground for this assertion: "Ever since the creation of the world his invisible nature, namely, his eternal power and deity, has been clearly perceived in the things that have been made. So they are without excuse."[38] In this sense, the

---

[34] Ibid., I, q. 1, a. 8, p. 55.
[35] Ibid., I, q. 1, a. 5, p. 49.
[36] Ibid., p. 48.
[37] EDP, p. 11.
[38] EDP, pp. 15-21.

Divine Principle is a natural theology as well. It is therefore both a revealed theology and a natural theology at once.

But what does this mean? Shall we, following Thomas, divide the whole system of the Divine Principle into two parts, one part natural theology and the other part revealed theology? Shall we thus distinguish between the two, saying that the former deals with the lower structure of nature (the created world) regardless of the human fall, and the latter the upper structure of the supernatural (God) for our redemption and restoration? With this Thomistic framework, the Principle of Creation, in so far as it tries to reach the truth of God from the created world regardless of the fall, would belong to natural theology, while the rest of the Divine Principle (Human Fall, Eschatology and Human History, Messiah, Predestination, Christology, Trinity, Principle of Restoration, etc.), in so far as it treats the process of our redemption and restoration centering on God, would belong to revealed theology. This would mean that although there is no contradiction between the two parts of the Divine Principle, nevertheless the Principle of Creation as natural theology is the "handmaid" of the rest of the Divine Principle as revealed theology, i.e., that the Principle of Creation is merely a preparation for the rest of the Divine Principle and an object which is to be augmented by the latter.

This, however, is far from correct. Far from being a "handmaid," the Principle of Creation is "the root principle by which humanity and the universe were originally created,"[39] and constitutes the essence and nucleus of the rest of the Divine Principle. The Human Fall teaches that the fall of Adam is the negation of the Principle of Creation, and the Principle of Restoration shows that the restoration of fallen humans is their re-creation based on the Principle of Creation. Thus the Divine Principle as a systematic theology possesses far greater consistency than the bifurcated relationship of revealed and natural theology as understood by Thomas.[40] We have no objection to distinguishing between revealed and natural theology, but we do not construe their relationship in the manner of Thomas.

From the standpoint of the Divine Principle, the supernatural (God) and nature (the created world) are to be completely united. In brief, the created world, as the substantial expression of God's own completely united "dual

[39] EDP, p. 15.

[40] Herbert W. Richardson talks about this kind of systematic power and consistency of the Divine Principle in his "A Lecture to Students at the Unification Theological Seminary in Barrytown, New York," in *A Time for Consideration: A Scholarly Appraisal of the Unification Church*, ed. M. Darrol Bryant and Herbert W. Richardson (New York: Edwin Mellen Press, 1978). See especially pp. 292, 295-98.

characteristics," is to assume the same dual characteristics within itself, which makes a complete unity possible not only within the created world but also between God and the created world. In other words, the Divine Principle, when maintaining both God and the world have the same dual characteristics, sees a perfect unity between them in what it calls the "four position foundation."[41] In Thomas' theology, however, God is not a God of dual characteristics but merely "pure act" (*actus purus*), a monopolar God of perfection in and by himself, aloof from the world, which, unlike God, is imperfect because it has the polarity of "act" and "potency."[42] Thomas, therefore, could not see the relationship between God and the created world as one of complete unity. At best, he could only recognize an "analogical" resemblance between them, as was seen above.

Because the Divine Principle thus sees a complete unity between God and the world, it also sees a complete unity between revealed and natural theology. The Divine Principle widens the definitions of revealed and natural theology to say that they actually mean religion and science, respectively. Religion focuses on "internal truth" about the "causal world of essence," while science searches for "external truth" about the "resultant world of phenomena."[43] Although religion and science have been pursuing two different paths until today, seeking internal and external truth, respectively, nevertheless they have a common purpose of leading humans to knowledge out of the "ignorance" that resulted from the human fall.[44] Until both unite, the whole picture of God's truth will not be seen, nor will their common purpose be accomplished. Therefore the unity of religion and science, the unity of revealed and natural theology, is necessary.

The Divine Principle, which is both a revealed theology and a natural theology at once, thus claims to "reconcile science and religion as one unified undertaking in order to overcome the internal and external aspects of people's ignorance."[45]

Consequently, it would be safe to say that the Principle of Creation, the Human Fall, the Messiah, the Principle of Restoration, etc. in the Divine

---

[41] For the notions of common "dual characteristics" in God and the created world and of the "four position foundation," see the first two sections of the Principle of Creation in EDP, pp. 15-32. Also, Chapter 4, Section 2 ("Advantages of Unification Theism") in the present book will enumerate eight advantages of Unification theism based on its notion of God's "dual characteristics," one of which is that it can secure the complete unity of God and the world.

[42] Vernon J. Bourke, ed., *The Pocket Aquinas* (New York: Washington Square Press, 1960), pp. 169-74.

[43] EDP, pp. 3-4.

[44] EDP, pp. 2-3.

[45] EDP, p. 105. See also pp. 3, 6-7.

Principle are each a unified teaching of revealed and natural theology. For example, when the Principle of Creation discusses the process of the creation of the universe, it unhesitatingly asserts that the revelation in the biblical account (revealed theology) and the findings of modern scientific research (natural theology) in that matter coincide with each other as truth: "Considering that the account of the creation of the universe recorded in the Bible thousands of years ago nearly *coincides* with the findings of modern scientific research, we are reassured that this biblical record must be a revelation from God."[46] Another example is the Human Fall, which is a combination of the biblical account of the fall (revealed theology) and a rational explanation of it through the universal notion of the "four position foundation" (natural theology), maintaining that even the fall of Adam and Eve consisted in relational, sexual give and take action in "the four position foundation centering on Satan" and not centering on God.[47] Here the distinction between revealed and natural theology is overcome.

Thomas Aquinas believed that revealed and natural theology are closely related to each other without any contradiction, but he was still aware of a real distinction or even tension between them because he only saw an "analogical," imperfect resemblance between God and the world. After all, he believed that God and the world do *not* "belong to the same order."[48] But the Divine Principle asserts that God and the world are completely united through their shared dual characteristics, so that revealed and natural theology are also completely united. Thus it can offer a solution to the problem of the tension between revealed and natural theology in the Thomistic system.

3. Recent Theological Trends

The Divine Principle's treatment of revealed and natural theology is not entirely novel. There is a trend in recent theologies to remove the distinction between the two types of theology. In removing this distinction, recent theologies take two different approaches.

One approach is to view both revealed and natural theology as starting from revelation. We can find revelation from God in the world of nature. Of course, this has traditionally been called "general revelation," as distinguished from "special revelation" which has the primary purpose of redemption. But we can enlarge the meaning of revelation by letting it contain both general and special revelation, i.e., by letting it cover the world of nature as well as the realm

---

[46] EDP, p. 40. Italics added.

[47] EDP, p. 68.

[48] Aquinas, *Summa Theologiae*, I, q. 13, a. 5, p. 209.

of God himself. If so, the distinction between revealed and natural theology can be transcended. Many contemporary theologians, liberal and conservative alike, take this approach.

For example, John Macquarrie (1919–2007), an existentialist theologian, adopts this approach in attempting to formulate what he calls a "new style natural theology." He calls for "the virtual abandonment of the old distinction between 'natural' and 'revealed' knowledge of God," seeking "a general possibility of revelation" or "a universal possibility of revelation."[49]

Process theology, with its "panentheistic" emphasis on the relatedness of God and the world, also "rejects the sharp contrast of general and special revelation" as it attempts to combine philosophy (natural theology) and theology (revealed theology) to constitute a "philosophical theology."[50] It is understandable, because process theology uses Alfred North Whitehead's (1861–1947) idea of God's dipolarity, which is similar to the Unification doctrine of God's dual characteristics.[51]

Even the approach of some American fundamentalist theologians fits into the first approach. Based on their belief that both the natural world and the Bible were authored by God, they firmly maintain that "true science" and revealed theology can go together and enrich each other, and that we should refrain from "locking them into two separate compartments in our minds."[52] This leads, for example, to so-called "scientific creationism," a position which holds that the biblical account of creation can be established scientifically.

What Ted Peters calls the "consonance" between science and religion, which has recently drawn the increasing attention of serious scientist-theologians such as Arthur Peacocke (1924–2006) in Britain and Robert John Russell (1946–) in America, falls under the first category, too, because it is "an attempt to uncover the domain of inquiry shared by science and theology" based on the theistic assumption that God created the world.[53]

---

[49] John Macquarrie, *Principles of Christian Theology*, 2nd ed. (New York: Charles Scribner's Sons, 1977), pp. 53-54, 57, 89.

[50] John B. Cobb, Jr. and David Ray Griffin, *Process Theology: An Introductory Exposition* (Philadelphia: Westminster Press, 1976), p. 159.

[51] For a comparative study of Whitehead's dipolar theism and the Divine Principle's doctrine of God's dual characteristics, see Theodore T. Shimmyo, "Dipolar Theism in Process Thought and Unificationism," in *Unification Theology: In Comparative Perspectives*, ed. Anthony G. Guerra (Barrytown, NY: Unification Theological Seminary, 1988), pp. 35-48.

[52] J. I. Packer, *'Fundamentalism' and the Word of God: Some Evangelical Principles* (Grand Rapids, MI: Wm. B. Eerdmans Publishing Co., 1958), pp. 134-35.

[53] Ted Peters, ed., *Science and Theology: The New Consonance* (Boulder, CO: Westview Press, 1998), p. 1. See excellent works such as Arthur Peacocke, *Theology for a Scientific Age*, enl. ed. (Minneapolis,

A second, and entirely opposite tack for removing the distinction between revealed and natural theology is to not consider revelation at all. It enlarges the concept of the existence of the world of nature to such an extent that it covers the whole of reality, including God. In this case, theology is to know the truth of this whole of reality in which God is already wholly immanent. This immanentist approach was popular among radical schools of theology such as secular theology and the "death of God" theology in the 1960s.[54] It is somewhat ironic that this approach emerged under the influence of Dietrich Bonhoeffer (1906–1945), a neo-orthodox theologian who, in an attempt to abandon the *deus ex machina* ("God from the machine," i.e., the convenient problem-solving God worshipped by irresponsible religious people) in favor of the God of the Bible (a God who helps us as we strive to tackle problems responsibly in the world), wrote from a Nazi prison that the world can be "religionless" because it has "come of age."[55] These radical schools attracted a lot of attention in the 1960s, but they have not developed much serious theology since then.

Both of these ways, whether liberal, conservative or radical, hold the important presupposition that there is a close relationship between God and the created world of nature. From the standpoint of the Divine Principle, their emergence is a sign that the time is very near when humans can completely resonate with God, overcoming their state of fallenness to realize the genuine unity of faith and reason and the complete unity of revealed and natural theology. When this sort of time comes, what will be our status as humans, and what will be the nature of theology? Thinking of these questions makes our hearts throb with excitement.

MN: Fortress Press, 1993); and John Polkinghorne, *Faith of a Physicist* (Princeton: Princeton University Press, 1994).

[54] See, for example, Harvey Cox, *The Secular City: Urbanization and Secularization in Theological Perspective* (New York: Macmillan Co., 1965); and Thomas J. J. Altizer and William Hamilton, *Radical Theology and the Death of God* (Indianapolis: Bobbs-Merrill, 1966).

[55] Dietrich Bonhoeffer, *Letters and Papers from Prison*, enl. ed., ed. Eberhard Bethge (New York: Macmillan Co., 1971), pp. 280-82, 359-61.

Chapter 3

God's Heart: Two Aspects of Love

Unification theism understands God in a new way. God is a God of "Heart" (*shimjeong* in Korean) who stands as the "True Parent" of human beings. God's Heart, which is parental, is defined as his "emotional impulse to seek joy through love."[1] With this Heart, God treats us as his true sons and daughters, unconditionally loving us, regardless of our situation, while at the same time being delighted to love any good things realized in us. In the end God becomes joyful as our Parent, when we as his sons and daughters, his partners of love, reflect him in some good way or other.

Traditional Christianity, of course, teaches that God is a God of love as our "Heavenly Father." But it still seems to be asserting that while God loves us unconditionally, he does not have to be delighted to love any good things realized in us, since he is in want of nothing as an absolutely sovereign, perfect God on his own. Christianity thus still seems to see some gap or distance between God and human beings, giving the impression that he may not be our True Parent completely. This may be due to the fact that traditional Christian theism, while originally biblical, was developed under the influence of the ancient Greek philosophical notion of God as a perfectly actualized, unmoved deity (e.g., Aristotle's "unmoved mover" or "pure form," and Neoplatonism's eternal, transcendent and unchanging God).

Anders Nygren (1890–1978) is the most commonly recognizable theologian to assert the above Christian position on God's love, as he sharply

---

[1] *New Essentials of Unification Thought: Head-Wing Thought* (Tokyo: Kogensha, 2006), p. 23. Henceforth abbreviated as NEUT.

separates between unconditional *agape*, which he believes to belong to God, and acquisitive *eros*, which he believes to belong to the human ego. But the present chapter will show that his position in this regard is only marginally biblical. We will show that Unification theism on God's Heart instead is unquestionably biblical. We will also briefly discuss Christian thinkers such as Jürgen Moltmann (1926–2024) and Nikolai Berdyaev (1874–1948), who reference something similar to God's Heart in Unification theism, because they are biblically grounded and want to distance themselves from the Greek notion of God.

§1. God's Heart

God's Heart is essentially altruistic, living for the sake of human beings and warmly relating with them, but also seeking joy by loving them. Unification theism thus sees within God's Heart two distinguishable, if inseparable, and successive aspects of love: 1) unconditionally loving and living for the sake of all humankind as his sons and daughters, regardless of their merits or lack thereof, to warmly encourage and help them to eventually realize the values of beauty and goodness in themselves; and then 2) loving them in the sense of appreciating and enjoying the values they realize in themselves in response to God's encouraging help. Both aspects of God's love involve "joy" on his part, although joy in the former case can be called the joy of "hope,"[2] and joy in the latter the joy of "fulfillment."[3]

What is important here is that the initial aspect of love in God's Heart comes first, and only after that does the second aspect come. In the first aspect of love God is active as the initiator and giver of love, but in the second aspect he can be passive in that he receives and enjoys the values of goodness and beauty from his object partners of love. God, therefore, gives first and receives next, while his object partners may receive first and give next: "In the relationship between God and human beings, God gives love as the subject partner and human beings return beauty as object partners."[4] This explains the

[2] NEUT, p. 251.

[3] Sun Myung Moon says: "Throughout history all mankind has been looking forward to the day of fulfillment when God could declare His joy and personally commemorate God's Day and Parents Day." See his "True Parents Day from the Historical Point of View," sermon delivered at Manhattan Center, New York, NY, April 18, 1977. http://www.tparents.org/Moon-Talks/sunmyungmoon77/SM770418.htm.

[4] *Exposition of the Divine Principle* (New York: H.S.A.-U.W.C., 1996), p. 38. Henceforth abbreviated as EDP.

reciprocal relationship of "give and take action" (or "give and receive action")[5] between God and his object partners. Therefore, when it is stated that God is the initiator of unconditional love, it never means that he refuses to be affected by any good input from his object partners of love subsequently. On the contrary, he is affected by it and rejoices over it as their True Parent.

Sun Myung Moon often talks about the two aspects of love in God's Heart. Regarding the first aspect, he highlights the "unconditional," "sacrificial," "giving" and "forgiving" nature of God's love:

> It is a love that gives and then forgets that it has given, that is, a love that gives unconditionally. It is sacrificial love… It is a love that is even forgiving and giving to an enemy. It is a love that gives, and then keeps on giving… It is a love of unlimited giving. This was the kind of love that God bestowed on human beings at the time He created us.[6]

This unconditional love of God encourages his object partners, regardless of their merits or lack thereof, to realize values in themselves. According to Rev. Moon, it "transforms everything, transforms ugliness into beauty and dirty smell into perfume,"[7] and "It is only His forgiveness, the giving and unconditional love of God, our parent, that can pull all peoples of the world into unity."[8]

Regarding the second aspect of love in God's Heart, Moon states that God especially loves human beings as his object partners in that he praises the values realized in them:

> God created human beings in such a way that… they have shared His essence and purpose. If there were prose or poetry with which God could praise human beings whom He had created in this way, it would be the greatest work of art, far beyond the level of any poets or writers of this world. The object of this praise is neither God nor all things of creation, but the representatives of all things, human beings.[9]

---

[5] EDP uses the term "give and take action," while NEUT makes use of the expression "give and receive action."

[6] Sun Myung Moon, "The Root of Peace Is in True Love," Founder's Address at Opening Ceremony of IIFWP Assembly on February 24, 2002. http://www.tparents.org/moon-talks/sunmyungmoon02/SM020215.htm.

[7] Sun Myung Moon, "Renewed Pride," sermon delivered in Washington, DC, December 4, 1977. http://www.tparents.org/Moon-Talks/sunmyungmoon77/771204.htm.

[8] Sun Myung Moon, "The Spirit World and Physical World," sermon delivered at Belvedere, Tarrytown, NY, February 6, 1977. http://www.tparents.org/Moon-Talks/sunmyungmoon77/SM770206.htm.

[9] Sun Myung Moon, *Cheon Seong Gyeong: Selections from the Speeches of True Parents* (Seoul, Republic of Korea: Sunghwa Publishing Co., 2006), p. 94.

This second aspect of God's love upholds valuable human beings as his object partners of love:

> God values human beings most. Why does He value them so? Because He needs an object partner for His love. No matter how much love He may have, He is unable to feel love without having a love partner. God can experience love only in a relationship with a partner. The reason God values human beings most is that they are His object partners whom He can love.[10]

God, however, has not been able to fulfill this second aspect of love due to the fall of Adam and Eve which made all human beings sinful and unlovable. God in the first aspect of love, of course, has always and unconditionally been loving the sinful and unlovable throughout history, hoping to be able to restore them as his sons and daughters. But he has not been able to experience the joy of fulfillment due to their continuous sinfulness. He has instead been feeling pain and suffering.[11]

§2. Old Testament Evidence

The important Hebrew word *chesed* in the Old Testament, which refers to God's love toward the people of Israel in his covenant with them, the English translation of which is usually "steadfast love," "loving-kindness" or "mercy," is equivalent to God's Heart in Unification theism in that it contains the above-mentioned two aspects of love.

First, God's *chesed* is unconditionally given in spite of the continual faithlessness of the people of Israel. Regardless of their disobedience, God "is ready to forgive, gracious and merciful, slow to anger and abounding in steadfast love (*chesed*), and didst not forsake them" (Neh. 9:17; cf. Ex. 34:6; Ps. 103:8; 145:8; Joel 2:13; Jon. 4:2; etc.). Although "the mountains may depart and the hills be removed," nevertheless "my steadfast love (*chesed*) shall not depart from you, and my covenant of peace shall not be removed" (Isa. 54:10). So God's "steadfast love (*chesed*) endures for ever" (1 Chron. 16:34, 41; 2 Chron. 5:13; 7:3, 6; 20:21; Ps. 100:5; 106:1; 107:1; etc.). It is also "forgiving" (Num. 14:19; Ps. 86:5; etc.). Thus the psalmist affirms: "thy steadfast love (*chesed*) is great above the heavens" (Ps. 108:4).

---

[10] Ibid., p. 93.

[11] NEUT, pp. 251-57.

The second aspect of love in God's *chesed*, too, is evident in that the Old Testament testifies that his *chesed* is also given to the people of Israel in return for the values of beauty and goodness they realize in themselves. God is "showing steadfast love (*chesed*) to thy servants who walk before thee with all their heart" (1 Kings 8:23; 2 Chron. 6:14). God is "abounding in steadfast love (*chesed*) to all who call on thee" (Ps. 86:5). It "is from everlasting to everlasting upon those who fear him" (Ps. 103:17). God "keeps covenant and steadfast love (*chesed*) with those who love him and keep his commandments" (Deut. 7:9; Neh. 1:5; Dan. 9:4; cf. Ex. 20:6; Deut. 5:10). God loves those who realize these values. Hence "those of blameless ways," "those who act faithfully," are God's "delight" (Prov. 11:20; 12:22), and "the prayer of the upright" is also "his delight" (Prov. 15:8). If they fail to positively respond to God, however, he suffers. When he saw much wickedness and evil in them, "the LORD was sorry that he had made man on the earth, and it grieved him to his heart" (Gen. 6:6). God even cried and shed "tears" over the plight of the people of Israel who disobeyed him (Jer. 14:17).

Norman H. Snaith (1898-1982), a British Bible and Judaica scholar, recognizes a tension between the two aspects of love in God's *chesed*, because while God unconditionally loves the people of Israel in spite of their waywardness, he also passionately desires to see value and goodness in them to his delight. Snaith, however, correctly believes that both aspects are interrelated and even inseparable within the same notion of *chesed*, and addresses the tension by saying that even though both are very strong, the former is "more insistent still" or "greater even" than the latter.[12] This explains the priority of the former over the latter in God's Heart, as understood in Unification theism.[13]

Besides *chesed*, the Old Testament uses additional words for different meanings of love. One is the verb *ahab*, which simply means to love without any context of the covenant, as in Deut. 7:8: "the LORD loves you." Yet a discussion here of *chesed* alone suffices to show the nature of God's love in the Old Testament.

In the Old Testament, God is not explicitly referred to as the True Parent of the people of Israel, as he is called *Yahweh* (translated "LORD"), *Adonai*

---

[12] Norman H. Snaith, "Loving-Kindness," in *A Theological Word Book of the Bible*, ed. Alan Richardson (New York: Macmillan Co., 1951), p. 137.

[13] Unification Thought says: "The impulse to seek joy is triggered by this impulse of love: the impulse of love is primary, and the impulse of joy is secondary. Thus, love is an unconditional impulse, rather than the means of joy. The necessary result of love is joy. Thus, love and joy are two sides of a coin, and the impulse to seek joy is the impulse to seek love that has manifested" (NEUT, p. 24).

(translated "Lord") or *Elohim* (translated "God"). But if we know the meaning of *chesed* truly, we can realize that he started his covenant with the people of Israel with a parental Heart.

§3. New Testament Evidence

The two aspects of God's love can be found in the New Testament as well. The following celebrated passage, "God so loved the world that he gave his only Son, that whoever believes in him should not perish but have eternal life" (Jn. 3:16; cf. 1 Jn. 4:9), expresses God's unconditional love. Again, God "loved us and sent his Son to be the expiation for our sins" (1 Jn. 4:10). This love of God is sacrificial, involving the death of Christ for us: "God shows his love for us in that while we were yet sinners Christ died for us" (Rom. 5:8). Thus it encourages us also to love one another, even by sacrificing our lives for others: "This is my commandment that you love one another as I have loved you. Greater love has no man than this, that a man lay down his life for his friends" (Jn. 15:13). It is also "forgiving" (Lk. 23:34; Eph. 1:7; 4:32), encouraging us also to forgive one another (Mt. 6:14; 18:21-22; Mk. 11:25; Lk. 6:37; Eph. 4:32) and love our enemies (Mt. 5:44; Lk. 6:27-30; Rom. 12:14). God's unconditional love is also impartial: "he makes his sun rise on the evil and on the good, and sends rain on the just and on the unjust" (Mt. 5:45).

However, after human beings receive this unconditional love of God, they are encouraged to realize the values of beauty and goodness in themselves, and God is delighted to love those who realize these values. Hence the second aspect of God's love in the New Testament as well. According to the Gospel of John, for example, if human beings realize these values by loving Jesus and keeping his word, then God loves them: "If a man loves me, he will keep my word, and my Father will love him" (Jn. 14:23; cf. 14:21; 12:26). God also loves the generous character of those who want to give: "God loves a cheerful giver" (2 Cor. 9:7). If we forgive others their trespasses, God will love us, by forgiving us also (Mt. 6:14; Mk. 11:25; Lk. 6:37). If we love our enemies, God will love us, by giving us the "reward" of being "sons of the Most High" (Lk. 6:35). This second aspect of God's love involves joy on his part, because he delights in the values of his object partners of love. This is why Jesus says in his parables of the lost sheep and the lost coin that God will feel "joy" over even one sinner who repents (Lk. 15:7, 10). In his parable of the prodigal son as well, Jesus says that the return of the prodigal son after his repentance makes his father (symbolizing God) "merry" and "glad" (Lk. 15: 32).

Human beings' failure to positively respond to God's will, however, makes God suffer. For example, when the rebellion of the people of Israel against Jesus made Jesus suffer (Mt. 23:37) and weep (Lk. 19:41-44), this meant God's own suffering, for Jesus said: "I am in the Father and the Father in me" (Jn. 14:11).

§4. Nygren's Mistake

In spite of the undeniable biblical witness to God's love having these two inseparable, if distinguishable, aspects, Anders Nygren sharply separates them from each other to maintain that God's love only consists in the former (unconditional love) and has nothing to do with the latter (appreciative love). According to the Swedish Lutheran theologian, appreciative love is not of God, but belongs to the human ego in want of something. In his influential book, *Agape and Eros*,[14] Nygren calls the two kinds of love *agape* and *eros* and determines that they are antithetical. He asserts that while *agape* is "overflowing," "unmotivated," "indifferent to value" and "sacrificial," *eros* is "evoked," "motivated," "acquisitive" and "egocentric."[15] He concludes that the latter does not belong to God who is absolute and sovereign.

Many may not be aware of the fact that before he began any work on theology and historical theology, Nygren for more than a decade had been quite seriously engaged in the philosophy of religion. It had led him to give priority to the discussion of fundamental formal categories of religion such as eternity and fellowship.[16] It was in response to these categories that he came up with three different motifs in history: *agape* in Christianity, *eros* in the Hellenistic civilization, and *nomos* (law) in Judaism.[17] He believed that these three motifs have clashed with one another in the course of history, and naturally he as a Christian was strongly in favor of the *agape* motif. It was on this schema of three conflicting motifs that he based his approach to the Bible.

This had at least two undesirable consequences. First, it led him to ignore what Martin Luther correctly acknowledged as the proper role of *nomos*, i.e., the role of the Law as the necessary background for the Gospel. Hence Nygren ignored the importance of the Old Testament and only focused on the New

---

14 Anders Nygren, *Agape and Eros*, trans. Philip S. Watson (London: SPCK, 1953).

15 See his own summary list of characteristics of *agape* and *eros* in his *Agape and Eros*, p. 210.

16 For this, see, for example, Gustaf Wingren, *Theology in Conflict: Nygren, Barth, Bultmann*, trans. Eric. H. Wahlstrom (Philadelphia: Muhlenberg Press, 1958), pp. 3-22.

17 Nygren, *Agape and Eros*, pp. 247 ff.

Testament. His book, *Agape and Eros*, therefore, has no real treatment of the Old Testament. For this reason, he could not appreciate the profound meaning of *chesed* in the Old Testament.

Second, when reading the New Testament, Nygren already presupposes that its motif is *agape* and not *eros*. Thus he could not realize that the New Testament speaks of the two aspects of God's love together, i.e., that the New Testament actually shows that God's love is evoked, motivated and acquisitive (if not egocentric) as well as overflowing, unmotivated, indifferent to value and sacrificial.

Because of the above two points, critics such as Gustaf Wingren (1910–2000), the successor of Nygren as professor of theology and ethics at the University of Lund, said that Nygren's position is hardly biblical. In the words of Wingren, "the method of approach in Nygren's theology clashes with the content of scripture,"[18] and "It is his very method of approach to the historical material [i.e., the Bible] that makes a correct interpretation of it impossible."[19]

By the way, when the New Testament describes the evoked and motivated side of God's love, which, strictly speaking, should be called God's *eros* according to Nygren's definition, it does not use the word *eros* but *agapao* (the verb form of *agape*), as in Jn. 14: 21, 23 and 2 Cor. 9:7. In fact, the New Testament never uses the word *eros* to describe any kind of love, whether from God or from humans. Instead, it mostly uses *agape* and sometimes *philia* (brotherly love), whether in noun or verb form. Therefore *agape* covers the meaning of *eros* as well; and *philia*, while it may still retain its brotherliness in some sense, is interchangeable with *agape*, thus containing the meaning of *eros* as well (as in Jn. 16:27 where God's *phileo*, the verb form of *philia*, is described as evoked by the values of Jesus' disciples). Thus Nygren's very narrow view of *agape* never reflects the New Testament's whole picture of love.

It is noteworthy that Nygren himself is actually aware that the Johannine literature in particular does not easily agree with him.[20] For one thing, the Gospel of John states that God loves (*agapao*) Jesus (Jn. 3:35; 15:9; 17:23-24). Whereas God's *agape* according to Nygren is unmotivated and therefore should only be given to the sinful and unlovable, here John apparently means that it is

---

[18] Wingren, *Theology in Conflict*, p. 18. For other critiques of Nygren's doctrine of *agape*, see Daniel Day Williams, *God's Grace and Man's Hope* (New York: Harper & Brothers Publishers, 1949), pp. 67-73; Thomas Jay Oord, *The Nature of Love: A Theology* (St. Louis, MO: Chalice Press, 2010), pp. 33-56; and Ádám Szabados, "Hellenistic Tendencies in John's Agape?: Andrew Nygren's Shipwreck on the Rocks of 1 John." http://szabadosadam.hu/divinity/wp-content/uploads/2010/09/HELLENISTIC-TENDENCIES-IN-JOHNS-AGAPE.pdf.

[19] Wingren, *Theology in Conflict*, p. 17.

[20] Nygren, *Agape and Eros*, pp. 150-59.

given to Jesus who is sinless, lovable and valuable. It thus seems to mean God's motivated *eros*. Nygren therefore blames John for having been influenced by the Hellenistic idea of *eros*.[21]

Yet it would be more reasonable to say that it is ironically Nygren himself who is Hellenistic, because his understanding of God's *agape* is well suited to the Hellenistic, Greek philosophical notion of God as an absolute and sovereign deity who is not acted upon by the world. When Nygren says that God's unmotivated *agape* is "sovereign,"[22] and that God is none other than "the sovereign Lord who has absolute authority over the ego,"[23] this God does not so much resemble the God of the Bible as Aristotle's "unmoved mover" or Neoplatonism's eternal, transcendent and unchanging God.

§5. Some Prominent Theologians on God's Desire

Unlike Nygren, some prominent theologians are profoundly aware of the second as well as the first aspect of God's love from the Bible. Thus they speak of God's love as his desire or longing for his object partners of love. For example, Jürgen Moltmann, a German Reformed theologian, says that it is "God's longing for 'his Other' and for that Other's free response to the divine love," so that he may find "bliss" in his Other that reflects the divine image.[24] This does not mean, of course, that the first aspect of God's love is absent in his longing for his Other. As Moltmann notes, "selflessness is part of love's very nature" and "God emptied himself by virtue of his love, out of the necessity of his being, going out to his 'Other', the world."[25]

The Russian religious thinker Nikolai Berdyaev, too, speaks of God's love as "the inner passionate divine thirst and longing for an other self."[26] It certainly refers to the second aspect of God's love, but it also contains the first aspect, because, as Berdyaev states, "God reveals Himself as freedom, love, sacrifice… suffers for man and strives together with man against the falsity and wrong of the world."[27]

---

21 Ibid., p. 150.
22 Ibid., pp. 74, 92, 126, 131, 210.
23 Ibid., p. 45.
24 Jürgen Moltmann, *The Trinity and the Kingdom: The Doctrine of God*, trans. Margaret Kohl (Minneapolis: Fortress Press, 1993), p. 106.
25 Ibid., pp. 106-7.
26 Nikolai Berdyaev, *The Meaning of History*, trans. George Reavey (New York: Charles Scribner's Sons, 1936), p. 48.
27 Nikolai Berdyaev, *Slavery and Freedom*, trans. R. M. French (New York: Charles Scribner's Sons, 1944), p. 89.

What Moltmann and Berdyaev understand to be God's love is very similar to God's Heart in Unification theism. Both thinkers apparently derived this understanding of God's love from the seventeenth-century German Lutheran mystic Jakob Böhme (1575–1624), according to whom God's *Ungrund* (Groundlessness, Abyss or Nothing), with its infinite potentiality, freedom and will, craves and longs for something: "The unground (*Ungrund*) is an eternal nothing, but makes an eternal beginning as a craving. For the nothing is a craving after something."[28] Berdyaev seriously studied and published on Böhme especially.[29] Moltmann's appreciative treatment of Berdyaev can be seen in his book, *The Trinity and the Kingdom*.[30]

The mystical theology of Böhme, as Berdyaev correctly observes,[31] is free from any influence from the Greek notion of God because the German mystic, a humble shoemaker who only studied the Bible and some works by local German visionaries such as Paracelsus (1493–1541) and Valentin Weigel (1533–1588), was never schooled to know Plato, Aristotle, Neoplatonism, Pseudo-Dionysios the Areopagite, and medieval scholasticism and mysticism. This may be the reason why Böhme was able to realize based on the Bible that God's love is a craving, a longing, a desire.

Berdyaev and Moltmann, too, are biblically grounded, distancing themselves from the Greek philosophical notion of God which influenced Christianity. Berdyaev is critical of Aristotle: "The Aristotelian conception of God as *actus purus* deprives God of that interior active life, and transforms Him into a lifeless subject."[32] In the following, rather lengthy quotation, Moltmann's criticism of Aristotle's conception of God devoid of divine suffering is quite striking:

> A God who cannot suffer is poorer than any man. For a God who is incapable of suffering is a being who cannot be involved. Suffering

---

[28] Jakob Böhme, "*Mysterium Pansophicum* or A Fundamental Statement Concerning Earthly and Heavenly Mystery." http://www.mystic.tlchrist.info/mysterium.html.

[29] At least two of these studies can be seen online. Nikolai Berdyaev, "Studies Concerning Jacob Boehme: Etude I. The Teaching about the Ungrund and Freedom," originally published in *Journal Put'* 20 (1930): 47-79, trans. S. Janos. http://www.berdyaev.com/berdiaev/berd_lib/1930_349.html. Also, "Studies Concerning Jacob Boehme: Etude II. The Teaching about Sophia and the Androgyne: J. Boehme and the Russian Sophiological Current," originally published in *Journal Put'* 21 (1930): 34-62, trans. S. Janos. http://www.berdyaev.com/berdiaev/berd_lib/1930_351.html.

[30] Moltmann, *The Trinity and the Kingdom*, pp. 42-47.

[31] Berdyaev, "Studies Concerning Jacob Boehme: Etude I. The Teaching about the Ungrund and Freedom."

[32] Nikolai Berdyaev, *The Destiny of Man*, trans. Natalie Duddington (London: The Century Press, 1937), p. 1.

> and injustice do not affect him. And because he is so completely insensitive, he cannot be affected or shaken by anything. He cannot weep, for he has no tears. But the one who cannot suffer cannot love either. So he is also a loveless being. Aristotle's God cannot love; he can only be loved by all non-divine beings by virtue of his perfection and beauty, and in this way draw them to him. The 'unmoved Mover' is a 'loveless Beloved'.[33]

§6. Common Theological Features

There are naturally some important theological features shared in common by Unification theism, Moltmann and Berdyaev, given their common understanding that God's love as his Heart or desire has two distinguishable, if inseparable, aspects. And these features are not shared by Nygren and much of traditional Christian theism.

First of all, they all teach that God and human beings have a reciprocal relationship. It is not a one-sided relationship in which God acts upon human beings but is not acted upon by them. Unification theism's understanding of the reciprocal character of the God-humanity relationship was already briefly touched upon above. According to Moltmann, the relationship between God and humanity is "reciprocal" as "a living relationship" and not one-sided.[34] God, therefore, gives us his "impress," and we in turn put our "impress" on God: "If God is love, then he does not merely emanate, flow out of himself; he also expects and needs love."[35] In a similar vein, Berdyaev states: "God desired another self and a reciprocal answer to His love."[36] Berdyaev also denies the one-sided relationship between God and humanity, stating: "God is not the master, the lord, the commander. God's management of the world is not an autocracy."[37]

Second, Unification theism, Moltmann and Berdyaev all agree that God is not a God of mere simplicity but rather a God of complexity, in order that he may act and also be able to be acted upon by us. A God of simplicity, like

---

[33] Jürgen Moltmann, *The Crucified God: The Cross of Christ as the Foundation and Criticism of Christian Theology*, trans. R. A. Wilson and John Bowden (New York: Harper & Row, 1974), p. 222.

[34] Moltmann, *The Trinity and the Kingdom*, p. 98.

[35] Ibid., p. 99.

[36] Nikolai Berdyaev, *Freedom and the Spirit*, trans. Oliver Fielding Clarke (New York: Charles Scribner's Sons, 1935), p. 21.

[37] Nikolai Berdyaev, *The Meaning of the Creative Act*, trans. Donald A. Lowrie (London: V. Gollancz, 1955), p. 126.

Aristotle's "pure form" or "unmoved mover" that is completely actualized, self-contained and in want of nothing, would not be able to receive our impress. But a God of complexity, who is in dynamic motion within himself, would be able to receive input from us. Unification theism, therefore, proposes that God is a God of the dual characteristics of *Sungsang* (original internal nature) and *Hyungsung* (original external form) centering on his Heart.[38] This Unification proposal is basically trinitarian, because God's Heart, *Sungsang* and *Hyungsang* constitute the Trinity in the Godhead, as will be shown in more detail in Chapter 5 in the present book. Both Moltmann and Berdyaev, too, use trinitarian language to argue for the complexity of God, by saying that God has the dual characteristics of the Father and the Son centering on his love, which is the Holy Spirit.[39] By contrast, traditional Christianity, opting for a God of simplicity as a completely actualized, sovereign deity under the influence of the Greek notion of God, has unfortunately allowed its doctrine of the Trinity to be "defeated" in favor of the simplicity of God.[40]

A third common theological feature shared by Unification theism, Moltmann and Berdyaev is the doctrine that God suffers when he cannot find the values of beauty and goodness in human beings. The Unification understanding of God's suffering will be explained in detail in Chapter 6 in the present book. Both Moltmann and Berdyaev are well known for their assertions about a suffering God.[41]

Fourth, Unification theism, Moltmann and Berdyaev take the Bible as their primary source. When they take the Bible seriously, they are disinterested in, or even critical toward, the ancient Greek notion of God and the conventional Christian conception of God formulated largely under its influence. Unification theism is free from any Hellenistic influence, because Rev. Moon was a serious student of the Bible[42] and apparently never schooled in Greek philosophy. It is also interesting to observe that although Unification theism basically resembles the thoughts of Moltmann, Berdyaev and Böhme regarding the nature of God's love, nevertheless apparently neither Moon nor the author of the official Divine Principle books was familiar with these

---

[38] NEUT, pp. 2-12.

[39] Moltmann, *The Trinity and the Kingdom*; Berdyaev, *The Meaning of History*.

[40] Catherine Mowry LaCugna, *God for Us: The Trinity and Christian Life* (New York: Harper Collins Publishers, 1991). See Part One: "The Emergence and Defeat of the Doctrine of the Trinity."

[41] Jürgen Moltmann, *The Crucified God* and *The Trinity and the Kingdom*. For Berdyaev's understanding of God's suffering, see especially his *The Meaning of History*.

[42] For this, see Chapter 1, Section 1, Subsection 1 ("Sun Myung Moon"), Section 2 ("Interpreting the Bible"), and Section 3 ("The Hermeneutical Circle") in the present book.

Western thinkers. What connects them all is the most important source they have in common, the Bible.

God's Heart, as understood in Unification theism, is biblical, conveying the Bible's whole picture of God's love as our True Parent in a coherent and undistorted way. Although God's Heart in Unification theism may sound new to much of Christianity, it is not actually new in that it is biblical.

Chapter 4

God and the World

The Unification notion of God's dual characteristics as presented here may initially sound unfamiliar to many, especially in the Christian tradition. As we proceed in this chapter, however, it will gradually become apparent that this notion was already present in the Judeo-Christian tradition in a profound way, even though it may not have been explicitly recognized due to the predominance throughout Christian history of what is called "classical theism."[1] So, please bear with the rather unfamiliar terminology of Unification theism at least in the beginning.

According to Unification theism, God has the dual characteristics of *Sungsang* (original internal nature) and *Hyungsang* (original external form), which are the root causes of the dual characteristics of *sungsang* (internal nature) and *hyungsang* (external form) of each and every creature in the world. God's *Sungsang* and *Hyungsang* correspond to the mind and body of a human person, which are that person's dual characteristics of *sungsang* and *hyungsang*. God also has another kind of dual characteristics, the dual characteristics of Yang (original masculinity) and Yin (original femininity), which are the sources of the yang (masculinity) and yin (femininity) characteristics of creatures in the world. The relationship between the dual characteristics of *Sungsang* and *Hyungsang* and the dual characteristics of Yang and Yin is that while the former

---

[1] A useful definition of classical theism is given in Veli-Matti Kärkkäinen, *The Doctrine of God: A Global Introduction* (Grand Rapids, MI: Baker Academic, 2004), pp. 53-59.

are "direct" attributes of God, the latter are "indirect" attributes of God by being attributes of the former.[2]

Unification theism thus holds that God is "dipolar" primarily because of the dipolarity of *Sungsang* and *Hyungsang*, and secondarily because of that of Yang and Yin. This is what makes Unification theism quite different from classical theism, which teaches that God is "monopolar"[3] rather than "dipolar" because God is believed to be "pure act" (or "pure form") devoid of any potentiality, and also because God is referred to only with masculine pronouns due to God's masculine names such as *Yahweh* in Hebrew.

It can be surmised fairly easily from the above that Unification theism considers God and the world to be much closer to each other than classical theism does. The purpose of this chapter is to show that Unification theism may be more advantageous than classical theism in explaining the close relationship of God and the world, because the world—which can already be understood to be dipolar due to its being composed of "form" and "matter" and also due to its possessing both masculine and feminine characteristics—resembles the dipolar God of Unification theism more than the monopolar God of classical theism.

Classical theism, which does not consider God and the world to be as close as Unification theism does, has long played an important role, of course, to make believers humble enough to acknowledge the apparently great power of God's grace needed for sinful, finite human beings. But Unification theism may be more suitable for us today than classical theism. For today a new age of our spiritual maturity has come when we can no longer be considered to be sinful recipients of divine grace but rather God's close "partners," "friends" or

---

[2] For this whole paragraph, see *New Essentials of Unification Thought: Head-Wing Thought* (Tokyo: Kogensha, 2006), pp. 2-19; and *Exposition of the Divine Principle* (New York: H.S.A.-U.W.C., 1996), pp. 15-19. These two books are henceforth abbreviated as NEUT and EDP, respectively.

[3] The use of the words "monopolar" and "dipolar" regarding God was popularized by Charles Hartshorne and other process thinkers. God is "monopolar," when God is, as in Thomas Aquinas' theology, treated as "an absolute exception" to the "Law of Polarity" which teaches that "ultimate contraries are correlatives, mutually interdependent, so that nothing real can be described by the wholly one-sided assertion of simplicity, being, actuality, and the like, each in a 'pure' form, devoid and independent of complexity, becoming, potentiality, and related contraries"; by contrast, God is "dipolar," when regarded as no exception to the Law of Polarity. For this, see Charles Hartshorne and William L. Reese, *Philosophers Speak of God* (Chicago: The University of Chicago Press, 1953), pp. 1-15. Prior to Hartshorne, the "dipolarity" of God as well as of each and every actual entity was discussed by Alfred North Whitehead in his *Process and Reality: An Essay in Cosmology* (New York: Macmillan Co., 1929); corrected ed., ed. David Ray Griffin and Donald W. Sherburne (New York: Free Press, 1978).

"sons and daughters,"[4] who can also be considered to be equally valued men and women without any gender discrimination.

Section 1 of this chapter will introduce the Unification doctrine of God's dipolarity in the context of existing biblical, theological and philosophical traditions, and explain how this Unification doctrine can secure the close relationship of God and the world. It will also discuss the *Hyungsang* (original external form) aspect of God in some detail. Also dealt with will be the gender of God, a rather complicated subject, as understood in Unification theism and also, by contrast, in classical theism.

Section 2 will make a comparison between Unification theism's doctrine of God's dual characteristics of *Sungsang* and *Hyungsang* and classical theism's monopolar view of God as "pure act," in order to see whether Unification theism is more advantageous than classical theism in explaining the God-world relationship. The following advantages of Unification theism will be explored: 1) Unification theism can affirm the similarity between God and the world better than classical theism. 2) It can secure the unity of God and the world better than classical theism. 3) It can say that God is a personal God better than classical theism. 4) It can explain God's purpose of creation more clearly than classical theism. 5) It can offer a better definition of God's perfection than classical theism. 6) It can present a better definition of God's omnipotence than classical theism. 7) It can explain the unity of individual creatures under God better than classical theism. 8) Finally, it can, much to our surprise, be more compatible with the very important traditional Christian notion of the Trinity than is classical theism, because it believes that God is a God of dipolarity centering on "Heart," constituting the threeness or complexity of God, rather than a God of monopolarity or simplicity.

Section 3 will address the question: How do you know, as Unification theism affirms, that God is a dipolar God? This question needs to be addressed well, lest any dipolar theism, including Unification dipolar theism, should be deemed heretical, given the predominance of classical theism to the virtual neglect of dipolar theism in Christian history. We will argue for dipolar theism from the authority of God's revelation, like Karl Barth (1886–1968) does

---

[4] Karl Barth talks about human beings as "covenant-partners" of God in his *Church Dogmatics*, III/2 (London: T&T Clark, 1960). Jürgen Moltmann treats human beings as God's "friends" in the kingdom of the Spirit in his *The Trinity and the Kingdom: The Doctrine of God*, trans. Margaret Kohl (Minneapolis: Fortress Press, 1993), pp. 219-22. According to Sun Myung Moon, human beings are supposed to become "true sons and daughters" of God; see his "Proclamation of True Sons and Daughters and Freedom," sermon delivered at Belvedere, Tarrytown, NY, June 10, 1990. http://www.tparents.org/Moon-Talks/ sunmyungmoon90/SM900610.htm.

through the "analogy of faith" (*analogia fidei*), which echoes Sun Myung Moon's dictum of "absolute faith, absolute love and absolute obedience."

In the long history of Christianity, insightful theological traditions and/or theologians such as primitive Hebraic (rather than later Platonic) Christianity, Eastern (rather than Western) Christianity, Karl Barth and Jürgen Moltmann (1926–2024) were already, at least to some degree, addressing what appeared to be the disadvantages of classical theism, whether deliberately or not. What they did naturally points toward Unification theism, and they will be appreciatively recognized throughout this chapter.

§1. God's Dual Characteristics

1. Heart

Unification theism refers to the essence of God's love as "Heart," and it is the inner core of God's *Sungsang* (original internal nature).[5] Heart is defined as the "emotional impulse to seek joy through love."[6] There are two distinguishable, if inseparable, and successive aspects of love in God's Heart: 1) unconditionally living for the sake of creatures to warmly encourage and help them to reach unity for the realization of the values of beauty and goodness in them; and then 2) loving them in the sense of appreciating and enjoying the values they realize in them in response to God's encouraging help. These two aspects of love in God's Heart are respectively unconditional love and appreciative love, so to speak, and they involve "joy" on the part of God, although joy in unconditional love can be called the joy of "hope,"[7] and joy in appreciative love the joy of "fulfillment."[8]

As has been shown in Chapter 3 in the present book, God's Heart of love in Unification theism is very similar to the Hebrew notion of God's *chesed* (usually translated as "steadfast love" or "loving-kindness") in the Old Testament, the Greek notion of God's *agape* (translated as "love") in the New Testament, and also to the notion of God's "longing" or "desire" in the theologies of Nikolai Berdyaev (1874–1948) and Jürgen Moltmann. The reason,

---

[5] NEUT, p. 25.
[6] NEUT, p. 23.
[7] NEUT, p. 251.
[8] Sun Myung Moon talks about "the day of fulfillment" as the time of God's "joy." See his "True Parents Day from the Historical Point of View," sermon delivered at Manhattan Center, New York, NY, April 18, 1977. http://www.tparents.org/Moon-Talks/sunmyungmoon77/SM770418.htm.

as has also been shown, is that these biblical notions of *chesed* and *agape* and Berdyaev and Moltmann's notion of God's longing or desire each contain the two inseparable aspects of God's love at once: unconditional and appreciative love. Anders Nygren (1890–1978), however, mistakenly separated these two inseparable aspects of God's love into "unmotivated love," which he called *agape*, and "acquisitive love," which he called *eros*, as if the former alone belonged to God and the latter to the human ego.

Heart is indeed God's "irrepressible desire" of love, which "wells up from within"; hence God cannot but have object partners of love to experience joy, and this constitutes God's "motive" for creating human beings as God's "direct" object partners of love and also all things as God's "indirect" object partners of love that God loves through human beings. Thus "creation was necessary, inevitable, and can never be considered as merely accidental."[9]

2. Dual Characteristics

God's Heart of love was first expressed at the time of creation. Centering on Heart in its feature of "purpose,"[10] God's dual characteristics of *Sungsang* and *Hyungsang* had complete "give and receive action" for the generation of "forming energy"[11] to create the world with its dual characteristics of *sungsang* and *hyungsang* endowed in resemblance to the divine dual characteristics.[12] God's *Sungsang* and *Hyungsang* are thus respectively the "root causes" of the *sungsang* and *hyungsang* of each and every creature, i.e., of its "intangible, functional aspect" and "tangible, material aspect."[13] The Korean terms *Sungsang* and *Hyungsang* in God are usually translated into English as "original internal nature" and "original external form" (and *sungsang* and *hyungsang* in each creature as "internal nature" and "external form"),[14] and they are respectively mental and physical in nature.

The *sungsang* and *hyungsang* of each creature are roughly equivalent to the "form" and "matter" of each substance in Aristotle's philosophy.[15] While the *sungsang* and *hyungsang* of each creature can ultimately be traced back

---

[9] For this whole paragraph, see NEUT, pp. 23-24.

[10] NEUT, p. 41.

[11] NEUT, p. 8.

[12] NEUT, pp. 105-10.

[13] NEUT, p. 2.

[14] EDP, pp. 17-18. Strictly speaking, God's "original internal nature" and "original external form" are actually *Bonsungsang* and *Bonhyungsang* in Korean, where *Bon* means "original" in the sense of being the cause of the *sungsang* and *hyungsang* of each creature. Here, however, we omit *Bon* to say that God has *Sungsang* and *Hyungsang* (with the initials capitalized). This is what NEUT does also.

[15] NEUT, p. 11.

respectively to the *Sungsang* and *Hyungsang* of God in Unificationism, the "form" and "matter" of each substance can ultimately be traced back respectively to "pure form" (God) and "prime matter" in Aristotelian philosophy. The difference here is that while in Unification theism the *Sungsang* and *Hyungsang* of God are "homogeneous" as "two forms of expression of one and the same essential element" of God, in Aristotelian philosophy "pure form" (God) and "prime matter" are two entirely different ultimate origins independently preexistent from all eternity.[16]

Unification theism holds that God is always perfect as a God of the already perfectly united dual characteristics of *Sungsang* and *Hyungsang*, and that a creature, too, can become perfect as long as its dual characteristics of *sungsang* and *hyungsang* become completely united in resemblance to the perfect unity of God's dual characteristics.[17] By contrast, classical theism, equating God with "pure form" in the manner of Aristotelian philosophy, and having this God create "prime matter" out of nothing in a Christian manner, believes that only God is perfect in the sense of being perfectly actualized "pure form" devoid of any unrealized potentiality or matter, and that the world, which is composite of "form" and "matter," is always imperfect.[18] Plato's philosophy, too, is known to have influenced classical theism; and according to his philosophy, God is perfect as the immaterial Idea or "highest form" of the Good, and the world is imperfect because it involves matter.[19]

Since the creation of the world, God's Heart of love has constantly been at work. Centering on Heart, God's dual characteristics of *Sungsang* and *Hyungsang* have always been having complete give and receive action to generate "acting energy" (or "Prime Force"), which is distinguished from the above-mentioned "forming energy."[20] This acting energy is a unifying thrust of love from God to act on the created world for its unity. It encourages the dual characteristics of *sungsang* and *hyungsang* within each individual creature (e.g., the mind and body of a human being) to be completely united individually, and also encourages different individual creatures (e.g., a man and a woman) to be completely united socially, so that the complete unity at individual and social levels in the world may resemble and reflect the complete unity of God's dual

---

[16] NEUT, pp. 9-12.
[17] NEUT, pp. 244-45.
[18] Thomas Aquinas, *Summa Theologiae*, vol. I, part 1, ed. Thomas Gilby (Garden City, NY: Image Books, 1969), I, q. 4, a. 1-3, pp. 89-95.
[19] According to Plato, is God the Idea of the Good, the Demiurge, or both? This debate is described in Frederick Copleston, *A History of Philosophy*, vol. I, pt. I (Garden City, NY: Image Books, 1962), pp. 215-18. But Neoplatonism certainly equates God with the Idea of the Good.
[20] NEUT, pp. 8, 26.

characteristics of *Sungsang* and *Hyungsang* to "stimulate" God to feel joy in Heart when God sees and loves it. God's joy in this regard is the "purpose of creation," although it should not be forgotten also that when the purpose of creation is realized, there is an experience of joy on the part of God's object partners of love as well.[21] If, however, the purpose of creation fails to be realized, God cannot see such unity and only sees disharmony in creatures, with the result that God feels sorrow and pain in Heart instead of joy and happiness.[22] Creatures, too, feel sorrow and pain in this case, needless to say.

There is actually another kind of dual characteristics in God, i.e., the dual characteristics of Yang and Yin, and Unification theism refers to Gen. 1:27 as its biblical evidence: "So God created man in his own image, in the image of God he created him; male and female he created them."[23] The dual characteristics of Yang and Yin, however, are "different in dimension" from those of *Sungsang* and *Hyungsang*, for while *Sungsang* and *Hyungsang* are God's "direct" attributes, Yang and Yin are God's "indirect" attributes, by being attributes of *Sungsang* and *Hyungsang.*[24] Each creature, too, has the dual characteristics of yang and yin, and again they are attributes of its *sungsang* and *hyungsang*, which directly make it up as a particular individual substance.[25] This means that just as God's *Sungsang* and *Hyungsang* each assume both Yang and Yin characteristics, a creature's *sungsang* and *hyungsang* each carry both yang and yin characteristics.

Unification theism has a notion of "Divine Image,"[26] which is the same as the biblical notion of the "image of God." Just like the image of God in the Bible is both male and female, the Divine Image in Unification theism is both masculine and feminine, containing the dual characteristics of Yang and Yin. Even more importantly, the Divine Image, as can be seen from the above, also contains God's dual characteristics of *Sungsang* and *Hyungsang.*[27] What about the image of God in the Bible, then? Does it also have a dipolarity of spiritual and physical aspects? While classical theism's answer is in the negative because of its monopolar understanding of God, the answer from the prominent German Old Testament scholar Gerhard von Rad (1901–1971) is in the affirmative, as he sees the whole man, both spiritual and physical, in the image of God:

---

[21] EDP, pp. 32-36; NEUT, pp. 95-96.
[22] EDP, pp. 8, 81, 196; NEUT, pp. 251-57.
[23] EDP, p. 19.
[24] NEUT, p. 13; cf. EDP, pp. 18-19.
[25] NEUT, pp. 13, 110-13.
[26] NEUT, pp. 1-2.
[27] NEUT, pp. 2-19.

> The marvel of man's bodily appearance is not at all to be excepted from the realm of God's image. This was the original notion, and we have no reason to suppose that it completely gave way… to a spiritualizing and intellectualizing tendency. Therefore, one will do well to split the physical from the spiritual as little as possible: the whole man is created in God's image.[28]

At this juncture, let us deal with the genders of creatures. Creatures differ from God regarding the gender issue. God's Yang and Yin are "in perfect harmony,"[29] implying that God has a kind of gender neutrality, as will be further discussed in the final subsection of the present section. Many creatures, however, such as human beings, animals, plants and ions, have either the masculine gender or the feminine gender, for they are either: 1) "with relatively more yang qualities" or 2) "with relatively more yin qualities" in their dual characteristics of yang and yin as attributes of their own *sungsang* and *hyungsang*. A creature of the former type, i.e., with the masculine gender, is called a "yang substantial being," while a creature with the latter, i.e., with the feminine gender, is called a "yin substantial being."[30] A man, for example, is a yang substantial being because his mind (*sungsang*) and body (*hyungsang*) are relatively more masculine than feminine, while a woman is a yin substantial being because her mind and body are comparatively more feminine than masculine.

When God's acting energy encourages two different individual creatures to be completely united socially, the two are usually a pair of yang and yin substantial beings. There are, of course, many other creatures that are basically gender-neutral (e.g., mountains, rivers and desks), but they, too, participate in "the relationship of subject and object"[31] to make social unity through the encouragement of God's acting energy. This social unity among individual creatures, whether gender-oriented or not, is still considered to resemble and reflect the unity of God's dual characteristics of *Sungsang* and *Hyungsang* to realize the purpose of creation.[32]

---

[28] Gerhard von Rad, *Genesis: A Commentary*, rev. ed., trans. John H. Marks (Philadelphia: Westminster Press, 1972), p. 58.

[29] EDP, p. 18.

[30] NEUT, pp. 111-12.

[31] NEUT, p. 123.

[32] To explain it more precisely according to Unification Thought, when the inner unity of *sungsang* and *hyungsang* of one individual creature is followed by its outer or social unity with another individual creature, that process is a reflection of the "Two-Stage Structure of the Divine Image" in which the "inner give and receive action" between "Inner *Sungsang*" (intellect, emotion, and will) and "Inner *Hyungsang*" (ideas, concepts and laws) within God's *Sungsang* is followed by the "outer give and receive action" between God's *Sungsang* and *Hyungsang*. Strictly speaking,

When creatures in the world realize complete unity at individual and social levels through the encouragement of God's acting energy coming from the complete give and receive action of God's dual characteristics of *Sungsang* and *Hyungsang* centering on Heart, the world completely resembles and reflects the inner unity of God at individual and social levels to make God joyful. Here God and the world reciprocate with each other: God provides acting energy for the unity of the world, and the world through its unity returns joy to God. Joy is experienced in this kind of reciprocal relationship between God and the world. In the words of Sun Myung Moon,

> Why did God create the universe? God is the absolute subject [partner], but, when alone, He cannot feel joy. Peace, happiness and joy do not come when one is alone, but occur through reciprocal relationships. Thus, on His own, God does not play the role of creator.[33]

When this reciprocal relationship happens between God and the world, they unite with each other to be completely present in each other. Hence the complete unity between God and the world is considered to be realized in what the Divine Principle calls the "four position foundation" of: 1) God, 2) a subject partner, 3) an object partner, and 4) their complete unity centering on God; and this four position foundation is indeed "the realization of God's purpose of creation."[34]

The complete unity of God and the world here involves at least two other important things. First, God's acting energy, when encouraging the world to be united individually and socially, is not coercive. It is rather an encouragement of unity coming out of God's Heart of love. Nor does the unity of the world occur automatically because of the divine input. Rather the world creatively responds to it in order to reach its unity. Hence creativity is not only on the part of God but also on the part of the world. "Creativity" here can be defined as the ability to have give and receive action between the dual characteristics of *Sungsang* and *Hyungsang* on the part of God, and between the dual characteristics of *sungsang* and *hyungsang* on the part of each individual creature.[35] Needless to say, the creativity of the world involves give and receive

---

therefore, the social relationship of unity between different creatures is considered to reflect the unity between God's *Sungsang* and *Hyungsang* (NEUT, pp. 49-52).

[33] Sun Myung Moon, *Sun Myung Moon's Philosophy of Peace.* http://www.tparents.org/Moon-Books/SM-Peace/SMM-PhilosophyOfPeace-3a.htm.

[34] EDP, p. 25.

[35] NEUT has quite a detailed explanation of God's creativity and human beings' creativity on pp. 33-39, 169-72. But it is yet to develop a sense in which it can be said that non-human creatures, too, have creativity as long as they have the dual characteristics of *sungsang* and *hyungsang.*

action among different individuals as well for their unity. Human beings have the highest level of creativity amongst creatures, and it is "their portion of responsibility" as compared with "God's portion of responsibility," which is God's own creativity.[36]

Second, although God and the world are discrete from each other, the complete unity between them is made possible because of the dynamic nature of give and receive action of the dual characteristics. Dynamism, being far from fixed, is open for input or impress. So even if God is a perfect God with the perfectly united dual characteristics of *Sungsanag* and *Hyungsang*, God is open to any impress from the world as long as the give and receive action of God's dual characteristics of *Sungsang* and *Hyungsang* is dynamic. The dynamic give and receive action of each creature's dual characteristics of *sungsang* and *hyungsang*, too, is open for any input from outside. So is the dynamic give and receive action between different individual creatures.

Rev. Moon explains the second point by using a metaphor of two tuning forks affecting each other through resonance, because each of them has two prongs like the dual characteristics in question:

> I have drawn here a man with two layers which work like two [prongs of a tuning fork]. When you hit a tuning fork it vibrates with a certain frequency, and its vibration will automatically cause the second tuning fork to vibrate in the same way. The sound waves travel and create the same reaction on the second tuning fork… Then together the mind and body will make up one tuning fork and God will be another tuning fork.[37]

Moon also says that a pair of a man and a woman centering on God's love are like the two prongs of a tuning fork which resonates with another tuning fork symbolizing God:

> As you become a vertical pair, the same wavelength will travel to God and He will respond to your vibration. Why are men and women a necessary unit? Because men and women vibrating on the same wavelength create one tuning fork that responds to God's tuning fork. Then the vibration between God and man and woman will produce ecstatic joy.[38]

---

[36] EDP, pp. 43-44, 157-58.

[37] Sun Myung Moon, "Mainstream of the Dispensation of God," sermon delivered at Belvedere, Tarrytown, NY, November 19, 1978. http://www.tparents.org/moon-talks/sunmyungmoon78/SM781119a.htm.

[38] Ibid.

3. The Hyungsang *of God*

The notion of the *Hyungsang* of God, the physical side of God, in Unification theism may be rather novel and even unacceptable to classical theism, which believes that God is purely spiritual as the "highest form" (Plato) or "pure form" (Aristotle) without any physicality. Therefore additional words of explanation are needed.

The *Hyungsang* of God is the fundamental cause of the corporeal, material aspect of all created beings. Today's science knows that the physical world is composed of fundamental particles, which in turn emerge from energy. This energy is dealt with by science. God's *Hyungsang* is considered to be the fundamental cause of this energy; so Unification theism terms God's *Hyungsang* "prior-stage energy" or simply "pre-energy."[39] As long as Unification theism teaches that the physical aspect of the world derives from God's "pre-energy," one may get the impression that Unification theism is not actually theism but a kind of material pantheism. But Unification theism is far from material pantheism, because it does not consider God's "pre-matter" to be the essence of God but rather only an attribute of God, out of which the world was created. More precisely, the world was created out of God's *Hyungsang* coupled with God's *Sungsang*, the spiritual side of God that is the other attribute of the divine dipolarity.

At least during the period of primitive Christianity, God was fairly commonly believed to be corporeal as well as spiritual, because the Old Testament—which was used as the Church's important scripture for the first hundred years as it took quite a while until the New Testament was canonized—describes God's appearances in human form, and this description was taken rather literally during that period. Although Platonic Christian theologians such as Clement of Alexandria (c. 150–c. 215) and Origen (c. 185–c. 254) presented a new view of God as a purely incorporeal deity and came up with an allegorical interpretation of the Old Testament, these new approaches by them were not spread yet among the earliest Christians who tended to be more Hebraic. Thus the noted Church historian Adolf von Harnack (1851–1930) in his major work, *History of Dogma*, reports about "the idea of a corporeality of God" held by primitive Christians based on the Old Testament during this period.[40]

---

[39] NEUT, p. 8.

[40] Adolf von Harnack, *History of Dogma*, vol. I, trans. Neil Buchanan (New York: Dover, 1961), p.180, n. 1. Harnack reports that the idea of a corporeality of God in those days was held also by those Christians who were under the influence of Stoic materialism.

The Old Testament indeed describes divine appearances in human form. For example, God spoke to Moses "face to face, as a man speaks to his friend" (Ex. 33:11). God said to Moses: "I will cover you with my hand until I have passed by; then I will take away my hand, and you shall see my back; but my face shall not be seen" (Ex. 33:23). God "put forth his hand and touched my mouth" (Jer. 1:9). God had "a form that had the appearance of a man" (Ezek. 8:2). Therefore the Old Testament scholar Terence E. Fretheim (1936–2020) believes that God, while being spiritual, must have some kind of form within the Godhead: "To speak of God as spirit does not necessarily entail formlessness."[41] He further explains: "it is probable that Israel did not conceive God in terms of formlessness, but rather that *the human form of the divine appearances constituted an enfleshment which bore essential continuities with the form which God was believed to have.*"[42]

For Fretheim, the main point here is that God, a spiritual being who at the same time has some kind of corporeality, can never be an impersonal Infinite or Absolute. God is rather a personal God who can, and wants to be truly accessible to people in the world: "God… has determined to be present in the world and to God's people in such an intensified way… [and] in as personal a way as possible."[43] From the viewpoint of Unification theism, this means that God with the dual characteristics of *Sungsang* and *Hyungsang* can establish a very close, reciprocal relationship of unity with human beings who have the dual characteristics of *sungsang* and *hyungsang.*

Classical theism would still insist that God is purely spiritual because the New Testament says that "God is spirit" (Jn. 4:24). But the Greek word *pneuma* for "spirit" literally means "air" or "wind"; so, as the incorporealist Origen reluctantly reported, the Christians of his day still believed this *pneuma* of God to be physical.[44] Furthermore, as Origen admitted, the Bible never describes God as purely incorporeal, given the absence in the Bible of the Greek word *asomatos* ("incorporeal").[45] Even St. Augustine (354–430) reported that there still were Christians in his day who believed God to be corporeal, and that it

---

[41] Terence E. Fretheim, *The Suffering of God: An Old Testament Perspective* (Philadelphia: Fortress Press, 1984), p. 102.
[42] Ibid., p. 105. Italics original.
[43] Ibid.
[44] Origen, "De Pricipiis," in Alexander Roberts, James Donaldson, and A. Cleveland Coxe, eds., *The Ante-Nicene Fathers: The Writings of the Fathers Down to A.D. 325*, American ed., vol. IV: *Fathers of the Third Century* (Grand Rapids, MI: Wm. B. Eerdmans Publishing Co., 1951), p. 242.
[45] Ibid., p. 241.

was the reason why for years he as a Neoplatonist originally could not accept the Christian faith.[46]

If Christianity had not been as much influenced by Hellenistic philosophical schools such as Platonism, Neoplatonism and Aristotelianism as it actually was, and if it had remained within the Hebraic tradition of the Old Testament, the God of Christianity would have continuously been believed to be corporeal in some sense as well as spiritual, and the anthropomorphic language of the Old Testament would have been accepted in Christianity without as much hesitation and resistance.

It should be mentioned here that classical theism seems to have a fundamental point of difficulty regarding the status of "prime matter," the material cause of the world, as long as it adheres to its assertion that God is purely incorporeal, for it maintains that God created or caused "prime matter": "God is the cause of prime matter."[47] The difficulty here is: If God is entirely immaterial, how can "prime matter" be created or caused by such a God? St. Thomas Aquinas (1225–1274), the most influential classical theist, replied that God must have had an idea of "prime matter" before its creation.[48] If so, however, wouldn't it be better to acknowledge "prime matter" as an attribute of God, just as Unification theism says that God's *Hyungsang* is a divine attribute? Perhaps Christianity could have affirmed this, if it had not been so influenced by Greek philosophy.

---

[46] Augustine refers to the corporealist Christians of his days as "carnal men, unable as yet to form spiritual conceptions, who think of God as having a human form," saying that what they do is a laughable folly; see his "Against the Epistle of Manichaeans," 23.25, in Philip Schaff, ed., *A Select Library of the Nicene and Post-Nicene Fathers of the Christian Church*, vol. IV: *St. Augustin: The Writings against the Manichaeans and against the Donatists* (Grand Rapids: Wm. B. Eerdmans Publishing Co., 1974), p. 139. He also finds them among "these foolish deceivers" and says: "I was ignorant of that other reality, true Being. And so it was that I was subtly persuaded to agree with these foolish deceivers when they put their questions to me [such as]… 'Is God limited by a bodily shape, and has he hairs and nails?'… In my ignorance I was much disturbed over these things and, though I was retreating from the truth, I appeared to myself to be going toward it… and how should I have seen this when the sight of my eyes went no farther than physical objects, and the sight of my mind reached no farther than to fantasms? And I did not know that God is a spirit who has no parts extended in length and breadth, whose being has no mass"; see his *Confessions* 3.7. http://faculty.georgetown.edu/jod/augustine/conf.pdf.

[47] Thomas Aquinas, *Summa Contra Gentiles*, II, 16, 12. https://isidore.co/aquinas/english/ContraGentiles2.htm#16.

[48] Thomas Aquinas, Questiones Disputatae de Veritate, q. 3, a. 5. https://isidore.co/aquinas/english/QDdeVer3.htm#5.

4. The Gender of God

According to Unification theism, God's Yang and Yin are in *chunghwa*, "perfect harmony." The Korean word *chunghwa* literally means neutralization without either of the two aspects being stronger than the other. Thus God's gender appears to be androgynous and neutral. This must be the reason why Mrs. Hak Ja Han Moon correctly announced in January 2013 that we should henceforth address God as "Heavenly Parent" (*Hanul Bumo*), a gender-neutral term, instead of "Heavenly Father."[49] The Korean word *bumo*, composed of *bu*, "father" and *mo*, "mother," usually means a couple, a father and a mother, but Mrs. Moon here must have meant only one gender-neutral Parent because God is only one.

Even before her announcement, sometimes Rev. Moon himself also called God "Heavenly Parent,"[50] although most often he and his Church called God "Heavenly Father." He also reminded us in the final years of his life that the "Heavenly Mother" side of God has long been forgotten in favor of the "Heavenly Father" side of God, and that the "Heavenly Mother" side needs to be restored.[51] Andrew Wilson, a Unificationist scholar, attempted to do so in an illuminating essay, "Heavenly Mother," asserting that "today as we seek to realize the full ideal of creation, it is now possible to appreciate Her [i.e., Heavenly Mother's] femininity, with the goal of attaining perfect balance."[52]

Unification theism's assertion that God has aspects of Heavenly Father and Mother because of the dual characteristics of Yang and Yin can be well supported not only by Gen. 1:27 but also by many other passages in the Bible. The Bible, on one hand, talks about the masculine side of God: God is "Father" (Ps. 89:26; Isa. 63:16; Mt. 6:9, 14; Jn. 14; etc.); God is like the "father" of the

---

[49] Douglas Burton and Lymha Kim, "Hak Ja Han: Address God as 'Heavenly Parents'." http://www.tparents.org/Moon-Talks/HakJaHanMoon-13/HakJaHan-130108.pdf. There is, however, a careless mistake which needs to be corrected here. "Parents" must be "Parent."

[50] See, for example, Sun Myung Moon, *Cheon Seong Gyeong: Selections from the Speeches of True Parents* (Seoul, Korea: Sunghwa Publishing Co., 2006), pp. 734, 912, 1151, 1470, 2141, 2523. Henceforth abbreviated as CSG.

[51] Sun Myung Moon, "Jesus Came to Be the True Parents," talk delivered at Cheongshim Youth Center, Korea, September 14, 2011. http://www.tparents.org/Moon-Talks/SunMyungMoon11/SunMyungMoon-110914.htm. "How Many Parents Are There?" comment during speech at Hoban Indoor Auditorium, Gangwon Province, Korea, January 11, 2012. http://www.tparents.org/Moon-Talks/SunMyungMoon12/SunMyungMoon-120111.htm. "January 18 Is the Saddest Day for Me," talk delivered at Cheon Jeong Gung, Korea, March 17, 2012. https://history.familyfed.org/tf-sermons/january-18-is-the-saddest-day-for-me. "The Fall, God, Lucifer, Adam and Eve: Compilation of Father's Words." http://www.tparents.org/Moon-Talks/SunMyungMoon12/SunMyungMoon-120701.htm.

[52] Andrew Wilson, "Heavenly Mother," *Journal of Unification Studies* X (2009): 74.

prodigal son (Lk. 15:11-32); God is "king forever and ever" (Ps. 10:16); and God is "like a mighty man" (Isa. 42:13). On the other hand, God's feminine side is also described: God is like a "mother" at whose breast a child is quieted (Ps. 131:2), and like a "mother" who comforts (Isa. 66:13); God is like a "woman" who cannot forget her sucking child, and who has compassion on the son of her womb (Isa. 49:15), and like the "woman" who found the lost coin (Lk. 15:8-10).

In our society, human beings are considered to have either the male gender or the female gender; so androgyny in any human being is usually regarded as a baffling gender disorder. One would, then, have much difficulty in accepting a God of an androgynously neutral gender, unless one is a pagan with whom androgynous deities are not unfamiliar. But it may be that Unification theism, while staying within the biblical tradition, believes that God, and only God, has this special neutral gender, as the Divine Principle teaches, concerning its idea of the process of "*origin-division-union action*," that "out of God, the [neutral] Origin [of dual characteristics], two entities are separately manifested" in the created world to be eventually "reunited in oneness" as two discrete entities.[53] Perhaps this is the way God can completely unite with men and women in the world to realize God's own lineage of love through them.

According to Rev. Moon, God, an invisible being, created Adam and Eve as two different visible substantiations of God in order to substantially realize God's ideal of love through the union of both of them.[54] If Adam and Eve had not fallen, God would have been able to love Eve through Adam, who was God's male substantiation, and God would also have been able to love Adam through Eve, who was God's female substantiation.[55] In other words, Adam as God's male substantiation would have loved Eve, and Eve as God's female substantiation, in turn, would have loved Adam: "Had Adam and Eve not fallen, the idea would have been formed here that Adam on behalf of God

---

[53] EDP, p. 24. Italics original.

[54] CSG, p. 95: "Why did God need Adam and Eve? He had two purposes: first, to realize the ideal of love, and second, for the invisible God to appear after assuming a form. For this reason, Adam and Eve are the base and core upon which the invisible God can assume a visible form and establish a relationship with the visible world." Note that God here is still referred to with the masculine pronoun of He.

[55] This love relationship of unity between God and Adam, and between God and Eve, is made possible, because God has the *dynamic* dual characteristics of *Sungsang* and *Hyungsang* and Adam and Eve each the similar dual characteristics of *sungsang* and *hyungsang*, as was mentioned above in Subsection 2 of the present section.

loves Eve, and Eve on behalf of God loves Adam."[56] This close-knit, intimate relationship of love among God, Adam and Eve is made possible only because God, and only God, has an androgynous neutral gender due to the dual characteristics of Yang and Yin. Perhaps this explains why it can be said that human beings "were created as God's object partners who can receive the love of God's *direct lineage*."[57]

While Unification theism holds that God has an androgynously neutral gender as explained above, classical theism holds that God has no gender. It should be noted that classical theism never maintains that God has a male gender, either. Those who think so misunderstand classical Christian theism. According to classical theism, God has no gender whatsoever, for the reason that God as "pure form" is purely spiritual, having no physical body and thus incapable of having a gender. Hence C. S. Lewis (1898–1963) says: "God is in fact not a biological being and has no sex,"[58] and the Catechism of the Catholic Church states: "God transcends the human distinction between the sexes. He is neither man nor woman: he is God."[59] Classical theism, therefore, regards the biblical descriptions of God as both male and female as mere allegories. Nevertheless, classical theism has long referred to God with only masculine names and pronouns. The reason for that will be explained shortly.

If God, as classical theism asserts, has no gender by reason of God having no physical body, there seem to emerge at least two problems: 1) that kind of God can hardly be a personal God; and 2) the notion of God's lineage is unthinkable. Unification theism, by contrast, does not have these problems.

Why, then, did the Unification Movement most often call God "Heavenly Father" before the announcement of 2013? The reason is that, given the initial creator-creature relationship between God and the world, God can at least initially be considered to stand comparatively with more masculine characteristics, and the world as a whole with more feminine characteristics.[60]

---

[56] This is the present writer's own translation from the original Korean version, although CSG, an English version, more simply reads: "Had Adam and Eve not fallen, they would have loved each other, but they would have loved each other in place of God" (p. 2245).

[57] Again, this is the present writer's own translation from the original Korean text, emphasizing the term "direct lineage" (직혜) here because CSG skips the word "lineage" as it reads: "we were created as God's object partners who can receive God's direct love" (p. 92).

[58] C. S. Lewis, *God in the Dock: Essays on Theology and Ethics* (Grand Rapids, MI: Wm. B. Eerdmans Publishing Co., 1971), p. 237.

[59] "Catechism of the Catholic Church," 239. http://www.vatican.va/archive/ccc_css/archive/catechism/p1s2c1p2.htm.

[60] Regarding this, the Divine Principle says that God has "the qualities of internal nature [*sungsang*] and masculinity," while the created world has "the qualities of external form [*hyungsang*] and femininity" (EDP, p. 19). This means also that the relationship of God and the world is a

Hence God can be called "Heavenly Father," as *Exposition of the Divine Principle* states.[61] But, after the full realization of God's ideal of creation is reached, going beyond the initial creator-creature relationship of God and the world and also overcoming their gap which was widened because of the fall of human beings, God and the world will now be completely united; and the reciprocal and complementary nature of their relationship will make their gender role distinction much less sharp. As a result, God will no longer be addressed exclusively as "Heavenly Father" but rather as "Heavenly Parent." The announcement of 2013 marked this.

Most likely, the same is the case with the Bible. The biblical writers, too, were aware of the initial creator-creature relationship between God and the world in which God was transcendent and initiating in relation to the created world. This must be the reason why they used only masculine names for God—*Yahweh*, *Elohim*, *El*, *Adonai* in Hebrew, and *Theos* in Greek—as well as masculine pronouns, although they were also aware that God is female as well as male. Thus "the Jewish revelation was distinctive in its exclusively masculine pronoun because it was distinctive in its theology of the divine transcendence… despite the fact that Scripture [also] ascribes to him feminine *attributes*."[62] Classical theism in Christianity, therefore, addresses God as "Heavenly Father." In fact, the Bible has about 170 references to God as "Father." But the question is: Can classical theism come to realize, like Unification theism does, that God, who is both male and female, will eventually have to be called "Heavenly Parent" rather than "Heavenly Father"?

Perhaps the answer to this question is in the negative, because classical theism, which believes that God has no gender as a purely spiritual being with no physical body, in the end is not interested in asking what God's gender is to be. Classical theists are rather satisfied with simply accepting God's exclusively masculine names and masculine pronouns as seen in the Bible, which for them are not an indication of God's male gender but merely allegorical. On this issue, therefore, classical theists typically talk about two

---

sungsang-hyungsang relationship as well. This echoes one of the themes of "panentheism" (not pantheism) that the world is "God's body." On this particular theme of panentheism, see Michael W. Brierley, "Naming a Quiet Revolution: The Panentheistic Turn in Modern Theology," in *In Whom We Live and Move and Have Our Being: Panentheistic Reflections on God's Presence in a Scientific World*, ed. Philip Clayton and Arthur Peacocke (Grand Rapids, MI: Wm. B. Eerdmans Publishing Co., 2004), pp. 6-7.

[61] EDP, p. 19: "In recognition of God's position as the internal and masculine subject partner, we can call Him 'Our Father'."

[62] Peter Kreeft and Ronald K. Tacelli, *Handbook of Christian Apologetics* (Downers Grove, IL: InterVarsity Press, 1994), p. 98. Italics original.

things which appear to be in some tension with each other, but which are accepted categorically: 1) that God has no gender; but 2) that God is allegorically revealed in the Bible exclusively in male form:

> In examining Scripture, two facts become clear: First, that God is a Spirit, and does not possess human characteristics or limitations; second, that all the evidence contained in Scripture agrees that God revealed Himself to mankind in a male form.[63]

In this sense, classical theists continuously insist on the importance of referring to God with masculine pronouns only, even if they do not believe in God's gender at all. Perhaps, therefore, they will not be able to have genuine dialogue with feminists who assert that the feminine side of God's gender, whether allegorical or not, has long been neglected and needs to be restored.

At this point, we would like to make a statement on our use (or non-use) at least in this chapter of pronouns for the God of Unification theism who has an androgynously neutral gender. We will not use double pronouns (e.g., "he or she," "his or her," "him or her" and "himself or herself") nor slashed pronouns ("he/she," "his/her," "him/her" and "himself/herself"), which are cumbersome, although they may be intended to be gender-neutral. Nor will we alternate between "he" and "she," lest it be confusing. Nor will we use impersonal pronouns such as "it," "its" and "itself." So far, we have tried not to use any pronoun for God, only repeating the words "God" and "God's," even though it, too, may be awkward. We will try as much as possible to stay with this option in this chapter, except when using quotations from Unification materials of the pre-2013 period which already used masculine pronouns. In Korean, by the way, this option of repeating the words God and God's is far from awkward and is commonly used, in part because gender-specific pronouns were not developed until the end of the eighteenth century or the beginning of the twentieth century. English seems not to have a very good alternative for our purpose.

§2. Advantages of Unification Theism

From the preceding section it is quite clear that Unification theism secures the close relationship of God and the world through its idea that God's dual characteristics of *Sungsang* and *Hyungsang* are resembled individually by each

[63] S. Michael Houdmann, ed., *Questions about God: The 100 Most Frequently Asked Questions about God* (Bloomington, IN: WestBow Press, 2014), p. 42.

creature's dual characteristics of *sungsang* and *hyungsang*, and socially by the give and receive action between different creatures. The present section will compare Unification theism and classical theism to see that the former is more advantageous than the latter in explaining the God-world relationship. The following several possible advantages of the former will be explored.

1. *Similarity between God and the World*

Unification theism can see the similarity between God and the world better than classical theism. For according to Unification theism, God has the dual characteristics of *Sungsang* and *Hyungsang*, and the world, in resemblance to God, has the dual characteristics of *sungsang* and *hyungsang* on the part of each creature. Moreover, God's dual characteristics of *Sungsang* and *Hyungsang* and their interaction resemble the give and receive action between different creatures. According to classical theism, by contrast, God is monopolar as "pure form," while the world is dipolar, being composite of "form" and "matter." Classical theism, therefore, is not as able to affirm the similarity of God and the world.

Thomas Aquinas, one of the most important architects of classical theism, maintains that God and the world are similar, if not perfectly similar, in that both have something in common: being. According to him, this is the case because the world receives being when it is created by God who is its cause: "things receiving existence from God resemble him."[64] This similarity between God and the world, according to Aquinas, is a proportional similarity. Therefore one's description of the God-world relationship, which normally starts from one's knowledge of the world that one applies to God, is "analogical." "Analogical" means that a word of description linguistically has "proportional" uses for God and the world due to a certain order they have; it is not "univocal" ("univocal" means that a word has "exactly the same meaning in different applications") in describing God and the world due to their total similarity; neither is it "equivocal" ("equivocal" means that a word has "different meanings in different applications") in describing God and the world due to their total dissimilarity.[65] This approach of Aquinas is usually termed the "analogy of being" (*analogia entis*).

Yet this approach ends up creating a large gulf between God and the world, when it concludes that God as pure form without any matter is "limitless" or infinite, while the world composed of form and matter is "limited"

[64] Aquinas, *Summa Theologiae*, I, q. 4, a. 3, p. 95.
[65] Ibid., I, q. 13, a. 5, pp. 205-9.

or finite.[66] Thus God and the world do not belong to the same order, although this does not mean that their relationship is to be described as equivocal.

Aquinas' assertion that one's description of the relationship of God and the world is analogical, not being univocal nor equivocal, may be generally acceptable. But the distance between God and the world, as understood by his analogy of being, seems to be way too large. Like Aquinas, Karl Barth also accepts the concept of "analogy" as "unavoidable" in order to stay away from the false thesis of "parity" between God and the world and also from the equally false thesis of "disparity" between them.[67] Nevertheless, Barth differs from Aquinas and resembles Unification theism when he recognizes more affinity between God and the world than Aquinas, by seeing the "analogy of relation" (*analogia relationis*) between the I–Thou "relation" within God, which can be viewed as equivalent to God's dual characteristics of *Sungsang* and *Hyungsang*, and the I–Thou "relation" between human beings in the world.[68] This point from Barth will be dealt with again in a different context in the final section.

2. Unity of God and the World

Unification theism can secure the real unity of God and the world better than classical theism. For it maintains that God and the world can reciprocally act upon each other: God provides acting energy to encourage the world to be united at individual and social levels, and the world, in turn, gives joy to God when it establishes its unity at individual and social levels. This is made possible because there is dynamism within the give and receive action between the dual characteristics of *Sungsang* and *Hyungsang* of God, between the dual characteristics of *sungsang* and *hyungsang* of each creature, and between different creatures. As was mentioned previously, this is like the unity of resonance of two different tuning forks, each of which has two dynamically vibrating prongs (equivalent to the dynamic dual characteristics) that make the resonance possible.

By contrast, the monopolar God of classical theism as pure act or pure form is completely actualized and immutable; so this God cannot be acted upon by the world at all, while being able to definitely act upon the world. In the words of Aquinas, God is the "first cause of change not itself being

---

[66] Ibid., I, q. 7, a. 1-2, pp. 117-21.

[67] Karl Barth, *Church Dogmatics*, II/1 (London: T&T Clark, 1957), p. 225.

[68] Karl Barth, *Church Dogmatics*, III/1 (London: T&T Clark, 1958), p. 196.

changed by anything."[69] There is thus no reciprocal relationship between God and the world. This means that there can be no real unity between them.

Theologians such as Jürgen Moltmann are critical of this aspect of classical theism. As in Unification theism, Moltmann holds that there is a real unity between God and the world through their reciprocal relationship by which they affect each other: "Just as God goes out of himself through what he does, giving his world his own impress, so his world puts its impress on God too, through its reactions, its aberrations and its own initiatives."[70] Moltmann says this because he believes that God has the dynamic inner relationship of love between the Father and the Son through the Holy Spirit, which may be equivalent to God's dual characteristics of *Sungsang* and *Hyungsang* centering on Heart, and that the world, too, has the dynamic relationship of love among human beings through the external works of the Trinity.[71] As long as the inner trinitarian relationship within God and the relationship of human beings in the world outside of God correspond and resonate with each other, it can be said that God and the world have a real unity.

If the Trinity as understood by Moltmann and others, is equivalent to God's dual characteristics of *Sungsang* and *Hyungsang* centering on Heart in Unification theism, and if the Trinity, just like God's dual characteristics centering on Heart, is believed to encourage the world to be united so that the world may resemble the inner unity of God, it is a very significant point. It will be discussed in the final subsection of the present section.

3. A Personal God

One issue which cannot be ignored when dealing with the reciprocal relationship between God and the world is this: Is God a personal being like human beings, and can God have a reciprocal relationship with them? According to Millard J. Erickson (1932–), an evangelical theologian, God is a personal God as "an individual being, with self-consciousness and will, capable of feeling, choosing, and having a *reciprocal* relationship with other personal and social beings."[72]

---

69 Aquinas, *Summa Theologiae*, I, q. 2, a. 3, p.68.

70 Moltmann, *The Trinity and the Kingdom*, p. 99.

71 See especially Chapter IV ("The World of the Trinity") of Moltmann, *The Trinity and the Kingdom*, pp. 97-128.

72 Millard J. Erickson, *Introducing Christian Doctrine*, 2nd ed., ed. L. Arnold Hustad (Grand Rapids, MI: Baker Academic, 2001), p. 93. Italics added.

Unification theism accepts Erickson's definition. The God of Unification theism can self-consciously feel and willfully choose like human beings do, because God's dual characteristics of *Sungsang* and *Hyungsang* are like the mind (*sungsang*) and body (*hyungsang*) of each human being. This God can also have a reciprocal relationship with human beings, because God with the dynamic dual characteristics of *Sungsang* and *Hyungsang* and human beings with the dynamic dual characteristics of *sungsang* and *hyungsang* can reciprocate with each other. In the words of Sun Myung Moon:

> If God exists, what kind of relationship does He have with human beings? To have a relationship with human beings, He must be a personal God. And to be a personal God, He must resemble human beings. People have the attributes of mind and body. Then God, as their Creator, has to have similar attributes if he is to share with them a common purpose. This point marks the origin of the concept of dual characteristics.[73]

But the God of classical theism, who is pure act or pure form, not only looks unlike human beings with mind and body, but also cannot be acted upon by them while being able to act upon them. There is, therefore, no reciprocal relationship between God and human beings. Strictly speaking, therefore, the God of classical theism cannot be a personal God based on the above definition by Erickson. In fact, Erickson is a classical theist who believes that God "is spirit" and "does not possess a physical nature";[74] his position as a classical theist contradicts his own definition of God above as a personal being. Classical theists like him may still assert that God as pure act or pure form can think and act like a personal being, but if so, there cannot be reciprocity between God and human beings. Thus the God of classical theism can hardly be a personal God. Unification theism, therefore, can say that God is a personal God more profoundly than classical theism.

The monopolarity of God as pure act or pure form in classical theism is usually called the "simplicity" of God. The basic argument for the divine simplicity according to Thomas Aquinas is that if God were composite of items such as form and matter without being simple, God would have to be caused by these component items and dependent on them, which would contradict God's status as "the first cause" of all beings.[75] Therefore the doctrine of the divine simplicity, which is derived from God being pure form,[76] also denies

---

[73] CSG, p. 61.

[74] Erickson, *Introducing Christian Doctrine*, p. 92.

[75] Aquinas, *Summa Theologiae*, I, q. 3, a. 4, and q. 3, a. 7, pp. 79, 85.

[76] Ibid., I, q. 3, a. 1-2, pp. 72-76.

God other kinds of composition such as the essence-properties composition.[77] This means to say, for example, that God is identical with each of the properties God has.

Alvin Plantinga (1932–), an American philosopher in the Reformed Christian tradition, takes issue with this simplicity doctrine, because according to him it ends up saying that God is not a personal being. For when we think of God's property of being good, for example, "God isn't merely good, on this view; he is goodness, or his goodness, or goodness itself."[78] If this is the case, complains Plantinga, God cannot be a personal being but an abstract object: "If God is a property, then he isn't a person but a mere abstract object; he has no knowledge, awareness, power, love or life. So taken, the simplicity doctrine seems an utter mistake."[79]

4. *God's Purpose of Creation*

Unification theism can explain God's purpose of creation more clearly than classical theism. When the unity of the dual characteristics of *Sungsang* and *Hyungsang* in God is resembled and reflected by the unity of the dual characteristics of *sungsang* and *hyungsang* of each creature individually, and also by the unity of different creatures socially, God appreciates and loves it to feel joy from it. God experiences joy, by having an object partner of love resembling God. And, given the irrepressible nature of God's Heart of seeking joy through love, God necessarily and inevitably created the world as God's object partner of love. Hence the "Heart Motivation Theory,"[80] which explains God's purpose of creation. It goes without saying that when the purpose of creation is realized, the world, too, feels joy, by resembling God and also by being appreciated and loved by God.

Classical theism usually pronounces that God created the world so that it might "glorify" God (Jn. 15:8). This does not mean, however, that God aimed at receiving something from the world. God, who is totally actualized as pure act, is in want of nothing, according to classical theism. Therefore, even though "all things are said to be good by divine goodness," as Aquinas says,[81] and the world thus may glorify God, nevertheless it adds nothing to the perfection of God. In the words of the Angelic Doctor, "Since… the divine goodness can be without other things, and, indeed, is in no way increased by other things, it

[77] Ibid., I, q. 3, a. 3-8, pp. 76-88.

[78] Alvin Plantinga, *Does God Have a Nature?* (Milwaukee: Marquette University Press, 1980), p. 46.

[79] Ibid., p. 47.

[80] NEUT, p. 24.

[81] Aquinas, *Summa Theologiae*, I, q. 6, a. 4, p. 116.

is under no necessity to will other things."[82] Thus God did not have to create, strictly speaking.

In classical theism, God, who is perfect, created the world freely and not out of any necessity.[83] God's freedom is so absolute that it is not constrained by any kind of external determination or even by God's own nature. Therefore God could also have freely decided not to create the world. "God did not have to create… He freely chose to create *for reasons not known to us*."[84] This means that for classical theism God's purpose of creation is unknown. Or at least it is not clear.

Jürgen Moltmann basically disagrees with classical theism and agrees with Unification theism on this matter. As was seen above, he believes that God has the inner relationship of love between the Father and the Son through the Holy Spirit, and that the world, too, has the relationship of love among human beings through the external works of the Trinity. This solidarity of people in the world becomes "the trinitarian glorification of the Father and the Son through the Spirit," expressing their joy to give God "bliss."[85] When the divine love is "responded to" by the world this way, God "rejoices over" it; and thus, God "needs" the world.[86]

5. God's Perfection

According to Unification theism, God is perfect because God's dual characteristics of *Sungsang* and *Hyungsang* are perfectly united. Human beings each have the dual characteristics of *sungsang* and *hyungsang* in resemblance to God's dual characteristics, and as long as they fully unite their dual characteristics of *sungsang* and *hyungsang*, they each also can become perfect like God, even acquiring "a divine nature."[87] This may be supported by the Eastern Orthodox notion of *theosis* ("deification"), which is a participation in the triune God.[88] This perfection is possible, as the Bible says: "You, therefore, must be perfect, as your heavenly Father is perfect" (Mt. 5:48). Even non-human creatures, whether animals, plants or minerals, also can reach perfection at their own respective levels, as long as their *sungasang* and *hyungsang* are fully united.

---

[82] Aquinas, *Summa Contra Gentiles*, I, 81, 2. https://isidore.co/aquinas/english/ContraGentiles1.htm#81.
[83] Ibid., II, 27. 1-3. https://isidore.co/aquinas/english/ContraGentiles2.htm#27.
[84] Erickson, *Introducing Christian Doctrine*, p. 122. Italics added.
[85] Moltmann, *The Trinity and the Kingdom*, pp. 126-27.
[86] Ibid., pp. 58-59.
[87] EDP, p. 34.
[88] John Meyendorff, *Byzantine Theology: Historical Trends and Doctrinal Themes* (New York: Fordham University Press, 1974), pp. 186-88.

According to classical theism, by contrast, God is perfect, as perfectly actualized pure act or pure form devoid of any unrealized potentiality or matter, while the world is always imperfect, as it is composite of form and matter. The perfect God is also immutable as pure act, while the imperfect world is mutable.

Unification theism's definition of God's perfection can allow creatures to become perfect, as long as they reach the full unity of their *sungasang* and *hyungsang* in resemblance to God. It also can allow the perfect God to be acted upon by the world. The reason is that God's Heart of love stands behind the whole creation. God's Heart is channeled through the unity of God's own dual characteristics of *Sungsang* and *Hyungsang* to emerge as a unifying thrust of love which encourages the world to be fully united. Out of love, God's Heart wants the world to fully resemble the inner unity of love within God, so that it may become a good and happy place, which God also can rejoice over. God wants the world to be perfect, and God does not mind being acted upon by such a perfect and happy world God loves so much.

Classical theism's definition of God's perfection, by contrast, does not allow creatures to be perfect. Nor does it allow the perfect God to be acted upon by the world. Its God seems to be a God of sovereignty over the world rather than a God of love for the world. Its concept of God's perfection seems not to go hand in hand with the divine love. Theologians such as Thomas Jay Oord (1965–), therefore, observe that classical theism's approach has largely neglected the centrality of God's love in favor of other things such as God's sovereignty, even though God's love should be the center of theology because it is biblical: "This approach often neglects the motive [of love] God might have for relationship and the motive we might have to respond lovingly."[89]

In Unification theism, the perfection of God is entirely compatible with God's Heart of love and even grounded on it. In classical theism, however, the perfection of God seems not to be compatible with God's love. Unification theism's definition of God's perfection, therefore, may be better than classical theism's.

6. God's Omnipotence

In Unification theism, God's Heart is understood to have an "irrepressible" desire of love, which wells up from within. It is not only unconditional love but also appreciative love to seek joy. Because of the irrepressible nature of Heart, God necessarily created the world as God's object partner of love. Even after the fall of humanity, at which God's Heart grieved, and in spite of their

---

[89] Thomas Jay Oord, *The Nature of Love: A Theology* (St. Louis, MO: Chalice Press, 2010), p. 4.

continuous rebellion in human history, because of which God's Heart has been aching again and again,[90] God has always been showing the unwavering Heart of love for fallen humanity to restore them. In this sense, "His Will for the providence of restoration, the goal of which is the accomplishment of the purpose of creation, must... be absolute, unique and unchanging."[91] God's will, therefore, will eventually be realized without fail. This "irrepressibility" of God's Heart is a new definition of the divine omnipotence suggested in Unification theism.[92]

Classical theism, however, is preoccupied with God being pure act when it defines the omnipotence of God. Anything in "actuality" possesses active power, while anything in "potentiality" has passive and receptive power. Now, God is pure act devoid of potentiality; so, God's active power is infinitely great, while creatures composite of act and potentiality are partially active and partially passive, thus having only limited active power. In the words of Aquinas, "God, who is pure actuality unmixed with potentiality, has active power infinitely beyond all things."[93] This defines God's omnipotence.

An important point of difference between Unification theism and classical theism here is that in Unification theism God who is omnipotent can still suffer from the miserable condition of the world, while in classical theism the omnipotent God, who cannot be acted upon by the world, cannot suffer, thus being an impassible God.

Many have taken issue with classical theism in this regard, notably Jürgen Moltmann, who states that the omnipotent God of classical theism "who is incapable of suffering is a being who cannot be involved" and "cannot love," and that this God "would be a being without experience, a being without destiny and a being who is loved by no one."[94] For Moltmann, as for Unification theism, divine omnipotence is the omnipotence of God's love of longing for the world expressed through God's self-limitation and self-humiliation for the world. God's love expressed this way is omnipotent because "God is nowhere greater than in his humiliation."[95] Moltmann talks

---

[90] How God's Heart suffers according to Unification theism will be explained in detail in Chapter 6 in the present book.
[91] EDP, p. 155.
[92] For this new definition of the omnipotence of God in Unification theism, see Chapter 6, Section 3, Subsection 2 ("The Inner Suffering of an Omnipotent God in His Heart") in the present book.
[93] Thomas Aquinas, *An Aquinas Reader: Selections from the Writings of Thomas Aquinas*, ed. Mary T. Clark (Garden City, NY: Image Books, 1972), p. 143.
[94] Jürgen Moltmann, *The Crucified God: The Cross of Christ as the Foundation and Criticism of Christian Theology*, trans. R. A. Wilson and John Bowden (New York: Harper & Row, 1974), pp. 222-23.
[95] Moltmann, *The Trinity and the Kingdom*, p. 119.

about this more explicitly: "It is not God's power that is almighty. What is almighty is his love."[96] The Jewish theologian Abraham J. Heschel (1907–1972), too, believes that divine omnipotence means the omnipotence of God's love and concern: "The most exalted idea applied to God is not infinite wisdom, infinite power, but infinite concern."[97]

7. Unity of Individual Creatures

Unification theism maintains that the unity of God's dual characteristics of *Sungsang* and *Hyungsang* centering on Heart generates acting energy, which encourages different individual creatures in the world to be united socially (as well as the dual characteristics of *sungsang* and *hyungsang* of each creature to be united within itself individually) to reflect the unity within God. Hence the unity of God's dual characteristics of *Sungsang* and *Hyungsang* centering on Heart is the source of the order of the world. Individual creatures are called "individual truth bodies," but because they are always ready to connect with each other under the acting energy coming from the unity within God, they are also called "connected bodies" at the same time.[98] This topic is discussed elsewhere in considerable philosophical detail by the present writer.[99]

In classical theism, by contrast, God is not dipolar but monopolar, as pure act or pure form. Therefore, while God's pure actuality supremely acts upon each and every creature directly, it does not necessarily coordinate the unity of different individual creatures in the world. Thomas Aquinas, of course, believes that the goodness of God, which includes "order,"[100] is the source of the order of the world,[101] and that creatures, each composite of form and matter, can cooperatively act upon, and be acted upon by, each other in conformity with that order: "things tend toward the divine likeness by the fact that they are causes of others."[102] But he offers no real explanation of the reason why the goodness of God should be the source of order. The God of Aquinas is not a

---

96 Jürgen Moltmann, "God's Kenosis in the Creation and Consummation of the World," in *The Work of Love: Creation as Kenosis*, ed. John Polkinghorne (Grand Rapids, MI: Wm. B. Eerdmans Publishing Co., 2001), p. 149.

97 Abraham J. Heschel, *The Prophets* (New York: Harper & Row, 1962), p. 241.

98 NEUT, p. 118.

99 Theodore T. Shimmyo, "Individuality and Relationship: A Unificationist View," in *Explorations in Unificationism*, ed. Theodore T. Shimmyo and David A. Carlson (New York: HSA-UWC, 1997), pp. 127-40.

100 Aquinas, *Summa Theologiae*, I, q. 6, a. 1, p. 111.

101 See, for example, Aquinas, *Summa Contra Gentiles*, III, 64, 2 and 10. https://isidore.co/aquinas/english/ContraGentiles3a.htm#64.

102 Ibid., III, 21, 4. https://isidore.co/aquinas/english/ContraGentiles3a.htm#21.

God of ordered dipolarity; so it may be rather difficult for him to explain the reason for order.

Although he may try to trace the order of the world to the trinitarian relationship within God, following Augustine's doctrine of *vestigia trinitatis in creatura* ("vestiges of the Trinity in creatures"),[103] nevertheless, as will be discussed in the following subsection, Aquinas's doctrine of God (and classical theism in general) actually ends up neglecting the importance of the trinitarian complexity of God in favor of the divine simplicity. Therefore classical theism is unable to secure the unity of individual creatures to the extent that Unification theism does.

8. Compatibility with the Trinity

Unification theism holds that God is a God of threeness because God's dual characteristics of *Sungsang* and *Hyungsang* have Heart as their center. As will be shown in Chapter 5, Heart (the "motive of creation"),[104] *Sungsang* (containing the "Logos")[105] and *Hyungsang* ("pre-energy")[106] in Unification theism are respectively equivalent to the Father, the Son and the Holy Spirit of the Trinity in the Christian tradition. Thus God's dual characteristics of *Sungsang* and *Hyungsang* centering on Heart actually refer to the intradivine relation of the three persons of the Trinity, meaning that the Son and the Holy Spirit are united centering on the Father.

By the way, Eastern Christianity is of the opinion that the Holy Spirit proceeds from the Father (single procession), while Western Christianity asserts that the Holy Spirit proceeds from the Father *and* the Son (double procession). Perhaps Unification theism is closer to the Eastern version than to the Western one, although a detailed exploration of it is beyond the scope of the present chapter. The main point here is that God's dual characteristics of *Sungsang* and *Hyungsang* centering on Heart in Unification theism refer to the intradivine relation of the Trinity in Christianity theology, whether Eastern or Western.

But the question to be asked here is: Does the intradivine relation of the Trinity in the Christian tradition, whether Eastern or Western, play the same important role as God's dual characteristics of *Sungsang* and *Hyungsang* centering on Heart in Unification theism? In other words, does the Trinity in the Christian tradition impart a unifying thrust of love to the world for its

---

[103] Aquinas, *Summa Theologiae*, I, q. 45, a. 7. http://www.newadvent.org/summa/1045.htm#article7.
[104] NEUT, p. 24.
[105] NEUT, pp. 27-33.
[106] NEUT, p. 8.

transformative unity, so that the world may be able to reflect the trinitarian unity within God to bring joy to God? This way, does the Trinity also unite God and the world closely? Actually, Jürgen Moltmann would answer the question in the affirmative, because this is what he asserts, if from a Western perspective, regarding the role of the Trinity, as was seen above. He seems to keep some distance from classical theism.

Classical theism especially in the West usually does not recognize this important role of the Trinity. Augustine, for example, was so preoccupied with the simplicity of God as a Neoplatonic Christian theologian that he tended to emphasize the oneness of God even to the neglect of the dynamic work of the three distinct persons of the Trinity for the transformation of the world. In Augustine's theology, therefore, the absolute oneness of God's essence directly impacts the world with irresistible divine power and authority, and the Trinity is basically pushed aside to become an esoteric concept of intradivine relations irrelevant and unrelated to the world.[107] Thomas Aquinas followed this tradition of Augustine regarding the Trinity. His *Summa Theologiae*, therefore, begins by treating the oneness of God first and then moves to the Trinity, rendering the Trinity less important. This meant the "defeat" of the Trinity, according to Catherine Mowry LaCugna (1952–1997).[108] In fact, classical theism may not be truly compatible with the Trinity. Unification theism is able to appreciate the role of the Trinity more fully than classical theism, being more compatible with the Trinity than classical theism is.

Classical theism in the East is a little different. While the West pushed aside the Trinity as something disconnected from the world, the East historically understood the importance of the threeness of the Trinity for the world to a considerable degree. Greek-speaking Eastern theologians such as the Cappadocian Fathers recognized the particularity and concreteness of each of the three *hypostases* ("realities") of the Father, the Son and the Holy Spirit within God. The three *hypostases* were considered to be different from the Latin expression of *tres personae* ("three persons") coined by Tertullian (c. 155–c. 240), in that the latter only meant three masks or ownerships, which in their view were not particular and concrete enough.

Unlike Augustine and others in the West, therefore, Eastern theologians did not push aside the Trinity. They understood its role to transform the world, even giving human beings *theosis* ("deification"), if within the limits of classical

---

[107] This can be known from Books V, VI, and VII of Augustine's *On the Trinity* (*De Trinitate*).
[108] Catherine Mowry LaCugna, *God for Us: The Trinity and Christian Life* (New York: HarperSanFrancisco, 1991), pp. 19-205.

theism.[109] In the West, the *theosis* of created human beings is unthinkable because the Trinity is isolated from the world. Unification theism accepts the *theosis* of human beings through the Trinity, as it maintains that each individual human being can acquire "a divine nature" with a complete mind-body unity under the encouragement of God's dual characteristics of *Sungsang* and *Hyungsang* centering on Heart, as was seen above. Eastern Christianity, therefore, is closer to Unification theism than its Western counterpart.

§3. Knowing God's Dual Characteristics

Classical theism, which believes in a monopolar God, has been predominant in Christianity and still is. Therefore dipolar theism in general, and the Unification doctrine of God's dual characteristics of *Sungsang* and *Hyunsang* in particular, (more than God's dual characteristics of Yang and Yin), may still face strong objection and even be deemed heretical. So the dipolarity of God needs to be defended.

To defend the dipolarity of God, the present section will first deal with the useful approach of Karl Barth, who according to Pope Pius XII (r. 1939–1958) was "the greatest theologian since Thomas Aquinas."[110] Barth's approach is that if we become faithful and humble enough in front of God, the dipolarity of God will be given us as a revelation from above, and that it is how we can know the analogical relationship between God and the world. This approach is called the "analogy of faith," and it is quite widely accepted among conservatives. So the dipolarity of God should not be heretical at all. The second subsection will discuss Rev. Moon's approach of "absolute faith, absolute love and absolute obedience," which, like Barth's analogy of faith, can lead us to know God's dual characteristics through revelation. The final, third subsection will explain that both Barth and Moon also have approaches to know God from the world below, but they ground such inductive approaches in their initial faith-based approaches.

The present section aims to show that Barth is a good defender of the Unification doctrine of God's dual characteristics, not in spite of, but rather because of, his emphasis on faith.

---

[109] Lynne Faber Lorenzen has a good explanation of this in her *The College Student's Introduction to the Trinity* (Collegeville, MN: Liturgical Press, 1999), pp. 7-23.

[110] Quoted in Karl Barth, *Fragments Grave and Gray*, ed. Martin Rumscheidt, trans. Eric Mosbacher (London: HarperCollins, 1971), p. i.

1. Barth's Analogy of Faith

As was mentioned previously, Barth agrees with Thomas Aquinas that God and the world have an "analogical" relationship. But they disagree on how to know that analogical relationship. Aquinas holds that we can know it by applying our knowledge of the being of the world to God, because God and the world, as cause and effect, must have being in common. But Barth maintains that we can know it only through God's own revelation based on our faith. Aquinas' approach is usually called the "analogy of being," and Barth's the "analogy of faith."[111] What is noteworthy here is that these two different approaches have two different results. Whereas Aquinas' analogy of being ends up seeing a large gulf between God and the world, Barth's analogy of faith finds much more affinity between them.

According to Barth, human beings as sinners have no inherent ability to know God: "We are not capable of conceiving Him."[112] Our knowledge of God, therefore, "does not begin in ourselves" but "in God's revelation and in faith to Him."[113] "It is by God Himself—namely, by His revelation—that we are led to the knowledge of Him, that we and our knowledge do not stand outside and afar off but in the very presence of God Himself," and this constitutes "the real knowledge of God."[114]

What God's revelation has shown us as "the real knowledge of God," according to Barth, is that God is a God of amazing "love," who stoops down especially through Jesus Christ to have close fellowship with us, while at the same time staying always as a transcendent God of absolute "freedom" from anything. Thus God has the dual characteristics of "freedom" and "love," to which Barth devotes a whole chapter entitled "The Reality of God" in his *Church Dogmatics*.[115] Whether this duality of freedom and love, as understood by Barth, is similar to the Unification notion of God's dual characteristics of *Sungsang* and *Hyungsang* may be a subject to be explored in the future. But, in the context of his discussion of this duality of God, Barth lists quite a few similar theological suggestions from the modern period on the dipolarity of God,[116] including the seventeenth-century orthodox Lutheran idea of God

---

[111] Hans Urs von Balthasar, *The Theology of Karl Barth: Exposition and Interpretation*, trans. Edward T. Oakes (San Francisco: Ignatius Press, 1992), has an excellent explanation of Barth's understanding of the analogy of faith (pp. 107-13) and of the analogy of being (pp. 161-67). Balthasar, however, was a Catholic theologian.

[112] Barth, *Church Dogmatics*, II/1, p. 190.

[113] Ibid., p. 192.

[114] Ibid.

[115] Ibid., pp. 257-677.

[116] Ibid., pp. 340-41.

being both "*interna* and *externa*" and O. Kirn's 1930 suggestion of God having both "formal" and "material" attributes. Some of them might fairly easily be able to be related to God's dual characteristics of *Sungsang* and *Hyungsang* in Unification theism.

What is extremely important here is that Barth's suggestion of God being a God of dynamic dipolarity marks a considerable departure from classical theism. In fact, Barth was not entirely satisfied with Aquinas' notion of God as *actus purus* ("pure act").[117] It is amazing that such a conservative theologian as Barth was able to go beyond classical theism, whereas Aquinas, another conservative, always stayed within the realm of classical theism. This was possible because of Barth's emphasis on the authority of divine revelation based on our humble faith, whereas Aquinas emphasized the analogy of being. This is the reason why Hendrikus Berkhof (1914–1995), another Reformed theologian, remarks: "Only the 20th century witnessed a profound change, mainly through Barth's exposition of the doctrine of God"; and "This fresh formulation of Barth in the doctrine of God has exerted a greater influence than any other part of his theology."[118]

This formulation of Barth, however, does not see as much correspondence between God's own dipolar unity and the unity of the world as we would expect. Thus it may not be as useful for our purpose here. But Barth actually suggests another kind of God's dipolarity, which turns out to be helpful for our purpose. It is none other than God's dipolarity of the I-Thou "relation" within the Godhead, which Barth believes is "reflected" and corresponded to by the I-Thou "relation" among human beings, especially "between male and female" human beings.[119] Barth explains this I-Thou relation within God as a kind of dynamic relation of reciprocity: "In God's own being and sphere there is a counterpart: a genuine but harmonious self-encounter and self-discovery; a free co-existence and co-operation; an open confrontation and reciprocity."[120] Then he says that it is "copied," "imitated," "repeated" and "reflected" by the horizontal relation between human beings in the created realm, as well as by God's vertical relation to each human being.[121]

There are two points of clarification regarding this. First, by God's dipolarity of the I-Thou reciprocal relation within the Godhead, Barth as a

---

[117] Ibid., p. 264.

[118] Hendrikus Berkhof, *Christian Faith: An Introduction to the Study of the Faith*, rev. ed., trans. Sierd Woudstra (Grand Rapids, MI: Wm. B. Eerdmans Publishing Co., 1986), pp. 118-19.

[119] Barth, *Church Dogmatics*, III/1, p. 196.

[120] Ibid., p. 185.

[121] Ibid.

Western theologian means, like Moltmann, the trinitarian relation of love between the Father and the Son in the Godhead.[122] Second, when the "correspondence" between God's own dipolar relation of the Father and the Son, on the one hand, and the relation between human beings, on the other, is referred to by Barth as the "analogy of relation" (*analogia relationis*),[123] this analogy of relation is still based on the analogy of faith, thus being unable to be equated with the analogy of being.[124]

To explain the second point further, although Barth sees a correspondence between the inner relation of the Trinity, on the one hand, and the relation between human beings in the created realm, on the other, acknowledging Augustine's expression of *vestigia trinitate in creatura*,[125] nevertheless he does not say that God's dipolarity, as the inner relation of the Trinity, can be known from our knowledge of various relations in the world. For Barth, only God's revelation in the Bible, and nothing else, is the "root" of the doctrine of the Trinity.[126] And, in order for us to receive the revelation of God's Word, we again need "faith,"[127] acknowledging that we by ourselves have no real ability to know God. Hence the analogy of faith again. This point may be related to Barth's assertion, which Unification theism may not necessarily be able to agree with, that the reflection of God's inner trinitarian relation by the world does not mean to bring any added joy to the "joy" God already has in that inner trinitarian relation.[128]

By the way, Barth's statement that the Trinity is known only from God's own revelation is not unusual in the Christian tradition. Aquinas states the same thing: "It is impossible to attain to the knowledge of the Trinity by natural reason."[129] But Barth is very different from Aquinas, in that while Barth is quite aware of the similarity and relevance of the Trinity to the world, Aquinas is basically not aware of it due to his emphasis on the simplicity of the absolute and transcendent God.

---

[122] Karl Barth, *Church Dogmatics*, III/2 (London: T&T Clark, 1960), pp. 219-20, 328.
[123] Barth, *Church Dogmatics*, III/1, p. 196. See also p. 185.
[124] Ibid., p. 195.
[125] Karl Barth, *Church Dogmatics*, I/1 (London: T&T Clark, 1936), pp. 333-47.
[126] Ibid., pp. 304-33.
[127] Ibid., pp. 227-47.
[128] Barth, *Church Dogmatics*, II/1, p. 661.
[129] Aquinas, *Summa Theologiae*, I, q. 32, a. 1. http://www.newadvent.org/summa/1032.htm.

2. Moon's Approach of Absolute Faith, Love and Obedience

Rev. Moon's approach of "absolute faith, absolute love and absolute obedience"[130] is epistemologically quite similar to Barth's analogy of faith. Just like Barth's analogy of faith encourages us to be humble in order to reach the real knowledge of God, Moon's approach encourages us to have absolute faith, love and obedience in order to know God truly. Just like Barth's approach involves God's revelation, Rev. Moon's approach also talks about God's revelation, through which we know the truth of God:

> This ultimate life-giving truth... cannot be discovered through an exhaustive investigation of scriptures or scholarly texts; nor can it be invented by any human intellect... This truth must appear as a *revelation* from God.[131]

Moon usually speaks about absolute faith, absolute love and absolute obedience together as a group, and his three-term dictum might be equivalent to Barth's key word: faith. Although the three terms themselves have their own distinctive tones, they are almost synonymous in that they are all related to one fundamental thing: to lower yourself to live for the sake of others in front of God. And, if you do so, you will be led to know God. Through absolute faith, love and obedience, therefore, we can "enter the realm of God's love" and "become one with Him,"[132] and "we are returning to the original position of God at the time of creation."[133]

But what kind of God is it that we can know this way? According to Rev. Moon, it is a God of absolute faith, love and obedience: "God also created with... absolute faith, absolute love and absolute obedience."[134] In other words,

> God started creating all things based on absolute faith. He began to create so that He could have object partners of absolute love. Absolute obedience means that there exists no awareness of "self." It is a state of complete zero—a complete nothingness. Once God returns to nothingness, a circular movement automatically begins. Since everything is given out, and there is no more to give, God returns to the bottom. This has become the origin of the movement of the universe.[135]

---

[130] See the whole section of "Through absolute faith, absolute love and absolute obedience" of CSG, pp. 2517-27.
[131] EDP, p. 11. Italics added.
[132] CGS, p. 2522.
[133] CGS, p. 2521.
[134] CSG, p. 2522.
[135] CGS, p. 2518.

What is important here is that God, as the God of absolute faith, love and obedience, participates in "a circular movement" for the sake of the created universe. The circular movement of God means that there is "give and take action between a subject partner and an object partner" within God, i.e., that God has dual characteristics:

> For anything to have an eternal nature it must move in a circle; give and take action between a subject partner and an object partner is necessary for any circular motion. This is true even for God; having dual characteristics allows Him to live eternally.[136]

These dual characteristics of God are nothing other than the dual characteristics of *Sungsang* and *Hyungsang*. As was seen previously, God, when uniting the dual characteristics of *Sungsang* and *Hyungsang* centering on Heart, generates forming energy for the creation of the world and acting energy for the unity of the created world. In doing so, God is in "a state of complete zero—a complete nothingness" to live for the sake of the world.

Consequently, Rev. Moon's approach of absolute faith, absolute love and absolute obedience leads us to realize that God is a dipolar God with the dual characteristics of *Sungsang* and *Hyungsang*. This is indeed similar to Barth's analogy of faith through which to be able to know that God is a dipolar God.

3. Knowing God from the World as Well?

Regarding how to know God truly, Barth's analogy of faith is entirely opposite to Aquinas' analogy of being. It relies on God's revelation coming from above, while Aquinas starts from human knowledge of the world and applies it to God. Barth, therefore, sharply criticizes the analogy of being for letting us encroach on God instead of having God encroach on us: "The real encroachment on our part consists in resisting the divine encroachment that takes place in the revelation of the truth, in thinking past it instead of our adapting our thinking to it."[137]

This is not the end of Barth's story, however. In the end, he comes to recognize some value in the analogy of being, as long as it is within the context of the overarching analogy of faith. If the analogy of being is grounded on God's revelation in the analogy of faith, it can legitimately describe God, if in a limited way:

> This work of ours [i.e., the analogy of being], grounded on God's revelation, can become a successful work. Our views, concepts and

136 EDP, p. 32.
137 Barth, *Church Dogmatics*, II/1, p. 70.

> words, grounded on God's revelation, can be legitimately applied to God, and genuinely describe Him even in this sphere of ours and within its limits. For all their unsuitability, they can still be correct and true.[138]

This means that Barth admits that we can know God from the world as well, as long as we are aware of the priority of the analogy of faith over the analogy of being. Because of this, Hans Urs von Balthasar (1905–1988), a Swiss Catholic theologian, tends to think that Barth's "analogy of relation" between God's dipolar relation of the Father and the Son and the relation between human beings in the world is already a part of the analogy of being based on the analogy of faith,[139] although Barth himself may not go so far as to say so.

Unification theism, too, holds that while God's truth can genuinely be known through God's revelation to our absolute faith, absolute love and absolute obedience, we can also know God's nature from our observation of the world as long as we are aware of the priority of absolute faith, love and obedience. Hence *Exposition of the Divine Principle* states that we can know "the divine nature of the invisible God" by "observing the world which He created," and that given our observation of the dual characteristics of *sungsang* and *hyungsang* and also the dual characteristics of yang and yin universally present in the natural world, we can come to know God to be a God of the dual characteristics of *Sungsang* and *Hyungsang* and of the dual characteristics of Yang and Yin.[140]

When talking about our knowledge of the world inductively leading to our knowledge of God's nature, Unification theism uses a New Testament passage to support it: "Ever since the creation of the world his invisible nature, namely, his eternal power and deity, has been clearly perceived in the things that have been made" (Rom. 1:20).[141] In fact, Aquinas uses the same passage for his analogy of being.[142] Thus there is definitely a similarity between this aspect of Unification theism and Aquinas' analogy of being. But at the same time there is quite a big difference between them. For while this inductive aspect of Unification theism leads us to know that God is a dipolar God, Aquinas' approach concludes that God is only a monopolar God. The reason for this difference is that while Unification theism's approach from below is already grounded in, and presupposed by, its other aspect which involves

---

138 Ibid., p. 227.
139 Balthasar, *The Theology of Karl Barth*, p. 163.
140 EDP, pp. 15-19.
141 EDP, p. 15.
142 Aquinas, *Summa Theologiae*, I, q. 5, a. 5, p. 208.

absolute faith, absolute love and absolute obedience, Aquinas' analogy of being is not grounded in anything like the analogy of faith. In this sense, the inductive aspect of Unification theism is similar to Barth's analogy of relation, which sees a link between God's dipolar relation and the relation between human beings in the world. Aquinas' analogy of being, by contrast, is dissimilar to Barth's analogy of relation.

Our discussion in the present section has been largely centered on Barth. We are aware that Barth may have some notoriety due to his initial emphasis on God's utter transcendence from us. He referred to God as the "Wholly Other" in his book, *The Epistle to the Romans*, whose first edition was published in 1919 in the aftermath of World War I to attack theological liberalism.[143] This initially very conservative position started to change and become more moderate around 1930, and it was after that that he expressed his view of God's dipolarity between "freedom" and "love" in *Church Dogmatics*, II/1 (1940), and his understanding of God's dipolarity between the Father and the Son in *Church Dogmatics*, III/1 (1945) and III/2 (1948). Barth's initial position in *The Epistle to the Romans* had such impact, "like a bombshell on the theologians' playground,"[144] that most of his critics have paid attention only to it, not giving enough study to his later theological development.

The present writer wants to draw our attention to the profound significance of the growth and development of Barth's theology, by saying that paradoxically it was because he was a conservative that he was able to outgrow his own initial conservatism. He was not a conservative for the sake of being a conservative but an authentic conservative, and he so faithfully humbled himself in front of the "hiddenness of God"[145] that God's dynamic dipolarity was apparently revealed to him beyond the hiddenness of God. Barth thus started to talk about the stooping down of the loving God to stay with human beings as God's partners. Eventually, therefore, he even qualified his initial reference to God as the Wholly Other:

> The God of the Gospel is no lonely God, self-sufficient and self-contained. He is no "absolute" God (in the original sense of absolute, i.e., being detached from everything that is not himself). To be sure, he has no equal beside himself, since an equal would no doubt limit, influence, and determine him. On the other hand, he is not imprisoned

[143] For references to God as the "Wholly Other," see *The Epistle to the Romans*, 6th ed., trans. Edwyn C. Hoskyns (London: Oxford University Press, 1968), pp. 49, 326, 380, 386, 452.
[144] Karl Adam, *Das Hochland*, June 1926, as referenced in J. McConnachie, "The Teaching of Karl Barth," *Hibbert Journal* 25 (1926–1927): 385.
[145] Barth, *Church Dogmatics*, II/1, pp. 179-204.

> by his own majesty, as though he were bound to be no more than the personal (or impersonal) "wholly other."[146]

It is interesting that such a conservative theologian as Barth can be enlisted as a defender of the Unification notion of God's dual characteristics of *Sungsang* and *Hyungsang* through his analogy of faith, which encourages us to receive the revelation of God's truth. What he teaches us is that if we first impose our own concepts and ideas upon God, we will not be able to know God's truth about the divine dipolarity. Rev. Moon would agree with Barth's approach, although this does not mean that Unification theism agrees with Barth's doctrine of God on every point.

---

[146] Karl Barth, *Evangelical Theology: An Introduction* (Grand Rapids, MI: Wm. B. Eerdmans Publishing Co., 1979), p. 10.

Chapter 5

The Trinity

The doctrine of the Trinity, which is central in Christianity, is one of the most difficult and mysterious doctrines. For one thing, the word "trinity" is not found in the Bible. Although the New Testament refers to the Father, the Son and the Holy Spirit together as a group, nowhere can we find the word "trinity" to describe their relations. "Trinity" is a technical term coined in a later era. Theophilus of Antioch (c. 120–c. 185) was the first to use the word *trias* in Greek, and Tertullian (c. 155–c. 240) used the word *trinitas* in Latin.

There is another difficulty more disturbing, for the word "trinity" contains a numerical contradiction when it indicates that the Father, the Son and the Holy Spirit are each God, and also at the same time that there is only one God. The three are equal to the one. This is beyond intellectual comprehension. Hence the doctrine of the Trinity has been called a *mysterium logicum*. St. Thomas Aquinas (c. 1225–1274) determined that this doctrine belongs to revealed theology which is to be accepted by faith beyond reason.

The doctrine of the Trinity is thus truly difficult to comprehend. Despite its central position in Christian theology, it has tended not to be dealt with very openly. In the words of a contemporary Catholic theologian, "Among the doctrines and symbols of Christianity perhaps none has been subject to theological neglect as that of the Trinity" due to its received status as a mystery.[1] According to another contemporary theologian, one widespread reaction to the doctrine of the Trinity is "one of hostility, dismissal or

[1] William J. Hill, *The Three-Personed God* (Washington, DC: Catholic University of America Press, 1982), p. xi.

indifference" because this inherited dogma is "of no interest or relevance to the modern mind."[2]

We will, however, attempt to solve the mystery of the doctrine of the Trinity, first by analyzing why it became a mystery historically when Tertullian proposed an obscure middle position between the two opposite heresies of Modalistic and Dynamistic Monarchianism in the third century, and then by explaining how the Unification understanding of the Trinity, which is comprehensive enough to contain both heresies without any contradiction, offers a good solution.[3] By so doing, we aim to restore the original central importance of the Christian doctrine of the Trinity, which should never be abandoned as an unintelligible or troublesome thing. We must reach its essence and understand what it was intended to teach. If we do so, we will be able to see what Christianity originally sought to accomplish through this doctrine.

In the twentieth century, theologians such as Karl Barth (1886–1968), Karl Rahner (1904–1984), Jürgen Moltmann (1926–2024) and Leonardo Boff (1938–) revived the doctrine of the Trinity by making it more relevant to the realm of the created world and thus more intelligible to the modern mind. Moltmann and Boff even proposed so-called "social trinitarianism," which understands the relevance of the Trinity in relation to the realm of creation more than Barth and Rahner did. These were important developments from our standpoint of restoring the original importance of the doctrine. Hence we will assess and appreciate their views on the Trinity from the viewpoint of Unificationism.

Another significant development about the doctrine of the Trinity in the twentieth century was a greater appreciation of the femininity of the Holy Spirit

---

[2] Colin E. Gunton, *The Promise of Trinitarian Theology* (Edinburgh: T&T Clark, 1991), p. 2.

[3] The Unification understanding of the Trinity can be found in *Exposition of the Divine Principle* (New York: H.S.A.-U.W.C., 1996), pp. 171-72. It can also be seen, if implicitly yet importantly, in "Theory of the Original Image," in *New Essentials of Unification Thought: The Head-Wing Thought* (Tokyo, Japan: Kogensha, 1992), pp. 1-102. These two books are henceforth abbreviated as EDP and NEUT, respectively. The Unification view of the Trinity is just briefly touched upon in Young Oon Kim's two books: *Unification Theology and Christian Thought* (New York: Golden Gate Publishing, 1975), pp. 127-28; and *Unification Theology* (New York: HSA-UWC, 1987), pp. 180-81. It is also briefly discussed in Sebastian Matczak, "God in Unification Philosophy and the Christian Tradition," in *A Time for Consideration: A Scholarly Appraisal of the Unification Church*, ed. M. Darrol Bryant and Herbert W. Richardson (New York: Edwin Mellen Press, 1978), pp. 241-44. It is again briefly dealt with in Sebastian Matczak, *Unificationism: A New Philosophy and Worldview* (New York: Learned Publications, 1982), pp. 305-9, 418-20. Kim and Matczak, however, have two very different assessments of the Unification teaching of the Trinity, perhaps because the former has a somewhat liberal Protestant bias and the latter a Roman Catholic perspective; nor do they suggest any Unification solution to the problem of the mystery of the traditional Christian doctrine of the Trinity.

by theologians such as Moltmann and Boff. From the Unification viewpoint, this was a healthy development, for if, as Unificationism asserts, the inner threeness within God is to be substantiated in the outer threeness in the realm of creation where women as well as men exist centering on God, then the discussion of the gender concerning the Trinity would be inevitable. These days the femininity of the Holy Spirit is an increasingly popular topic. So we will discuss a brief history of the gender of the Holy Spirit as well.

§1. Why the Doctrine of the Trinity Became a Mystery

The reason why the doctrine of the Trinity became a mystery beyond intellectual comprehension stems from the Church's combat with the two different heresies of Monarchianism in the third century.

Monarchianism, in describing the relations of the Father, the Son and the Holy Spirit, sought to defend the unity of God and his sole rule or monarchy (*monarchia*). In so doing, it had its laudable motive of combating the error of pagan polytheism. Despite its laudable motive, however, Monarchianism unfortunately ended up being heretical. It had two different schools: Modalistic Monarchianism and Dynamistic (or Dynamic) Monarchianism. Adherents to the former included Noetus, Praxeas and Sabellius, while Theodotus of Byzantium and Paul of Samosata were among the adherents to the latter.

These two heretical positions can be described concisely as follows: Modalistic Monarchianism defended the unity of God by maintaining that the Father, the Son and the Holy Spirit are three different successive "modes" of one and the same God. As modes of God the three are all one and the same and equally divine. By contrast, Dynamistic Monarchianism defended the unity of God by regarding the Father alone as God and deciding that the Son and the Holy Spirit are merely creatures, although very close to God.

Modalistic Monarchianism, because of its teaching of the Father, the Son and the Holy Spirit as three successive modalities of one and the same God, held that God the Father suffered as the Son at the time of the crucifixion; hence this Monarchian school is also called "patripassianism." Still another name of this school is Sabellianism, named after Sabellius. By contrast, Dynamistic Monarchianism asserted that the Son, a created man subordinate to God the Father, received a power (*dynamis*) from the Father at the time of his baptism to be adopted as the Son of God. Hence this school is also called "subordinationism" or "adoptionism." By the way, Arius (c. 256–336) emerged later within this tradition of Dynamistic Monarchianism.

Although these two Monarchian schools had the good purpose of defending the unity of God in their own ways, their views especially on the Son sounded extreme to many in the Church. The former regarded the Son as one mode of God himself, neglecting his human nature, while the latter viewed the Son merely as a man, disregarding his divine nature. Therefore Christian leaders such as Tertullian, St. Hippolytus (c. 170–c. 235) and Novatian (c. 200–258) vigorously opposed both schools. According to Novatian, "the Lord is… crucified between two thieves [i.e., these two heresies], even as He was formerly placed; and thus from either side He receives the sacrilegious reproaches of such heretics as these."[4]

Historically, Modalistic Monarchianism became more popular than Dynamistic Monarchianism. Even so, the former was still a heresy in the eyes of the Church, which therefore sought to refute it. Tertullian's refutation was outstanding and accepted by the Church. In a nutshell, his refutation rejected both Monarchian schools by going beyond the two extreme positions to pioneer a middle position belonging to neither of them. As will be seen, this middle position turned out to be obscure and difficult (perhaps profound, if taken positively). In our opinion, this is the reason why the Christian doctrine of the Trinity became a mystery beyond intellectual comprehension.

§2. Tertullian's Doctrine of the Trinity

The trinitarian position of Tertullian became the orthodox formulation of the Trinity. The mainstream of the Church, being unable to accept either of the two Monarchian schools, thought that Tertullian's formulation succeeded in properly representing the Church by avoiding both. Apparently, he was the first to use terms such as *persona* and *trinitas* which became indispensable in later formulations of the doctrine. He was influential as the "founder of theology in the West."[5]

Tertullian first refuted Modalistic Monarchianism in his treatise *Against Praxeas*, which, according to a German Catholic scholar of patristics, "represents the most important contribution to the doctrine of the Trinity in

---

[4] Novatian, *On the Trinity*, chap. 30. https://www.newadvent.org/fathers/0511.htm.

[5] J. Tixeront, *History of Dogmas*, vol. I: *The Antenicene Theology*, trans. H. L. B. (St. Louis, MO: B. Herder, 1910), p. 304.

the Ante-Nicene period."[6] Tertullian complained that Modalistic Monarchianism favored the monarchy of God over his dispensation or economy (*oikonomia*). He asserted, therefore, that the Father, the Son and the Holy Spirit are not one and the same, as the Modalistic view suggested, but that they are three persons (*tres personae*) that are distinct from one another in the divine economy. According to Tertullian, this distinction (*distinctio*) among the three persons of the Trinity should be clearly understood and definitively established in the context of the divine economy in which the salvific activities of the Trinity historically occur. In this sense, the word "person" (*persona*), as used by Tertullian, assumed much more individuality than the Modalistic word "mode."

What we have to note carefully here, however, is that the Latin word *persona* in the day of Tertullian never meant what the modern English word "person" means, i.e., a self-conscious individual person. The term meant only legal ownership or a mask used at the theater. According to Tertullian, therefore, there is no separation (*separatio*) among the three persons (*tres personae*), although there is a clear distinction (*distinctio*) among them, given the divine economy. Tertullian decided that the three persons are of one substance (*una substantia*). In this way he also criticized Dynamistic Monarchianism's error of separating the three from one another.

To explain his own position further, Tertullian gave illustrations from nature, referring to the relations of root, tree and fruit, of fountain, river and stream, and of sun, ray and apex.[7] In each of these cases, the three elements involved are distinctly three by procession, but they are inseparable from one another because they are correlatively joined. To these relations he likened those of the three persons, which he called *trinitas*, Trinity.

§3. The Doctrine of the Trinity after Tertullian

The trinitarian formulation presented by Tertullian determined the course of the development of the doctrine of the Trinity for centuries to come. The terms he coined, *una substantia* and *tres personae*, had a considerable influence on the Councils of Nicea (325) and of Constantinople (381), the first two

---

[6] Johannes Quasten, *Patrology*, vol. II: *The Ante-Nicene Literature after Irenaeus* (Westminster, MD: Christian Classics, Inc., 1986), p. 285. For Tertullian's *Against Prexeas*, see "Against Praxeas," in Alexander Roberts, James Donaldson, and A. Cleveland Coxe, eds., *The Ante-Nicene Fathers: The Writings of the Fathers Down to A.D. 325*, American ed., vol. III: *Latic Christianity: Its Founder, Tertullian* (Grand Rapids, MI: Wm. B. Eerdmans Publishing Co., 1973), pp. 597-627.

[7] Tertullian, "Against Praxeas," pp. 602-3.

Ecumenical Councils in the history of Christianity. The Council of Nicea affirmed the consubstantiality (*homoousion*) of the Son with the Father against Arianism, and the Council of Constantinople in turn upheld the consubstantiality of the Holy Spirit with the Father and the Son against Semi-Arianism. The Cappadocian Fathers, i.e., St. Basil of Caesarea (330–379), St. Gregory of Nazianzus (c. 329–390) and St. Gregory of Nyssa (c. 335–c. 395), were instrumental in the decision of the Council of Constantinople.

In support of the orthodoxy of the *homoousion* of the Father, the Son and the Holy Spirit, the Cappadocian Fathers by the end of the fourth century made a distinction between the two similar Greek words of *ousia* and *hypostasis* to have them roughly mean *substantia* and *persona* in Tertullian's terminology, respectively; they made this distinction because they wanted to maintain, in the spirit of unity between East and West, that God has only one *ousia* (*substantia* in Latin) but three *hypostases* (*personae* in Latin).[8] Strictly speaking, however, what they meant by three *hypostases* in the East and what Tertullian meant by three *personae* in the West were not completely the same: the three *hypostases* were understood to be three different players that are a little more individual and concrete than the three *personae*, thus leaning toward what is social trinitarianism with more emphasis on the threeness in the East vis-à-vis what is Latin trinitarianism with more emphasis on the oneness. In any case, although since the time of the Cappadocian Fathers many people have made various statements about the Trinity, nevertheless the fundamental trinitarian teaching about one substance (or *ousia*) and three persons (or *hypostases*) has never altered.

But what does it really mean to say that God has *one* substance, while there are *three distinct* persons? How can there be three distinct persons, each one God, and yet be just one God? As was noted previously, it seems that this notion cannot escape the apparent numerical contradiction between the threeness and the oneness of God. Neither of the two schools of Monarchianism had this problem. The problem was created because Tertullian avoided both Monarchian schools and came up with a middle position which

---

[8] See, for example, Basil of Caesarea, "Letter 214": "I shall state that *ousia* has the same relation to *hypostasis* as the common has to the particular. Every one of us both shares in existence by the common term of essence (*ousia*) and by his own properties is such an one and such an one. In the same manner, in the matter in question, the term *ousia* is common, like goodness, or Godhead, or any similar attribute; while *hypostasis* is contemplated in the special property of Fatherhood, Sonship, or the power to sanctify. If then they describe the Persons as being without *hypostasis*, the statement is *per se* absurd; but if they concede that the Persons exist in real *hypostasis*, as they acknowledge, let them so reckon them that the principle of the *homoousion* may be preserved in the unity of the Godhead." https://www.newadvent.org/fathers/3202214.htm.

turned out to be rather unintelligible. Thus Millard J. Erickson (1932–), a prolific American evangelical writer, admits: "By way of a quick evaluation, we note that there is something of a vagueness about this view of the Trinity [by Tertullian]. Any effort to come up with a more exact understanding of just what it means will prove disappointing."[9]

At least three significant attempts were made during the early centuries of Christian history to solve the problem of the Trinity's numerical contradiction. Yet each one ended up compromising the real distinction among the three persons by securing some kind of additional unity among them in view of the one substance of God. Therefore each of these attempts ended up with a tendency toward Modalistic Monarchianism, leading to a strong tendency especially in the Latin tradition to emphasize the intradivine unity of the three persons in God. Hence none of them really succeeded in solving the problem. Let us briefly look at these attempts, however.

One attempt to address the problem, put forth by St. Athanasius (c. 296–373), the Cappadocian Fathers and St. Augustine (354–430), was to propose the mutual indwelling or interpenetration of the three persons. According to this, one person is as inevitably in the other two as they are in the one. This mutual indwelling of the persons was later called *perichoresis* in Greek and *circumincessio* (or *circuminsessio*) in Latin. This proposal emerged from mysticism rather than from any serious logical thinking of the matter.

Second, as a natural result of the first proposal, medieval theologians after Augustine suggested that although God's three main external operations of creation, redemption and sanctification may be attributed primarily to the Father, the Son and the Holy Spirit, respectively, nevertheless these external operations of the Trinity are indivisible (*opera trinitatis ad extra indivisa sunt*), so that all the three persons are involved in each of those operations. But this suggestion makes it difficult for us to have any understanding of the real distinction of the three persons.

A third attempt to address the problem in question was Augustine's doctrine of relations in the Trinity, which encourages us to say that in God there are not three particular persons but only one person:

> Because the Father is a person, the Son a person, and the Holy Spirit a person, there are assuredly three persons; because the Father is God, the Son God, the Holy Spirit God, why, therefore, are there not three gods? Or since these three together are one God on account of their

[9] Millard J. Erickson, *Introducing Christian Doctrine*, 3rd ed., ed. L. Arnold Hustad (Grand Rapids, MI: Baker Academic, 2015), p. 113.

> ineffable union, why are they not also one person, so that we cannot say three persons, even though we call each singly a person, just as we do not say three gods, even though we call each singly God, whether the Father, or the Son, or the Holy Spirit?[10]

This approach by Augustine clearly had a strong tendency toward Modalistic Monarchianism, even though he himself was aware that he should be on guard against that heresy.

§4. The Unification Doctrine of the Trinity

How does Unificationism propose to solve the difficult mystery of the traditional doctrine of the Trinity? Tertullian avoided both heresies of Modalistic and Dynamistic Monarchianism to take an obscure middle position between them, but Unificationism *contains* both schools of Monarchianism without any contradiction in its comprehensive doctrine of the Trinity. This is how the mystery of the traditional doctrine of the Trinity can be solved.

1. Containing Both Schools of Monarchianism

First of all, the Unification doctrine of the Trinity contains Modalistic Monarchianism. Recall that this Monarchian school regarded the Father, the Son and the Holy Spirit as three modes of God which are all divine. In a similar vein, the Unification doctrine of the Trinity talks about three main attributes of God which are all divine: Heart, *Sungsang* (original internal nature) and *Hyungsang* (original external form).[11] They are deemed equivalent to the Father, the Son and the Holy Spirit within God. First, God's Heart is equivalent to the Father, because it, as the irrepressible "emotional impulse to seek joy through love," makes it "absolutely necessary" to create human beings and all things as his object partners of love.[12] Next, God's *Sungsang* is equivalent to the Son, because it as "the mind of God" entails the formation of the "Logos" within itself.[13] Finally, God's *Hyungsang* is equivalent to the Holy Spirit, because it is "pre-energy" in God.[14] When within God the *Sungsang* (the Son) and the *Hyungsang* (the Holy Spirit) engage in "give and receive action" centering on

[10] Augustine, *The Trinity*, trans. Stephen McKenna (Washington, DC: Catholic University of America Press, 1963), 7.4.8, p. 232.

[11] To get acquainted with these terms, read NEUT, pp. 2-12, 23-33.

[12] NEUT, pp. 23-24.

[13] NEUT, pp. 3, 27-28.

[14] NEUT, p. 8.

Heart (the Father), they form a "union."[15] The present writer calls this union of the three within God the "inner Trinity."[16] This threeness within God is acknowledged also in the Divine Principle: "God is the one absolute reality in whom the dual characteristics interact in harmony; therefore, He is a Being of the number three."[17]

At the same time, the Unification doctrine of the Trinity also contains Dynamistic Monarchianism. As was previously seen, Dynamistic Monarchianism regarded God alone as the Father, saying that the Son and the Holy Spirit are merely creatures. In much the same way, Unificationism treats God alone as the Father and places perfected Adam and perfected Eve outside of God as the Son and the Holy Spirit in the realm of creation. When perfected Adam (the Son) and perfected Eve (the Holy Spirit) engage in give and receive action to form a harmonious union centering on God (the Father), these three constitute what the present writer calls the "outer Trinity."[18] And perfected Adam and Eve are also called the "True Parents of humankind" centering on God in the outer Trinity. Regarding this, the Divine Principle says:

> Originally, God's purpose for creating Adam and Eve was to form a[n] [outer] trinity by raising them to be the True Parents of humankind united in harmonious oneness as husband and wife centered on God in a four position foundation. If Adam and Eve had not fallen, but had formed this [outer] trinity with God and become the True Parents who could multiply good children, their descendants would have also become good husbands and wives with God as the center of their lives. Each couple would thus have formed a trinity with God.[19]

Despite this equivalence between the Unification notion of the outer Trinity and Dynamistic Monarchianism, however, it should be noted that the two traditions significantly differ from each other regarding the creaturely status of the Son and the Holy Spirit. For the sense in which Unificationism says that perfected Adam (the Son) and perfected Eve (the Holy Spirit) of the outer Trinity are creatures is quite different from the sense in which Dynamistic Monarchianism says that the Son and the Holy Spirit are creatures. According to Unificationism, perfected Adam and Eve of the outer Trinity are created

---

[15] NEUT, p. 41.

[16] For the terms "inner Trinity" and "outer Trinity" coined by the present writer, see Theodore T. Shimmyo, "Unification Christology: A Fulfillment of Niceno-Chalcedonian Orthodoxy," in *Explorations in Unificationism*, ed. Theodore T. Shimmyo and David A. Carlson (New York: HSA-UWC, 1997), pp. 30-31.

[17] EDP, p. 41.

[18] Shimmyo, "Unification Christology: A Fulfillment of Niceno-Chalcedonian Orthodoxy," pp. 30-31.

[19] EDP, p. 172.

human beings who are perfected with full divinity in complete unity with God. By contrast, the Son and the Holy Spirit in Dynamistic Monarchianism are creatures with no divinity, no matter how great they are. The reason for this difference will be explained in the following subsection.

2. Unification Ontology of Complete Unity of God and the World

The reason for this difference comes from the fact that Unificationism has a unique theological ontology of complete unity between God and the world, whereas Dynamistic Monarchainism (as well as Christianity in general) has no such ontology.

According to Unificationism, God has the dual characteristics of *Sungsang* (original internal nature) and *Hyungsang* (original external form), and the created world in resemblance to God has the similar dual characteristics of *sungsang* (internal nature) and *hyungsang* (external form). When God's *Sungsang* and *Hyungsang* have their give and receive action centering on Heart to completely unite with each other, "acting energy" (or "Prime Force")[20] is generated in God to encourage the dual characteristics of *sungsang* and *hyungsang* of each created being to completely unite with each other at the individual level, and this acting energy of God also encourages two or more created beings to completely unite with each other at the social level. When complete unity in the created world is thus made at the individual and social levels, it completely reflects the complete unity of God's own dual characteristics of *Sungsang* and *Hyungsang*, enabling God to feel "joy" in his Heart from the stimulation of this reflection and thus having God's "purpose of creation" realized.[21] In this way, God and the world mutually act upon each other, and it is how the complete unity of God and the world is realized.[22]

When it comes to perfected Adam and Eve as human beings who each have completely realized the purpose of creation at the individual level, their respective complete unity of mind and body, i.e., of the dual characteristics of *sungsang* and *hyungsang*, completely reflects and resembles God's dual characteristics of *Sungsang* and *Hyungsang*, so they each acquire full divinity.[23] The full divinity of human beings may sound unheard of. But full divinity here refers to the state of complete unity of the dual characteristics in total

---

[20] NEUT, pp. 8, 26.

[21] EDP, p. 33.

[22] The complete unity of God and the world is treated as one of the eight advantages of Unification theism based on its notion of God's dual characteristics of *Sungsang* and *Hyungsang*, in Chapter 4, Section 2 ("Advantages of Unification Theism") in the present book.

[23] EDP, pp. 34, 164.

investment of love and sacrifice for the sake of others, as will be discussed also in Chapter 9 on Christology. God certainly has it already, and human beings, too, can have it because they were created in the image of God to completely resemble and reflect God through the dual characteristics in total investment of love and sacrifice for others. By contrast, Dynamistic Monarchianism, not having this kind of theological ontology of complete unity between God and creation due to its lack of knowledge of anything like the Unification idea of God's dual characteristics of *Sungsang* and *Hyungsang*, regards the Son and the Holy Spirit as creatures without any divinity. Because of this fundamental ontological difference between the two traditions, perfected Adam and Eve of the outer Trinity in Unificationism, in spite of their creaturely discreteness from God, are each fully divine and exceedingly much closer to God than are the Son and the Holy Spirit in Dynamistic Monarchianism.

And, if perfected Adam and Eve of the outer Trinity completely unite with each other at the social level, this complete social unity, too, reflects and resembles God's dual characteristics of *Sungsang* and *Hyungsang*, realizing the purpose of creation at the social level. In that state, perfected Adam and Eve become an ideal couple that is fully divine. This means that the outer Trinity, as the outer substantial manifestation of the inner Trinity as a result of God's act of creation, is fully divine in its complete unity with the inner Trinity, although it is undoubtedly discrete from the inner Trinity.

In the Unification doctrine of the Trinity, therefore, it is not only the three members of the inner Trinity (God's Heart, *Sungsang* and *Hyungsang*) but also the three members of the outer Trinity (God, perfected Adam and perfected Eve) as well that are fully divine. But, although perfected Adam and Eve of the outer Trinity are fully divine, they are human beings who have perfected the purpose of creation. They are not Gods. It is clear, therefore, that Unificationism does not allow for tritheism.

3. Jesus' Death and the Doctrine of the Trinity

We have learned that the Church adopted Tertullian's middle position between Modalistic and Dynamistic Monarchianism. The question remains: Why this adoption? From the viewpoint of Unificationism, theologians such as Tertullian had no choice but to take such a middle position because Jesus, who was supposed to be the first to be in the position of perfected Adam, prematurely died on the cross 2,000 years ago, thereby forming only what the Divine Principle calls the "spiritual Trinity": "the resurrected Jesus [after his death] and the Holy Spirit in oneness with God could form only a spiritual trinity."[24] This spiritual Trinity can be located somewhere between the inner and the outer Trinity in Unificationism, thus also taking a middle position between Modalistic and Dynamistic Monarchianism in Christianity.

God's original will during the life of Jesus Christ was that the inner Trinity be substantially manifested to constitute the outer Trinity in the realm of creation. Specifically, Jesus as the Logos incarnate was expected to become the Son of the outer Trinity as the second, perfected Adam and to find his Bride who was to be the Holy Spirit of the same outer Trinity as the second, perfected Eve. Unfortunately, however, he was murdered on the cross, thus losing his physical body. Therefore the outer Trinity, which is the substantial manifestation of the inner Trinity, was not formed with respect to the Son. For the same reason, this substantial manifestation was not formed with respect to the Holy Spirit as well. That is to say, Jesus was not able to find his Bride in the position of perfected Eve in the outer Trinity.

Under those circumstances, Jesus, who lost his physical body, could only unite with a manifestation of the Holy Spirit whose locus and identity were not clear. Therefore the status of the spiritual Trinity was not very clear. The spiritual Trinity is, strictly speaking, neither the inner Trinity nor the outer Trinity. Also, it is neither Modalistic Monarchianism nor Dynamistic Monarchianism. The mysterious and obscure nature of the traditional doctrine of the Trinity can, in actuality, be attributed to this status of the spiritual Trinity.

In the last days, however, Jesus must return in order to complete the outer Trinity, which involves himself as the third, perfected Adam and his Bride as the third, perfected Eve centering on God:

> Christ must return in the flesh and find his Bride. They will form on the earth a perfect trinity [i.e., the outer Trinity] with God and become True Parents both spiritually and physically. They will give fallen people rebirth both spiritually and physically, removing their original sin and enabling them to build trinities on earth with God as the center.[25]

According to Unificationism, the "marriage of the Lamb" (Rev. 19:7) means the real marriage between the Christ of the Second Coming as the third, perfected Adam and his Bride as the third, perfected Eve centering on God, in order for them to stand as the True Parents of all humankind.

Here, at least three additional points of importance in the Unification doctrine of the Trinity are to be mentioned. First, if God's original will is that

---

[24] EDP, p. 172.

[25] Ibid.

the inner Trinity be substantially manifested to constitute the outer Trinity for all humankind, then the original importance of the doctrine of the Trinity must lie in aiming at this constitution of the outer Trinity, in which perfected Adam and Eve transformatively "give fallen people rebirth both spiritually and physically, removing their original sin." As long as this original importance of the Trinity is thus recognized in the Unification doctrine of the Trinity, it can be said that the Unification doctrine of the Trinity is thoroughly trinitarian, even being more trinitarian than the traditional Christian doctrine of the Trinity which has not recognized it.

Second, our salvation/restoration is to be accomplished completely through the outer Trinity, as it is brought forth through transformative rebirth given by perfected Adam and Eve. This means, and it is very important, that in Unificationism soteriology and Christology are inseparably connected with the doctrine of the Trinity especially with respect to the outer Trinity. This may be somewhat similar to the Eastern Christian tradition in which salvation has been believed to be *theosis* (deification), which is brought forth to everybody thorough the joint trinitarian work of the Son and the Holy Spirit centering on God the Father. Eastern Christianity has held that the divine Son of God became human in the incarnation, so that we humans might be transformed to become divine, and that this *theosis* as our salvation is to be made definite through the spiritual grace of the Holy Spirit after the Son's resurrection.[26] In the East, therefore, salvation is closely linked to what Unificationism calls the "spiritual Trinity," if not to the outer Trinity. In the West, by contrast, from the death of Christ on the cross, which stopped the outer Trinity from being realized, has issued the idea that salvation comes forensically only from his substitutionary death itself and not necessarily from the Trinity, so that soteriology and Christology have little to do with the doctrine of the Trinity. In the West, therefore, the universal availability of the Trinity for salvation has been replaced by the idea that only the one sovereign God, rather than the Trinity in its threeness, determines election and predestination for salvation by Christ's crucifixion, as can be seen in Augustine's theology, for example.[27]

A third point is about the gender of the Holy Spirit. If the outer Trinity is the substantial manifestation of the inner Trinity, then perfected Adam and Eve of the outer Trinity are the substantial manifestations of the Son and the Holy Spirit of the inner Trinity, respectively. Hence perfected Eve of the outer

---

[26] For an excellent explanation of this point, see, for example, Lynne Faber Lorenzen, *The College Student's Introduction to the Trinity* (Collegeville, MN: The Liturgical Press, 1999), pp. 11-13, 19, 21.

[27] This point is well made in Lorenzen, ibid., pp. 26-28.

Trinity corresponds to the Holy Spirit of the inner Trinity, whose gender therefore must be feminine. At least in theory, of course, the Holy Spirit of the inner Trinity as God's *Hyungsang* can be both masculine and feminine because it can have the dual characteristics of Yang and Yin as its attributes;[28] but when "acting energy" is generated from the unity of God's *Sungsang* and *Hyungsang* centering on Heart to encourage perfected Adam and Eve of the outer Trinity to completely unite with each other at the social level, we can find a certain correspondence between God's *Hyungsang* of the inner Trinity and perfected Eve of the outer Trinity. In this sense, God's *Hyungsang*, i.e., the Holy Spirit of the inner Trinity, can be said to be feminine. It becomes more evident when Unificationism refers to the Holy Spirit of the "spiritual Trinity" as the "feminine counterpart" of Jesus.[29]

4. The Immanent and the Economic Trinity

As was discussed above, the Unification doctrine of the Trinity has within its scope both the inner and the outer Trinity. In truth, however, this is not exclusive to Unificationism; something quite similar to it can be seen also in the Christian tradition. There are two sorts of the Trinity in the Christian tradition, called the "immanent Trinity" and the "economic Trinity."

The immanent Trinity refers to the relations of the Father, the Son (the eternal Logos) and the Holy Spirit immanent within the essence of God; hence it is also called the "essential Trinity." By contrast, the economic Trinity pays attention to the economic operations of creation by the Father, salvation by the Son, and sanctification by the Holy Spirit, as the outward expressions of God's essence and purpose; hence it refers to the relations of the Father, the Son (the Logos incarnate) and the Holy Spirit as they work in the divine economy. The Bible, early creeds and liturgical doxologies are understood to be much more concerned with the economic Trinity than the immanent Trinity.

It can easily be understood that the immanent and the economic Trinity in the Christian tradition are respectively equivalent to the inner and the outer Trinity in Unificationism. Strictly speaking, however, the economic Trinity in Christianity is not completely similar to the outer Trinity in Unificationism. This divergence between the two traditions concerns the identity of the Son and also that of the Holy Spirit. The Son of the outer Trinity in Unificationism is perfected Adam as a discrete, self-conscious individual man who has perfected the purpose of creation, acquiring full divinity. By contrast, the Son

---

[28] NEUT, p. 13.
[29] EDP, p. 170.

of the economic Trinity in Christianity as the Logos incarnate is *not* discrete from the eternal Logos yet, for the human nature of the Logos incarnate is merely a *physis anhypostatos* ("impersonal or non-hypostatic nature") in the sense of having *no* separate *hypostasis* or person of its own, so that it is a *physis enhypostastos* ("in-hypostatic nature") in the sense of finding its *hypostasis* or person only *in* the *hypostasis* of the eternal divine Logos within God.[30]

Similarly, while the Holy Spirit of the outer Trinity in Unificationism is perfected Eve as a discrete, self-conscious individual woman with full divinity who stands as the Bride of perfected Adam in the domain of creation, the Holy Spirit of the economic Trinity in Christianity, by contrast, is not really discrete from the Holy Spirit within God himself, still with the gender of masculinity, just slightly emerging out of God to work in the outer realm of economy.

This divergence of Christianity from Unificationism is derived from the fact that due to the death of Jesus on the cross, Christianity has not yet been able to find perfected Adam and perfected Eve as Bridegroom and Bride in the realm of creation, as was mentioned in the preceding subsection. Therefore, whereas the outer Trinity in Unificationism is completely economic, the economic Trinity in Christianity is *not*. This means that in the Christian tradition the economic Trinity is not discrete from the immanent Trinity yet. Both are still identical, although the same identical Trinity simply comes to be called the "economic Trinity" as soon as it begins to turn toward the divine economy.

According to Unificationism, the inner Trinity, which is within God, and the outer Trinity, which is completely economic in the realm of creation, are not identical. The two are discrete from each other, although they are completely united with each other. Hence perfected Adam and Eve of the outer Trinity are discrete from God, thus not being Gods, although they have full divinity as perfect human beings. There is no tritheism at all here, therefore, as was previously mentioned.

But if you keep to the traditional Christian idea of the identity of the immanent and the economic Trinity, while at the same time trying to put much emphasis on the importance of the economic Trinity, then you might be critiqued for supporting tritheism. For in that case, you most likely lean toward the belief of so-called "social trinitarianism," that the three members of the Trinity are a society of three distinct centers of self-consciousness. The

---

30 For this doctrine of the *physis anhypostastos* and the *physis enhypostatos*, which was established by theologians such as Leontius of Byzantium in the sixth century, see, for example, G. W. H. Lampe, "Christian Theology in the Patristic Period," in *A History of Christian Doctrine*, ed. Hubert Cunliffe-Jones (Philadelphia: Fortress Press, 1981), p. 144.

Cappadocian Fathers in the East in the fourth century already had this belief, when they talked about the three distinct *hypostases* as compared with the three less distinct *personae* in the West. In the twentieth century, theologians such as Jürgen Moltmann and Leonardo Boff upheld similar beliefs of social trinitarianism. Again, social trinitarians might be criticized for supporting tritheism—criticized especially by those leaning toward traditional Latin trinitarianism. But if they knew the outer Trinity in Unificationism, they would be free from this criticism

The identity of the immanent and the economic Trinity, as understood in Christianity, was a natural result of Tertullian's obscure middle position between Modalistic and Dynamistic Monarchianism. Therefore, although he originally recognized the importance of the economic Trinity in opposition to Modalistic Monarchianism, nevertheless it gradually faded away, and theologians became more and more inclined to downplay the economic Trinity while engaging in ever more discussion of the intradivine unity of the immanent Trinity. Thus they ended up making the Trinity basically irrelevant to the world and our real life of faith, and they even tended to separate the Trinity from the discussion of the atonement by Christ especially in the West. This unfortunately constituted what Catherine Mowry LaCugna (1952–1997) calls "the defeat of the doctrine of the Trinity."[31] This tendency was more noticeable in the Latin West than in the Greek East, because the West was more interested in the priority of the oneness over the threeness of the triune God.

§5. A New Direction

In spite of its importance in Christian dogma, the doctrine of the Trinity, with all its obscurity and mystery, has long been neglected as not very useful and relevant. Even the Reformers of the sixteenth century were not particularly interested in it. They simply accepted the past trinitarian tradition. They had little new to comment on it from the viewpoint of the Bible which they so emphasized. To that degree, the doctrine of the Trinity has not been a matter of much concern.

This changed with the twentieth century, as new departures in formulating the doctrine of the Trinity emerged from theologians including Karl Barth,

[31] Catherine Mowry LaCugna, *God for Us: The Trinity and Christian Life* (New York: Harper Collins Publishers, 1991), p. 9.

Karl Rahner, Jürgen Moltmann and Leonardo Boff. These thinkers reemphasized the economic Trinity as they sought to overcome the failure of the traditional trinitarian doctrine to be economic enough. From the viewpoint of Unificationism, their theologies moved in a healthy direction, helpful for addressing the mystery of the doctrine of the Trinity. This new direction in twentieth-century thought about the Trinity helped to revive theological interest. Since the time of Karl Barth there has been much serious theology written on the Trinity, and many books and articles on the Trinity have been published. It seems that today people throughout the Christian world are more and more recognizing the significance of the doctrine.

The new approaches of Barth, Rahner, Moltmann and Boff will each be briefly discussed. It should be noted at this point, however, that we cannot expect them to find a perfect solution. None of their formulations of the doctrine is as thoroughly economic as we desire. But as they are moving in the right direction, we treat them with appreciation.

1. Karl Barth

Karl Barth, perhaps the most important Protestant theologian since Friedrich Schleiermacher (1768–1834), was instrumental in establishing the importance of the doctrine of the Trinity in systematic theology by treating it in the prolegomena to his entire multivolume work of *Church Dogmatics*. The doctrine of the Trinity had not received as much attention in the Protestant tradition before him. Schleiermacher treated the Trinity merely as an appendix to his systematic theology.

Barth dealt with the Trinity in the context of God's revelation which he took very seriously as the founder of neo-orthodoxy in the beginning of the twentieth century. God's self-revelation in his economy is such that "God Himself in unimpaired unity yet also in unimpaired difference is Revealer, Revelation, and Revealedness,"[32] referring to the Father, the Son, and the Holy Spirit, respectively. And Barth did not see any subordinationism in this economic dimension of God's revelation.

Therefore, although he distinguished the economic Trinity of revelation from the immanent Trinity of eternity by saying that the latter is the "basis" and "prototype" of the former,[33] and that the former does not result from the latter out of necessity but rather through God's own freedom to reveal himself,[34] nevertheless he did not believe that these two kinds of the Trinity

[32] Karl Barth, *Church Dogmatics*, I/1, trans. G. W. Bromiley (Edinburgh: T&T Clark, 1975), p. 339

[33] Ibid., p. 383.

[34] Ibid., pp. 172, 371.

are discrete from each other: "the reality of God which meets us in revelation [as the economic Trinity] *is* His reality in all the depth of eternity [as the immanent Trinity]."[35]

Another important thing is Barth's suggestion that when the Father, the Son and the Holy Spirit in revelation are each God and have their essential oneness in God, it should not mean tritheism. To avoid the possibility of tritheism, he suggested not to use for each of the three members of the Trinity the word "person," which today is taken to mean a self-conscious individual entity.[36] Thus he proposed that we not say three persons but three "modes of being" (*Seinsweisen*).[37] By this, however, he never meant to support Modalistic Monarchianism.[38]

Barth's idea that the economic Trinity is not discrete from the immanent Trinity may be disappointing for our purpose. But his appreciation of the economic Trinity in the context of God's economic self-revelation eventually gave rise to a more appropriate understanding of the status of the Son of the economic Trinity. Thus in his 1956 lecture *The Humanity of God*, he acknowledged that Jesus Christ is God's "loyal partner" as true man (while at the same time being man's loyal partner as true God).[39] For Christ to be God's loyal partner as true man would mean that Christ is now more inclined to be different from God himself. Also, in his 1962 lecture *Evangelical Theology: An Introduction*, Barth made an appropriate distinction between God and Jesus Christ, saying that the former is "the primary partner of the covenant" while the latter is "the other, the secondary, partner of the covenant."[40] This was a celebrated shift in his later years.[41] It evinced a considerable tendency toward the idea of the Son of the economic Trinity as a discrete, perfected individual man. While he showed no shift or change regarding the status of the Holy Spirit, Barth's appreciation of the economic Trinity coupled with his later, new Christological understanding is very encouraging and noteworthy.

---

[35] Ibid., p. 548. Italics added.
[36] Ibid., pp. 349-51.
[37] Ibid., pp. 355, 359.
[38] Ibid., p. 355.
[39] Karl Barth, *The Humanity of God*, trans. John Newton Thomas and Thomas Wieser (Atlanta, GA: John Knox Press, 1960), p. 46.
[40] Karl Barth, *Evangelical Theology: An Introduction,* trans. Grover Foley (Grand Rapids, MI: William B. Eerdmans Publishing Co., 1985), pp. 19-20.
[41] This shift of Barth in his later years is covered well in Klaas Runia, *The Present-day Christological Debate* (Leicester, England: Inter-Varsity Press, 1984), pp. 20-21.

2. Karl Rahner

Karl Rahner was the Catholic counterpart of Karl Barth to reawaken interest in the doctrine of the Trinity in the twentieth century. Like Barth, Rahner treated the Father, the Son and the Holy Spirit in the context of God's revelation which he preferred to call the "self-communication of God":

> The absolute self-communication of God to the world… is Father as the absolutely primordial and underivative; it is Son as the principle which itself acts and necessarily must act in history in view of this free self-communication; it is Holy Spirit, as that which is given, and accepted by us.[42]

From this we can see Rahner's appreciation of the economic Trinity, which is grounded in the immanent Trinity. According to Rahner, however, the economic Trinity is so closely related to the immanent Trinity that they are not discrete from each other. They are still identical in spite of their distinction. Hence his famous dictum, called "Rahner's Rule": "*The 'economic' Trinity is the 'immanent' Trinity and the 'immanent' Trinity is the 'economic' Trinity.*"[43]

One might criticize this dictum of Rahner for teaching that the economic Trinity, identical with the immanent Trinity, is still far from economic. That criticism might be legitimate from the perspective of Unificationism. But it is important to know that Rahner's real intention of this dictum was to address the problem of what LaCugna calls "the defeat of the doctrine of the Trinity," mentioned at the end of the preceding section. Rahner was concerned about this problem, i.e., the unfortunate fact that Christian theologians for many centuries, by not appreciating the economic Trinity enough, were isolating the Trinity from the rest of Christian dogma that deals with the economy of salvation in the world:

> The treatise on the Trinity occupies a rather isolated position in the total dogmatic system. To put it crassly, and not without exaggeration, when the treatise is concluded, its subject is never brought up again. Its function in the whole dogmatic construction is not clearly perceived. It is as though this mystery has been revealed for its own sake, and that even after it has been made known to us, it remains, *as a reality*, locked up within itself. We make statements about it, but as a reality it has nothing to do with us at all.[44]

---

[42] Karl Rahner, "The Concept of Mystery in Catholic Theology," *Theological Investigations*, vol. IV, trans. Kevin Smith (New York: Crossroad, 1982), p. 70.

[43] Karl Rahner, *The Trinity*, trans. Joseph Donceel (New York: Seabury Press, 1974), p. 22. Italics original.

[44] Ibid., p. 14.

So his intention of the dictum was to connect the immanent Trinity with the economic Trinity.

But did his avowed recognition of the importance of the economic Trinity in close connection with the immanent Trinity lead Rahner to go so far as to say, as the Unification doctrine does, that the Son and the Holy Spirit of the economic Trinity are discrete, self-conscious human individuals? The answer is No. Regarding the Son, Rahner still basically followed the Niceno-Chalcedonian tradition, maintaining that the Son of the economic Trinity, in spite of his human nature assumed through the incarnation, is identical with the Son of the immanent Trinity: "here the Logos with God and the Logos with us, the immanent and the economic Logos, are strictly the same."[45] Regarding the Holy Spirit, Rahner did not believe the Holy Spirit can be incarnated. It is in this context that he tried to avoid tritheism, proposing that we not say three persons but rather three distinct "manners of subsisting" (*Subsistenzweisen*).[46] This proposed term is similar to Barth's "modes of being" (*Seinsweisen*).

This may seem a bit disappointing. But the language of Rahner's discussion of the theology of symbols in his *Theological Investigations* has a tendency toward the idea of Jesus Christ as a discrete exteriorization of God: "in [God's] self-exteriorization he goes out of himself into that which is other than he."[47] This may have resulted from his emphasis on the economic Trinity. And, although his celebrated dictum talked about the identity of the two sets of the Trinity, it actually has had a great impact on theology, and as a result many theologians have started paying more attention to the economic Trinity.

3. Jürgen Moltmann

Jürgen Moltmann accepted Rahner's axiom that the economic Trinity is the immanent Trinity and vice versa, but his way of doing so was uniquely eschatological because his position was meant to take up the economic Trinity into the immanent Trinity upon the eschatological completion of the former in history: "The economic Trinity completes and perfects itself to immanent Trinity when the history and experience of salvation are completed and perfected."[48]

---

[45] Ibid., p. 33.

[46] Ibid., pp. 103-15.

[47] Karl Rahner, *Theological investigations*, vol. IV, trans. Kevin Smyth (London: Darton, Longman & Todd, 1966), p. 239.

[48] Jürgen Moltmann, *The Trinity and the Kingdom*, trans. Margaret Kohl (Minneapolis, MN: Fortress Press, 1993), p. 161.

What is really unique about Moltmann's eschatological affirmation of the identity of the economic and the immanent Trinity is that it comes from his keen interest in the theology of the cross and also in the history of God's economy. On the cross Jesus experienced the agony of being forsaken by the Father. The Father in turn experienced the suffering of separation from the Son. But, by surrendering to this kind of misery for the sake of the salvation of sinful humanity, the Father and the Son experienced a new unity with each other in the Holy Spirit. Thus the economic involvement of the Trinity is constitutive of the intradivine life of the immanent Trinity. Moltmann also believed that the identity of the immanent and the economic Trinity is such that the Son had already carried the cross within the immanent Trinity as well, and that the cross in the economic Trinity has "a retroactive effect" on the cross within the immanent Trinity.[49]

Moltmann in his appreciation of economic history regarded the three persons of the Trinity as three "distinct centres of consciousness and action,"[50] thereby avoiding Barth's "modes of being" and Rahner's "manners of subsisting." Moltmann wanted to see the genuine work of each person of the Trinity in the economy of the salvific love of a suffering God. Thus he critiqued Barth and Rahner for being still too preoccupied with the monotheistic oneness of the Trinity despite their openness to the economic Trinity.[51] The God of monotheism, according to Moltmann, is cold and uninvolved in the suffering of humans. He declared that monotheism should be replaced by genuine trinitarianism, i.e., social trinitarianism, which comprehends the love of God. He, however, did not believe that this means tritheism, although many people took issue with his possible tritheism. If he had known the Unification idea of the completely economic, outer Trinity in which perfected Adam (the Son) and perfected Eve (the Holy Spirit) are not God but perfect human beings with full divinity, he would have been free from that problem.

Moltmann's new emphasis on the real threeness of the Trinity in his social trinitarianism was a very good development in the history of the doctrine of the Trinity. One positive outcome of it was his idea that the real threeness of the Trinity provides a model for human community: "the Trinity's relations of fellowship... are open to men and women, and open to the world."[52] Hence "the open Trinity."[53] This echoes the Unification teaching that the relationship

---

[49] Ibid., p. 160.
[50] Ibid., p. 146.
[51] Ibid., pp. 139-48.
[52] Ibid., p. 19.
[53] Ibid., pp. 94-96.

within the inner Trinity, which is the give and receive action between God's *Sungsang* and *Hyungsang* centering on Heart, provides a model of unity which encourages two or more human beings to unite at the social level in the world. Even so, however, due to his basic adherence to the identity of the immanent and the economic Trinity, he did not go so far as to say, as Unificationism would, that the Son and the Holy Spirit of the economic Trinity are discrete, self-conscious human individuals.

Another notable thing in Moltmann's doctrine of the Trinity is his recognition of the femininity of the Holy Spirit: "If believers are 'born' again from the Holy Spirit [as in Jn. 3:3-5], then the Spirit is 'the mother' of God's children and can in this sense also be termed a 'feminine' Spirit."[54] This coincides with Unificationism, which teaches that the Holy Spirit is the "feminine counterpart" of Jesus in the spiritual Trinity,[55] and that perfected Eve is the feminine counterpart of perfected Adam in the outer Trinity.[56]

4. *Leonardo Boff*

Leonardo Boff, a Brazilian liberation theologian, studied with Karl Rahner at the University of Munich in Germany, obtaining his doctorate in 1970. Thus he knew Rahner's Rule and accepted it, if in a qualified way. According to Boff, "the economic Trinity is the immanent Trinity, but not the whole of the immanent Trinity," i.e., "not the whole immanent Trinity is the economic Trinity."[57] The reason is that the "self-bestowal [of the immanent Trinity] is made within the framework of space and time and the limits of created perception, distorted by the dark waters of sin."[58] Thus Boff did not fully believe in the identity of the immanent and the economic Trinity, seeing more distinction or distance between them, although he unquestionably believed in the deep connection between them.

For this reason, Boff, to the surprise of many, believed in the incarnation of the Holy Spirit in Mary as well as that of the Son in Jesus: "The Holy Spirit, coming down on Mary, 'pneumatized' her, taking on human form in her, in the same manner as the Son who... set up his tent amongst us in the figure of Jesus of Nazareth."[59] For this, he appealed to the annunciation to Mary in the

---

[54] Jürgen Moltmann, *The Spirit of Life: A Universal Affirmation*, trans. Margaret Kohl (Minneapolis, MN: Fortress Press, 1993), p. 157.
[55] EDP, p. 170.
[56] EDP, p. 172.
[57] Leonardo Boff, *Trinity and Society*, trans. Paul Burns (Eugene, OR: Wipf & Stock Publishers, 1988), p. 215.
[58] Ibid.
[59] Ibid., p. 210-11.

Lukan narrative: "The Holy Spirit will come upon you" (Lk. 1:35).[60] The Church does not officially teach such a thing, but Boff presented it as "a *theologoumenon* (theological hypothesis), based on correlating the biblical narrative with other related truths of faith," some of which are:

> that woman as well as man is made in the image and likeness of God (Ge. 1:27); that there is a call to divinization; that femininity reveals God; that the feminine dimension present in [the humanity of] Jesus through the incarnation was taken on hypostatically, so that a feminine element has been divinized eternally; that the feminine as well as the masculine will in eternity participate on the highest level in the communication of the Trinity.[61]

In this connection, Boff also talked about the femininity of the Holy Spirit, by saying that the Holy Spirit has a "maternal-virginal womb."[62]

The *theologoumenon* of Boff was actually a great development from the perspective of the Unification doctrine of the Trinity, according to which the Holy Spirit of the inner Trinity was to be substantially manifested in perfected Eve of the outer Trinity, in the same way as the Son of the inner Trinity was substantially manifested in perfected Adam of the outer Trinity, who was the Jesus of Nazareth. The difference is that whereas Boff identifies Mary as the incarnation of the Holy Spirit, Unificationism does not. Unificationism instead believes that someone else as perfected Eve in the position of Jesus' Bride and not in the position of his mother was to be the incarnation of the Holy Spirit. But both Boff and Unificationism agree that a created female human being is the substantial manifestation/incarnation of the Holy Spirit.

Boff's position is social trinitarianism, recognizing the real "differentiation" of the three members of the Trinity in their perichoretic "union."[63] Like Moltmann, therefore, he understood that the real threeness of the Trinity in union within God provides a model for human community. As a liberation theologian in Latin America, he took this trinitarian model seriously to help solve the problem of oppression in society: "It is also experienced as hope and anticipated in this hope whenever the oppressed and their allies fight against tyranny and oppression."[64]

Boff was able to talk about this trinitarian model for human community more persuasively than Moltmann because the Brazilian theologian maintained,

---

[60] Ibid., p. 210.
[61] Ibid., p. 211.
[62] Ibid., p. 147.
[63] Ibid., p. 5.
[64] Ibid., p. 163.

albeit as a theological hypothesis but in much resemblance to Unificationism, that the incarnations of the Son and the Holy Spirit are Jesus and Mary in the created world. According to Boff, from Mary as the Holy Spirit incarnate, "the presence of the Spirit would flood out" over all "humanity on its journey toward the Kingdom, a journey through change and liberation processes that make creation progressively more like its ultimate goal of communion in the Trinity."[65]

§6. The Gender of the Holy Spirit

The gender of the Holy Spirit is quite confusing. While the Hebrew word for "spirit" in the Old Testament is *ruach* (breath), whose grammatical gender is feminine, the Greek word for that in the New Testament is *pneuma* (air, wind), whose grammatical gender is neuter, but for which the masculine pronoun is used. From a different angle, given the Greek masculine term *logos* (word) and its feminine counterpart *sophia* (wisdom), if the Son is related to the Logos, then perhaps the Holy Spirit is related to *sophia*, being feminine, like the personification of wisdom in Proverbs 8:12. But the Latin word for "spirit" is *spiritus*, whose gender is masculine. Additionally, the God of Christianity from the beginning was seen as Father who is masculine, and the Church organization became increasingly patriarchal. Under these circumstances, the gender of the Holy Spirit was deemed decisively masculine.

Let us, however, consider a widespread tradition of the earliest Christians, who were Jews. They decided that the Holy Spirit is feminine because of the grammatical femininity of *ruach*, the Hebrew word for "spirit," and also of *rucha*, the Aramaic word for the same. Hence the *Gospel of the Hebrews*—which was written in Hebrew or Aramaic for Jewish Christians around the end of the first century or in the early second century but was lost apart from some quotations made by Church Fathers such as Origen (c. 185–254) and St. Jerome (c. 342–420)—has Jesus identify the Holy Spirit as his Mother. Also, the *Book of Elchasai*, a Jewish Christian book of prophesy—which was originally written in Aramaic in the beginning of the second century but was lost except for some quotations made by Christian writers such as Hippolytus—speaks of the Holy Spirit as feminine.

In Syriac, a dialect of Aramaic, *rucha*, the word for "spirit," is again grammatically feminine. Therefore old Syriac documents, which remain in

---

[65] Ibid., p. 212.

today's Syriac Orthodox Church, regard the Holy Spirit as feminine. For example, the *Gospel of Thomas*, which was written in Syriac in the second half of the second century and translated into Greek and Coptic later, regards the Holy Spirit as True Mother; by the way, this gospel became part of the New Testament Apocrypha. The *Acts of Thomas*, which was written in Syriac sometime before the middle of the third century and translated into Greek later, has the concept of the Holy Spirit as the Mother, and this writing also became part of the New Testament Apocrypha. The *Fifty Homilies of St. Macarius the Egyptian*, which was most likely written by St. Symeon (c. 390–459), a Syrian monk, refers to the Holy Spirit as our Mother. The *Sinaitic Palimpsest*, a late fourth-century Syriac translation of the four canonical Gospels, describes the Holy Spirit as feminine.

But, under the influence of the Greek and Roman Church's adherence to the masculinity of the Holy Spirit, the Syriac New Testament of the fifth century, known as part of the *Peshitta*, altered the gender of the Holy Spirit to masculinity in several spots. And the early seventh-century Syriac version of the New Testament, known as the *Harklean*, treated the Holy Spirit entirely as masculine, because of its reliance on the Greek New Testament.

Western Protestants such as Nicolaus Zinzendorf (1700–1760), bishop of the Moravian Church in the Pietistic tradition, and John Wesley (1703–1791), who associated with Zinzendorf and gave rise to the Methodist Church, were influenced by the *Fifty Homilies of St. Macarius the Egyptian*, translated into German in the seventeenth century. Zinzendorf referred to the Holy Spirit as our Mother, believing that the Trinity is like a family which can be the prototype for the community of brothers and sisters on the earth.

In the twentieth century, besides Moltmann and Boff, other prominent theologians such as the French Dominican friar Yves Congar (1904–1995) and the North American evangelical theologian Clark H. Pinnock (1937–2010) described the Holy Spirit as feminine. It seems that the theological trend of recognizing the femininity of the Holy Spirit is growing, as our appreciation of the importance of the economic Trinity of Christianity and therefore of the outer Trinity of Unificationism is increasing.

Conclusion: Importance of the Doctrine of the Trinity

Tertullian originated the traditional Christian doctrine of the Trinity by taking an obscure middle position between Modalistic and Dynamistic Monarchianism.

According to Unificationism, this middle position was inevitable because of the premature death of Jesus on the cross, i.e., because the outer Trinity was not realized through him in the realm of creation. This also means that what is called the economic Trinity in Christianity has not been able to be completely economic, so that no real discreteness of the economic Trinity from the immanent Trinity has been reached in Christianity. Hence follows what LaCugna calls "the defeat of the doctrine of the Trinity," which is the problem of the Trinity not being really relevant to the created world and our real life of faith.

In the twentieth century, new trinitarian insights emerged from theologians such as Barth, Rahner, Moltmann and Boff as good attempts to reappreciate the importance of the economic Trinity. It was a welcome development, in spite of the fact that these theologians basically still believed in the identity of the immanent and the economic Trinity (Rahner's Rule). Moltmann and Boff, however, appreciated the economic Trinity more than Barth and Rahner; they appreciated it to such a degree that they believed in social trinitarianism, holding that the real threeness within God is a model for human community in the created world. Furthermore, Moltmann and Boff recognized the femininity of the Holy Spirit. As for Boff, he even held, by accepting Rahner's Rule only in a qualified way, that the Holy Spirit was incarnate in Mary just as the Son was incarnate in the Jesus of Nazareth.

All these developments in the twentieth century seem to indicate that the time has come when the outer Trinity of Unificationism is not unacceptable at all in Christianity. The outer Trinity as the complete substantial manifestation of the inner Trinity of God is thoroughly economic. So it is discrete from the inner Trinity, while being so closely related to it as to be divine as its substantial reflection in the realm of creation. And perfected Adam, who is male, and perfected Eve, who is female, of the outer Trinity are discrete from the Son and the Holy Spirit of the inner Trinity, while being so closely related to them as to be divine.

According to Unificationism, God's purpose of creation is the complete realization of the outer Trinity for all humankind in the realm of creation. It was supposed to be realized through Adam and Eve in the Garden of Eden. But it was not realized due to their fall. It was also supposed to be realized though Jesus as perfected Adam and his Bride as perfected Eve. But again, it was not realized due to the premature death of Jesus on the cross. The "spiritual Trinity" instead was realized, and especially in the West salvation unfortunately has been considered to come only from the substitutionary death of Jesus and not necessarily from the spiritual Trinity as a whole. Furthermore, this non-trinitarian type of salvation has been understood to be given only to the elect. In the last days, therefore, the Christ of the Second Advent as perfected Adam and his Bride as perfected Eve must come to realize the outer Trinity for all humankind. It is to be understood that the Christian doctrine of the Trinity was originally developed for this ultimate purpose of completely realizing the outer Trinity, whether Christianity has been aware of it or not. The original importance of the doctrine of the Trinity consists exactly in this.

The Christian tradition may still have some difficulty in understanding the need for perfected Adam and Eve of the outer Trinity. That is to say, there may still remain a gap between the economic Trinity in Christianity and the outer Trinity in Unificationism. A way to address this gap could be found in the liberal, Arian idea of theologians such as Edward Schillebeeckx (1914–2009), Hans Küng (1928–2021), Hendrikus Berkhof (1914–1995) and John Hick (1922–2012) that Jesus Christ is a man discrete from God without real divinity.[66] But this idea is unacceptable, as it denies Jesus' divinity, placing him too distant from God. Thus Christianity would have to find a good way to make the economic Trinity completely economic like the outer Trinity in Unificationsim, in order to be able to say, like Unificationism does, that the Son and the Holy Spirit of the economic Trinity are human beings discrete from God yet fully divine. The Eastern notion of *theosis* (deification) would be of great help for this.

In conclusion, it can be understood that the doctrine of the Trinity serves to point us toward the realization of the outer Trinity, which is the completion of the divine economy to realize the kingdom of God on earth. The real importance of the doctrine of the Trinity lies in this.

---

[66] For the liberal views of Christ, see, for example, Runia, *The Present-day Christological Debate*, and John Hick, ed., *The Myth of God Incarnate* (Philadelphia: Westminster Press, 1977).

Chapter 6

The Suffering of God

Christianity has long taught as an axiom that God is omnipotent and perfect, and therefore cannot suffer, even though one finds that the Bible, especially the Old Testament in its account of the Exodus, Hebrew prophecy, etc., gives many indications that God suffers. Many scholars agree that this discrepancy between traditional classical theism and the biblical account exists because classical theism, while it undeniably had the Bible as a most important source, was actually developed under the strong influence of ideas from ancient Greek philosophy such as the Stoic virtue of *apatheia* (freedom from emotions), the Neoplatonic view of the eternal, transcendent and unchanging God, and the Aristotelian notion of God as the unmoved mover. The axiom of classical theism, that a God of omnipotence and perfection cannot suffer, still exerts a strong influence in Christianity today, including both Roman Catholicism and Protestantism as well as Eastern Orthodoxy.

In reaction to classical theism, however, a new theological trend arose especially among British theologians toward the end of the nineteenth century, and it spoke about the suffering of God. J. K. Mozley's (1883–1946) book, *The Impassibility of God* (1926), lists 22 such theologians, mostly British and American, from the period between 1866 and 1926, including William Temple (1881–1944) and Horace Bushnell (1802–1876).[1] With more careful research, Michael W. Brierley identifies many more such theologians (46 of them) from

[1] J. K. Mozley, *The Impassibility of God: A Survey of Christian Thought* (London: Cambridge University Press, 1926), Chapter 2.

the same period.[2] Since then, and especially after the Second World War, this theological trend spread not only in Britain but also in other parts and traditions of Christendom. It has involved numerous theologians of various persuasions including Karl Barth (1886–1968), Alfred North Whitehead (1861–1947), Kazoh Kitamori (1916–1998; a Japanese Lutheran theologian), James Cone (1938–2018; an American black theologian), Jürgen Moltmann (1926–2024) and Hans Küng (1928–2021). A 1986 article by Ronald Goetz (1933–2006) in *The Christian Century* even describes this trend as "the rise of a new orthodoxy," although Goetz himself is not in sympathy with it.[3]

Writing in 1988, Paul S. Fiddes (1947–), a British Baptist theologian at Oxford, refers to four general reasons why recent theology is convinced that God suffers.[4] First, the modern meaning of love, as affirmed in modern psychology, holds that true love involves suffering as the one who loves shares in the suffering of the loved, whereas according to traditional theology the love of God just wills and achieves the good of his objects of love without any feeling of suffering with them. Second, the appreciation of God's relationship to the cross has led to the recent conviction that God suffers. This appreciation is first seen in Anglo-Saxon theology toward the end of the nineteenth century (mentioned in Mozley's book above), which recognizes God's eternal cross within the entire cosmic process. This comes to an entirely new phase, when the twentieth-century German "theology from the cross" (*Kreuzestheologie*) focuses on the cross of Jesus as a decisive place of God's suffering, by following Martin Luther's (1483–1546) "theology of the cross" (*theologia crucis*), according to which God is known most clearly in the suffering and humiliation of the cross of Jesus. Third, recent treatments of theodicy dealing with the problem of human suffering hold that a suffering (yet eventually victorious) God would be a consolation to those who suffer. Fourth, a new model of the God-world relationship has arisen, according to which God and the world are interconnected and affect each other.

In spite of the widespread popularity of the notion of God's suffering among many theologians in the twentieth century and thereafter, it seems that most of them have not adequately explained with theological rigor how an omnipotent and perfect God can actually suffer. Warren McWilliams (1946–), author of *The Passion of God* (1985), agrees: "More theologians are confronting

---

[2] Michael W. Brierley, "Introducing the Early British Passibilists," *Journal for the History of Modern Theology* 8 (2001): 218-33.

[3] Ronald Goetz, "The Suffering God: The Rise of a New Orthodoxy," *The Christian Century* 103 (1986): 385-89.

[4] Paul S. Fiddes, *The Creative Suffering of God* (New York: Oxford University Press, 1988), pp. 16-45.

the issue [of divine suffering], but many still fail to explore the issue as carefully as necessary."[5]

Fiddes' more careful analysis, which explains the meaning of suffering at two distinct dimensions, is available, and it is useful for our discussion at our intended level of theological rigor. Referring to a well-received medical distinction between the experience of *mental* pain and the sensation of *bodily* pain, he holds that suffering has two dimensions: 1) an emotion of suffering within, and 2) a constraint or impact received from outside. Applying this distinction to God, he holds that "although God has no pain sensation, since he does not have a body and a mass of nerve endings, he can still suffer in a way analogous to" these two dimensions of suffering.[6] (As will be seen later, Unification theism believes that God indeed has a kind of body, if not exactly the same as the human body, as well as a mind, given his dual characteristics of *Sungsang* and *Hyungsang*; thus Unification theism would be in a better position to argue that God can suffer at these two dimensions.) These two dimensions of suffering in God are usually closely connected to each other, according to Fiddes: "To *feel* suffering is to be *under constraint* from external forces, and so for God to suffer means that he is changed by the world."[7] We will use his proposed two dimensions of suffering as we deal with biblical theism, classical theism and Unification theism.

We will find that classical theism, which considers God to be infinite and perfect "pure act," holds that, given this infinity of act (omnipotence) and perfection of actualization in God, God is both impassible (incapable of passion) and immutable (incapable of change), respectively, with the result that he is far from suffering at the first and second dimensions, respectively. Unification theism, by contrast, maintains that God can suffer both at the first and second dimensions because he is both passible (capable of passion) and mutable (capable of change), while being omnipotent and perfect, respectively. The fundamental difference between classical theism and Unification theism is that while the former, with the help of St. Thomas Aquinas' (1225–1274) use of Aristotle's (384–322 BC) metaphysics, ultimately regards God as "pure form" (or "pure act") without any "matter" (or "potency"), the latter asserts that God has within himself the dual characteristics of *Sungsang* and *Hyungsang*, which are

[5] Warren McWilliams, *The Passion of God: Divine Suffering in Contemporary Protestant Theology* (Macon, GA: Mercer University Press, 1985), p. 5.
[6] Fiddes, *The Creative Suffering of God*, pp. 47-49.
[7] Ibid., p. 63. Italics added.

roughly parallel to Aristotle's "form" and "matter."[8] While the former derives God's omnipotence (*qua* his infinite active power) and his perfection from its view of God as "pure form," the latter proposes newly and uniquely that God's omnipotence consists in the "irrepressible" nature of the impulse of his Heart of love for the world,[9] and his perfection the complete unity of his dual characteristics of *Sungsang* and *Hyungsang* centering on Heart.[10]

The thesis of the present chapter is that according to Unification theism, a God of omnipotence and perfection can suffer both at the first and the second dimensions: 1) God, while being always omnipotent because of his irrepressible Heart, can emotionally suffer within his same Heart when he fails to find his true object partners of love; and 2) God, while being always perfect because of his completely united dual characteristics of *Sungsang* and *Hyungsang*, can, through these same dual characteristics of his, can receive and suffer a negative impression or impact from the fallen world where he fails to find his true object partners of love. Based on this thesis, it will also be shown that God, while always suffering throughout the history of fallen humanity, suffered tremendously especially when Adam, who was supposed to realize the purpose of creation, fell in the Garden of Eden, and also when Jesus as the second Adam was killed on the cross.

To support the above thesis, we will use as helpful references the formulations of three prominent twentieth-century Christian thinkers: Karl Barth, Jürgen Moltmann and Alfred North Whitehead. Barth is widely recognized as the most important theologian of the twentieth century. Moltmann is famous for his book, *The Crucified God* (1972), which is considered by many to be a significant turning point in the process by which the idea of God's suffering becomes the new orthodoxy. Whitehead is well known for "dipolar theism" in his philosophy of organism or process philosophy, which has given rise to the school of process theology. These three theologians each have developed in their own ways two essential concepts that support the argument for God's suffering at the two dimensions: 1) God's love as desire, which somehow explains his inner suffering even as a God of omnipotence; and 2) God's dual characteristics, which somehow explain his suffering from an external constraint even as a God of perfection.

These three thinkers, of course, do not agree with Unification theism on every point. For example, while Barth, Moltmann and Whiteheadian process

---

[8] *New Essentials of Unification Thought: Head-Wing Thought* (Tokyo, Japan: Kogensha, 2006), p. 11. Henceforth abbreviated as NEUT.

[9] The "irrepressible" nature of God's Heart is explained in NEUT, pp. 23-24.

[10] NEUT, p. 244.

theologians agree with Unification theism in taking the death of Jesus Christ on the cross seriously for understanding God's suffering, they do not support Unification theism in featuring the fall of Adam as a basis for knowledge about God's suffering. Barth, Moltmann and Whitehead also naturally differ from one another. Barth's formulation is perhaps less distant from classical theism than the other two. Moltmann's approach is more explicitly trinitarian than Barth's. Whitehead's philosophy of organism deals more generally with the interdependence of God and the world to explain God's suffering. In spite of these differences, however, all the three quite surprisingly have two things in common: 1) God's love as desire, and 2) God's dual characteristics. Therefore, in addition to marking an important departure from classical theism toward appreciating God's suffering, they also constitute helpful references in support of the thesis of Unification theism.

§1. Biblical Theism

According to the Bible, God is omnipotent: "our God the Almighty" (Rev. 19:6); "with God all things are possible" (Mt. 19:26). God is also "perfect" (Mt. 5:48; Deut. 32:4).

Yet many passages, especially in the Old Testament, show that God suffers in terms of the above-mentioned two dimensions: God has internal emotions such as sorrow and frustration in response to what is going on in the fallen world, and God suffers an external constraint in dealing with the world. According to Genesis 6:5-6, for example, when God "saw that the wickedness of man was great in the earth, and that every imagination of the thoughts of his heart was only evil," he "was sorry that he had made man on the earth, and it grieved him to his heart." This passage indicates that: 1) God is grieved internally; and 2) he even changes his mind, at least temporarily, about the appropriateness of his creation of human beings, after having received a negative impression from the fallen world.

There is no doubt that the wickedness of humans God saw at that time resulted from the fall of Adam and Eve in the Garden of Eden (Gen. 3). If so, it is reasonable to think that God was also sorry about the creation of Adam and Eve because of their fall. This would mean that God suffered at their fall as well, although it is not explicitly indicated in Genesis 3.

More biblical passages express, or at least imply, God's suffering. In the interest of brevity, the passages in the following list will not be technically analyzed in terms of the two dimensions of suffering. Nor is this list meant to be exhaustive.

The Exodus story shows that God suffers together with the Israelites who suffer under slavery in Egypt, and that he responds to their situation by liberating them from the slavery: "I have seen the affliction of my people who are in Egypt, and have heard their cry because of their taskmasters; I know their sufferings, and I have come down to deliver them out of the hands of the Egyptians" (Ex. 3:7-8). Later, God is angry at the Israelites when he sees them worshipping a molten calf, and thinks about destroying them in response, but in the end he changes his mind and decides not to destroy them thanks to Moses' plea for them (Ex. 32:7-14). During their 40-year wilderness period, God quite often gets frustrated and angry in response to the people's faithlessness (Num. 11:1; 14:11; 20:12; 21:6). God suffers, because anger is a kind of suffering that entails sorrow.

At one point during the period of judges, God is "provoked to anger" by his faithless people (Judg. 2:12) to such a degree that he hands them over to their plunderers and enemies for their possible destruction (Judg. 2:14), but he changes his mind and saves them because "he was moved to pity by their groaning" in that miserable situation (Judg. 2: 18). Then, when he is disappointed with King Saul's disobedience, God indicates to Samuel the change of his mind about the appropriateness of his initial appointment of Saul as king: "I repent that I have made Saul king; for he has turned back from following me, and has not performed my commandments" (1 Sam. 15:11).

God's suffering is seen most strikingly in Hebrew prophecy. Because of his love and concern for his people, God suffers when they suffer, even though it is the result of their faithlessness, and he wants to redeem them: "In all their affliction he [i.e., God] was afflicted, and the angel of his presence saved them; in his love and in his pity he redeemed them" (Isa. 63:9). God agonizes over their faithlessness, but he does so because of his love: "How can I give you up, O Ephraim! How can I hand you over, O Israel! … My heart recoils within me, my compassion grows warm and tender. I will not execute my fierce anger, I will not again destroy Ephraim" (Hos. 11:8-9). The tears of Jeremiah (Jer. 9:1) are a reflection of God's own tears over the plight of his beloved people who disobey him: "Let my eyes run down with tears night and day, and let them not cease, for the virgin daughter of my people is smitten with a great wound, with a very grievous blow" (Jer. 14:17). The Hebrew prophets also quite often indicate that God changes his attitude or intention depending on whether his people are faithfully obedient or not: "It may be they will listen, and everyone turn from his evil way, that I may repent of the evil which I intended to do to them because of their evil doings" (Jer. 26:3; cf. 18:7-10; 26:13, 19; 42:10; Joel 2:13; Amos 7:3; Jon. 3:10; 4:2).

The Bible does not deny God's omnipotence and perfection. Why, then, does it say that God suffers? Classical theologians usually respond to this question by saying that God's situation is beyond our human level, and that the biblical data about God's apparent grief and the apparent change of his mind are just anthropomorphic descriptions from human points of view meant to be intelligible to less developed minds. These descriptions, therefore, are not to be taken literally but only metaphorically. But is that response satisfactory? Does classical theism take the Bible seriously enough? Is classical theism so preoccupied with its own definitions of God's omnipotence and perfection that it fails to truly appreciate what the Bible says about God's suffering?

The Old Testament scholar Terence E. Fretheim (1936–2020), author of *The Suffering of God: An Old Testament Perspective* (1984), believes that as long as we do not ascribe to God very limited or ungodly aspects of human nature such as death and sinfulness, anthropomorphism is acceptable. He argues that if human beings are created in the image of God, we have "permission to reverse the process and, by looking at the human, learn what God is like."[11] For Fretheim the "relationship of reciprocity" between God and the world is a key to understanding God's suffering in the Old Testament, because in that relationship God affects and is affected by the world.[12] The Jewish theologian Abraham J. Heschel (1907–1972), famous for his book, *The Prophets* (1962), also defends anthropomorphism, here more precisely anthropopathism, as an important hermeneutical key to the theology of the prophets, although he knows from Isaiah 55:8-9 that the level of God's pathos is "higher" than that of human beings.[13]

Does the New Testament also show God's suffering? This question can be answered in the affirmative when we consider the life, death and resurrection of Jesus. Through Jesus, God shows his love and care for humanity (Jn. 3:16; 1 Jn. 4:8-9), and especially for the poor, outcast, underprivileged and sinful, who are unusually suffering (Mk. 2:14-17; Lk. 7:36-50; Jn. 8:1-11; etc.). The life of Jesus is full of tribulations because of the persecutions he receives. His life of suffering culminates in his death on the cross, which is extremely painful, although he is resurrected thereafter. If Jesus says that "I am in the Father and the Father in me" (Jn. 14:11), then his

[11] Terence E. Fretheim, *The Suffering of God: An Old Testament Perspective* (Philadelphia: Fortress Press, 1984), p. 11.

[12] Ibid., p. 35.

[13] Abraham J. Heschel, *The Prophets* (New York: Harper & Row, 1962), p. 276.

suffering must be God's suffering. Although this may sound like the heretical idea of Sabellian "patripassianism" in the third century (that the Father suffers in the modality of the Son), and although this may also sound like the Alexandrian idea of "theopaschism" in the fourth century and thereafter (that God suffers his own death in the death of the Son), which is still deemed heretical by many Christians today in spite of its official acceptance at the Second Council of Constantinople (553),[14] nevertheless it seems that the Bible speaks about God's suffering without necessarily being patripassian or theopaschite. According to Moltmann, the Bible avoids both patripassianism and theopaschitism by showing that God's suffering and Jesus', while being equally important, are different in kind from each other, because while "Jesus suffers dying in forsakenness..., [God] the Father who abandons him and delivers him suffers the death of the Son in the infinite grief of love."[15]

§2. Classical Theism

Classical theism wholeheartedly accepts the biblical passages on God's omnipotence and his perfection. It also wholeheartedly accepts the biblical passages on God's immutability: "The LORD has sworn and will not change his mind" (Ps. 110:4); "For I the LORD do not change" (Mal. 3:6); "the Father of lights with whom there is no variation or shadow due to change" (James 1:17). But it does not accept the biblical data about God's suffering at the two dimensions, unless it does not take them literally. It says slightly pejoratively that the biblical account is just anthropomorphic, and by doing so it admits of a great gulf between God who does not suffer and humans who suffer. Church Fathers in the tradition of classical theism such as St. Jerome (c. 342–420) even strongly criticized the fourth-century anthropomorphite group of Audians for promoting a "foolish heresy."[16]

As mentioned above, classical theism was developed under the influence of schools of Greek philosophy such as Stoicism and Neoplatonism. Its definition of God's perfection, however, was most clearly expressed by Thomas Aquinas using Aristotelian metaphysics. According to him, God's

---

[14] The Second Council of Constantinople will be discussed in Chapter 9, Section 1, Subsection 3 ("Second Council of Constantinople") in the present book.

[15] At least this is what Jürgen Moltmann says about his own interpretation of the Bible. See his *The Crucified God: The Cross of Christ as the Foundation and Criticism of Christian Theology*, trans. R. A. Wilson and John Bowden (New York: Harper & Row, 1974), p. 243.

[16] St. Jerome, "Letter to Pammachius against John of Jerusalem." http://www.catholic-forum.com/saints/stj06001.htm.

"perfection" means that he is pure act, which is the "first actual principle," being "most actual" with no "potentiality" or "matter":

> Now God is the first principle, not material, but in the order of efficient cause, which must be most perfect. For just as matter, as such, is merely potential, an agent, as such, is in the state of actuality. Hence, the first active principle must needs be most actual, and therefore most perfect; for a thing is perfect in proportion to its state of actuality, because we call that perfect which lacks nothing of the mode of its perfection.[17]

This perfect God as pure act without any potentiality is completely actualized and in want of nothing, with the following two results: 1) that he in his eternal, untroubled bliss does not have any inner feeling of suffering and even of additional happiness (thus being impassible); and 2) that he in his uncaused self-existence does not need to process any potentiality in the Godhead to receive an impression from outside, whether it is a negative or positive impression (thus being immutable). So this perfect God without any unrealized potentiality is: 1) "impassible,"[18] free from "passions of the sensitive appetite" such as anger and additional joy, which imply imperfection;[19] and also 2) "immutable," since "everything which is in any way changed, is in some way in potentiality."[20] This clearly means that God is incapable of suffering at both dimensions suggested by Fiddes. Furthermore, according to Aquinas, this God is also "omnipotent" in that his "active power" as pure act unmixed with potentiality is "infinite"; the divine omnipotence thus means God's "infinite" power to do everything (except what implies contradiction).[21]

There is one point of caution we have to keep in mind, however, when trying to understand Aquinas. When he says that God is immutable as pure act, Aquinas does not mean that God is inert and static, but rather that he acts without having to achieve anything. He acts effortlessly, because he is already completely actualized as pure act. His activity, therefore, is not an activity of passions that still presupposes potentiality, but rather "acts of understanding, and willing, and loving" without involving any effort to realize potentiality.[22] The love of God, therefore, is passionless: "He loves without passion."[23]

---

[17] Thomas Aquinas, *Summa Theologiae*, I, q. 4, a. 1. http://www.newadvent.org/summa/1004.htm.
[18] Ibid., I, q. 25, a. 3. http://www.newadvent.org/summa/1025.htm.
[19] Ibid., I, q. 20, a. 1. http://www.newadvent.org/summa/1020.htm.
[20] Ibid., I, q. 9, a. 1. http://www.newadvent.org/summa/1009.htm.
[21] Ibid., I, q. 25, a. 2. http://www.newadvent.org/summa/1025.htm.
[22] Ibid., I, q. 9, a. 1. http://www.newadvent.org/summa/1009.htm.
[23] Ibid., I, q. 20, a. 1. http://www.newadvent.org/summa/1020.htm.

Addressing the criticism from the new orthodoxy to the effect that the God of Aquinas is static, inert and inactive because of his immutability as pure act, Thomas G. Weinandy (1946–), a leading Catholic theologian, argues in his 2000 publication, *Does God Suffer?*, that this criticism misses the mark because God being pure act actually means that he is "supremely active and dynamic and cannot ontologically become more in act." [24] Regarding God's impassibility, Weinandy similarly argues that it means that God as pure act is "supremely passionate and cannot become any more passionate."[25] Thus, according to Weinandy, God who is "supremely active" and "supremely passionate" due to his immutability and impassibility is truly related to the world as a radically active and passionate God. But his arguments seem simply rhetorical, unable to clearly elucidate the matter. Thus he finally confesses that "we cannot comprehend" it, as it is still a mystery of faith.[26] He also admits that when he argues that God is supremely passionate because of his impassibility, he oversteps the position of Aquinas: "Aquinas does not say this."[27] As was noted above, according to Aquinas, God's activity is a passionless activity.

The idea that the love of God is passionless leads to a difficult paradox in classical theism, because when God loves someone, he does not share in the suffering of the loved at all, although he may will and achieve the good of the loved one. This paradox is well expressed by St. Anselm of Canterbury (c. 1033–1109):

> But how are You at once both merciful and impassible? For if You are impassible You do not have any compassion; and if You have no compassion Your heart is not sorrowful from compassion with the sorrowful, which is what being merciful is. But if You are not merciful whence comes so much consolation for the sorrowful?[28]

Classical theism, therefore, believes that while God loves human beings in the world, he paradoxically does not suffer when they suffer or go astray. God did not suffer, therefore, when Adam fell in the Garden of Eden. And God did not suffer when Jesus Christ suffered his painful death on the cross. Even Jesus Christ did not suffer in his divinity; he only suffered in his humanity.

---

[24] Thomas G. Weinandy, *Does God Suffer?* (Notre Dame, IN: University of Notre Dame Press, 2000), p. 123.
[25] Ibid., p. 127.
[26] Ibid., p. 145.
[27] Ibid., p. 126.
[28] Anselm of Canterbury, "Proslogion," in *Anselm of Canterbury: The Major Works*, trans. Brian Davies and Gillian Evans (New York: Oxford University Press, 1998), p. 91.

What is the purpose of creation, then, according to classical theism? Aquinas maintains that God creates the world because he wills to "communicate" the divine goodness to others "by likeness," so that they as partakers in it may be ordained to him as their "end."[29] Creatures, which thus receive the divine goodness in likeness, are to glorify God. The glorification of God as the purpose of creation has long been accepted in Christianity: "For from him and through him and to him are all things. To him be glory forever" (Rom. 11:36). But the glorification of God from creatures is understood to add nothing to his perfection because he as pure act without any potentiality is completely actualized and in want of nothing. Strictly speaking, therefore, God does not even need the created world for himself. He creates the world under no necessity: "Since… the divine goodness can be without other things, and, indeed, is in no way increased by other things, it is under no necessity to will other things."[30] This leads many theologians to confess that the purpose of creation is really unknown. According to the American evangelical theologian Millard J. Erickson (1932–), "God did not have to create. He had to act in a loving and holy fashion in whatever he did, but he was not required to create. He freely chose to create for reasons *not known* to us."[31]

Classical theism, while it is most clearly expressed by Aquinas, has been dominant throughout the history of Christianity, not only among earlier Church Fathers such as St. Irenaeus (c. 130–c. 202), St. Augustine (354–430) and Anselm but also in the Protestant tradition. The first article of the Thirty-nine Articles of Religion finalized by the Church of England in 1571 states that God is "everlasting, without body, parts, or passions."[32] And the first chapter of the Westminster Confession of Faith, originally drawn up in 1646, similarly says that God is "infinite in being and perfection, a most pure spirit, invisible, without body, parts, or passions, immutable."[33] These two influential documents in Protestant history strongly echo the Thomistic formulation.

---

[29] Aquinas, *Summa Theologiae*, I, q. 19, a. 2. http://www.newadvent.org/summa/1019.htm#article2.
[30] Aquinas, *Summa Contra Gentiles*, I, 81, 2. http://dhspriory.org/thomas/ContraGentiles1.htm#81.
[31] Millard J. Erickson, *Introducing Christian Doctrine*, 2nd ed., ed. L. Arnold Hustad (Grand Rapids, MI: Baker Academic, 2001), p. 122. Italics added.
[32] "Articles of Religion." http://www.eskimo.com/~lhowell/bcp1662/articles/articles.html.
[33] "The Westminster Confession of Faith A.D. 1647." http://www.ccel.org/ccel/schaff/creeds3.iv.xvii.ii.html.

§3. Unification Theism

1. God's Perfection as the Unity of His Dual Characteristics

Unification theism defines God's perfection in connection with the perfection of an individual human person. According to the Divine Principle, the perfection of an individual human person consists in the unity of that person's mind and body centering on God, i.e., the God-centered unity of that person's dual characteristics of *sungsang* (internal nature) and *hyungsang* (external form), which thereby resembles and reflects the unity of God's dual characteristics of *Sungsang* (original internal nature) and *Hyungsang* (original external form). In this state, a human being is able to return "joy" to God.[34] Unification Thought, a more philosophical development of the Divine Principle, explicitly states that God's perfection is none other than this unity of his dual characteristics: "In God, the *Sungsang* and *Hyungsang* are in harmonious give and receive action in the relationship of subject and object centering on Heart, and are united in oneness. This state is perfection."[35] The *Sungsang* and *Hyungsang* in God (or the *sungsang* and *hyungsang* in the created world) are respectively mental and physical in nature. Aristotle's "form" and "matter" respectively are said to "correspond to" them,[36] although there are fundamental differences between the two systems of Unificationism and Aristotelianism.

Unification theism's definition of divine perfection is very different from classical theism's. Whereas classical theism holds that God is perfect because he is pure form only, Unification theism believes that God is perfect because he has both his *Sungsang* and *Hyungsang* completely united within himself. God's *Sungsang* and *Hyungsang* in Unification theism are "homogeneous," thus being able to be completely united within himself (so are the *sunsang* and *hyungsang* in the world, by reason of their homogeneity).[37] But Aristotle's form and matter are not homogeneous,[38] thus not being able to stay together in God who is already perfect as pure form, but only in the imperfect world. This means that Unification theism consistently sees the dual characteristics in the whole of reality including both God and the world, whereas classical theism, under the influence of Aristotle's metaphysics among others, does not consistently apply the theory of the duality of form and matter (hylomorphism) to the whole of

---

[34] *Exposition of the Divine Principle* (New York: H.S.A.-U.W.C., 1996), pp. 33-34. Henceforth abbreviated as EDP.

[35] NEUT, p. 244.

[36] NEUT, p. 11.

[37] NEUT, pp. 9-11.

[38] NEUT, p. 11.

reality as it exempts God from that theory. This difference is a crucial one, because it leads one school (Unification theism) to understand, as will be shown below, that a God of perfection can be acted upon by the world, while it leads the other school (classical theism) not to do so.

2. The Inner Suffering of an Omnipotent God in His Heart

"Heart," as referred to in the above quotation in the preceding subsection, is the core of God's *Sungsang*, and it is defined as his "emotional impulse to seek joy though love."[39] It is basically God's desire of love for the created world. From this Heart, God makes "a total investment" to the process of creation in order to create the world.[40] He then seeks to love his created object partners of love to feel "joy" from them.[41] To draw the above example of a perfected human person, God, when beholding this person as his object partner of love, is "stimulated" to feel the unity of his own *Sungsang* and *Hyungsang* reflected in this person's God-centered mind-body unity, thereby feeling the "fullness of joy." For God to feel joy this way is the very "purpose of creation," although it should be noted that this perfected person, too, can experience joy.[42] The purpose of creation based on God's impulse of love in his Heart is such that "an object partner of love was absolutely necessary for God."[43]

But if this human person fails to realize a God-centered unity of mind and body and instead shows a unity of mind and body centering on a purpose contrary to the purpose of creation, as is the case in the fallen world, then God in his Heart cannot feel joy but instead feels suffering and pain. This frustrates the purpose of creation. In this case, what usually occurs is the fallen physical body's dominion over the mind instead of the mind's God-centered dominion over the body, resulting in a conflict between mind and body. In this case, God emotionally suffers because he cannot connect with this human person. In the words of Sun Myung Moon:

> Are your mind and body in complete harmony now, so that you can detect God? You must be composed of subject and object like everything else in creation, but the problem is whether they are united… In this situation would God want to stay with you or escape from you? It is almost certain that God would like to escape from you.

---

[39] NEUT, p. 23.
[40] NEUT, p. 251.
[41] NEUT, pp. 23-24.
[42] EDP, pp. 33-34.
[43] NEUT, p. 24.

> God is really at a loss because He desires to stay with man, but instead He is driven to escape.[44]

What is important here, however, is that whether this person as God's object partner of love succeeds or fails to reflect the unity of God's dual characteristics, i.e., whether God in his Heart feels joy or suffering from that person, his Heart of love is consistently so strong that "it is impossible to repress it."[45] So even after the fall of humanity, and in spite of our continuous rebellion against the purpose of creation, God has been showing his unwavering Heart of love for fallen humanity to restore them, even as he has been suffering at the same time. The purpose of creation, therefore, will eventually be realized. In this sense, "His Will for the providence of restoration, the goal of which is the accomplishment of the purpose of creation, must… be absolute, unique and unchanging."[46] In the opinion of the present writer, this "irrepressibility" of God's Heart of love gives rise to a new definition of divine omnipotence. As such, given this unique nature of Heart, there is no incompatibility between God's omnipotence and his inner suffering.

Rev. Moon's insight into why God's Heart is irrepressible is to be noted here. Using the analogy of air pressure in the atmosphere, he says that God in his sacrificial Heart of "living for the sake of others" lowers himself to make a "vacuum," so to speak, in front of them. Hence they cannot help but eventually give back of themselves to him, just like "high-pressure air" has no choice but to flow to the area of low pressure surrounding the vacuum:

> Suppose we take a volume of air where pressure is evenly distributed and create a vacuum in one place. The more the air pressure in that area approaches a vacuum, the faster the high-pressure air will rotate around the area of low pressure… When God has invested Himself over and over again in search of His objects of love, He can simply remain in His place and everything will naturally come back to Him.[47]

This analogy explains why no one can repress or resist God's Heart. It therefore explains God's omnipotence in his Heart.

This new definition of God's omnipotence in Unification theism is not clearly articulated yet in the official texts of the Divine Principle and Unification Thought, as they seem to rather customarily attribute omnipotence

---

[44] Sun Myung Moon, "Where God Resides and His Course," sermon delivered at Belvedere, Tarrytown, NY, March 19, 1978. http://www.tparents.org/moon-talks/sunmyungmoon78/780319.htm.

[45] NEUT, p. 24.

[46] EDP, p. 155.

[47] Andrew Wilson, ed., *World Scripture and the Teachings of Sun Myung Moon* (Tarrytown, NY: Universal Peace Federation, 2007), pp. 51-52.

to God without defining the term.[48] But the present writer contends that this is what the texts mean to say after all.

This new definition of the divine omnipotence derived from the nature of God's irrepressible Heart is very different from the Thomistic definition of the divine omnipotence as the infinite active power of God who is pure act. Yet it is supported by a number of theologians—not only by Barth, Moltmann and Whitehead, who will be dealt with in detail in Section 4 below, but also by other thinkers such as Geddes MacGregor (1909–1998) and Abraham Heschel (1907–1972).

For MacGregor, who believes that a God of kenotic love can suffer, "To say that God is omnipotent can only mean that nothing diminishes his love."[49] Again, he says:

> The power of God is not to be conceived as an infinite degree of power understood as the ability to do everything (*omnipotere*) or to control everything (*pantokratein*)... The divine power should be conceived as, rather, the infinite power that springs from creative love.[50]

In a similar vein, Heschel remarks: "The most exalted idea applied to God is not infinite wisdom, infinite power, but infinite concern."[51]

3. God Can Be Acted Upon, While Perfect in His United Dual Characteristics

The preceding subsection has mainly explained the inner suffering of an omnipotent God in his Heart, the first dimension of suffering suggested by Fiddes. What, then, about God's suffering at the second dimension, i.e., his receiving of an external constraint? To answer this question correctly, we have to know how God's dual characteristics of *Sungsang* and *Hyungsang* and a creature's dual characteristics of *sungsang* and *hyungsang* can affect and act upon each other.

It is easier to know how God's dual characteristics of *Sungsang* and *Hyungsang* can affect and act upon a creature's dual characteristics of *sungsang* and *hyungsang*, because according to Unification Thought, when the *Sungsang* and *Hyungsang* of the perfect God are united centering on his Heart, the "pre-energy" of his *Hyungsang* will be coupled with the "force of love" from his

---

[48] EDP, pp. 10, 42, 76, 81; NEUT, pp. 1, 22, 164, 253.

[49] Geddes MacGregor, *He Who Lets Us Be: A New Theology of Love* (New York: Seabury Press, 1975), p. 128.

[50] Ibid., p. 15.

[51] Heschel, *The Prophets*, p. 241.

Heart, the core of his *Sungsang*, thus generating "acting energy" (or "Prime Force"),[52] which acts upon a creature's dual characteristics of *sungsang* and *hyungsang*. This way a creature (especially a human person) is inspired and moved to realize the unity of its own dual characteristics of *sungsang* and *hyungsang* to "reflect" God's united dual characteristics of *Sungsang* and *Hyungsang*.

But the real question is: How can this reflection from a creature (especially from a human person) affect and act upon the dual characteristics of *Sungsang* and *Hyungsang* of the perfect God? The Divine Principle says that it "stimulates" the dual characteristics of God.[53] According to Unification Thought, however, a perfect human person is "a being of heart," and that person's "heart" resembles God's Heart because that person knows God's Heart.[54] So, when that person completely realizes the unity of mind and body centering on that person's own heart, some kind of energy of love can issue from that person. This energy of love can affect and act upon God's dual characteristics of *Sungsang* and *Hyungsang* to such a dramatic degree that even the perfect God "surrenders," according to the founder of the Unification Church:

> God is invisible, but we know through Divine Principle that God has internal and external characteristics, *sung sang* and *hyung sang*. Even though God is invisible, He has two parts which work together 100 per cent. When you love someone with your mind and body in total oneness, you are completely flexible and can penetrate anything. The heart of God is perhaps the most impenetrable of all things, but when a bullet of gold love hits it, even God surrenders. When true love hits the heart of God, it causes the greatest thunder and lightning.[55]

This quoted passage says that God in his Heart surrenders, but it also strongly suggests that it happens because God's united dual characteristics of *Sungsang* and *Hyungsang* are affected and acted upon by your God-centered oneness of mind and body.

We still have to explain, however, how God through his dual characteristics of *Sungsang* and *Hyungsang* can also suffer a negative constraint from the fallen world. When a human person fails to realize the God-centered unity of mind and body and instead realizes a mind-body unity centering on a purpose entirely contrary to the purpose of creation, say, a Satan-centered

---

52 NEUT, pp. 8, 26.

53 EDP, p. 33.

54 NEUT, pp.164-67.

55 Sun Myung Moon, "Thanksgiving to God's Will," sermon delivered at Belvedere, Tarrytown, NY, July 8, 1979. http://www.tparents.org/Moon-Talks/sunmyungmoon79/SM790708.htm.

purpose, that undesirable mind-body unity is still a unity yielding a negative kind of energy. That energy can give a negative impact upon God's dual characteristics. According to Moon, "When these children [i.e., Adam and Eve] fell, the consequences had a direct impact on God."[56] He explains right away that one of the consequences of the human fall is the loss of God's temple,[57] which according to the Divine Principle means the loss of an individual human person with God-centered mind-body unity.[58] Thus God, while being perfect because of the complete unity of his dual characteristics of *Sungsang* and *Hyungsang*, can still suffer a negative impact or constraint from each individual human person in the fallen world. This is God's suffering at the second dimension.

4. Our Social Relationships and God's Suffering

Thus far our discussion has only been at the individual level, only dealing with whether or not an individual human person can realize what the Divine Principle calls "God's first blessing" or "individual perfection" with that person's mind-body unity reflecting the unity of God's dual characteristics of *Sungsang* and *Hyungsang.*[59] According to the Divine Principle, however, the purpose of creation has two other blessings of God, because Genesis 1:28, after saying, "Be fruitful" (first blessing), goes on to say, "multiply and fill the earth" (second blessing), and "subdue it and have dominion over" all things (third blessing).[60]

God's second blessing is for a perfected man and woman to love each other as husband and wife to create an ideal family, multiplying and raising their children. "A family or society" thus formed "is patterned after the image of a perfect individual," reflecting not only that individual person's mind-body unity but also the unity of God's dual characteristics of *Sungsang* and *Hyungsang*, with the result that God and also humans feel "joy."[61] And God's third blessing is for a perfected human person and the natural world to "share love and beauty to become completely one." In this case, the dual characteristics of *sungsang* and *hyungsang* in the natural world reflect that human person's mind-body unity. Furthermore the complete oneness of love as a whole between that human person and the natural world is also considered to reflect the unity of

[56] Sun Myung Moon, "The Pinnacle of Suffering," sermon delivered at Belvedere, Tarrytown, NY, June 26, 1977. http://www.tparents.org/Moon-Talks/sunmyungmoon77/770626.htm.
[57] Ibid.
[58] EDP, p. 34.
[59] EDP, pp. 33-34.
[60] EDP, p. 32.
[61] EDP, p. 34.

God's dual characteristics of *Sungsang* and *Hyungsang*, with the result that God and humans as well experience "joy."[62]

When the Divine Principle discusses the mind-body unity of an individual human person (first blessing), it naturally says that it reflects the unity of God's dual characteristics of *Sungsang* and *Hyungsang*. It is interesting to observe, however, that even when it discusses social relationships such as that between a perfected man and woman (second blessing) and that between a perfected human person and the natural world (third blessing), it still says that they reflect the unity of God's dual characteristics of *Sungsang* and *Hyungsang*, hardly saying that they reflect the unity of God's other dual characteristics of Yang and Yin. The reason for this is that it is *Sungsang* and *Hyungsang* that are God's "direct" attributes, while Yang and Yin, which are merely attributes of *Sungsang* and *Hyungsang*, are God's "indirect" attributes.[63]

Unification Thought more clearly explains how social relationships still reflect God's dual characteristics of *Sungsang* and *Hyungsang*, rather than those of Yang and Yin, by its notion of the "Two-Stage Structure of the Divine Image." When the inner mind-body unity of an individual human person is followed by that person's outer unity with other persons or beings, that process is a reflection of the Two-Stage Structure of the Divine Image in which the "inner give and receive action" between "Inner *Sungsang*" (intellect, emotion and will) and "Inner *Hyungsang*" (ideas, concepts and laws) within God's *Sungsang* is followed by the "outer give and receive action" between God's *Sungsang* and *Hyungsang*.[64] Strictly speaking, therefore, social relationships are considered to reflect the unity of God's *Sungsang* and *Hyungsang*.

Consequently, if social relationships of unity are realized as God's second and third blessings, they give a positive impact upon God's dual characteristics of *Sungsang* and *Hyungsang*, with the result that God feels joy in his Heart. But if these social relationships are realized centering on a purpose entirely contrary to the purpose of creation, they give a negative impact upon God's dual characteristics of *Sungsang* and *Hyungsang*, leading him to suffer at the second dimension, with the result that he also suffers in his Heart at the first dimension. For example, when Adam and Eve fell in the Garden of Eden, they realized their relationship of love centering on the purpose of Satan, and this Satan-centered social relationship between a man and a woman, as well as the loss of

---

[62] EDP, pp. 35-36.

[63] NEUT, p. 13. Cf. EDP, p. 19.

[64] NEUT, pp. 49-52.

an individual human person with God-centered mind-body unity, had "a direct impact on God."[65]

5. The Fall of Adam and Eve and God's Suffering

Rev. Moon describes God's tremendous suffering at the fall of Adam and Eve as follows:

> How sorrowful God was when Adam and Eve committed the Fall and sank away from Him! They were to have been the ideal partners for God, who embodies the pure essence of love. God's sorrow exceeded that of any person. He grieved so very deeply. The deeper and greater the value of what was lost, the deeper the sorrow.[66]

Perhaps Moon more than any other theologian teaches such a great degree of God's agony and sorrow over the fall of Adam. Needless to say, theologians of classical theism entirely deny God's suffering. Even those theologians who teach about God's suffering do not take the fall of Adam as seriously as Moon does, either by negating the historicity of the fall of Adam, or by denying the social nature of the fall even if they may believe in its historicity. The fall of Adam and Eve, if it happened historically, has traditionally been believed to have consisted in the voluntary act of disobedience on the part of each individual involved rather than in any wrong social relationship of love between them. Belief in the individualist or atomistic, rather than social, nature of the fall generally seems unable to appreciate the gravity of God's suffering, for it usually fails to recognize the value of what was lost through the fall, i.e., the value of what the Divine Principle calls the second blessing, ideal families centering on God's love. This perhaps gives classical theism still another reason why it denies God's sorrow over the fall. By contrast, the Divine Principle teaches that the fall consisted in a social, and more precisely, premature sexual relationship of Adam and Eve centering on the purpose of Satan,[67] affecting and acting upon God's dual characteristics of *Sungsang* and *Hyungsang*, with the result that he was truly grieved in his Heart.

But there is something more to be mentioned about the value of what was lost. According to Moon, the second blessing, which God expected the first human ancestors to realize, was supposed to be the most intimate substantiation of God's own Heart of love, because it was to be realized

---

[65] Moon, "The Pinnacle of Suffering."

[66] Sun Myung Moon, *Cheon Seong Gyeong: Selections from the Speeches of True Parents* (Seoul, Korea: Sunghwa Publishing Company, 2006), p. 138.

[67] EDP, pp. 53-78. These pages are the chapter on "The Human Fall."

through the God-centered intimate love relationship between Adam and Eve—to God's joy and to the joy of Adam and Eve as well:

> He [i.e., Adam] would have loved his wife [i.e., Eve] as God loved her and Eve would have loved her husband as God loved him. Therefore, Adam and Eve united in perfection would have been the walking God, living God's way of life, God's life itself. It was the Principle of Creation that Adam and Eve feel the joy of God. When they feel joy, God feels joy; when God feels joy, they feel joy.[68]

God lost that precious opportunity, however, because it was taken away by Satan's love which entered the sexual union of Adam and Eve, establishing the "lineage" and "sovereignty" of Satan.[69] This indeed explains the unspeakable suffering of God.

By the way, it is helpful to note that the Divine Principle's sexual interpretation of the fall, while mostly unheard of in the Christian tradition, is not entirely alien in that tradition, for at least two famous early Church Fathers, i.e., St. Clement of Alexandria (c. 150–c. 215) and St. Ambrose (c. 340–397), accepted the idea of the sexual fall,[70] although they, adhering to classical theism, did not believe that God suffered due to this sexual fall of Adam and Eve.

6. The Cross of Jesus Christ and God's Suffering

Since the fall of Adam and Eve, God has been continuously suffering throughout history because of fallen humanity's sinful social relationships under Satan's sovereignty. But especially when Jesus was killed on the cross due to the faithlessness of the Jewish leaders, God suffered tremendously again, and his suffering at that time was no less great than at the fall of Adam. For although he expected Jesus as the second Adam to restore the second blessing lost due to the fall of the first Adam, nevertheless Jesus was killed on the cross before restoring it.

In other words, God suffered because he again could not see the realization of the second blessing, which at that time was to create an ideal family with "Jesus and his [human] Bride" as the first ideal husband and wife to multiply sinless children in "God's direct lineage."[71] God also suffered because he saw the sinful social structure of Jewish leaders and Roman leaders

---

[68] Sun Myung Moon, "Renewed Pride," sermon delivered in Washington, DC, December 4, 1977. http://www.tparents.org/Moon-Talks/sunmyungmoon77/771204.htm.

[69] EDP, p. 68.

[70] For the sexual interpretations of the fall by Clement of Alexandria and Ambrose, see Chapter 10, n. 16 as well as Chapter 7, Section 4, Subsection 2, Subsubsection b ("Clement of Alexandria and Ambrose") in the present book

[71] EDP, p. 284.

under the sovereignty of Satan working strongly to destroy Jesus.[72] And God also suffered when he saw his beloved Son, with his perfect mind-body unity, suffering and dying on the cross: "In the end, when Jesus was crucified, how deep the grief in the heart of God [was] as He watched His beloved son, Jesus, miserably dying!"[73]

Although Christ's death on the cross based on his sacrificial love at that time brought forth what the Divine Principle calls "spiritual salvation," spiritually restoring the second blessing with the resurrected Jesus and the Holy Spirit as spiritual parents of humanity, it was not "full salvation," which is supposed to come "both spiritually and physically."[74] Thus God's suffering continues to exist until Christ comes back in the last days to completely restore the second blessing as well as the first and third blessings here on the earth. The day on which the Christ of the Second Coming and his Bride completely realize the second blessing is the day of God's joy. According to the Divine Principle, the last days are at hand.[75]

At this juncture, it would be appropriate to reiterate the Unification doctrine of the Trinity.[76] God's Heart, *Sungsang* and *Hyungsang* are the three *indiscrete* members of what is called the "inner Trinity," being respectively equivalent to the Father, the Son and the Holy Spirit of that Trinity, while God, perfected Adam and perfected Eve are the three *discrete* members of what is called the "outer Trinity," being respectively equivalent to the Father, the Son and the Holy Spirit of that Trinity in the divine economy. The latter as the outer manifestation or realization of the former is to constitute an ideal family of perfected Adam and Eve centered on God's love, completely reflecting the former to return joy and glory to it. But the latter failed to be realized when Adam fell in the Garden of Eden and when Jesus Christ as the second Adam was killed on Golgotha. This is why God suffered tremendously over the fall of Adam and the death of Jesus Christ on the cross. What was realized after Jesus Christ's death and resurrection was only the "spiritual Trinity" of God, Christ and the Holy Spirit in the divine economy, and the outer Trinity, therefore, is to be realized substantially by the Christ of the Second Coming.

---

[72] EDP, pp. 122-31. This idea that the social structure of evil under the reign of Satan killed Jesus is also echoed in J. Denny Weaver, *The Nonviolent Atonement* (Grand Rapids, MI: Wm. B. Eerdmans Publishing Co., 2001).

[73] NEUT, p. 257.

[74] EDP, pp. 118, 171-72.

[75] EDP, pp. 96-103.

[76] For a detailed discussion of this, see Chapter 5 in the present book.

§4. God's Dual Characteristics as Described by Other Theologians

1. Karl Barth

In criticizing Thomas Aquinas' view of God as *actus purus* ("pure act")[77] and even suggesting that "In God all potentiality is included in His actuality and therefore all freedom in His decision,"[78] Karl Barth proposes a doctrine of God's dual characteristics of "freedom" and "love."[79] According to Barth, while God in his "freedom" is absolutely free from anything, thus being impassible and immutable (unconditioned), he in his "love" reveals himself through Jesus Christ to seek and create fellowship with us in the finite world, thus becoming even passible and mutable (conditioned). God in his love "has limited Himself"[80] to be a suffering God.

The point of connection between divine freedom and love exists when God absolutely freely chooses to love and suffer with us. For Barth, this connection or unity between God's freedom and love means divine perfection: "God's being consists in the fact that He is the One who *loves* in *freedom*. In this He is the perfect being."[81] From this perfection of God are derived various divine perfections (traditionally called attributes) classified under two groups: perfections of the divine freedom such as holiness, on the one hand, and perfections of the divine love such as grace, on the other. God's perfection itself consists in the "complete reciprocity" of these two different sides in him, in which "each of the opposing ideas [i.e., perfections] not only augments but absolutely fulfills the other."[82] This is somewhat similar to the Unification definition of divine perfection as the unity of God's dual characteristics of *Sungsang* and *Hyungsang*, although how much God's dual characteristics of freedom and love in Barth's theology correspond to God's dual characteristics of *Sungsang* and *Hyungsang* in Unification theism needs to be studied more carefully.[83]

---

77 Karl Barth, *Church Dogmatics*, II/1(Edinburg: T&T Clark, 1957), p. 264. His criticism is that the Thomistic view of God as *actus purus* lacks the particularity of each revelatory act of God in the world. He, therefore, suggests to replace this insufficient description with *actus purus et singularis* ("pure and singular act").

78 Ibid., I/1, p. 157.

79 Ibid., II/1, pp. 257-677.

80 Ibid., II/1, p. 518.

81 Ibid., II/1, p. 322. Italics added.

82 Ibid., II/1, p. 343.

83 In *Church Dogmatics*, II/1, pp. 340-41, Barth shows quite a substantial list of those theologians who have suggested God's dual characteristics in various ways from the seventeenth to twentieth

It is in the context of this divine perfection that Barth discusses divine omnipotence. Divine omnipotence, as one of the perfections of the divine love, is not the same as the "omnicausality" of God which would automatically make him the cause of everything above and apart from us.[84] Rather, it is "the omnipotence of love" only in his fellowship of love with us in which he even allows for our freedom.[85] Barth's discussion of omnipotence in relationship to love is again somewhat similar to the Unification notion of Heart of love, wherein the divine omnipotence lies. In fact, Barth couples "constancy" with the omnipotence of God's love,[86] and it is like Unification theism, which attributes "irrepressibility" to the omnipotence of God's Heart.

God, who is thus omnipotent and perfect, chooses in his freedom to suffer for us in Jesus Christ: "For the sake of this choice and for the sake of man He hazarded Himself wholly and utterly. He elected our suffering... as His own suffering. This is the extent to which His election is an election of grace, an election of love."[87]

Perhaps the following two quotations from Barth can be taken to mean that God can suffer at the two dimensions proposed by Fiddes, because they respectively refer to God's passibility and conditionedness in spite of his initial impassibility and unconditionedness:

> He is absolute, infinite, exalted, active, impassible, transcendent, but in all this He is the One who loves in freedom, the One who is free in His love, and therefore not His own prisoner. He is all this as the Lord, and in such a way that He embraces the opposites of these concepts even while He is superior to them.[88]

---

centuries, including the orthodox Lutheran theologians of the seventeenth century (of *attributa negativa* and *positiva*, or *quiescentia* and *operativa*, or *interna* and *externa*, or *absoluta* and *relativa*, or *immanentia* and *transeuntia*, or *primitiva* and *derivata*, or *metaphysica* and *moralia*), the older Reformed theologians (of *attributa incommunicabilia* and *communicabilia*), R. A. Lipsius (of metaphysical and psychological attributes), Wichelhaus (of Elohim and Yahweh), O. Kirn (of formal and material attributes) and E. Troeltsch (of holiness and love). After showing the list, he comments: "In spite of all the differences of nomenclature, basis and arrangement in this classification, and in spite of all the doubts which we can and must feel almost everywhere in matters of detail, it is impossible to overlook or deny the fact that in the last resort it is the same thing which is here perceived and meant with greater or lesser acuteness, so that we have a certain broad consensus of Christian theological opinion at this not unimportant point." One can guess that he would probably have included the Unification doctrine of God's dual characteristics of *Sungsang* and *Hyungsang*, if he had lived long enough to learn it.

[84] Barth, *Church Dogmatics*, II/1, pp. 527-28.

[85] Ibid., II/1, pp. 598-99.

[86] Ibid., II/1, p. 522.

[87] Ibid., II/2, p. 164.

[88] Ibid., IV/1, p. 187.

> God has the prerogative to be free without being limited by His freedom from external conditioning, free also with regard to His freedom, free not to surrender Himself to it, but to use it to give Himself to this communion and to practise this faithfulness in it... God must not only be unconditioned but, in the absoluteness in which He sets up this fellowship, He can and will also be conditioned.[89]

This does not mean, however, that Barth distinguishes clearly enough between God's passibility and conditionedness to speak of them, as Unification theism does, in the context of God's omnipotence in his love, on the one hand, and in the context of God's perfection in the unity of his dual characteristics, on the other.

Barth's doctrine of God's dual characteristics of freedom and love can be traced back to Martin Luther's insightful distinction between the *deus absconditus* (hidden God) and the *deus revalatus* (revealed God). And it, following the Reformer's position, constitutes quite a big step toward understanding God's suffering. It goes well beyond classical theism's assertion that God cannot suffer at all. According to Hendrikus Berkhof (1914–1995), "This fresh formulation of Barth in the doctrine of God has exerted a greater influence than any other part of his theology... Even many who in no way follow him know that on this point they cannot disregard Barth."[90]

But there seem to be at least three difficulties in Barth's formulation. What follows may be a lengthy explanation of them, but it is important to know them well in order to see how different Barth's theology is from Unification theism.

A first difficulty in Barth's formulation is that God in his absolute freedom could have chosen not to seek and create fellowship with us, staying alone as a God without love. In Barth's own words, "He could have remained satisfied with Himself and with the impassible glory and blessedness of His own inner life."[91] This would be a contradiction to God's love Barth is talking about as an "overflowing of His goodness."[92] This is exactly the issue Jürgen Moltmann raises: "Is this concept of absolute freedom of choice not a threat to God's truth and goodness? Could God really be content with his 'impassible glory'?"[93] In criticizing Barth, therefore, Anna Case-Winters goes so far as to say that "although Barth does make efforts in the direction of modifying the

---

89 Ibid., II/1, p. 303.

90 Hendrikus Berkhof, *Christian Faith: An Introduction to the Study of the Faith*, revised ed., trans. Sierd Woudstra (Grand Rapids, MI: Wm. B. Eerdmans Publishing Co., 1986), p. 119.

91 Barth, *Church Dogmatics*, II/2, p. 166.

92 Ibid., IV/2, p. 346.

93 Jürgen Moltmann, *The Trinity and the Kingdom: The Doctrine of God*, trans. Margaret Kohl (Minneapolis, MN: Fortress Press, 1993), p. 53.

scope of divine power, he leaves the [traditional] *meaning* for power… unaltered."[94]

Second, Barth in a very christocentric manner holds that God in his absolute freedom decides from eternity to elect Jesus Christ (who is eternally one with him in the unity of the Godhead) for the creation of the world[95] and also for the salvation of sinful humans.[96] In doing so, he mingles creation, fall and redemption together to attribute their occurrences to the eternal election of Jesus Christ. If God so decides, all humans are to be created through Jesus Christ, all are to commit sin equally, and all without exception are to be redeemed by Jesus Christ. This entails three things, with which some people may take issue: 1) since all humans are to sin, the fall of Adam is not necessarily a historical event but merely a "saga" which generally points to how every human equally sins;[97] 2) God's suffering at the fall of Adam, therefore, is not to be considered at all as a particular historical experience of seriousness for God, although God's general suffering starts from the moment of creation and culminates in the suffering of the Son on the cross; and 3) the death of Jesus Christ on the cross is part of the eternal election within God's freedom of decision. All these three things are basically unacceptable to the Unification tradition.

Critics such as the Catholic theologian Hans Urs von Balthasar (1905–1988) observe that Barth's idea of God's eternal election of Jesus Christ for creation, fall and redemption may have resulted from his own reading of the Bible from his undeniable background of German Idealism, in spite of his desire to avoid bringing in any philosophical system to theology.[98] If so, Barth may be guilty of distorting the biblical message.

Third, although for Barth "the purpose and therefore the meaning of creation" is so that God in his love may have fellowship or "covenant" with us,[99] he does not believe that the realization of that purpose of creation gives any additional joy to God. While Barth calls the world, created by God as a finite world, "an object of His joy,"[100] this divine joy is already within God's own inner life even before the creation of the world. God simply shares it with

---

94 Anna Case-Winters, *God's Power: Traditional Understandings and Contemporary Challenges* (Louisville, KY: Westminster/John Knox Press, 1990), p. 97. Italics hers.
95 Barth, *Church Dogmatics*, II/2, p. 94.
96 Ibid., II/2, p. 116.
97 Ibid., IV/1, p. 508.
98 Hans Urs von Balthasar, *The Theology of Karl Barth: Exposition and Interpretation*, trans. Edward T. Oakes (San Francisco: Ignatius Press, 1992), pp. 218-19.
99 Barth, *Church Dogmatics*, III/1, p. 42.
100 Ibid., III/1, p. 102.

the world, if to a limited degree, at the time of creation, to "affirm" the world as a world of "benefit."[101] Hence, even though our relationships of love, whether between an individual human person and God or between different humans, are each a "copy" or "reflection" of the inner "reciprocity" between the Father and the Son in the unity of love which is the Holy Spirit in the immanent Trinity within God,[102] they do not give any additional joy to God. Even the economic Trinity, which mirrors the immanent Trinity because the redemptive obedience of Jesus Christ in the economic Trinity "reflects" and "corresponds" to the obedience of the eternal Son in the inner Trinity,[103] does not add any joy to the inner life of blessedness in the immanent Trinity.

In spite of these difficulties, however, Barth should be appreciated for going beyond classical theism to present quite a serious theology of God's suffering.

The third point above about the purpose of creation shows that Barth talks about the polarity of the Father and the Son within God as still another kind of God's dual characteristics besides his dual characteristics of freedom and love. This is somewhat confusing. Moltmann, however, addresses the confusion by opting for the polarity of the Father and the Son as God's dual characteristics. It is to him that we turn next.

2. *Jürgen Moltmann*

In criticizing classical theism's idea that God cannot suffer, Jürgen Moltmann says that such a God is completely insensitive and even loveless:

> A God who cannot suffer is poorer than any man. For a God who is incapable of suffering is a being who cannot be involved. Suffering and injustice do not affect him. And because he is so completely insensitive, he cannot be affected or shaken by anything. He cannot weep, for he has no tears. But the one who cannot suffer cannot love either. So he is also a loveless being.[104]

This shows that Moltmann seriously believes God to be a God of love who can suffer. It is from this perspective that he criticizes Barth's idea, described above, that God in his absolute freedom of choice could have chosen not to love and suffer with us. According to Moltmann, if God is a God of love, then "he does not have the choice between being love and *not* being love," and "his liberty" only "lies in doing the good which he himself is, which means

---

[101] Ibid., III/1, p. 331.
[102] Ibid., III/1, p. 185.
[103] Ibid., IV/1, pp. 200-4.
[104] Moltmann, *The Crucified God*, p. 222.

communicating himself."[105] Moltmann thus sees no tension whatsoever between freedom and love in God, while Barth's view of the unity of freedom and love in God may still suggest the priority of freedom over love. This leads Moltmann to develop two significant ideas.

First, he propounds a new understanding of God's love as his undeterred desire for his objects of love. It is "God's longing for 'his Other' and for that Other's free response to the divine love."[106] Thus when God decides to communicate himself to his Other, he does so "out of the inner pleasure of his eternal love" and not out of any arbitrary freedom of choice or out of any compulsion.[107] God, therefore, needs his object partners of love: "God 'needs' the world and man. If God is love, then he neither will nor can be without the one who is his beloved."[108] When God's love is responded to by the Other, "it finds its echo, its answer, its image, and so its bliss in freedom and in the Other";[109] hence God's "joy" in the fulfillment of his love.[110] Until his love is fulfilled, however, God continues to "suffer"; and according to Moltmann, God's suffering is there even at the time of creation because his act of creation involves his "self-limitation" and "self-humiliation" out of love.[111] This new understanding of God's love, developed under the influence of Nikolai Berdyaev (1874–1948),[112] is very similar to the Unification notion of God's Heart of longing, in which God can emotionally feel joy or suffering, depending on how his object partners of love respond.

Moltmann couples this new understanding of God's love with a new definition of divine omnipotence. According to him, when God's love involves his self-limitation and self-humiliation for the sake of his object partners of love, even by withdrawing his omnipotence in the traditional sense of the term, he is paradoxically so powerful that "he has confidence in the free response of men and women." In this sense, "God is nowhere greater than in his humiliation."[113] Giving this new meaning to the divine omnipotence, Moltmann rejects the traditional view of divine omnipotence that has nothing to do with suffering.[114] His understanding of divine omnipotence based on

---

[105] Moltmann, *The Trinity and the Kingdom*, pp. 54-55.
[106] Ibid., p. 106.
[107] Ibid., p. 58.
[108] Ibid.
[109] Ibid., p. 59.
[110] Ibid., pp. 59-60.
[111] Ibid.
[112] Ibid., pp. 42-47.
[113] Ibid., p. 119.
[114] Moltmann, *The Crucified God*, p. 223.

God's love is similar to the Unification idea that God is omnipotent because his Heart of love is so sacrificial for the sake of others as to be irrepressible.

The second idea Moltmann puts forth in criticizing Barth's doctrine of God's dual characteristics of freedom and love is his new doctrine of God's dual characteristics of the Father and the Son. It is trinitarian in the tradition of Western Christianity because Moltmann believes that the Father and the Son are united by love which is the Holy Spirit. But it is still primarily about the relationship of the two poles of God: the Father and the Son. According to Moltmann, "divine perfection" consists in the "movement" of love in God's united dual characteristics of the Father and the Son.[115] Moltmann's definition of divine perfection as the unity of the Father and the Son in God is similar to the Unification view of God's perfection as the unity of his dual characteristics of *Sungsang* and *Hyungsang*, although whether or not the Father and the Son in God in Moltmann's theology correspond to God's *Sungsang* and *Hyungsang* in Unification theism is a different question which needs to be addressed through a more careful study.[116]

Moltmann believes that God, through his unified dual characteristics which constitute his perfection, can be affected and acted upon by the world just as he affects and acts upon the world: "Just as God goes out of himself through what he does, giving his world his own impress, so his world puts its impress on God too, through its reactions, its aberrations and its own initiatives."[117] In what Moltmann calls "the history of the triune God with the world,"[118] God affects and acts upon the world, especially when he, through his dual characteristics of the Father and the Son, creates the world, has the Son incarnated for the redemption of humans in the world, and pours out the Holy Spirit after the Son's death and resurrection to transform the world for the eschatological kingdom of God. The world, in turn, affects and acts upon God, when its creation has God "rejoice" over it and "have pleasure" in it because it is "good";[119] when the incarnate Son redemptively has humans assume the "image of God" and "gathers them into his relationship of sonship to the Father";[120] and when the Holy Spirit renews the world and brings about the "new solidarity and fellowship" of humans to partake of the "inner-

[115] Moltmann, *The Trinity and the Kingdom*, pp. 45-46.

[116] Chapter 5 in the present book sees that the Father, the Son and the Holy Spirit in the immanent Trinity in the Christian tradition correspond respectively to God's Heart, *Sungsang* and *Hyungsang* in the inner Trinity in Unification theism.

[117] Moltmann, *The Trinity and the Kingdom*, p. 99.

[118] Ibid., p. 97.

[119] Ibid., pp. 58, 112.

[120] Ibid., pp. 117-18.

trinitarian life" of God, giving "joy" and "bliss" to God.[121] What is important here is that the image of God is none other than his inner-trinitarian image,[122] which is the relationship of love between the Father and the Son through the Holy Spirit within God, and that when this relational image of God is realized and reflected in human relationships in the world as a result of the external works of the Trinity, God becomes happy. According to Moltmann, the glorification of God, which has traditionally been referred to as the "purpose of creation," really means that "the world [reflecting this image of God] becomes the bliss of God the Father and the Son."[123]

Since the very time of creation, however, the world has never fully reflected the image of God. Hence God has always been receiving and suffering a negative impact from the world. Even God's creation of the world through his love involves his suffering because it involved his acceptance of the finitude of that world as an impact in his self-limitation and self-humiliation in his dual characteristics of the Father and the Son: "Creative love is always suffering love as well."[124] God's suffering reached its peak at the time of the incarnate Son's death on the cross. Moltmann's explanation of it is again trinitarian, using God's dual characteristics between the Father and the Son in the Holy Spirit.[125] In response to the sinful world which needs to be redeemed, the Father forsook the Son on the cross. Thus the Son experienced the agony of being forsaken by the Father, who in turn experienced the suffering of separation from the Son. But the Father and the Son, by surrendering to this painful situation, experienced a new unity with each other in the Holy Spirit. And "What happens on Golgotha reaches into the innermost depths of the Godhead, putting its impress on the trinitarian life in eternity."[126]

Moltmann is quite often criticized for disregarding the immanent Trinity in favor of the economic Trinity because his book, *The Crucified God* (1972), does not talk about the Trinity apart from the historical event of the cross.[127] But his later, more mature work, *The Trinity and the Kingdom* (1980), tones down this initial approach and makes a distinction between the two kinds of the Trinity by mentioning the eternal "inner-trinitarian love" as distinguished from

---

121 Ibid., pp. 126-27.
122 Ibid., pp. 198-200.
123 Ibid., p. 113.
124 Ibid., p. 59.
125 Ibid., pp. 80-83.
126 Ibid., p. 81.
127 Moltmann, *The Crucified God*, p. 207: "Anyone who really talks of the Trinity talks of the cross of Jesus, and does not speculate in heavenly riddles."

the process of the world.[128] By this, however, he does not mean that the immanent and the economic Trinity are two discrete sets of the Trinity, like the inner and the outer Trinity in Unification theism. They are rather "the relationship of the triune God to himself" and "the relationship of the triune God to the world," respectively, referring to only one and the same Trinity in God from two different perspectives. And these two have a mutual relationship: "The economic Trinity not only reveals the immanent Trinity; it also has a retroactive effect on it."[129] In the last days in which "everything is 'in God' and 'God is all in all'," however, the economic Trinity is completed and perfected to be "raised into and transcended in the immanent Trinity."[130]

Another related criticism quite frequently directed toward Moltmann is that he tends to be tritheistic because he regards members of the Trinity as three subjects or "distinct centres of consciousness and action."[131] But he is not a tritheist, as he does not understand them to be three discrete divine individuals. He simply wants to treat them relationally and dynamically in a "social doctrine of the Trinity" because he is critical toward the traditional doctrine of the Trinity for tending to treat them merely as three modes of being. He criticizes the traditional trinitarian idea of *una substantia–tres personae* (one substance–three persons) for having disintegrated into "abstract monotheism" that is unable to explain their relationships of *perichoresis* (mutual indwelling) and their dynamic activities in the divine economy.[132] Moltmann's understanding of the three members as three centers of conscious activity, as the present writer argues elsewhere,[133] is "a very good development in the history of the doctrine of the Trinity" from the perspective of Unification theism, which pursues the completion of the divine economy in which the three members of the "outer Trinity" (God, perfected Adam and perfected Eve) are discrete self-conscious beings but unite with one another to completely reflect the "inner Trinity."

Moltmann's theology of God's suffering is an important development from the thesis of Luther's theology of the cross (*theologia crucis*) that "God is not to be found except in sufferings and in the cross."[134] He reports that Luther's theology of the cross is more or less accepted ecumenically among

---

[128] Moltmann, *The Trinity and the Kingdom*, pp. 58, 106.
[129] Ibid., p. 160.
[130] Ibid., p. 161.
[131] Ibid., p. 146.
[132] Ibid., pp. 16-20.
[133] See Chapter 5, Section 5, Subsection 3 ("Jürgen Moltmann") in the present book.
[134] Martin Luther, *Luther: Early Theological Works*, trans. and ed. James Atkinson (Philadelphia: Westminster Press, 1962), p. 291.

twentieth-century Catholic and Protestant theologians such as Karl Rahner (1904–1984), Hans Urs von Barthasar, H. Mühlen (1927–2006), Hans Küng, Karl Barth, Eberhart Jüngel (1934–2021) , and H.-G. Geyer (1929–1999).[135]

Yet there seems to be at least one major problem in Moltmann's influential position. It is that he mingles creation and redemption together to attribute the occurrences of both of them to the immanent Trinity in the Godhead. It is fine to attribute the occurrence of creation to it, because God is the creator anyway. But it would be problematic to attribute the occurrence of redemption to it, as Moltmann does, when he says: "the Son's sacrifice of boundless love on Golgotha is from eternity already included in the exchange of the essential, the consubstantial love which constitutes the divine life of the Trinity."[136] A God of love would not want his created object partners of love from the beginning to sin for their redemption. As was shown above, Barth has the same problem. The difference is that while Barth believes that the eternal election of the Son in God's freedom makes all these occur, Moltmann argues that the close relationship of the two sets of the Trinity makes whatever is in the immanent Trinity happen in the economic Trinity as well. This problem in Moltmann yields three undesirable corollaries, as in Barth: 1) all humans are to sin for their redemption through the Son, which is also to occur, so that the fall of Adam does not have to be singled out as a particular historical event but rather has to be treated as a "saga" or "myth";[137] 2) God's suffering at the fall of Adam, therefore, does not have to be considered at all; and 3) the tragic death of the Son on the cross, which causes the Father to suffer, is already planned within the immanent Trinity.

In spite of this, Moltmann's formulation, which is much more innovative than Barth's, should be appreciated for its deep theological insights into God's suffering, consistent with an important biblical theme.

3. Alfred North Whitehead

While Barth and Moltmann have their particular Christian perspectives on God's suffering, Alfred North Whitehead has a broader philosophical system to explain it. According to his philosophy of organism or process philosophy, God and the world are interconnected with each other and affect each other because of the dual characteristics of mental and physical poles that can be found in the whole of reality including God and the world. Basic units of reality

---

[135] Moltmann, *The Crucified God*, pp. 200-3.

[136] Moltmann, *The Trinity and the Kingdom*, p. 168.

[137] Moltmann, "Justice for Victims and Perpetrators," *Reformed World* 44 (March 1994). http://www.warc.ch/pc/rw941/01.html.

are called "actual entities." Each actual entity in the world is "essentially dipolar with its physical and mental poles."[138] God, who is an actual entity "not to be treated as an exception to all metaphysical principles" but as "their chief exemplification," [139] is therefore also dipolar, having "primordial" and "consequent" natures, which are respectively mental and physical.[140] This is very similar to God's dual characteristics of *Sungsang* and *Hyungsang* in Unification theism.[141]

Whitehead also has a notion of God's "appetition" or "Eros," which somehow resembles the Unification notion of God's Heart. God's "appetition," belonging to his primordial nature, constitutes his "purpose" or "aim," which is to seek "intensity" or "depth of satisfaction" in each actual entity in the world eventually for "the fulfillment of his own being."[142] Thus his appetition is also called his "subjective aim."[143] God's "Eros," another name of his appetition, is defined as "the living urge towards all possibilities, claiming the goodness of their realization."[144] In short, it is God's desire of love for the world.

When God's two natures are "integrated" centering on his subjective aim,[145] his input for unity is yielded as an "initial aim" for each actual entity in the world.[146] Hence each actual entity, using that input from God as well as its own self-creativity, may realize a unity or integration of its own mental and physical poles[147] and also its unity with other actual entities in its process of "concrescence" to reach the final phase of "intensity of satisfaction" promoted by "order" among these components.[148] Each and every actual entity finally "enjoys" this "self-realization,"[149] and thereafter avails itself to be "objectified" for other actual entities.[150]

---

138 Alfred North Whitehead, *Process and Reality: An Essay in Cosmology*, corrected ed., ed. David Ray Griffin and Donald W. Sherburne (New York: Free Press, 1985), p. 239.
139 Ibid., p. 343.
140 Ibid., p. 345.
141 Regarding the similarity between God's "primordial" and "consequent" natures in Whitehead's thought and God's *Sungsang* and *Hyunsang* in Unification theism, see Theodore T. Shimmyo, "Dipolar Theism in Process Thought and Unificationism," in *Unification Theology: In Comparative Perspectives*, ed. Anthony Guerra (Barrytown, NY: Unification Theological Seminary, 1988), pp. 35-48.
142 Whitehead, *Process and Reality*, p. 105.
143 Ibid., p. 344.
144 Alfred North Whitehead, *Adventures of Ideas* (New York: Macmillan Co., 1933), p. 381.
145 Whitehead, *Process and Reality*, p. 345.
146 Ibid., pp. 244, 344.
147 Ibid., p. 266.
148 Ibid., pp. 84-85.
149 Ibid., p. 51.
150 Ibid., pp. 23, 25, 41.

Intensities of satisfaction thus created in the world constitute values of beauty, and they are received by God through his two natures centering on his subjective aim. The manner by which God receives these values is this: first, God physically feels them in his consequent nature, and then, he integrates them with his primordial nature.[151] If the world shows him its values of beauty which reflect the unity of his two natures centering on his subjective aim, God experiences his own satisfaction and enjoyment. If, however, the world creates "disorder" among its components, which "enfeebles" the intensity of satisfaction in each actual entity,[152] God may not experience as much enjoyment, but he still receives it with "infinite patience"[153] and "love."[154] It is in this context that Whitehead says: "God is the greatest companion—the fellow-sufferer who understands."[155] It can be said, therefore, that God can emotionally suffer in his appetition or Eros, while he can suffer an external constraint from the world through the dual characteristics of his primordial and consequent natures. Hence God's suffering includes the two dimensions.

But is this God omnipotent and perfect? Whitehead does not think so in classical theism's sense of the terms. Maintaining that God is not "coercive" but "persuasive,"[156] Whitehead criticizes classical theism's idea that omnipotence is a monopoly of power: "the deeper idolatry, of the fashioning of God in the image of the Egyptian, Persian, and Roman imperial rulers, was retained. The Church gave unto God the attributes that belonged exclusively to Caesar."[157] He also critiques classical theism's view of divine perfection as "eminently real" that comes from Aristotle's notion of God as the unmoved mover.[158]

According to the Whiteheadian scholar Charles Hartshorne (1897–2000), however, the God of Whitehead is omnipotent and perfect in a new sense. First, God is omnipotent because his creative power is "all-inclusive" and "all-surpassing" in the whole of reality in which all self-creative actual entities are interconnected in give and take.[159] God's power is "all-inclusive" in that it influences all other self-creative actual entities under any circumstances; and

[151] Ibid., p. 345.

[152] Ibid., p. 84.

[153] Ibid., p. 346.

[154] Ibid., p. 351.

[155] Ibid.

[156] Whitehead, *Adventures of Ideas*, p. 213.

[157] Whitehead, *Process and Reality*, p. 342.

[158] Ibid.

[159] Charles Hartshorne, *Omnipotence and Other Theological Mistakes* (Albany, NY: State University of New York Press, 1984), p. 44.

his power is "all-surpassing" in that it is greater than the power of all other actual entities because all other actual entities may be unable to influence others as much under some circumstances. This kind of omnipotence, in the judgment of the present writer, seems to be derived from God's penetrating love from Eros.

Next, Hartshorne gives a new definition of God's perfection. According to this new definition, God is perfect by reason of his "dual transcendence,"[160] which means that God as a God of the dual characteristics of primordial and consequent natures is the supreme and chief exemplification of each pair of metaphysical contraries such as infinite/finite and absolute/relative, providing his vision of unity to the world based on the complete unity of his own two natures.

From the above, it can be understood that in Whitehead's thought God's omnipotence and perfection are respectively derived from his Eros and his dual characteristics, and that God, who is thus omnipotent and perfect, can suffer at the first and second dimensions, respectively.

Whitehead is not a theologian, but by applying his process philosophy to Christian theology, process theologians have developed their views of sin, Christ, redemption, Trinity, church, etc. Process theologians believe that God suffered at the death of Jesus Christ on the cross,[161] thus being in agreement on this point with Barth and Moltmann. But they do not believe, as Barth and Moltmann do, that the cross of Jesus Christ was foreordained. In this regard, they agree with Unification theism. For process theologians, Jesus is genuinely a human just like all other humans. But he as the Christ is different from all of them in that he feels God's initial aim to a "full"[162] or "unsurpassable"[163] degree, while they only feel it to lesser degrees because of their imperfection. The salvific work of Christ, therefore, means that he encourages them to feel the divine initial aim more, by having them unite with him, so that they may be transformed. Thus salvation is incarnation-oriented rather than crucifixion-oriented. The crucifixion of Jesus Christ took place because other humans unfortunately rejected him against God's ideal: "Process theology understands the cross in relational terms as the result of human decisions rather than divine necessity, sacrifice, or coercion"; and "God also experienced… the stark

---

160 Ibid., pp. 45-47.

161 Daniel Day Williams, *The Spirit and the Forms of Love* (New York: Harper & Row, Publishers, 1968), pp. 166-67. See also Bruce G. Epperly, *Process Theology: A Guide for the Perplexed* (New York: T&T Clark International, 2011), pp. 51, 73-74.

162 Marjorie Suchocki, *God, Christ, Church: A Practical Guide to Process Theology* (New York: Crossroad, 1982), pp. 95-96.

163 David R. Griffin, *A Process Christology* (Philadelphia: Westminster Press, 1973), p. 216.

realities of Jesus' encounter with Pilate and the Jewish leaders. Like us, these religious leaders and political leaders could have chosen differently; they could have welcomed God's vision of Shalom embodied in Jesus' words and deeds."[164] Hence God's tremendous disappointment and pain was there, even though through the cross of Jesus Christ the divine love, which was even stronger than the power of death, was still shown to continuously transform people.[165]

But process theology as it developed based on Whitehead's philosophy has at least three difficulties. First, while this school of theology quite profoundly understands God's suffering at the death of Jesus Christ on the cross, it is silent about God's suffering at the fall of Adam, unlike Unification theism. The reason is that process theologians do not accept the historicity of Adam's fall at all, as they follow Whitehead's idea that human beings are already naturally imperfect because they inherit the imperfections of their antecedents in a very long evolutionary process from lower-grade actual entities to higher-grade ones and organisms, although this process of evolution is generally guided by God's initial aim. Thus the fall of Adam is a "myth."[166] This does not mean that process theologians have no theory of sin at all. On the contrary, according to them, sin is related to our imperfection, and it is to volitionally turn away from God's aim for us to realize values of beauty in our lives.[167] And when God sees us sinning that way, he suffers.

A second difficulty in process theology is that it as yet has no clear doctrine of the Trinity. Although several process theologians have developed their views of the Trinity, they have not reached a consensus regarding the identities of the three trinitarian members in relationship to the two natures of God.[168] Everyone in the process school seems to agree that Jesus Christ is a discrete human being who fully feels God's initial aim, and who therefore could well be a member of the so-called economic Trinity. But they do not address the question of whether the Holy Spirit should eventually be discrete from God just like Jesus Christ is. Adding to this lack of clarity, John B. Cobb, Jr. (1925–

---

164 Epperly, *Process Theology*, pp. 73-74.

165 Suchocki, *God, Christ, Church*, p. 106.

166 Suchocki, "Original Sin Revisited." http://www.religion-online.org/showarticle.asp?title=2817.

167 Epperly, *Process Theology*, pp. 87-90.

168 Lewis S. Ford, for example, identifies the Father, the Son and the Holy Spirit as God himself, his primordial nature and initial aim, respectively in his *The Lure of God: A Biblical Background for Process Theism* (Philadelphia: Fortress Press, 1978), pp. 103-4. But Joseph A. Bracken tends to identify the three as God's primordial nature, consequent nature and initial aim, respectively in his *The Triune Symbol: Persons, Process, and Community* (New York: University Press of America, 1985).

2024) and David Ray Griffin (1939–2022) are reluctant to develop a process doctrine of the Trinity because they believe that there are only two natures of God, i.e., his primordial and consequent natures, and not three: "process theology is not interested in formulating [three] distinctions within God for the sake of conforming with traditional Trinitarian notions."[169] For this reason, process theology has not yet developed any argument to say that the immanent Trinity is reflected by some kind of the Trinity in the divine economy (one of whose members could be Jesus Christ as a discrete human being) to receive joy from that reflection.

A third difficulty concerns Whitehead's idea that the world exists from all eternity without any beginning in time: God "is not *before* all creation, but *with* all creation."[170] Whitehead rejects the traditional doctrine of creation *ex nihilo*, and asserts that God creates the world only in the sense that he provides his initial aim to the existing world in its evolutionary process from simpler forms of order to more complex forms to enhance values of beauty for enjoyment: "He does not create the world, he saves it: or, more accurately, he is the poet of the world, with tender patience leading it by his vision of truth, beauty, and goodness."[171] Although this appears to explain the purpose of creation in the name of God's initial aim, it cannot explain why God had to bring the world into existence with that purpose of creation. Furthermore, if there is no beginning of the world, there is no final end of the world either, as the process of evolution continues for eternity: "Process eschatology, or the vision of the ultimate future of human and planetary life, is open-ended. Following Whitehead, process theologians do not envisage any predetermined terminus point for planetary history."[172] Perhaps this problem is related to Whitehead's other problematic idea that God himself is not the ultimate cause of creative power but merely an exemplification of that creative power which he believes is located outside of God as the "ultimate metaphysical principle."[173]

Conclusion

The present study has shown that Barth, Moltmann and Whitehead, unlike classical theism, understand God's suffering, if in their own ways: Barth, by

---

[169] John B. Cobb, Jr. and David Ray Griffin, *Process Theology: An Introductory Exposition* (Philadelphia: Westminster Press, 1976), p. 110.
[170] Whitehead, *Process and Reality*, p. 343. Italics original.
[171] Ibid., p. 346.
[172] Epperly, *Process Theology*. p, 132.
[173] Whitehead, *Process and Reality*, p. 21.

having God in his freedom choose to suffer; Moltmann, by bringing God's longing love to the fore; and Whitehead, through his philosophical system which affirms the interdependence between God and the world. Among them, perhaps Barth is the least distant from classical theism while Whitehead may be the most distant. Moltmann is the most trinitarian while Whitehead (together with process theologians) is the least trinitarian.

In spite of these differences, however, the three thinkers all have two things in common: 1) God's love, because of which he is omnipotent, but in which he can suffer internally; and 2) God's dual characteristics, because of whose unity he is perfect, but through which he can suffer an external constraint from outside. The first thing in common, which is referred to by Barth, Moltmann and Whitehead as God's love, desire and Eros, respectively, is very different from God's "passionless" love in classical theism. And the second common point mentioned by the three thinkers is God's unified dual characteristics, conceived of as freedom and love, as the Father and the Son, and as his primordial and consequent natures, respectively. This is very different from classical theism's concept of God's "simplicity" as pure spirit or pure actuality. Thus the three disagree with classical theism and converge with the thesis of Unification theism that: 1) God suffers emotionally in his irrepressible and therefore omnipotent Heart; and 2) God suffers an external constraint from outside through his perfectly unified dual characteristics of *Sungsang* and *Hyungsang*.

It is interesting to note that this convergence exists despite the fact that Rev. Moon developed Unification theism entirely independently from the three, who in turn established their formulations entirely apart from Moon. Also, Whitehead developed his philosophy entirely separately from Barth and Moltmann. This might be taken as proof that these two common points, although unacceptable to classical theism, should be taken seriously as important and promising conceptualities in theology. Furthermore, with these two conceptualities in common, these thinkers and Unification theism may be more appealing than classical theism because they more adequately explain the biblical notion of God's suffering.

Unification theism, however, takes God's suffering more seriously than Barth, Moltmann and Whitehead do, for it talks about God's unspeakable suffering at the fall of Adam, while they are entirely silent about it. Unification theism understands the importance of the purpose of creation, especially of the second blessing, which is for Adam and Eve to create an ideal family that God can rejoice over as his abode of love. Unification theism understands, therefore, that when God lost that ideal family through the sexual fall of Adam and Eve centering on Satan, it caused him devastating suffering. By contrast, Barth, Moltmann and Whitehead do not see the purpose of creation that way, and they even ignore the historicity of Adam's fall in the name of the universal sinfulness of humanity—whether due to the eternal election of Jesus Christ for redemption (Barth), what happens in the immanent Trinity (Moltmann), or the evolutionary process of the world (Whitehead).

Further, although Barth, Moltmann and process theologians estimably understand God's suffering at the death of Jesus Christ on the cross, they do not believe, as Unification theism does, that God suffered because the chance of creating an ideal family was lost again due to the death of the second Adam on the cross. They rather limit their scope to a focus on God's own choice to suffer with Jesus Christ (Barth), the Father's inseparable love for the Son (Moltmann), or the philosophical interdependence of God and Jesus Christ in the world (process theologians). Also, Barth's and Moltmann's knowledge of God's suffering at the cross of Jesus Christ might be somewhat jeopardized by their idea that the cross was foreordained by the eternal election of Jesus Christ (Barth), or by the immanent Trinity (Moltmann), although process theology might not have this problem

The knowledge of God's suffering is one of the striking characteristics of the Unification Church. It is not just a doctrine. It is also a part of praxis in Unification spirituality, and Unification members are encouraged to work hard to become God's sons and daughters in his ideal family in order to comfort God and liberate him from his suffering. In this context, Moon explains what kind of prayer we should offer to God:

> We will say to God, "For the first time in history You have sons and daughters who truly understand Your suffering. Heavenly Father, please be comforted by us, because we understand Your broken heart. God, take comfort and rest because Your sons and daughters are determined to gratefully go over greater suffering than You have." That is our prayer.[174]

It seems, however, that the notion of God's suffering has not been theologically articulated enough in the Unification tradition. While God's Heart of suffering has always been taught,[175] the omnipotence of his Heart of love behind that suffering has not explicitly been referred to in connection with it. Regarding the unity of God's dual characteristics of *Sungsang* and *Hyungsang*

---

[174] Sun Myung Moon, "The Pinnacle of Suffering," sermon delivered at Belvedere, Tarrytown, NY, June 26, 1977. http://www.tparents.org/Moon-Talks/sunmyungmoon77/770626.htm.

[175] See, for example, NEUT, pp. 252-57; EDP, pp. 8, 81, 196; and *Cheon Seong Gyeong* (2006), pp. 132-43.

centering on his Heart, while this has been clearly identified as God's perfection by Unification Thought, it has not been explicitly articulated anywhere, if implicitly discussed, as the channel through which God can suffer an external constraint from the fallen world or receive a delightful impact from an ideal world giving him joy in his Heart. The present chapter is an attempt to address this need. Interestingly, we have realized that the study of Barth, Moltmann and Whitehead can help address this need in Unification theism.

Chapter 7

The Fall

The traditional Christian doctrine of the fall as a whole has two different components: 1) the doctrine of Adam's fall, and 2) the doctrine of original sin proper. The reason is that Adam's fall as his primal sinful act is usually distinguished from original sin proper, which is considered to be a sinful condition subsequently given to him and his offspring as a punishment for his primal sin.[1]

It is to be pointed out at the outset that these two components of the traditional Christian doctrine of the fall seem to be inconsistent with each other because their approaches are inconsistent: Whereas the former component has an *atomistic, individualist* approach, the latter, in talking about the transmission of original sin, has a *relational* and even *sexual* approach.

In other words, according to the former component in its atomistic, individualist approach, the three figures of Adam, Eve and Lucifer (originally

---

[1] St. Augustine coined the term "original sin" (*peccatum originale*) in his early treatise of 397, "Miscellany of Questions in Response to Simplician," 1:1:10; see *The Works of Saint Augustine: A Translation for the 21st Century*, vol. I/12: *Responses to Miscellaneous Questions*, ed. Raymond Canning, trans. Boniface Ramsey (Hyde Park, NY: New City Press, 2008), p. 179. At that time, he actually meant by it the primal sin of Adam. As will be shown later, however, he in his later years distinguished this primal sin of Adam from original sin proper, saying that original sin proper is now a sinful condition subsequently imposed upon Adam and his offspring as a punishment for his primal sin. Original sin in this latter sense, which Augustine used later, has become what the term, original sin, usually signifies. More precisely, it is *peccatum originale originatum* ("originated" original sin), while the primal sin of Adam may well be called *peccatum originale originans* ("originating" original sin). Augustine was aware of this distinction, although there is a confusion of the two quite often among many people.

a good angel)[2] individually fell because each of them, with free will given as a gift of God, severally made the wrong choice of disobeying God's commandment that the fruit of the tree of the knowledge of good and evil not be eaten. Even before Lucifer's temptation to Eve and her temptation to Adam were able to make any appeal to the real act of eating the fruit, each of them had already fallen because of disobedience through free will. Thus the fall was basically an individual matter. In contrast to this, however, the latter component in its relational, even sexual approach affirms the close relationship of all members of the human race, saying that original sin has been transmitted from one generation to another through the sexual union of parents for procreation at each generation since the time of Adam and Eve under the influence of Satan.

This apparent inconsistency can be explained by the historical situation of the time of St. Augustine (354–430), largely by whom the traditional Christian doctrine of the fall as a whole was established. In his earlier years as a Christian leader he was involved in the Manichaean controversy and developed a rather libertarian doctrine of the fall of Adam based on the notion of free will against the Manichaean determinism. In his later years, he involved himself in the Pelagian controversy and developed a basically pessimistic doctrine of original sin against the Pelagian optimism, by paying more attention to the reality of the shared fallenness of humankind. This shift of emphasis resulted in the inconsistency in question.

This inconsistency actually means that whereas the latter component in its relational, sexual approach clearly presupposes the inheritance of original sin, the historicity of Adam and the existence of Satan, the former component in its atomistic, individualist approach does not need to, as it amounts to believing that one's sin is basically caused only by one's own free will and not by the influence of anyone else. Like it or not, therefore, this inconsistency has given rise to three quite serious problems of theological ambiguity: 1) that the inheritance of original sin is affirmed, on the one hand, but obscured, on the other; 2) that the historicity of Adam is regarded as a necessary component, on

[2] Strictly speaking, there is no biblical evidence that there was a good angel or archangel called Lucifer, who fell to become a fallen angel. "Lucifer" in the Bible only refers to the King of Babylon (Isa. 14:12 in KJV). Even in the days of Augustine, therefore, Lucifer was not yet a common name for the devil or Satan, the chief of the fallen angels. But St. Jerome (c. 342–420) and some other Fathers started to identify Lucifer with Satan, by taking Isaiah 14:12 ("How art thou fallen from heaven, O Lucifer, son of the morning!") in conjunction with Luke 10:18 ("I saw Satan fall like lightening from heaven"). This identification later became just customary in the history of Christianity. Part of the custom is also to say that Lucifer as the chief of the fallen angels was an archangel.

the one hand, but deemed not absolutely needed, on the other; and 3) that the existence of Satan is required, on the one hand, but not necessarily required, on the other.

These three problems of theological ambiguity were made more serious and unsolved historically by the emergences of modern liberal theology under the influence of the Enlightenment and of evolutionary theology under the influence of Darwinism, which explicitly denied the inheritance of original sin, the historicity of Adam and the existence of Satan. Liberal and evolutionary theologians argued that original sin is merely a figurative expression of the very universal fact that everybody sins because of imperfect and even fallen human nature, or animal nature, which everyone has from the beginning, and not because of the fall of a first human ancestor nor because of a Satan. Currently, the three problems are far from being settled and involve continuing debate. A recent Catholic writer confesses that the whole question about original sin is "far from being a theologically settled question."[3]

The Unification doctrine of the fall adopts a relational, sexual approach consistently *both* with respect to the fall of Adam *and* the transmission of original sin. The fall involved two consecutive sexual relationships of illicit love: 1) a spiritual sexual relationship of illicit love in which Lucifer seduced Eve; and 2) a physical sexual relationship of illicit love in which Eve seduced Adam. The act of eating the fruit meant having an illicit sexual relationship, although Adam and Eve, according to the Divine Principle, were supposed to eventually eat the fruit as husband and wife in their God-given blessed marriage after reaching a point of individual maturity. Freedom on the part of each was not the cause of the fall; rather, freedom was "lost" by the fall as it was overwhelmed by "the stronger power of unprincipled love."[4] As for the transmission of original sin, the Divine Principle teaches that because Adam and Eve committed their sexual fall under Satan, they formed "a four position foundation yoked to Satan," which gave rise to "the lineage of Satan."[5] Throughout history this fallen lineage has always involved Satan-centered procreational sex on the part of parents, giving birth to sinful children. This is how original sin has been sexually transmitted from one generation to another,

In the present study, the first and second sections will respectively discuss the traditional Christian and Unification doctrines of the fall. The third section will, in more detail, deal with how the three problems of theological ambiguity,

[3] Ralph J. Lawrence, "Creation," in *Principles of Catholic Theology: A Synthesis of Dogma and Morals*, ed. Edward J. Gratsch (New York: Alba House, 1981), p. 81.
[4] *Exposition of the Divine Principle* (H.S.A.-U.W.C., 1996), p. 75. Henceforth abbreviated as EDP.
[5] EDP, p. 68.

which resulted from the inconsistency of the traditional Christian doctrine of the fall, were made more serious and unsolved by modern liberal theology and evolutionary theology. The fourth, final section will show that the Unification doctrine of the fall does not have these problems at all, as it takes a relational, sexual approach consistently both on the fall of Adam and on the transmission of original sin. The final section will also show that the Unification doctrine of Adam's fall in its relational, sexual approach has several allies in the Judeo-Christian tradition: some writers in Jewish pseudepigrapha and rabbinical literature and early Church Fathers such as St. Clement of Alexandria (c. 150–c. 215) and St. Ambrose (c. 340–397), all of whom sexually interpreted Adam's fall. A certain historical-critical approach to Genesis 3 will be shown as another ally, as it asserts that Genesis 3 was a Yahwist critique of the Canaanite sex cults of fertility. The historicity of Adam and Eve will also be argued for from the nature of the Divine Principle as a "systematic theology" and from "Unification evolutionary creationism" which involves modern paleoanthropology.

§1. The Traditional Christian Doctrine of the Fall

Although prior to the time of Augustine there had been a basic Christian understanding of Adam's fall and its great influence on his offspring, the traditional Christian doctrine regarding these was systematized and established largely by him.

1. Augustine's Doctrine of Adam's Fall

Before his conversion to Christianity in Milan in 386, Augustine was involved in Manichaeism in Carthage for some nine years and then with Neoplatonism in Milan for about two years. It was natural, then, that he as a Christian utilized his past experiences of Manichaeism and Neoplatonism to address the problem of evil and thereby formulate his doctrine of Adam's fall during the Manichaean controversy, although the Bible was the primary source for him.

Augustine used to be much drawn to Manichaeism, because its cosmic dualism of God and Satan, making God a finite and limited God, offered what he thought to be a good explanation of the virulent evil he himself was going through as a young man, and also because its determinism, making substantial evil necessary, freed immoral human beings such as him from any responsibility for evildoing. But he, now as a responsible Christian, critiqued Manichaeism, and in doing so, drew upon Neoplatonism to assert that there is only one God, who is good, infinite and supreme, that all being (*esse*) in the world, coming from such a God, is good, and that evil is therefore "non-being" (*non esse*).

a. Creation out of nothing

Augustine, however, was not simply a Neoplatonist but a Christian Neoplatonist. So he abandoned the Neoplatonic theory of emanation in favor of the Christian doctrine of "creation out of nothing" (*creatio ex nihilo*), which had been gradually developed since the second century.[6] By "creation out of nothing," Augustine meant that the transcendent and omnipotent God of Christianity does not use his own substance nor any preexisting independent material to create the world, as he creates it only "by word and command."[7] Therefore, whereas for the Neoplatonists there is a monistic continuity between God and the world, for Augustine there is a deep gap between God and the created world.

This gap means that while God is supreme and unchangeable, all created beings, as long as they are created out of nothing and thereby participate in nothing, are changeable.[8] This changeability or mutability of created beings, in turn, means that it is possible for them to fall away from their own given natural places to lower ones, thus being able to corrupt, although originally they, whether great or small, are all good creatures of God in and of themselves, with each of them given its proper "measure, form, and order" of goodness in the hierarchy of being in the entire world.[9] This possible "falling away" from, or "corruption" of, the properly given measure, form and order of any creature is none other than "evil" for Augustine.[10] Evil is therefore a privation, a diminution, a loss, or a lack of the goodness proper to any created being. Augustine's most well-known definition of evil is "a privation of good" (*privatio*

[6] James Noel Hubler reports that the doctrine of *creation ex nihilo* "was a position taken by the apologists of the late second century, Tatian and Theophilus, and developed by various ecclesiastical writers thereafter, by Irenaeus, Tertullian, and Origen"; see his "Creatio ex Nihilo: Matter, Creation, and the Body in Classical and Christian Philosophy Through Aquinas" (Ph.D. dissertation, University of Pennsylvania, 1995), p. 102.

[7] Augustine, "Concerning the Nature of Good, against the Manichaeans," 26, in Philip Schaff, ed., *A Select Library of the Nicene and Post-Nicene Fathers of the Christian Church*, vol. IV: *St. Augustin: The Writings against the Manichaeans and against the Donatists* (Grand Rapids, MI: Wm. B. Eerdmans Publishing Co., 1974), pp. 356-57.

[8] Ibid. 1, p. 351.

[9] Ibid. 3, p. 352.

[10] Ibid. 4, p. 352.

boni).[11] At least three things about this anti-Manichaean definition of evil are to be noted. First, evil thus defined is non-substantial; it is "not a substance."[12] Second, evil is only possible and not necessary; creatures are only "liable to hurt through falling away."[13] Third, "God is not the author of evil," as he is none other than "the author of all natures and substances."[14]

What is the relevance of all this to Augustine's doctrine of the fall of Adam? When he applies this privative conception of evil to moral evil which possibly emerges from free will as sin, the relevance becomes clear.

b. Free will

According to Augustine, the "free will" (*liberum arbitrium*) of each of the rational creatures (angels and humans) is also a mutable thing which God created out of nothing; so it is possible for free will to fall away from its proper and natural state, resulting in moral evil. Thus free will contains the possibility of moral evil, but not its necessity. Moral evil in this regard is "not... forced" but "voluntary."[15] Free will in its proper state is expected to adhere to God as its end, but moral evil possibly occurs when it falls away, by choosing to prefer the material to the spiritual, the temporal to the eternal, and creatures to the Creator.[16] Needless to say, for Augustine, God is not the author of moral evil or sin: "Sin [is] not from God, but from the will of those sinning."[17]

How, then, did the fall of Adam take place, according to Augustine? To begin with, an originally good angel fell and became the devil or Satan by his own free will: "it was by his own perverse will that the devil himself, after being a good angel, became a devil";[18] "the devil [was]... good by God's creation, wicked by his own will."[19] There were also some other angels who fell in the same way as the first fall of the devil, their chief, although the other angels did

---

[11] See, for example, Augustine, *The Confessions of St. Augustine*, trans. Rex Warner (New York: New American Library, 1963), 3:7, p. 60.

[12] Augustine, "On the Morals of the Manichaeans," 8.11, in Schaff, ed., *A Select Library of the Nicene and Post-Nicene Fathers of the Christian Church*, vol. IV, p. 72.

[13] Ibid., 4.6, p. 71.

[14] Ibid., 2.3, p. 70.

[15] Augustine, *On Free Choice of the Will*, trans. Anna S. Benjamin and L. H. Hackstaff (Indianapolis, IN: Bobbs-Merrill Co., 1964), 3.1, p. 87.

[16] Augustine, *The Confessions*, 2.5, p. 46.

[17] Augustine, "Concerning the Nature of Good," 28, p. 357.

[18] Augustine, *The Confessions*, 7.3, p, 139.

[19] Augustine, *The City of God*, trans. Marcus Dods (New York: The Modern Library, 1993), 11.17, p. 361. The fall of Adam is described by Augustine in more detail in *The City of God*, which was written later during the period of the Pelagian controversy, than in his earlier, anti-Manichaean writings. But his atomistic, individualist, libertarian and non-sexual approach to the fall of Adam basically stayed without any substantial change even during this later period.

not fall. The difference between the fallen and unfallen angels arose "not from a difference in their nature and origin… but from a difference in their wills and desires."[20]

How did the first human ancestors fall, then? According to Augustine, they were not fallen yet, when the devil fell on his own. So their "unfallen condition provoked him [i.e., the devil] to envy now that himself was fallen," and out of his envy of them he used the serpent, a real animal, as his mouthpiece to "insinuate his persuasive guile into the mind of [Adam and Eve],"[21] so that they might eat the forbidden fruit. The devil first tried to deceive Eve because she was "the weaker part of that human alliance," and then tried to deceive Adam through Eve because Adam would more easily "yield to the error of the woman," who was "his only companion," than to the direct deception of the devil himself.[22]

Eve and Adam actually ended up eating the fruit. But what is important in Augustine's thought is that, strictly speaking, the devil's temptation did not cause Eve to fall, nor did Eve's enticement cause Adam to fall. After all, their free wills caused them to fall. For it was *of their own accord* that they chose to yield to the temptations they respectively received from outside. In this scenario, one "yields, *of his own will*, to evil persuasion from outside."[23] Hence the fundamental libertarianism of Augustine. This means that the notion of satanic temptation is secondary because the final determining factor of one's act is one's own free will.

If, therefore, Eve and Adam had willed not to fall, the devil's temptation would have had no impact on them at all: "if the will had remained steadfast in the love of [God]… the woman would not have believed the serpent spoke the truth, nor would the man have preferred the request of his wife to the command of God";[24] "The devil, then, would not have ensnared man in the open and manifest sin of doing what God had forbidden, had man not already begun to live for himself."[25]

Here the Bishop of Hippo makes a distinction between the internal dimension of free will and the external dimension of act, arguing that the former is more essential and important than the latter because the latter does not happen without the direction of the former which precedes it: "Our first

---

20 Ibid., 12.1, p. 380.
21 Ibid., 14.11, p. 458.
22 Ibid., pp. 458-59.
23 Augustine, *On Free Choice of the Will*, 3.10, p. 111. Italics added.
24 Augustine, *The City of God*, 14.13, p. 460.
25 Ibid., 14.13, p. 461.

parents fell into open disobedience because already they were secretly corrupted [in their free wills]; for the evil act had never been done had not an evil will preceded it";[26] "The wicked deed, then—that is to say, the transgression of eating the forbidden fruit—was committed by persons who were already wicked [in their free wills]."[27]

Augustine has a further explanation of why the temptation from the devil was less essential. According to him, while God was the "originator" of the movement of Adam's free will toward good, it cannot be said that the devil was the originator or efficient cause of Adam's evil will, for it was "[Adam's] own will [that] was the originator of its evil."[28] Thus his evil will had no efficient cause whatsoever except his own free will itself: "Let no one… look for an efficient cause of the evil will; for it is not efficient, but *deficient*, as the will itself is not an effecting of something, but a defect," when it falls away from God.[29] Hence the Augustinian doctrine of *deficient* causation regarding the evil will. This is why the evil will of Adam, as well as that of Eve, was not caused by the devil. Augustine confesses that the cause of the evil will is unknowable, as long as it is deficient: "Let no one, then, seek to know from me what I know that I do not know."[30]

But, although the evil will had no efficient cause, there was certainly a motive within Adam and Eve which led them each to willfully choose to fall away. This motive as the origin of the evil will was nothing other than "pride" according to Augustine, and he defines it as "the craving for undue [self-]exaltation," which emerges when "the soul willfully abandons Him [i.e., God] to whom it ought to cleave as its end, and becomes an end to itself,"[31] by thinking of becoming like God to the neglect of its own creaturely status. The devil, too, willfully chose to abandon the truth of God by his "pride."[32] It is to be noted, however, that pride is not an efficient cause of the evil will; it might rather be just a potential desire inherent within free will.

2. Augustine's Doctrine of Original Sin

In his later years, however, Augustine had to deal with the new heresy of Pelagianism. The Pelagians, named after Pelagius (c. 360–418), a Christian moralist from Britain, stressed the unfailing ability of free will so much that

---

[26] Ibid., 14.13, p. 460.
[27] Ibid.
[28] Ibid., 13.15, p. 423.
[29] Ibid., 12.7, p. 387. Italics added.
[30] Ibid.
[31] Ibid., 14.13, p. 460.
[32] Ibid., 11.15, p. 359.

they thought little of the reality of human sinfulness and ignored the need for God's grace. Naturally, this extreme version of libertarianism in Pelagianism was not acceptable to Augustine and the Church.

In order to address the problem of Pelagianism, Augustine affirmed the following points: 1) that all the descendants of Adam have received original sin as a punishment for his fall; 2) that original sin is transmitted from one generation to another through procreation; and 3) that the free will of any descendant of Adam is so weakened that it needs the help of God's grace. As he was incorporating these points, Augustine went beyond his initial atomistic, individualist approach of libertarianism in his doctrine of the fall of Adam in favor of a relational, sexual approach to deal with the post-fall situation of human beings.

a. Original sin

In his earlier years as a Christian leader in which he was still involved in the Manichaean controversy, Augustine was already (in 395, for example)[33] aware of the importance of the Christian idea of what would later be called "original sin" inherited from Adam. But when he actually coined the term "original sin" (*peccatum originale*) in 397, he meant by it the primal sin or fall of Adam.[34] It was only in his later years that he meant by it a resultant, sinful condition which God imposed on Adam and his descendants as a punishment for his primal sin: "the voluntary transgression of the first man is the cause of original sin";[35] "Owing, indeed, to God's justice, who punishes… men are born with the fault of original sin."[36] To be terminologically precise, original sin in this latter sense is *peccatum originale originatum* ("originated" original sin), while the primal sin of Adam may well be called *peccatum originale originans* ("originating" original sin).[37]

Augustine referred to physical death as a punishment for Adam's primal sin, but he did not regard it as part of original sin. So let us focus on what Augustine understood to be two elements of original sin: 1) guilt (*reatus*), and 2) corrupted human nature, which means carnal concupiscence (*carnalis*

---

[33] Augustine, *On Free Choice of the Will*, 3.19, pp. 129-30.

[34] See n. 1.

[35] Augustine, "On Marriage and Concupiscence," 2.26.43, in Philip Schaff, ed., *A Select Library of the Nicene and Post-Nicene Fathers of the Christian Church*, vol. V: *Saint Augustin: Anti-Pelagian Writings* (Grand Rapids, MI: Wm. B. Eerdmans Publishing Co., 1975), p. 300.

[36] Augustine, "On the Grace of Christ, and on Original Sin," 2.39.46, in Schaff, ed., *A Select Library of the Nicene and Post-Nicene Fathers of the Christian Church*, vol. V, p. 254.

[37] Tatha Wiley, *Original Sin: Origins, Developments, Contemporary Meanings* (New York: Paulist Press, 2002), pp. 5, 56, 72.

concupiscentia).[38] Guilt, a first element, means that because of a just punishment of God all the descendants of Adam as well as Adam himself have been made guilty of his primal sin, thus becoming his "condemned stock"[39] or the "mass of perdition."[40] This is the case because all of them, who were seminally "present in his [i.e., Adam's] loins,"[41] are considered to have fallen when Adam fell. Augustine's own reading of Romans 5:12 is, therefore, that "all men are understood to have sinned in that first 'man,' because all men were in him when he sinned."[42]

Corrupted human nature as carnal concupiscence, on the other hand, is the disordering of the whole person of Adam or any of his descendants in which the flesh disobeys the soul—a disordering which has come about as still another just punishment of God for Adam's disorderly fall in which his soul disobeyed the law of God: "When the first man [in his soul] transgressed the law of God, he began to have another law in his [fleshly] members which was repugnant to the law of his mind, and he felt the evil of his own disobedience when he experienced in the disobedience of his flesh a most righteous retribution recoiling on himself";[43] "God… condemns man because of the fault [i.e., the fall] wherewithal his nature is disgraced."[44] This disgraced state of our nature is a "corruption," a "wound," a "pollution" of that human nature which otherwise "came from him [i.e., God]" originally.[45] Augustine calls this corrupted human nature "carnal concupiscence"[46] or simply "concupis-

---

[38] That Augustine believed original sin to consist in these two elements is what people such as Jesse Couenhoven suggest. See his treatment of what Augustine understands to be the "two forms" of original sin in his "St. Augustine's Doctrine of Original Sin," *Augustinian Studies* 36:2 (2005): 363, 369-72, 376-79. Many Catholic thinkers, however, would disagree, as they usually would believe concupiscence to be separate from original sin.

[39] Augustine, "On the Grace of Christ, and Original Sin," 2.38.43, p. 252.

[40] Ibid., 2:31:36, p. 250.

[41] Augustine, *The Works of Saint Augustine: A Translation for the 21st Century*, vol. I/25: *Unfinished Work in Answer to Julian (Answer to the Pelagians, III)*, ed. John E. Rotelle, trans. Roland J. Teske (Hyde Park, NY: New City Press, 1999), 1.48, p. 75.

[42] Augustine, "Against Two Letters of the Pelagians," 4.4.7, in Schaff, ed., *A Select Library of the Nicene and Post-Nicene Fathers of the Christian Church*, vol. V, p. 419. This reading of Romans 5:12 by Augustine was based on its key phrase "because in him [i.e., Adam] all men sinned" in the then available Latin text, although the original Greek text simply reads "because all men sinned," without referring to Adam.

[43] Augustine, "On Marriage and Concupiscence," 1.6.7, p. 266.

[44] Augustine, "On the Grace of Christ, and on Original Sin," 2.39.46, p. 254.

[45] Augustine, "On Marriage and Concupiscence," 1.23.26, p. 274.

[46] Ibid., 1.1.1, p. 264; 1.17.19, p. 271; 1.18.20, p. 272, for example.

cence."[47] He even calls it the "lust of the flesh."[48]

As for the regenerate people, however, this "concupiscence is not itself sin any longer, whenever they do not consent to it for illicit works,"[49] and even "a concupiscence of the spirit which craves wisdom"[50] is considered to exist. This shows that Augustine is aware of the original state of human nature in which the body would unite with the soul, which in turn would unite with God. Nevertheless, his primary awareness is of the fallen state of concupiscence in the above sense of disordering.

At this point, it would be pertinent to know Augustine's understanding of why a God of goodness punishes us by imposing original sin on us. But first, we have to know that as early as during the period of the Manichaean controversy, Augustine was already speaking of natural evil in all things as God's "penalty of sin," saying that all things in the world, which were originally supposed to "serve" us if we also "had willed to serve God," have now become "adverse" to us because of our refusal to serve God, and that this natural evil has occurred because "He is just in taking vengeance on sin" as a God who originally had "all things... ordered in the best possible way."[51] This penalty from God is "an appointed distribution of things and times" by which we "are called to return" and also the "corrupted" things are to be "restored," so that we may "have consolations mingled with punishments" and "take refuge in Him when tried by experience of evils."[52] By applying this basic principle of retribution, Augustine was also saying even during the Manichaean controversy that the undesirable corruption of the human nature of rational beings, too, is God's "punishment" of justice for their own willful sins of disobedience.[53] When the Pelagian controversy started, Augustine now said the same thing about the occurrence of original sin, which is guilt as well as carnal concupiscence, as God's punishment for Adam's first sin, as was seen above.

It can be said as a point of difference between guilt and carnal concupiscence that while guilt is qualitative and objective, as it is forensic, carnal concupiscence is quantitative and subjective, as it concerns the inner

---

[47] Ibid., 1.23.25, p. 274, for example.

[48] Augustine, "On the Grace of Christ, and on Original Sin," 2.37.42, p. 252; "On Marriage and Concupiscence," 1.19.21, p. 272.

[49] Augustine, "On Marriage and Concupiscence," 1.23.25, p. 274.

[50] Ibid., 2.30.52, p. 304.

[51] Augustine, "Acts or Disputation against Fortunatus the Manichaean," 15, in Schaff, ed., *A Select Library of the Nicene and Post-Nicene Fathers of the Christian Church*, vol. IV, p. 116.

[52] Augustine, "Against the Epistle of Manichaeus Called Fundamental," 37.43, in, Schaff, ed., *A Select Library of the Nicene and Post-Nicene Fathers of the Christian Church*, vol. IV, p. 148.

[53] Augustine, "Concerning the Nature of Good," 7, p. 352.

human nature of each person. While the former is all or nothing, therefore, the latter is measurable, being able to increase or decrease. So, while the former can be taken away all at once by regeneration through baptism, the latter remains even after baptism until the body passes away to be physically resurrected eventually: "Although its guilt is taken away, it [i.e., carnal concupiscence] still remains until our entire infirmity be healed by the advancing renewal of our inner man, day by day, when at last our outward man shall be clothed with incorruption."[54] Therefore, even if it can still be said that carnal concupiscence "is remitted, indeed, in baptism," it does not really mean that "it is put out of existence" but only that "it is not to be imputed for sin" in the regenerate. It actually still remains "just as languor does after recovery from disease," and it therefore can still be "increasing" if we yield a wicked service to it, and can be "lessened" if we stay in continence or get older agewise.[55]

b. The transmission of original sin

Given this persistent nature of carnal concupiscence, we can now look into Augustine's understanding of how it has been instrumental in transmitting original sin from one generation to another since the time of Adam and Eve. Fallen Adam and Eve were not regenerate yet, nor was anyone else in the Old Testament age regenerate yet, for Christ was not yet available. Suppose, however, that there are a regenerate man and woman in the Christian era who are married to each other in holy matrimony. Even their children will be born with original sin, according to Augustine. For when the regenerate parents have a sexual intercourse for procreation, even they cannot stop the noticeable activation of carnal concupiscence which is otherwise inactive in them: "the connubial intercourse and lust [i.e., carnal concupiscence] are at the same time in action,"[56] bringing forth "a certain amount of bestial motion, which puts human nature to the blush."[57] The reason is that concupiscence still somehow remains in them even after baptism, as was seen above. It is this activation of concupiscence in the sexual union even of the regenerate parents that is indeed instrumental in transmitting original sin from them to their infants: "infants, although incapable of sinning, are yet not born without the contagion of [original] sin… on account of that which is unseemly [i.e., carnal

---

[54] Augustine, "On Marriage and Concupiscence," 1.25.28, p. 275.
[55] Ibid.
[56] Augustine, "On the Grace of Christ, and on Original Sin," 2.37.42, p. 252.
[57] Ibid., 2.38.43, p. 253.

concupiscence]";[58] "Now from this concupiscence whatever comes into being by natural birth is bound by original sin."[59]

When original sin is transmitted this way, it is not only concupiscence but also guilt that is transmitted. Both are transmitted together because they are interconnected with each other, in that carnal concupiscence makes us feel guilty, experiencing the "guilt of this concupiscence." [60] Although the regenerate themselves may be cleansed of Adam's guilt by virtue of baptism, they have no choice but bequeathing it to their children through carnal concupiscence. This is why Augustine can also say that all of us "who were in his [i.e., Adam's] loins and were destined to enter this world through concupiscence of the flesh were condemned at the same time."[61]

Hence even children of regenerate parents in holy matrimony are born with original sin, and they stay with it until they themselves are regenerated through baptism. Does this mean that marriage is evil according to Augustine? His answer is in the negative. He believes that marriage is still good in that it involves three gifts of God: offspring (procreation), chastity (fidelity) and sacramental bond (no separation). [62] So the conjugal intercourse for procreation, even if it unavoidably involves the evil of carnal concupiscence, is not sinful in itself, as long as it is for a good purpose of procreation: "the [sexual] embrace is not after all a sin in itself, when reason applies the concupiscence to a good end [of procreation]." [63] Augustine, therefore, distinguishes between "the good of marriage" and "the evil of carnal concupiscence from which man who is born therefrom contracts original sin."[64] By the way, Augustine says, quoting 1 Corinthians 7:3-6, that the conjugal intercourse which is not for procreation but merely "for the pleasure of concupiscence" involves "some amount of sin," but that it is still "permissible" as a venial sin because it can avoid "damnable sins" such as fornications and adulteries.[65]

What is important in Augustine's doctrine of the transmission of original sin is that the devil is involved in it as the dominator over all of us: "of whatever kind of parents they are born, they are still under the dominion of the devil";[66]

---

[58] Ibid., 2.37.42, p. 252.
[59] Augustine, "On Marriage and Concupiscence," 1.24.27, p. 275.
[60] Ibid., 1.19.21, p. 272.
[61] Augustine, *Unfinished Work in Answer to Julian*, 6.22, p. 660.
[62] Augustine, "On Marriage and Concupiscence," 1.10.11, p. 268; 1.11.13, p. 269; 1.17.19, p. 271.
[63] Augustine, "On the Grace of Christ, and on Original Sin," 2.38.43, p. 253.
[64] Augustine, "On Marriage and Concupiscence," 1.1.1, p. 264.
[65] Ibid., 1.14.16, p. 270.
[66] Ibid., 1.1.1, p. 263.

the devil "was able to hold all men in his grasp through one [i.e., Adam]."[67] Of course, the fall of the devil, Eve and Adam, as volitional disobedience to God's commandment on the part of each of them, was neither relational nor sexual in nature; so, strictly speaking, the devil would have no dominion whatsoever over Adam and Eve. But when God afterwards imposed original sin on Adam, Eve and all their descendants as his just punishment for the first sin committed, it actually means that God permitted the devil to encroach on them. This must be the reason why Augustine now said during the Pelagian controversy that the devil who "approached the man [i.e., Adam] through the woman [i.e., Eve]" actually "holds" their descendants.[68] The devil holds them especially through their wounded carnal concupiscence, as it is instrumental in transmitting original sin. Augustine states: "This wound which the devil has inflicted on the human race compels everything which has its birth in consequence of it to be under the devil's power."[69]

Here we can see quite a modification of his original libertarianism. Instead of his earlier idea that Adam alone was responsible for his own fall, he now says that it was the devil who deceived as well as Adam who consented that led to the fall: "of the [first] sin the author is the subtlety of the devil who deceives, and the will of the man who consents."[70] It should be understood, however, that this modified, more relational view of the primal fallen act of Adam on the part of the later Augustine is still far from sexual, involving no sexual act, while his relational view of the transmission of original sin is definitely sexual.

c. Free will and grace

According to Augustine, Adam before his fall in the Garden of Eden had free will by which he was "able not to sin" (*posse non peccare*), although it was not yet the perfect, much better freedom of "not to be able to sin" (*non posse peccare*).[71] The *posse non peccare* which Adam had was such that if he had willed not to sin, he would not have fallen. He, however, fell actually. This means that his original free will contained both the ability not to sin (*posse non peccare*) and the alternative possibility of sinning, which was the ability to sin (*posse peccare*): "man should be at first so created, as to have it in his power both to will what was

---

[67] Augustine, "On the Grace of Christ, and on Original Sin," 2.39.45, p. 253.
[68] Ibid.
[69] Augustine, "On Marriage and Concupiscence," 1.23.26, p. 274.
[70] Augustine, "On the Grace of Christ, and on Original Sin," 2.37.42, p. 252.
[71] Augustine, "On Rebuke and Grace," 12.33, in Schaff, ed., *A Select Library of the Nicene and Post-Nicene Fathers of the Christian Church*, vol. V, p. 485.

right and to will what was wrong."[72] And, while the *posse non peccare* was lost after the fall, the *posse peccare* still remained. Free will in the latter sense, therefore, did not perish even after the fall: "free will in the sinner up to this extent did not perish,—that by it all sin, especially they who sin with delight and with love of sin."[73] This is how Augustine at least theoretically addresses Julian the Pelagian's (c. 388–c. 465) criticism to the effect that the Bishop of Hippo and his fellow believers in the Church were erroneously believing, like the Manichaeans, that after the fall free will completely "perished."[74]

In actuality, however, Julian the Pelagian's criticism may not have been entirely wrong. For Augustine admits that free will in the sense of being the *posse peccare* alone after the fall always leads to sinning, unless it is aided by the grace of God: "it [i.e., the *posse peccare*] avails for sinning in men subjected to the devil; while it is not of avail for good and pious living, unless the will itself of man should be made free by God's grace, and assisted to every good movement of action, of speech, of thought."[75] Hence Augustine admits of "a certain necessary tendency to sin" on the part of fallen human beings,[76] who are therefore "unable to avoid sin" (*non posse non peccare*).[77] Throughout his anti-Pelagian writings, therefore, Augustine asserts that we cannot escape from this evil necessity except with the assistance of God's grace. This way he criticized the Pelagian exaltation of free will and emphasized the need for our absolute dependence on God's grace.

What, then, is the relationship between free will and grace according to Augustine? After the fall, free will is incapacitated and weakened in that the *posse non peccare* is lost, although the *posse peccare* remains. In this situation, there is nothing in us to merit the grace of God. So the divine grace "is not rendered for any merits [of us], but is given *gratis* [i.e., gratuitously or freely], on account of which it is also called *grace*."[78] At this initial stage, the grace of God unmeritedly operates to heal our incapacitated will by restoring the *posse non peccare* for us. At the next stage, however, the divine grace works co-operatively with our now healed and strengthened will to fulfill the law of God. Regarding

---

[72] Augustine, "The Enchiridion," 105, in Philip Schaff, ed., *A Select Library of the Nicene and Post-Nicene Fathers of the Christian Church*, vol. III: *St. Augustin: On the Holy Trinity, Doctrinal Treatises, Moral Treatises* (Grand Rapids, MI: Wm. B. Eerdmans Publishing Co., 1974), p. 271.
[73] Augustine, "Against Two Letters of the Pelagians," 1.2.5, p. 378.
[74] Ibid., 1.2.4, p. 378.
[75] Ibid., 2.5.9, p. 395.
[76] Augustine, "On Nature and Grace," 66.79, in, Schaff, ed., *A Select Library of the Nicene and Post-Nicene Fathers of the Christian Church*, vol. V, p. 149.
[77] Ibid., 49.57, p. 140.
[78] Ibid., 4.4, p. 122. Italics original.

these two distinctive yet successive stages of the work of God's grace, Augustine says: "He [i.e., God] operates… without us, in order that we may will; but when we will, and so will that we may act, He co-operates with us."[79] And, the initial grace of "operation" and the subsequent grace of "co-operation" correspond, respectively, to our initial "small and weak" will, which is "unable," and our subsequent "great and robust" will, which has become "able."[80] In both stages, we need the grace of God: "We can… ourselves do nothing to effect good works of piety without Him either working that we may will, or co-working when we will."[81]

When Augustine maintains that we can do nothing good without the grace of God, whether it is gratuitously operating to heal our incapacitated will at the initial stage or co-operatively working with our healed and strengthened will at the next stage, his anti-Pelagian idea of free will in this regard is far less libertarian and far more deterministic than his earlier, anti-Manichaean idea of free will that only free will decides outcomes. Thus there seems to be a theological inconsistency between his earlier and later years, i.e., between his anti-Manichaean and anti-Pelagian years.

In order to explain this inconsistency away, Augustine in his *Retractations*, written near the end of his life, said among others that the incapacitated will, a certain necessary tendency to sin, is the penalty of the sin committed freely. Nevertheless, Albert H. Newman, in his translation of Augustine's "On Two Souls, against the Manichaeans," observes that Augustine's "efforts to show the consistency of his earlier with his later models of thought" in his *Retractations* "are to be pronounced only partially successful."[82]

3. Later Developments of the Doctrine of Original Sin

Augustine's doctrine of original sin became the official position of the Church through the Council of Carthage (418) and the Second Council of Orange (529). Since then, however, it went through several stages of noticeable modification and development in the history of Christianity, while his doctrine of the fall of Adam per se was generally accepted without any real modification. In the present subsection, therefore, let us see the later developments of his doctrine of original sin.

---

[79] Augustine, "On Grace and Free will," 17.33, in Schaff, ed., *A Select Library of the Nicene and Post-Nicene Fathers of the Christian Church*, vol. V, p. 458.

[80] Ibid., 17.33, p. 457.

[81] Ibid., 17.33, p. 458.

[82] Augustine, "On Two Souls, against the Manichaeans," trans. Albert H. Newman, in Schaff, ed., *A Select Library of the Nicene and Post-Nicene Fathers of the Christian Church*, vol. IV, p. 102, no. 1.

Augustine's doctrine of original sin appeared to be in favor of the traducianist idea that human souls, being tainted, are generated together with physical bodies at the time of conception by fallen parents. He himself admitted of it: "the practice of infant baptism gives greater weight to the opinion of those [i.e., traducianists] who hold that souls are generated by parents."[83]

This apparently caused a problem, however, because traducianism, originally coming from Tertullian (c. 155–c. 240), carried with itself materialist overtones. Augustine, who believed the soul not to be material at all, could therefore not really accept traducianism.[84] Creationism, which believes that human souls are directly created by God, was generally more popular than traducianism in the Church, and especially in the Eastern Church. Therefore Augustine himself in his earlier years leaned toward creationism, although in his later years he was more open, if reluctantly, to traducianism. In the end, he could not choose between creationism and traducianism, and honestly confessed to be "ignorant" of the origin of the soul, saying that only God can teach it eventually.[85]

a. Anselm of Canterbury and Thomas Aquinas

This is why a new development made by St. Anselm of Canterbury (c. 1033–1109) was significant. Although he was Augustinian in many ways, Anselm subtly reoriented the doctrine of original sin in favor of creationism. He newly defined original sin as the "deprivation of due justice,"[86] and considered it to be transmitted without the involvement of concupiscence. He stopped talking about concupiscence altogether.

According to him, humans were originally given "justice" (*justitia*) as a supernatural gift added to their human nature (reason and will) in the natural order in which the soul is a direct creature of God. This original justice constitutes the "rectitude of the [human] will" to conform with the will of God.[87] But its deprivation (original sin) occurred due to Adam's primal sin of disobedience to God, and as a result human nature became somewhat

---

[83] Augustine, *The Literal Meaning of Genesis*, trans. John Hammond Taylor (Mahwah, NJ: Paulist Press, 1982), vol. 2, 10.23.39, p.127.

[84] Ibid., 10.24.40-25.41.

[85] Augustine, "On the Soul and Its Origin," 4.4.5, in Schaff, ed., *A Select Library of the Nicene and Post-Nicene Fathers of the Christian Church*, vol. V, p. 355.

[86] Anselm, "The Virgin Conception and Original Sin (Selections)," 27, in *A Scholastic Miscellany: Anselm to Ockham*, ed. and trans. Eugene R. Fairweather (Philadelphia: Westminster Press, 1956), p. 199.

[87] Ibid., 3, p. 187.

impoverished and wounded. This straightforwardly applied to the human nature of all the descendants of Adam. It is in this sense and in this sense alone that Adam's sin passed over into them all as original sin:

> Thus in Adam the person despoiled the [human] nature of the [supernatural] good of justice, and the [human] nature, once impoverished, makes every person it engenders from itself sinful and unjust, by virtue of that same poverty. In this way the personal sin of Adam passes over into all those who are naturally propagated from him, and becomes original or natural in them.[88]

Note that Anselm seems not to have made a clear distinction between Adam's sin and original sin. Note also that human nature impoverished by Adam's sin, being instrumental for the transmission of original sin, was not called "concupiscence" by Anselm yet, although it was later so called at the Council of Trent in 1546[89] and in the *Catechism of the Catholic Church* in 1992.[90] If so, it can be said that even though Anslem stopped referencing concupiscence as the vehicle for the transmission of original sin, he virtually did not stop doing so. By the way, original sin, as understood by Anselm, seems not to involve the inheritance of Adam's guilt.

Anselm's view of original sin as the deprivation of the supernatural gift of original justice from human nature was accepted by St. Thomas Aquinas (1225–1274), the best-known of the medieval schoolmen, who too was in favor of creationism as the origin of the soul. But Aquinas was also aware of Augustine's significant view of concupiscence as part of original sin. Therefore he synthesized Anselm and Augustine, by saying, based on the Aristotelian notions of form and matter, that while the deprivation of original justice, as understood by Anselm, is the "formal element" of original sin, concupiscence, as understood by Augustine, is the "material element" of original sin,[91] the "effect" of original sin.[92]

So, while agreeing with Anselm as to the transmission of original sin in terms of all mankind's sharing of "one common nature" with Adam,[93] Aquinas also referenced physical procreation more explicitly than Anselm: "Original sin

---

[88] Ibid., 23, pp. 197-98.

[89] The Council of Trent, the Fifth Session, "Decree Concerning Original Sin," Canon 5. https://history.hanover.edu/texts/trent/ct05.html.

[90] *Catechism of the Catholic Church* (English translation, 1994), 405. http://www.scborromeo.org/ccc/p1s2c1p7.htm#405.

[91] Thomas Aquinas, *Summa Theologiae*, I-II, q. 82, art. 3. http://www.newadvent.org/summa/2082.htm#article3.

[92] Ibid., I-II, q. 85, art. 3. http://www.newadvent.org/summa/2085.htm#article3.

[93] Ibid., I-II, q. 81, art. 1. http://www.newadvent.org/summa/2081.htm#article1

is caused by the semen as instrumental cause."[94] This Thomistic synthesis may appear somewhat obscure, but it became an important part of the Catholic tradition.

b. Martin Luther

Martin Luther (1483–1546) believed the scholastic theologians' definition of original sin as the deprivation of the supernatural gift of original justice to be lukewarm, in that it does not take the corruption of human nature seriously: "to think that original sin is merely the lack of righteousness in the will is merely to give occasion for lukewarmness and a breakdown of the whole concept of penitence."[95] He even criticized them for being Pelagian because he thought they believed that "the Law can be fulfilled by our powers" without the grace of God.[96]

Unlike the scholastic theologians, therefore, Luther considered original justice *not* to be a supernatural gift added to human nature but rather *an integral part* of human nature itself in the natural order. For him, then, original sin as the loss of original justice due to the fall of Adam means the total corruption of human nature, by reason of which we cannot help sinning. Thus original sin is "a total lack of uprightness and of the power of all faculties both of body and soul and of the whole inner and outer man."[97] He went on to say that original sin is "a propensity toward evil," "a nausea toward the good," "a loathing of light and wisdom," etc., calling it "universal concupiscence."[98] Hence concupiscence is the essence of original sin, although Luther did not forget that the inheritance of Adam's "guilt" is also part of original sin.[99]

Luther, who experienced his own sinfulness, was attracted to the existential approach of Augustine, and in order to talk about the seriousness of concupiscence, he appealed to the authority of the Bishop of Hippo's thesis that concupiscence persistently remains even after baptism, although it is not imputed to those who call upon God and cry out for deliverance.[100]

The Reformer, however, went even further than Augustine, in that while Augustine said that concupiscence remains only as something like languor after

---

[94] Ibid., I-II, q. 83, art. 1, reply to obj. 2. http://www.newadvent.org/summa/2083.htm#article1.
[95] Martin Luther, *Luther's Works*, vol. 25: *Lectures on Romans*, ed. Hilton C. Oswald (St. Louis, MO: Concordia Publishing House, 1972), p. 300.
[96] Ibid., p. 262.
[97] Ibid., p. 299.
[98] Ibid.
[99] Martin Luther, *Luther's Works*, vol. 37: *Word and Sacrament III*, ed. Robert H. Fischer (Philadelphia: Muhlenberg Press, 1961), p. 362.
[100] Luther, *Luther's Works*, vol. 25: *Lectures on Romans*, p. 261, cf. pp. 259-61.

baptism, Luther stated that it still remains as real sin even after baptism.[101] (Needless to say, guilt is removed by baptism, according to Luther, who followed Augustine in this regard.[102]) Therefore, while Augustine could not decide between creationism and traducianism, Luther was clearly in favor of traducianism.[103]

c. The Council of Trent

In reaction to Luther, the Catholic Church convened the Council of Trent from 1545 to 1563, announcing a decree concerning original sin in 1546. The Council disagreed with Luther on the seriousness of concupiscence; it held that concupiscence is itself not sin,[104] whereas the Reformer considered it to be sin. Trent rather agreed with Augustine, by saying that "in the baptized there remains concupiscence... which [however]... cannot injure those who consent not, but resist manfully by the grace of Jesus Christ."[105] Trent also followed Anselm in formally defining original sin as the deprivation of supernatural justice and holiness as well.[106] This means that the Council of Trent followed both Augustine and Anselm like Aquinas did.

Also, in order to address Luther's criticism of the Catholic tradition for being Pelagian, Trent clearly made the following anti-Pelagian statement: "this sin of Adam" is "transfused into all by propagation, not by imitation," nor is it "taken away... by the power of human nature."[107] Original sin is only taken away by the grace of Christ conferred in baptism.[108]

From the above, it can be observed that the seriousness of original sin, as understood by Augustine, was toned down by Anselm's new approach, but that it was somewhat reappropriated by Aquinas when he synthesized Anselm with Augustine. Luther took original sin even more seriously than Augustine, and critiqued the scholastic theologians for being lukewarm. But the Council of Trent countered Luther's criticism and reaffirmed the position of Aquinas. Trent's decree on original sin then became a dogma of the Catholic Church.

---

[101] Martin Luther, *Luther's Works*, vol. 32: *Career of the Reformer II*, ed. George W. Forell (Philadelphia: Muhlenberg Press, 1958), pp. 19-31.
[102] Ibid., p. 27.
[103] David Albert Jones, *The Soul of the Embryo: An Enquiry into the Status of the Human Embryo in the Christian Tradition* (London: Continuum, 2004), p. 143.
[104] The Council of Trent, the Fifth Session, "Decree Concerning Original Sin," Canon 5. https://history.hanover.edu/texts/trent/ct05.html.
[105] Ibid., canon 5.
[106] Ibid., canons 1 and 2.
[107] Ibid., canon 3.
[108] Ibid., canon 5.

d. Assessment

Many people quite often say, as a point of difference between the Catholic tradition and Luther's position regarding original sin, that the former separated concupiscence from original sin, referring to concupiscence merely as an effect of original sin, while the latter collapsed the two to identify concupiscence with original sin.[109] Anselm's position is usually considered to have been a good example of this Catholic separation of concupiscence from original sin, because he newly defined original sin as the deprivation of original justice, thinking little of concupiscence. Even Aquinas' synthesis of Augustine and Anselm, which had a little more understanding of concupiscence, is considered to have been another example of this Catholic separation of concupiscence from original sin, because it still regarded concupiscence as an effect of original sin. Trent is also considered to have been still another example of the Catholic separation, because it held that concupiscence is itself not sin. This Catholic separation is usually quite sharply contrasted with Luther's identification of concupiscence with original sin.

In the opinion of the present writer, this is a misconceived exaggeration resulting from the confusion between Adam's primal sin (*peccatum originale originans*) and original sin (*peccatum originale originatum*)—a confusion that happens commonly. We should not confuse Adam's primal sin with original sin. As Augustine said in his later years, original sin is not identical with Adam's primal sin or fall in the Garden of Eden; it is rather a resultant condition which God imposed on Adam and his descendants as a punishment for his primal sin. If so, original sin, which is thus a resultant condition, and concupiscence, which is also resultant, cannot be as separate as one would think. In fact, Augustine believed that concupiscence is part of original sin, while guilt is another part of original sin. Therefore Luther's identification of concupiscence with original sin is not as strange as one would think.

Perhaps we should read Anselm, Aquinas, Luther and Trent from the viewpoint of Augustine to avoid any unnecessary sharp contrast between the Catholic tradition and Luther regarding original sin. The difference between the Catholic tradition and Luther seems to be just the difference of degrees to which concupiscence, which is part of original sin according to Augustine, is emphasized: Anselm with the least emphasis on it; Aquinas and Trent with a little more emphasis on it; and Luther with the most emphasis on it, even going beyond Augustine.

---

[109] See, for example, Wiley, *Original Sin*, pp. 90, 95-96.

§2. The Unification Doctrine of the Fall[110]

The Unification doctrine of the fall can be learned mainly from *Exposition of the Divine Principle* and the words of Rev. Sun Myung Moon, founder of the Unification movement. And like the Christian doctrine, it has two different components: 1) a doctrine of Adam's fall, and 2) a doctrine of original sin proper. It consistently treats both components by the same relational, sexual approach. In the present section, the Unification doctrine of the fall will be discussed with occasional comparisons to the Christian doctrine.

1. The Unification Doctrine of Adam's Fall

a. Sexual fall

The Divine Principle, which is Rev. Moon's new interpretation of the Bible,[111] teaches that Adam and Eve sexually fell because of illicit love centered on Archangel Lucifer.[112] Michael Breen (1952–) reports that "Moon's search for the [Divine] Principle… lasted for nine years from his encounter with Jesus in 1935," and that "at the end of this period" he was able to finally discover the sexual nature of the fall, by "confront[ing] Lucifer" and also by being tested by God, who initially "denied" Moon's interpretation.[113] In spite of God's initial denial, says Breen, Moon with his "monumental conviction and determination" insisted on the rightness of his own interpretation, and only thereafter did God approve it as the truth, so that Moon might able to claim his ownership of the truth, avoid being accused by Satan, and heal the broken heart of God who had suffered rejection from fallen humanity.[114]

---

[110] This particular section on the Unification doctrine of the fall, in its original version published in *Journal of Unification Studies*, was reviewed by Vassilios Bebis, Professor of Eastern Orthodox and Ecumenical Theology at Graduate Theological Foundation, Sarasota, Florida. His review constitutes a useful supplementary note to show three points of similarity between the theology of St. Irenaeus and Unification theology on the fall: 1) that Adam and Eve were not created as perfect beings but had the ability to achieve perfection gradually; 2) that Lucifer was responsible for the fall of Adam and Eve out of his envy for them; and 3) that while the sexual interpretation of the fall and original sin, seen in Unification theology, may not appear directly in Irenaeus' writings, it appears indirectly in his *The Demonstration of the Apostolic Preaching* at least. See his "The Unification Doctrine of the Fall and the Writings of Irenaeus of Lyon," *Journal of Unification Studies* 24 (2023):105-9. See also Theodore Shimmyo's "A Rejoinder to Dr. Bebis," ibid.:111-15.

[111] In order to understand that the Divine Principle is Rev. Moon's interpretation of the Bible, see Chapter 1 in the present book.

[112] The Divine Principle just follows the Christian custom of regarding Lucifer as an archangel, although there is no biblical evidence to support it. See n. 2.

[113] Michael Breen, *Sun Myung Moon: The Early Years 1920-53* (Hurstpierpoint, U.K.: Refuge Books, 1997), pp. 36-37.

[114] Ibid., p. 37.

In the short history of Christianity in Korea, Sun Myung Moon was actually not the first to assert that the fall of Adam and Eve was sexual. Moon acknowledges that Sung Do Kim (c. 1884–1944), female founder of a new spiritual Christian group, the Holy Lord Church, was "the first person who understood the root of sin [to be sexual]," and that she thus made a great preparation "for the Messiah [of the Second Advent] to appear."[115] Her understanding of the sexual fall of Adam and Eve was revealed about twenty years earlier than Rev. Moon's, although hers was just "an approximate outline" which was "not detailed," according to him.[116]

The Divine Principle teaches that Lucifer, symbolized by a serpent, "was the channel of God's love to the angelic world" and "virtually monopolized the love of God," but that after God created Adam and Eve as his children, Lucifer as God's servant realized that God loved them "many times more than" him.[117] So Lucifer, "feeling as though he were receiving less love than he deserved, wanted to grasp the same central position in human society as he enjoyed in the angelic world."[118] At that point, Eve, as the beloved daughter of God, looked so beautiful that he wanted to seduce her. In her initial response to his temptation, she "wanted to open her eyes and become like God before the time was ripe."[119] This led him to feel even a stronger stimulation of love from her. This way the two "formed a common base and began give and take action. The power of the unprincipled love generated by their give and take led them to consummate an illicit sexual relationship on the spiritual plane."[120] This was the spiritual fall between Lucifer and Eve.

It is to be noted that this understanding of the spiritual fall between Lucifer and Eve by the Divine Principle is quite different from Augustine's understanding. The Divine Principle maintains that Lucifer, who tempted Eve out of his jealousy of the children of God, and Eve, who responded to his temptation, spiritually fell together simultaneously through a reciprocal relationship of illicit love, which was symbolized by the act of eating the fruit. According to Augustine, by contrast, Lucifer first fell by himself through his own free will, becoming the devil or Satan, and then, out of his envy of the

---

115 Su Wong Chung, "Seung Do Kim, the Holy Lord Church and My Life as a 36 Couple." https://www.tparents.org/Library/Unification/Talks1/Chung/Chung-860400.htm. Su Wong Chung is a grandson of Sung Do Kim.

116 Sun Myung Moon, *Makotono Gofubosama no Shogai Rotei* [The Life Course of True Parents], vol. 2 (Tokyo: Kogensha, 2000), pp. 37-38.

117 EDP, p. 63.

118 EDP, p. 64.

119 Ibid.

120 Ibid.

unfallen condition of Adam and Eve, tried to tempt Eve through the serpent, a real animal, to eat the fruit, although in actuality she, by herself, decided to eat it through her own free will. The Divine Principle's approach is relational and sexual, whereas Augustine's is atomistic and individualist, without being sexual.

As for Eve's next fall which was her physical fall with Adam, the Divine Principle holds that Eve, through her spiritual fall with Lucifer, received from him "feelings of dread arising from the pangs of a guilty conscience" and "a new wisdom that her originally intended spouse was not the Archangel but Adam."[121] At that point, Adam, who was not fallen yet, looked beautiful to her. So she, who now stood in the position of Lucifer toward Adam, "seduced Adam with the hope that by uniting with him, her intended spouse, she could rid herself of the dread and once again stand before God."[122] Adam responded. The two, then, "formed a common base" and "began give and take action with each other," with the result that the "power of the unprincipled love generated in their relationship induced Adam to abandon his original position and brought them together in an illicit physical relationship of sexual love."[123] This was the physical fall between Eve and Adam, although it should be pointed out at this juncture that after the time was ripe without the fall, they were to marry each other and have sexual relations, "joining as true husband and wife and bearing and raising [sinless] children in God's love."[124]

Again, the Divine Principle view of the physical fall between Eve and Adam is relational and sexual, being quite different from Augustine's atomistic and individualist view, according to which Adam decided to eat the fruit by himself through his own free will, not directly influenced by Eve's temptation. The Divine Principle, therefore, teaches that eating the fruit in the Garden of Eden meant having a sexual relationship of illicit love, and that the fruit signified the "love of Eve"[125] or, more specifically, her "reproductive organ."[126]

Consequently, Lucifer, using the power of illicit love, first dominated Eve sexually and became Satan, and then dominated Adam sexually through Eve who was in the position of Satan to him. Thus "Adam and Eve formed a family through the husband and wife relationship centered on Satan rather than

---

121 EDP, p. 65.

122 Ibid.

123 Ibid.

124 EDP, p. 67.

125 EDP, p. 60.

126 Hak Ja Han Moon and Sun Myung Moon, *The Holy Scripture of Cheon Il Guk: Cheon Seong Gyeong* (Seoul, Korea: Seonghwa Publications, 2014), p. 408.

God."[127] This was how Satan was able to claim Adam and Eve and all their descendants as his "children" in "the lineage of Satan, not the lineage of God."[128] To support this point on the lineage of Satan, the Divine Principle uses biblical passages such as John 8:44, which reads: "You are of your father the devil, and your will is to do your father's desires."[129]

The Divine Principle gives further reasons why the fall of Adam and Eve was sexual and not from literally eating the fruit of the tree of the knowledge of good and evil: 1) because something you eat would not cause a sin which can be transmitted to your descendants;[130] 2) because the fruit, instead of being a food, must have been "something so extraordinarily stimulating that even the fear of death did not deter them [i.e., Adam and Eve] from grasping it";[131] 3) because Adam and Eve, after the fall, became ashamed of their lower parts, covering them with fig leaves;[132] 4) because fornication has been regarded as a cardinal sin by religions in pursuit of purity;[133] and 5) because "no one can prevent the plague of sexual promiscuity," although we may be able to eradicate all other evils by moral codes, education, and betterment of socio-economic systems.[134] Rev. Moon says that this sexual interpretation is therefore "more logical"[135] and "much more plausible"[136] than the traditional, non-sexual and literal interpretation.

By the way, when the Divine Principle says that the "fear of death" did not deter Adam and Eve from sexually falling, it holds that their death, which is mentioned in Genesis 2:17 ("in the day that you eat of it you shall die"), and which actually happened after their fall, was not physical death but spiritual death. Physical death is not a punishment for the fall. According to the Divine Principle, regardless of the fall, human beings are all to physically die, then go to the spirit world to live there forever: "When we shed our physical bodies after our life in the physical world, we enter the spirit world as spirits and live there for eternity."[137]

---

[127] Sun Myung Moon, "Blessing and Ideal Family," in *Blessed Family and the Ideal Kingdom* (New York: HSA-UWC, 2000), p. 234.
[128] EDP, p. 60.
[129] EDP, p. 59.
[130] EDP, p. 54.
[131] Ibid.
[132] EDP, p. 59.
[133] EDP, p. 61.
[134] Ibid.
[135] Sun Myung Moon, *Way of Unification*, part 1 (Washington, DC: Family Federation for World Peace and Unification, 1998), p. 4.
[136] Moon, "Blessing and Ideal Family," p. 232.
[137] EDP, p. 46.

b. Free will

One might ask if the Divine Principle espouses free will at all, given its relational and sexual interpretation of the fall, which seriously considers the role of temptation. The traditional atomistic and individualist interpretation emphasizes the role of free will (free choice of the will) in the fall, even to the virtual neglect of temptation, as was seen previously. But does the Divine Principle acknowledge any role of free will? This question should be answered in the affirmative.

In fact, the Divine Principle believes that the "free will" of an original, sinless person is "an expression of the mind" which "cannot operate outside of God's Word, that is, the Principle," and that this free will, therefore, never generates "free action" apart from the Principle.[138] Also, in order to realize God's purpose of creation, this free will of a sinless person ceaselessly pursues, through free action, the fulfillment of responsibility and concrete results which bring joy to God.[139] Thus, if "freedom" means a harmonious combination of free will as "internal nature" and free action as "external form," as the Divine Principle defines it,[140] then there is no freedom without the Principle, nor any freedom without responsibility, nor any freedom without good results.[141]

If this is the case, then freedom or free will, to begin with, never causes the fall: "it cannot be that freedom caused the human Fall."[142] This is unlike the traditional Augustinian thesis that free will caused the fall. Here we see a fundamental difference between the Divine Principle view and the Augustinian view on free will. The former believes that the free will of an original, sinless person always results in good choices, whereas the latter holds that the free will of Adam and Eve before their fall was no more than the ability not to sin (*posse non peccare*), which necessarily included the ability to sin (*posse peccare*) as well, i.e., that it had both possibilities of good and bad choices from the very beginning. Therefore the former maintains that the fall was only "caused by the stronger power of unprincipled love, which overwhelmed the freedom of the original mind,"[143] suggesting that Lucifer the tempter was behind that power of unprincipled love, whereas the latter asserts that it was not Satan's temptation but the free will of Adam and Eve itself that caused their fall.

---

[138] EDP, p. 74.
[139] Ibid.
[140] Ibid.
[141] EDP, pp. 74-75.
[142] EDP, p. 75.
[143] Ibid.

Both the Divine Principle and the traditional Augustinian position, of course, admit of the possibility of the fall of Adam and Eve. But they do so in two very different ways. The former says that if the power of love, which is "stronger than" the power of the Principle (on which the free will of Adam and Eve was based), collides with it "from a different direction and with an unprincipled purpose," then it can overwhelm their free will and freedom, inducing them to fall.[144] As a result, they can lose their freedom, and actually they "lost" it.[145] The latter, by contrast, holds that Adam and Eve before the fall already had the possibility of falling (*posse peccare*) within their free will itself.

Thus the Divine Principle teaches that Adam and Eve fell because their free will or freedom did not fully and perfectly function, as they were still in the process of growth in the growing period, during which they needed to obey God's commandment of not eating the fruit, in order to avoid falling.[146]

The Divine Principle explains the reason why God made the power of love stronger than that of the Principle, even though it made room for the possibility of the fall. The reason is as follows. God's love is "truly the source and wellspring of our life and happiness," because without it there is no establishment of the true "four position foundation," in which our love also functions centered on God; so, "in order for love to fulfill its proper role, its power must be stronger than the power of the Principle."[147]

If Adam and Eve had become perfect and created an ideal family under the direct governance of God's absolute love, therefore, "their conjugal love would have become absolute," and "No person, no power in the universe could ever break that bond of love."[148] And there would have been no fall.

2. The Unification Doctrine of Original Sin

a. Original sin distinct from the fall

The Divine Principle takes original sin seriously. But what needs to be clarified is whether or not original sin is to be differentiated from the primal sin of Adam and Eve, i.e., whether or not it is to be considered as a resultant condition imposed on all humanity as a punishment for the fall of the first human ancestors. There is a passage from a speech of Rev. Moon which initially appears to differentiate between the original sin of human beings and

---

144 EDP, p. 66.
145 EDP, p. 75.
146 EDP, pp. 66-67.
147 EDP, p. 66.
148 EDP, p. 67.

the fall of their first ancestors itself, as it says that "we human beings came to have original sin through the fall of the first human ancestors"; but almost immediately thereafter it seems to equate the two with each other, as it references "this original sin which Adam and Eve committed."[149] In a couple of other places as well, we receive the impression that the two are to be equated with each other: "The original sin of the first human ancestors was that Adam and Eve broke God's commandment and engaged in an illicit sexual relationship";[150] "the root of sin," another name of original sin in the Divine Principle, "was… that they had an illicit sexual relationship with an angel."[151]

But if we read the Unification materials more carefully, we find many, many more passages which differentiate between original sin as a resultant state and the fall of Adam and Eve as its cause: "Since the fall was an accident related to blood lineage, it *resulted in* the original sin which has been passed on until today";[152] "The Fall began from a motivation denying the lineage. Therefore people have inherited the *consequences* of the Fall as the original sin until the present day";[153] "The ancestors of humankind, Adam and Eve, fell with the wrong kind of love… In this way, by establishing the love relationship not permitted by God, what happened to humankind was that the original sin *came about*";[154] "the first human ancestors fell *and* acquired the original sin."[155]

In the case of Augustine, while initially equating original sin with the fall of Adam in the year 397, he later distinguished between the two, saying that original sin is a resultant punishment of God for the primal sin of Adam. It was a good move on his part. As was previously mentioned,[156] the present writer suggests that Anselm, Aquinas, Luther and the Council of Trent should be read from the viewpoint of Augustine's later distinction between original sin and Adam's fall, in order to avoid any unnecessary sharp contrast between the Catholic tradition and Luther regarding the relationship of original sin and concupiscence.

---

149 Sun Myung Moon, *Bun Senmei Sensei no Mikotoba ni Manabu Touitsu Genri* [Learning the Divine Principle from the Words of Rev. Sun Myung Moon], part 1 (Tokyo: Kogensha, 2012), p. 182.

150 Sun Myung Moon, "Becoming the Leaders in Building A World of Peace," delivered at Little Angels Performing Arts Center, Seoul, Korea, August 24, 1992. https://www.tparents.org/Moon-Talks/SunMyungMoon92/SM920825.HTM.

151 EDP, p. 61. The "root of sin" is another name for "original sin" in the Divine Principle (EDP, p. 72).

152 Moon, *Way of Unification*, part 1, p. 5. Italics added.

153 Sun Myung Moon, *Cheon Seong Gyeong: Selections from the Speeches of True Parents* (Seoul, Korea: Sunghwa Publishing Company, 2006), p. 1139. Italics added

154 Moon, "Blessing and Ideal Family," p. 408. Italics added.

155 EDP, p. 181. Italics added.

156 See Section 1, Subsection 3.

In the same way, the present writer would suggest, concerning Unificationism as well, that in order for it to avoid any confusion, original sin should be differentiated from the fall of Adam and Eve itself and be regarded as its resultant condition. There is much textual evidence to support this, although there also are some passages which seem to equate or confuse the two with each other. Another merit of this distinction would be that it can make it easier for Unificationism to engage the Augustinian doctrine of original sin which has been very influential in the Christian tradition. But the real merit of distinguishing original sin from the fall of Adam and Eve in Unificationism is that the definition of original sin becomes clearer than otherwise, as will be seen immediately below.

b. Original sin

What, then, does original sin really mean, as differentiated from the fall of Adam and Eve in the Divine Principle? It means that *after* their sexual fall involving illicit love centered on Satan, they and their descendants were now put in the state in which they were linked to the lineage of Satan: "What is the original sin? It is love gone wrong. Our love should have been connected to God's love, life and lineage. Instead, it was connected to satanic love, life and lineage";[157] "What is original sin? We have inherited the enemy's blood lineage."[158] Original sin thus means that "due to the Fall of the first human ancestors, human beings are of the lineage of Satan,"[159] and that "all humanity became the children of Satan" based on the "four position foundation yoked to Satan,"[160] i.e., the Satan-centered four position foundation of: 1) Satan, 2) fallen Adam and Eve, and 3) children.

Original sin, therefore, also means that "Satan came to dominate human beings" based on the four position foundation "under the sovereignty of Satan."[161] It, then, also means the state in which if we attempt to get away from Satan's dominion, he claims us, by attacking or invading us: "A fallen person with original sin is stained with the condition through which Satan can attack him";[162] "the conditions by which Satan can attack us… stem from the original sin."[163]

---

157 *Cheon Seong Gyeong* (2006), p. 135.

158 Sun Myung Moon, "70 Points to Live By," delivered at a 12-Day Seminar in Hawaii, July 2001. https://www.tparents.org/Moon-Talks/SunMyungMoon01/SunMyungMoon/010700.htm.

159 EDP, p. 68.

160 Ibid.

161 Ibid.

162 EDP, p. 168.

163 EDP, p. 118.

In this situation, Satan has always been "accusing" Adam, Eve and all their descendants in front of God, saying: "This is my society, my world. These people are immoral, selfish, and changing so they are my property. Where are Your people, God?"[164] Original sin, therefore, also means that we are in the state of being always accused by Satan in front of God: "Satan is constantly accusing all people before God… in order to drag them into hell."[165]

Now we have understood that according to the Divine Principle original sin means that we, including Adam and Eve, are of the lineage of Satan, under the domination of Satan, and in the state of being attacked, invaded and accused by Satan. We carry this original sin because we are *guilty* of the primal sin of Adam and Eve, of which the first ancestors themselves, too, are guilty. Original sin, therefore, actually means our guilt in this regard.

Rev. Moon quite often talks about "guilt": "we will not be able to help but repent taking on ourselves the sinful guilt of humankind"; we "cannot help but repent for our historical guilt, and we cannot help but repent for the guilt of the present age"; "having him [i.e., the precious son of heaven] be able to atone for the suffering and guilt of history."[166] The word "guilt," used by Moon here, shows something which all humankind has, which has historically existed and still exists now, and which is to be atoned for by the son of heaven; so it must be original sin. Although the Korean word for "guilt" here is 죄상, which can also be translated simply as "sin" or "crime," it is to be differentiated from the primal "sin" or "crime" of Adam and Eve, as our guilt here means that we are guilty of the primal sin of the first human ancestors.

Also, if we are guilty of the primal sin of Adam and Eve, we are also responsible for it. For we are guilty of their failure to fulfill their portion of responsibility at their fall. Hence Rev. Moon says:

> Adam and Eve were unable to fulfill their portion of responsibility. Nevertheless, the fact that they could not fulfill this did not just end with them. Adam and Eve became the root and all the descendants became the trunk, branches and leaves, and as a consequence all human beings were unable to fulfill their responsibility.[167]

Augustine spoke about original sin in terms of guilt (as well as concupiscence). It is interesting to observe that both the Augustinian tradition

---

164 Sun Myung Moon, "Heaven's Side and Satan's Side," sermon delivered at Belvedere, Tarrytown, NY, February 20, 1983. https://www.tparents.org/Moon-Talks/SunMyungMoon83/830220.htm.
165 EDP, pp. 68-69.
166 All the three passages are found in "Sun Myung Moon, Prayers: A Lifetime of Conversation with Our Heavenly Father." https://www.tparents.org/Moon-Books/Prayers/Prayers.pdf.
167 *Cheon Seong Gyeong* (2006), p. 1117.

and the Divine Principle understand original sin as the state in which we are guilty of the primal sin of Adam and Eve. This is certainly the case, although both understand the content of guilt in two different ways: in the Augustinian tradition we are guilty of the literal act of individually eating the fruit in disobedience, whereas according to the Divine Principle we are guilty of the relational, sexual crime of illicit love.

c. The transmission of original sin

How is original sin transmitted from one generation to another? According to the Divine Principle, when sinful parents in the Satan-centered four position foundation of: 1) Satan, 2) sinful parents, and 3) children, give birth to and multiply children, these children are already automatically within the lineage of Satan. Thus they immediately inherit the original sin of guilt from their parents. The transmission of original sin naturally occurs through the sexual relationship of sinful parents for procreation centered on Satan, and it started from the very first human parents, Adam and Eve.

This sexual interpretation of the transmission of original sin is quite similar to Augustine's, according to which original sin is transmitted through the agency of concupiscence which unavoidably awakens to emerge in the sexual union of parents for procreation under the dominion of Satan, whether or not the parents are regenerate through baptism. But there seem to be at least two points of difference between the Divine Principle and Augustine. First, whereas the Divine Principle explicitly talks about the lineage of Satan, Augustine fell short of doing so, only talking about the dominion of Satan in general, perhaps for the reason that he did not believe that the primal sin or fall of Adam, Eve and Lucifer was sexual.

A second point of difference between the Divine Principle and Augustine is that whereas the Divine Principle believes that those parents who have received "rebirth both spiritually and physically" from "True Parents" (perfected Adam and Eve),[168] thus having no original sin at all, do not transmit original sin to their children, Augustine taught that those parents who are regenerate through baptism, thus being with no guilt (one element of original sin) but with concupiscence (another element of original sin) remaining, transmit the entirety of original sin to their children through the agency of concupiscence unavoidable in their sexual relationship for procreation. By the way, according to the Divine Principle it is possible that those parents who are cleansed of original sin through True Parents still have what the Divine

---

[168] EDP, p. 172.

Principle calls "fallen nature." ("Fallen nature" will be discussed a little later as something which is different from original sin in the Divine Principle but which is equivalent to concupiscence in Augustine.) If so, do they transmit their fallen nature to their children? The right answer would be that they do, although they do not transmit original sin, which they do not have, to their children.

Given the Divine Principle's sexual interpretation of the transmission of original sin, which addresses the lineage of Satan, the question is: Is the Divine Principle traducianist regarding the origin of the soul? No, it isn't. It is creationist instead, as it rather clearly holds that "while in the womb, the child does not have a spiritual body; God imparts the spirit with the first breath."[169] If so, how is the child's new soul going to be contaminated with the original sin of its sinful parents? To answer the question, it would be safe to say that the moment at which the soul is imparted by God with the first breath, it cannot help getting contaminated with original sin by virtue of the Satan-centered four position foundation of: 1) Satan, 2) the sinful parents, and 3) the new soul.

d. Removing original sin

How can we remove original sin? If original sin means that we as children of Satan are linked to the satanic lineage based on the Satan-centered four position foundation of: 1) Satan, 2) fallen Adam and Eve, and 3) children, then removing it means that we cut off our linkage to the satanic lineage. We receive "rebirth" to become children of God by being engrafted with the lineage of God based on the God-centered four position foundation of: 1) God, 2) "True Parents" (perfected Adam and Eve), and 3) children.[170] This is done through the rite of the Blessing officiated by True Parents (perfected Adam and Eve) or any officiator couples who represent them, and it involves drinking the Holy Wine and sprinkling the Holy Water. We are to receive the Blessing either as a newly married couple or as an already married couple. Either way, the bridegroom and bride as a couple are to receive the Blessing together in order to remove their inherited guilt of the sexually fallen couple of Adam and Eve.

The Blessing in the Unification movement is equivalent to baptism in Christianity because Christian baptism, too, removes the element of guilt in original sin according to Augustine and Luther. (In the later Catholic tradition, original sin does not mean guilt but the deprivation of original justice, but

---

[169] *Tradition*, book 1 (New York: Rose of Sharon Press, 1985), p. 163.
[170] EDP, p. 172.

original sin in this sense, too, is considered to be removed through baptism.) The Blessing in the Unification movement, however, is different from Christian baptism in two ways. First, the Blessing is given to couples, as was mentioned above, while Christian baptism is given to individuals because Christianity understands the fall of Adam and Eve to be individual and atomistic. Second, through the Blessing from True Parents "we must be cleansed of original sin by being born again both spiritually and physically," while through Christian baptism we are cleansed of original sin only by receiving "spiritual rebirth" from "spiritual True Parents" (Jesus and the Holy Spirit).[171]

This second point is the reason why in spite of the Christian claim that baptism cleanses original sin, the Divine Principle holds that through baptism, strictly speaking, Christians are not cleansed of original sin: "Even the most devout Christian still has the original sin and gives birth to children who also carry the original sin."[172] Spiritual rebirth through baptism alone is not enough according to the Divine Principle. We have to be reborn "both spiritually and physically." That is the reason why Jesus and the Holy Spirit as spiritual True Parents must return to earth to become substantial True Parents who can give both spiritual and physical rebirth.

e. Fallen nature

The Divine Principle includes a doctrine of "fallen nature." Fallen nature is not original sin. It rather signifies "all the proclivities incidental to" the fall of Adam and Eve centered on Lucifer, and it has been "inherited" to all humanity.[173] The fundamental motivation which engendered this fallen nature was the "envy" which Lucifer felt toward Adam and Eve, the beloved children of God. Fallen nature has the following "four types of primary characteristics: 1) "failing to take God's position" in loving others, thus being jealous and self-centered; 2) "leaving one's proper position" with an excessive desire; 3) "reversing dominion" with arrogance; and 4) "multiplying the criminal act," shifting responsibilities to others.[174]

In order to investigate the real meaning of fallen nature, however, let us see what the Divine Principle calls "original nature," which is opposite to fallen nature. Original nature is our "original God-given nature" in which we can

---

[171] EDP, p. 171.
[172] EDP, p. 118.
[173] EDP, p. 72.
[174] EDP, pp. 72-74.

"cultivate a give and take relationship with God."[175] But our give and take relationship with God is realized when our "mind and body become one through give and take action with God as their center," reaching the "perfection of individual character."[176] Original nature, therefore, is our original human nature in which our mind and body are united centered on God. Fallen nature, then, should refer to the fallen state of our human nature which experiences "the struggle between mind and body."[177] In this state, "Your mind and body struggle because of the Fall," having a "rebellion against God."[178]

This is actually very similar to Augustine's notion of "concupiscence," which, as was seen previously, means the disordering of human nature in which the flesh disobeys the soul—a disordering that occurred as a result of the fall, which was the disobedience of Adam's soul to God. Interestingly, therefore, fallen nature in the Divine Principle is equivalent to the notion of concupiscence in Augustine. It is also equivalent to the notion of concupiscence in the Council of Trent and the *Catechism of the Catholic Church* and, of course, to Luther's idea of concupiscence.

In spite of this great similarity between fallen nature in the Divine Principle and concupiscence in Christianity, there is a noticeable difference. It is that the Divine Principle does *not* regard fallen nature as part of original sin, while Augustine and Luther regarded concupiscence as part of original sin. The Divine Principle, therefore, resembles the later Catholic tradition which did not include concupiscence as part of original sin.

According to the Divine Principle, fallen nature, being just "incidental" to the fall, may not be as serious as original sin, which is our guilt of Adam's serious sexual fall which brought about our linkage to the lineage of Satan. This may be why the Divine Principle does not include fallen nature in original sin. By contrast, for Augustine and Luther, who had no sexual interpretation of the fall, our guilt for Adam's non-sexual sin of disobedience may be no more serious than concupiscence, and furthermore Augustine and Luther personally experienced the seriousness of concupiscence in their own lives. This may be the reason why Augustine and Luther included concupiscence as well as guilt in original sin.

---

[175] EDP, p. 23.

[176] EDP, pp. 33-34.

[177] Sun Myung Moon, "Declaring the Era of the Peace Kingdom," March 23, 2004, Address to the United States Congress, Washington, DC https://www.tparents.org/Moon-Talks/SunMyungMoon04/SM040323.htm.

[178] Sun Myung Moon, *The Way for Young People* (Seoul, Korea: Family Federation for World Peace and Unification International, 1998), p. 37.

Is fallen nature, which is different from original sin itself, transmitted from one generation to another like original sin? It is transmitted to later generations whenever original sin is transmitted to them. The reason is that fallen nature, which is our mind-body disunity as well as our disunity with God, always accompanies original sin, which is our guilt of the primal sexual sin of Adam and Eve that brought forth our mind-body disunity as well as our disunity with God.

How can we remove fallen nature? While we can remove original sin instantaneously at the moment of being engrafted with the lineage of God through the Blessing, we cannot remove fallen nature in the same way. It is not to be removed through the Blessing. (This is similar to the traditional Christian teaching that while original sin with respect to guilt can be removed through baptism, concupiscence cannot.) Instead, fallen nature can only gradually be removed in the somewhat lengthy "process" of the growth of the "spirit self," called "resurrection,"[179] which can be done by believing and practicing God's Word on this earth.[180] Believing and practicing God's Word to gradually remove fallen nature usually involves establishing the so-called "foundation of substance," in which a Cain figure loves, unites with, and submits to an Abel figure for reconciliation to overcome their struggle.[181] This reconciliation actually begins with the individual level at which the body (Cain) submits to the mind (Abel), and even expands to various social levels at which Esau (Cain), for example, submits to Jacob (Abel). Therefore the Divine Principle says:

> In relationships at every level of society—from those between individuals to those at the level of families, communities, societies, nations and the world—we find that one party is in the role of Abel and the other is in the role of Cain. In order to restore society at each level to the state originally envisioned by God, those in the Cain position should respect and obey those in the Abel position.[182]

The Divine Principle idea that fallen nature cannot be removed through the Blessing but through a long process of spiritual growth echoes the general Christian assertion that concupiscence cannot be removed through baptism but through a process of the regenerate striving not to consent to it.

---

179 EDP, p. 136.
180 EDP, p. 138.
181 EDP, pp. 192-94.
182 EDP, p. 194.

§3. Three Problems of the Christian Doctrine of the Fall

Section 1 above dealt with the traditional Christian doctrine of the fall, formulated largely by Augustine. We saw that the two components of the Christian doctrine of the fall, which are the doctrine of Adam's fall and the doctrine of original sin proper, are inconsistent with each other because they have two inconsistent approaches. The former component has an atomistic, individualist approach, believing that Adam, Eve and Lucifer individually fell because each of them, with free will, severally made the wrong choice of disobeying God's commandment. Thus it already implies that you alone are responsible for the sin you commit, and that you need no one else, neither a first human ancestor nor a Satan, in order for you to commit your own sin. By contrast, the latter component has a relational, sexual approach, affirming the solidarity of all members of the human race to say that original sin has been transmitted from one generation to another through the sexual union of parents for procreation with the involvement of Satan after the fall of Adam and Eve. Thus it affirms the hereditary nature of original sin, the historicity of Adam and the existence of Satan.

It is in this basic inconsistency between the two components of the doctrine of the fall in their inconsistent approaches that we can find at least three quite serious problems of theological ambiguity: 1) that the inheritance of original sin is affirmed, on the one hand, but obscured, on the other; 2) that the historicity of Adam is regarded as a necessary component, on the one hand, but deemed not absolutely needed, on the other; and 3) that the existence of Satan is required, on the one hand, but not necessarily required, on the other.

The present section will see how modern liberal theology and evolutionary theology, which emerged respectively under the influence of the Enlightenment and Darwinism, explicitly denied the inheritance of original sin, the historicity of Adam and the existence of Satan, thus making the above three problems more serious and unsolved.

1. Denial of the Inheritance of Original Sin

Although the inheritance of original sin has long been unquestionably believed to be true, its denial was already implicitly hinted at by the atomistic, individualist approach on the fall of Adam and Eve in traditional Christianity. This denial was also reinforced by liberal theology and evolutionary theology which emerged in modern times.

Friedrich Schleiermacher (1768–1834), the father of modern theology, attempted a theological reconstruction in the beginning of the nineteenth century (even before the emergence of evolutionism) by integrating traditional Christianity with the Enlightenment tradition. In this context, he reinterpreted original sin, denying its biological inheritance.

His view of sin was psychological, as he understood it within the framework of the relationship between the spiritual and the sensual functions of human beings, i.e., between the "higher self-consciousness" (the God-consciousness) and the "sensible self-consciousness" (the world-consciousness): Sin freely occurs when the sensual functions gain power before the spiritual.[183] Sin, as understood this way, always exists in human nature as "innate sinfulness"[184] or "prior sinfulness"[185] regardless of the fall of Adam and Eve: "human nature in the first pair was the same before the first sin as it appears subsequently alike in them and in their posterity," and "we cannot say that human nature was changed as a result of the first sin."[186] Therefore there was no golden age of innocence for Adam and Eve before their fall. For Schleiermacher, this timeless, innate sin in human nature is what is original sin in Christianity, and it as "an incapacity for good" is "the universal state of men" before and after the fall of Adam and Eve.[187]

This modern reinterpretation of original sin by Schleiermacher was adopted by many other prominent, liberal, modern theologians such as Albrecht Ritschl (1822–1889) and Walter Rauschenbusch (1861–1918). Interestingly, however, even the conservative theologian Karl Barth (1886–1968), who inaugurated the school of neo-orthodoxy as a staunch critic of Schleiermacher, had quite a similar idea of the universality of sin. He was apparently somewhat influenced by the Schleiermachian tradition in that regard, because he initially received a liberal theological education within that tradition before becoming a conservative critic of it. According to Barth, sin essentially as "pride" always exists in human nature: "Pride goes before a fall."[188] Thus there never was a point in time in which human beings were unfallen: "There never was a golden age. There is no point in looking back to one."[189]

---

[183] Friedrich Schleiermacher, *The Christian Faith*, English trans. of 2nd ed., ed. H. R. Mackintosh and J. S. Stewart (Philadelphia: Fortress Press, 1976), p. 293.
[184] Ibid., p. 295.
[185] Ibid., p. 294.
[186] Ibid., p. 296.
[187] Ibid., p. 301.
[188] Karl Barth, *Church Dogmatics*, IV/1 (Edinburg: T&T Clark, 1956), p. 478.
[189] Ibid., IV/1, p. 508.

But Barth's reason for saying so was unique. According to him, the occurrences of the creation, fall and redemption of human beings are all to be attributed to God's eternal plan, as God in his absolute freedom decided from eternity to elect Jesus Christ (who is eternally one with him in the unity of the Godhead) for the creation of the world[190] and the salvation of sinful human beings.[191] This christocentric, predestinarian approach of Barth logically necessitates the fall and redemption of *all* human beings, so there needs to be no moment of "fall" within time. The fall of Adam does not have to be a historical event; it is rather a "saga" (*Geschichte* in German) which, using "intuition and imagination," points to how all human beings generally and equally sin.[192] In God's Word "all men are continually as the first man Adam, for what God continually sees them do is what Adam first did [in the saga]."[193] In this idea of the solidarity of the human race, the "hereditary" transmission of original sin is rejected,[194] and thus the notion of individual "responsibility" on the part of each human being is maintained.[195]

Reinhold Niebuhr (1882–1971) was another prominent conservative theologian in the twentieth century who denied original sin, as traditionally understood, although he took it very seriously in his own way. According to him, sin can be occasioned by "anxiety" or "insecurity" which arises from the "tension" or "paradox" between the dual characteristics of "spirit" (self-transcendence) and "nature" (natural creatureliness) which every human being has as the God-given human composition.[196] While this anxiety itself is not sin yet, it is definitely "the precondition of sin," or else "the basis of all human creativity."[197] If we in the midst of this anxiety humbly accept our situation and find security in God, we can stay as creative humans who do not sin; but if we do not find security in God, we will sin in two different ways: 1) by finding security in the exaltation of our finite, natural creatureliness to the level of infinite significance (the sin of "pride"); or 2) by finding security in the escape from our infinite possibilities of spirit toward finite creatureliness (the sin of "sensuality").[198]

---

190 Ibid., II/2, p. 94.
191 Ibid., II/2, p. 116.
192 Ibid., IV/1, p. 508.
193 Ibid., IV/1, p. 509.
194 Ibid., IV/1, p. 511.
195 Karl Barth, *Christ and Adam: Man and Humanity in Romans 5*, trans. T. A. Smail (New York: Collier Book, 1962), p. 113.
196 Reinhold Niebuhr, *The Nature and Destiny of Man: A Christian Interpretation*, vol. I: *Human Nature* (New York: Charles Scribner's Sons, 1964), pp. 179-82.
197 Ibid., pp. 182-83.
198 Ibid., pp. 185-86.

Sin thus understood is "not necessary," although it may be "inevitable,"[199] thus being able to be called original sin. If so, we are not entirely exempt from responsibility for sinning. Sin is, therefore, not a hereditary taint from the fall of Adam, but rather something which inevitably exists in our human nature from the very beginning. So there is no golden age of innocence or perfection before the fall.[200] The fall of Adam, then, is not an event in history but rather "a symbol of an aspect of every historical moment in the life of man."[201] Again, the fall of Adam, not being historical, is simply "representative" of the sinful condition of all humans at all times.[202] Here again, some influence from Schleiermacher can be seen.

Let us now proceed to evolutionary theology, which was developed within Christianity under the influence of Charles Darwin's (1809–1882) theory of evolution expressed in *On the Origin of Species* (1859) and *The Descent of Man* (1871). His theory that the human species originated through a very long process of random mutation and natural selection apart from God was a serious challenge to traditional Christianity. But it became so widespread that many Christian theologians of a more liberal bent tried to integrate it with theology. Hence evolutionary theology. Also called "evolutionary creationism" or "theistic evolutionism,"[203] it believed that "God used the process of evolution to create living things, including humans."[204] There have been various versions of evolutionary creationism, ranging from a deistic, polygenistic one, through a monotheistic, polygenistic one, to a more conservative, monogenistic one, the last one of which is a minority position among evolutionary creationists.

The first major attempt to integrate evolution with theology in evolutionary creationism or theistic evolutionism on the Protestant side was made by the Anglican theologian F. R. Tennant (1866–1957) in his *The Origin and Propagation of Sin* (1902).[205] He argued that our capacity to sin, which consists of "instincts, appetites and impulses" in our common human nature,

---

[199] Ibid., pp. 150, 263.
[200] Ibid., p. 268.
[201] Ibid., p. 269.
[202] Ibid., p. 261.
[203] The terms "evolutionary creationism" and "theistic evolutionism" are usually interchangeable. But the emphasis of the former is on "creationism" with "evolutionary" merely as an adjective, and that of the latter is on "evolutionism" with "theistic" merely as an adjective. Thus the former may sound slightly less liberal than the latter.
[204] Ted Davis, "Theistic Evolution: History and Beliefs." https://biologos.org/articles/theistic-evolution-history-and-beliefs.
[205] This book was published after his Hulsean Lectures at the University of Cambridge in 1901-1902.

came from our animal ancestors in the process of evolution under God, and that while it by itself is the morally neutral "raw material for the production of sin,"[206] from it "sin, as the activity of the individual will, is produced" as moral consciousness awakens in the same evolutionary process.[207] This is original sin for him. Thus he denied the historicity of the primal fall of a first human ancestor.

His reinterpretation of original sin from the viewpoint of evolution has been followed and further developed by many other Protestant evolutionary creationists such as Francis S. Collins (1950–),[208] founder of BioLogos whose mission is "to present an evolutionary understanding of God's creation";[209] Denis O. Lamoureux (1954–),[210] a professor of science and religion at St. Joseph's College at the University of Alberta; and Peter Enns (1961–),[211] a former professor at Westminster Theological Seminary. Enns had to resign from the seminary because his 2005 book criticized the traditional evangelical doctrine of biblical inerrancy.[212]

Within Catholicism, the French Jesuit priest Pierre Teilhard de Chardin (1881–1955) was the first to take evolution seriously. Although he did not develop any extensive treatment of original sin itself, he generally saw sin as an inevitable result of the finite nature of all creation, including free will, in the evolutionary process: "Original sin, taken in its widest sense, is not a malady specific to the earth, nor is it bound up with human generation. It simply symbolizes the inevitable chance of evil... which accompanies the existence of *all* participated being."[213] Teilhard was censured by the Catholic Church for this view in the mid-1920s.

Afterwards, Pope Pius XII's (r. 1939–1958) encyclical *Humani Generis* (1950) showed a bit of openness to evolution, by cautiously saying that any research of it by competent persons is not forbidden, as long as it does not

---

[206] F. R. Tennant, *The Origin and Propagation of Sin*, 2nd ed. (Cambridge: Cambridge University Press, 1906), p. 95.
[207] Ibid., p. 75.
[208] Francis S. Collins, *The Language of God: A Scientist Presents Evidence for Belief* (New York: Free Press, 2006).
[209] https://biologos.org/about-us#our-mission.
[210] Denis O. Lamoureux, *Evolutionary Creation: A Christian Approach to Evolution* (Eugene, OR: Wipf & Stock, 2008).
[211] Peter Enns, *The Evolution of Adam: What the Bible Does and Doesn't Say about Human Origins* (Grand Rapids, MI: Brozos Press, 2012).
[212] Peter Enns, *Inspiration and Incarnation: Evangelicals and the Problem of the Old Testament* (Grand Rapids, MI: Baker Academic, 2005).
[213] Pierre Teilhard de Chardin, *Christianity and Evolution: Reflections on Science and Religion*, trans. René Hague (New York: A Harvest Book, 1969), p. 40. Italics added.

infringe upon the Catholic faith in God's immediate creation of the human soul[214] and also in monogenism.[215] But the Dutch Jesuit theologian Piet Shoonenberg (1911–1999) had a much more open appreciation of evolution in the spirit of Teilhard. According to Schoonenberg, we have to pay attention to "the slow development of order [in the evolutionary process] and all the travail involved in it" from the beginning as the basis of original sin.[216] Thus there was no paradise at the beginning: "Paradise lies not at the beginning, but at the end."[217] This sin, which is already there in the process of evolution, naturally occurs in each and every human being, and it has three manifestations: punishment, the inability to love, and the inclination to evil.[218] Thus this sin as original sin is not transmitted from a primeval fall of a first man. There is a situation of the world in which human sins are accumulated by socially affecting one another—a situation which John 1:29 calls "the sin of the world."[219] This is the meaning of the transmission of sin: "Man possesses a *situated* freedom; every human choice is conditioned by past decisions and restricts future possibilities."[220]

Karl Rahner (1904–1984), Schoonenberg's fellow Jesuit theologian from Germany, stood for the gradual creation of the human soul in the evolutionary process centered on God rather than for its immediate creation by God which had been affirmed by Pius XII's *Humani Generis*.[221] His understanding of original sin was very similar to Schoonenberg's, as he believed that original sin does not refer to something which has been transmitted from some primeval act of sin to all subsequent generations but rather refers to the fact that we are situated in a sinful world. Original sin thus means the undeniable fact that "the guilt of others is a permanent factor in the situation and realm of the individual's freedom,"[222] although this guilt felt is also always accompanied with "grace" due to what Rahner called "the supernatural existential."[223]

---

214 *Humani Generis*, 36. http://www.papalencyclicals.net/pius12/p12human.htm.
215 Ibid., 37.
216 Piet Schoonenberg, *Man and Sin: A Theological View*, trans. Joseph Donceel (Notre Dame, IN: University of Notre Dame Press, 1965), p. 193.
217 Ibid., p. 194.
218 Ibid., pp. 63-80.
219 Ibid., p. 101.
220 Piet Schoonenberg, "Original Sin and Man's Situation," *Theology Digest* 15 (1967): 204. Italics original.
221 Karl Rahner, *Hominisation: The Evolutionary Origin of Man as a Theological Problem*, trans. W. J. O'Hara (Freiburg: Herder, 1958; London: Burns & Oates, 1965), pp. 108f.
222 Karl Rahner, *Foundations of Christian Faith: An Introduction to the Idea of Christianity*, trans. William V. Dyck (New York: Seabury Press, 1978), p. 109.
223 Ibid., p. 114.

Since the Second Vatican Council (1962–1965), many other influential Catholic thinkers such as the Dutch Augustinian theologian Ansfried Hulsbosch (1912–1973),[224] the Loyola University professor Stephen J. Duffy (1931–2007),[225] the Scottish Jesuit theologian Jack Mahoney (1931–2024)[226] and the Catholic systematic theologian John F. Haught (1942–)[227] showed much interest in the modern synthesis of evolution and creation and thus denied the traditional notion of the inheritance of original sin. Even so, Pope Paul VI's *Credo of the People of God* (1968) and the *Catechism of the Catholic Church* (1992) reaffirmed the traditional doctrine of original sin.[228]

2. Denial of the Historicity of Adam

The atomistic, individualist approach on the fall of Adam and Eve in traditional Christianity already implied that we do not necessarily need a first human ancestor from whom to receive a sinful influence, if we can all sin individually anywhere and anytime. This implication was made explicit by modern theology and evolutionary theology, which denied the historicity of Adam.

Friedrich Schleiermacher was not interested in the question of whether or not Adam and Eve historically existed, although he may have believed in their historicity. He believed that sin has always existed in human nature as "innate sinfulness" regardless of their fall. For him, therefore, their fall was a trivial event: "the first appearance of sin in the first pair… was in itself a single and trivial event."[229] And our dogmatics "cannot be expected to determine how the said record [of the fall including the existence of Adam and Eve] is to be interpreted, and whether it purports to be *history* or *allegory*."[230] We can only use the story of Adam and Eve "in illustration of the universal process of the rise of sin as something always and everywhere the same."[231] Thus Schleiermacher in effect denied the historicity of Adam, if not positively. It goes without saying

---

[224] Ansfried Hulsbosch, *God in Creation and Evolution*, trans. Martin Versfeld (New York: Sheed and Ward, 1965).

[225] Stephen J. Duffy, "Our Hearts of Darkness: Original Sin Revisited," *Theological Studies* 49 (1988): 597-622. Also see his "Genes, Original Sin and the Human Proclivity to Evil," *Horizons* 32, no. 2 (2005): 210-34.

[226] Jack Mahoney, *Christianity in Evolution: An Exploration* (Washington, DC: Georgetown University Press, 2011).

[227] John F. Haught, *God after Darwin: A Theology of Evolution*, 2nd ed. (Boulder, CO: Westview Press, 2000); Ernst M. Conradie, "John Haught on Original Sin: A Conversation," *HTS Theological Studies* 72, no. 4 (2016): 1-10.

[228] *Credo of the People of God* 16. http://w2.vatican.va/content/paul-vi/en/motu_proprio/documents/hf_p-vi_motu-proprio_19680630_credo.html. *Catechism of the Catholic Church* 402-405.

[229] Schleiermacher, *The Christian Faith*, p. 302.

[230] Ibid., p. 302. Italics added.

[231] Ibid., p. 303.

that many other modern theologians in the tradition of Schleiermacher, too, denied the historicity of Adam in the same way.

Karl Barth maintained that "the coming into being of Adam and his corresponding individual existence" is "not history but only saga," and that "if we try to read and understand it as history," we "miss the unprecedented and incomparable thing which the Genesis passages tell us."[232] This unprecedented and incomparable thing is none other than "prophetic witness to what has taken place by virtue of the Word of God in the (historical or pre-historical) sphere where there can be no historical proof,"[233] and it cannot be comprehended with a historical approach. Adam simply "denotes the being and essence of all other men."[234] This is related to Barth's other idea that sin always exists in human nature.

Reinhold Niebuhr believed that because sin inevitably occurs from the very beginning due to "anxiety" arising from the tension between "spirit" and "nature" in human beings, there is no golden age of perfection before the fall. It is a "literalistic error" to insist on the fall "as an historical event."[235] Thus the historicity of Adam is to be denied.

Most evolutionary theologians (theistic evolutionists), too, basically denied the historicity of Adam. There are two reasons: 1) because they held that there was no paradise of innocence which preceded a primal fall in the evolutionary process, as was seen above; and 2) because they accepted the very compelling evidence of genomics about ancestral population sizes that modern human beings were descended from a population of at least several thousand individuals and not from a single ancestral couple like Adam and Eve.[236] They thus have considered Adam not to be a historical individual person but rather a symbolic name representing multiple people or even all humankind. In fact, as is well known, "Adam" is translated as "persons" in Numbers 31:28, 30, 35, 40 in the Old Testament.

Here we will not enumerate many evolutionary theologians to show how they have denied the historicity of Adam. Only a few examples will suffice. On the Protestant side, Francis Collins denied Adam's historicity when saying: "Many sacred texts do indeed carry the clear marks of eyewitness history... Others, such as the stories of Job and Jonah, and of Adam and Eve, frankly do

232 Barth, *Church Dogmatics*, IV/1, p. 508.
233 Ibid., IV/1, p. 508.
234 Ibid., IV/1, pp. 507-8.
235 Niebuhr, *Human Nature*, pp. 267-68.
236 Dennis Venema and Darrel Falk, "Does Genetics Point to a Single Primal Couple?" https://biologos.org/articles/does-genetics-point-to-a-single-primal-couple.

not carry the same historical ring."[237] Denis Lamoureux explicitly denied Adam's historicity: "Adam never actually existed."[238] So did Peter Enns: "The symbolic nature of the garden story would be even clearer if we see Adam as a proto-Israel figure, not the first human."[239]

On the Catholic side, Pierre Teilhard de Chardin questioned the historicity of Adam when he said: "if we accept the hypothesis of a *single, perfect* being [i.e., Adam] put to the test *on only one occasion*, the likelihood of the Fall is so slight that one can only regard the Creator as having been extremely unlucky."[240] For Piet Schoonenberg and Karl Rahner as well, the historicity of Adam is not important. Schoonenberg even remarked that the Council of Trent was not officially teaching monogenism, as it only took it for granted.[241] In case of Rahner, although he as an evolutionary theologian was still in favor of monogenism in 1954 when he wrote on the subject,[242] nevertheless in a later article published in 1967 he shifted his position from monogenism to polygenism, saying that if monogenism in the context of evolution allows for the creation of the first couple of Adam and Eve without the body of Eve being derived from Adam, then the creation of many more than the two, which would mean polygenism, is also possible; and that polygenism does not necessarily have a conflict with original sin.[243] Jack Mahoney and John Haught, too, denied the historicity of Adam.[244]

3. Denial of the Existence of Satan

The atomistic, individualist approach on the fall of Adam and Eve in traditional Christianity already implied that we do not necessarily need a Satan in order for us to sin, as we can all sin individually anywhere and anytime through our own free will. This implication was made explicit by modern theology and evolutionary theology, which denied the existence of Satan.

Already in the eighteenth century, the denial of the existence of Satan was made by Enlightenment thinkers such as Voltaire (1694–1778) and Denis

---

237 Collins, *The Language of God*, p. 209.
238 Lamoureux, *Evolutionary Creation*, p. 315.
239 Enns, *The Evolution of Adam*, p. 119.
240 Teilhard de Chardin, *Christianity and Evolution*, p. 193. Italics original.
241 Wiley, *Original Sin*, p. 124.
242 Karl Rahner, "Theological Reflections on Monogenism," in *Theological Investigations*, vol. I, trans. Cornelius Ernst (Baltimore, MD: Helicon Press, 1965), pp. 229-96.
243 Karl Rahner, "Evolution and Original Sin," in *The Evolving World and Theology*, ed. Johannes Metz (New York: Paulist Press, 1967), pp. 61-73.
244 Mahoney, *Christianity in Revolution*, p. x; Haught, *God after Darwin*, p. 137.

Diderot (1713–1784).[245] In the beginning of the nineteenth century, Friedrich Schleiermacher, not interested in the historicity of the fall of Adam, denied the existence of Satan, saying that explaining our sin by tracing it back to the temptation of Satan is "no explanation at all."[246] According to him, the biblical idea of the devil was *not* "acquired through Divine revelation" but only "drawn from the common life of the period just as it is still present more or less in all our minds in spite of our utter ignorance as to the existence of such a being," and "the question as to his existence is not one for Christian Theology but for Cosmology."[247]

Karl Barth had a very unique notion of Satan. Satan is not a fallen angel. Demons including Satan are not fallen angels, nor are they any kind of creatures of God. Indeed, demons' "origin and nature lie in nothingness (*Das Nichtige*)."[248] According to Barth, this "nothingness" is that which God chose not to create, while all other things are what God chose to create: "Nothingness is that from which God separates Himself and exerts His positive will," and therefore it "has no existence and cannot be known except as the object of God's activity as always a holy activity."[249] This nothingness, even if it has no existence, can function as the devil with his legions, however. Our correct response, therefore, must be that we have "resolute unbelief" in Satan and demons.[250] This was how Barth was trying to deny the existence of Satan.

We can recall Reinhold Niebuhr's thesis that human beings sin inevitably, if not by necessity, due to "anxiety" which arises from the tension between "spirit" and "nature" in their God-given human situation. If they in the midst of this anxiety humbly accept their situation and find security in God, they will not sin. But if they misinterpret their God-given situation and try to find security outside of God on their own, they will sin. According to Niebuhr, therefore, this tendency of human beings to misinterpret their situation and find security and transcendence on their own is already there in their situation, before they sin; and it can be called the devil. The devil is therefore "a principle or force of evil antecedent to any evil human action."[251] This devil is not what the Bible literally describes as a personality who is actively evil. It is merely an impersonal principle or force of evil.

---

245 W. Scott Poole, *Satan in America: The Devil We Know* (New York: Rowman & Littlefield Publishers, 2009), p. 10.

246 Schleiermacher, *The Christian Faith*, pp. 162-63.

247 Ibid., p. 167.

248 Barth, *Church Dogmatics*, III/3, ibid., p. 522.

249 Ibid., p. 351.

250 Ibid., p. 530.

251 Niebuhr, *Human Nature*, p. 180.

What about evolutionary theologians? They naturally denied the literal existence of Satan. According to a member of BioLogos, Satan merely represents "those inclinations [within us]—such as selfishness, the need for control, and the like—that often tempt us to do evil."[252] Piet Schoonenberg, too, showed his great skepticism about the existence of demons including Satan, saying that it is not a dogmatic necessity.[253] In a similar vein, Karl Rahner stated that "it would be untheological levity to look on Satan and his devils as a sort of 'hobgoblins knocking about the world,'" and went on to say: "rather it may be assumed that they are the powers *of* the world in so far as *this* world is a denial of God and a temptation to man."[254]

The Catholic Church today officially believes in the literal existence of Satan, as is indicated in its *Catechism*.[255] Recently, therefore, a controversy was stirred within the Church, when Arturo Sosa (1948–), Superior General of the Society of Jesus, regarded Satan as a symbolic figure, as can be seen in his expression of "symbolic figures such as the devil," in his 2017 interview with a Spanish newspaper.[256] This only means that in spite of the official doctrine, Catholics, including leaders such as Sosa, cast doubt on the existence of Satan today.

§4. The Unification Doctrine of the Fall Not Having the Three Problems

1. Consistency of the Unification Doctrine of the Fall

a. Consistent use of a relational, sexual approach

The Unification doctrine of the fall consistently uses a relational, sexual approach *both* on the fall of Adam *and* on the transmission of original sin.

According to this relational, sexual approach by the Unification doctrine, the fall of Adam involved two consecutive sexual relationships of illicit love: 1) a spiritual sexual relationship of illicit love in which Lucifer seduced Eve;

---

[252] Ted Davis, "Evolution and Original Sin: The Historical/Ideal View." https://biologos.org/articles/evolution-and-original-sin-the-historical-ideal-view.

[253] Piet Schoonenberg, *God's World in the Making* (Pittsburgh: Duquesne University Press, 1964), pp. 8-9.

[254] Karl Rahner and Herbert Vorgrimler, *Theological Dictionary*, ed. Cornelius Ernst, trans. Richard Strachan (New York: Herder and Herder, 1965), p. 127. Italics original.

[255] *Catechism of the Catholic Church* 391.

[256] "Satan Seen Increasingly as a Myth, Even within the Church Itself." https://fsspx.news/en/news/satan-seen-increasingly-myth-even-within-church-itself-16859.

and 2) a physical sexual relationship of illicit love in which Eve in the position of Lucifer (now Satan) seduced Adam. The act of eating the fruit meant having an illicit sexual relationship. Freedom on the part of each was not the cause of the fall; rather, freedom was "lost" by the fall as it was overwhelmed by the power of unprincipled love even stronger than that of freedom.

As for the transmission of original sin as well, the Unification doctrine uses the same relational, sexual approach, holding that because Adam and Eve through their sexual fall centering on Satan bound themselves with the satanic lineage based on the Satan-centered four position foundation, they could not help giving birth to sinful descendants under the sovereignty of Satan, and that the descendants have been repeating the same kind of sexual relationship for procreation in the lineage of Satan, thus transmitting original sin from one generation to another.

b. Free from the three problems of ambiguity

It is because of its consistent use of a relational, sexual approach both on the fall of Adam and on the transmission of original sin that the Unification doctrine of the fall, having no atomistic, individualist approach on the fall of Adam, is free from the above-mentioned three problems of theological ambiguity. Thus it can unequivocally believe in the inheritance of original sin, the historicity of Adam and the existence of Satan, even in face of the challenges coming from modern theology and evolutionary theology which denied these three points.

First, that the Unification doctrine of the fall takes the inheritance of original sin very seriously because of its consistent use of a relational, sexual approach can be seen in many words of Rev. Moon such as the following passage:

> What does it mean that Adam and Eve fell as a family? Nothing other than love could have made Adam and Eve fall as a family. What kind of fruit would make thousands of future generations become sinners? This is a blood relationship. If a root of sin is planted in the blood lineage, it would continue eternally according to the law of inheritance. Only the problem of love could make this happen.[257]

Second, the Unification doctrine of the fall affirms the historicity of Adam, because it holds that the inheritance of original sin through procreation does not start without the real existence of Adam who fell. Moon evidently has the historicity of Adam in mind when he talks about how God actually created

---

[257] Moon, "Blessing and Ideal Family," p. 232.

Adam and Eve as "babies" and not as adults, meaning that they were supposed to go through the growing period toward maturity: "God created them [i.e., Adam and Eve] as babies, in the formation stage, with the destiny to grow into perfection." [258] According to the Divine Principle, Adam and Eve unfortunately "fell during their growing period, when they were still immature."[259]

Third, the Unification doctrine of the fall affirms the existence of Satan, as it believes that the inheritance of original sin can best be understood through the sexual fall of Adam and Eve which involved Satan. Rev. Moon is very clear about the existence of Satan, therefore, when he states: "The Unification Church is clearly making a declaration about the existence of both God and Satan."[260] He even deplores the fact that many people, especially in the West, do not understand the existence of Satan as "an entity."[261] Needless to say, however, the Divine Principle denies cosmic dualism's assertion of the independent preexistence of Satan: "the spiritual being represented by the serpent was originally created with a good purpose, but later fell and became Satan."[262]

2. Allies of the Relational, Sexual Approach on the Fall of Adam

Although Christianity especially after Augustine has not accepted the consistent use of a relational, sexual approach, using it only on the transmission of original sin and not on the fall of Adam, nevertheless if we carefully look at the longer and wider, Judeo-Christian history, we can find several writers or theologians who consistently used a relational, sexual approach on the fall of Adam as well, like Unificationism does. They can thus be allies of Unificationism and can join together to unhesitatingly believe in the inheritance of original sin, the historicity of Adam and the existence of Satan

a. Jewish pseudepigrapha and rabbinical literature

The Second Book of Enoch, also known as the Book of the Secrets of Enoch, is a Jewish pseudepigraphic text written in the first century A.D., and interestingly it said that Satan "conceived thought against Adam," and that "in

---

[258] Sun Myung Moon, "The Day of All Things 1982," sermon delivered at Belvedere, Tarrytown, NY, June 21, 1982. https://www.tparents.org/Moon-Talks/SunMyungMoon82/820621.htm.

[259] EDP, p. 42.

[260] Sun Myung Moon, "Heaven's Side and Satan's Side," sermon delivered at Belvedere, Tarrytown, NY, February 20, 1983. https://www.tparents.org/Moon-Talks/SunMyungMoon83/830220.htm.

[261] Sun Myung Moon, "Leaders Conference, April 8, 1989." https://www.tparents.org/Moon-Talks/SunMyungMoon89/SM890408.htm.

[262] EDP, p. 57.

such form he entered and seduced Eva (Eve), but did not touch Adam."[263] This would definitely mean that when Satan seduced Eve, he touched her sexually. It meant a sexual fall between Satan and Eve. This is confirmed by F. R. Tennant, who, in spite of being an evolutionary theologian, did substantive research on the doctrines of the fall and original sin in Judeo-Christian history before Augustine: "We have, in fact, in this passage another example of the association of the Fall with the sin of unchastity, and an allusion to the tradition that Satan *seduced* Eve, in the narrower sense of that word."[264]

Tennant also reports that rabbinical literature commonly held that Satan envied Adam on account of Eve, whom he therefore desired to possess. According to Tractate Sotah, a part of the Talmud, for example, Satan said: "I will kill Adam and marry Eve; but now, I will put enmity between thee [i.e., God] and the woman, and between thy seed and her seed."[265] Tennant therefore observes that this sexual interpretation of the fall of Adam and Eve centering on Satan was "both widespread and ancient among the Jews," and that "this is rather the sense in which... the Fall is associated in rabbinical writings with evil concupiscence."[266]

Robert Gordis (1908–1992), a conservative rabbi in America, suggests that "the knowledge of good and evil [as part of the name of the tree whose fruit was eaten at the fall] is 'sexual consciousness,'" adding that notable Jewish scholars such as Abraham ibn Ezra (1089–c. 1167), Arnold Ehrlich (1848–1919) and Ludwig Levy (1854–1907) had the same assertion.[267]

b. Clement of Alexandria and Ambrose

Among the Church Fathers, St. Clement of Alexandria and St. Ambrose are known to have had a sexual interpretation of the fall, although the difference between the two was that while the former was pro-marriage, the latter was basically against marriage, emphasizing the importance of pure virginity.

Clement of Alexandria, referring to all humans as "lovers of pleasure," said: "the first man of our race did not bide his time, desired the favor of marriage before the proper hour, and fell into sin by not waiting for the time of God's will; 'for everyone who looks upon a woman to lust after her has

---

263 The Book of the Secrets of Enoch 31:5. http://www.pseudepigrapha.com/pseudepigrapha/enochs2.htm#Ch31.

264 F. R. Tennant, *The Sources of the Doctrines of the Fall and Original Sin* (New York: Schocken Books, 1968), p. 209. Italics original.

265 Sotah 9b. https://halakhah.com/sotah/sotah_9.html.

266 Tennant, *The Sources of the Doctrines of the Fall and Original Sin*, p. 156.

267 Robert Gordis, *The Word and the Book: Studies in Biblical Language and Literature* (New York: Ktav Publishing House, 1976), p. 79.

already committed adultery with her.'"[268] The irony, however, is that Clement hardly developed a doctrine of the inheritance of original sin, given the nature of his own days in Alexandria in which the seriousness of sin was not understood yet. Thus his sexual interpretation of the fall might not be as useful for our purpose. But it still is worth mentioning.

Ambrose's sexual interpretation was based on Philo's psychological reading of the serpent, Eve and Adam: "The serpent is a type of the pleasures of the body. The woman stands for our senses and the man, for our minds. Pleasure stirs the senses, which, in turn, have their effect on the mind. Pleasure, therefore, is the primary source of sin."[269] Ambrose, as the godfather of Augustine, strongly influenced Augustine regarding the inheritance of original sin, although unfortunately Augustine, unlike Ambrose, did not use a relational, sexual approach on the fall of Adam and Eve itself.

The idea of the sexual fall by both Clement of Alexandria and Ambrose is rejected by Ludwig Ott (1906–1985) in his *Fundamentals of Catholic Dogma*, a standard reference work on Catholic dogmatics.[270]

c. The historical-critical approach

A historical-critical understanding of the Genesis account of the fall was proposed by scholars such as the Belgian priest J. Coppens (1896–1970)[271] and the Italian biblical scholar J. Alberto Soggin (1926–2010),[272] and it has been fairly widespread and received among biblical scholars. It argues that Genesis 3 was a polemic of the Yahwist against the Canaanite fertility cult which worshipped the serpent god as the deity of sexual ecstasy, procreation, health and immortality. Thus Soggin, finding in the story of the fall sexual motifs such as "the meaning of the verb ['to know']; the fruit, so easily susceptible to aphrodisiac implications; the fig leaf, which is normally connected with sexual (religious) orgies; [and] the shame flooding the couple after the act,"[273] concluded that:

---

[268] Clement of Alexandria, *Stromateis* III.14.94; see John Ernest Leonard Oulton and Henry Chadwick, eds., *Alexandrian Christianity: Selected Translations of Clement and Origen* (London: SCM Press, 1954), p. 84.

[269] Ambrose, *De Paradiso* 15.73; see his *Hexameron, Paradise, and Cain and Abel*, trans. John J. Savage (Washington, DC: Catholic University of America Press, 1961), pp. 351-52.

[270] Ludwig Ott, *Fundamentals of Catholic Dogma*, trans. Patrick Lynch, ed. James Canon Bastible (Rockford, IL: Tan Books and Publishers, 1974), p. 107.

[271] J. Coppens, *La connaissance du bien et du mal et le péché du Paradis* (Gembloux: J. Duculot, 1948).

[272] J. Alberto Soggin, *Old Testament and Oriental Studies* (Rome: Biblical Institute Press, 1975).

[273] Ibid., p. 101.

> The only reasonable explanation for these [sexual] elements [found in the Genesis story of the fall] is the assumption that an original Canaanite account disclosing the rites of fertility was taken over by Israel and turned completely around as a direst polemic against those same rites, accusing them of producing not life and fertility, but death and sterility.[274]

He therefore wanted to argue that the fall of Adam and Eve was sexual.[275] Unification theologians such as Young Oon Kim (1914–1989) and Andrew Wilson (1950–) appreciatively acknowledge this historical-critical approach.[276] This approach is credible, although some scholars such as John Day (1948–), Old Testament Professor at Oxford, may be cautious about it, thinking that the Canaanite fertility cult was quite unrelated to the theme of the knowledge of good and evil.[277]

3. The Historicity of Adam and Eve

There are at least two more ways to argue for the historicity of Adam and Eve: 1) from the perspective of the nature of the Divine Principle as a systematic theology; and 2) from evolutionary creationism as accepted by Unificationism, involving modern paleoanthropology.

a. From the Divine Principle as a systematic theology

All the contents of the Divine Principle as a systematic theology are naturally seamless and consistent with one another. The Divine Principle view of the fall of Adam and Eve, therefore, must be consistent with its soteriology, for example. This means that it is because Adam and Even historically existed and sexually fell centering on Satan to give birth to sinful children with original sin in the lineage of Satan that True Parents must come as perfected Adam and Eve to give rebirth to humankind and free them from original sin in the lineage

---

[274] Ibid., pp. 107-8.

[275] Soggin refers to those scholars who have the sexual interpretation around the middle of the twentieth century and those who are against it; see ibid., p. 102, n. 35.

[276] Young Oon Kim, *Unification Theology*, revised ed. (New York: The Holy Spirit Association for the Unification of World Christianity, 1987), pp. 98-100. Andrew Wilson, "The Sexual Interpretation of the Human Fall," in *Unification Theology in Comparative Perspectives*, ed. Anthony Guerra (Barrytown, NY: Unification Theological Seminary, 1988), pp. 51-70.

[277] John Day says that "The knowledge of good and evil which the serpent tempts the first humans to acquire is quite unrelated to the fertility cult," and that "the fertility cult is not depicted as an important concern of the Yahwist source elsewhere"; see his "The Serpent in the Garden of Eden and its Background," adapted and expanded from his *From Creation to Babel: Studies in Genesis 1-11* (London: T&T Clark, 2013), pp. 35-37. https://www.bibleinterp.com/articles/2015/04/day398028.shtml.

of Satan. Hence in the words of Rev. Moon, "Since human beings began from false parents [Adam and Eve, who sexually fell], they must go back and make a new beginning from the True Parents."[278]

The argument here is that given the fact that True Parents, who restore fallen humankind to the lineage of God, actually emerged, it would be consistent to maintain that Adam and Eve historically existed and sexually fell at the beginning of human history. Rejecting the historicity of Adam and Eve and their sexual fall would mean rejecting the whole point about the mission of True Parents.

Christian theology, too, similarly argues from the consistent nature of systematic theology for the historicity of Adam and his fall and the inheritance of original sin, as can be seen in the article, "Threads in a Seamless Garment: Original Sin in Systematic Theology," written by Michael Reeves and Hans Madueme in 2014: "if we are to be theologically consistent, rejecting a historical Adam and original sin would leave us without a recognizable Christian gospel";[279] "The doctrine of original sin directly affects what it means to say that Jesus is Savior."[280] This is the case with traditional Christianity, although traditional Christianity, unlike Unificationism, has not even used a relational, sexual interpretation on the fall of Adam itself.

As was seen above, however, many modern theologians and evolutionary theologians have denied the historicity of Adam and his fall, regarding Adam merely as what figuratively denotes all humankind that is imperfect and even sinful from the very beginning. Without recognizing a historical Adam and a historical first fall, then, they have not looked to Adam but to Christ, "the last Adam" (1 Cor. 15:45), for the benchmark by which to determine what sin is and also what sinless perfection is. It is thus not Adam but Christ who is the original standard. In this case, one should not talk about the Adam-Christ parallel but rather about the Christ-Adam parallel in which Christ is the original and Adam merely a figurative indication of all imperfect humankind.[281]

This Christological focus has been accepted by many modern theologians such as Schleiermacher, Barth and Niebuhr. For example, Niebuhr, denying the historicity of Adam and the golden age of pre-fall innocence, said: "it is not possible to define the lost perfection of Adam, the ideal possibilities of human

---

[278] *Cheon Seong Gyeong* (2006), p. 1162.

[279] Michael Reeves and Hans Madueme, "Threads in a Seamless Garment: Original Sin in Systematic Theology," in *Adam, the Fall, and Original Sin*, ed. Hans Madueme and Michael Reeves (Grand Rapids, MI: Baker Academic, 2014), p. 210.

[280] Ibid., p. 223.

[281] See, for example, Barth, *Church Dogmatics*, IV/1, pp. 512-13.

life, except in terms drawn from the perfection of Christ."[282] This Christological focus has also been accepted by many evolutionary theologians. Thus Jerry D. Korsmeyer (1930–2015), an evolutionary Catholic theologian himself, says:

> The concept of "original sin" needs to be understood from the perspective of our redemption in Jesus Christ, not the other way around. The Father did not send the Son to patch up some broken divine plan for humanity. God's self-communication in love points us toward the kingdom ahead, not a paradise lost.[283]

This way of reversing the Adam-Christ parallel to come up with the Christ-Adam parallel is very popular these days. But is it legitimate? The answer should be in the negative. For if the historicity of Adam and his fall is rejected in favor of the timeless innate sinfulness of human nature, then God as the Creator should be ultimately responsible for this innate human sinfulness, and that scenario would not be acceptable:

> If we remove a historical Adam and fall from the theological picture, then sin becomes a side effect of evolution, a part of natural ontology of created human beings. [And]... human sinfulness is no longer contingent but emerges from the very structure of the material world... The creator God is rendered ultimately responsible for sin.[284]

In order to uphold the goodness of God, therefore, we have to assert that Adam and Eve were created to historically exist for a good purpose of God, but that they unfortunately fell in spite of that good purpose. This means that sin is a contingency. The Divine Principle talks about the possibility of Adam and Eve *not* falling but having a great result: "If Adam and Eve had not fallen, but had... become the True Parents who could multiply good children, their descendants would have also become good husbands and wives with God as the center of their lives."[285] Christ, then, would not have been needed: "If our [first] ancestors had not fallen, there would have been no necessity for the savior."[286] This means that the Adam-Christ parallel rather than the Christ-Adam parallel is to be maintained, although one may be tempted to favor the

---

[282] Reinhold Niebuhr, *The Nature and Destiny of Man: A Christian Interpretation*, vol. II, *Human Destiny* (New York: Charles Scribner's Sons, 1964), p. 77.

[283] Jerry D. Korsmeyer, *Evolution and Eden: Balancing Original Sin and Contemporary Science* (New York: Paulist Press, 1998), pp. 54-55.

[284] Reeves and Madueme, "Threads in a Seamless Garment," pp. 210-11.

[285] EDP, p. 172.

[286] Sun Myung Moon, "The New Messiah, and the Formula of God in History," lecture delivered at Lisner Auditorium, George Washington University, Washington, DC, February 21, 1972. https://www.tparents.org/Moon-Talks/SunMyungMoon72/ SM720221.htm.

Christ-Adam parallel under the influence of modern theology and evolutionary theology, and although, as the Orthodox Presbyterian theologian Carl R. Trueman (1967–) aptly states, "There has been no temptation through the centuries to which theology has been more exposed than this temptation."[287] We have to overcome this powerful temptation.

b. Evolutionary creationism as accepted by Unificationism

The Divine Principle follows modern science to say that "The age of the earth is calculated to be several billion years," and that the biblical period of six days of creation, instead of being six literal days, "symbolizes six [long] ordered periods of time in the creation process."[288] And while not accepting the atheistic theory of evolution itself, it does accept the aspect of progression in the theory and combines it with God's creation, holding that the stage-by-stage progression from low-level to more complex, higher-level creatures with the culmination of human beings happens through the purposeful input of God's energy. Hence Rev. Moon says:

> The theory of evolution seems to be logical, but the process of the stage-by-stage progression of all things can never convincingly be explained through the theory of random mutation. Without outside energy added [from God], this progression into more valuable and higher dimensions is absolutely impossible. The evolution of all animals has culminated in man, and we can say that man is the ultimate purpose of the first causal being [i.e., God].[289]

This position is in line with so-called "evolutionary creationism" or "theistic evolutionism," which believes that God creates through evolution. Hence comes what can be called "Unification evolutionary creationism."

But unlike most evolutionary creationists (such as F. R. Tennant, Pierre Teilhard de Chardin and Francis Collins), who deny the historicity of Adam and Eve in favor of polygenism, Unification evolutionary creationism accepts the historicity of Adam and Eve in favor of monogenism. It holds that Adam and Eve were born as the first human babies from their physical parents that were not human beings but previously existent hominids, i.e., that when they were born as babies, God infused human spirits into them, while their physical

---

[287] Carl R. Trueman, "Original Sin and Modern Theology," in *Adam, the Fall, and Original Sin*, ed. Hans Madueme and Michael Reeves (Grand Rapids, MI: Baker Academic, 2014), p. 186.

[288] EDP, p. 40.

[289] Sun Myung Moon, "The Search for Absolute Values: Harmony Among the Sciences," Founder's Address at The Fifth International Conference on the Unity of the Sciences, Washington, DC, November 25-28, 1976. https://www.tparents.org/Moon-Talks/SunMyungMoon76/SunMyungMoon-761125.htm.

parents as their surrogate parents without spirits provided only physical bodies to them. This is not an unusual idea; it can actually be found as one of the various views of evolutionary creationism or theistic evolutionism,[290] although it is just a minor position among them.

This position is supported by the following words of Rev. Moon: "Adam and Eve were produced by exactly the same process as we produce a child. By strong love and energy of father and mother, a child is conceived and grows, first within the womb, then outside of it."[291] In this scenario, God's infusion of human spirits occurred as a result of what Rev. Moon refers to as "outside energy added" from God. The Unification theologian/biologist Jonathan Wells (1942–2024) accepts this scenario, identifies the "surrogate parents" of Adam and Eve as "animals with features that were intermediate between apes and humans—such as those found in the fossil record," and adds that they "nourished and protected the babies until the latter were able to fend for themselves, and then that species went extinct."[292]

Adam and Eve, then, are understood to be the first ancestors of our own species, *Homo sapiens*, also described as "anatomically modern humans." Their surrogate parents perhaps belonged to the previous yet now extinct species of *Homo heidelbergensis*, whose fossils were found in Africa as well as in Heidelberg, Germany. In modern paleoanthropology, the fossils of *Homo sapiens* from Kibish, Ethiopia are deemed the earliest ones, being dated to about 200,000 years ago.[293] It is likely, then, that Adam and Eve were born in East Africa about 200,000 years ago (although it does not match the fairly popular idea that the Garden of Eden was located in Mesopotamia).

---

[290] Thomas J. Centrella shows that within evolutionary creationism or theistic evolutionism there are six different views: 1) "total atheistic or pantheistic evolution," 2) "deistic evolution," 3) polygenistic theistic evolution," 4) monogenistic theistic evolution; broad natural transformism," 5) "monogenistic theistic evolution: natural transformation for Adam only," and 6) "monogenistic theistic evolution: special transformation." See his "Is Theistic Evolution Truly Plausible?" http://kolbecenter.org/is-theistic-evolution-truly-plausible/. Unification evolutionary creationism would belong to the fourth view, while most evolutionary creationists, denying monogenism, belong to the third view. By the way, Centrella himself adheres to none of the six, saying that evolutionary creationism is not truly plausible.

[291] Sun Myung Moon, "The Master Speaks on Creation," March and April 1965. https://www.tparents.org/Moon-Talks/SunMyungMoon65/SunMyungMoon-650404.htm.

[292] Jonathan Wells, "God's Creation of Adam and Eve," December 11, 2013. https://www.tparents.org/Library/Unification/Talks/Wells/Wells-131211.pdf.

[293] This is shown in Ian McDougall, Francis H. Brown, and John G. Fleagle, "Stratigraphic Placement and Age of Modern Humans from Kibish, Ethiopia," *Nature* 433 (2005): 733-36. Although the fossils from Jebel Irhoud, Morocco, considered to be those of *Homo sapiens*, are dated to as early as about 300,000 years ago, their classification as *Homo sapiens* is still questioned due to the lack of genomic evidence.

Most evolutionary creationists would have much difficulty in accepting this monogenistic scenario, because they, as was previously mentioned, adhere to polygenism based on the compelling evidence from genomics that modern humans were descended from a population of at least several thousand individuals and not from a single ancestral couple like Adam and Eve, i.e., that the extreme population bottleneck of just a single ancestral couple is impossible. Interestingly, however, Professor Kenneth W. Kemp of the University of St. Thomas has addressed this issue in favor of monogenism, by proposing that the first couple of Adam and Eve emerged from "a population of 5,000 hominids, beings which are in many respects like human beings, but which lack the capacity for intellectual thought," and that because the descendants of Adam and Eve can be considered to "continue, to some extent, to interbreed with the non-intellectual hominids among whom they live," all modern humans born this way with the endowment of human spirits would have both the hominids and the first human couple among their ancestors, with the result that they "would be descended from a single original human couple (in the sense of having that human couple among their ancestors) without there ever having been a population bottleneck in the human species."[294] Here the key is interbreeding, and with the initial population of 5,000 hominids included this way, the problem of the population bottleneck of only a single ancestral couple can be evaded.

By the way, according to the "Out of Africa" theory, which is well received among paleoanthropologists today, the species of *Homo sapiens* originated in Africa, whether polygenistically or monogenistically,[295] and all non-African modern humans are descendants of those members of that species who got out of Africa in a few different waves of dispersal starting from around 120,000 years ago to migrate to the other parts of the world.[296] This theory, as long as it is interpreted monogenistically, is acceptable to Unification evolutionary creationism, which stands for monogenism.

The exposition of Unification evolutionary creationism here, however, does not mean to argue with absolute certainty for the historicity of Adam and Eve. Rather, it means to say that the historicity of Adam and Eve is *not*

---

[294] Kenneth W. Kemp, "Science, Theology, and Monogenesis," *American Catholic Philosophical Quarterly*, vol. 85, no. 2 (2011): 231-32.

[295] The "Out of Africa" theory, which is uniregionalism, is not necessarily monogenistic, still quite strongly leaning toward polygenism, whereas multiregionalism, which holds that the species of *Homo sapiens* arose in different multiple regions, is inherently polygenistic. See Kemp, "Science, Theology, and Monogenesis": 221-23.

[296] See, for example, David W. Cameron and Colin P. Groves, *Bones, Stones and Molecules: "Out of Africa" and Human Origins* (Burlington, MA: Elsevier Academic Press, 2004).

contradictory to the science of paleoanthropology which presupposes evolution. In the words of Wells, "God's creation of Adam and Eve is inconsistent with materialistic 'science,' but (I would argue) it is *not* contrary to evidence-based science."[297]

In conclusion, in spite of the challenging emergences of liberal theology after the Enlightenment and of evolutionary theology after Darwinism, the Unification doctrine of the fall, which consistently uses its relational, sexual approach both on Adam's fall and on the transmission of original sin, can effectively defend the inheritance of original sin, the historicity of Adam and the existence of Satan. By contrast, it is considerably difficult for the traditional Christian doctrine of the fall to defend them in face of the challenges of liberal theology and evolutionary theology in modern times, because of its inconsistent use of two different approaches: an atomistic, individualist approach on Adam's fall and a relational, sexual approach on the transmission of original sin. The Unification doctrine of the fall is not alone, however, in having its relational, sexual approach on Adam's fall as well as well as on the transmission of original sin; it has some good allies regarding this in the Judeo-Christian tradition. The historicity of Adam and Eve can also be argued for from the nature of the Divine Principle as a systematic theology and from the Unification version of evolutionary creationism which involves modern paleoanthropology.

---

[297] Wells, "God's Creation of Adam and Eve." Italics added.

Chapter 8

The Problem of Evil

We experience evil in the world, whether it is "natural" or "moral" evil.[1] We also experience suffering, which is physical or mental pain caused by evil. If, however, there is an omnipotent and perfectly good God, as theism believes, then why is it that evil, and suffering as well, exists in the world? Wouldn't such a God have the power and character to prevent it? This is the problem of evil raised as a serious challenge to theism.

The problem of evil consists simply in a logical contradiction between the following three propositions: 1) God is omnipotent; 2) God is perfectly good; and 3) evil exists in the world.[2] The three cannot all be true; the truth of any two of them can mean the falsity of the third. So, if God is both omnipotent and perfectly good, then evil cannot exist; if God is omnipotent, and evil really

---

[1] It is usually understood that there are two kinds of evil: 1) natural evil, and 2) moral evil. Natural evil refers to disasters and obstacles by natural causes without the intention of a moral agent; they are, for example, hurricanes, tornados, earthquakes and incurable diseases. Moral evil, by contrast, is evil which arises from the intentional action or inaction of an intelligent, conscious and moral agent; examples of it are murder, cruelty, theft, lying and adultery. The dividing line between the two may sometimes not be absolutely clear, because some natural evils such as global warming may arise from our wrong moral decisions. The dividing line is virtually removed by St. Augustine, who maintains that natural evil, which is nature's disobedience to us, is the consequent punishment for our moral evil, which is our disobedience to God: "When thou sinnest, that is, disobeyest thy Lord, the things [in nature] thou before ruledst over are made instrumental in thy punishment." See St. Augustine, "Against the Epistle of Manichaeus Called Fundamental," 37:43, in Philip Schaff, ed., *A Select Library of the Nicene and Post-Nicene Fathers of the Christian Church*, vol. IV: *St. Augustin: The Writings against the Manichaeans and against the Donatists* (Grand Rapids, MI: Wm. B. Eerdmans Publishing Co., 1974), p. 148.

[2] The present chapter does not consider the proposition that God is omniscient.

exists, then God cannot be perfectly good; and if God is perfectly good, and evil really exists, then God cannot be omnipotent.

This problem of evil in relation to theism is longstanding. Any attempt to solve this problem, especially in the monotheistic tradition, is called "theodicy" (from Greek *theos*, God; *dikē*, justice), which means to justify God in face of the existence of evil. The term was coined in 1710 by the German philosopher Gottfried Leibniz (1646–1716) in his work *Théodicée.*

The history of theodicy shows that there have generally been three types of theodicies: 1) *simple* theodicies, 2) *aesthetic* theodicies, and 3) *practical* theodicies.

Simple theodicies *simply* deny one of the above three propositions to remove their logical contradiction. Thus they are of three different kinds: 1) simple theodicies that deny the omnipotence of God; 2) simple theodicies that deny the perfect goodness of God; and 3) simple theodicies that deny the reality of evil. Simple theodicies of the first kind, as in Zoroastrianism, make God a finite God by having an independent, ultimate principle of evil challenge and limit the power of the good God, so that evil in the world cannot be avoided by God. This is dualism. Simple theodicies of the second kind limit the goodness of God by believing, as in staunch Calvinism, that God is so powerful as to cause evil as well as good. This is despotism. Simple theodicies of the third kind deny the reality of evil in the world by basically equating the world with an omnipotent and good God, as in the theology of Christian Science. This is panentheism.

All the three kinds of simple theodicies, however, have at least two difficulties: 1) that they are not acceptable to most theists, who still somehow believe that none of the above three propositions should be denied; and 2) that these simple, logical attempts to solve the contradiction between the three propositions are unable to actually eradicate evil from the world at all; evil is still there.

Aesthetic theodicies have therefore been developed to go beyond simple theodicies, based on the belief that all the three propositions must be affirmed. To affirm all the three propositions beyond their apparent logical contradiction, they usually add a supplementary proposition to them. This supplementary proposition usually refers to a greater purpose of God which it believes to be realized by evil. They thus argue that an omnipotent and perfectly good God allows evil to exist to serve his greater purpose. Therefore, evil, no matter how real it may be, is regarded as *aesthetically* harmonious with that purpose of God. The "best of all possible worlds" theodicy of Gottfried Leibniz (1646–1716), the "free will" defense of Alvin Plantinga (1932–), and the "soul-making" theodicy of John Hick (1922–2012) are among the most well-known ones of this aesthetic type.

These aesthetic theodicies are an improvement upon, and more plausible than, simple theodicies, and have therefore come to constitute "theodicy's canonical tradition."[3] But even they have been criticized for carrying at least four difficulties, which are related to one another: 1) that their theoretical rationalization of evil through an aesthetic harmonization of it with God's greater purpose cannot eradicate evil from the world—evil is still there; 2) that so-called "gratuitous evil," which is pointlessly excessive evil, may be too cruel to be aesthetically rationalized or justified even by God's greater purpose; 3) that aesthetic theodicists, when theoretically explaining away evil by God's greater purpose, are just theoreticians who are not necessarily in a state of inner conversion or salvation; and 4) that the omnipotence and perfect goodness of God, which are affirmed here, would lack the depth of their true meanings, as they are basically of the God of the philosophers rather than of the God of the Bible who, out of love, suffers for human salvation.

These difficulties of aesthetic theodicies have led *practical* theodicies to be proposed. Dorothee Soelle (1929–2003) and Jürgen Moltmann (1926–2024) are the chief practical theodicists. They suggest that we should accomplish the *practical* task of removing evil, including gratuitous evil, by showing the suffering love of God through our Christ-like commitment to, presence in, and solidarity with, the victims of evil. They often show far deeper insights into the meanings of God's omnipotence and perfect goodness than do proponents of philosophical theism.

This constitutes a context in which we can show the relevance of Unification theodicy. Unification theodicy, like practical theodicies and unlike simple theodicies or aesthetic theodicies, asserts that evil, including gratuitous evil, should and can be eradicated from the world rather than just logically and/or aesthetically explained away. Also, Unification theodicy, like practical theodicies, teaches about the need for our conversion through Christ centering on God's suffering love, so that we may be able to willingly and creatively serve the world by removing evil in order to build the kingdom of God.

Unification theodicy as a new, practical theodicy, however, may have a good advantage over existing practical theodicies in that it provides a theological clarification of their new insights into God's omnipotence and perfect goodness because of its unique yet biblically developed theological notions of God's "Heart" and God's "dual characteristics of *Sungsang* and

[3] Kenneth Surin, *Theology and the Problem of Evil* (New York: Basil Blackwell, 1986), p. 2.

Hyungsang."[4] Other practical theodicies, perhaps with the exception of Moltmann's, have not yet developed these notions. It may have another advantage in that its sexual interpretation of the historical fall of Adam can make more sense of the origin of evil and its connection with the role of Christ, and our role as well, to eradicate evil. Other practical theodicies are less clear about the origin of evil because they do not recognize historicity in the fall of Adam, let alone any sexual element in it.

This chapter has four sections. Section 1 will discuss the three kinds of simple theodicies. Section 2 will discuss the aesthetic theodicies of Leibniz, Plantinga and Hick, and Section 3 the practical theodicies of Soelle and Moltmann. Unification theodicy will be treated in the final, fourth section. It will be shown by the end of the chapter that there have been an evolution of theodicy and an evolution of the doctrine of God along with it, going beyond philosophical theism to reach a new understanding of God's omnipotence and perfect goodness, which resembles Unification theism.

§1. Simple Theodicies: Three Kinds

1. Denying God's Omnipotence: Dualism

Simple theodicies of the first kind deny God's omnipotence, asserting that the power of God is limited by the existence of an ultimate principle of evil that independently pre-exists from eternity. This dualistic assertion can be seen in the Christian heresies of Gnosticism and Manichaeism as well as in the pre-Christian religion of Zoroastrianism. It seems to be quite an appealing solution to the problem of evil. Its adherents have included many nineteenth-century and twentieth-century intellectuals such as John Stuart Mill (1806–1873), F. C. S. Schiller (1864–1937), J. M. E. McTaggart (1866–1925), H. G. Wells (1866–1946), C. E. M. Joad (1891–1953), and Edwin Lewis (1881–1959). Here we will examine the dualism of C. E. M. Joad, a British philosopher.

For thirty years following his student days at Oxford, Joad was an "agnostic."[5] As an agnostic, he could not really believe in "an omnipotent and

---

[4] *Sungsang* and *Hyungsang* as God's dual characteristics are Korean terms, which mean the "original internal nature" and "original external form" of God. But when *sungsang* and *hyungsang* (not capitalized) are used, they are the dual characteristics of each and every created being, meaning "internal nature" and "external form." For a detailed explanation of God's Heart and God's dual characteristics of *Sungsang* and *Hyungsang*, see Chapter 4, Section 1 ("God's Dual Characteristics") in the present book.

[5] C. E. M. Joad, *God and Evil* (London: Farber & Farber, 1943), pp. 9, 62.

benevolent God," given what he called the "obtrusiveness of evil."[6] He was eventually able to go beyond this agnosticism in favor of a dualism which he thought would be able to explain the stark facts of evil very well:

> If we are to go beyond a simple agnosticism, then what must be surmised is that there are two Gods, a good one and a bad; or, since the notion of a bad God is revolting and not absolutely necessary, there must be a good God and an obstructive hampering principle in and through and in spite of which He seeks to work. This is what a plain reading of the facts seems to require.[7]

A good God and his evil adversary are "two equally real and conceivably equally powerful antagonists," and between them "a perpetual battle is fought in the hearts of men for the governance of the world"; thus, even if God is a good God, his power is "limited."[8]

Joad was aware that this dualism "has always been regarded as a heresy" in the Christian tradition, but he decided that this "would seem more nearly to accord with the facts of experience."[9] Thus Joad's "mind came to rest" in this conclusion.[10]

Besides this form of *external* dualism, there is another form of dualism which is *internal* dualism. Internal dualism also limits the power of God in order to address the problem of evil, but it does so by locating the two conflicting principles of good and evil within God. This internal dualism was adhered to by thinkers such as Edgar S. Brightman (1884–1953) and William Pepperell Montague (1873–1953). Here we will take a look at the thought of Edgar S. Brightman, an American philosopher.

According to Brightman, the internal dualism of God consists in two conflicting aspects of what he calls "The Given" within God: 1) "the eternal, uncreated laws of reason"; and 2) "equally eternal and uncreated processes of nonrational consciousness which exhibit all the ultimate qualities of sense objects (*qualia*), disorderly impulses and desires, such experiences as pain and suffering, the forms of space and time, and whatever in God is the source of surd evil."[11] The two can be equated respectively with the Ideas and the Receptacle in Plato's cosmology.[12] The difference is that while the two aspects

---

[6] Ibid., pp. 24-62.
[7] Ibid., p. 101.
[8] Ibid., pp. 85-86
[9] Ibid.
[10] Ibid., 101.
[11] Edgar Sheffield Brightman, *A Philosophy of Religion* (New York: Prentice-Hall, 1940), p. 337.
[12] Ibid., p. 339.

of The Given in Brightman's view are both included in God, the Ideas and the Receptacle in Plato's cosmology are external to God.

Brightman is of the opinion that God as the creator wills to combine the two aspects of The Given to realize the ideal good, but the two can never be completely and perfectly combined, given their chaotic conflict between good in the former and "surd evil" in the latter. Here, surd evil means intrinsic evil which can never become instrumentally good.[13] Therefore, although "his [i.e., God's] will for love and goodness is unlimited," nevertheless "the power of his will is limited by The Given."[14] The Given as a whole, then, becomes an obstacle to God's will. This finite God, therefore, cannot prevent evil from occurring in the world.

2. Denying God's Perfect Goodness: Despotism

Simple theodicies of the second kind deny the perfect goodness of God by arguing that God is all powerful, like a despot, and that he is authorized to cause evil as well as good. Theodicies of this kind may appear to agree with Brightman that God causes both good and evil. But there is a striking disagreement, for while Brightman holds that evil is caused by the limited power of God due to The Given, theodicies of the despotist kind believe that evil is caused by God's absolutely unlimited power.

Let us look at the despotist theodicy of the staunch American Calvinist Gordon H. Clark (1902–1985). According to Clark, God is sovereign to the extent that he causes all things in the world, including evil human acts. God is thus the "cause of sin":

> Let it be unequivocally said that this view certainly makes God the cause of sin. God is the sole ultimate cause of everything. There is absolutely nothing independent of him. He alone is the eternal being. He alone is omnipotent. He alone is sovereign.[15]

For Clark, however, being the cause of sin does *not* mean being the author of sin. Although God is the "ultimate cause" of sin, he is not the "immediate cause of sin," i.e., the "author of sin."[16] It is human beings that are authors of sin, committing sin. God does not commit sin nor can he commit sin, for the reason that "whatever God does is just and right. It is just and right simply in

---

13 Ibid., pp. 245-46.
14 Ibid., p. 337.
15 Gordon H. Clark, *Religion, Reason, and Revelation* (Philadelphia: Presbyterian and Reformed Pub. Co., 1961), pp. 237-38.
16 Ibid., pp. 238-39.

virtue of the fact that he does it."[17] Thus human sinners are responsible for sin, and "God is neither responsible nor sinful, even though he is the only ultimate cause of everything."[18]

When God is regarded as the ultimate cause of sin from human perspectives, his perfect goodness is denied, and it explains the occurrence of evil in the world. But at the same time it is believed that whatever God does, including our sin, is "just and right" because it is what he does, while our sin, caused by God, is evil on our part for which we are held accountable. This would mean that what is good to God is sometimes what is evil to us. Millard J. Erickson (1932–) comments: "In Clark's scheme, the statements 'God does good' and 'man does good' are so dissimilar that we virtually cannot know what it means to say, 'God is good.'"[19] It seems that the word "good" here is used "equivocally," according to the terminology of Thomas Aquinas, because it has different meanings in its applications to a very transcendent God and to the world.[20]

3. Denying the Reality of Evil: Pantheism

Simple theodicies of the third kind deny the reality of evil by holding that evil is merely an illusion in the context of pantheism. Here we will deal with Benedict Spinoza (1632–1677), a Dutch pantheistic philosopher, and Mary Baker Eddy (1821–1910), the founder of Christian Science, as simple theodicists of this kind.

According to Spinoza's pantheism, there is only one substance, which both God and the world of nature share. His famous formula of *Deus sive Natura* ("God or Nature")[21] shows that these two words of God and Nature are interchangeable. The only distinction between them is that while God is that single substance with infinite attributes ("thought" and "extension" included), all things in the natural world are simply "modes" of the attributes of that substance.[22] Thus the world is not really distinct from God but *is* God, expressed in various modes of God's attributes.

Also, God's being is considered to be necessary and not contingent; hence all the modes in the world flow forth from God by necessity: "Nothing in the

---

[17] Ibid., p, 239.

[18] Ibid.

[19] Millard J. Erickson, *Christian Theology*, vol. 1 (Grand Rapids, MI: Baker Book House, 1983), p. 419.

[20] Thomas Aquinas, *Summa Theologiae*, vol. I, part 1, ed. Thomas Gilby (Garden City, NY: Image Books,1969), p. 205.

[21] Benedict de Spinoza, *The Ethics*, trans. R. H. M. Elwes (London: George Bell & Sons, 1891), Part IV, preface.

[22] Ibid., Part I, prop. 25, corollary.

universe is contingent, but all things are conditioned to exist and operate in a particular manner by the necessity of the divine nature."[23] In this sense nothing in the world is free, whereas God may be free in the sense that he is not conditioned by anything outside of himself, but not free in the sense that he could have created a different kind of world. He necessarily had to create just what he did.

This pantheistic vision clearly holds that everything in the world is divine. In this world, then, evil does not exist, nor can it possibly exist. Of course, we seem to often experience "evil" as "every kind of pain, especially that which frustrates our longings";[24] however this is simply due to our inadequate knowledge of the whole system of nature centering on God: "The knowledge of evil is an inadequate knowledge," and "if the human mind possessed only adequate ideas, it would form no conception of evil."[25] After all, therefore, what appears to be evil is part of the natural order, and thus is not really evil.

Let us now turn to Mary Baker Eddy's pantheistic position. According to her, God is completely spiritual as "incorporeal, divine, supreme, infinite Mind, Spirit, Soul, Principle, Life, Truth, Love,"[26] and "There is no life, truth, intelligence, nor substance in matter. All is infinite Mind [i.e., God] and its infinite manifestation, for God is All-in-all."[27] Thus her pantheism is a radical form of philosophical idealism. The whole of reality is purely spiritual and entirely good.

Hence the material world does not exist, and to think that it exists is just an error of one's mortal mind: "Matter is the falsity, not the fact, of existence."[28] The concept of matter is merely derived from "the subjective condition of mortal mind,"[29] and it is "an error of statement" as "a human concept."[30]

Interestingly, Eddy denies that her theology is pantheistic. Her denial is based on her definition of pantheism as the belief that "God, or Life, is in or of matter."[31] This definition certainly does not apply to her theology as it does to the pantheism of Spinoza which involves both "thought" and "extension"

[23] Ibid., Part I, prop. 29.
[24] Ibid., Part III, prop. 39, note.
[25] Ibid., Part IV, prop. 64.
[26] Mary Baker Eddy, *Science and Health with Key to the Scriptures*, authorized ed. (Boston, MA: Christian Science Board of Directors, 2011), p. 465.
[27] Ibid., p. 468.
[28] Ibid., p. 127.
[29] Ibid., p. 189.
[30] Ibid., p. 277.
[31] Ibid., p. 27.

together. Hence her position is not pantheistic in the Spinozistic sense. But it is unquestionably pantheistic in the sense of equating God with the world, even though in such a radically idealist way as to believe the world to be purely spiritual and good and not material.

What, then, is Eddy's answer to the problem of evil? According to her, evil appears to occur when the material world, which does not exist, occurs to one's mortal mind as an error. Therefore evil is an illusion without any reality: "Evil has no reality. It is neither person, place, nor thing, but is simply a belief, an illusion of material sense."[32] All forms of evil such as disharmony, sin, suffering, sickness and death are illusions in this sense. Therefore "evil, disease, and death" can be overcome "by understanding their nothingness and the allness of God, or good."[33]

4. Difficulties

The three kinds of simple theodicies that we have viewed thus far seem to have at least two difficulties: 1) that their denials of the omnipotence of God, the perfect goodness of God, or the reality of evil in the world, respectively, are unacceptable to most theists, who believe that God is omnipotent and perfectly good, while at the same time evil really exists in the world; and 2) that these simple theodicies are merely logical solutions to the problem of the contradiction between the three original propositions, without being able to eradicate evil from the world.

The first difficulty is related to the fact that most theists do not accept dualism, despotism, or pantheism. That they do not accept dualism and pantheism is unquestionable, but is it really true that they do not accept despotism, either? The answer should be in the affirmative, as long as despotism means to say that whatever God does, including our sin, is "just and right" because it is what he does. Alan Richardson (1905–1975) is typical, when he says: "the idea that a thing is right because it is willed by God rather than that it is willed by God because it is right will appear offensive to the moral sense of most Christians today."[34]

The second difficulty is self-evident. Evil, which is just a topic of their discussion, can never be removed from the world by simple theodicies. Even if pantheists may assert that there is no evil at all, and that evil is merely an

[32] Ibid., p. 71.
[33] Ibid., p. 450.
[34] Alan Richardson, "Evil, The Problem of," in *The Westminster Dictionary of Christian Theology*, ed. Alan Richardson and John Bowden (Philadelphia: Westminster Press, 1983), p. 195.

illusion, that is not acceptable. There still exists the "illusion of evil" at least in case of Christian Science, and "the problem is shifted, but is no less difficult."[35]

Aesthetic theodicies address the first difficulty well, by accepting all the three original propositions of the omnipotence of God, the perfect goodness of God, and the reality of evil in the world. They, however, cannot address the second one, as they aesthetically explain away evil, not being able to actually remove evil from the world. Practical theodicies well address not only the first difficulty but also the second one, being committed to eradicating evil from the world.

Unification theodicy joins practical theodicies in addressing both difficulties well. Let us see here how it addresses the first difficulty. (How it addresses the second one will be seen later in Section 4.) Unification theodicy clearly affirms the omnipotence of God (the denial of which is dualism), the perfect goodness of God (the denial of which is despotism), and the reality of evil (the denial of which is pantheism), thus rejecting dualism, despotism and pantheism.

The Divine Principle rejects the dualism of God and Satan, saying that Satan did not exist "before the creation of the universe" to have "a purpose contrary to that of God."[36] It therefore states quite often that God is "omnipotent."[37] Now, God's "dual characteristics of internal nature and external form," i.e., his dual characteristics of *Sungsang* and *Hyungsang*, in the Divine Principle[38] may look like the internal dualism of God in Brightman's philosophy which limits the power of God. However, the "original external form" of God, i.e., his *Hyungsang*, in the Divine Principle is not evil at all, unlike the second aspect of The Given which is the source of surd evil in Brightmen's view. Also God's dual characteristics are always harmoniously united, unlike the two aspects of The Given which can never be completely combined. Thus God's dual characteristics in the Divine Principle do not mean an internal dualism of the Brightmanian type which would limit the power of God.

The Divine Principle also rejects despotism, because it never believes that God is so sovereign as to cause evil as well as good. God is always "the source of goodness"[39] or "the Subject of goodness,"[40] thus never predestining anything evil even from the viewpoint of human beings:

---

[35] Erickson, *Christian Theology*, vol. 1, p. 421.

[36] *Exposition of the Divine Principle* (New York: H.S.A.-U.W.C., 1996), p. 57. Henceforth abbreviated as EDP.

[37] EDP, pp. 10, 42, 76, 81.

[38] EDP, pp. 16-18.

[39] EDP, p. 42.

[40] EDP, p. 84.

> God is the Author of goodness. Hence, His purpose of creation is good; likewise, the purpose of the providence of restoration and His Will to accomplish its purpose are good. For this reason, God does not intend anything that obstructs or opposes the fulfillment of the purpose of creation. In particular, He could not have predestined the human Fall or sins which make fallen human beings liable to judgment. Nor could He predestine such events as the destruction of the cosmos. If such evils were the inevitable result of God's predestination, then God could not be the Author of goodness.[41]

It goes without saying that the Divine Principle also rejects pantheism. Even if it affirms the close relationship between God and the world, it does not mean a pantheistic relationship. The Divine Principle believes that God created the world not out of the divine substance but only in the image of God, i.e., in what Unification Thought calls the "Divine Image."[42] Therefore the Divine Principle is not a pantheism but rather what Unification Thought calls a "Pan-Divine-Image theory."[43] By the way, the Divine Image here refers to two things: 1) "Universal Images" of the dual characteristics of *Sungsang* and *Hyungsang* and the dual characteristics of Yang and Yin, and 2) "Individual Images," which are their "individualizations"[44] The Divine Principle thus rejects pantheism and does not teach that evil is just an illusion. It teaches that evil is as substantial as good. Good emerges as a substantial "force" resulting from the "give and take of love and beauty" between a subject partner and object partner in the "four position foundation" centering on "God's purpose of creation."[45] Evil emerges the same way, albeit completely opposite to God's purpose of creation: it is substantial as "an act or its result… [which] violates God's purpose of creation by forming a four position foundation under the dominion of Satan."[46]

---

[41] EDP, p. 155.

[42] *New Essentials of Unification Thought: Head-Wing Thought* (Tokyo: Kogensha, 2006), pp. 2-22. Henceforth abbreviated as NEUT.

[43] NEUT, p. 557.

[44] NEUT, pp. 19-22.

[45] EDP, pp. 25, 39.

[46] EDP, p. 39.

§2. Aesthetic Theodicies

1. Gottfried Leibniz: The "Best of All Possible Worlds" Theodicy

The German philosopher Gottfried Leibniz is well known not only for the word "theodicy" that he coined but also for the phrase, the "best of all possible worlds." Representing the optimism of the eighteenth century, he, while acknowledging the existence of evil, thinks that evil is aesthetically compatible with a greater purpose of God.

According to Leibniz, an omnipotent and good God, before creating the world, used his divine mind to go through all the "forms" within it to set up every possible combination or set of possibilities that are compatible with one another for the realization of God's goodness. Each and every possible combination of compatible possibilities would comprehensively constitute a complete possible history from creation onwards until the present. God surveyed all these possible combinations or sets, and when creating the world, he decided to choose from among them one particular set of compatible possibilities which would bring forth the best possible value of goodness. Hence this world is the "best of all possible worlds,"[47] consisting of those possibilities "which, being united, produce most reality, most perfection, most significance."[48] In other words, "The result of all these comparisons and deliberations is the choice of the best from among all these possible systems, which wisdom makes in order to satisfy goodness completely; and such is precisely the plan of the universe as it is."[49]

The divinely chosen set of compatible possibilities which is this actual world includes all the free actions of free beings in a complete sequence of events for the history of the world, whether these free actions are morally good or wrong ones. For Leibniz, however, God's prior choice of that set of possibilities does not contradict the free actions of free beings in the world. The reason is that the world, which contains all possibilities involving free beings, was already decreed by God:

> This decree changes nothing in the constitution of things: God leaves them just as they were in the state of mere possibility, that is, changing nothing either in their essence or nature, or even in their accidents,

---

[47] G. W. Leibniz, *Theodicy: Essays on the Goodness of God, the Freedom of Man and the Origin of Evil*, trans. E. M. Huggard (London: Routledge & Kegan Paul, 1952), para. 168.
[48] Ibid., para. 201.
[49] Ibid., para. 225.

> which are represented perfectly already in the idea of this possible world.[50]

Leibniz is aware of three kinds of evil: 1) "metaphysical evil" consisting in "imperfections" or "monstrosities and other apparent irregularities of the universe"; 2) "physical evil" in suffering; and 3) "moral evil" in sin.[51] Metaphysical evil here seems to be equal to what is usually called "natural evil." Leibniz believes that while physical evil is the consequent "punishment" of moral evil,[52] metaphysical evil is not. (St. Augustine would say that natural evil, too, is the consequent punishment of moral evil.[53])

The heart of Leibniz' theodicy is that God permits evil—whether it is metaphysical, physical or moral—even in the best possible world, so that it may aesthetically serve "greater goods" and even "the greatest goods": "Not only does he [i.e., God] derive from them [i.e., evils] greater goods, but he finds them connected with the greatest goods of all those that are possible: so that it would be a fault not to permit them."[54] Thus all kinds of evil contribute to the best of all possible worlds, the realization of which is God's purpose.

In this context, Leibniz approvingly refers to the hymn of praise sung on the eve of Easter in the Roman Catholic Church:[55]

> *O certe necessarium Adae peccatum, quod Christi morte deletum est!*
> [O truly necessary sin of Adam, which is cancelled by Christ's death!]
> *O felix culpa, quae talem ac tantum meruit habere Redemptorem!*
> [O happy fault, which merited such and so great a redeemer!]

This aesthetic view echoes Augustine's statement on the usefulness of evil for good: "God judged it better to bring good out of evil than not to permit any evil to exist."[56]

Some observe[57] that the God of Leibniz may not be as omnipotent as expressed, because the German philosopher himself quite honestly admits that "the source of evil lies in the possible forms, anterior to the acts of God's will."[58] Apparently, God's will to create the world had to be in conformity with,

---

[50] Ibid., para. 52.
[51] Ibid., paras. 21, 241,
[52] Ibid., para. 155.
[53] See n. 1.
[54] Leibniz, *Theodicy*, para. 127.
[55] Ibid., para. 10.
[56] Augustine, *Enchiridion: On Faith, Hope, and Love*, trans. Albert C. Outler (1955), VIII.27. http://www.tertullian. org/fathers/augustine_enchiridion_02_trans.htm.
[57] For example, John Hick. See his *Evil and the God of Love*, rev. ed. (San Francisco: Harper & Row, 1978), pp. 164-66.
[58] Leibniz, *Theodicy*, para. 381.

thus limited by, "the source of evil" which was already permitted to lie in the best possible set of possibilities within his mind.

Leibniz, however, addresses that concern by saying that "God cannot but be all-powerful, even though he can do no better than produce the best, which includes the permission of evil."[59] He also says that God brought the best possible world into existence "by means of the all-powerful word *Fiat*."[60]

2. Alvin Plantinga: The "Free Will" Defense

The American analytic philosopher Alvin Plantinga believes that there is no contradiction between an omnipotent and perfectly good God and the existence of evil in the world, because "God would have a good reason for permitting evil."[61] When it comes to moral evil, it results from wrong choices we make through our God-given "free will"; and God permits this moral evil to occur, so that it may contribute to the greater good of the universe. This aesthetic view of Plantinga, too, is Augustinian. He states:

> Augustine tries to tell us *what God's reason is for permitting evil.* At bottom, he says, it's that God can create a more perfect universe by permitting evil. A really top-notch universe requires the existence of free, rational, and moral agents; and some of the free creatures He created went wrong. But the universe with the free creatures it contains and the evil they commit is better than it would have been had it contained neither the free creatures nor this evil.[62]

Plantinga, however, draws a distinction between his position and Augustine's, calling the former a "Free Will Defense" and the latter a "Free Will Theodicy," because the former only attempts to say "what God's reason [for permitting evil] *might possibly be*," while the latter intends to say with more certitude "what God's reason *is*."[63] Thus his free will defense proposes the following two points: 1) it is *possible* that God permits moral evil for the reason that it can contribute to the greater good of the world; and 2) it is *possible* that even if God creates free beings who are completely free to choose between good and evil, God is not responsible for their evil choices. Plantinga clarifies the second point by explaining the nature of free will: Whether a free person performs an action or refrains from performing it is completely "within his

---

[59] Ibid., para. 333.
[60] Ibid., para. 52. Italics original.
[61] Alvin Plantinga, *God, Freedom, and Evil* (Grand Rapids, MI: Wm. B. Eerdmans Publishing Co., 1977), p. 26.
[62] Ibid., p. 27. Italics original.
[63] Ibid., p. 27-28. Italics original.

power," and "no antecedent conditions and/or causal laws [including God] determine" it.[64]

Prior to Plantinga's free will defense, Antony Flew (1923–2010) and J. L. Mackie (1917–1981) famously developed their ideas which would be objections to it. Flew thought that if free will in theism is a God-given nature out of which we behave as we do, then an omnipotent and good God could have created "people who would always as a matter of fact freely have chosen to do the right thing."[65] Mackie similarly held that in spite of the available possibility of God creating people who would always in fact freely have chosen to do the right thing, God failed to "avail himself of this possibility," so that God is "inconsistent with his being both omnipotent and wholly good."[66] Flew and Mackie were atheists when they presented these ideas.

Plantinga naturally expressed his disagreement with Flew and Mackie.[67] In this context, he further explained his free will defense by stating that it is *possible* that even if God is omnipotent, "it was not within His power to create a world containing moral good but no moral evil."[68] God could have created any other possible world, but what happens in this world in terms of us freely choosing evil would also happen in any other possible world. Plantinga calls this universal malady "transworld depravity."[69]

So far we have dealt with Plantinga's understanding of moral evil. What about natural evil? According to him, natural evil, which involves hurricanes, earthquakes, etc., is not due to the free activity of human beings, but *possibly* "due to the free actions of nonhuman persons," i.e., "Satan and his cohorts"; hence "*natural* evil significantly resembles *moral* evil in that, like the latter, it is the result of the activity of significantly free persons."[70] Needless to say, Plantinga believes that God would have the same good reason for permitting natural evil as well as moral evil.

Plantinga's free will defense initially does not specifically reference the "*O felix culpa*" hymn, in spite of its basically aesthetic treatment of evil. But, in an article, "Supralapsarianism, or '*O Felix Culpa*,'" written much later,[71] he

---

[64] Ibid., p. 29.

[65] Antony Flew, "Divine Omnipotence and Human Freedom," in *New Essays in Philosophical Theology*, ed. Antony Flew and Alasdair C. MacIntyre (London, SCM Press, 1955), p. 152.

[66] J. L. Mackie, "Evil and Omnipotence," *Mind* 64, no. 254 (April 1955): 209.

[67] Plantinga, *God, Freedom, and Evil*, pp. 31-33.

[68] Ibid., p. 45.

[69] Ibid., pp. 49-53.

[70] Ibid., pp. 58-59. Italics original.

[71] Alvin Plantinga, "Supralapsarianism, or '*O Felix Culpa*,'" in *Christian Faith and the Problem of Evil*, ed. Peter van Inwagen (Grand Rapids, MI: Wm. B. Eerdmans Publishing Co., 2004), pp. 1-25.

develops a "*felix culpa*" theodicy, which is somewhat similar to the theodicy of Leibniz but which emphasizes the importance of the Incarnation and Atonement for the actualization of "a really good possible world" as a happy result of our falling into sin.

3. John Hick: The "Soul-making" Theodicy

The English philosopher of religion John Hick also holds that evil aesthetically serves a greater purpose of an omnipotent and perfectly good God. In this, he seems similar to Leibniz and Plantinga, but there is a difference. While Leibniz and Plantinga believe that evil just generally contributes to the greatest or greater good of the universe, Hick has in mind a more specific purpose of God, which is to have immature human souls grow ("soul-making") through their experiences of evil in the world, so that they can develop an ultimately perfect personal relationship with God.[72] Evil is understood to be useful in this teleological and eschatological context.

According to Hick, humans are created as immature and imperfect children at an "epistemic distance" from God,[73] and they are therefore to go through a very long process of growth to eventually realize their mature unity with God. Hick apparently borrows this idea from the second-century Church Father St. Irenaeus (c. 130–c. 202), rejecting St. Augustine's view that Adam was created "in a finished state, as a finitely perfect being."[74]

Hick criticizes the Augustinian tradition on this issue for being incoherent because in order to preserve God from any responsibility for the existence of evil in the world, it believes that Adam, in spite of having been wonderfully created as a "free and finitely perfect" being, freely sinned: "It is impossible to conceive of wholly good beings in a wholly good world becoming sinful."[75]

Augustine's free will theodicy, of course, has its own aesthetic reason why God permits free creatures to sin, as was seen in the preceding subsection on Plantinga; but Hick does not accept it. He instead develops an "Irenaean" theodicy, whose aesthetic treatment of evil focuses on God's more specific purpose of our "soul-making." For him, the fall of Adam is simply a myth, which intends to convey the fact that God created immature and imperfect free humans whose fall is virtually inevitable: "A fall… [is] rendered virtually inevitable by the basic features of man's divinely appointed situation."[76] (Note,

---

[72] Hick, *Evil and the God of Love*, pp. 253-61.
[73] Ibid., pp. 281-82, 285-88.
[74] Ibid., p. 253.
[75] Ibid., pp. 249-50.
[76] Ibid., p. 285.

however, that Irenaeus himself believed in the historicity of the fall of Adam.) God, then, is responsible for this vulnerable situation in which imperfect humans are placed, namely, "a hazardous adventure of individual freedom" they have to pass through.[77] But as they pass through it, even making many wrong choices of their own as well as some good ones and as a result experiencing much suffering as well as some joy, they can gradually, if very slowly, grow to be perfect "by meeting and eventually mastering temptations, and thus by rightly making choices in concrete situations."[78] For "the paradox of creaturely freedom is that only those who are initially against Him [i.e., God] can of their own free volition choose to be for Him."[79]

The usefulness of moral evil for our soul-making is, according to Hick, "in agreement with... the profound medieval insight of the 'O felix culpa.'"[80] This means that he agrees with Leibniz and Plantinga on the aesthetic effect of evil for good, although his understanding of it is more specific than the other two.

Physical pain, and other forms of suffering resulting from it, also serve the purpose of soul-making. Our natural world is not intended to be a paradise, but rather an environment that provides us with physical pain and suffering due to the general laws of nature, so that we as moral beings, by experiencing them, may be fashioned into mature children of God:

> This is a world of rough edges, a place in which man can love only by the sweat of his brow, and which continually presents him with challenges, uncertainties, and dangers; and yet... just these features of the world seem, paradoxically, to underlie the emergence of virtually the whole range of the more valuable human characteristics.[81]

Hick is aware, of course, that our soul-making process may not be completed during our lifetime on the earth. Therefore he suggests the hopeful idea of "an after-life" beyond this world, in which a "decisive bringing of good out of evil" can be done, so that we might experience our final blessedness as "the fulfillment of God's good purpose."[82]

---

[77] Ibid., p. 256.
[78] Ibid., p. 255.
[79] Ibid., p. 287.
[80] Ibid., pp. 287, 364.
[81] Ibid., pp. 326-27.
[82] Ibid., pp. 337-40.

4. Difficulties

The aesthetic theodicies of Leibniz, Plantinga and Hick have quite often been criticized for having at least four difficulties: 1) that their theoretical rationalization of evil through an aesthetic harmonization of it with God's greater purpose cannot eradicate evil from the world; 2) that gratuitous evil, pointlessly excessive evil, may be too severe and cruel to be rationalized even by God's greater purpose; 3) that when aesthetic theodicists theoretically rationalize evil with God's greater purpose, they may not necessarily be in a state of inner conversion or salvation; and 4) that God's omnipotence and perfect goodness, though affirmed, are not grasped deeply enough to be able to accommodate the biblical notion of God's suffering love for human salvation; in aesthetic theodicies God is basically still the God of the philosophers.

The first difficulty unquestionably exists in Leibniz and Plantinga, who assume that evil should exist even forever for the sake of good. Leibniz' best possible world, which is this world, always contains evil for the realization of the best possible value of goodness, and Plantinga's notion of "transworld depravity" assumes that rational beings in any possible world always make wrong choices as well as right ones for the greater good of that world. However, does the first difficulty exist in Hick's theodicy, which hopes that with time the perfection of soul-making will finally come? Will evil, which is instrumental for soul-making, disappear when the final blessedness is reached? Hick himself admits that it is "an exceedingly difficult question to meet," for "if only challenges and obstacles and sufferings can evoke the highest moral qualities within us, will not these evils still be necessary in heaven?"[83] The process theologian David Ray Griffin (1939–2022) observes that Hick does not understand "genuine evil," which is evil "without which the world would have been a better place."[84] If Griffin's observation is correct, what Hick thinks to be evil should remain forever even in the final kingdom of God.

What about the second difficulty? An example of gratuitous evil is mentioned by Ivan in the novel of Fyodor Dostoevsky (1821–1881), *The Brothers Karamazov*. An army general angrily and mercilessly let his numerous hunting hounds chase after an eight-year-old boy, catch him and tear him to pieces before his mother's eyes, simply because the poor child had thrown a stone in play and accidently hurt the paw of the general's favorite hound. Ivan

---

[83] Ibid., p. 351.

[84] David Ray Griffin, *God, Power, and Evil: A Process Theodicy* (Philadelphia: Westminster Press, 1976), p. 200.

complains that this evil is too cruel to be aesthetically harmonized with any greater purpose of God: "Listen! If all must suffer to pay for the eternal harmony, what have children to do with it, tell me, please? It's beyond all comprehension why they should suffer, and why they should pay for the harmony." He also says that if "too high a price is asked for harmony," then "it's beyond our means to pay so much to enter on it." Thus he would rather "give back my entrance ticket" to God. Not that he does not believe in God, but that he cannot accept the strange fact that there are even cruel human beings who invent the idea of the need of an omnipotent and good God for the occurrence of such intolerable evil: "the marvel is that such an idea, the idea of the necessity of God, could enter the head of such a savage, vicious beast as man."[85]

Ivan's "rebellion" here devastatingly discredits all aesthetic theodicies that attempt to rationalize and domesticate even gratuitous evil. It should also be noted in this connection that evil which is rationalized and domesticated by aesthetic theodicies is pejoratively dubbed an "aesthetic phantom" by the French philosopher Paul Ricoeur (1913–2005), who observes that they only triumph over this phantom and not over real evil at all.[86]

Now the third difficulty. Very few aesthetic theodicists would be what Ivan refers to as "savage, cruel" human beings. But according to Kenneth Surin (1948–), who is a practical theodicist, aesthetic theodicists seem not to have any real inner conversion, transformation or evidence of salvation centering on God when they aesthetically rationalize evil.[87] For example, Job's comforters in the Book of Job are aesthetic theodicists, when they plausibly attribute his afflictions to his ancestral sins, unknown sins, forgotten sins, and sins of the community, so that everything may be harmonized with God's will. Their apparent problem is that they are not internally transformed enough to be able to know God's wisdom behind the afflictions of Job, an upright and pious servant of God. Job himself strongly disagrees with them. Furthermore, God finally appears in a whirlwind to challenge all plausible human explanations by declaring: "Who is this that darkens council by words without knowledge?" (Job 38:2)

In the Book of Job, therefore, we are strongly challenged to first connect humbly with God for inner transformation rather than proudly present our

---

[85] Fyodor Dostoevsky, *The Brothers Karamazov*. http://www.planetpublish.com/wp-content/uploads/2011/11/The_Brothers_Karamazov_NT.pdf. All quotations come from this.
[86] Paul Ricoeur, "The Hermeneutics of Symbols and Philosophical Reflection: I," in *The Conflict of Interpretations*, ed. Don Ihde (Evanston, IL: Northwestern University Press, 1974), p. 312.
[87] Surin, *Theology and the Problem of Evil*, pp. 11, 23.

own superficial explanations on evil. According to Surin, our conversion, our inner connection with God is the only foundation on which we can address the problem of evil properly:

> So it is conversion—which comes about when the human will co-operates with divine grace—that solves the 'problem of evil'. Without conversion, the very *process* of seeking an answer to the question 'whence is evil?' will be undermined by the distorted thinking of a crippled intellect.[88]

The fourth and final difficulty of aesthetic theodicies concerns their understanding of God. When they try to solve the problem of the logical contradiction between an omnipotent and perfectly good God and the existence of evil in the world by adding another proposition concerning a greater purpose of God that evil serves, they deal with God rather intellectually and philosophically. Thus their God is the God of philosophical theism rather than the God of the Bible. God is treated as an object of philosophical thinking rather than as a living God for the faithful. God is understood as a being, object or entity "possessing a number of clearly specifiable characteristics," and based on that understanding of God, "the things of the world" are rendered "rational, meaningful and explicable."[89] Such philosophical theism entered into Christian theology under the influence of Greek philosophy from nearly the beginning of the Christian era, but it became more visible since the seventeenth and eighteenth centuries when the aesthetic theodicy of Leibniz emerged.

According to Surin, however, this tradition of treating God merely as an object of philosophical thinking has "the most profound misunderstanding of who God is. It is to leave theological utterance in irreparable disarray."[90] The God of the philosophers is basically a "unipersonal" God, the measure of whom does not have to involve significant theological issues such as Incarnation, redemption, Holy Spirit and Trinity.[91] God's omnipotence and perfect goodness, which are important components in philosophical aesthetic theodicy, are hardly discussed in relationship to these theological issues. Thus these divine attributes are not grasped deeply enough to be able to accommodate the biblical notion of God's suffering love for human salvation.

We will see in the following section that the practical theodicies of Dorothee Soelle and Jürgen Moltmann address the above four difficulties of aesthetic theodicies in quite profound ways. We will also see in the final section

---

[88] Ibid., p. 11. Italics original.
[89] Ibid., pp. 6-7.
[90] Ibid., p. 7.
[91] Ibid., pp. 4-7.

that Unification theodicy is a practical theodicy which addresses these difficulties of aesthetic theodicies in an even more acceptable way.

§3. Practical Theodicies

1. Dorothee Soelle

The German political theologian Dorothee Soelle has quite a radical approach to the problem of evil and suffering, which primarily deals with social suffering. She sharply criticizes traditional aesthetic approaches, saying that when they aestheticize or harmonize suffering with God's greater purpose, they mean to encourage believers to "masochistically" endure their suffering for their purification in front of a "sadistic" God:

> The [traditional] Christian interpretations of suffering... amount to a recommendation of masochism... Affliction has the intention of bringing us back to a God who only becomes great when he makes us small... Suffering is understood to be a test, sent by God, that we are required to pass. It is considered a punishment that follows earlier sins... or as a refining from which we come out purified.[92]
>
> [There is also] a companion piece of a sadistic God. The libidinal and flexible impulses of pious sufferers are now sadistically fixed by the theologians, who make the wrath of God their essential motif. The God who produces suffering and causes affliction becomes the glorious theme of a theology that directs our attention to the God who demands the impossible and tortures people.[93]

Soelle also complains that God's omnipotence and perfect goodness mentioned in this context are of a sadistic God, and that God's love therefore tends to be minimized.[94] She points to still another problem resulting from this, and it is that we become apathetic and insensitive to other people's misery in front of an apathetic God.[95] In this situation, suffering is far from being eradicated.

What Soelle suggests, therefore, is that we should become people who can practically strive to abolish suffering, including gratuitous suffering, instead of staying as apathetic bystanders: "It is axiomatic for me that the only

---

[92] Dorothee Soelle, *Suffering*, trans. Everett R. Kalin (Philadelphia: Fortress Press, 1975), p. 19.
[93] Ibid., p. 22.
[94] Ibid., pp. 24-25.
[95] Ibid., pp. 33-59.

humanely conceivable goal is the abolition of circumstances under which people are forced to suffer, whether through poverty or tyranny."[96]

How, then, can we abolish suffering? Soelle's answer as a Christian is that we go to the sufferers and bear their pain with them, like Jesus Christ did on the cross. She finds this answer particularly in the stance of Alyosha, Ivan's younger brother, who is a novice in a monastery in Dostoevsky's *The Brothers Karamazov*. Thus Soelle describes Alyosha as follows:

> Alyosha directs his attention not to the power above but to the sufferers. He puts himself beside them. He bears their pain with them. During this conversation he says almost nothing. He listens in agony as Ivan introduces examples of suffering he had assembled as witnesses against the compassion of God. Later Alyosha arises, goes up to Ivan, the rebel and insurrectionist, and kisses him silently on the lips. It is the same gesture with which Christ departed in the legend of the Grand Inquisitor.[97]

It is in this *imitatio Christi* stance of Alyosha that Soelle finds at least two amazing things: 1) "Alyosha's strength is the silent sharing of suffering"; and 2) "God is not over Alyosha… [but] within him."[98]

When Jesus, who was going to the cross, bore the pain of the sufferers by drinking the "cup of suffering," it became the "cup of strengthening" which "conquered all fear" because of the emergence of "love unbounded" there.[99] If we follow Christ in this regard, then we can experience the power of love by which we can be strengthened enough to be able to overcome and even eradicate suffering.

Soelle does not assert that from the beginning there is a God of omnipotence and perfect goodness, based on whom we just rationally explain away the existence of suffering. She rather means to argue that we first throw ourselves into the painful situation of the sufferers to be with them, with the result that we, together with God who is now "within us," can experience love unbounded in the midst of the suffering which is to be overcome. God also suffers with us even in such miserable places as Auschwitz: "Between the victim and the executioner, God… is on the side of the sufferer. God is on the side of the victim, he is hanged."[100] This way the nature of God can gradually yet truly be discovered. In this sense, says Seolle, God is "one who certainly is

---

[96] Ibid., p. 2.
[97] Ibid., p. 175.
[98] Ibid., pp. 175-76.
[99] Ibid., pp. 85-86.
[100] Ibid., p. 148.

not over us like a perfect being [from the beginning] but one who is in the process of becoming."[101]

Soelle's theodicy certainly poses a challenge to traditional philosophical theism. She has not fully developed a doctrine of God, but her theodicy can potentially develop a new, practical understanding of God's omnipotence and perfect goodness based on the tremendous power of love, by which we are able to eventually abolish evil and suffering.

2. Jürgen Moltmann

Jürgen Moltmann, too, takes seriously Ivan Karamazov's rebellious complaint of traditional aesthetic theodicy which harmonizes evil with a greater purpose of an omnipotent and perfectly good God. Thus the German Reformed theologian says: "The suffering of an innocent child is an irrefutable rebuttal of the notion of the almighty and kindly God in heaven."[102]

In this context he criticizes any aesthetic explanation for its inability to obliterate suffering from the world: "There is no explanation of suffering which is capable of obliterating his [i.e., the sufferer's] pain, and no consolation of a higher wisdom which could assuage it."[103] Again, with this "highly questionable" traditional explanation, the sufferer has to "come to terms with" his suffering, without being able to overcome it:

> The desire to explain suffering is already highly questionable in itself. Does an explanation not lead us to justify suffering and give it permanence? Does it not lead the suffering person to come to terms with his suffering, and to declare himself in agreement with it? And does this not mean that he gives up hope of overcoming suffering?[104]

Moltmann therefore proposes an entirely new approach which is both "practical" and "eschatological." It is practical in that we, together with God, strive to overcome suffering, and it is eschatological in that it seeks a future when the overcoming of suffering will be completed, i.e., "the future in which the desire for God will be fulfilled, suffering will be overcome, and what has been lost will be restored."[105]

---

[101] Ibid., p. 92.

[102] Jürgen Moltmann, *The Trinity and the Kingdom: The Doctrine of God*, trans. Margaret Kohl (New York: Harper & Row, 1981), p. 47.

[103] Ibid.

[104] Ibid., p. 52.

[105] Ibid., p. 49.

His approach involves a *theologia crucis* (theology of the cross), which he believes to be the only answer to the question of severe torments in places like Auschwitz:

> Any other answer [than the *theologia crucis*] would be blasphemy. There cannot be any other Christian answer to the question of this torment. To speak here of a God who could not suffer would make God a demon. To speak here of an absolute God would make God an annihilating nothingness. To speak here of an indifferent God would condemn men to indifference.[106]

Soelle's approach also involves a *theologia crucis*. But Moltmann's *theologia crucis* has a more developed doctrine of God than hers, because it directly incorporates the passion of Christ on the cross into the inner being of the Godhead. According to Moltmann, God is a God of the Trinity in whom there is a dynamic relationship of love between the Father and the Son centering on the Holy Spirit. Hence, when the Father forsakes the Son on the cross for the redemption of the sinful world of suffering, the Son experiences the agony of being forsaken by the Father, who in turn experiences the suffering of separation from the Son. By surrendering to this painful situation together, however, the Father and the Son experience a new unity of love with each other in the Holy Spirit.[107] Thus "What happens on Golgotha reaches into the innermost depths of the Godhead, putting its impress on the trinitarian life in eternity."[108]

When God, through the cross of the Son on Golgotha, makes our suffering his own within his inner-trinitarian life, we feel that our suffering is healed. It is on the basis of this crucified God of suffering that we as believers are now empowered to crucify ourselves together with Christ to practically bear the pain of others who are still suffering: "The crucifixion of the believer with Christ takes its meaning from Christ's death on the cross for the godless."[109] This is how suffering is overcome; and when we are engaged in this task, it is no longer the case in which we are apathetic to others in front of an apathetic God. We are instead "sympathetic" to others in front of a sympathetic God, being "filled with the spirit of God":

> In the sphere of the apathetic God man becomes a *homo apatheticus*. In the situation of the *pathos* of God he becomes a *homo sympatheticus*. The

---

[106] Jürgen Moltmann, *The Crucified God: The Cross of Christ as the Foundation and Criticism of Christian Theology*, trans. R. A. Wilson and John Bowden (New York: Harper & Row, 1974), p. 274.
[107] Moltmann, *The Trinity and the Kingdom*, pp. 82-83.
[108] Ibid., p. 81.
[109] Moltmann, *The Crucified God*, p. 62.

> divine *pathos* is reflected in man's participation, his hopes and his prayers. Sympathy is the openness of a person to the present of another. It has the structure of dialogue. In the *pathos* of God, man is filled with the spirit of God. He becomes the friend of God, feels sympathy with God and for God. He does not enter into a mystical union but into a sympathetic union with God. He is angry with God's wrath. He suffers with God's suffering. He loves with God's love. He hopes with God's hope.[110]

The removal of suffering from the world, however, cannot be completed until the last days. The cross of Christ is just the beginning. After the Son's death and resurrection, the Holy Spirit is poured out to transform us all, so that we may eventually come up with our "new solidarity and fellowship" among ourselves to partake of the "inner-trinitarian life" of God, thus giving "joy" and "bliss" to God.[111] This signifies "the completion of the trinitarian history of God and the end of world history" in which "the history of man's sorrow" is overcome and "his history of hope" fulfilled.[112]

According to Moltmann, God is a God of sympathy who suffers for us. Thus he rejects traditional theism's idea that God is "an omnipotent God who cannot suffer."[113] His theology, however, seems to have a new, profound understanding of God's omnipotence as the omnipotence of God's love. When God suffers for the sake of love, by limiting and emptying himself and even withdrawing his omnipotence in the traditional sense of the term, "he has confidence in the free response of men and women"; and that confidence of God is nowhere more powerful than in his kenosis of love: God is "nowhere greater than," "nowhere more glorious than," and "nowhere more divine than" there.[114]

Moltmann also seems to have a new understanding of God's perfection. Unlike traditional philosophical theism's understanding, it does not mean God' immutability. Instead, the inner dynamic unity of love between the Father and the Son centering on the Holy Spirit is "the very proof of divine perfection."[115]

3. Assessment

Let us assess how Soelle and Moltmann address the four difficulties of aesthetic theodicies. Both of them address the first difficulty well, boldly stating that we

---

110 Ibid., p. 272.
111 Moltmann, *The Trinity and the Kingdom*, pp. 126-27.
112 Moltmann, *The Crucified God*, p. 278.
113 Ibid., p. 223.
114 Moltmann, *The Trinity and the Kingdom*, p. 119.
115 Ibid., pp. 45-46.

have to commit ourselves to removing evil and suffering from the world. The abolishment of suffering is "axiomatic" for Soelle, and any explanation of suffering which cannot obliterate it is "highly questionable" for Moltmann. Both theologians also take the example of Ivan's rebellion very seriously, and this means that they address the second difficulty for the eventual removal of gratuitous evil and suffering.

They address the third difficulty well, saying that we have to be internally converted and empowered through the cross of Jesus Christ, which shows God's suffering love for human salvation, and that on that basis we can be ready to bear the suffering of victims in order to help them to remove it through the power of God's love. Thus apathy to the victims of evil is the last thing we should have, according to both theologians.

They address the fourth difficulty by critically challenging the traditional philosophical understanding of God's omnipotence and perfect goodness and also by restating these divine attributes in the context of the *theologia crucis* which holds that God can only be known through the cross of Christ who suffers for us out of love. Both theologians are aware of God's unbounded kenosis of love, and they believe that only in connection with it can we start talking about the divine omnipotence and perfection.

The difference between Soelle and Moltmann is that Moltmann has a more developed doctrine of God than Soelle, in that he directly incorporates the passion of Christ on the cross into the inner-trinitarian life of the Godhead. Thus he connects the theodicy problem with Incarnation, redemption, Holy Spirit and Trinity more than Soelle does. By contrast, aesthetic theodicies for the most part are not interested in doing this.

Unification theodicy as a practical theodicy addresses the four difficulties of aesthetic theodicies in much the same way as the practical theodicies of Soelle and Moltmann. Especially notable is Unification theodicy's convergence with them in believing that because of his unbounded love for us, God is a God of suffering, while at the same time being a God of omnipotence and perfect goodness. How Unification theodicy addresses the difficulties of aesthetic theodicies will be seen in more detail in the next section.

But there is one quite important difference between Unification theodicy and the existing practical theodicies. That is, while Unification theodicy is very interested in finding out the origin of evil, they are not. They do not seriously try to seek the origin of evil in spite of their intended noble task of abolishing evil. They already presuppose the existence of evil as an undeniable universal reality which does not have to be explained or traced back to any particular historical event like the fall of Adam. This is a modern liberal view that is widespread among scholars, including Soelle and Moltmann. For Soelle the fall of Adam is a myth and its narrative in Genesis 3 simply "describes how the human being is—and always was."[116] For Moltmann as well, it is just a "myth" or "saga" without any historicity.[117] Yet if they are thus not necessarily interested in finding out the origin of evil, how are they able to say that Christ is absolutely needed to abolish evil?

Unification theodicy answers this question by tracing evil back to the fall of Adam, which it believes to be a historical event. Augustine is famous for tracing evil in the same way, although he is not a practical theodicist but basically an aesthetic theodicist who ends up harmonizing evil, even if its origin is found out, with God's greater purpose. Unification theodicy traces the origin of evil in the sexual fall of Adam, as will be seen below, while Augustine traces it in the free will of Adam.

§4. Unification Theodicy

1. The Fall of Adam

Unification theodicy believes that the fall of Adam gave rise to the problem of evil, so that Jesus Christ came as "the last Adam" (1 Cor. 15:45) to tackle this problem, i.e., to abolish evil. This parallelism between Adam and Christ is mentioned by St. Paul: "As one man's trespass led to condemnation of all men, so one man's act of righteousness leads to acquittal and life for all men" (Rom. 5:18). Irenaeus' doctrine of "recapitulation" reinforces this point by saying that Christ "summed up all things" since the time of Adam in order to renew them all for the future.[118] Given this parallelism, then, the historicity of the life and work of Christ would reinforce the historicity of Adam and his fall. The Unificationist scholar Jonathan Wells (1942–2024) with Ph.Ds. in both theology and molecular and cell biology rejects Darwinism and supports the idea that Adam and Eve actually existed, by saying: "There is no *scientific* reason—that is, no reason based on evidence as opposed to philosophical or theological assumptions—to abandon the traditional view that our species began with one male and one female."[119]

---

[116] Dorothee Soelle et al., *Great Couples of the Bible*, trans. Brian McNeil (Minneapolis, MN: Fortress Press, 2006), p. 28.

[117] Jürgen Moltmann, "Justice for Victims and Perpetrators," *Reformed World* 44 (March 1994): 2-12.

[118] Irenaeus, *Against Heresies* 5.21.1. http://www.ccel.org/ccel/schaff/anf01.ix.vii.xxii.html.

[119] Jonathan Wells, "Evolution and Unification Thought," *Journal of Unification Studies* 12 (2011): 134. Italics original.

While Unification theodicy affirms the historicity of Adam's fall, this does not mean that it believes that the fall of Adam was a historical necessity. That Adam would fall was only a possibility. If he had not fallen in the Garden of Eden, God's will would have been realized there completely with no need for the coming of Christ. Unification theodicy, therefore, rejects the *O felix culpa* clause which aesthetic theodicies cherish. Thus Unification theodicy diverges from aesthetic theodicies, as well as from the practical theodicies of Soelle and Moltmann which deny the historicity of Adam's fall.

What, then, is the Unification interpretation of Adam's fall?[120] According to the Divine Principle, Archangel Lucifer first seduced Eve sexually (the "spiritual fall") and became Satan, and then Eve seduced Adam sexually ("physical fall"), giving birth to sinful children. God originally intended Adam and Eve not to fall but to realize the God-centered "four position foundation" and the "lineage of God" through their conjugal love supported by the divine words of blessing: "Be fruitful and multiply, and fill the earth and subdue it" (Gen. 1:28). Instead, they realized the "four position foundation" centering on Satan and the "lineage of Satan" for all humankind. Through this lineage of Satan, the "original sin" of Adam has been transmitted from generation to generation, and the whole world has been under the "sovereignty of Satan" instead of "God's sovereignty."

The idea that Adam and Eve sexually fell may sound very unfamiliar in the Christian tradition, but early Church Fathers such as St. Clement of Alexandria (c. 150–c. 215) in the East and St. Ambrose (c. 340–397) in the West actually believed in the sexual fall of the first human ancestors.[121] Also, the notions of the lineage of Satan and the sovereignty of Satan may sound novel to many in the Christian tradition. But it should be noted that at least during the first eleven centuries of the Christian era before the appearance of St. Anselm's (c. 1033–1109) "satisfaction theory" of the atonement, the sovereignty of Satan was a commonsensical notion. It was considered to be something that had to be defeated in favor of the sovereignty of God through the death of Christ on the cross, according to the classic "ransom theory" of the atonement widespread during the first eleven centuries of the Christian era. Regarding the notion of the lineage of Satan, it was, strictly speaking, not present even during those centuries, but still it can be considered to be somewhat similar to the notion of the sovereignty of Satan, in that both

---

[120] For the Unification doctrine of the fall of Adam, see EDP, pp. 53-78. See also Chapter 7, Section 2, Subsection 1 ("The Unification Doctrine of Adam's Fall") in the present book.
[121] See Chapter 10, n. 16, as well as Chapter 7, Section 4, Subsection 2, Subsubsection b ("Clement of Alexandria and Ambrose") in the present book.

concern the solidarity of human beings centering on Satan, if at different levels.[122]

The lineage of Satan is a central notion in the Unification understanding of Adam's fall, which holds that the fall took place through a sexual relationship of "illicit love"[123] or "unprincipled love"[124] between Adam and Eve centering on Satan. This resulted in the formation of a Satan-centered family of all humanity as intimated in the verse: "You brood of vipers! how can you speak good, when you are evil?" (Mt. 12:34)

Hence, according to the Unification understanding, the fall was "caused by the stronger power of unprincipled love, which overwhelmed the freedom of the original mind."[125] The fall was *not* caused by "freedom."

The meaning of freedom as understood in the Divine Principle needs to be explained here. Freedom functions perfectly when "both free will and the free actions pursuant to that will" are "in harmony" with each other (i.e., mind-body unity) centering on "God's Word"; hence there is no freedom without "the Principle," no freedom without "responsibility," and no freedom without "accomplishment" bringing "joy to God."[126] Freedom as a gift of God, therefore, always purports to accomplish the purpose of creation, not just by staying at the individual level of mind-body unity but by going to the higher levels of making relationships of unity with others to make God joyful. Closely associated with this freedom is the notion of "creative nature" or "creatorship" which human beings are endowed with in resemblance to God.[127] Therefore this freedom, which is called the "freedom of the original mind," never caused the fall of Adam.[128] It was rather squashed and lost, when Adam and Eve fell through their illicit love relationship which overpowered it.

Interestingly, the Unification notion of the freedom of the original mind as the freedom to make only the right choice for the purpose of creation coincides with what Flew and Mackie, the aforementioned atheist philosophers, perceived free will to be if there were an omnipotent and perfect God. This means that the Unification view of freedom is very different from the received notion of free will as the ability to freely choose between right and wrong, which is adhered to by aesthetic theodicists such as Leibniz, Plantinga and Hick.

---

[122] For this discussion, see Chapter 10 in the present book.
[123] EDP, p. 67.
[124] EDP, pp. 64-67, 75-76.
[125] EDP, p. 75.
[126] EDP, p. 74.
[127] EDP, pp. 43-44, 67, 77-78.
[128] EDP, p. 75.

This received notion of free will was, needless to say, theologically established and popularized by Augustine, who was combating Manichaean fatalism. According to the Bishop of Hippo, the fall of Adam as a historical event was caused by free will (*liberum arbitrium*), when it freely made the wrong choice: "Free will is the cause of our doing evil."[129] Therefore the fall means that Satan, Eve and Adam severally and individually had already fallen because of the free will of each of them, before Satan's temptation to Eve to eat the fruit of the tree of the knowledge of good and evil was able to make any appeal to her and her temptation to Adam to eat the fruit was able to make any appeal to him. With Augustine's atomistic, non-relational and non-sexual interpretation, the notion of the lineage of Satan is unthinkable. This is the interpretation that has been prevalent and dominant throughout the history of Christianity. Although Augustine also said correctly that the original sin of Adam has been relationally and sexually transmitted from generation to generation,[130] nevertheless he adhered to his non-relational and non-sexual interpretation of how evil originated in the fall of Adam. This is an inconsistency in his theology.

2. *Christ's Role and Ours*

Both Unification theodicy and the existing practical theodicies are aware of the important role of Christ for the removal of evil. But Unification theodicy is more advantageous in that it has a clearer view of Christ's role based on its understanding of a historical parallelism between Adam and Christ.

According to the Divine Principle, Adam and Eve fell sexually, realizing the Satan-centered four position foundation and the lineage of Satan for all humanity. Although they were originally supposed to realize the "three great blessings" of individual perfection, multiplication of children, and dominion over creation based on the God-centered four position foundation,[131] they failed to do so. Therefore the role of Christ as the last Adam was to restore the God-centered four position foundation and the lineage of God based on which to realize the three great blessings. For that purpose, Christ came as "the Son

---

129 Augustine, *The Confessions of St. Augustine*, trans. Rex Warner (New York: New American Library, 1963), p. 138.

130 For his doctrine of the transmission of original sin, see Augustine, "On Original Sin," and "On Marriage and Concupiscence," in Philip Schaff, ed., *A Select Library of the Nicene and Post-Nicene Fathers of the Christian Church*, vol. V: *Saint Augustin: Anti-Pelagian Writings* (Grand Rapids: MI: Wm. B. Eerdmans Publishing Co., 1971), pp. 237-55, 261-308.

131 EDP, pp. 32-36.

of God"[132] and as "the incarnation of the Word,"[133] born "without the original sin"[134] to be able to "redeem" our sins first.[135] Through the lineage of God, he was to multiply sinless children in the world. To be sure, the existing practical theodicies are also well aware that Christ came as the sinless Son of God and the incarnation of the Word to redeem us, but they do not know that his real role was to restore the God-centered four position foundation and the lineage of God as the basis for realizing the three great blessings. They do not explain the origin of evil, as they do not recognize historicity in the fall of Adam, let alone any sexual element in it.

Nevertheless, Unification theodicy is in basic agreement with the existing practical theodicies in holding that the essence of Christ's approach was love and sacrifice: "Love your enemies" (Mt. 5:44); "Greater love has no man than this, that a man lay down his life for his friends" (Jn. 15:13). Unification theodicy agrees that Christ knew the importance of that approach, because he was well aware that God could only be truly experienced through love, sacrifice and the cross: "If any man would come after me, let him deny himself and take up his cross daily and follow me" (Mt. 16:24; Mk. 8:34; Lk. 9:23). With this approach of generating God's immense power of love, Christ was to abolish evil, including gratuitous evil, in the world to build the kingdom of God on earth. Thus Unification theodicy clearly possesses a *theologia crucis* in the broader sense of the term, meaning that Christ was carrying the cross daily on the earth because of God's love. In this connection, Sun Myung Moon states of Christ: "He could overcome any difficulties for God and His will, and could even give up his own life. That is why God's love could dwell with him, and for the first time in human history, he could personally incarnate the love of God."[136]

In fact, Christ received so much opposition from the Israelite leaders that he had to walk the path of the real cross and be literally crucified. Even so, his approach was the same. Out of utmost love and forgiveness, he shouldered the evil of his opponents and of sinful humankind as well, even when he was thrown to the hand of Satan at the crucifixion. Because of this, God exerted his power for the resurrection of Christ. Thus the Divine Principle states: "God exercised His maximum power and resurrected Jesus," opening "the way for

---

[132] EDP, pp. 23, 128, 284.
[133] EDP, pp. 92, 95, 167, 180, 283.
[134] EDP, p. 168.
[135] EDP, pp. 56, 392.
[136] Sun Myung Moon, "Jesus' True Heart for God," in *Sermons of Reverend Sun Myung Moon*, vol. 2 (New York: HSA Publications, 1994), p. 270. The book shows that this sermon was originally delivered in Korean at Chung Pa Dong Church, Seoul, Korea, August 4, 1957.

all humanity to be engrafted with the resurrected Jesus and thereby receive salvation and rebirth."[137]

But this was only "spiritual salvation";[138] it necessarily could not include physical salvation because Christ lost his physical body on the cross. This is the reason why he must return in the last days to completely accomplish his original role, bringing joy to God. The Divine Principle claims that today is the last days,[139] and calls the returning Christ "the third Adam," while referring to the Christ of the first coming "the second Adam."[140] The existing practical theodicies, too, talk about the return of Christ, but they seem not to know the real reason why Christ must return. They are not aware that the real mission of the Christ of the first coming, which was to restore the God-centered four position foundation and the lineage of God based on which to realize the three great blessings, was actually left unaccomplished due to his premature death on the cross.

What, then, is our role? According to Unification theodicy, it is to imitate Christ (*imitatio Christi*) in bearing the cross daily for the sake of those who suffer from evil, so that God's power of love may overwhelm evil to abolish it. We are supposed to work together with the returning Christ (as well as with the Christ of the first coming) to quicken the time of the realization of the kingdom of God. To do so, after he redeems us, each of us is supposed to restore and realize, together with him, God's original three great blessings of individual perfection, multiplication of children, and dominion over creation.

We are expected to reach the first blessing of individual perfection first, before we are qualified to play our role of removing evil from the world. Individual perfection means that our mind and body are united centering on God, experiencing the "Heart of God" as if it were our own.[141] We are thus internally transformed. As was seen above, the God-centered mind-body unity is also the state in which we are able to exercise the "freedom of the original mind." Therefore we can voluntarily and creatively serve and help others to overcome evil and suffering. That way we can fulfill the "human portion of responsibility" which Adam and Eve could not fulfill.[142]

---

137 EDP, p. 279.
138 EDP, p. 118.
139 EDP, pp. 96-103.
140 EDP, p. 202.
141 EDP, p. 34.
142 EDP, p. 77.

From a trinitarian perspective, the role of Christ can be described as follows:[143] The inner Trinity of God (Heart, *Sungsang* and *Hyungsang*)[144] was supposed to be substantially manifested as the outer "trinity" of God, Adam and Eve, with Adam and Eve as the "True Parents of humankind" giving birth to all humankind in the lineage of God. That way, the kingdom of God on earth fulfilling God's three great blessings was to be realized at that time. But instead, the "fallen trinity" of Satan, Adam and Eve was formed due to their sexual fall, giving birth to all humanity in the lineage of Satan. At the time of Jesus Christ, therefore, the original inner Trinity of God was supposed to be substantiated as the outer "trinity" of God, Christ and his Bride, with Christ and his Bride as the True Parents giving rebirth to humankind on the earth. Due to the crucifixion of Christ, however, only the "spiritual trinity" of God, the resurrected Christ and the Holy Spirit was formed, with the resurrected Christ and the Holy Spirit as the "spiritual True Parents" giving only "spiritual rebirth." Therefore Christ must return, so that the "perfect trinity" of God, the returning Christ and his Bride may be substantially formed, with the returning Christ and his Bride as the True Parents of humanity giving "rebirth both spiritually and physically."

It goes without saying that the substantial, outer trinity of God, True Father and True Mother, which constitutes the God-centered four position foundation when the children reborn through them are added to it as a fourth position, brings forth the stage where all the stakeholders (God, True Father, True Mother and children) practice love and sacrifice toward one another for their victory over evil in the world.

3. Addressing the Difficulties of Aesthetic Theodicies

At this juncture, let us address the difficulties of aesthetic theodicies from the perspective of Unification theodicy.

As was already mentioned at the end of Subsection 4 of Section 1, the Divine Principle believes that evil's emergence as a substantial force is the result of a violation of God's purpose of creation, "forming a four position foundation under the dominion of Satan."[145] Evil, therefore, will cease to exist in the heavenly kingdom only under the dominion or sovereignty of God. Hence evil, including gratuitous evil, will be completely removed from the

---

143 EDP, pp. 171-72.

144 For how God's dual characteristics of *Sungsang* and *Hyungsang* centering on Heart can be equated with the Trinity within the Godhead, see Chapter 5, Section 4, Subsection 1 ("Containing Both Schools of Monarchianism") in the present book.

145 EDP, p. 39.

world when Christ and we who follow him restore and realize the original three great blessings based on the four position foundation under God's sovereignty. This is how Unification theodicy addresses aesthetic theodicies' first difficulty (i.e., the inability to eradicate evil from the world) and their second difficulty (i.e., the difficulty in aestheticizing gratuitous evil).

Unification theodicy may sometimes teach, echoing Hick's soul-making theodicy, that evil is useful for our character formation in the process of restoration through indemnity, as Rev. Moon himself says: "You become an important person through suffering."[146] But evil, including gratuitous evil, is definitely something "without which the world would have been a better place," to use David Ray Griffin's phrase. And it should never exist in the kingdom of God.

The Divine Principle also teaches that the eradication of evil from the world only begins with the "individual perfection" of Christ and of each human person who follows him. The individual perfection of persons is the state of personal transformation in which they are one with God through complete unity of mind and body centering on God. Naturally, therefore, they will voluntarily show up, like Christ does, with a spirit of love and sacrifice, at places where victims of evil exist, in order to shoulder their suffering for the removal of evil and suffering. They will thus contribute to building ideal families, societies, nations and eventually the kingdom of God. These people would never be satisfied with just theoretically and logically explaining away evil. Regarding Jesus Christ in this matter, Rev. Moon says: "He did not talk about the definition of love or its logic. He represented human history in the light of actualizing love. He did not mention anything that he personally did not feel or actualize."[147] This is how Unification theodicy addresses aesthetic theodicies' third difficulty (i.e., the lack of personal transformation on the part of the theodicist).

How does Unification theodicy address aesthetic theodicies' fourth difficulty (i.e., the lack of ability to deeply grasp the meaning of God's omnipotence and perfect goodness)? Unification theodicy does not treat God only as an object of philosophical thinking. It, as mentioned above, holds that God is a God of omnipotence and perfect goodness, but it also believes that God is a God of Heart who suffers as our Parent to work for our salvation and restoration. Therefore God's omnipotence and perfect goodness should be understood more deeply and even restated in the context of God's suffering

---

[146] Sun Myung Moon, *The Way of God's Will* (New York: HSA-UWC, 1980), p. 140.
[147] Moon, "Jesus' True Heart for God," p. 270.

Heart of love, which is expressed through the dynamic give and take action of God's dual characteristics of *Sungsang* (original internal nature) and *Hyungsang* (original external form).

Thus, unlike philosophical theism, Unification theodicy does not see God's omnipotence simply as his infinite sovereign power but rather as the "irrepressibility" of God's Heart of love,[148] nor does it define God's perfection as his immutable character but rather as the "unity" of the dynamic give and take action of God's dual characteristics of *Sungsang* and *Hyungsang*.[149] Therefore, while God is omnipotent in that his Heart is absolutely irrepressible, he can still feel an inner emotion of suffering when there is evil in the world; and while God is perfect in that his dual characteristics are completely united in their dynamic give and take action, he can still suffer from a constraint coming from the sinful world.[150]

The Unification theologian Young Oon Kim (1914–1989) quite clearly states that "God is not omnipotent,"[151] but this statement apparently comes from her reliance on the traditional definition of God's omnipotence in philosophical theism as his infinite sovereign power, without recognizing the possibility of the newly defined omnipotence of God's Heart here.

Unification theodicy also connects the problem of evil with redemption and the Trinity, in that it relates the redemptive role of the incarnated Christ and the Trinity with the abolition of evil. God's dual characteristics of *Sungsang* and *Hyungsang* centering on Heart, which make the threeness of God, constitute the "inner Trinity" of the Godhead, which in turn is economically manifested to constitute the "outer Trinity" of God and the True Parents of humanity, forming the God-centered four position foundation for the salvation and restoration of human beings and the world.[152]

4. Why God Did Not Intervene in the Fall

Exposition of the Divine Principle in its second chapter on "The Human Fall" has a section entitled "The Reason God Did Not Intervene in the Fall of the First Human Ancestors."[153] The main reason stated there is that human beings,

---

148 The "irrepressible" nature of God's Heart is mentioned in NEUT, pp. 23-24.
149 NEUT, p. 244.
150 For a more detailed discussion on this, see Chapter 6 in the present book.
151 Young Oon Kim, *Unification Theology* (New York: The Holy Spirit Association for the Unification of World Christianity, 1980), p. 67. In the revised edition of 1987, the language of "not omnipotent" about God is erased.
152 For the distinction between the inner and the outer Trinity, see Chapter 5, Section 4, Subsection 1 ("Containing Both Schools of Monarchianism") in the present book.
153 EDP, pp. 76-78.

created in the image of God and thus endowed with the "creative nature of God" in accordance with the "Principle of Creation" which is "absolute and perfect," must grow to perfection "by fulfilling their portion of responsibility" during the "period of their growth" without God's intervention.[154] This relates clearly to the "freedom of the original mind."

At a glance, this might look the same as Augustine's free will theodicy or Alvin Plantinga's free will defense or any other aesthetic theodicy's free will defense of God. But we have to be reminded that the Divine Principle's notion of the "freedom of the original mind" is different from the received notion of "free will" in aesthetic theodicies.[155] The former means our ability to always make the right choice, while the latter refers to our ability to freely choose between right and wrong. The former, unless it is clearly impeded to be overwhelmed by any undesirable, strong power from outside during the period of its growth, is only headed for the right choice, while the latter in and of itself is neutral in that it can go either right or wrong. Additionally, the former, being designed to work for the realization of God's purpose of creation, does not have to be aestheticized with it at all, while the latter, when making the wrong choice, needs to be theoretically justified to be harmonized and aestheticized with it. Therefore it would be inadequate to say that Unification theodicy is a free will defense.

Adam and Eve fell not because of the wrong choice of the will according to the received notion of free will, but because the freedom of the original mind that should be accompanied by the Principle was not fully developed or exerted in unbreakable oneness with God's realm of love. The fall of Adam and Eve took place because their freedom, not fully developed or exerted, was overwhelmed by the stronger power of illicit or unprincipled love.

Why, then, did God make the power of love "stronger" than the power of the Principle, thus making the sexual fall a possibility from the beginning? The reason is that "love [when centering on God] is truly the source and wellspring of our life and happiness," and that "in order for love to fulfill its proper role, its power must be stronger than the power of the Principle."[156]

God created the world in which love is stronger than the Principle. In a sense, therefore, it can be said that God was responsible for the possibility of the fall. Thus the Divine Principle talks about the "ninety-five percent

---

[154] EDP, p. 77.

[155] Young Oon Kim seems not to be very aware of this difference when she says that "human freedom," as understood in Unification theology, is "freedom of choice." See her *Unification Theology*, p. 119.

[156] EDP, p. 66.

responsibility" of God as the creator in comparison with the "five percent responsibility" of human beings.[157] But God was not directly responsible for the fall itself. Adam and Eve were responsible for it because they could not fully develop nor exercise their freedom.

In the course of our restoration, however, God's Heart of love for us is available through his dual characteristics of *Sungsang* and *Hyungsang*. Also, it has been made substantially available through Christ who suffered for us. Therefore, as long as we imitate Christ by bearing the cross for the sake of others, the power of the love of God, which is even stronger than the power of the Principle, will overwhelmingly help our freedom of the original mind to grow strong enough to overcome evil: "Since fallen people can also relate with God in freedom, if they follow the words of truth, form a common base and engage in give and take with Him, then the power of principled love can revive their original nature."[158] This seems to be another unique way of defending God in Unification theodicy. This is certainly related to the *theologia crucis* in which the power of the suffering love of God is a major theme.

Conclusion

Unification theodicy is not a *simple* theodicy, which denies one of the following three propositions: the omnipotence of God, the perfect goodness of God, and the reality of evil in the world. Nor is it an *aesthetic* theodicy, which, after accepting the above three propositions, adds a supplementary proposition to aesthetically harmonize evil with a greater purpose of God.

Rather, Unification theodicy is a *practical* theodicy. It agrees with the practical theodicies of Dorothee Soelle and Jürgen Moltmann that evil, including gratuitous evil, must be abolished instead of being logically and/or aesthetically explained away; that the theodicist must practice a *theologia crucis* to be equipped with God's suffering love for us, expressed in the cross of Christ, in order to be able to be qualified to tackle the problem of evil; and that God's omnipotence and perfect goodness, as understood in philosophical theism, should be challenged and restated in the context of God's suffering love for us seen in the Bible, so that they may be understood more profoundly.

Unification theodicy, however, differs from the practical theodicies of Soelle and Moltmann on at least three points. First, as was mentioned above,

---

[157] EDP, p. 157.
[158] EDP, p. 76.

Unification theodicy accepts the historicity of Adam's fall as the origin of evil, whereas the theodicies of the German theologians do not do so. Second, Unification theodicy understands that the role of Christ was to undo what Adam did historically, i.e., his sexual fall, his failure to realize the lineage of God for all humanity, whereas the theodicies of Soelle and Moltmann do not sufficiently address that role of Christ as they are not interested in knowing the origin of evil, by denying historicity to the fall of Adam. Third, Unification theodicy holds that Christ must return as the third Adam in the last days to finally complete his mission, together with his Bride, of realizing the lineage of God for all humankind to completely remove evil from the world, whereas the theodicies of Soelle and Moltmann do not go so far as to say this.

Even so, the emergence of the practical theodicies of these German theologians in the evolution of theodicy is very significant in that it provides a new understanding of God which, going beyond philosophical theism, converges very much with the Unification understanding of God. Especially when Moltmann newly proposes that God's omnipotence and perfect goodness respectively mean the omnipotence of God's love and the perfect unity of the Father and the Son within God, this echoes the Unification understanding that God's omnipotence and perfect goodness respectively mean the omnipotence of God's irrepressible Heart of love and the perfect unity of the dual characteristics of *Sungsang* and *Hyungsang* within God.

Chapter 9

Christology

In the history of Christian theology, there has been a conflict between two types of Christology: "high" and "low" Christology. High Christology, which is orthodox Christology, holds that Christ, as the *divine* Logos "consubstantial" (*homoousios*) with God the Father, is actually God who assumes a human nature merely added as a "nature in the person" (*physis enhypostatos*) of that divine Logos after the incarnation.[1] Christ, then, is not a human being in the same sense that we are human beings. By contrast, low Christology, which is liberal Christology, believes that Christ is a real man with a real human nature who assumes only some or no divinity.

According to Unification Christology in *Exposition of the Divine Principle*, Jesus is "a man who has completed the purpose of creation."[2] This certainly gives the impression that Unification Christology is a low Christology. In actuality, however, Unification Christology is far from being a low Christology, as it *recognizes* Christ's full divinity unlike low Christology which does *not.* Unification Christology firmly believes that Jesus as a man possesses "the same divine nature as God," by completing "the purpose of creation" at the individual level, i.e., by becoming "a person of perfect individual character"

---

[1] This will be further explained below in Section 1, Subsection 3 ("Second Council of Constantinople").

[2] *Exposition of the Divine Principle* (New York: H.S.A.-U.W.C., 1996), p. 166. Henceforth abbreviated as EDP.

who is "perfect as God is perfect"[3] and who is in "inseparable oneness with" God, assuming "a divine value, comparable to God."[4]

If Unification Christology is not a low Christology, it is obviously not a high Christology, either, since it holds, as seen above, that Jesus is "a man who has completed the purpose of creation." Unification Christology thus goes beyond the tension between the two types of Christology. It is "head-wing" Christology, so to speak,[5] and it can put an end to the never-ending conflict between high and low Christology (which may well be considered to be right- and left-wing, respectively), by uniting them.

The reason Unification Christology can unite both types of Christology is that Unification ontology uniquely asserts that God and created human beings as his true children can be *completely* united because both have "dual characteristics" in common. God's "dual characteristics" of *Sungsang* (original internal nature) and *Hyungsang* (original external form) and human beings' "dual characteristics" of *sungsang* (internal nature) and *hyungsang* (external form) can completely reflect, resonate with, and act upon, each other for the inseparable unity of God and human beings.[6]

Through dynamic dual characteristics, God completely lowers, denies and sacrifices himself to show love, and so do human beings such as Jesus. This is how they can be completely united.

But the reason why there has always been the conflict between high and low Christology in Christianity is that traditional Christian ontology has found it extremely difficult to affirm that God and human beings can be completely united. For, unlike Unification ontology, it has not believed that God and the world have something like the above-mentioned "dual characteristics" in common. It rather has believed, under some influence of Platonism and Aristotelianism, that God is "pure act" or "pure form" without "matter," thus being infinite, absolute and immutable, whereas the world has the dual characteristics of "form" and "matter," thus being finite, relative and mutable. Hence a deep gulf between God and the world. This is a difficult issue which has not been overcome in traditional Christian ontology. In the honest words of the American evangelical theologian Millard J. Erickson (1932–), "The

---

[3] EDP, p. 166.

[4] EDP, p. 164.

[5] The term "head wing" was coined by Sun Myung Moon, and by it he means a central position which has the capacity of uniting together the left and right wings.

[6] This point will be explained in more detail below in Section 2, Subsection 2 ("Unification Ontology"). For the meanings of the Korean words of *Sungsang* and *Hyungsang* in God (and also of *sungsang* and *hyungsang* in the created world), see Chapter 4, Section 1, Subsection 2 ("Dual Characteristics") in the present book.

separation of God and the human race is still a difficulty that has not been overcome."[7] According to him, Christology in this regard is "one of the most difficult of all theological problems, ranking with the Trinity and the relationship of human free will and divine sovereignty."[8]

However, the Christology of Martin Luther (1483–1546) considerably resembles Unification Christology, which is considered to have a solution to the difficult problem of the separation between God and human beings. As a biblical scholar, Luther was not interested in the Ecumenical Councils' ontological speculation of the divine Logos becoming incarnate so much as in the biblical depiction of how the concrete person of the historical Jesus as a man, when despised, lowers himself out of love for the sinful world in resemblance to God who, in turn, lowers himself to the level of the despised man Jesus. This way Luther was able to assert a real unity between God and the historical Jesus, thus being able to say that Jesus is fully divine as well as fully human. Significantly, it is related to his unique doctrine of God's dual characteristics: the "hidden God" (*deus absconditus*) and the "revealed God" (*deus revelatus*).[9] This, which is somewhat similar to the Unification doctrine of God's dual characteristics of *Sungsang* and *Hyungsang*, makes God truly relatable to the world, as the Unification doctrine does.

The present chapter has three sections, which will deal with orthodox Christology, Unification Christology, and the Christology of Luther, respectively. Section 1 will explain in some detail how orthodox Christology was established as high Christology through at least the following three of the first seven Ecumenical Councils: First Council of Nicea (325), Council of Chalcedon (451) and Second Council of Constantinople (553). Section 2 will argue that Unification Christology can well address both the problem of the gap between God and human beings and the problem of the conflict between high and low Christology, which have not been successfully addressed in the Christian tradition yet. Section 3 will show how the Christology of Luther resembles Unification Christology, thus being an important forerunner of Unification Christology, although there are understandably some significant differences between the two.

---

[7] Millard J. Erickson, *Introducing Christian Doctrine*, 3rd ed., ed. L. Arnold Hustad (Grand Rapids, MI: Baker Academic, 2015), p. 260.

[8] Ibid.

[9] This will be further explained below in Section 3, Subsection 3 ("Luther's *Theologia Crucis*").

§1. Orthodox Christology

This section will discuss, in some detail, three of the first seven Ecumenical Councils through which orthodox Christology was officially established as a high Christology: First Council of Nicea (325), Council of Chalcedon (451) and Second Council of Constantinople (553).

1. First Council of Nicea

The First Council of Nicea, the very first Ecumenical Council, was called by the Roman Emperor Constantine the Great (r. 306–337) in 325, and approximately 300 bishops participated. Against the teachings of Arius (c. 250–336), it proclaimed that the Son is "of one substance" (*homoousios*) with the Father.

According to Arius, who was the main figure in the Arian controversy, the Son is not of one substance with the Father: "He is neither part of God, nor of any substance."[10] The Son is not related to the Father by essence but only by will. Like other creatures, the Son was created *ex nihilo* by the Father: "there was a time when He was not."[11] God created the Son as the first-born of creatures and then created the whole world with the Son as his agent of creation. Hence the Son is the intermediary between God and the world, being neither true God nor part of the world. Even though he is the Son of God, he as a created being is "mutable" and "subject to change."[12] Arius was apparently interested in protecting the oneness of God as a monotheist when he decided that the Son is not part of God but a created being. He was also a follower of Origen (c. 184–c. 253) in this matter, because the great Alexandrian had held the Son to be "a second God"[13] and a creature.[14]

But those who were against the teachings of Arius appealed to Origen's other line of thought which had affirmed the eternal generation of the Son.[15] (Thus it is easy to see how Origen could be quoted on either side in the controversy.) The Council of Nicea, led by those who were against Arianism, officially condemned this heresy. This happened largely under the theological leadership of St. Athanasius (c. 296–373). Nicea formulated its creed as follows:

---

[10] Joseph Cullen Ayer, Jr., *A Source Book for Ancient Church History* (New York: AMS Press, 1970), p. 302.
[11] Ibid., p. 303.
[12] Ibid., pp. 303-4.
[13] Origen, *Contra Celsum*, trans. Henry Chadwick (Cambridge: Cambridge University Press, 1980), p. 296.
[14] Ibid., p. 294.
[15] In his *First Principles*, trans. G. W. Butterworth (London: S.P.C.K., 1936), p. 18, Origen says: "This is an eternal and everlasting begetting, as brightness is begotten from light."

> We believe in one God, the Father almighty, maker of all things, visible and invisible;
>
> And in one Lord Jesus Christ, the Son of God, begotten from the Father, only-begotten, that is, from the substance of the Father, God from God, light from light, true God from true God, begotten not made, of one substance with the Father, through Whom all things came into being, things in heaven and things on earth, Who because of us men and because of our salvation came down and became incarnate, becoming man, suffered and rose again on the third day, ascended to the heavens, and will come to judge the living and the dead;
>
> And in the Holy Spirit.
>
> But as for those who say, There was when He was not, and Before being born He was not, and that He came into existence out of nothing, or who assert that the Son of God is from a different hypostasis or substance, or is created, or is subject to alteration or change—these the Catholic Church anathematizes.[16]

The four anathemas in the last paragraph of the creed were specifically directed against the Arian teachings.

Noteworthy in the creed are the expressions regarding the Son, such as: "God from God, light from light, true God from true God," "begotten not made," and "of one substance (*homoousios*) with the Father." The Greek word *homoousios*, although it had not occupied a prominent place in the Christian theological vocabulary prior to Nicea due to its associations with the Gnostics and Paul of Samosata, was nevertheless used in the creed as a test word to express the Latin *consubstantialis*. In the West, the consubstantiality between the Son and the Father had long been an orthodox teaching thanks to the work of Tertullian (c. 155–c. 240) and Novatian (c. 200–258).

It is to be noted that after speaking of the Son's *homoousios* relationship with the Father within the Godhead, the creed says that the Son "came down and became incarnate, becoming man." This is indeed an approach "from above" in high Christology. After that passage we, of course, read something a little different, i.e., that the Son "suffered and rose again on the third day, ascended to the heavens," which may give the impression that Nicea also has an approach "from below" as in low Christology; but we should say that no real approach from below exists here. The reason is that according to the creed the Son is still "God from God, light from light, true God from true God," who would not have to ascend to the heavens in the sense in which someone

[16] J. N. D. Kelly, *Early Christian Doctrines*, rev. ed. (New York: Harper & Row, Publishers, 1978), p. 232.

other than God does. It can still be said, therefore, that the creed only has an approach from above.

2. *Council of Chalcedon*

While the First Council of Nicea decided that the Son is consubstantial with the Father, the Council of Chalcedon, the fourth Ecumenical Council, which was convoked by the Eastern Roman Emperor Marcian (r. 450–457) to be held in 451, and in which more than 500 bishops participated, took the incarnation further, affirming that the Son is consubstantial not only with the Father in divinity but also with us human beings in humanity except sin as a result of the incarnation. In this sense, Chalcedon was "the necessary complement and result of the discussion that led to the definition of Nicaea."[17]

But if the Son is thus both fully divine and fully human at the same time, what would be the relationship between the two in his person? In the fifth century, prior to Chalcedon, this was the biggest Christological issue, over which there were two different heretical positions: Nestorianism and Eutychianism. (Note, however, that these two heresies did not reject Nicene orthodoxy.) While Nestorianism made a real distinction between the divine and human natures of the Son by saying that they are separate from each other, Eutychianism confused the two. The Council of Chalcedon condemned both extremes, taking a position midway between them.

Nestorianism, named after Nestorius (c. 386–c. 450), is well summarized in his own words: "With the one name Christ we designate at the same time two natures… The essential characteristics in the nature of the divinity and in the humanity are from all eternity distinguished."[18] In other words, Nestorius held that Christ has only one person but two separate natures of divinity and humanity in it—separate in such a way that the integrity of each of the natures is always retained. It was for this reason that he rejected the description of Mary as the *Theotokos*, "Mother of God." Of course, he spoke of the relationship of the two natures in Christ in terms of "conjunction" (*synapheia*), but he preferred not to use the word "union" (*enosis*), except as a union of the will. Thus he seemed to endanger the essential unity of the person of Christ. His teachings were, therefore, strongly criticized by Cyril of Alexandria (c. 376–444), who proposed the "hypostatic union" of the two natures and stood for the *communicatio idiomatum* (communication of properties) in the two. Nestorianism

---

[17] Ayer, *Source Book*, p. 516.
[18] Ibid., p. 502.

was also officially condemned in the Council of Ephesus (431), the third Ecumenical Council, which was presided over by Cyril.

Nestorius was a member of the school of Antioch, which appreciated the historical humanity of Christ much more than the school of Alexandria; thus he separated the human nature from the divine nature in the person of Christ, affirming two separate natures. But he would not accept the more extreme idea of Diodorus of Tarsus (c. 330–c. 390), founder of the school of Antioch, that there are in Christ two separate persons.

The other heresy, Eutychianism, was named after Eutyches (c. 380 –c. 456). He came from the school of Alexandria, whose Platonic, mystical tradition led him to see in Christ the full making divine of the human, thereby confusing the two natures of Christ to say that there is only one nature after their union: "I confess that our Lord was of two natures before the union… but after the union one nature."[19] When he thus spoke of one nature after the union, Eutyches completely absorbed Christ's humanity into his divinity basically in line with the Alexandrian tradition. Therefore he naturally denied that the body of Christ was consubstantial with us. Because of his formula of one nature after the union, Eutyches became the real founder of "monophysitism" (*monos*, one; *physis*, nature). He was condemned at a local synod in Constantinople (448) and also criticized by Pope Leo I's (r. 440–461) *Tome* (449), which set forth the Latin orthodox formula of the *communicatio idiomatum* (communication of properties), according to which properties of the two distinct natures of Christ are united and communicated to each other in his one person. Eutyches was temporarily rehabilitated at the Robber Council (449), but was officially condemned again at the Council of Chalcedon (451).

Avoiding the two extremes of Nestorianism and Eutychianism, Chalcedon attempted to offer an orthodox settlement to the Christological controversy. The definition of Chalcedon reaffirmed the creed of Nicea as the standard of orthodoxy, setting the so-called Niceno-Constantinopolitan creed beside it. The definition also approved Cyril's two Letters (against Nestorianism) and Leo's *Tome* (against Eutychianism). The essential part of the Chalcedonian definition was what is shown below:

> In agreement, therefore, with the holy fathers, we all unanimously teach that we should confess that our Lord Jesus Christ is one and the same Son, the same perfect in Godhead and the same perfect in manhood, truly God and truly man, the same of a rational soul and body, consubstantial with the Father in Godhead, and the same

[19] Ibid., p. 514.

> consubstantial with us in manhood, like us in all things except sin; begotten from the Father before the ages as regards His Godhead, and in the last days, the same, because of us and because of our salvation begotten from the Virgin Mary, the *Theotokos*, as regards His manhood; one and the same Christ, Son, Lord, only-begotten, made known in two natures without confusion, without change, without division, without separation, the difference of the natures being by no means removed because of the union, but the property of each nature being preserved and coalescing in one *prosopon* and one *hupostasis*—not parted or divided into two *prosopa*, but one and the same Son, only-begotten, divine Word, the Lord Jesus Christ, as the prophets of old and Jesus Christ Himself have taught us about Him and the creed of our fathers has handed down.[20]

According to this, Christ has two perfect natures of divinity and humanity, as he is "consubstantial with the Father" and "consubstantial with us"; and these two perfect natures are united in his one person (*prosopon* or *hypostasis*) "without confusion, without change, without division, without separation" (*asynchytos*, *atreptos*, *adiairetos*, *achoristos*). Of the four celebrated negative adverbs, the first two were directed against the heresy of Eutychianism, and the last two against that of Nestorianism. Thus it affirmed both the unity and the distinction of the two natures in Christ at once with a good balance.

The unity of the two natures is seen not only in the anti-Nestorian expressions, "without division, without separation," but also in the repetitive use of the words "the same" for one and the same person of Christ and in the adoption of the title *Theotokos* for Mary. (Note, however, that the definition did not use the Cyrilline expression of "hypostatic union.") The distinction of the two natures, on the other hand, is seen not only in the anti-Eutychian expressions, "without confusion, without change," but also in the phrase, "in (*en*) two natures," of the final version of the definition, which replaced the first draft's phrase, "from (*ek*) two natures."[21]

This decision by Chalcedon was apparently as satisfactory a position as was possible at that time of theological controversies. It was a balanced, middle position between Nestorianism and Eutychianism, and more generally, between the schools of Antioch and Alexandria. Frankly, however, the use of the four negative expressions, "without confusion, without change, without division, without separation," was no positive, real explanation of the relationship of the two natures at all. Apparently, it was very difficult to explain

---

20 Kelly, *Early Christian Doctrines*, pp. 339-40.

21 Later, the expression, "from two natures," became the slogan of monophysitism.

it positively. Even Cyril of Alexandria said that it is "indescribable and inconceivable" and also "inexpressible and inexplicable."[22]

According to J. N. D. Kelly (1909–1997), therefore, "Chalcedon failed to bring permanent peace."[23] Although the West stayed loyal to Chalcedon, various kinds of monophysites in the East were still hostile to it as it was difficult for them to accept its explicit use of the "dyophysite" (*dyo*, two; *physis*, nature) term of "two natures," which seemed to them to be the triumph of Nestorianism. They felt that Chalcedon had in effect repudiated Cyril and his achievement at Ephesus in 431, although Chalcedon's use of "two natures" had never contradicted his Christology. The struggle was not just theological but political as well.

In order to reconcile especially with moderate monophysites, therefore, the Second Council of Constantinople was convoked by the Byzantine Roman Emperor Justinian the Great (r. 527–565) in 553, and it "subtly shifted the bias of the council [of Chalcedon], interpreting its teaching in a positive Cyrilline sense."[24] The two distinct natures in the person of the Son were now interpreted to be considerably less distinct. This new position is called "neo-Chalcedonianism."[25]

As will be shown in the following subsection, this neo-Chalcedonian interpretation was about the relationship of the two full natures of divinity and humanity in the person of the divine Logos incarnate, not considering the human nature apart from the incarnation.

3. Second Council of Constantinople

The First Council of Nicea and the Council of Chalcedon were the two most important Ecumenical Councils in the history of the Christian Church. The former "has always lived in Christian tradition as the most important in the history of the church,"[26] and the latter's definition is "theologically second only to that [of Nicea] in importance."[27]

But the Second Council of Constantinople took place in 553 to address the above-mentioned new tension between Chalcedonians and various kinds

---

[22] Henry Bettenson, ed., *Documents of the Christian Church*, 2nd ed. (London: Oxford University Press, 1963), p. 47.
[23] Kelly, *Early Christian Doctrines*, p. 342.
[24] Ibid., p. 343.
[25] The term, "neo-Chalcedonianism" was coined by the Belgian Catholic theologian Joseph Lebon (1879–1957) in 1909.
[26] Williston Walker, *A History of the Christian Church* (New York: Charles Scribner's Sons, 1970), p. 108.
[27] Ayer, *Source Book*, p. 516.

of monophysites. For their reconciliation, the council decided to be positively Cyrillian, showing its opposition to Nestorianism through its posthumous condemnation of the so-called "Three Chapters": 1) the person and work of Theodore of Mopsuestia (d. 428), the precursor of Nestorianism; 2) certain writings of Theodoret of Cyrus (c. 393–c. 458) against Cyril of Alexandria; and 3) the letter of Ibas of Edessa (d. 457) to Maris, which was against Cyrillianism and the Council of Ephesus. Pope Vigilius (r. 537–555), in spite of his initial refusal to participate, eventually approved the council.

As a result, Christological orthodoxy now asserted the "hypostatic union" of the two natures and allowed the phrases, "from two natures" (as well as "in two natures") and "one incarnate nature," provided that "these are recognized as asserting unity of person and not confusion of natures or essences."[28]

The council's assertion of the "hypostatic union" also resulted in an endorsement of "theopaschism," which teaches that when the incarnate Christ, who is the second person of the Trinity, suffers on the cross, God also suffers. Regarding this, the council stated: "If anyone does not confess that our Lord Jesus Christ who was crucified in the flesh is true God and the Lord of Glory and one of the Holy Trinity; let him be anathema."[29]

In the sixth century, even before the Second Council of Constantinople, theologians such as Leontius of Byzantium (485–543) made a more careful theological explanation, which greatly assisted Emperor Justinian's neo-Chalcedonian cause. Based on the Aristotelian categories, Leontius argued that a "nature" (*physis*) is a species which cannot be conceived of except as exemplified in a "person" (*hypostasis*) which is a particular subsisting entity, so that no nature should really be impersonal or non-hypostatic. Therefore the human nature of the Son would be a mere abstraction or a "non-hypostatic nature" (*physis anhypostatos*) unless it could be exemplified or individualized in the person of the divine Logos incarnate, so that it is indeed an "in-hypostatic nature" (*physis enhypostatos*) in the sense of being a nature which finds its person only *in* the particular person of the divine Logos incarnate.[30] Hence it is clearly in the person of the divine Logos incarnate and nowhere else that the two full natures are united.

---

[28] G. W. H. Lampe, "Christian Theology in the Patristic Period," in *A History of Christian Doctrine*, ed. Hubert Cunliffe-Jones (Philadelphia: Fortress Press, 1981), p. 144.
[29] See "The Anathemas of the Second Council of Constantinople." http://www.grace.org.uk/faith/2cconst.html.
[30] Lampe, "Christian Theology in the Patristic Period," p. 144. He indicates that Leontius expressed this argument in his *Contra Nestorianos et Eutychianos*.

This explanation by Leontius was able to well address the question of the status of the human nature of the Son in relationship to his person. This question, which had long been left unaddressed since Chalcedon, was: If the divine nature of Christ is clearly derived from the person of the divine Logos consubstantial with that of the Father from the beginning, what kind of relationship does his human nature, being added later in the incarnation, have with the person of the divine Logos? Chalcedon had no clear answer to this question: "The definition [of Chalcedon] was… not preceded by any clear understanding of what was to be understood by [human] nature in relation to hypostasis. This was left for later discussion."[31] This was finally taken care of by the neo-Chalcedonian clarification by Leontius.

Thus far we have dealt with the First Council of Nicea, the Council of Chalcedon and the Second Council of Constantinople, through which orthodox Christology was established. We realize here that this orthodox Christology turned out to endorse high Christology. It first started from above, by talking about the full divinity of Christ (Nicea I), and then went on to the addition of his full humanity (Chalcedon). And it was decided thereafter (Constantinople II) that his human nature is a "non-hypostatic nature" (*physis anhypostatos*), which has no person of its own, so that its real personhood is only in the person of the divine Logos incarnate as an "in-hypostatic nature" (*physis enhypostatos*). Christ, then, is not a man in the same sense that we are human beings. Some say that Christ is "not a man, but Man."[32] Thus he has traditionally been called the "God-Man" (*Theanthropos*).

This was actually a *tacit* admission of the secondary status of the human nature of the Son in spite of Chalcedon's *explicit* recognition of his full humanity as well as his full divinity. For his human nature, even if it was said to be fully human, has no person of its own unlike ours. This marked the official victory of high Christology over low Christology. As a result, Christologists in orthodoxy have not been open to low Christology at all.

But the fact is that low Christology, which starts from the level at which Christ is a real man, has continuously revolted against high Christology. Low Christology has historically been advocated by adoptionism, Ebionites, Dynamistic Monarchianism, Arianism, eighth-century Spanish adoptionism and some medieval theologians. After the Enlightenment, the influence of low Christology became much stronger. As has already been mentioned, the reason

---

[31] Ayer, *Source Book*, p. 516.

[32] Nels F. S. Ferré, "Know Your Faith." https://www.religion-online.org/book-chapter/chapter-2-the-son-of-his-love/.

for the never-ending conflict between high and low Christology is that traditional Christian ontology has not been able to solve the problem of the gap between God and human beings, and more generally, between God and the world.

§2. Unification Christology

Unification Christology claims to be able to offer a solution to the problem of the gap between God and human beings based on Unification ontology, which talks about the dynamic give and take action between "dual characteristics" shared commonly by both God and human beings. This is how Unification Christology unites high and low Christology.

1. Neither a High Christology nor a Low Christology

Unification Christology holds that Jesus "is not God Himself,"[33] and that he is "a man who has completed the purpose of creation."[34] This certainly gives the impression as if Unification Christology were a low Christology and not a high Christology. In fact, many Christians and Unificationists alike have received this impression, thinking that Unification Christology is a low Christology.[35] And orthodox Christologists, who are not open at all to anything other than high Christology, would immediately react to Unification Christology negatively, determining that it, not being a high Christology, is totally unacceptable.

But it should be clearly stated here that Unification Christology, while not being a high Christology, is not a low Christology, either. The reason is that it has a way to recognize the full divinity of the man Jesus unlike low Christology which does not. Unification Christology firmly believes that Jesus as a man possesses "the same divine nature as God," by completing "the purpose of creation" at the individual level, i.e., by becoming "a person of perfect

---

[33] EDP, p. 167.

[34] EDP, p. 166.

[35] Durwood Foster, a Christian theologian, for example, says that Unification Christology is "typically a 'low' Christology of the Antiochen type"; see his "Unification and Traditional Christology," in *Ten Theologians Respond to the Unification Church*, ed. Herbert Richardson (New York: Rose of Sharon Press, 1981), p. 183. Young Oon Kim, a Unification theologian, also thinks Unification Christology to be a low Christology, when she says that "Unificationism agrees with the recent trends in Christology that Jesus was human, as well as somehow divine"; see her *Unification Theology* (New York: HSA-UWC, 1987), p. 162.

individual character" who is "perfect as God is perfect"[36] and who is in "inseparable oneness with" God, assuming "a divine value, comparable to God."[37] Thus he "may well be called God because, as a man who has realized the purpose of creation and who lives in oneness with God, he has a divine nature."[38]

One might wonder if created human beings can really become fully divine like God. But we can be reminded that Eastern Orthodox Christianity, if not Catholic and Protestant Christianity in the West, has the idea of "deification" (*theosis*), according to which human beings can be made divine because of what happens in the incarnation. In the incarnation the divine Logos becomes flesh, taking on our human nature, so that we may become divine, taking on God's divine nature. In the words of Athanasius, "he was incarnate that we might be made god."[39] We can even become fully divine like God through the incarnation, as it "makes man God to the same degree as God Himself became man" according to St. Maximus the Confessor (c. 580–662).[40]

Consequently, Unification Christology's assertion that Jesus as a created human being can be fully divine is not entirely novel, although there are at least two recognizable differences between Unification Christology and the position of Eastern Christianity. A first difference is that whereas Eastern Orthodox Christianity is still based on high Christology in holding that the divine Logos taking on a human nature can make human beings fully divine, Unification Christology is not a high Christology in maintaining that Jesus is the first real human being to become fully divine before all other humans can become fully divine.

A second difference is that whereas Eastern Orthodox Christianity may have no clear ontological explanation of how human beings can be fully divine other than its faith in the high Christology of the incarnation, Unification Christology has a unique explanation through Unification ontology, which holds that God and a human being, while being discrete from each other, can completely be united, so that the human being may be able to be fully divine. This Unification ontology will be explained in the following subsection.

From the above, it is very clear that Unification Christology, which asserts the full divinity of Jesus, is not a low Christology. Nor is it a high Christology.

---

36 EDP, p. 166.
37 EDP, p. 164.
38 EDP, p. 167.
39 Athanasius of Alexandria, *On the Incarnation*, trans. John Behr (Yonkers, NY: St. Vladimir's Seminary Press, 2011), p. 167.
40 G. E. H. Palmer et al., eds., *The Philokalia*, vol. II (London: Farber and Faber, 1981), p. 178.

Unification Christology, then, is "head-wing" Christology to unite high and low Christology, putting an end to the never-ending conflict between the two different types of Christology.

2. Unification Ontology

Unification ontology maintains that the whole of reality is characterized by what it calls "dual characteristics." God has the dual characteristics of *Sungsang* (original internal nature) and *Hyungsang* (original external form); and the created world, in resemblance to God, has the similar dual characteristics of *sungsang* (internal nature) and *hyungsang* (external form).[41]

When God totally invests and sacrifices himself out of love for the world, he makes complete give and take action between his dual characteristics of *Sungsang* and *Hyungsang* centering on his Heart. When he does so, he can send his "acting energy,"[42] his vibration of love, as a divine input of encouragement for give and take action to completely occur not only between the dual characteristics of *sungsang* and *hyungsang* of each and every created being at the individual level, but also between two or more different created beings at the social level.

The world thus encouraged by God to be a unified world at the individual and social levels, then, responds to God on its part, by reflecting the complete unity of God's dual characteristics of *Sungsang* and *Hyungsang*. When God thus receives the stimulation of the world's reflection of himself, he feels "joy,"[43] and so does the world, of course. God would not be able to feel the stimulation of joy from the world if the world were not discrete from him but identical with him. This joy is indeed "God's purpose of creation."[44] The realization of the purpose of creation this way means that God and the world reciprocally act upon each other to have the relationship of complete unity with each other, although they are discrete from each other.

A good analogy of this unity between God and the world would be the unity of resonance between two different tuning forks, each of which has two prongs which would be equivalent to dual characteristics. When one tuning fork with its two prongs sends a vibration of sound, the other one with its two prongs receives it with the same frequency to start vibrating and sends it back to the first one. The first one, in turn, receives it to keep vibrating and sends it

---

[41] EDP, pp. 17-18.

[42] *New Essentials of Unification Thought: Head-Wing Thought* (Tokyo: Kogensha, 2006), p. 8. Henceforth abbreviated as NEUT.

[43] EDP, p. 33.

[44] Ibid.

back to the other one. Thus the two discrete tuning forks continue to act upon each other, creating the unity of resonance with each other. Sun Myung Moon very often talks about the analogy of tuning forks because Unification ontology teaches the role of dual characteristics for the unity of love between God and the world. For example, he says:

> When you live completely for others, you are reaching the very essence of God's own being. God's vibrations become your vibrations. God's feelings are naturally transmitted to you. Living this way, you become a resonant body of God's heart and love. As much as two tuning forks resonate together, you and God always resonate together.[45]

In the case of Jesus, when the complete unity of God's dual characteristics of *Sungsang* and *Hyungsang* is given to the man Jesus as a divine encouragement of unity, and then reflected by his added effort to complete the unity of his own dual characteristics of *sungsang* (mind) and *hyungsang* (body) at the individual level, and also by his added effort to complete his relationship of love with other human beings at the social level, God feels joy, and so do Jesus and other human beings, of course. What is important here is that God would not feel the stimulation of joy from Jesus if Jesus were not discrete from him but identical with him. This joy is God's purpose of creation. The realization of the purpose of creation here means that God and Jesus as a created man mutually act upon each other to bring forth their relationship of complete unity with each other, although they may be discrete from each other. In this complete unity between them, Jesus can fully assume God's divinity; hence his full divinity as well as his full humanity.

"Divinity," then, would not be something which is exclusively God's. It would be something that human beings, as the image of God, also can possess when their dual characteristics completely resonate with God's. If so, divinity must be referring to the state of the complete unity of dual characteristics in total investment of love and sacrifice for the sake of others. God certainly has it already, and human beings, too, can have it because they were created to completely resemble and reflect God through the dual characteristics.

What is to be noted here is that when the complete unity of God's dual characteristics of *Sungsang* and *Hyungsang* is reflected by Jesus' complete unity of his dual characteristics of *sungsang* (mind) and *hyungsang* (body) at the individual level, and also by his complete relationship of love with other human

[45] Sun Myung Moon, "True Unification and One World." Founder's Address at World Media Conference, Moscow, USSR, April 10-11, 1990. https://www.tparents.org/Moon-Talks/sunmyungmoon90/SM900410.HTM.

beings at the social level, it means that Jesus as a man of the complete unity of his mind and body centered on God is able to completely invest and lower himself to love all other human beings even including his enemies. This is well attested in the Gospels of the New Testament. In the same manner, God as a God of the complete unity of *Sungsang* and *Hyungsang* entirely lowers himself to love Jesus and all other human beings in the world.

At this juncture, the suffering of God can be mentioned briefly.[46] If God feels joy when the unity of his dual characteristics of *Sungsang* and *Hyungsang* is reflected in the world at the individual and social levels, then God suffers when that is not the case and there are undesirable situations of disunity or even unity centered on Satan in the world. So, when the Jewish leaders' unfaithful disunity with Jesus caused him to suffer and die on the cross, God also suffered. In the words of Rev. Moon, "Who knew the miserable mind and heart of God who had to turn a blind eye to the death of His beloved son, Jesus?"[47] The suffering of God, however, does not mean that God is not omnipotent. God still is omnipotent, in that his Heart of love in its persuasive power of love is so "irrepressible"[48] that he will win over any undesirable situations in the world in the end, no matter how much time it may take.

3. As Compared with Traditional Christian Ontology

In order to understand Unification ontology better, it will be good to compare it with traditional Christian ontology.

Traditional Christian ontology, under the influence of prominent ancient Greek philosophers such as Plato and Aristotle, puts God in a very transcendent position distant from the created world, although the Bible often talks about God's intimate relationship of love with human beings in the world. Traditional Christian ontology even uses the terminology of ancient Greek philosophy quite often, saying that God is "pure form" (or "pure act") without "matter," thus being purely spiritual and completely actualized apart from the world, which, by contrast, is always imperfect because it has "matter" as well as "form." So God is not a God of dual characteristics, while the world has the dual characteristics of "form" and "matter." There is, then, a sharp contrast between God and the world. God is perfect, infinite and immutable on his own, while the world is always imperfect, finite and mutable. God basically cannot

---

[46] For a fuller treatment of God's suffering from a Unificationist perspective, see Chapter 6 in the present book.
[47] Sun Myung Moon, "Sun Myung Moon's Insights on the Heart of God (Part 1 of 3)." http://www.tparents.org/moon-talks/moon-other/SunMyungMoon-Heart-1.htm.
[48] NEUT, pp. 23-24.

be acted upon by the world, while the world can be acted upon by God. God, therefore, does not suffer at all, no matter what may happen in the world; for example, God did not suffer, when Jesus suffered on the cross in the world. There can be no reciprocal relationship between God and the world. God and the world, then, cannot become completely one.

This also means that God and human beings as part of the created world cannot become completely one, either. Thus God cannot be human, and human beings cannot be divine. This deep gulf between God and human beings has not been overcome in traditional Christian ontology, as Erickson admits: "The separation of God and the human race is still a difficulty that has not been overcome."[49]

Consequently, if Jesus is divine, he must be none other than God; and if he is human, he must be none other than a created man. He cannot be both God and a man at the same time, nor can he be both divine and human at the same time. Sounding contradictory to this, however, Chalcedon proclaimed that the Son is both fully divine and fully human at the same time, and that his two full natures of divinity and humanity are united in his person "without confusion, without change, without division, without separation."

Chalcedon decided to follow the idea of Nicea that the Son is already consubstantial with God the Father. Thus the only way for the Son to be both fully divine and fully human at the same time would be that he is God, who takes on a full human nature, and not a human being in the same sense that we are human beings. His human nature, therefore, would have no personhood of its own as a "non-hypostatic nature" (*physis anhypostatos*), finding its real personhood only in the person of the divine Logos as an "in-hypostatic nature" (*physis enhypostatos*), as was decided by neo-Chalcedonians such as Leontius of Byzantium in the sixth century.

Even so, the unity of the two full natures of divinity and humanity in the person of the divine Logos was believed by Chalcedonian orthodoxy to be "without confusion, without change, without division, without separation." Apparently, the use of the four negative adverbs, no matter how satisfactory they may have sounded for the refutation of the heresies of both Nestorianism and Eutychianism at that time, was still an indication that Chalcedon was puzzled with how the two natures are united. This is why Erickson says that "the relationship between these two natures in the one person" is "one of the

[49] Erickson, *Introducing Christian Doctrine*, p. 260.

most difficult of all theological problems, ranking with the Trinity and the relationship of human free will and divine sovereignty."[50]

Unification Christology has no such problem, as it can assert, based on the Unification ontology of dual characteristics, that Jesus as a man can completely unite with God, thus being able be fully divine, while at the same time being fully human.

Furthermore, when Unification Christology affirms the two full natures of divinity and humanity of the Son equally, it is neither a high Christology nor a low Christology. It can unite both types of Christology. For it affirms the reciprocal relationship of unity between God and Jesus, which encompasses both a movement from above and a movement from below at the same time. The movement from above descends from God to Jesus, as the complete unity of God's dual characteristics of *Sungsang* and *Hyungsang* is given to Jesus as a divine input for unity. At the same time, the movement from below goes up from Jesus to God, as the unity of Jesus' dual characteristics of *sungsang* and *hyungsang* at the individual level and his unity of love with others at the social level reflect God's dual characteristics of *Sungsang* and *Hyungsang* for God to be stimulated to feel joy.

4. *Assessing Chalcedon's Four Negative Adverbs*

When Unification Christology maintains that God and the created man Jesus are completely united with each other, it presupposes that they are discrete from each other. For there would be no real relationship of unity without discreteness of the relata.

The presupposition that God and Jesus are discrete from each other means that their unity is "without confusion" and "without change"; thus Unification Christology is not Eutychian. Also, the conclusion that they are completely united with each other with the presupposition of their discreteness means that their unity is "without division" and "without separation"; thus Unification Christology is not Nestorian, either. Therefore Unification Christology can support Chalcedon's two anti-Eutychian adverbs, "without confusion, without change," and its two anti-Nestorian adverbs, "without division, without separation," although Unification Christology is about the unity of the two discrete figures of God and Jesus, while Chalcedon was concerning the unity of the two distinct natures of divinity and humanity in the person of the divine Logos.

---

[50] Ibid.

Another difference between Unification Christology and Chalcedon, which is an important one, is that Unification Christology gives a positive explanation of the meanings of Chalcedon's four negative adverbs based on the Unification ontology of dual characteristics, whereas Chalcedon does not show any positive explanation of them, given traditional Christian ontology's lack of ability to explain the real unity of the two natures.

§3. The Christology of Martin Luther

Something similar to Unification Christology's solution to the problem of the gap between God and human beings can be seen in the Christology of Martin Luther, because his Christology includes a doctrine of God's dual characteristics between the "hidden God" (*deus absconditus*) and the "revealed God" (*deus revelatus*) based on his "theology of the cross" (*theologia crucis*) in resemblance to the Unification doctrine of God's dual characteristics of *Sungsang* and *Hyungsung*. Therefore, for Luther's Christology as well as for Unification Christology, Jesus is a man who is completely united with God to assume the full divine nature as well as the full human nature. In this sense, Luther's Christology is a significant forerunner of Unification Christology.

1. Luther's Soteriological Orientation

Luther believed that Christ has the two distinct, full natures of divinity and humanity united in his one person. In this sense he was Chalcedonian. He was actually knowledgeable of the contents of the Ecumenical Councils including Chalcedon. However, he was not interested in the Ecumenical Councils' ontological speculation of how the divine Logos became human in the incarnation so much as in the biblical depiction of what the historical Jesus, already with the two full natures of divinity and humanity, did for our salvation. This point is evident in his following words:

> Christ has two natures. What has that to do with me? If he bears the magnificent and consoling name of Christ, it is on account of the ministry and the task which he took upon himself; it is that which gives him his name. That he should by nature be both man and God, that is for him. But that he should have dedicated his ministry and poured

> out his love to become my savior and my redeemer, it is in that that I find my consolation and well-being.[51]

Thus Luther was basically disinterested in the traditional speculation on who Christ is *in himself* in favor of a more soteriological appreciation of who Christ is *for me.* His soteriological interest in Christ apparently came from his deep awareness of the helpless situation of sinful human beings including himself. When he was an Augustinian monk, he existentially struggled because he could not feel confident of his own Christian salvation. That led him to the Bible, from which he learned that the grace of God replaces the wrath of God through one's faith in Christ who, like God, chose to be despised on the cross out of love for sinners. Hence came his *theologia crucis*, which became the very foundation of his Protestant Reformation.

2. Free from High Christology

As long as he was not particularly interested in the Ecumenical Councils' ontological speculation on Christ, Luther was basically free from traditional high Christology. Whereas high Christology starts from the divine Logos above and then has him take on a human nature, Luther believed that the concrete person of the historical Jesus, as seen in the Bible, is a man somehow composite of divine and human natures already. Hence, whereas orthodox Christology believes Christ to be the immutable divine Logos taking on a new manner of existence which contains a human nature, Luther believed Christ to be the historical Jesus who is already God in a substantial union with a man.

This means that whereas traditional high Christology tacitly acknowledges a second-rate status of the human nature of Christ which as a later addition would be a mere abstraction or a "non-hypostatic nature" (*physis anhypostatos*) apart from the incarnation, Luther understood that the full human nature of the historical Jesus is the starting point of Christology: his human nature is "the holy ladder" to his divine nature.[52] This does not mean that he proposed a low Christology. In fact, he was very critical toward Arius.[53] Thus, if he was free from high Christology, he was also free from low Christology.

What is important is that Luther's Christology actually went beyond the tension between high and low Christology, even being able to unite them. He

---

[51] Martin Luther, *Luthers Werke. Kritische Gesamtausgabe* (Weimar: Herman Böhlaus Nachfolger, 1883), 16, 217, 33ff. Henceforth referred to as WA. Also cited in Thomas G. Weinandy, *Does God Change?* (Still River, MA: St. Bede's Publications, 1985), pp. 101-2.

[52] Martin Luther, *Luther's Works*, vol. 29, ed. Jaroslav Pelikan (St. Louis, MO: Concordia Publishing House, 1968), p. 111. Henceforth abbreviated as LW.

[53] LW 12, pp. 54-55.

maintained that God and Jesus as a man are truly united because God sacrifices and lowers himself together with Jesus, who, in turn, sacrifices and lowers himself on the cross out of love for sinners. This is evident from Luther's idea contained in his *theologia crucis* that God is "hidden in the despised man Christ" on the cross. This is highlighted by the Swedish Lutheran theologian Gustaf Aulén (1879–1977), when he talks about Luther's Christology's unique ability to go beyond the tension between high and low Christology:

> The characteristic viewpoint of faith is well expressed in Luther's words that it is most vital to perceive that God who is "hidden in the despised man Christ [on the cross]." These words contain the whole inner tension of the confession of Christ—God in the humble circumstances of man. *Here no attempt is made to escape the tension by means of a Christology of separation* [which is a low Christology] *or theophany* [which is a high Christology]. The revelation of God is a revelation "in secret." The eye beholds a human figure who lived under historical conditions and was crucified on Golgotha, but in this lowliness faith sees nothing less than the incarnation of love. *Christian faith thus preserves its twofold front* [of high and low Christology].[54]

Needless to say, the ability of Luther's Christology to unite high and low Christology is related to his view of the real unity of the two natures of Christ, which is his new interpretation of the *communicatio idomatum* beyond Chalcedon.

3. Luther's Theologia Crucis

What, then, is Luther's *theologia crucis*, from which we can see his soteriological appreciation of Christ, his Christology's ability to unite high and low Christology, and his view of the real unity of the two natures in his new interpretation of the *communicatio idiomatum*?

His *theologia crucis*, succinctly expressed in his *Heidelberg Disputation* of 1518,[55] is a theology which believes that God is revealed only in the suffering and death of Christ on the cross: "God can be found only in suffering and the cross";[56] "the visible and manifest things of God [are] seen through suffering and the cross."[57] For God's grace for us sinners is such that his only way to substantiate it is by stooping down to the lowly level of the despised man Christ in suffering, who sacrifices himself on the cross to love us.

---

[54] Gustaf Aulén, *The Faith of the Christian Church*, trans. Erick H. Wahlstrom (Philadelphia: Fortress Press, 1983), p. 193. Italics added. Also bracketed words added.

[55] Martin Luther, *Heidelberg Disputation*. https://bookofconcord.org/sources-and-context/heidelberg-disputation/. Henceforth abbreviated as HD.

[56] HD, proof of thesis 21.

[57] HD, thesis 20.

This work of God in the lowliness of Christ can be understood and appreciated by those who truly despair of their sinful nature and who therefore humbly lower and deny themselves to be faithful in fear of God: "It is certain that man must utterly despair of his own ability before he is prepared to receive the grace of Christ."[58] However those who seek to ascend to the level of glorious accomplishment through their own "attractive and good" human works[59] cannot understand it. To them it is always "unattractive" and even appears "evil."[60] It looks foolish to them, as they have no fear of God. They hate suffering and the cross in favor of the glory of their human works including human intellect. Hence Luther's distinction between the "theology of the cross" (*theologia crucis*) and the "theology of glory" (*theologia gloriae*).[61] Paradoxically, while the former eventually leads to graceful victory over sin, the latter leads to sin.

What we can notice here is the polarity between the "hidden God" (*deus absconditus*) and the "revealed God" (*deus revelatus*), as understood by Luther. The hidden God stays in his absolute majesty, thus being transcendent and hidden from the world, but the revealed God is revealed to the world through Christ. The hidden God "in his own nature and majesty" is so transcendent that "nothing can be exalted" above him and "all things are under his majesty"; but the revealed God "is known to us and has dealing with us."[62] The hidden God is unapproachable and even terrifying with his wrath, but the revealed God is approachable and graceful through Christ. So there is a tension between these two aspects of one and the same God.

According to Luther, this tension between the hidden God and the revealed God disappears when the former is overcome by the latter for their unity. The former is overcome by the latter for their unity when the latter works in such a gracious way that the believer is grasped by the latter who is revealed in Christ. But the unity of the two sides of God may not happen when there are those who are not grasped by the latter. They are not grasped by the latter, as they are not faithful and humble enough to be able to understand the work of Christ who died on the cross. (In this sense, even the revealed God in Christ is still "hidden" from them.[63]) And they do not understand the grace of Christ

---

[58] HD, thesis 18.
[59] HD, thesis 3.
[60] HD, thesis 4.
[61] HD, thesis 21.
[62] LW 33, p. 139.
[63] The sense in which even the revealed God of love in Christ is "hidden" from those who are far from faithful and humble is to be distinguished from the sense in which the hidden God in his absolute majesty is literally hidden from the world. It can be seen in Luther's writings. For

which comes from the revealed God, with the result that they are only left with the hidden God who is unapproachable, terrifying and wrathful.

Luther holds that for the unity between the two sides of God to happen, those of us who are grasped by the revealed God are to begin by relating to Christ, in whom the revealed God is working; we begin from Christ: "Begin from below, from the Incarnate Son… Christ will bring you to the Hidden God… If you take the revealed God, he will bring you to the Hidden God at the same time."[64]

Here we can see the dynamic relationship between the hidden God and the revealed God for the making of God's close relationship with the despised man Christ and also for the making of Christ's close relationship with the believer. This point by Luther was something unthinkable in traditional Christian ontology. For, as was already stated, traditional Christian ontology believes that God as "pure form" (or "pure act") is an absolute and immutable God of simplicity without having any dynamic polarity within himself, who therefore cannot have any close relationship with the created world.

Luther's new thinking in this regard is considerably similar to Unificationism, as his view of the polarity between the hidden God and revealed God resembles the Unification doctrine of God's dual characteristics of *Sungsang* and *Hyungsang*. In both cases, the real unity between God and human beings is established when the give and take action between the two distinguishable sides of God centering on the selfless commitment of love and sacrifice for the sake of others is reflected by the same kind of give and take action at the level of human beings centering on Christ.

4. Real Unity between God and Christ (and Human Beings)

Consequently, Luther's *theologia crucis* would affirm the relationship of real unity between the infinite God and the finite human nature, supporting the idea that the finite is capable of carrying the infinite (*finitum capax infiniti*).[65] The full divinity of God can be embodied in the full humanity of Christ.

This is related to Luther's new view of the *communicatio idiomatum*. Whereas Chalcedon and the Christian tradition thereafter simply meant by the *communicatio idiomatum* that the properties of the two distinct natures of Christ are each predicated of his person, thus being still distinct from each other in

---

example, the proof of thesis 21 of the *Heidelberg Disputation* says: "He who does not know Christ does not know God *hidden* in suffering"; italics added.

[64] Luther's words, as cited in Dennis Ngien, *The Suffering of God according to Marin Luther's 'Theologia Crucis'* (Vancouver, British Columbia: Regent College Publishing, 1995), p. 121.

[65] Ngien, *The Suffering of God*, p. 57.

their communication, Luther in a non-traditional way used the formula to mean that they can have their own mutual participation, interchange and intercommunication directly with each other: "Those things, which are human, are correctly predicated of God, and on the other hand, those things which are divine are correctly predicated of the *homo*."[66]

Suffering, for example, is undoubtedly a property of the human nature of Christ, and according to the Chalcedonian tradition, it is distinct from his divine nature, so that while Christ does not suffer in his divine nature, he suffers in his human nature. According to Luther, however, suffering as a property of the human nature can directly be predicated of the divine nature, so that Christ suffers in his divine nature as well. According to Luther, therefore, God suffers. Hence he says: "This is the communication of attributes. Those things which Christ suffered are attributed to God since they are one."[67] This certainly echoes the Unification understanding of God's suffering. It should be recalled, however, that the Second Council of Constantinople, because of its Cyrillian reinterpretation of Chalcedon, was able to talk about the suffering of God long before Luther.

The reason for Luther's new view of the *communicatio idiomatum* was that he believed that as the cross completely unites God and the man Christ in accordance with his *theologia crucis*, the divine and human natures are no longer abstract concepts in separation from each other but things which are actively involved in the concrete person of Christ united with God. In the words of Luther himself, "Abstract concepts should not be cut loose, or our faith will become false. But one believes in a concrete sense (*in concreto*) saying that this man is God, etc. Then the properties are attributed."[68] Going beyond the abstract level, all properties of the two distinct natures of Christ acquire new meanings to be interchangeable.

5. Differences between Luther's Christology and Unification Christology

In spite of the above-mentioned important similarities between Luther's Christology and Unification Christology, however, there are a few significant differences between them.

First, the hidden God and the revealed God in Luther's Christology may not be exactly the same as God's *Sungsang* and *Hyungsang* in Unification Christology. Luther's theory of the polarity of God tends to be existential,

---

66 Cited in Dennis Ngien, "Chalcedonian Christology and Beyond: Luther's Understanding of the *Communicatio Idiomatum*," *The Heythrop Journal* XLV (2004): 62. Italics original.

67 WA 39.2, 120, 21-22.

68 WA 40.3, 707, 22-27.

whereas the Unification doctrine of God's dual characteristics is more ontological and scientific. Luther's spiritual journey started with his experience of the wrath of the hidden God as a struggling Augustinian monk, and it was followed by his discovery of the tremendous grace of the revealed God in Christ. But God's dual characteristics of *Sungsang* and *Hyungsang* in Unificationism are induced from our observation of the created world that each and every being in it has the dual characteristics of *sungsang* and *hyungsang*.

So, how the two sides of God are united is explained rather differently by Luther and Unificationism (although the selfless commitment of love and sacrifice is recognized similarly by both as the center of the unity of God's two sides). According to Luther, their unity is reached when the hidden God is overcome by the revealed God who grasps the believer in Christ. But according to Unificationism, the unity of the two sides of God is made centering on his Heart of love, giving a divine encouragement of unity for Christ and the believer to unite.

A second difference is related to the first. It is that although both Luther's Christology and Unification Christology similarly involve the dynamics of dual characteristics for the real unity of God and Jesus (and other human beings), nevertheless both approaches have quite different presuppositions. Luther's Christology presupposes the helplessly sinful condition of human beings to argue for the need of the grace of the revealed God in Christ, from which a theory of God's dual characteristics is developed, whereas Unification Christology presupposes the idea of God's dual characteristics as part of the principle of creation in the ideal world and applies it even to the salvific providence as a legitimate principle. It is interesting to observe that this difference between Luther's Christology and Unification Christology still results in the same kind of dynamics of dual characteristics which involves the commitment of love and sacrifice.

Third, Luther's Christology affirms the necessity of Christ's particular cross of Golgotha as its core, whereas Unification Christology does not, as it treats the cross as a more generic and universal symbol of all Christ's acts of sacrificing and lowering himself out of love for others (including the cross of Golgotha). Unification Christology holds that Christ could have lived much longer on the earth, continuously bearing the cross to live for the sake of others for the transformation of the world, without dying at Golgotha at such a young age.[69]

---

[69] Regarding this, see Chapter 10 in the present book.

A fourth difference concerns married messiahship. We know that Luther married Katharina von Bora (1499–1552), a former nun, and positively talked about God-centered marriage: "It is the highest grace of God when love continues to flourish in married life."[70] Perhaps it was a good step toward appreciating married messiahship. Understandably, however, Luther still fell short of addressing it, just focusing on the mission of Christ as a single Messiah without marriage, although marriage would not be entirely strange to the historical Jesus, who is a man completely united with God, as seen by Luther. Unification Christology, by contrast, holds that Jesus as a man was to marry to complete his messianic mission.[71] Thus it believes that after his crucifixion "the resurrected Jesus and the Holy Spirit" became "spiritual True Parents" to give "spiritual rebirth" to believers.[72] It also contends from the biblical description of the "marriage of the Lamb" (Rev. 19:7-10) that the Christ of the Second Coming goes beyond the individual level to marry his Bride at the social level to be "True Parents" to give "rebirth both spiritually and physically" to humankind.[73] If Christ is "a man who has completed the purpose of creation," his Bride must be a woman who, too, has completed the purpose of creation. This is a unique yet important feature of Unification Christology. It was already dealt with in our discussion of the Trinity in Chapter 5, and it will be further explored in the context of the atonement to be discussed in Chapter 10.

In conclusion, Unification Christology asserts, based on Unification ontology, that Jesus is a man who has full divinity as well as full humanity by being able to completely unite with God. Unification Christology, therefore, is neither a high Christology nor a low Christology. It is a Christology which can unite both types of Christology, putting an end to their never-ending conflict which has been caused by traditional Christian ontology's lack of ability to solve the problem of the gap between God and created human beings. Luther's Christology has a unique theory of God's dynamic dual characteristics in his *theologia crucis* in resemblance to the Unification ontological doctrine of God's dual characteristics which involves the selfless spirit of carrying the cross out of love. Thus Luther's Christology maintains that the historical Jesus is a man

---

70 "Christian History Sampler: Martin Luther on Marriage." https://christianhistoryinstitute.org/magazine/article/christian-history-sampler-martin-luther-on-marriage.

71 Even within Christianity, there are some scholars who seriously argue for the marriage of Jesus. See, for example, William E. Phipps, *Was Jesus Married?: The Distortion of Sexuality in the Christian Tradition* (New York: Harper & Row, Publishers, 1970).

72 EDP, p. 172.

73 Ibid.

who has full divinity as well as full humanity by completely uniting with God through the cross. In this sense, Luther's Christology is an important forerunner of Unification Christology, although there are still some significant differences between them.

Chapter 10

The Atonement

In Christian theology the atonement is the work of Christ, which is usually considered to be accomplished through his death on the cross. The English word "atonement," derived from "at-one-ment," was coined by William Tyndale (c. 1494–1536) to correspond to the Greek word καταλλαγη (meaning "reconciliation") in biblical passages such as Romans 11:15 in his translation of the New Testament in 1526. Thus the atonement means that God and alienated fallen humans become one by being reconciled through the work of Christ.

Historically, there have been a variety of theories of the atonement. Among them, there are four major ones: 1) the "classic" theory, widespread amongst early Church Fathers and in the Church in the first eleven centuries of the Christian era; 2) the "satisfaction" theory in the Catholic Church since the eleventh century; 3) the "penal substitution" theory in the Reformation tradition; and 4) the "moral influence" theory amongst liberal Christians. Other theories are usually variations of them. This chapter will discuss the Unification doctrine of the atonement mainly in the context of these four major ones.

If one reviews all the major Christian theories of the atonement, one is faced with at least three areas of ambiguity or uncertainty. Many serious believers and theologians have pointed these out.

First, given the variety of competing theories, there is no official consensus about the atonement. Regarding this ambiguity, the Anglican theologian John Macquarrie (1919–2007) observes: "The Church has never formulated a doctrine of the atonement with the same precision with which it has tried to define the person of Christ."[1] The work of Christ should be one of the most important topics in Christian theology because it is related to our redemption and salvation. And yet, this ambiguity is the reality. In the words of the prominent Oxford theologian J. N. D. Kelly (1909–1997), "Indeed, while the conviction of redemption through Christ has always been the motive force of Christian faith, no universally accepted definition of the manner of its achievement has been formulated to this day."[2]

A second area of ambiguity is that while many Christians agree with St. Paul that the resurrection of Christ as well as his death is "of first importance" (1 Cor. 15:3-5), these major theories of the atonement put so much emphasis on his death on the cross that most fail to appreciate the value of his resurrection. One prime example of this is the satisfaction theory, developed by St. Anselm of Canterbury (c. 1033–1109) around the end of the eleventh century. When it maintains that for the atonement the death of Christ successfully "satisfied" the honor of God offended since the time of the fall of Adam, it does not indicate any role for the resurrection of Christ at all. Wouldn't this create ambiguity or uncertainty for our faith in Christ? Perhaps the only exception is the classic theory, which appreciates not only the death of Christ but also his resurrection and even all the other things that happened in his entire life on the earth since the Incarnation.

A third area of ambiguity concerns those who contributed to Christ's death on the cross such as his own faithless disciples, Jewish leaders, and Roman officials and soldiers. According to all the major theories, his death for the atonement was in accordance with God's will from the beginning. If so, all those who helped to kill Christ helped God's will to be done. They should, then, be praised as "agents of divine will," so to speak. However, is this conclusion really acceptable? Perhaps not. They have always been blamed and held accountable for what they did. Were they, then, agents in opposition to God's will? Here is a tremendous amount of uncertainty. The typical Church response has been that the death of Christ, which is a great event planned by God, is a mystery of faith anyway. But recent scholarship, involving especially a new school of theology inspired by the French philosophical anthropologist René Girard (1923–2015),[3] intriguingly exposes this inner disjuncture behind the crucifixion.

---

[1] John Macquarrie, *Principles of Christian Theologies*, 2nd ed. (New York: Charles Scribner's Sons, 1977), p. 314.

[2] J. N. D. Kelly, *Early Christian Doctrines*, revised ed. (New York: Harper & Row, Publishers, 1978), p. 163.

[3] René Girard is, strictly speaking, not a theologian, but his own theological application of his anthropological theory of "mimetic desire," which will be discussed later in this chapter, can be

The present chapter will see how the Divine Principle, which is the doctrinal teaching of the Unification Church based on a new interpretation of the Bible,[4] addresses the above three areas of ambiguity or uncertainty. In the process of having the Divine Principle address them, we will elaborate the Divine Principle view of the atonement, i.e., the Unification doctrine of the atonement, in the context of the Christian tradition. Whether or not the Unification doctrine of the atonement is acceptable will depend on how well the Divine Principle addresses the areas of ambiguity. It will also depend on whether or not any new and unique contributions the Divine Principle makes are convincingly reasonable.

§1. Four Major Theories

1. The Classic Theory

The classic theory was developed by early Church Fathers such as St. Irenaeus (c. 130–c. 202) and Origen (c. 184–c. 253). It was the standard view in Christianity until the eleventh century. It maintains that because humans became the children of the devil under his dominion due to the fall of Adam, Christ was offered as a "ransom" (Mt. 20:28; Mk. 10:45; 1 Tim. 2:6) to the devil to liberate them from his dominion. Thus it is also called the ransom theory. This theory is about Christ victoriously defeating Satan's dominion to bring a complete change in the relationship between God and humans; thus it points to the "kingly" mission of Christ. It should be noted that Satan is not a mythological figure for early Church Fathers, who literally believed in his actual existence.

After the eleventh century the classic theory was forgotten in the West, although it basically continued to be adhered to in the East. The reason was that the satisfaction theory newly emerged in the West in the eleventh century

---

seen in his books such as: *Things Hidden Since the Foundation of the World*, trans. Stephen Bann and Michael Metteer (Stanford, CA: Stanford University Press, 1987); and *I See Satan Fall Like Lightning*, trans. James W. Williams (Maryknoll, NY: Orbis Books, 2001). So-called Girardian theologians, who are inspired by Girard, include Raymund Schwager, James G. Williams, Robert G. Hamerton-Kelly and Anthony W. Bartlett. For their works on the atonement, see, for example, Raymund Schwager, *Jesus in the Drama of Salvation: Toward a Biblical Notion of Redemption*, trans. James G. Williams and Paul Haddon (New York: Crossroad, 1999); Robert G. Hamerton-Kelly, *Sacred Violence: Paul's Hermeneutic of the Cross* (Minneapolis, MN: Fortress Press, 1992); and Anthony W. Bartlett, *Cross Purposes: The Violent Grammar of Christian Atonement* (Harrisburg, PA: Trinity Press International, 2001).

[4] For this new interpretation of the Bible which constitutes the Divine Principle, see Chapter 1 in the present book.

and became very popular since then. It was finally in 1930 that the classic theory was rehabilitated from oblivion in the West through special lectures at Uppsala University in that year by the Swedish Lutheran theologian Gustaf Aulén (1879–1977). His lectures became a book entitled *Christus Victor*, whose English translation, published in the following year, turned out to be groundbreaking, drawing attention to the classic theory.[5] So this theory has "Christus Victor" ("Christ the Victor") as another name.

What is interesting about this theory is its assertion that all the things that happened in the entire life of Christ, including the Incarnation, his three temptations, his Sermon on the Mount, his miracle performances and his death, resurrection and ascension, were equally redemptive because they all had the same purpose of battling against the devil's dominion. Although the theory holds that Christ had to die on the cross, it does not emphasize his death in such a way as to neglect the importance of other things that happened in his life. Thus, in the words of Aulén, there is "a continuous line from the Incarnation, through the entire earthly life of Christ, and His death, to His resurrection and exaltation," and "no one point in this line claims anything like an exclusive emphasis."[6]

2. The Satisfaction Theory

The satisfaction theory was formulated by Anselm in his book *Cur Deus Homo* ("Why the God-Man") written 1098, and since then it has been spread widely in the Catholic Church. Anselm explicitly rejected the then accepted idea that Christ was offered as a ransom to the devil for the deliverance of fallen humans. He rejected it because he could not believe that the devil had any right to hold humans, given the almighty power of God.

According to Anselm, the fall of Adam offended the honor of God, incurring an infinite debt to divine justice. As a consequence, someone needs to "satisfy" the offended honor of God, by paying the debt. Fallen humans cannot do that work because of their grave sinfulness; the infinite debt can be

---

[5] Gustaf Aulén, *Christus Victor: An Historical Study of the Three Main Types of the Idea of the Atonement*, trans. A. G. Herbert (New York: Macmillan Co., 1969). According to Aulén, the classic theory was restored by Martin Luther in the sixteenth century, but that Luther's followers did not accept it. This thesis of Aulén on Luther, however, has been disputed by many because in Luther's writings passages in support of the penal substitution theory can also be found.

[6] Ibid., p. 28. This observation by Aulén stands, especially when we look at Irenaeus' theory of recapitulation in Christ, which juxtaposes his life as the Incarnation of the Word and his death on the cross as equally important for the undoing of the effects of the disobedience of Adam; see Irenaeus, "Against Heresies," II.22.4, V.16.2-3, in Alexander Roberts, James Donaldson, and A. Cleveland Coxe, eds., *The Ante-Nicene Fathers: The Writing of the Fathers Down to A.D. 325*, American ed., vol. I: *The Apostolic Fathers with Justin Martyr and Irenaeus* (Grand Rapids, MI: Wm. B. Eerdmans Publishing Co., 1981), pp. 391, 544.

paid only by God. But since it is humans who owe it, it must be paid by someone who is also human. Christ as the God-Man, therefore, had to die on the cross on our behalf to pay the debt, in order to satisfy God's honor. Christ voluntarily did this act of "giving His life, or laying down His life, or delivering Himself up to death for the honor of God."[7]

The work of Christ is thus propitiation or appeasement to God on our behalf, and it points to the "priestly" mission of Christ. It is an "objective" atonement because it is for the satisfaction of God, our "object" of faith, outside and independent of us, "subjects" of faith, although God's satisfaction eventually brings us forgiveness and a new life.

One noteworthy point about this theory is that it regards the death of Christ on the cross as the only way for the atonement, leaving out of sight all the other events that happened in his life even including his resurrection: "[Its] whole emphasis is on the death as an isolated fact, and as in itself constituting the satisfaction."[8] This makes this theory very different from the classic theory that maintains that all the events in his life are equally important for the atonement. Another thing that makes the satisfaction theory very different from the classic theory is its removal of the devil from the equation.

3. The Penal Substitution Theory

The penal substitution theory, adhered to by John Calvin (1509–1564) and other Reformers,[9] is very similar to the satisfaction theory, in that it points to the "priestly" mission of Christ as an another "objective" theory. It holds that Christ died on the cross on behalf of us, yet outside and independent of us, to propitiate and appease the wrath of God (caused by the fall of Adam), although the propitiation eventually brings us forgiveness. Justice demands that our sin inherited from the fall of Adam deserves "death" as the "wages of sin" (Rom. 6:23). As our "substitute," however, Christ received this "penalty" of death on the cross. "Christ," in the words of Calvin, "interposed, took the punishment upon himself, and bore what by the just judgment of God was impending over sinners."[10]

---

[7] *Cur Deus Homo* II.7; see Anselm, *Why God Became Man and The Virgin Conception of Original Sin*, trans. Joseph M. Colleran (Albany, NY: Magic Books, 1969), p. 136.

[8] Aulén, *Christus Victor*, p. 89.

[9] Whether Martin Luther should be included among the Reformers in support of the penal substitution theory is debatable, because Gustaf Aulén strongly asserts that Luther stood for the classic theory while many believe that he was more for the penal substitution theory than for the classic theory.

[10] John Calvin, *Institutes of the Christian Religion*, trans. Henry Beveridge, rev. ed. (Peabody, MA: Hendrickson Publishers, 2008), 2.16.2, p. 325.

While this theory is very similar to the satisfaction theory, its legal notion of penalty for the atonement makes it quite different from the latter where voluntary obedience rather than penalty is stressed for the satisfaction of God's honor in accordance with the Catholic doctrine of penance.

But the penal substitution theory is again similar to the satisfaction theory, as it isolates the death of Christ from all the other events that took place in his life such as the Incarnation, his Sermon on the Mount and his resurrection, seeing the crucifixion as the only way for the atonement. This theory also does not involve the devil in its discussion of the atonement.

4. The Moral Influence Theory

This theory was originally developed by Peter Abelard (1079–1142) in his book *Expositio in Epistolam ad Romanos* ("Commentary on the Epistle to the Romans") and accepted by liberal theologians in the nineteenth and twentieth centuries such as Horace Bushnell (1802–1876) and Hastings Rashdall (1858–1924).[11] Like Anselm, Abelard rejected the classic theory's assertion that the death of Christ was a ransom paid to the devil for the deliverance of fallen humans. But Abelard also rejected Anselm's idea that the death of Christ was a debt-payment to satisfy God's offended honor. Abelard was not so much interested in how to satisfy God to have him change his attitude toward sinful humans as in how to let sinful humans see the love of God that is ever present. God's love is so abundant that he overrules his need for satisfaction.

For Abelard, therefore, the sacrificial death of Christ on the cross is a demonstration of God's abundant love, so that that love may be morally awakened in sinful humans as they respond to it as a supreme "example" (1 Pet. 2:21). Regarding the benefit of the death of Christ, Abelard states: "Every man is made… juster, that is to say, more moving to the Lord after the passion of Christ than he was before, because a benefit actually received kindles the soul into love more than one merely hoped for."[12]

It is a "subjective" atonement because it exercises an impression and influence on us, "subjects" of faith. It points to the "prophetic" mission of Christ for our moral awakening. This theory presupposes optimism with respect to human nature and discusses the atonement in personal terms.

This theory believes that the death of Christ was necessary as the ultimate way of displaying God's love for the moral inspiration of humans. While other events that took place in his life also displayed the love of God, his death was the supreme exhibition of that love.

---

[11] Hastings Rashdall expounds the moral influence theory in his well-known book, *The Idea of Atonement in Christian Theology* (Charleston, SC: BiblioBazaar, 2009), originally published in 1919.
[12] Quoted in Rashdall, ibid., p. 358.

§2. The Divine Principle View and the Classic Theory

How does the Divine Principle view the atonement? It maintains that due to the fall of Adam and Eve all their descendants became children of Satan under his "sovereignty."[13] Therefore it naturally views the atonement as our deliverance from the dominion of Satan to the dominion of God. It thus resembles the classic theory and differs from the other major theories, which have removed Satan from the equation.

But the Divine Principle seems to have a more detailed explanation of the nature of Satan's dominion than the classic theory because it maintains that sinful humans are of "the lineage of Satan" after Adam and Eve sexually fell and "bound themselves in blood ties with Lucifer."[14] The word "lineage" used here to explain about dominion would be similar to what Calvinism calls Adam's "natural headship" (rather than "federal headship") under Satan,[15] which connotes a tighter relationship than the word "dominion" generally would indicate. Also, the word "lineage" derives from the idea of the sexual fall of Adam and Eve, which is quite a unique idea, although it is not entirely alien in the Christian tradition, given the fact that early Church Fathers such as St. Clement of Alexandria (c. 150–c. 215) and St. Ambrose (c. 340–397) accepted it.[16]

---

[13] *Exposition of the Divine Principle* (New York: H.S.A.-U.W.C., 1996), p. 68. Henceforth abbreviated as EDP.

[14] Ibid.

[15] For the meaning of Adam's "natural headship" as compared with his "federal headship" in Calvinism, see, for example, Millard J. Erickson, *Introducing Christian Doctrine*, 2nd ed., edited by L. Arnold Hustad (Grand Rapids, MI: Baker Academic, 2001), pp. 229-30.

[16] Clement of Alexandria's idea of the sexual fall of Adam and Eve can be seen when he refers to all humans as "lovers of pleasure" and states that "the first man of our race did not bide his time, desired the favor of marriage before the proper hour, and fell into sin by not waiting for the time of God's will; 'for everyone who looks upon a woman to lust after her has already committed adultery with her'" (*Stromateis* III.14.94); see John Ernest Leonard Oulton and Henry Chadwick, eds., *Alexandrian Christianity: Selected Translations of Clement and Origen* (London: SCM Press, 1954), p. 84. Ambrose, following Philo's psychological reading of the serpent, Eve and Adam, proposes a sexual interpretation of the fall: "The serpent is a type of the pleasures of the body. The woman stands for our senses and the man, for our minds. Pleasure stirs the senses, which, in turn, have their effect on the mind. Pleasure, therefore, is the primary source of sin" (*De Paradiso* 15.73); see his *Hexameron, Paradise, and Cain and Abel*, trans. John J. Savage (Washington, DC: Catholic University of America Press, 1961), pp. 351-52. The idea of the sexual fall put forth by both Clement of Alexandria and Ambrose is rejected in Ludwig Ott, *Fundamentals of Catholic Dogma*, trans. Patrick Lynch, ed. James Canon Bastible (Rockford, IL: Tan Books and Publishers, 1974), p. 107.

According to the Divine Principle, Jesus Christ came as "the second Adam"[17] to defeat Satan's lineage and dominion and restore God's lineage and sovereignty on the earth. He continuously made efforts to accomplish that task. But he eventually realized that it was impossible to accomplish it due to unspeakably strong opposition from the Jewish leaders in the chosen nation. He, then, believed that the only way left was for him to sacrifice his own life out of love for his opponents and all humanity, so that this act of love on his part might be able to lay a foundation for the future accomplishment of that original task at his Second Coming.[18] That foundation for the future was none other than his *resurrection* following his death.

When the Jewish leaders rebelled against Christ instead of accepting him, Satan decisively took possession of them and all humanity. At that moment, God decided to still save them all even by "delivering Jesus into the hands of Satan," who in turn wanted to kill Jesus "even though he might have to hand back all of humanity, including the Jewish people, to God."[19] The release of all sinful humans from Satan was made possible by the resurrection of Christ arranged by God after he was killed by Satan. The Divine Principle explains it as follows:

> Because Satan had already exercised his maximum power in killing Jesus, according to the principle of restoration through indemnity, God was entitled to exercise His maximum power. While Satan uses his power to kill, God uses His power to bring the dead to life. As compensation for Satan's exercise of his maximum power in killing Jesus, God exercised His maximum power and resurrected Jesus. God thus opened the way for all humanity to be engrafted with the resurrected Jesus and thereby receive salvation and rebirth.[20]

Here the Divine Principle and the classic theory agree that humans are to be delivered from the dominion of Satan through the resurrection of Jesus following his death, but there is a difference between the two positions. It is that while the classic theory holds that the death of Jesus was in accordance with God's will from the beginning, the Divine Principle does not. According to the Divine Principle, the death of Jesus was never in accordance with God's original will. Satan killed Jesus through those who were against God's will, and God had to permit it to happen. This issue of responsibility for Jesus' death will be further discussed later when our third area of ambiguity above is addressed.

---

[17] EDP, p. 203.
[18] EDP, p. 121.
[19] EDP, p. 278.
[20] EDP, p. 279.

The Divine Principle also differs from the classic theory in that while the classic theory holds that the atonement in terms of the release of sinful humans from Satan's dominion, brought by the death and resurrection of Christ, was complete, the Divine Principle does not. The Divine Principle holds that the atonement brought by the death and resurrection of Christ was not yet complete and was only partial. (In this regard, the Divine Principle is also different from the other major theories because they all believe in their own ways that the atonement by Christ 2000 years ago was complete.)

The original task of Christ, according to the Divine Principle, was to bring a "full" atonement[21] by completely delivering sinful humans from the lineage of Satan, which the Divine Principle believes to be the real meaning of the dominion of Satan. What if Jesus had been wholeheartedly accepted instead of being rebelled against? He would have had an alternative course of life on the earth, and it would have been able to bring the full atonement, involving the creation of the lineage of God. Then all the events that took place and would have taken place in his entire earthly life would have been instrumental for this atonement. The full atonement, however, became what must be accomplished at his Second Coming. This full atonement is a uniquely important topic in the Divine Principle, but it can only be understood properly after we first address the three areas of ambiguity mentioned above.

§3. Addressing the Three Areas of Ambiguity

1. Integrating the Various Theories

Reviewing the four major theories, we recognize the above-mentioned first area of ambiguity, which is that there is no real unanimity on the atonement in Christianity. The classic theory talks about the atonement in terms of defeating the reign of Satan, whereas the others, having removed Satan from the equation, are preoccupied with what happens to God first or what happens to sinful humans first. Preoccupied with what happens to God first are the objective theories (satisfaction theory and penal substitution theory), whereas the subjective theory (moral influence theory) is more interested in what happens to sinful humans first.

These various theories are also each prone to criticism. The objective theories are usually criticized for emphasizing Christ's propitiation of God's offended honor or wrath so much that they fail to understand any essential connection of love between Christ and sinful humans. They are also criticized

[21] EDP, p. 118.

for picturing God not as a loving God but rather as a harsh God who demands justice by sending Christ to the cross. Thus the Yale theologian George Barker Stevens (1854–1906) blames the satisfaction theory, stating that "it would be difficult to name any prominent treatise on atonement, whose conception of sin is so essentially unethical and superficial."[22] John Macquarrie critiques the penal substitution theory for being "sub-Christian" in its idea that Christ was punished by God for the sins of humans.[23] More recently, Steve Chalke (1955–), an insider of British evangelical circles where the penal substitution theory is regarded as an essential teaching, has denounced the theory for being "morally dubious and a barrier of faith" because of its image of God as "a vengeful Father."[24] Chalke's denunciation stirred a great controversy amongst evangelicals, leading to a public debate in London in 2005.[25]

On the other hand, the moral influence theory is criticized for an opposite reason, i.e., for being simply subjective, referring to the work of Christ as "manward" and not "Godward," in spite of the fact that the Bible also says that it is Godward: "Christ loved us and gave himself up for us, a fragrant offering and sacrifice to God" (Eph. 5:2).[26] This theory is also critiqued by St. Bernard of Clairvaux (1090–1153), a contemporary of Abelard, for teaching humanistically that if the death of Christ is merely an example, the actual work of salvation is done by the efforts of humans.

Even the classic theory is not free from criticism. Anselm's critique of it, which says that it wrongfully acknowledges certain rights of the devil, is quite well known. Also, many modern people criticize its belief in the actual existence of the devil.

If John Wesley (1703–1791) is right when he says, "Nothing in the Christian system is of greater consequence than the doctrine of the atonement,"[27] then how can we tolerate the fact that different atonement theories just compete with one another and are also each prone to criticism, without there being any officially agreed-upon position? To address this question, many have recently admitted that each and every one of the various theories actually conveys some truth about the work of Christ. Thus the

---

[22] George Barker Stevens, *The Christian Doctrine of Salvation* (Edinburgh: T&T Clark, 1905), p. 242.
[23] Macquarrie, *Principles of Christian Theologies*, p. 315.
[24] Steve Chalke and Alan Mann, *The Lost Message of Jesus* (Grand Rapids, MI: Zondervan, 2003), p. 182.
[25] Published as a result of this public debate is Derek Tidball, David Hilborn, and Justin Thacker, eds., *The Atonement Debate: Papers from the London Symposium on the Theology of Atonement* (Grand Rapids, MI: Zondervan, 2008).
[26] H. D. McDonald, *The Atonement of the Death of Christ: In Faith, Revelation, and History* (Grand Rapids, MI: Baker Book House, 1985), p. 180.
[27] John Wesley, *A Compend of Wesley's Theology*, ed. Robert W. Burtner and Robert E. Chiles (Nashville: Abingdon Press, 1954), p. 79.

American evangelical theologian Millard J. Erickson (1932–), while believing the penal substitution theory to be "the most basic" of all, states: "Each of the theories… seizes upon a significant aspect of his [i.e., Christ's] work," and "each one possesses a dimension of the truth."[28]

The Scottish Presbyterian theologian John McIntyre (1916–2005), however, went one step further, by "making a plea for an inclusive treatment of the theories of the atonement" where all of them are retained to the exclusion of none because "they mutually influence and condition one another" within "the coherence of the system" of Christ's work.[29] His position implies that the various theories can be integrated in one coherent system. But the question is: What would be that one coherent system? It would not be the penal substitution theory, contrary to Erickson's claim that it is the most basic of all, as it is no more than an objective view. Macquarrie answers that it would be the classic theory because it can integrate both the objective and subjective theories within itself, transcending their distinction: "The classic view of atonement gathers up in itself the most important elements in both the subjective and objective views, thus transcending them."[30]

Maquarrie, of course, is deeply aware that "subjective and objective accounts are by themselves inadequate and misleading," but he still believes that "they both make useful contributions toward understanding the atonement when they are brought into relation to the classic view and treated as supplementary models."[31]

According to him, the classic theory includes an objective element in itself in so far as it holds that "the self-giving of God for his creation" is really involved through the self-giving of Christ, and it also contains a subjective element in itself in so far as it "shows us a life of perfect obedience, overcoming every temptation to idolatry and remaining faithful even to the cross."[32] Macquarrie also says that the kingly office of Christ finding expression chiefly in the classic theory can embrace the priestly and prophetic offices finding expression in the objective and subjective theories, respectively:

> Christ the king, who wins his victory over the enslaving forces, is also Christ the prophet who gives us the "example" of obedience, but still more he is the priest who utterly gives himself as sacrificial victim and

---

[28] Erickson, *Introducing Christian Doctrine*, p. 254.

[29] John McIntyre, *The Shape of Soteriology: Studies in the Doctrine of the Death of Christ* (Edinburgh: T&T Clark, 1992), pp. 28, 82.

[30] Macquarrie, *Principles of Christian Theologies*, p. 320.

[31] Ibid.

[32] Ibid.

> thereby brings right into human history the reconciling activity of God in a new and decisive manner.[33]

There is, however, an even better way of describing how the classic theory is both objective and subjective at once—better than Macquarrie's description. It is by stating that the classic theory refers to a completely new relationship between God and human beings after they are delivered from the dominion of Satan, for in that new relationship both God and humanity are equally in a changed status through the work of Christ. Irenaeus, an important advocate of the classic theory, mentions this new divine-human relationship when he says in his *Against Heresies* that Christ being resurrected after his death "poured out the Spirit of the Father to bring about the union and communion of God and man."[34] It should be noted here that the resurrection of Christ, along with the work of the Holy Spirit, is essential for the atonement in the classic theory.

The Divine Principle agrees with Irenaeus' description of the classic theory that the atonement means to liberate humans from the dominion of Satan to bring about a completely new divine-human relationship under the dominion of God. It agrees, therefore, that the atonement is both objective and subjective at once, involving both God and humans together in that new relationship. This point is evident when it asserts that the "spiritual rebirth" of sinful humans occurs in their new relationship with God through the mediation of the resurrected Jesus and the Holy Spirit.[35]

According to the Divine Principle, this scheme of spiritual rebirth shows that humans, when reborn spiritually, stand in front of the "spiritual Trinity" of: 1) God, 2) the resurrected Jesus, and 3) the Holy Spirit, and that this spiritual Trinity and humans constitute a "four position foundation" centering on God.[36] The relationship of four positions within the four position foundation is such that all of them affect one another.[37] Therefore the Divine Principle view of the atonement is objective as well as subjective, being able to unite both within the four position foundation.

The Divine Principle use of the Trinity and the four position foundation for the integration of the various theories of the atonement is not entirely novel. Robert Sherman in his book, *King, Priest, and Prophet*, develops a trinitarian theology of atonement, which associates "the three commonly recognized

[33] Ibid., p. 321.

[34] Irenaeus, "Against Heresies," V.1.1, in Roberts, Donaldson, and Coxe, eds, *The Ante-Nicene Fathers*, vol. I, p. 527.

[35] EDP, pp. 171-72.

[36] Ibid.

[37] For this mutual relationship of the four positions, see the notion of "three object purpose" in EDP, p. 25.

models" of the atonement, i.e., the "kingly" classic theory, "priestly" objective theory, and "prophetic" subjective theory, with the Father, Son, and Holy Spirit, respectively, to argue that the three models are undivided as long as the three persons are undivided, as the tradition affirms: *Opera trinitatis ad extra indivisa sunt* ("The external works of the Trinity are undivided").[38] Although associating the threefold office of Christ with the Trinity may be a little too simplistic and may not be entirely legitimate, his general idea that the atonement should be grounded in the Trinity is correct.

When the Divine Principle uses the four position foundation based on the spiritual Trinity to integrate the objective and subjective theories, it does not mean to accept these theories as they are. It agrees with Macquarrie that they "are by themselves inadequate and misleading." They are by themselves merely partial, by being objective or subjective. At the same time, even the classic theory, through which they can be integrated, is not enough, for the reason that it does not offer another alternative of the life of Christ in which he would have been able to continuously live, without being rebelled against and killed by the people of his day, to bring what the Divine Principle calls the full atonement. If so, unfortunately even the Divine Principle's four position foundation on the foundation of the spiritual Trinity is not enough, either, as it does not encompass the full atonement. (Again, the full atonement will be discussed below once the three areas of ambiguity are addressed.)

But it is safe to say at this juncture that best elements in the objective, subjective and classic theories are gathered up in the four position foundation on the basis of the spiritual Trinity. The strongest element of the objective theories (satisfaction theory and penal substitution theory) is their idea that God is affected by what Christ does on behalf of humans in accordance with the divine will, although what the divine will truly means may still be debatable. The strongest element of the subjective theory is its assertion that sinful humans are encouraged by Christ on behalf of God to repent and improve themselves. The strongest element of the classic theory is its description of how the resurrected Christ and the Holy Spirit work together to bring about a new divine-human relationship under the spiritual dominion of God. All these elements are gathered up in the God-centered four position foundation, because, according to the Divine Principle, the four positions of that foundation (God, the resurrected Christ, the Holy Spirit, and humans) relate to and affect one another. It should be noted that the Divine Principle teaches that even the omniscient and omnipotent God is so affected as to feel "joy"

[38] Robert Sherman, *King, Priest, and Prophet: A Trinitarian Theology of Atonement* (New York: T&T Clark International, 2004), pp. 8-23.

from what is done in accordance with "the purpose of creation,"[39] and also that humans are always encouraged by God to fulfill "their own portion of responsibility."[40] Thus sinful humans are expected to make efforts to stand engrafted into the spiritual Trinity prepared for their spiritual rebirth.

2. Appreciating the Resurrection of Christ

Our second area of ambiguity concerns the role of the resurrection of Christ for the atonement. It is usually believed that Christ was resurrected with a glorified and imperishable "spiritual body" (1 Cor. 15:42-44) after his death on the cross.[41] The problem is that while people such as St. Paul strongly believe the resurrection of Christ as well as his death to be important for the atonement, quite surprisingly the objective and subjective theories of the atonement do not appreciate the value of his resurrection. This causes ambiguity in our faith in Christ.

The satisfaction theory, as developed by Anselm, goes to the extreme, because his *Cur Deus Homo*, his major work on the atonement, has no reference whatsoever to the resurrection of Christ. This theory is so much preoccupied with describing how the death of Christ satisfies the offended honor of God that it forgets about his resurrection. Perhaps it does not even think that his resurrection is needed for the atonement. The Catholic theologian Thomas G. Weinandy (1946–) is aware of this weakness of the satisfaction theory, when he says: "Anselm provided no account of the importance of the resurrection of Christ."[42] Weinandy also talks about a second weakness resulting from the first within this theory: the complete absence of the Holy Spirit because of the neglect of the risen Christ:

> Because of his [i.e., Anselm's] failure to grasp the importance of the Resurrection, he gave the impression that the merits of Christ are dispersed as if they were monetary increments given to individual believers. Rather, the merit of Christ is that new resurrected life, which the believer shares in by being united to the risen Christ and so shares in the benefits of being a member of his body, the Church. Thus, the role of Holy Spirit, who is the fruit of the cross and the life of Christ's body, is completely absent within Anselm's soteriology.[43]

How about the penal substitution theory? This theory, too, is preoccupied with explaining how the death of Christ propitiates God for the atonement. It

---

39 EDP, p. 33.

40 EDP, p. 43.

41 Resurrection is not resuscitation, which is the reanimation of a corpse that will eventually die again.

42 Thomas G. Weinandy, *Jesus the Christ* (Huntington, IN: Our Sunday Visitor, 2003), p. 157.

43 Ibid.

asserts that only the death of Christ can handle retribution for sin that flows from the wrath of God against sinners. Thus it fails to recognize the real importance of the resurrection of Christ. Even the American conservative Calvinist theologian Richard B. Gaffin, Jr. (1936–) , who is an advocate of the penal substitution theory, observes that "in the history of doctrine, especially in soteriology, Christ's resurrection has been relatively eclipsed," and he correctly goes on to admit this problem in Western Christianity and especially in the penal substitution theory in the Reformation tradition:

> In Western Christianity (both Roman Catholic and Protestant)... attention has been focused heavily and at times almost exclusively on Christ's death and its significance. The overriding concern, especially since the Reformation, has been to keep clear that the Cross is not simply an ennobling and challenging example but a real atonement—a substitutionary, expiatory sacrifice that reconciles God to sinners and propitiates his judicial wrath. In short, the salvation accomplished by [the death of] Christ and the atonement have been virtually synonymous. My point is not to challenge the validity or even the necessity of this development, far less the conclusions reached. But in this dominating preoccupation with the death of Christ, the doctrinal or soteriological significance of his resurrection has been largely overlooked. [44]

According to Calvin, who is the most well-known advocate of the penal substitution theory, the atonement is already completed through the death of Christ: "in his death we have an effectual completion of salvation, because by it we are reconciled to God, satisfaction is given to his justice, the curse is removed, and the penalty paid." So the resurrection of Christ has only a secondary role of bestowing "the power and efficacy" of his death upon us and renewing "righteousness" in us.[45]

The moral influence theory does not appreciate the resurrection of Christ as much as his death, either. According to this theory, his death on the cross is already the supreme exhibition of God's love, to which his resurrection cannot be superior. This theory, of course, considers all events surrounding Christ including his resurrection to be exhibitions of God's love; but it still believes that the death of Christ is the ultimate exhibition of divine love.

The moral influence theory is advocated by liberal Christians, many of whom usually deny the historicity of supernatural phenomena such as the resurrection of Christ. Even though the resurrection of Christ is not a historical

---

[44] Richard B. Gaffin, Jr., "Redemption and Resurrection." http://11nk.org/part-i-background-biblical-theology.

[45] Calvin, *Institutes of the Christian Religion*, 2.16.13, p. 334.

event for them, they still cherish its demythologized version, saying that it means a rejuvenation of the tradition of love which was evident in his life and which therefore could be put to death. Thus the Episcopal theologian John Shelby Spong (1931–2021), who is well known for his liberal stance, states that even though Easter "is not an event that takes place inside human history," it "becomes for us a timeless invitation to enter the meaning of God by living for others, expecting no reward, loving wastefully no matter what the cost."[46] This kind of interpretation has actually led many liberals to engage in social action ministries. Nevertheless, this does not mean that they reject the supremacy of the death of Christ in favor of what they mean by his resurrection; they rather uphold the former strongly by means of the latter.

The general neglect of the resurrection of Christ in the objective and subjective theories, as seen above, is not in accordance with Paul's assertion that the resurrection of Christ as well as his death is "of first importance" (1 Cor. 15:3-5). According to Paul, the resurrection of Christ is essential to the atonement: "if you confess with your lips that Jesus is Lord and believe that God raised him from the dead, you will be saved" (Rom. 10:9); "If Christ has not been raised, your faith is futile and you are still in your sins" (1 Cor. 15:17). Also, the Acts of the Apostles reports that the apostles enthusiastically testified to the resurrections of Christ (Acts 2:31; 4:33; 17:18; 26:23).

By reviewing all the major theories of the atonement, one can realize that only the classic theory seems to understand the value of the resurrection of Christ for the atonement because only this theory believes that his resurrection finalizes his spiritual victory over the dominion of Satan that brings the atonement. The other theories do not treat the atonement in terms of Christ's victory over the reign of Satan but rather in terms of a vicarious debt-payment through his death or a demonstration of an example of love through his death; they assume that his death basically did everything for the atonement, thus not appreciating his resurrection. Regarding the resurrection of Christ, as appreciated by the classic theory, Aulén says that it is "the manifestation of the decisive victory over the powers of evil, which was won on the cross; it is also the starting-point for the new dispensation, for the gift of the Spirit, for the continuation of the work of God in the souls of men."[47] Therefore the classic theory "lay[s] emphasis not merely on the death of Christ, but also on His victory, His triumph, His passage through death to life."[48]

---

[46] John Shelby Spong, *Resurrection: Myth or Reality?: A Bishop's Search for the Origins of Christianity* (San Francisco: Harper San Francisco, 1994), p. 143.
[47] Aulén, *Christus Victor*, p. 32.
[48] Ibid., p. 42.

The Divine Principle again agrees with the classic theory that the resurrection of Christ finalized his spiritual victory over the dominion of Satan for the deliverance of humans. But while the classic theory appreciates both the death and resurrection of Christ equally, the Divine Principle seems to have a much stronger appreciation of his resurrection than of his death, as it asserts that when Satan exercised "his maximum power in killing Jesus," God, as compensation for that, exercised "His maximum power and resurrected Jesus" for the spiritual rebirth of fallen humans.[49] This assertion means to say that while Satan caused the death of Christ, his victorious resurrection was brought by God. In other words, it was not through his death, caused by Satan, but rather through his victorious resurrection, brought forth by God, that the atonement was able to occur.

According to the Divine Principle, there was actually another element behind the reason why God was able to resurrect Jesus, and it was that even in face of the crucifixion caused by Satan and his cohorts, Jesus never complained nor vindicated himself but forgave and loved his opponents until the end, adhering to God's principle of love. In the words of Rev. Sun Myung Moon:

> He did not complain or despair just because he had to die on the cross. Even when he entered the position of death, he did not speak in his own defense. As you all know, Jesus did not try to vindicate himself even while he was passing through the court of Pilate, even on the hill of Golgotha to be crucified on the cross. He was the champion of no self-vindication. He could feel that even the opposition that he received from the people was his own responsibility... Jesus did not become a friend of life but a friend of death. Although countless people walked the path of death in the course of history, Jesus is the only one who became the friend of death on behalf of the deaths of all people. He died on behalf of all people... you must understand, it was the course of Jesus to love without any grudges.[50]

The classic theory, too, is, of course, aware of this great love of Christ for his opponents, but that theory usually explains his resurrection mainly by contending that it occurred because the ransom payment satisfied or even exceeded Satan's rights, or because the offering of Christ tricked Satan when he preyed on his flesh without knowing that the presence of God or the divinity of Christ was hidden under his humanity just like a fishhook under bait.

Thus the Divine Principle's much stronger appreciation of the resurrection of Christ than of his death results from its understanding of God's

[49] EDP, p. 279.

[50] Sun Myung Moon, *Sermons of the Reverend Sun Myung Moon* (New York: HSA Publications, 1994), vol. 1, pp. 240-41.

maximum power to override Satan's maximum power for the resurrection of Christ and also from its understanding of Christ's unchanging love for his enemies and his nonviolent and obedient response to his death plotted by his enemies. Something similar to this is actually shared by some contemporary theologians such as the Mennonite thinker J. Denny Weaver (1941–). Weaver's "narrative Christus Victor" theory, a fairly recently developed version of the classic theory ("Christus Victor") from the perspective of the nonviolent tradition of Mennonitism, says: "In this giving of himself [i.e., Christ] for the reign of God, the nonviolent confrontation of his enemies has high theological significance. It displays the love of God for enemies, a making visible of the reign of God that is even willing to suffer rejection at the hands of its enemies."[51] Weaver goes on to say: "When Jesus was executed, the powers of evil enjoyed a momentary triumph—Jesus' very existence was removed. However, God raised Jesus from death, thereby revealing the reign of God as the ultimate power in the cosmos."[52] Thus, while his death itself "accomplished nothing for the salvation of sinners,"[53] his resurrection liberates us from the reign of the powers of evil for our atonement.

This point can be seen in Rev. Moon's more explicit statement that Christianity "came into existence not by the principle of the cross, but by the principle of the resurrection," and also that "Because Christianity began on the foundation of Jesus' resurrection, Christianity has been strictly spiritual."[54]

The above assertion that Satan and his cohorts, constituting the powers of evil, triumphantly killed Christ (although immediately afterwards his victorious resurrection took place) may not sound very familiar, for throughout Christian history it has been held that his death on the cross was directed and executed by God's plan from the beginning. Was it, then, God who killed Christ? If so, did all those who helped to kill him help God to kill him? Or were they rather agents of Satan? This brings us to our third area of ambiguity.

3. Satan Killed Christ

This third area of ambiguity exists in all the major theories of the atonement, because they believe that his death was in accordance with God's will from the beginning. Especially the satisfaction theory and the penal substitution theory

---

[51] J. Denny Weaver, *The Nonviolent Atonement* (Grand Rapids, MI: Wm. B. Eerdmans Publishing Co., 2001), p. 42.

[52] Ibid., p. 43.

[53] Ibid., p. 72.

[54] Sun Myung Moon, "The Life of Jesus as Seen from God's Will, and God's Warning to the Present Age, the Period of the Last Days," speech delivered at the banquet held in honor of the 20th Anniversary of *The Washington Times*, May 21, 2002. http://www.unification.net/2002/20020521_2.html.

overemphasize the importance of the death of Christ by isolating his death from all the other events that happened in his whole life. If, however, it was God's will from the beginning for Christ to die, then those who helped to kill him such as his faithless disciples, Jewish leaders, and Roman officials and soldiers should be praised for what they did in accordance with God's will. In reality, however, they have been blamed and held responsible. For example, St. Stephen accused those Jews who killed Christ of "betraying and murdering" him (Acts 7:52). Paul criticized "the rulers of this age" for having "crucified the Lord of glory" because of their ignorance of a "hidden wisdom of God" (1 Cor. 2:7-8). Even Jesus, when still alive, brokenheartedly blamed the people of Jerusalem for not accepting him, by saying: "O Jerusalem, Jerusalem, killing the prophets and stoning those who are sent to you! How often would I have gathered your children together as a hen gathers her brood under her wings, and you would not" (Mt. 23:37).

This discrepancy is pointed out by scholars such as the Swiss Jesuit theologian Raymund Schwager (1935–2004). According to Schwager, the discrepancy arises when one believes that while Christ stood in his mission with the divine will, his opponents also at the same time acted as "agents of divine will" to help to kill him. To avoid this "contradictory opposition," one should conclude that "the will of his opponents was not similarly in agreement with that of the Father, for they acted… in the most shameful and reprehensible way."[55] In other words, the opponents of Christ were never agents of divine will. Rather, they killed him through what René Girard (1923–2015) calls the "single victim mechanism" (*mécanisme victimaire*) that was "the work of Satan."[56] Thus they were agents of Satan, and Satan killed Christ through them. By the way, Schwager is one of the so-called "Girardian theologians" who apply Girard's anthropological theory to theology.

According to Girard, the single victim mechanism is the universal mechanism in any civilization or community through which a scapegoat is singled out to be victimized and murdered, being blamed for all social chaos and disorder, so that this scapegoating may bring peace and order to the chaotic and disorderly community. Social chaos and disorder consists in violent rivalries which result from people's "mimetic desire," i.e., their desire to imitate one another in pursuit of the same object. Although "we should not conclude that mimetic desire is bad in itself," it is "responsible for most of the violent acts that distress us,"[57] and the resulting "single victim mechanism," through

---

[55] Schwager, *Jesus in the Drama of Salvation*, p. 163.

[56] René Girard, *I See Satan Fall like Lightning*, trans. James W. Williams (Maryknoll, NY: Orbis, 2001), p. 36.

[57] Ibid., p. 15.

which scapegoating takes place for the purpose of peace, is the work of Satan. To show that this universal mechanism killed Christ, Girard refers to the high priest Caiaphas' statement in John 12:50: "It is better that one man die and that the whole nation not perish."[58]

J. Denny Weaver, who has developed "narrative Christas Victor," is not a Girardian theologian, but he, too, clearly states that the death of Christ was not the act of God but "the product of the forces of evil that oppose the reign of God,"[59] whether these forces of evil are "understood as Satan, or in terms of earthly structures such as Rome, which is the symbolic representative of Satan in Revelation, or as the powers of death, sin, the law, and the flesh."[60]

The Divine Principle agrees with Girard and Weaver that Satan was behind the death of Christ on the cross. The Divine Principle, noting that after the three temptations Satan departed from Jesus until an opportune time (Lk. 4:13), says that Satan now came back to kill him when his opponents betrayed him:

> It is written that Satan, who was defeated in the three temptations, left Jesus' side "until an opportune time," indicating that Satan had not left Jesus for good but might confront him at a future date. As a matter of fact, Satan did confront Jesus, working primarily through the Jewish leadership, the priests and scribes who disbelieved in Jesus. In particular, Satan confronted Jesus through Judas Iscariot, the disciple who betrayed him.[61]

Hence Rev. Moon states: "The crucifixion was not God's victory. Instead, it was Satan's victory."[62] Right after this statement, Moon refers, as proof for that, to what Jesus said to the Jewish religious leaders before his arrest: "this is your hour, and the power of darkness" (Lk. 22:53). Interestingly, to prove that "the Cross and the mechanism of Satan are one and the same thing," Girard, too, refers to the same biblical passage and says: "This hour, the moment of the power of darkness, is the hour of Satan."[63]

But if it was not God but Satan who was behind the death of Christ, the question would naturally arise: What, then, was God's real purpose of sending Christ? Weaver answers that "God did not send Jesus to die, but to live, to make visible and present the reign of God."[64] This answer is very interesting because it mentions about Christ's other alternative which has nothing to do

---

[58] Ibid., p. 36.
[59] Weaver, *The Nonviolent Atonement*, p. 45.
[60] Ibid., pp. 73-74.
[61] EDP, p. 277.
[62] Moon, "The Life of Jesus as Seen from God's Will."
[63] Girard, *I See Satan Fall Like Lightning*, pp. 36-37.
[64] Weaver, *The Nonviolent Atonement*, p. 74.

with the crucifixion. Weaver, however, has no further explanation of what would have happened if Christ had lived without being killed or opposed at that time. He simply says that the death of Christ was "inevitable."[65]

What is Girard's view of Christ's other possible alternative which would be for him to live if God was not behind his death? It seems that Girard has no thought of the other alternative. His thought is that although the cycle of mimetic violence as the continuous pattern of society was used by Satan to kill Christ, nevertheless after his murder that cycle or pattern was abolished and the spell of Satan ("violent contagion") broken through his resurrection: "The Resurrection is not only a miracle, a prodigious transgression of natural laws. It is a spectacular sign of the entrance into the world of a power superior to violent contagion."[66] According to Girard, this explains the uniqueness of Christianity because in other civilizations or communities the cycle of mimetic violence naturally repeats itself in such a way as to have peace followed by chaos again. As an apologist for traditional Christianity, therefore, he stops at this point without exploring Christ's other possibility of living without the cross.

§4. The Full Atonement

The Divine Principle acknowledges the value of the "spiritual" atonement brought by the resurrection of Christ, but the uniqueness of the Divine Principle is its assertion that the spiritual atonement is *not* a full atonement, no matter how great the victory of his resurrection may have been. If the people of his time had accepted him in accordance with the will of God and not with Satan's, the atonement through his work on the earth would have been a full atonement or "full salvation," both spiritual and physical: "Had the people believed in Jesus and so united with him in both spirit and flesh, they would have received salvation both spiritually and physically."[67] God originally sent Jesus as the second Adam, not to be crucified but to live for the realization of God's kingdom on earth where this full atonement would take place. The Divine Principle, therefore, can draw on Weaver's general idea that God sent Jesus to live to make the reign of God visible and present, although unfortunately Weaver himself does not explore it further.

This general idea of Weaver is actually echoed by other theologians who are not related to the Mennonite tradition nor to the Girardian school. The

---

[65] Ibid.
[66] Girard, *I See Satan Fall Like Lightning*, p. 189.
[67] EDP, p. 118.

Italian-born German Catholic priest Romano Guardini (1885–1968), for example, insightfully says: "Jesus ushered in the kingdom. It would have come in full bloom had the people accepted it. But the people failed and lost the kingdom which in the new order of things should have been theirs."[68] Another interesting point by Guardini is that the people's acceptance of Jesus "would have cancelled Adam's sin," but that their failure to accept him became "the second fall."[69] The German New Testament scholar Willi Marxsen (1919–1993), a central figure in the controversy in Germany from 1964 to 1968 on the resurrection of Christ, believes that "the purpose of Jesus" (*Sache Jesu*), that of the earthly Jesus, continues to be such an important thing that what is perceived to be his resurrection cannot be established as an actual historical event,[70] and maintains that "Jesus did not see his death as a saving event," given his important earthly activity for the eschaton.[71]

The same idea can be found among radical feminist and womanist theologians in America. The feminist theologians Joanne Carlson Brown and Rebecca Parker believe that the death of Jesus on the cross consists in "divine child abuse" because God the Father apparently killed the Son, and they complain that although the cross is thus a symbol of abuse which the forces of oppression too easily use to subjugate women, nevertheless all the historical theories of the atonement parade this abusive image of the cross as salvific. Thus Brown and Parker want to "do away with" all these atonement theories, simply asserting that Jesus "did not choose the cross" and lived "in opposition to unjust, oppressive cultures."[72]

The womanist theologian Delores Williams (1937–2022) observes that African-American women, who have been suffering under males and white females alike, can relate to the exploited experience of Hagar as Sarah's surrogate in the house of Abraham, and she criticizes the satisfaction theory and the penal substitution theory for making Jesus "the ultimate surrogate figure," who on behalf of humans takes their sin upon himself and suffers to die on the cross. According to Williams, this image of redemption through the ostensibly sacred surrogacy of Jesus is wrong because it expects African-

---

[68] Romano Guardini, *The Lord*, trans. Elinor Castendyk Briefs (Washington, DC: Gateway Editions, 1982), p. 250.

[69] Ibid., p. 247.

[70] Willi Marxsen, "The Resurrection of Jesus as a Historical and Theological Problem," in C. F. D. Moule, ed., *The Significance of the Message of the Resurrection for Faith In Jesus Christ*, trans. Dorothea M. Barton and R. A. Wilson (London: SCM Press, 1968), pp. 38-39.

[71] Quoted in Walter Kasper, *Jesus the Christ*, trans. V. Green (New York: Paulist Press, 1977), p. 115.

[72] Joanne Carlson Brown and Rebecca Parker, "For God So Loved the World?" in *Christianity, Patriarchy and Abuse: A Feminist Critique*, eds. Joanne Carlson Brown and Carole R. Bohn (New York: Pilgrim Press, 1989), pp. 1-30.

American women to "passively accept the exploitation that surrogacy brings."[73] She believes instead that Jesus, without dying on the cross, was supposed to resist the system of exploitation to bring a real atonement between God and humans and also among humans through his work on the earth:

> It seems more intelligent and more biblical to understand that redemption had to do with God, through Jesus, giving humankind new vision to see the resources for positive, abundant relational life—a vision humankind did not have before. Hence the kingdom-of-God theme in the ministerial vision of Jesus does not point to death... Rather, the kingdom of God is a metaphor of hope God gives those attempting to right the relationship between self and self, between self and others, between self and God as prescribed in the sermon on the mount, in the golden rule and in the commandment to show love above all else.[74]

Because of her emphasis on the importance of the work of Jesus on the earth, Williams does not want to see any value of his death and resurrection, somewhat resembling Marxsen who puts so much emphasis on the purpose of the earthly Jesus that he questions the historicity of the resurrection of Christ.

While the Divine Principle cannot agree with Marxsen and Williams when they completely neglect the importance of the resurrection of Christ, it appreciates them (and, of course, others such as Weaver, Guardini, Brown and Parker) for their understanding of Jesus' other alternative course of life without the crucifixion, i.e., his earthly ministry for what is expected to be the full atonement. Especially Williams' notion of the atonement as the realization of "the relationship between self and self, between self and others, between self and God" is a very good point.

According to the Divine Principle, the full atonement, which is both spiritual and physical, is the restoration of the relationship between God and humans in accordance with God's original purpose of creation. Following God's original blessing of "Be fruitful and multiply, and fill the earth and subdue it" (Gen. 1:28), Adam and Eve in the Garden of Eden were supposed to realize a God-centered ideal family based on the "four position foundation," which would involve the unity of love of four positions: 1) God, 2) Adam as Father, 3) Eve as Mother, and 4) their sinless children,[75] the first three of whom would constitute an original Trinity.[76] This way, Adam and Eve as "the True

---

[73] Delores S. Williams, *Sisters in the Wilderness: The Challenge of Womanist God-Talk* (Maryknoll, NY: Orbis Books, 1993), p. 162.
[74] Ibid., pp. 165-66.
[75] EDP, pp. 34, 172.
[76] EDP, p. 172.

Parents of humankind"[77] were supposed to create "the lineage of God" in which all their descendants would be born as "the children of God" and the kingdom of God on earth would be built under his "sovereignty." Unfortunately, however, Adam and Eve succumbed to the "sexual" temptation of the Archangel Lucifer,[78] and "bound themselves in blood ties with" him, creating "the lineage of Satan" in which all their descendants became "the children of Satan" and "this world has come under Satan's sovereignty."[79] As a result of this, the God-centered four position foundation was lost, and it was replaced by a Satan-centered four position foundation: 1) Satan, 2) Adam as fallen Father, 3) Eve as fallen Mother, and 4) their fallen children, the first three of whom formed a "fallen" Trinity.[80] The full atonement, therefore, means to completely defeat this Satan-centered four position foundation to restore the God-centered four position foundation through someone who is in the position of the unfallen Adam and someone who is in the position of the unfallen Eve.

Two thousand years ago Jesus came in this position of the unfallen Adam to bring the full atonement, according to the Divine Principle. If the leaders at that time had accepted him, not killing him on the cross, he would have been able to bring the full atonement by realizing an ideal family to restore the lineage of God and the sovereignty of God based on the God-centered four position foundation. When Weaver, Guardini, Marxsen, Brown, Parker and Williams reference Jesus' other alternative course of life without the crucifixion, they all allude to this full atonement from the viewpoint of the Divine Principle.

When the Divine Principle claims that Jesus was supposed to create an ideal family, it means to say that he was supposed to be married. But it does not mean to say that he was actually married. The Divine Principle, therefore, does not agree with Dan Brown's (1964–) popular yet controversial idea in his 2003 novel, *The Da Vinci Code*, that Jesus was married to Mary Magdalene,[81] nor does it accept William E. Phipps' (1930–2010) assertion in his 1970 book, *Was Jesus Married?*, that Jesus may have already been married, given the Jewish view of his day that marriage was a sacred duty for everyone, and also given the silence of the New Testament about his marital status.[82] Yet the Divine Principle does agree with Phipps that Jesus, as described in the Gospels, had a

---

[77] EDP, p. 172.
[78] EDP, pp. 63-65.
[79] EDP, p. 68.
[80] EDP, p. 172.
[81] Dan Brown, *The Da Vinci Code* (New York: Doubleday, 2003).
[82] William E. Phipps, *Was Jesus Married?: The Distortion of Sexuality in the Christian Tradition* (New York: Harper & Row, Publishers, 1970).

deep understanding and appreciation of the role of women, and that unfortunately the traditional view of Jesus as a celibate savior was established under the influence of Greek asceticism that came into Christianity.

The Divine Principle holds that Jesus' mission as the second Adam to be married was frustrated by his death on the cross due to the faithlessness of leaders behind whom Satan stood. As was already discussed previously, however, his victorious resurrection in spite of his undesirable death on the cross brought the spiritual atonement, by making the spiritual four position foundation: 1) God, 2) the resurrected Jesus as spiritual Father, 3) the Holy Spirit as spiritual Mother,[83] and 4) their spiritually reborn children (i.e., Christians), the first three of whom formed a "spiritual" Trinity. By the way, this Divine Principle idea that the spiritual atonement at the Christian level is connected with the spiritual Trinity coincides with the Eastern Christian idea that soteriology and Christology are quite deeply connected with the doctrine of the Trinity in the classic theory. This connection of the atonement with the Trinity has been basically absent in the West where Jesus' death on the cross has been far more emphasized than his resurrection and the Holy Spirit due to the satisfaction theory and the penal substitution theory.[84]

Even if the spiritual Trinity may have been acknowledged in the East because of the classic theory, however, the resurrected Jesus and the Holy Spirit "could fulfill only the mission of spiritual True Parents" according to the Divine Principle.[85] Therefore Christ must come back to the earth to bring the full atonement, which is both spiritual and physical, by creating an ideal family based on the God-centered four position foundation: 1) God, 2) the Christ of the Second Coming as Father, 3) his Bride as Mother, and 4) their own direct children and also all humankind as their children, the first three of whom form a "perfect" Trinity where the Christ of the Second Coming and his Bride are the True Parents of humankind who give rebirth both spiritually and physically for the removal of original sin: "Christ must return in the flesh and find his Bride. They will form on the earth a perfect trinity with God and become True Parents both spiritually and physically. They will give fallen people rebirth both

---

[83] The idea of the Holy Spirit as spiritual Mother is not totally alien in the Christian tradition. In Aramaic (and hence in the dialect known as Syriac), the gender of the word "spirit" was feminine; hence Syriac documents, which remain in today's Syrian Orthodox Church, refer to the Holy Spirit as feminine. Some Eastern Christian theologians such as St. Clement of Alexandria, Origen and St. Jerome identified the Holy Spirit as the Mother. So did Zinzendorf (1700-1760), bishop of the Moravian Church. For all this, see Chapter 5, Section 6 ("The Gender of the Holy Spirit") in the present book.

[84] This difference between East and West was already touched upon in Chapter 5, Section 4, Subsection 3 ("Jesus' Death and the Doctrine of the Trinity") in this book.

[85] EDP, p. 172.

spiritually and physically, removing their original sin."[86] This is how God's original purpose of creation is restored and accomplished, and it is referred to as "the marriage of the Lamb" in the Bible (Rev. 19:7).

The idea in the Divine Principle that the Christ of the Second Coming and his Bride fulfill God's will here on the earth is biblical. To begin with, God gave Adam and Eve his blessing to be realized on the earth: "Be fruitful and multiply, and fill the earth and subdue it" (Gen 1:28). God also promised Abraham and his seed the inheritance of "the land" as a blessing (Gen. 12:1-3, 7; 13:14-17). Abraham, however, never received the promise as he always stayed as a sojourner. So, according to Irenaeus, as the seed of Abraham "those who fear God and believe in him" in the Church will receive the inheritance of the land in the last days, if not now.[87] Jesus, who talked about the meek inheriting the earth (Mt. 5:5), had to die on the cross without fulfilling the inheritance of the land. Commenting on Jesus' statement at the Last Supper that "I shall not drink again of this fruit of the vine until that day when I drink it new with you in my Father's kingdom" (Mt. 26:29), Irenaeus says that drinking new of the fruit of the vine in the future kingdom means the inheritance of the land in the last days when Jesus returns.[88] This idea of Irenaeus is more understandable if one is reminded that he was a sharp critic of Gnosticism.

In accordance with the biblical teaching on the inheritance of the land, traditional apocalyptic eschatology generally asserts that God's will is to be realized on the earth in the last days at his initiative, although it may also hold that after the final judgment to destroy the earthly world, the eternal order will be otherworldly. According to premillennialism, adhered to by early Church Fathers in the first three centuries of the Christian era and also by many evangelical Christians today, in the last days earthly believers (together with the dead in Christ who are resurrected) are "caught up... in the clouds to meet the Lord in the air" (1 Thess. 4:17), and then the Lord as king and they as his royal subjects come back to the earth to inaugurate and reign the earthly millennial kingdom, making Satan surrender (Rev. 20:2-6).

According to postmillennialism, advocated by many Americans during the Great Awakenings from the eighteenth to the twentieth century, Christ will return at the culmination or conclusion of the successful development of the earthly millennial kingdom through the growth of the church in the world (Mt. 24:14), which had already started long before.

---

[86] EDP, p. 172.

[87] Irenaeus, "Against Heresies," V.32.2, in Roberts, Donaldson, and Coxe, eds, *The Ante-Nicene Fathers* series, vol. I, p. 561.

[88] Ibid., V.33.1, p. 562.

Amillennialism, accepted by the Catholic Church and mainline Protestant denominations as well as by the Eastern Orthodox Church, may be less earthly than the other two schools because it denies a literal 1000-year earthly kingdom and holds that the millennial kingdom only symbolically means the church as it exists on the earth now, imperfectly pointing to God's kingdom in heaven (Lk. 17:20-21); but it still does believe that Christ will return to the earth, after the age of the church, for the general bodily resurrection (Acts 24:14) and the final judgment.

Needless to say, according to non-apocalyptic eschatology in the German liberal tradition of Albrecht Ritschl (1822–1889), Adolf von Harnack (1851–1930), etc. and in the Social Gospel of Walter Rauschenbusch (1861–1918) in America, the kingdom of God on earth will be realized primarily by human efforts, and it will constitute the earthly eternal order with little appreciation of the otherworldly eternal order. As will be discussed in Chapter 12 in the present book, Unification eschatology mediates between traditional apocalyptic and liberal non-apocalyptic eschatology, maintaining that after the kingdom of God on earth is completely realized through the cooperation of God and humanity, the kingdom of God in heaven will be realized in the other world, and that the kingdom of God both on earth and in heaven will last for eternity.

§5. A Not Easy Task

From the God-given original task of Adam and Eve, through their failure to accomplish it due to Satan's invasion, to the spiritual atonement by the resurrected Jesus and the Holy Spirit, we find two basic metaphysical notions of the Divine Principle: the four position foundation and the Trinity. That these basic notions of the Divine Principle are related to the atonement is nothing new because theologians such as Robert Sherman have developed a theology of the atonement grounded on the Trinity to integrate all the major atonement theories, as was seen above in Section 3, Subsection 1. But when we apply these basic metaphysical notions also to the task of the Christ of the Second Coming and his Bride to bring the full atonement, the story may sound somewhat mechanical and simplistic, without being able to convey the involvement of a difficult process through which the task is going to be accomplished. Therefore this chapter will end with some words on this matter.

To begin with, when the Christ of the Second Coming comes in the last days, he will be misunderstood and persecuted by the world: "But first he must suffer many things and be rejected by this generation" (Lk. 17:25). This is exactly what happened also to the Christ of the First Coming two thousand years ago, and he ended up being killed on the cross by the forces of Satan. But the Christ of the Second Coming as "the third Adam"[89] is expected to continuously live, in order to defeat the reign of Satan. Of course, the Christ of the First Coming became spiritually victorious over Satan through his resurrection that was made possible by his unspeakable love and forgiveness even for his opponents at the time of the crucifixion; but the Christ of the Second Coming will become both spiritually and physically victorious by continuously living on the earth and making efforts in his entire life to show his utmost love for his enemies in spite of tremendous opposition from them. This full victory by the Christ of the Second Coming can be understood when Weaver's narrative Christus Victor's understanding of the power of Christ's love at the time of the crucifixion is applied to the *entire* earthly life of the Christ of the Second Coming that lasts as he continues to live in face of opposition. This full victory can also be understood well when the perspective of feminist and womanist theology, according to which Jesus was supposed to live to resist the system of exploitation on the earth for the purpose of atoning between God and human beings and also among human beings, is applied to the Christ of the Second Coming.

Building the God-centered four position foundation substantially on the earth, which was once shattered into pieces and lost due to the fall of Adam and Eve, is not that easy. Even the resurrected Christ and the Holy Spirit, after his noble sacrifice out of love, were able to build only the spiritual Trinity, forming the four position foundation only spiritually, with the result that the substantial four position foundation still stayed shattered and lost. This must be the reason why Christianity had to witness a variety of fragmented atonement theories called "subjective" or "objective" theories without being able to have any agreed-upon official atonement doctrine, although the classic theory (as well as the Divine Principle view of the resurrected Christ, of course) has the ability to integrate the theories. So, when the substantial four position foundation is constructed, involving the unity among God, the Christ of the Second Coming, his Bride, and all humankind, it should be able to reassemble those fragmented theories by lifting them up to the substantial level. This unity and reassembling can be done through love and sacrifice on the part of all parties involved in the new relationship of the lineage of God, which fully defeats the reign of Satan.

Contributing to this full atonement, then, is not only what the Christ of the Second Coming as the mediator does together with his Bride, but also what God does and what humans do. The Divine Principle teaches that God as the

[89] EDP, p. 203.

Creator has always been investing himself and still does so to realize the full atonement, that humans are also expected to fulfill their portion of responsibility to join this atonement by overcoming various challenges, and that God and humans relate to and affect each other in their relationship of love through the mediation of the Christ of the Second Coming and his Bride. This is how the substantial four position foundation is formed, and in that four position foundation in which all the stakeholders are finally united, humans are fully atoned with God.

A. G. Herbert in his "Translator's Preface" to Gustaf Aulén's *Christus Victor* states that the classic theory, rehabilitated by Aulén, can bring the "Reunion" of the Catholic and Protestant traditions, overcoming the division between them by integrating objective and subjective theories within each tradition (i.e., Anselm's satisfaction theory and Abelard's moral theory in the Catholic tradition, and the penal substitution theory and the moral influence theory in the Protestant tradition).[90] If that is true, the Unification doctrine of the atonement, which integrates objective and subjective theories in the four position foundation for the full atonement defeating the dominion of Satan fully, should be able to bring that Reunion of the Catholic and Protestant traditions.

[90] Aulén, *Christus Victor*, p. xxvi.

Chapter 11

Providential History of Modern Thought

The Divine Principle talks about the "Period of Preparation for the Second Advent of the Messiah," which is the "four-hundred-year period from the Protestant Reformation in 1517 to the end of World War I in 1918."[1] During this period, there were three stages of division into "Cain-type" and "Abel-type" views of life: 1) the Renaissance vs. the Reformation, 2) the Enlightenment vs. Pietism, etc., and 3) communism vs. a "third reformation" of Christianity. This was so that the "foundation of substance," or reintegration through love and surrender, between the Cain-type and Abel-type camps might be able to be laid worldwide three times, eventually to receive Christ at the Second Advent in the last days.[2]

The Divine Principle says that in the period in question all this started when God divided the "guiding medieval ideology" into the Renaissance and the Reformation because it had been defiled by Satan due to the failure of the popes and emperors of the ninth century and thereafter to be faithful enough to establish the foundation of substance for the Second Advent of the Messiah.[3] This division was like that in Adam's family, where "God had divided fallen Adam into Cain and Abel to separate Satan,"[4] so that the foundation of

---

[1] *Exposition of the Divine Principle* (New York: H.S.A.-U.W.C., 1996), p. 347. Henceforth abbreviated as EDP.
[2] EDP, pp. 347-79. The reference to a "third reformation" of Christianity can be seen in EDP, p. 364.
[3] EDP, pp. 338-39.
[4] EDP, p. 350.

substance between the two sons, i.e., their reintegration involving Abel's love for Cain and Cain's natural surrender to Abel, might be able to be laid to receive the Messiah, a restored Adam, on the family level.

It is important to note that this Cain-Abel typology of the Divine Principle is quite different in nature from the celebrated Cain-Abel typology of St. Augustine (354–430). The former contends that both the Cain-type and Abel-type camps, after establishing the foundation of substance between them to receive the Messiah, will equally be saved and restored through him, while the latter holds that on the day of final judgment after continuous struggles between the two throughout history, only the Abel-type camp will be saved and the Cain-type camp damned for eternity.[5]

Regarding how this period started and developed, thinkers such as Paul Tillich (1886–1965) and Reinhold Niebuhr (1892–1971), too, observe that the "medieval synthesis" was divided into the Renaissance and the Reformation, and that this division was repeated basically three times during this period. Tillich reports[6] that the three stages of division were: 1) the Renaissance vs. the Reformation, 2) the Enlightenment vs. Pietism, etc., and 3) Marxism vs. the neo-orthodoxy of Karl Barth (1886–1968). In a similar vein Niebuhr observes[7] that they were: 1) the Renaissance vs. the Reformation, 2) the Enlightenment[8] vs. the continuing Reformation tradition,[9] and 3) Marxism vs. the dialectical theology of Karl Barth. Tillich and Niebuhr also talk respectively about "new

---

[5] Augustine, *The City of God*, trans. Marcus Dods (New York: The Modern Library, 1993), books 21-22.

[6] Paul Tillich, *A History of Christian Thought: From Its Judaic and Hellenistic Origins to Existentialism*, ed. Carl E. Braaten (New York: Simon and Schuster, 1967), pp. 134-541.

[7] Reinhold Niebuhr, *The Nature and Destiny of Man: A Christian Interpretation*, vol. II: *Human Destiny* (New York: Charles Scribner's Sons, 1964), pp. 127-212.

[8] The Enlightenment, according to Niebuhr, is "a second chapter" of the Renaissance. See his *Human Destiny*, p. 165.

[9] It should be noted that according to Niebuhr the continuing Reformation tradition here does not refer to Pietism and Methodism. Surprisingly, he believes that Pietism and Methodism belong to the Renaissance tradition (whose second chapter is the Enlightenment) rather than to the Reformation tradition because he thinks that their "perfectionist claims" are based on the "immanent *logos*" principle of the Renaissance. See his *Human Destiny*, pp. 169-76.

ways of mediation"[10] and a "new synthesis"[11] needed between the two conflicting camps.

What is interesting is that while the Divine Principle is ambiguously silent about what the foundation of substance, or reintegration, between the Renaissance and the Reformation in the first stage would be, Tillich clearly identifies it as "Protestant orthodoxy" (or "Protestant scholasticism") in the late sixteenth and seventeenth centuries.[12] And again, while the Divine Principle is silent about what the foundation of substance, or reintegration, between the Enlightenment and Pietism in the second stage would be, Tillich clearly identifies it as the "theological synthesis" of Friedrich Schleiermacher (1768–1834)[13] or the "universal synthesis" of Georg W. F. Hegel (1770–1831).[14] Another interesting thing is that what the Divine Principle calls the "third reformation" of Christianity in the third stage, both Tillich and Niebuhr unambiguously identify as the theology of Barth.[15]

The advantage of the Divine Principle, of course, is that it gives a much clearer explanation of the reason for the Cain-Abel typology than Tillich and Niebuhr, because of its teaching that after the fall of Adam the foundation of substance between Cain and Abel has to be established to be able to receive the Messiah, a restored Adam. But we will use the insightful and reliable observations of Tillich and Niebuhr in order to a little more accurately interpret the "four-hundred-year period of preparation for the Second Advent of the Messiah" in the Divine Principle. This interpretation will therefore do the following things, among others:

---

[10] Tillich, *A History of Christian Thought*, p. 504. Although what he refers to as "new ways of mediation" here refers primarily to various schools of mediation from the late nineteenth century and the earliest part of the twentieth century before World War I as a continuation of the second stage of reintegration, nevertheless he is unquestionably a theologian of mediation to overcome polarities in the post-World War I period in the third stage of reintegration as well. According to him, any "theology of mediation" is "mediating the tradition to the modern mind," without "compromising the message with the modern mind" (ibid., p. 505). Cf. Langdon Gilkey, "Tillich: The Master of Mediation," in *The Theology of Paul Tillich*, ed. Charles W. Kegley (New York: The Pilgrim Press, 1982), pp. 26-58.

[11] Niebuhr's "new synthesis" between the two traditions (*Human Destiny*, p. 207) is quite a humble one, far from perfectionist or utopian, as it constitutes "the twofold emphasis upon the obligation to fulfill the possibilities of life [following the Renaissance tradition] and upon the limitations and corruptions in all historic realizations [following the Reformation tradition]," implying "that history is a meaningful process but is incapable of fulfilling itself and therefore points beyond itself to the judgment and mercy of God for its fulfillment" (ibid., p. 211).

[12] Tillich, *A History of Christian Thought*, pp. 276-83, 305-11. Although Tillich says, "Orthodoxy," capitalizing it, we say, "orthodoxy," using the lower case.

[13] Ibid., pp. 386-410.

[14] Ibid., pp. 410-31.

[15] Ibid., pp. 469, 535-39. Niebuhr, *Human Destiny*, p. 159.

First, it will touch upon Protestant scholasticism as the foundation of substance between the Renaissance and the Reformation, the theology of Schleiermacher as part of the foundation of substance between the Enlightenment and Pietism, and the theology of Barth as a main Abel-type view of life in the third stage, none of which is discussed in the Divine Principle.

Second, it will treat Hegel as a philosopher of synthesis between the Enlightenment and Pietism, rather than merely a representative of the Abel-type view of life as the Divine Principle seems to indicate.[16] It will also regard Immanuel Kant (1724–1804) as another philosopher of synthesis between the Enlightenment and Pietism as will be seen later, rather than another representative of the Abel-type view of life as the Divine Principle seems to suggest.[17]

Third, it will argue that it was actually Protestant scholasticism that was divided into the Enlightenment and Pietism in the second stage, whereas the Divine Principle does not say what was divided into the two. It will also show that it was Hegel's universal synthesis along with Kant's synthesis and Schleiermacher's theological synthesis that was divided into communism and Barth's theology in the third stage, whereas again the Divine Principle does not indicate what was divided into the two.

Fourth, it will suggest that the foundation of substance, or reintegration, between communism and Barth's theology in the third stage was manifest in important pre-1960s theologies of synthesis such as the theologies of the later Barth, Reinhold Niebuhr, H. Richard Niebuhr (1894–1962) and Paul Tillich. This is a suggestion that will need to be more carefully examined elsewhere by historians of theology.

Finally, it will mention a *fourth* stage of division, which occurred mainly in America in the turbulent 1960s but about which the Divine Principle is silent: the division of the pre-1960s theological synthesis into Cain-type radical theologies such as "death of God" theology, black theology and feminist theology vs. Abel-type theological views such as neo-fundamentalism and neo-Pentecostalism.[18] Accordingly, a *fourth* stage of reintegration, which followed the fourth stage of division, will also be discussed as the foundation of substance laid in the 1970s through the 1990s to receive what Sun Myung

---

[16] EDP, p. 356.

[17] Ibid.

[18] Neo-fundamentalism and neo-Pentecostalism are to be distinguished from fundamentalism and Pentecostalism, which emerged in the early twentieth century, supposedly belonging to the third reformation along with the theology of Karl Barth.

Moon calls the "fourth Adam."[19] It will be seen that several schools of reintegrative theology, such as evangelical theology, reconstructive postmodernism, and the theologies of Karl Rahner (1904–1984) and Jürgen Moltmann (1926–2024), as well as the "head-wing"[20] thought of Rev. Moon, contributed to the fourth stage of reintegration.

It is clear, therefore, that the "modern" period does not just mean the four-hundred-year period between 1517 and 1918 but the longer period from the Reformation to the present.[21]

§1. Medieval Scholasticism and Its Breakdown

1. Formation of Medieval Scholasticism

Medieval scholasticism was an attempt to unify everything centering on God. In order to solve all the practical problems of human beings, it attempted to synthesize faith and reason, theology and philosophy, religion and culture, and church and state centering on God. In the Middle Ages it was common sense to understand that all are to be united under the authority of God and under the authority of the Church representing God. God was as natural to everyone as the air we breathe. It was indeed a noble ideal. Unless we understand this point well, we may be inclined to think rather simplistically that the Middle Ages were "Dark Ages."

Medieval scholasticism started from around the ninth century and enjoyed its golden age in the thirteenth century. It had two major schools: the Augustinian and Thomistic. Both had one thing in common: they attempted

---

[19] For an explanation of the "fourth Adam," see the very end of the present chapter.

[20] Moon has coined the term "head wing," and by it he means a central position which has the capacity of uniting together the left and right wings, which are Cain-type and Abel-type, respectively. See his "Reflection of 1986," sermon delivered at Belvedere, Tarrytown, NY, December 28, 1986: "Godism is the 'head wing.' That is a new word. The human body has a head and two arms, the right and the left. Godism is like the head, while the arms are the left wing and the right wing… the right wing and the left wing, representing Abel and Cain, have continued to struggle. The right and left wings will not settle their conflict until the 'head wing' comes forward and says, 'You two guys, instead of fighting, you must cooperate!'… Thus the ideology of heaven and earth has emerged. We stand neither on the right nor on the left, but rather are vertically uniting upper and lower, heaven and earth." http://www.tparents.org/Moon-Talks/sunmyungmoon86/861228.htm.

[21] By the adjective "modern," Christopher Ben Simpson means "what comes after the mediaeval," including things happening today. See his *Modern Christian Theology* (London: Bloomsbury T&T Clark, 2016), p. 7. We follow his definition.

to synthesize everything centering on God. But their approaches were quite different from each other.[22]

The Augustinian school inherited the tradition of St. Augustine, and its representatives included St. Bonaventure (1221–1274) of the Franciscan order. This school taught the unity of faith and reason based on its basic assertion that faith precedes reason. Because God as the Creator knows this world much better than we do, we first have to unite with God and accept the world by faith before we eventually know the world well by reason. This school had the same attitude toward the authority of the Church, and it tried to first unite with God to accept the Church by faith before understanding it by reason.

By contrast, the Thomistic school was formed by St. Thomas Aquinas (1225–1274) of the Dominican order, who used the then rediscovered philosophy of Aristotle for doing theology. This school taught the unity of faith and reason, saying that while they are independent of each other, they support each other without contradiction. Therefore, while accepting revelation and the traditional teaching of the Church on God by faith, it also observed the created world by reason to induce God's existence and attributes from it. Thus it taught that these two independent ways of understanding God—by faith and by reason—are not contradictory but complementary.

According to the Divine Principle, the formation of this medieval synthesis, whether Augustinian or Thomistic, was providential preparation for the Second Advent of the Messiah, through whom the "new truth" would be brought forth to "resolve the problems of religion and science as an integrated human endeavor, guiding religion, politics and economy to progress in one unified direction based on God's ideal."[23]

The Second Advent of the Messiah was initially supposed to take place based on the foundation of substance to be made between Emperor Charlemagne (r. 800–814), in the position of Abel, and Pope Leo III (r. 795–816), in the position of Cain, when the latter crowned the former Emperor of the Holy Roman Empire in 800.[24] The coronation of Charlemagne was very significant from the viewpoint of the Divine Principle. This must be why many historians talk about it in appreciative ways, even if they may not realize its connection with an expected Second Advent of the Messiah. The British academic James Bryce (1838–1922), for example, goes so far as to say that the coronation was not only "the central event of the Middle Ages" but also "one

---

[22] For an excellent explanation of this, see Tillich, *A History of Christian Thought*, pp. 180-87.
[23] EDP, p. 338.
[24] EDP, pp. 321, 338.

of those very few events" without which "the history of the world would have been different."[25]

2. *Breakdown of Medieval Scholasticism*

The approaches of the two major schools in medieval scholasticism were at the zenith of their reputation in the thirteenth century. For some time, the Thomistic school was dominant over its Augustinian counterpart. Eventually, however, radical members of the Augustinian school such as John Duns Scotus (c. 1266–1308) and William of Ockham (c. 1287–1347) challenged and dissolved the synthetic approach of the Thomistic school, separating faith and reason.

Opposing Aquinas' intellectualism, Scotus believed that in God and also in human beings the will has primacy over the intellect. God's will is thus absolutely free. If so, no possible reason for God's free choices can be found. Our intellectual observation of the created world, therefore, can never ascertain the reason for his actions. This means that there is no intellectual way to know God from the created world.

Ockham, while accepting Scotus' voluntarism, also adhered to nominalism, according to which what truly exist are only particular individuals. It holds that universal concepts are merely names made from thinking on their existence, rejecting the view that they exist in the mind of God. Thus our knowledge of particular individuals in the world does not lead us to any reality beyond that experience, and in particular it does not lead us to God.

The assertions of Scotus and Ockham resulted in this: God can only be reached by faithful submission to the biblical and ecclesiastical authorities and not from the created world, while the created world can be known only by direct observation through reason. This helped to destroy the Thomistic school and even the Augustinian school. This led to the breakdown of medieval scholasticism, and a separation between the religious and secular realms.

But the problem was that in spite of this breakdown the Church still wanted to continue to exert its authority over the secular realm as well. Hence, according to Tillich, by the end of the Middle Ages "the desperate fight between autonomous secularism and religious heteronomy developed."[26] Heteronomy means a state in which a finite and limited authority, exalting itself to the level of the infinity of God, "claims absolute authority and demands the

---

[25] James Bryce, "The Coronation as a Revival of the Roman Empire in the West," in *The Coronation of Charlemagne: What Did It Signify?* ed. Richard E. Sullivan (Boston: D. C. Heath and Co., 1959), p. 41.

[26] Tillich, *A History of Christian Thought*, p. 188.

submission of every other reality," and it is therefore "demonic."[27] The Catholic Church, says Tillich, had this heteronomous trait.[28] The Church, therefore, had to be deprived of its power by the Renaissance and the Reformation. In the words of Tillich, "The Renaissance and the Reformation were the means by which the church was deprived of this power."[29]

Regarding this, the Divine Principle, too, references the effect of the demonic: "The popes and emperors... in the Carolingian period" were supposed to lay the foundation for the Second Advent of the Messiah, but they became "faithless," and "their faithlessness and immorality allowed Satan to corrupt the guiding medieval ideology [i.e., the medieval synthesis]," with the result that "for the separation of Satan," God "divided" it into "two trends of thought: Cain-type Hellenism and Abel-type Hebraism," which "bore fruit in the Renaissance and the Reformation, respectively."[30]

a. The Renaissance

According to the Divine Principle, the Renaissance and the Reformation respectively emerged as people's "external" and "internal" pursuits of the "original human nature" because it had been "repressed" in medieval feudal society.[31] Pursuits of that original nature are inevitably both internal and external, for the reason that human beings have the dual characteristics of "internal nature" and "external form," being created in resemblance to God's dual characteristics of "original internal nature" and "original external form," and that "we exist and thrive" based upon the give and take action between these dual characteristics.[32]

Regarding the reason for the emergence of the Renaissance, therefore, the Divine Principle says it is because "it is the calling of our original nature [from an external point of view] to pursue freedom and autonomy" when "repressed," as "we are created to attain perfection by fulfilling our given responsibility of our own free will, without God's direct assistance"[33] The Divine Principle goes on to say:

---

[27] Paul Tillich, On *the Boundary: An Autobiographical Sketch* (New York: Charles Scribner's Sons, 1966), p. 40.

[28] Ibid., p. 39. See also Paul Tillich, *Systematic Theology*, vol. I: *Reason and Revelation: Being and God* (Chicago: The University of Chicago Press, 1951), p. 85.

[29] Tillich, *A History of Christian Thought*, p. 188.

[30] EDP, p. 350.

[31] EDP, pp. 351-52.

[32] EDP, p. 348.

[33] EDP, p. 351.

> The Renaissance came to life in fourteenth-century Italy, which was the center of the study of the classical Hellenic heritage. Though it began as a movement imitating the thought and life of ancient Greece and Rome, it soon developed into a wider movement which transformed the medieval way of life. It expanded beyond the sphere of culture to encompass every aspect of society, including politics, economic life and religion. In fact, it became the external driving force for the construction of the modern world.[34]

Reinhold Niebuhr has a similar characterization of the Renaissance, saying that it "opposes the ecclesiastical control of all cultural life in the name of the autonomy of human reason and thereby lays the foundation for the whole modern cultural development."[35]

b. The Reformation

The Reformation, by contrast, was more internal and faith-oriented. The Divine Principle says that the Reformation was "to restore our spirituality through religion,"[36] calling for "the revival of the spirit of early Christianity, when believers zealously lived for the Will of God, guided by the words of Jesus and apostles."[37] It was initiated by Martin Luther (1483–1546), who posted his "Ninety-five Theses" on the castle door at Wittenberg on October 31, 1517, with the first thesis stating: "When our Lord and Master, Jesus Christ, said 'Repent,' He called for the entire life of believers to be one of penitence."[38] Other famous Reformers were Huldrych Zwingli (1484–1531) and John Calvin (1509–1564).

According to Niebuhr, it was not only the Renaissance but also the Reformation that sought freedom. Freedom, as understood by the Reformation, primarily means "the right and the ability of each soul to appropriate the grace of God by faith without the interposition of any restrictive institution of grace."[39] Consequently,

> The Reformation opposes the dogmatic control of religious thought by the church in the name of the authority of Scripture, insisting that no human authority (not even that of the church) can claim the right

---

[34] EDP, pp. 351-52.
[35] Niebuhr, *Human Destiny*, p. 150.
[36] EDP, p. 349.
[37] EDP, p. 352.
[38] John Dillenberger, ed., *Martin Luther: Selections from His Writings* (Garden City, NY: Anchor Books, 1961), p. 490.
[39] Niebuhr, *Human Destiny*, p. 152.

of possessing and interpreting the truth of the gospel, which stands beyond all human wisdom.[40]

3. Protestant Scholasticism: Foundation of Substance between the Renaissance and the Reformation

The Divine Principle acknowledges the possibility of the Renaissance and the Reformation uniting with each other to establish the foundation of substance with the former "submitting to" the latter,[41] but observes that the former actually "took a dominant position over" the latter with no sign of the establishment of the foundation of substance.[42] Niebuhr agrees with this observation by the Divine Principle, referring to the "defeat" of the Reformation by the Renaissance for two reasons: 1) because of the "moral pessimism and cultural indifference" of the Reformation; and 2) because "the phenomenal development of all the sciences and social techniques, of the conquest of nature and of the general extension of human capacities in the modern period" were advantageous for the Renaissance.[43]

Unlike the Divine Principle, however, Tillich and other scholars seem to be of the opinion that the Renaissance and the Reformation were somehow reintegrated to constitute Protestant scholasticism in the late sixteenth and seventeenth centuries. John Dillenberger (1918–2008) and Claude Welch (1922–2009), for example, characterize Protestant scholasticism as a sort of reintegration between revelation and reason. When talking about its similarity to medieval scholasticism in that regard, they say: "There was similarity… in emphasis upon a natural knowledge of God, supplemented by revelation."[44] In fact, Johann Gerhard (1582–1637), a Lutheran, developed a theological system of grand synthesis in the seventeenth century "comparable" to that of Thomas Aquinas in thirteenth-century Roman Catholicism—a two-structure theory of reality: the superstructure of revelation and the substructure of reason, distinguishable yet without contradiction.[45] Hence we can safely posit that Protestant scholasticism was supposed to be the foundation of substance between the Renaissance and the Reformation.

In a way, Protestant scholasticism within the Lutheran tradition started with Philip Melanchthon (1497–1560), who "as a man of broad cultural,

---

[40] Ibid., p. 150.
[41] EDP, p. 351.
[42] EDP, p. 350.
[43] Niebuhr, *Human Destiny*, p. 156.
[44] John Dillenberger and Claude Welch, *Protestant Christianity: Interpreted through Its Development* (New York: Charles Scribner's Sons, 1954), p. 97.
[45] Tillich, *A History of Christian Thought*, pp. 279, 310.

humanist and classical interests" systematically and intellectually explained Luther's more unsystematic and prophetic teachings and coped with theological controversies by using "the utmost of tact and mediation in every situation."[46] Melanchthon in his thinking gradually became more humanistic and synergistic than Luther. After the death of Luther, therefore, quite a hostile split emerged between extremely conservative followers of Luther (known as "Gnesio-Lutherans") and followers of Melanchthon (called "Philippists"). Controversies intensified on issues such as the presence of Christ in the Lord's Supper, the relationship of the activities of the Spirit and human beings, and the place of law and works in the context of faith. But these issues were finally settled in the Formula of Concord in 1577, which marked a victory for the basically conservative wing (neither for extremely conservative Gnesio-Lutheranism nor for Philippism) and became an authoritative Lutheran statement of faith. In 1580, the Book of Concord, containing the Formula of Concord as well as the Augsburg Confession drafted by Melanchthon in 1530, the catechisms of Luther, etc., was published.

Regarding this development of Lutheran scholasticism, Dillenberger and Welch state: "The Bible as Bible, understood through the Book of Concord, was synonymous with the Word of God."[47] They go on to say about the scholastic nature of this development:

> Faith in revelation meant assent to statements which had been given in an infallible form in a book. God's truth meant propositions about God. Thus the initial warmth and freedom of Lutheranism gave way to a stress upon statements derived from the Bible. And these were set forth with the rigor of a theological method in which sensitive spirituality was often lacking. Men were now more concerned with being correct than with the revivifying power of the Spirit.[48]

Within the Reformed tradition as well, theological controversies occurred after Calvin published the first edition of *Institutes of the Christian Religion* in 1536. To address the controversies, several confessions of faith such as the Belgic Confession of 1561 were formulated. "People were asked to believe the confessions, and the faith these were meant to safeguard often took second place";[49] this was how Reformed scholasticism started to be created. After the emergence of Arminian liberalism, controversies intensified on issues such as predestination as God's decree, Christ's death for the elect only or for all

---

[46] Dillenberger and Welch, *Protestant Christianity*, p. 80.
[47] Ibid., p. 85.
[48] Ibid.
[49] Ibid., p. 89.

people, and the possibility or impossibility of rejecting God's grace. The Synod of Dort in Holland in 1618-1619 officially settled these issues in favor of the conservative side. Also in defense of the Synod of Dort, the Formula Consensus (Helvetic Consensus) was formulated in the Swiss Reformed Church in 1675, having the "most elaborate and scholastic official expression" of the Calvinism of the day.[50] In this context, the Reformed tradition, too, established a doctrine of biblical inerrancy, equating the Bible itself with the Word of God. One of the authors of the Formula Consensus was Francis Turretin (1623–1687), whose major work, *Institutes of Elenctic Theology*, adopted the scholastic method of Thomas Aquinas. This constituted the culmination of Reformed scholasticism, and was widely used as a textbook in the Reformed tradition for the next two or three centuries.

Tillich interestingly encourages us to take Protestant orthodoxy seriously, because it "was and still is the solid basis of all later [theological] developments, whether these developments... were directed against Orthodoxy, or were attempts at restoration of it."[51] From the viewpoint of the Divine Principle, it can be said that Protestant scholasticism was very significant. Although the Divine Principle is silent about its existence, it was providentially supposed to be the foundation of substance for the Second Advent of the Messiah.

§2. Protestant Scholasticism and Its Breakdown

1. Breakdown of Protestant Scholasticism

Protestant scholasticism broke down into Cain-type and Abel-type views of life in the late seventeenth and eighteenth centuries: the Enlightenment vs. Pietism, etc. Although the Divine Principle falls short of identifying Protestant scholasticism as the foundation of substance between the Renaissance and the Reformation, the reason for its breakdown is obvious from the viewpoint of the Divine Principle: it is because it was defiled by Satan, like medieval scholasticism had been. In the language of Tillich, Protestant scholasticism, too, became demonic because of its heteronomous trait.[52]

In fact, Protestant scholasticism, whether Lutheran or Reformed, was heteronomously absolutist and dogmatic. Lutheran theologians dogmatically

---

[50] Arthur Cushman McGiffert, *Protestant Thought before Kant* (London: Duckworth & Co., 1911), p. 153.
[51] Tillich, *A History of Christian Thought*, pp. 276-77. See also pp. 306-8.
[52] Tillich, *Systematic Theology*, vol. 1: *Reason and Revelation: Being and God*, p. 86.

decided that the truth was "already fully given and unalterably fixed" in the Formula of Concord, and that "to depart from it or correct it in any way was out of the question."[53] As for the Reformed tradition, its authoritarianism was such that after the Synod of Dort, the Arminian Dutch statesman Johan van Oldenbarnevelt (1547–1619) was executed and all Arminian pastors, about 200 of them, were deposed as heretics.

Originally, Protestant scholasticism was supposed to be a reintegration between the Cain-type Renaissance and the Abel-type Reformation, with the former "submitting to" the latter for the establishment of the foundation of substance.[54] In fact, however, the former "took a dominant position over" the latter.[55] So their reintegration, if any, to form Protestant scholasticism seems to have been done in an imperfect way and even in a reverse way. This is the problem of "reversing dominion," one of the primary characteristics of the "fallen nature," explained in the Divine Principle.[56] This problem in the reintegration seems to have been found in both Lutheran and Reformed scholasticism, given what we know about how they were formed and how badly they treated their dissenters. So Protestant scholasticism, which was now heteronomous and demonic, disintegrated into the Cain-type Enlightenment and Abel-type Pietism.

The Enlightenment and Pietism into which Protestant scholasticism was disintegrated, were two different ways of revolting against it. Thus Tillich says: "Historically, Pietism and the Enlightenment both fought against Orthodoxy [i.e., Protestant scholasticism]."[57] The Enlightenment and Pietism respectively stood for two kinds of autonomy: "rational autonomy" and "mystical autonomy," which were both against the heteronomy of Protestant scholasticism.[58]

a. The Enlightenment

In explaining about the emergence of the Enlightenment as a revolt against Protestant scholasticism, Tillich talks about Protestant scholasticism's two-story theory of reality which, like Thomas Aquinas' theological synthesis, distinguished between the upper story of revealed theology and the lower story of natural theology. According to Tillich, the autonomous rationalism of the

---

[53] McGiffert, *Protestant Thought before Kant*, p. 145.
[54] EDP, p. 351.
[55] EDP, p. 350.
[56] EDP, pp. 73, 193.
[57] Tillich, *A History of Christian Thought*, p. 286.
[58] Ibid., pp. 286-87.

Enlightenment emerged as "a revolution… by the lower story fighting against the upper story"; to break down Protestant scholasticism, "the lower claimed the right to become the whole building of theology and denied the right to have any independent upper story at all."[59]

It may be that the two-story theory of reality in Protestant scholasticism was established in such an intellectual way as to make the upper story of non-intellectual revealed theology ironically claim its absolute intellectual authority. Therefore the upper story had to be challenged by the lower, which became the Enlightenment.

Tillich also explains the value of Enlightenment concepts such as autonomy, reason, harmony and tolerance. Autonomy is the "natural law given by God, present in the human mind and in the structure of the world," thus being in opposition to the "arbitrariness" of heteronomy; reason is the "awareness of the principles of truth and justice"; harmony follows "from the principles of autonomy and reason"; and tolerance is something to be proposed against the "religious wars" of "various confessional groups."[60]

The Divine Principle's description of the Enlightenment as the Cain-type view of life is as follows:

> By the turn of the eighteenth century, the Cain-type view of life had broken down the verities enshrined by history and tradition. All matters in human life came to be judged by reason or empirical observation. Anything deemed irrational or other-worldly, including belief in the God of the Bible, was thoroughly discredited. People's energies were narrowly directed toward the practical life. Such was the ideology of the Enlightenment.[61]

A distinction can be made between non-religious and religious rationalism in the Enlightenment. Non-religious rationalists were atheistic, and they included Denis Diderot (1713–1784), Jean le Rond d'Alembert (1717–1783) and Baron d'Holbach (1723–1789) in the French Enlightenment. Religious rationalists were theistic, but they reduced religion to those essentials which can be rationally defended, such as certain moral principles like tolerance and a few universally held beliefs about God, and regarded all the other elements as not really necessary ecclesiastical trappings, such as sacraments, rituals and doctrines of incarnation, atonement, resurrection and Trinity. They included Edward Herbert (1583–1648), John Toland (1670–1722), Matthew Tindal (1655–1733), Voltaire (1694–1778), Gottfried Leibniz (1646–1716), Christian

---

59 Ibid., pp. 310-11.
60 Ibid., pp. 289-91.
61 EDP, p. 355.

Wolff (1679–1754) and G. E. Lessing (1729–1781). Many of the religious rationalists were also "deists," who believed that God, after creating the world, has no dealings with it. According to the Divine Principle, all these Enlightenment figures, atheistic and theistic alike, belonged to what it calls the "second renaissance."[62]

b. Pietism

As was mentioned a little earlier, the upper story of non-intellectual revealed theology in the two-story theory of Protestant scholasticism ironically claimed its absolute intellectual authority, losing its God-centered religious subjectivity and assuming an authoritarianism of objectivity instead. Pietism, founded by the Lutheran pastor Philip Spener (1635–1705), was a revolt against it to restore the subjective side of religion which was lost. According to Tillich, Pietism was "the reaction of the subjective side of religion against the objective side."[63] In a similar vein, Dillenberger and Welch state: "Such dissatisfaction [with Protestant scholasticism or orthodoxy] expressed itself in Pietism and in a kind of general revulsion against orthodoxy."[64]

Pietism put such an emphasis on the subjective side of religion that it believed that there is no *theologia irregenetorum* (theology of the unregenerate), i.e., that unless you have the experience of regeneration, you cannot be a theologian; whereas Protestant orthodoxy apparently maintained that whether you are regenerated or not, you can still write a fully valid theology.

The Pietist nobleman Nicolaus Zinzendorf (1700–1760) helped to organize the Moravian Church, which stressed the importance of spiritual renewal through the Holy Spirit. Under the Moravian influence, the Methodist Church of John Wesley (1703–1791) started.

In addition to Spener and Wesley, the Divine Principle mentions George Fox (1624–1691), who founded Quakerism, and Emanuel Swedenborg (1688–1772), from whose writings the New Church was established, and says that they all started "new movements" which "stressed the importance of religious zeal and the inner life," valuing "mystical experience over doctrine and rituals."[65] According to the Divine Principle, they all belonged to what it calls the "second reformation."[66] Jonathan Edwards (1703–1758) and George

---

[62] EDP, p. 364.
[63] Tillich, *A History of Christian Thought*, p. 284.
[64] Dillenberger and Welch, *Protestant Christianity*, p. 98.
[65] EDP, pp. 356-57.
[66] EDP, p. 364.

Whitefield (1714–1770), who were among the main figures of the First Great Awakening in America, were part of this trend also.

Reinhold Niebuhr disagrees that these movements of religious renewal belonged to the Abel-type tradition of the Reformation. According to him, they, which he refers to as "sects" in Protestantism, rather belonged to the Renaissance tradition, part of which was the Enlightenment, because their "perfectionist impulse" was based on the "immanent *logos*" principle belonging to the Renaissance.[67] Tillich, too, recognizes a similarity between Pietism and the Enlightenment: both of them stood for the principle of autonomy, i.e., the immanence of God's law in us, if in two somewhat different ways. Nevertheless, Tillich never neglects the important connection of Pietism with Luther's Reformation and observes that Spener was aware of the presence of "all the elements of Pietism" in the earlier Luther, and wanted to restore it because it had been lost due to Protestant orthodoxy.[68] Perhaps, therefore, Niebuhr's mapping of Pietism, Methodism, etc. within the Enlightenment is misplaced. Niebuhr is basically a theologian of transcendence who is reluctant to approve any theology which "obscures the real dialectic between the historical and the eternal."[69]

2. *Nineteenth-Century Theology: Foundation of Substance between the Enlightenment and Pietism*

Although the Divine Principle is silent again about what would be the foundation of substance, or reintegration, between the Enlightenment and Pietism in the second stage, Tillich identifies it as the theological synthesis of Friedrich Schleiermacher and the universal synthesis of Georg W. F. Hegel.[70] The moral religion of Immanuel Kant can also be added as another candidate of synthesis for the foundation of substance between the Enlightenment and Pietism. The importance of these three thinkers in this regard can be seen from the following words of James C. Livingston (1930–2011): "Those [works] of Kant, Schleiermacher, and Hegel alone determined the course of theology for the next century and beyond."[71] The projects of synthesis by these three thinkers actually determined the generally synthetic and optimistic character of nineteenth-century theology as a whole.

---

[67] See n. 9.

[68] Tillich, *A History of Christian Thought*, p. 284.

[69] Niebuhr, *Human Destiny*, p. 176.

[70] See nn. 13, 14.

[71] James C. Livingston, *Modern Christian Thought*, vol. 1: *The Enlightenment and the Nineteenth Century*, 2nd ed. (Upper Saddle River, NJ: Prentice Hall, 1988), p. 116.

At this point, it would be pertinent to mention just briefly about the American Revolution as a synthesis between the "American Enlightenment"[72] (Cain-type) and the First Great Awakening (Abel-type) in the eighteenth century. Its importance lies in the fact that it marked a significant spread from Europe to America of the efforts to establish the foundation of substance to receive the Messiah. This point will be discussed in a little more detail below, when the importance of America as a Christian nation where the foundation of substance in the third stage was to be laid is dealt with later.

a. Moral religion of Immanuel Kant

Kant experienced both the Enlightenment and Pietism. He started his career as a disciple of the Enlightenment rationalism of Gottfried Leibniz and Christian Wolff in Germany, appreciating the theme of rational autonomy. Also, as his parents were devout Pietists, he was aware of the good qualities of Pietism such as moral integrity after regeneration. But he gradually became dissatisfied with both, because he felt that the Enlightenment was overemphasizing the capacity of human reason, while Pietism was a little too emotional and even hypocritical.

In order to critique the Enlightenment confidence on human reason, he argued in his *Critique of Pure Reason* (1781) that since our *a priori* forms of intuition (space and time) and forms of thought (twelve categories such as plurality and causality) are only applicable to the physical world of "phenomena," we cannot know by "pure reason" things-in-themselves ("noumena") behind the physical world. This was his agnosticism.

He then published *Critique of Practical Reason* (1788) to show an alternative way of establishing religion, which is to base religion on "practical reason" instead of pure reason. Practical reason is the rational faculty concerning human conduct, apprehending the moral law (the categorical imperative) within oneself. Autonomous obedience to this moral law within oneself always results in right action. For the sake of morality, practical reason can postulate God, freedom and immortality. For Kant, practical reason in this sense is faith. He destroyed speculative knowledge in order to make room for this faith: "I have therefore found it necessary to deny *knowledge* in order to make room for *faith*."[73]

---

[72] The term "American Enlightenment" was not used in the eighteenth century, but was coined by historians and philosophers after World War II.

[73] Immanuel Kant, *Critique of Pure Reason*, trans. Norman Kemp Smith (New York: St. Martin's Press, 1965), p. 29. Preface to second edition, Bxxx. Italics original.

As can be seen in his *Religion within the Limits of Reason Alone* (1793), Kant reinterpreted traditional Christian doctrines in terms of his moral philosophy. For him, Jesus is a moral teacher who has reached moral perfection, and his divinity means his perfect humanity that is pleasing to God. Original sin means "radical evil," our innate propensity to evil, whose origin is an inscrutable mystery, although it is at least *not* an inheritance from Adam but something for which we have moral responsibility. Justification means that we, with the help of Jesus, choose to have the right disposition to atone for past misdeeds, although we can even do this on our own because we already have the moral law within us. When we all have the right disposition this way, we can build an "ethical commonwealth," which is the kingdom of God on earth.

Kant was criticized by many including King Frederick William II of Prussia (r. 1786–1797) for distorting Christianity, but his moral religion turned out to be a synthesis of the Enlightenment and Pietism. From the Enlightenment it borrowed the theme of autonomy, while denying its overconfidence on human reason. From Pietism it adopted the theme of autonomous spiritual maturity after regeneration, while negating its emotional fervor. Kant was actually the first to synthesize the Enlightenment and Pietism in the second stage. To use the terminology of the Divine Principle, his synthesis was for the realization of the foundation of substance between them. The Divine Principle, therefore, may not be accurate, when it says that he was a representative the Abel-type view of life.[74]

The importance of Kant as the first synthesizer in the second stage was such that only with him did the eighteenth century start to understand "its limitations," so that he stood "at the turning-point of his age."[75] The Kantian tradition of synthesis in morality was inherited by many in the nineteenth and early twentieth centuries, although it eventually disintegrated into Cain-type and Abel-type views of life in the third stage in the early twentieth century.

b. Theological synthesis of Friedrich Schleiermacher

Schleiermacher, too, experienced both the Enlightenment and Pietism. He was exposed to Moravian Pietism through his father who encountered the Moravian Brethren because the Prussian troops he served as a Reformed army chaplain were stationed at the place where there was a Moravian community. He and his father learned that religion cannot be taught but should be awakened. At age 17, he enrolled in a Moravian seminary. Later, being drawn

---

74 EDP, p. 356.

75 Karl Barth, *Protestant Thought: From Rousseau to Ritschl*, trans. Brian Cozens (New York: Simon and Schuster, 1959), p. 150.

to the humanism and rationalism of the Enlightenment, he left the seminary and matriculated at Halle University to study in a more open environment. He then felt a great tension between Pietism and the Enlightenment.

In coping with the tension, Schleiermacher at one point was impressed with the Kantian synthesis which understood religion on a moral ground. But after he was exposed to Romanticism, he gradually realized that even the Kantian synthesis is not sufficient, because moral volition seems to contain a sort of unnatural manipulation, like the intellectual manipulation of Enlightenment rationalism, which makes gaps between God and us and among us.

Schleiermacher opted for neither intellect nor moral volition but feeling (*Gefühl*) as a ground on which the deep religious experience of God can occur: "It [i.e., religion] is to have life and to know life in *immediate feeling*, only as such… [a finite and temporal] existence in the Infinite and Eternal."[76] Thus he went beyond the Enlightenment tradition of intellectual reason, while retaining its theme of autonomy. He also went beyond the Kantian way of moral synthesis, while keeping its theme of autonomy coming from Pietism as well as from the Enlightenment. Thus he concluded that feeling is an appropriate ground on which the Enlightenment and Pietism can be reconciled. His new synthesis based on feeling was evidently under some influence from Pietism, because he later remarked: "After all I have passed through I have become a Moravian again, only of a higher order."[77] His synthesis was well expressed in his *On Religion: Speeches to its Cultured Despisers*, published in 1799.

Based on his new synthetic approach, he published his systematic theology book, *The Christian Faith* (1821), to argue that Christian doctrines are accounts of our Christian religious affections set forth in speech. Thus God's attributes of eternity, omnipresence, omnipotence and omniscience are not to be taken as actually describing God but as how our experience of God-consciousness is related to him. Sin means our lack of God-consciousness. Original sin does not mean a first sin of the first human parents; it only refers to the fact that the whole human race lacks God-consciousness. Redemption comes only by divine grace, when the perfect God-consciousness of Christ is communicated to us. If we each have God-consciousness and have a fellowship of love among ourselves, then the kingdom of God on earth can come.

---

[76] Friedrich Schleiermacher, *On Religion: Speeches to its Cultured Despisers*, trans. John Oman (New York: Harper Torchbooks, 1958), p. 36. Italics added.

[77] Friedrich Schleiermacher, *The Life of Friedrich Schleiermacher, as Unfolded in His Autobiography and Letters*, vol. 1, trans. Frederica Rowan (London: Smith, Elder and Co., 1860), pp. 283-84.

It is to be noted that Schleiermacher was in favor of the 1817 announcement by King Frederick William III of Prussia (r. 1797-1840) on the union of the Lutheran and Reformed Churches, although he later disagreed with the king on his further claim on his sovereignty over the Union.

"Schleiermacher," says Tillich, "represents what I call the great synthesis in the theological realm."[78] Even Barth, a staunch critic of Schleiermacher, admits that "Schleiermacher's achievement" was a "historical necessity" well fitting "the whole spirit of 19th and 20th centuries," so that it is hard to reject it even if you may be equipped "with a positive counter-argument."[79] This indicates the immense influence of his theological synthesis in the nineteenth century and beyond.

From the viewpoint of the Divine Principle, his significance is due to the fact that as a theologian he seriously tried to establish the foundation of substance, if imperfectly, between the Enlightenment and Pietism, although his name and his work are not mentioned in the Divine Principle. The Unification theologian Young Oon Kim (1914–1989) seems to regard Schleiermacher as part of the Pietistic tradition in the second reformation,[80] but he should rather be considered as a theological synthesizer of the Enlightenment and Pietism.

The theological tradition of Schleiermacher was to be greatly challenged by the neo-orthodoxy of Barth in the early twentieth century.

c. Universal synthesis of Georg W. F. Hegel

Hegel was yet another important thinker who synthesized the Enlightenment and Pietism. To be precise, after entering the seminary at Tübingen in 1788 at age 18 he was actually trying to synthesize Enlightenment religion and Greek folk religion. Greek folk religion, however, was quite closely connected with and appreciated by German Romanticism, which in turn, according to scholars such as Isaiah Berlin (1909–1997), was rooted in Pietism.[81] Thus it would not be wrong to say that Hegel was pursuing a synthesis between the Enlightenment and Pietism.

---

[78] Tillich, *A History of Christian Thought*, p. 388.

[79] Karl Barth, *The Theology of Schleiermacher: Lectures at Göttingen, Winter Semester of 1923/24*, ed. Dietrich Ritschl and trans. Geoffrey W. Bromiley (Grand Rapids, MI: Wm. B. Eerdmans Publishing Co., 1982), p. 260.

[80] Young Oon Kim, *Unification Theology and Christian Thought*, rev. ed. (New York: Golden Gate Publishing, 1976), pp. 267-69.

[81] Isaiah Berlin, *The Roots of Romanticism*, ed. Henry Hardy (Princeton, NJ: Princeton University Press, 1999).

As a young theologian during his formative ten-year period from 1788 to 1799, he was faced with various polarities of experience such as the Enlightenment, Pietism, Romanticism, Greek folk religion and Kant's moral religion. He tried to develop the theological concept of the true religion by dialectically reconciling them into a higher unity.

To begin with, he as a Romantic seminarian at Tübingen found a tension between Enlightenment religion, an objective religion of the head, and Greek folk religion, a subjective religion of the heart. He was, of course, in favor of the latter. But after graduating from the seminary, he became a Kantian, identifying Kant's moral religion with the true religion of Jesus in order to go beyond the tension between Enlightenment religion and Greek folk religion. Toward the end of this formative ten-year period, however, he came to see a tension even between Kant's moral religion and Greek folk religion. To solve it, he found a third way: Christianity. It seemed to him that the Christian teaching of love as embodied in Jesus is able to overcome any dichotomy.

Yet he came to realize that even the Christian teaching of love as a subjective feeling is not enough, unless it is manifested in objective forms such as virtue and worldly action, and that unfortunately the "fate" of Christianity is that its manifestation in objective forms can never happen completely.

This led Hegel to make a shift from theology to philosophy after 1800. He now developed a more penetrating form of logic in his absolute idealism, affirming an identity between thought and being, i.e., an identity between the rational and the real. As expressed in his works such as *Phenomenology of the Spirit* (1804) and *Science of Logic* (1812–1816), this means that we can know the essence of reality by logically moving from the "thesis" to the "antithesis" to be *aufgehoben* as a new "synthesis" of the two. The past participle of the German verb *aufheben* has the double meaning of being "done away with" and at the same time "preserved" at a higher level.

God as the Absolute Spirit, therefore, discloses himself in the world through his self-development of Becoming (synthesis) of his Being (thesis) and Not-Being (antithesis). Also particular things in the world, each with its self-development of becoming (synthesis) of its being (thesis) and not-being (antithesis), disclose themselves with each other; and this process in the world continues until it ends in the Absolute Spirit. Thus God and the world are united, and all things in the world are united centering on God. God thus comes to self-awareness through the world. Hegel claimed that through this method we can explain and know everything in its rational necessity. This made him different from Kant and Schleiermacher, who were agnostic when it came to pure reason in that they were aware of its limitation.

Hegel reinterpreted many traditional Christian doctrines by applying his philosophy. For example, the fall of Adam is a necessary dialectical movement from innocence or the insensate (thesis) to blamable knowledge or consciousness of estrangement (antithesis) in order to reach reconciliation (synthesis). The Incarnation means a necessary dialectical movement from Being (thesis) to Not-Being (antithesis) within the Infinite to reach the self-disclosure of Becoming (synthesis) in the finite. In this way Hegel's philosophy made the Christian faith more reasonable and acceptable to the modern world.

Hegel's final understanding of Christian doctrines may sound a little too simplistic to be plausible. But if his initial attempt to synthesize Enlightenment religion and Pietism (even under the guise of Greek folk religion) and his later universal synthesis through his absolute idealism were for the establishment of the foundation of substance for the Second Advent of the Messiah, he was providentially a very significant thinker. He was not simply a representative of the Abel-type view of life, as the Divine Principle says he was.[82] From this point of view, Tillich's statement that Hegel, along with Schleiermacher, "had a tremendous impact on the whole history of thought to the present day,"[83] can be appreciated even more deeply.

d. Kant, Schleiermacher and Hegel as "head-wing" thinkers

As was noted previously,[84] Rev. Moon has coined the term "head wing," by which he means a central position having the capacity of uniting together the left and right wings, which are Cain-type and Abel-type, respectively. If so, Kant, Schleiermacher and Hegel, all of whose thoughts aimed at uniting the Cain-type Enlightenment and Abel-type Pietism for the establishment of the foundation of substance, may well be called "head-wing" thinkers.

According to Rev. Moon, the head wing usually has a wider perspective of God to be able to go beyond the struggle between Cain-type and Abel-type camps to unite both. Thus he also calls it "Godism."[85] Godism is indeed a godly and noble position. It is fitting, therefore, that Stanley J. Grenz (1950–2005) and Roger E. Olson (1952–) describe Kant, Schleiermacher and Hegel as "three intellectual giants,"[86] although Grenz and Olson may have had no concept of the foundation of substance.

---

[82] EDP, p. 356.
[83] Tillich, *A History of Christian Thought*, p. 301.
[84] See n. 20.
[85] Moon, "Reflection of 1986."
[86] Stanley J. Grenz and Roger E. Olson, *20th-Century Theology: God and the World in a Transitional Age* (Downers Grove, IL: InterVarsity Press, 1992), p. 25.

Also, Protestant scholasticism, which attempted to integrate the Cain-type Renaissance and the Abel-type Reformation in the late seventeenth and eighteenth centuries, may well be called a "head-wing" movement. This must be the reason why Tillich encourages us to take Protestant scholasticism seriously, as was noted previously.[87]

In the history of Christian thought, however, Kant, Schleiermacher and Hegel have been regarded as the shapers of so-called "liberal theology" in Protestantism.[88] Especially Schleiermacher, a full-fledged theologian and preacher, has been called the "father of liberal theology." The problem here is that the word "liberal" has the pejorative connotation of being so progressive as to *deviate* from the traditional orthodoxy of Christianity. The three thinkers' head-wing reinterpretations of Christianity, as was seen above, certainly looked quite different from, and even quite unacceptable to, traditional Christian orthodoxy, thus appearing to have deviated from it. Therefore they may well be pejoratively regarded as liberal from the viewpoint of traditional orthodoxy. (By contrast, Protestant scholasticism, which may have been a head-wing movement in the first stage, has hardly been regarded as liberal even from the viewpoint of traditional orthodoxy; this is perhaps due to the absence at that time of the influential Enlightenment, which was later a component of the head-wing positions of the three thinkers in the second stage.)

It should be pointed out, however, that the three thinkers were courageously broadminded and generous when they accommodated the Enlightenment in their head-wing enterprises. This noble and positive sense of being liberal on their part should not be forgotten. It should probably be distinguished from other, irresponsible deviations from traditional Christianity. Roger E. Olson, a prolific writer of the evangelical Baptist yet Arminian persuasion, is aware of this distinction when he says that liberal theology is "not just any deviation from orthodoxy but an elevation of modern reason and discovery, the 'modern mind,' to a source and norm for theology."[89]

Hopefully, a true head-wing thought will eventually have to appear and go beyond both Cain-type and Abel-type views of life to integrate them so completely that its originally intended liberalism, in the noble and positive sense of the term, will no longer be questioned or critiqued by either of the two sides. Perhaps it can be said that the syntheses made by Kant, Schleiermacher and Hegel were not perfect yet, and that this may be the reason

---

[87] See n. 51.

[88] Grenz and Olson, *20th-Century Theology*, p. 25.

[89] Roger E. Olson, "What Is 'Liberal Theology'?" http://www.patheos.com/blogs/rogereolson/2013/10/what-is-liberal-theology/.

why they have been blamed by traditional orthodox Christians for being liberal in the pejorative sense.

§3. Nineteenth-Century Theology and Its Breakdown

1. Breakdown of Nineteenth-Century Theology

Kant's moral synthesis, Schleiermacher's theological synthesis, and Hegel's universal synthesis all helped to form the synthetic nature of nineteenth-century theology as a whole, which created a culture of optimism.

Kant's moral religion could be found especially in the value-judgment practical theologies of Albrecht Ritschl (1822–1889) and his followers such as Adolf von Harnack (1851–1930) and Wilhelm Herrmann (1846–1922) in Germany. The Ritschlians were usually supporters of the Prussian Union of Churches which united both the Lutheran and Reformed Churches in opposition to Confessional Lutheranism. The Social Gospel theology of Walter Rauschenbusch (1861–1918) in America, which tried to apply Pietistic faith to social issues, emerged under the influence of the Ritschlian school.

Schleiermacher's theological synthesis was repeated in the nineteenth-century "mediating theologies" of Friedrich August Tholuck (1799–1877), Isaak August Dorner (1809–1884) and others, who attempted to reconcile the Christian faith with modern culture in Schleiermachian ways. They, too, were usually supporters of the Prussian Union of Churches. The philosopher and poet Samuel Taylor Coleridge (1772–1834) was the English equivalent of Schleiermacher, who on his own attempted to synthesize Romanticism and the Enlightenment. The American theologian Horace Bushnell (1802–1876) drew significantly on the work of Coleridge and also was acquainted with the theology of Schleiermacher; he was dubbed the "American Schleiermacher."[90] Even Roman Catholic theologians such as Johann Sebastian von Drey (1777–1853) at the Tübingen School of Catholic Theology in Germany were Schleiermachian, as they believed in our innate capacity of God-consciousness and regarded the Church as a place of Christian nurture.

Hegel's philosophy of universal synthesis, after his death in 1831, continued to be a major school of thought for a time. It was inherited by the so-called Right Hegelians in the Continent. The popularity of Hegel's thought declined in the second half of the nineteenth century, although his influence

---

[90] Sydney E. Ahlstrom, *A Religious History of the American People*, 2nd ed. (New Haven, CT: Yale University Press, 2004), p. 610.

later extended not only into philosophy and theology but also into the political arena in the twentieth century. In the nineteenth century, "Hegel's own direct influence was shortest lived," compared with the two other thinkers of synthesis in question here.[91] In fact, Hegel's synthesis started breaking down in the 1840s, much earlier than those of Kant and Schleiermacher which broke down in the early twentieth century. Hence we will first deal with the breakdown of Hegel's system, and after that the syntheses of Schleiermacher and Kant.

At this juncture, it should be mentioned that the synthetic nature of nineteenth-century thought, attributable to Kant, Schleiermacher and Hegel, was far from perfect, perhaps because, as mentioned above, their respective syntheses were not perfect. Thus the nineteenth century, in spite of its basically mediating and synthetic nature, still witnessed the existence of very diverse schools of thought, both progressive and conservative.

On the more progressive side, biblical historical criticism, which had originated from Enlightenment rationalism in the eighteenth century, developed in the nineteenth century, producing scholars such as Wilhelm Martin Leberecht de Wette (1780–1849), who began historical criticism of the Pentateuch, and Julias Wellhausen (1844–1918), who proposed the documentary hypothesis for the composition of the Pentateuch. In the area of natural science, in 1859 Charles Darwin (1809–1882) published *On the Origin of Species*, presenting his theory of evolution.

In response to these progressive schools, there arose conservative movements such as Confessional Lutheranism in Germany, the Oxford Movement in the Church of England, and in America, Princeton Theology by Calvinist theologians such as Charles Hodge (1797–1878) and Benjamin Warfield (1851–1921).

a. Breakdown of Hegel's universal synthesis

The breakdown of Hegel's universal synthesis was "a historic event," according to Tillich.[92] It can be said that his synthesis initially broke down into the atheistic anthropology of Ludwig Feuerbach (1808–1872), a Cain-type view of life, and the God-centered existentialism of Søren Kierkegaard (1813–1855), an Abel-type view of life. This happened in the middle of the nineteenth century, although its final breakdown occurred in the early twentieth century when the communist revolution of Russia, inheriting the Feuerbachian

---

[91] Livingston, *The Enlightenment and the Nineteenth Century*, p. 137.
[92] Tillich, *A History of Christian Thought*, p. 413.

tradition in a certain way, emerged as a Cain-type movement, and Barth's theology of crisis, inheriting the Kierkegaardian tradition in a certain way, emerged as an Abel-type view of life.

Tillich says that the initial breakdown of the Hegelian system in the middle of the nineteenth century occurred when "Hegel was attacked from all sides and removed from the throne of providence on which he had placed himself," because "the finished system [of Hegel] cut off all openness to the future."[93] What is the meaning of "the throne of providence on which he had placed himself"? It apparently means the absolute status of Hegel's finished system, which claimed to have secured the complete historical actualization of the coming into being of the Absolute Spirit, although historical Christianity never made that absolutist claim, always believing instead that God is distant and transcendent from us. Hegel's finished system thus put itself "in the state of *hybris*" (by this Greek word Tillich does not simply mean "pride" but, more to the point, "self-elevation toward the realm of the divine"), but "then this *hybris* was followed by the tragedy of his system," i.e., its tragic breakdown.[94]

To put it another way, Hegel's "essentialism" was attacked by "existentialists" such as Feuerbach and Kierkegaard, whether they were atheistic or theistic: "It was in protest to Hegel's perfect essentialism that the existentialism of the nineteenth and twentieth centuries arose."[95] The all-embracing character of Hegel's system saw no gap between existence and essence, as it asserted that existence is the expression of essence. But existentialists, whether atheistic or theistic, were concerned about the gap between existence and essence, looking upon human existence as a dehumanized state of estrangement or alienation from its essential nature.

Although Tillich nowhere specifically uses the word "demonic" to characterize Hegel's system, nevertheless it can perhaps be said that Hegel's finished system turned out to be "demonic" in the Tillichian sense that it, even if it was a finite system, exalted itself to the level of the infinite, i.e., placed itself in the state of *hybris*. If so, it can be said, using the Divine Principle terminology, that Hegel's system suffered from the invasion of Satan, and that it therefore had to be divided into Cain-type and Abel-type views of life.

From the Cain-type camp, therefore, Ludwig Feuerbach, one of the so-called Left Hegelians, rebelled against Hegel's absolute idealism by turning it upside down. This was well expressed in his *The Essence of Christianity*, published

---

[93] Ibid., p. 414.

[94] Ibid.

[95] Paul Tillich, *Systematic Theology*, vol. II: *Existence and the Christ* (Chicago: The University of Chicago Press, 1957), p. 24.

in 1841. Whereas for Hegel God comes to know himself in human beings in the world, for Feuerbach human beings come to know themselves in God. From Feuerbach's existentialist point of view, this means that we, whose existence is estranged or alienated from our own essence that is our own infinite nature, dream of worshipping God by projecting our own infinite nature, while being aware of our own self-alienation. God is therefore none other than the projection of our own infinite self-consciousness from which we are estranged: "God is the manifested inward nature, the expressed self of a man,—religion the solemn unveiling of a man's hidden treasures."[96] We thus create the infinite and perfect God, instead of God creating us. In this way Feuerbach reduced theology to anthropology. The Christian doctrine of the Incarnation, for example, simply means a reflection of our desire to address our self-alienation by seeing the non-alienated human nature in Christ. Feuerbach even went so far as to say that true religion will eventually be found in true human communion of non-alienation, and that human beings in this true communion can be called God. Perhaps in a way this still represented nineteenth-century optimism.

From the Abel-type camp, Kierkegaard sharply criticized Hegel's absolute idealism by objecting that it has no room whatsoever for the importance of the individual commitment of faith in God. Hegel's system only attempts to reach the truth by logical deduction and rational necessity with all-encompassing objectivity centering on God, thus attempting to solve even the real problems of life only in pure theory. According to Kierkegaard, however, there is no truth or no solution in such objective information or knowledge. The real problems of life actually come from our estrangement from the true self, which is our estrangement from God due to our sinfulness and guilt—an estrangement which Kierkegaard calls the "infinite qualitative difference" between God and humanity.[97] The problems can only be solved by the passionate, subjective inwardness of faith on the part of each of us, which fills the gap between God and oneself, between the eternal and the historical. "Truth," therefore, "is subjectivity."[98] Kierkegaard was a very important Abel-type theologian at that time, even though his name is not mentioned in the Divine Principle.

---

[96] Ludwig Feuerbach, *The Essence of Christianity*, trans. George Eliot (New York: Harper Torchbooks, 1957), pp. 12-13.

[97] Søren Kierkegaard, *The Sickness unto Death: A Christian Psychological Exposition for Upbuilding and Awakening*, ed. and trans. Howard V. Hong and Edna H. Hong (Princeton: Princeton University Press, 1983), p. 126.

[98] Søren Kierkegaard, *Concluding Unscientific Postscript*, trans. David F. Swenson and Walter Lowrie (Princeton: Princeton University Press, 1968), pp. 169-224.

Feuerbach's atheistic Cain-type view of religion was inherited by Karl Marx (1818–1883), another Left Hegelian. Marx appreciated Feuerbach's definition of religion as a projection. But while Feuerbach's definition just psychologically focused on individual human beings, Marx expanded religion to the socioeconomic level because of his increasing awareness of the problem of injustice and exploitation brought forth by the Industrial Revolution. Religion is, for Marx, merely the assurance of an eternal fulfillment in the imaginary realm of heaven which the oppressed people illusorily embrace, yet it is no more than their projection of true humanism which does not exist in the estranged and dehumanized society of exploitation. In a way, the ruling classes, with which the Christian churches are allied, have invented religion to prevent the masses from seeking fulfillment on the earth by diverting their attention to imaginary life after death. "Religion," therefore, "is the sigh of the oppressed creature, the heart of a heartless world, and the soul of soulless conditions. It is the opium of the people." [99] Marx, then, suggested to overthrow, through revolutions, these unjust social conditions that produce this religious illusion. To justify this, he developed historical materialism based on Hegel's dialectics of progress and Feuerbach's materialism.

It is to be noted that the Divine Principle correctly identifies Feuerbach and Marx's Cain-type views of life.[100] The Divine Principle also says that Marx' historical materialism, from which communism developed, belonged to what it calls the "third renaissance."[101] In fact, Russia's communist revolution in 1917 occurred in opposition to the optimism of the nineteenth century in general and the class society of the Russian Empire of that time in particular.

Kierkegaard's theistic Abel-type view of religion, on the other hand, was bequeathed to Karl Barth in the early twentieth century. Barth's theology on the Abel side, together with communism on the Cain side, completely finalized the Hegelian system's breakdown that had begun in the middle of the nineteenth century.

Barth, going through the tragic time of World War I, felt that the whole of nineteenth-century theology, which was synthetic in nature because of Hegel as well as Kant and Schleiermacher, is too optimistic and humanistic to seriously understand the radical transcendence of God in Christianity. Barth, therefore, challenged it by making Kierkegaard's notion of the "infinite

---

99 Karl Marx, *Critique of Hegel's 'Philosophy of Right,'* ed. and trans. Joseph O'Malley (Cambridge: Cambridge University Press, 1977), p. 131.
100 EDP, p. 355. It also mentions about D. F. Strauss, another Left Hegelian, and Friedrich Engels, Marx' co-worker.
101 EDP, p. 364.

qualitative distinction" between God and humanity a cornerstone of his theology.[102] Barth expressed his own criticism of Hegel by saying that in the Hegelian system "the identification of God with the dialectical method" brought forth the abolition of God's sovereign freedom, making God subject to necessity, such that "This God, the God of Hegel is at the least his own prisoner."[103] For Barth, God must be so "wholly other" that we are incapable of knowing him. The only way that we know him is through revelation, which God initiates to give us in faith. This was clearly expressed in the second edition in 1922 of his *The Epistle to the Romans*, which turned out to be a bombshell. It marked the rise of a new theological era associated with his name.

Besides the new theological movement coming from Barth, fundamentalism and Pentecostalism arose in America in the early twentieth century. Although they were not directly related to Barth, they, too, were concerned about the secular trend of the time. So they, too, can probably be considered part of the third reformation. They will, however, be explained in our later discussion of neo-fundamentalism, which arose in the 1970s, and neo-Pentecostalism, which arose in 1960, as Abel-type views of life in the fourth stage of division.

b. Breakdown of Schleiermacher's theological synthesis

Schleiermacher's theological synthesis, too, broke down into Cain-type communism and Abel-type Barthianism, which respectively expressed themselves in history as the communist revolution of Russia in 1917 and the publication of the second edition of Barth's *The Epistle to the Romans* in 1922.

It seems that Marx and his successors in Russia did not specifically study the theology of Schleiermacher to react against it. The only possible link we can think of between Schleiermacher and Karl Marx was that Schleiermacher was deeply involved in the newly started Prussian Union of Churches, which included the Lutheran Church where Heinrich Marx (1777–1838), Karl's father, converted from Judaism in 1817 or 1818 to eventually have Karl baptized as a young boy in 1824. But Karl grew radical and atheistic by associating with the Left Hegelians at the University of Berlin from 1837, and he apparently started resenting the Prussian Union of Churches when the Prussian state censored his journalistic activities in Cologne in 1842 and 1843.

Marx eventually decided that the Church, whether in Prussia, Belgium or England, was allied with the ruling classes and complicit in exploiting the

---

102 Karl Barth, *The Epistle to the Romans*, 6th ed., trans. Edwyn C. Hoskyns (London: Oxford University Press, 1968), p. 10.

103 Barth, *Protestant Thought*, p. 304.

masses in its system of capitalism. Furthermore, while Schleiermacher believed that religion has an essence, to which it can be reduced, namely the feeling of absolute dependence, Marx held that religion has no essence since, as the opium of the people, it is just an illusory product of the socioeconomic conditions of exploitation. For Marx, therefore, if these conditions are overthrown, there is no need for religion. Vladimir Lenin (1870–1924), who seriously studied the works of Marx during his Kazan State University days, agreed with Marx that religion is the opium of the people, and decided that the Russian Orthodox Church, allied with the ruling classes, was a great obstacle for the people. He was the main leader behind the communist revolution in Russia in 1917.

How about Barth's relationship to Schleiermacher? Barth studied the theology of Schleiermacher very carefully, as he was originally trained in nineteenth-century liberal theology. Barth's *The Theology of Schleiermacher* contains the "Concluding Unscientific Postscript on Schleiermacher," which autobiographically reports that he was deeply involved with Schleiermacher over many decades.[104] But he eventually reacted against Schleiermacher. He decided that Schleiermacher's theology is too much bound to human experiences to appreciate the transcendence of God, which is sorely needed to overcome various crises of human beings. Theology should not speak of God by speaking of human beings. It should speak of God *from* God. Its task is to hear and witness the challenging Word of God instead of listening to our own words: "Religion confronts every human competence, every concrete happening in this world, as a thing incomprehensible, which cannot be tolerated or accepted."[105] The living truth of God cannot be found in our own man-made synthesis between God and us. Thus Barth was against Schleiermacher's theological synthesis of the Enlightenment and Pietism. In order to make these points, Barth numerous times critically referenced Schleiermacher in his major work, *Church Dogmatics*.

c. Breakdown of Kant's moral religion

Kant's moral religion, too, broke down into Cain-type communism and Abel-type Barthianism, which both reacted against it in two very different ways.

Marx, in his *The German Ideology* (1846) which was co-authored with Friedrich Engels (1820–1895), sharply criticized Kant by saying that Kant's theory of autonomous "good will" could not have any revolutionary result,

---

104 Barth, *The Theology of Schleiermacher*, pp. 261-79.

105 Barth, *The Epistle to the Romans*, p. 258.

because it was unable to address the impact of the world coming from nature and also from the material relations of production in industrial societies. Rather, it was simply a reflection of the impotence and wretchedness of the German burghers of his days. Also, when Marx criticized the Prussian Union of Churches for being allied with the ruling classes to oppress the masses, he was indirectly critical toward the Kantians of his day, who were Ritschlians in support of the Union.

Lenin also criticized Kant, in his *Materialism and Empirio-criticism* (1909), saying that while Kant initially appeared to lean considerably toward "materialism" when talking about the knowability only of the physical world ("phenomena") by our sensation, his materialism was actually compromised by his "idealist" decision to declare things-in-themselves ("noumena") outside of our sensations to be "unknowable, transcendental, other-sided."[106] Lenin further observed in the same work that Feuerbach, Marx and Engels turned from Kant to the Left because of his quasi-materialism. This work of Lenin became an obligatory subject of study at all schools of higher education during the Soviet era.

What about Barth's Abel-type reaction against Kant? According to Barth, Kant's moral religion means to say that each of us as the agent of practical reason is the measure of religion and even the measure of God. This, according to Barth, gives rise to the problem of a gap or discrepancy between Kant's own religion based on the moral law within us and the revealed positive religion of Christianity centering on God. Kant himself sees no discrepancy between the two, said Barth, as he simply reinterprets the latter from the viewpoint of the former. But his reinterpretation results in a problematic distortion of the latter by the former, according to Barth. Therefore Barth suggested that we should question Kant's approach and believe that it is not each of us humans but God who is the measure of religion. Our religion should spring from God, and theology should recognize "the point of departure for its method in revelation" to be God, who is "not identical with quintessence of human reason, with the 'God in ourselves.'"[107]

On October 4, 1914, two months after the outbreak of World War I, ninety-three prominent German intellectuals, including fourteen Nobel laureates, signed a manifesto in support of Kaiser Wilhelm II's (r. 1888–1918) war policy. Barth was much dismayed that Adolf von Harnack and Wilhelm

---

[106] Vladimir Lenin, "The Criticism of Kantianism from the Left and from the Right," which is chap. 4, sec. 1 of his *Materialism and Empirio-criticism*. https://www.marxists.org/archive/lenin/works/1908/mec/four1.htm.

[107] Barth, *Protestant Thought*, p. 191.

Herrmann, who used to be his great teachers at Berlin and Marburg, were among them. Harnack and Herrmann were members of the Ritschlian school, which Albrecht Ritschl founded through the publication of his influential *The Christian Doctrine of Justification and Reconciliation* in the early 1870s to reconstruct Christian theology in a Kantian way. Ritschl's Kantian way combined itself with serious historical research on Jesus in the New Testament. It therefore had its own way of synthesis, refusing to go back to any of the previous traditions of the nineteenth century, whether the Enlightenment, Pietism, Schleiermacher's theological synthesis, or Hegel's speculative synthesis. For the Ritschlians, the main task of religion was to enable us to actualize ourselves as moral human beings in the kingdom of God on earth. Apparently they equated the highly developed culture in Germany with the kingdom of God on earth.

Barth in his *The Epistle to the Romans* vehemently criticized this *Kulturprotestantismus* (culture-Protestantism) for exalting human culture to the point of obscuring the distance between God and us: "Thinking of ourselves what we can be thought only of God, we are unable to think of Him more highly than we think of ourselves."[108]

2. Pre-1960s Theology: Foundation of Substance between Communism and Barthianism

In order for the foundation of substance to be established in the third stage, Cain-type communism and Abel-type Barthianism should be synthesized. Let us see several attempts to synthesize the two prior to the 1960s. They included at least the theologies of the later Barth, Reinhold Niebuhr, H. Richard Niebuhr and Paul Tillich.

a. The later Barth

As was seen above, Barth reacted strongly against the synthetic nature of nineteenth-century theology as a whole by asserting the complete transcendence of God. Thus God can truly be known only through his revelation to us, as we deny ourselves to be faithful. God can never be known from the viewpoint of what is regarded as our own *a priori* religious nature. This was Barth's initial, very conservative position during the period of 1916 to 1930. After that period, however, he came to realize that the God we can truly know only through his revelation is actually a God of love who through Jesus Christ stoops down to stay with us, while at the same time staying as a God of

[108] Barth, *The Epistle to the Romans*, p. 45.

transcendence. Thus the later Barth started talking about God's immanence grounded in Jesus Christ as well as his transcendence.

This change to a more moderate stance explains how he became interested in worldly political affairs, joining the German Social Democratic Party in 1931. Prior to his conservative period, during his younger days as a liberal pastor he was engaged in socio-political issues such as injustice and poverty, even joining the Swiss Social Democratic Party. The later Barth, now showing his interest in politics again, actively opposed Nazism in Germany and spearheaded the writing of the Barmen Declaration in 1934.

The later Barth's involvement in political affairs did not weaken after World War II, even when communism became a big issue in the Cold War. In 1949 he stated that the tension between East and West is God's "concern," thus being the "concern" of the Church as well, and that "the Church must seek an answer to the problem."[109] His answer was that the Church, which stands for the Word of the living God, should assume "a third way,"[110] not taking sides with either communism or capitalism as both are idolatrously materialistic and inhumane to the people. The Church, from the perspective of the Word of God, should encourage not only the East but also the West to do the work of "reconstruction"[111] to enhance democracy, freedom, justice and peace within each bloc, so that the mutual hatred and anger between East and West may disappear to allow the coming of the kingdom of God. Consciously or unconsciously, therefore, Barth was talking about what in the Divine Principle is the foundation of substance. Thus the later Barth can be regarded as a head-wing thinker.

There seem to be at least two issues here that need to be addressed. First, isn't it our task to understand and explain how the later Barth synthesized between communism and Barthianism rather than between communism and capitalism? The answer, of course, is yes. But Barthianism here means earlier Barthianism, the conservative theological position of the earlier Barth (1916–1930). It stood in sharp contrast with communism, and even can be deemed to be part of the capitalist West vis-à-vis the communist East. Barth himself admitted as much: "something inside us [including the earlier Barth] instinctively joins in the battle-hymn of the West, whilst it goes against the grain for us to listen to the chorus of the East at all."[112] So, when the later

---

[109] Karl Barth, "The Church between East and West," in *Against the Stream: Shorter Post-War Writings 1946-52*, ed. Ronald Gregor Smith (New York: Philosophical Library, 1954), p. 127.
[110] Ibid., pp. 132, 136, 145.
[111] Ibid., pp. 143-46.
[112] Ibid., p. 135.

Barth was trying to synthesize communism in the East and capitalism in the West centering on the Word of God, he was not far from trying to synthesize communism and his earlier Barthianism.

A second issue is whether the later Barth constructed any theology specifically to synthesize Cain-type communism and his own earlier Barthianism. The answer is most likely no. Perhaps, however, he believed that his mature theology, expressed in his multi-volume *Church Dogmatics* published between 1932 and 1967, was sufficient to address the importance of the Word of God for the "reconstruction" needed for the synthesis of the two.

b. Reinhold Niebuhr

Let us now proceed to the theological school of "Christian realism" in America, of which Reinhold Niebuhr and his younger brother H. Richard Niebuhr were the most prominent members. Christian realism was Barthian in that it accepted radical monotheism and the biblical view of human sin and predicament in opposition to the optimistic anthropology of nineteenth-century European thought. At the same time, Christian realism was very much interested in dealing with various social issues caused by the sinful human situation—social issues which communism also was concerned about. Christian realists, then, were relating radical monotheism and the biblical view of sin to social issues. In this sense, it can be said that American Christian realism was exploring a unique synthesis between earlier Barthianism and communism.

Reinhold Niebuhr was initially involved with the optimistic, liberal theological tradition of the nineteenth and early twentieth centuries, notably the Social Gospel coupled with the educational philosophy of John Dewey (1859–1952). But during the period from 1915 to 1928 when he was serving as pastor of Bethel Evangelical Church in Detroit, he witnessed the sad reality of the exploited workers of the Ford Motor Company, and realized that liberal theology's naïve optimism about moral progress was not at all competent to solve the serious problem of injustice in capitalism. In order to address this problem, he explicitly abandoned liberal theology in the 1930s in favor of two alternative solutions which, though actually opposite to each other, co-existed within his new thought: the Barthian (and Augustinian) idea of human sinfulness in front of a transcendent God of love, on the one hand, and the Marxist analysis and solution of the problem of inequality, on the other.

This unique tension between the two opposing solutions within Niebuhr's thought showed itself in his influential book, *Moral Man and Immoral Society* (1932), published just a few years after he was called in 1928 to teach ethics at Union Theological Seminary in New York City. The book argued that there is an irreconcilable tension between individual moral life and social life, because individual morality alone cannot handle the problems of injustice and unrestrained egoism which unavoidably exist in social groups. These social problems need to be handled by external political measures such as "self-assertion, resistance, coercion, and perhaps resentment," [113] and even "violence."[114] He thus accepted some insights from Marxism. (In 1930, he had helped to found the League of Christian Socialists.)

It can be said, therefore, that Niebuhr's own initial liberal theology had been divided into Abel-type Barthianism and Cain-type communism *within* himself. Eventually, however, he became aware of the unacceptable, bloody tyranny of Soviet Russia's communist regime. Thus his real position was one of a reintegration, if still with a considerable tension, between Barthianism and communism. His 1935 book, *An Interpretation of Christian Ethics*, was meant to construct such a reintegration with a prophetic fervor: "Only a vital Christian faith, renewing its youth in its prophetic origin, is capable of dealing adequately with the moral and social problems of our age." [115] This reintegration, according to him, is still far from perfect due to our original sin.

Niebuhr also proposed a "new synthesis" between the Renaissance and the Reformation,[116] the respective culminations of which were Marxism and Barthianism for him. This new synthesis of the Renaissance and the Reformation, therefore, must contain a synthesis of Marxism and Barthianism. For him, this new synthesis is again far from perfect, given the limits as well as possibilities of human beings in history. It will not bring thereby the utopian kingdom of God on earth but rather a world in which at least "tolerance" and proximate "justice" can be maintained.[117] The kingdom of God will not come within history by human action. It will come rather as God's gift from beyond.

Niebuhr was concerned about the Cold War after World War II. While he was aware of the malignancy of communism, he also warned in his *The Irony of American History* (1952) that America as a Christian nation should avoid "a fanatic anti-communism" based on the idea of American innocence because it ironically "can become so similar in its temper of hatefulness to communism itself."[118] As late as 1969, he even stated that "we've all followed [George F.

[113] Reinhold Niebuhr, *Moral Man and Immoral Society* (New York: Charles Scribner's Sons, 1932), p. 257.
[114] Ibid., p. 259.
[115] Reinhold Niebuhr, *An Interpretation of Christian Ethics*, Living Age ed. (New York: Meridian Books, 1956), p. 38.
[116] See n. 11.
[117] Niebuhr, *Human Destiny*, pp. 213-87.
[118] Reinhold Niebuhr, *The Irony of American History* (New York: Charles Scribner's Sons, 1962), p. 170.

Kennan] in shifting subtly from the containment of Communism to the partnership of the two superpowers for the prevention of nuclear war."[119] It is noteworthy that Reinhold Niebuhr, hailed as "the greatest Protestant theologian in America since Jonathan Edwards,"[120] was trying to establish, if incompletely still, the foundation of substance, whether or not he was aware of the meaning of this Divine Principle term.

c. H. Richard Niebuhr

H. Richard Niebuhr, too, was initially a theologian within the nineteenth-century liberal tradition of Schleiermacher and Ritschl, writing his Ph.D. dissertation at Yale in 1924 on Ernst Troeltsch (1865–1923), a Ritschilian whose conception of sociological and historical development had been profoundly influenced by Karl Marx.[121] In the 1930s, however, H. Richard Niebuhr rediscovered radical monotheism by studying Barthianism. Thus in his *The Meaning of Revelation* (1941), he tried to "combine" Troeltsch and Barth, who were "frequently set in diametrical opposition to each other."[122] These two can be combined or synthesized, according to Niebuhr, if our awareness of the limitation of our knowledge of God resulting from historical relativity and conditionedness, as shown in the historical relativism of Troeltsch (and in the religious relativisms of Schleiermacher and Ritschl as well), leads us to be "critical" of ourselves, "humble," "faithful," [123] "communal" [124] and "confessional"[125] enough to be able to receive what Barth understands to be "revelation" from God, which, of course, is subject to progressive validation through our communal life.

What is to be noted here is that Niebuhr also spoke about the historical relativism of Marx and Engels in "economic history" in the context of Troeltsch's historical relativism, by saying that "the point of such Marxian analysis" is that we, in all our thinking and acting, are "deeply influenced" not simply by the fact that we are economic people but rather by the fact that we are "men living amid certain, definite economic relations, who think as pastoral,

---

119 Ronald H. Stone, "An Interview with Reinhold Niebuhr," *Christianity and Crisis*, March 17, 1969, p. 48.

120 "Death of a Christian Realist," *Time*, June 14, 1971.

121 Regarding his connection with Marx, see Ernst Troeltsch, *Der Historismus und seine Probleme* (Tübingen: J. C. B. Mohr, 1922).

122 H. Richard Niebuhr, *The Meaning of Revelation* (New York: Macmillan Co., 1960), p. x.

123 Ibid., p. 17.

124 Ibid., pp. 36-37.

125 Ibid., pp. 18, 40-43.

agricultural, industrial, or bourgeois men."[126] For Niebuhr, therefore, the synthesis between Barthianisn and Troeltschianism is, in this respect, the synthesis between Barthianism and Marxism. According to Niebuhr, this synthesis is liberating as an "approach to universality,"[127] and it can address the problems of idolatry, self-aggrandizement, self-defense and self-justification that have plagued human society very much.

This synthesis was also expressed in his classic work, *Christ and Culture* (1951), which discussed five different models of the relationship between Christ and culture: 1) Christ against culture, 2) the Christ of culture, 3) Christ above culture, 4) Christ and culture in paradox, and 5) Christ the transformer of culture. Niebuhr apparently stood for the fifth model of "Christ the transformer of culture," and given that Marxism was part of culture, he must have had in mind Christ as the "transformer" of Marxism. It was a transformative synthesis of Christianity and communism that would not support the "[otherworldly] Christian attitude [that]... arouses Marx and Lenin to hostility" such that they object that "Christian faith is a religious opiate used by the fortunate to stupefy the people, who should be well aware that there is no life beyond culture."[128]

After World War II, H. Richard Niebuhr warned that it is not appropriate to simplistically regard America, a Christian nation, and the Soviet Union, a communist nation, as the epitomes of "good" and "evil." America needs to repent for her shortcomings when confronted by the Soviet Union, as Israel was supposed to do when confronted by Assyria during the Old Testament period. For God transcends the illusions of both sides.[129] This indicated Niebuhr's profound sense of an eventual synthesis between Christianity and communism.

d. Paul Tillich

Paul Tillich was another theologian who experienced the age of turmoil in which World War I broke out and the communist revolution of Russia took place. He initially associated with neo-orthodoxy, being an early follower of Barth's theology. But Tillich showed much interest in Marxism as well, knowing the miserable conditions of the proletariat in Germany. While teaching at universities such as Berlin and Frankfurt from 1919 to 1933, he developed a synthesis between conservative Christianity and Marxism, which

---

[126] Ibid., pp. 13-14.

[127] Ibid., p. 45.

[128] H. Richard Niebuhr, *Christ and Culture* (New York: Harper & Row, Publishers, 1951), p. 6.

[129] H. Richard Niebuhr, "The Illusions of Power," *Pulpit* 33 (April 1962): 100-3.

constituted his "religious socialism."[130] Religious socialism is compatible with Christian love, not losing sight of God and therefore being "theonomous," whereas the class struggle in capitalism is "demonic." Religious socialism, however, has to be careful about itself, lest it should become as materialistic and ideological as communism and capitalism. The proletariat is the bearer of the future for the fulfillment of Christian eschatological expectation, although it should be ready to go beyond its own status to reach the theonomous classless society.

After persecution from Nazism led him to move to America in 1933 where, with the help of Reinhold Niebuhr, he received a teaching position at Union Theological Seminary, Tillich joined the League of Christian Socialists. But he came to realize the bloody tyranny of the Soviet Union. During the Cold War, he stopped writing about Karl Marx in order to avoid sounding anti-American. He now focused on theology. Even so, he became well known as a theological synthesizer, using the "method of correlation," which brings together insights from Christian revelation with issues raised in human existence.[131]

e. The nouvelle théologie

We have been observing that the foundation of substance for the Second Advent of the Messiah was prepared mainly by Protestants after the breakdown of medieval scholasticism. But it would be wrong to say that Catholics have had nothing to do with this preparation. At this point, therefore, we would like to note an important Catholic movement called *nouvelle théologie* ("new theology") that occurred from the 1930s through the 1950s among reformist French theologians such as Marie-Dominique Chenu (1895–1990), Henri de Lubac (1896–1991), Yves Congar (1904–1994) and Jean Daniélou (1905–1974); this was also good preparation for the Second Advent. Although it was a movement outside of America, it soon became internationally influential.

The *nouvelle théologie* was critical of "neo-Thomism" ("neo-scholasticism"), which, having enshrined Thomism as absolute and timelessly true, was dominant in the Catholic Church since the middle of the nineteenth century, standing behind the First Vatican Council in 1869–1870 and also spearheading

---

130 Some of Paul Tillich's articles written during the period between 1919 and 1933 are included in his *Political Expectation*, ed. James Luther Adams (New York: Harper & Row, Publishers, 1971). See also his *The Socialist Decision*, trans. Franklin Sherman (New York: Harper & Row, Publishers, 1977), which was originally published in Germany in 1933.

131 Tillich, *Systematic Theology*, vol. 1: *Reason and Revelation: Being and God*, p. 64.

the persecution of "Catholic modernists" such as the English Jesuit George Tyrrell (1861–1909) and the French theologian Alfred Loisy (1857–1940) who were trying to find a synthesis between the Catholic faith and modern historical-critical culture. The *nouvelle théologie* tried to overcome the authoritarianism of neo-Thomism by "returning to the sources" (*ressourcement*) of the old tradition of Christianity to study the early and later Church Fathers including Thomas Aquinas in their real historical contexts, so that the deeper, more lively and open-minded tradition of the past might be recovered. In this sense it helped to mediate between the Catholic tradition and the rest of the world, and it prepared the ground for the Second Vatican Council,[132] which started in 1962 under the leadership of Pope John XXIII (r. 1958–1963) and continued until 1965. More importantly, it was a Catholic preparation for the Second Advent.

3. The Second Advent of the Messiah

The Divine Principle teaches that the Messiah comes after the foundation of substance is established between Cain and Abel camps. This teaching is quite similar to the "postmillennial" assertion in the Great Awakening tradition in America in the eighteenth and nineteenth centuries that the Second Advent of the Messiah takes place *after* Christians work hard and establish a good foundation involving social and political transformations, which itself means the millennial kingdom. This similarity between Unification eschatology and American postmillennialism, with respect to the non-apocalyptic foundation on which the Second Advent is to occur, is well pointed out by M. Darrol Bryant (1942–2025).[133]

Unification eschatology, therefore, has difficulty accepting the exceedingly apocalyptic claim of "premillennialism" that the Messiah returns in such a cataclysmic way as to bring a sharp break from the awfully evil condition of the world to inaugurate the millennial kingdom. Nevertheless, regarding the eschatological timeline, Unification eschatology disagrees with postmillennialism and rather agrees instead with premillennialism, because it still believes that the Messiah at the Second Advent, while coming only after

---

132 For the connection of the *nouvelle théologie* with Vatican II as well as its connection with Catholic modernism, see Jürgen Mettepenningen, *Nouvelle Théologie – New Theology: Inheritor of Modernism, Precursor of Vatican II* (New York: T&T Clark International, 2010).

133 M. Darrol Bryant, "Unification Eschatology and American Millennial Traditions," in *A Time for Consideration: A Scholarly Appraisal of the Unification Church*, ed. M. Darrol Bryant and Herbert W. Richardson (New York: Edwin Mellen Press, 1978), pp. 261-74.

the establishment of the foundation of substance between Cain and Abel camps, actually comes *before* the millennial kingdom which he is to inaugurate.

As has been seen so far, the foundation of substance was established in three stages during the period of preparation for the Second Advent of the Messiah and a little beyond it, with the foundation of substance in the final, third stage having been laid through the pre-1960s mediating Protestant theologies of the later Barth, the Niebuhr brothers and Tillich, and even the Catholic *nouvelle théologie* in France. These pre-1960 theologies of mediation had already emerged by the end of World War II basically. This coincided with the time when Sun Myung Moon, who Unificationists believe had the messianic mission, started his public ministry: 1945.

Rev. Moon was born in Korea in 1920 and became a Presbyterian around age 10 when his family joined a Presbyterian church. By that time, Korea was already a nation where Christianity was rapidly growing. He went through certain conditions in his own country to emerge as a Christian leader with a messianic consciousness. Moreover, according to the Divine Principle, after the Cain-type fascist nations of Germany, Japan and Italy surrendered to the Abel-type democratic nations of America, Great Britain and France at the end of World War II, "the age for building a new heaven and new earth under the leadership of Christ at the Second Advent had begun."[134]

Moon believed that America is the modern-day Rome, relating to Korea as the modern-day equivalent of biblical Israel, and that America therefore has the crucial mission of realizing the God-given purpose of Christianity for the sake of the world.[135] He sent missionaries to America in 1959, visited America in 1965 and 1969 on his world tours, and spent much of his life working in America after moving there in December 1971. Given Moon's belief in America's important mission, it is interesting to observe that although Barth was a Swiss and the *nouvelle théologie* a French movement, the Niebuhr brothers and Paul Tillich (an immigrant to America) were prominent American theologians who helped to make the foundation of substance in America in the last days.

America actually had already been prepared in the eighteenth century as a place to pave the way for the Second Coming. In this regard, the American Revolution (1765–1783) can be considered a historic event that integrated the American Enlightenment (Cain-type) and the First Great Awakening (Abel-

---

[134] EDP, p. 375.

[135] Sun Myung Moon, "The mission of America as the world-level Rome," in *Cheon Seong Gyeong: Selections from the Speeches of True Parents* (Seoul, Republic of Korea: Sung Hwa Publishing Company, 2006), pp. 1200-04.

type) to help to establish the foundation of substance in the second stage. The American Enlightenment of the eighteenth century, which developed in the British colonies of America under the influence of the European Enlightenment, encouraged the use of human reason in various fields such as religion, philosophy, literature, arts, politics and science, unaffected by any authorities outside of oneself. Many of the Founding Fathers such as Benjamin Franklin (1706–1790) were, in fact, deists within this Enlightenment tradition. By contrast, the First Great Awakening, whose main preachers were Jonathan Edwards and George Whitefield, stressed the importance of rebirth and spiritual conversion on the part of each individual person in a pious way. Its religious revivals made the Christian faith intensely personal to many people throughout the colonies, thus inspiring them to obliterate class lines and change the existing landscape of hierarchical order religiously and even politically.

The American Enlightenment's appreciation of individual integrity through human reason, on the one hand, and the First Great Awakening's understanding of personal maturity through piety and conversion, on the other, were apparently integrated to give rise to the American Revolution, whereby America obtained independence from the authoritarian monarchy of the United Kingdom centering on King George III (r. 1760–1801) and became a new republic. Franklin was deeply impressed with Whitefield's sermon at a revival meeting in Philadelphia in 1739, and their lifelong close friendship thereafter[136] was perhaps a good symbol of the unity in the American Revolution between the Enlightenment tradition and the First Great Awakening.

The foundation of substance established through the American Revolution in the second stage and the foundation of substance established through the mediating theologies of the Niebuhr brothers and Tillich in America (as well as by that of the later Barth in Europe) in the third stage are hardly regarded as liberal, while the theologies of integration by Kant, Schleiermacher and Hegel in the second stage are usually regarded as liberal. One reason for this difference was that the American Revolution in the eighteenth century and the mediating theologies of the Niebuhr brothers and Tillich in the twentieth century put somewhat more emphasis, in their synthetic projects, on the Abel-type views of life (the First Great Awakening and Barthianism) than on the Cain-type views of life (the American Enlightenment

---

[136] Regarding the friendship of the two people, see, for example, Larry Gragg, "A Mere Civil Friendship: Benjamin Franklin and George Whitefield," *History Today* 28 (1978): 574-79.

and communism), while the theologies of integration by Kant, Schleiermacher and Hegel could not do so, given the tremendous impact of the Enlightenment.

§4. Pre-1960s Theology and Its Breakdown

1. Breakdown of Pre-1960s Theology

But something apparently went wrong with the providence of Rev. Moon. After his public ministry started in 1945, he went through a 10-year period of tremendous difficulties until the founding of the Holy Spirit Association of the Unification of World Christianity (a.k.a. the Unification Church) in 1954. During this period, he was rejected by Christianity in his own country of Korea. According to him, therefore, Christianity then started to decline, not only in Korea but also in America and other parts of the world, and it even began to be invaded by Satan.[137]

If his viewpoint is correct, it can explain why the pre-1960s theology of synthesis, formed by the later Barth, the Niebuhr brothers and Tillich, broke down. This in fact happened in the 1960s, as it disintegrated into Cain-type radical theologies such as "death of God" theology, black theology and feminist theology, on the one hand, and Abel-type theologies such as neo-fundamentalism and neo-Pentecostalism, on the other. It turned out to be a fourth stage of division. In fact, Satan's invasion of Christianity, which resulted in its division during the 1960s, was alluded to by the black theologian James H. Cone (1938–2018), who spoke of its "satanic" racism, and the feminist theologian Mary Daly (1928–2010), who spoke of its "demonic" sexism, as the reason for their revolt against it. And, needless to say, neo-fundamentalists and neo-Pentecostals often talked about Satan standing behind mainline Protestantism. No wonder that *Life* magazine in a special double issue of December 26, 1969 called the 1960s the "Decade of Tumult and Change."

Let us now look at the affiliations of Barth, the Niebuhr brothers and Tillich, who helped to establish the foundation of substance in the third stage as preparation for the Second Advent of the Messiah. Barth was a pastor of the Swiss Reformed Church, which is similar to American mainline Protestantism. The Niebuhr brothers were ordained ministers of the German

---

137 Sun Myung Moon stated: "Korean Christianity was invaded by Satan, causing Christians all over the world to ignore God's Will," in his "The Unification of My Country," God's Day 1990 midnight address at Chungpadong Church, Seoul, Korea, January 1, 1990. http://www.tparents.org/Moon-Talks/SunMyungMoon90/SunMyungMoon-900101Mid.htm.

Evangelical Synod of North America, the American branch of the Prussian Union of Churches in Germany, which in 1934 became part of the Evangelical and Reformed Church and in 1957 became part of the United Church of Christ, a mainline Protestant denomination today. Tillich was an ordained pastor of the Lutheran Church in Germany, and after coming to America he remained a Lutheran, thus being part of mainline Christianity. From this, it can be said that pre-1960s synthetic theology as theological preparation for the Second Advent of the Messiah was born from mainline Protestantism in America, which therefore had a very important mission.

Mainline Protestant churches had been central to the whole history of America since the arrival of the Pilgrim Fathers in 1620. Puritans and Anglicans were the first mainline Protestants, and other denominations joined later. The evangelical approach of the First Great Awakening in the 1730s and the 1740s reshaped Congregational, Presbyterian and Reformed churches and strengthened Baptist and Methodist churches. The Second Great Awakening in the first half of the nineteenth century helped Baptist and Methodist congregations to rapidly increase their membership. The term "mainline Protestantism" was coined in the beginning of the twentieth century as it started to have tension and friction with the rise of fundamentalism. But it can be said that mainline Protestant denominations, which today include the Episcopal Church, the United Church of Christ, the Presbyterian Church (USA), the Evangelical Lutheran Church in America, the United Methodist Church, the American Baptist Churches USA, and the Christian Church (the Disciples of Christ), originally constituted America's Protestant Christianity that was prepared by God for the Second Coming in the last days. They peaked in membership in the 1950s, constituting a majority of all American Christians. Many of the mainline Protestants were well educated, wealthy and influential in society.

But in the 1960s, mainline Protestant churches started to rapidly decline in membership and in faith, as the pre-1960s synthetic theology of mainline Protestant Christianity broke down into Cain-type and Abel-type theologies. This coincided with the decline of Christianity in America as well as in Korea mentioned by Rev. Moon. After the 1960s, mainline Protestants became a minority among Protestants, while evangelicals, neo-fundamentalists, and neo-Pentecostals increased in number as well as in zeal.

a. Radical theologies in the 1960s

The Cain-type radical theologies of the 1960s in America included "death of God" theology, black theology and feminist theology. They were Cain-type because they put more emphasis on the importance of humans and this world than on God, although it should be remembered according to the Divine Principle that after they reconcile with their Abel-type counterparts, thus establishing the foundation of substance, they and their counterparts both would equally connect with God for salvation and restoration.

Death of God theology was developed mainly by William Hamilton (1924 –2012) and Thomas J. J. Altizer (1927–2018), who belonged to mainline Protestant Christianity. Hamilton, an ordained Baptist pastor who taught at Portland State University for many years, challenged mainline Protestantism by saying that the idea of God itself should be abolished because it has ironically contributed to human suffering and evil. By contrast, Altizer, an Episcopalian who taught at Emory University and Stony Brook University, argued in his *The Gospel of Christian Atheism* (1966) that God is dead in that the transcendent God now disappeared to become totally immanent in humanity. In this way Altizer affirmed the profane to the neglect of the transcendently sacred.

The spearhead of black theology was James H. Cone, an ordained minister of the African Methodist Episcopal Church, a mainline denomination, who taught at Union Theological Seminary since 1970. He shared the plight of oppressed blacks through his upbringing in the South. His *Black Theology and Black Power* (1969) and *A Black Theology of Liberation* (1970) developed black theology as a theology of liberation of black people from "satanic whiteness" in mainline Protestantism.[138] According to him, as the biblical tradition shows that "God has been revealed in the history of the oppressed Israel and decisively in the Oppressed One, Jesus Christ," so black theology regards God as "the God of and for the oppressed [black], the God who comes into view in their liberation."[139] This posed a big challenge to established mainline Protestantism which was predominantly white.

Still another challenge came from feminist theology, which was developed by female scholars such as Mary Daly and Letty M. Russell (1929–2007). Although Daly was a Catholic who taught at Boston College for more than thirty years, her influence on mainline Protestant women was great. In her *The Church and the Second Sex* (1968), Daly discussed the existence of "the 'demon' of sexual prejudice in the Church" and the need for its exorcism.[140] Her *Beyond God the Father* (1973), using controversially strong language, suggested that because the masculine God is the source of all kinds of aggression including

---

[138] James H. Cone, *A Black Theology of Liberation* (Maryknoll, NY: Orbis Books, 1986), p. 64.
[139] Ibid., pp. 60-61.
[140] Mary Daly, *The Church and the Second Sex* (New York: Harper & Row, Publishers, 1975), p. 193.

sexism, we should "castrate" him.[141] Her radical feminism eventually went so far as to abandon Christianity, by asserting that God is only feminine like the pagan Goddess of antiquity.

In contrast, Russell, a Presbyterian, was among more moderate, reformist feminist theologians. Initially working as a religious leader in East Harlem, New York, Russell experienced the problems of racism and sexism. Thus she felt the need for both justice and partnership that can overcome barriers, and published *Christian Education in Mission* (1967). Her later publications such as *Human Liberation in a Feminist Perspective: A Theology* (1974), written after she began serving as a faculty member of Yale Divinity School, showed her feminist ideas more explicitly. According to her, Jesus was a "feminist" in that he considered both men and women "equal," severally having their own "total personhood."[142] Women are not inferior to men. Based on this kind of biblical interpretation, she wanted Christianity to reject what she considered to be its patriarchal and oppressive tradition and go through a reformation.

Even more influential than Russell in the area of moderate feminist theology was Rosemary Radford Reuther (1936–2022), a Catholic. But she started writing seriously as a feminist theologian in the 1980s, far later than the 1960s.

b. Neo-fundamentalism and neo-Pentecostalism

Any discussion of "neo-fundamentalism" needs a prior explanation of "fundamentalism." Fundamentalism initially emerged in the early twentieth century as an angry and militant trans-denominational movement within American Protestantism in opposition to biblical criticism, Darwinism and modern secularism, and even to mainline Protestantism itself. It can be considered part of the Abel-type third reformation according to the Divine Principle. While it arose independently from Barthianism, it shared with it grave concern about the liberal trend of the nineteenth century. The term "fundamentalism" was coined in 1920, deriving its name from *The Fundamentals*, a series of pamphlets published from 1910 to 1915. Fundamentalists had two chief pillars of their theology: 1) biblical inerrancy, coming from the Princeton Theology of Charles Hodge and Benjamin Warfield, and 2) pretribulational premillennialism, inherited from the Anglo-Irish dispensationalist John Nelson Darby (1800–1882). Although fundamentalists won in the Scopes Trial of 1925

[141] Mary Daly, *Beyond God the Father: Toward a Philosophy of Women's Liberation* (Boston: Beacon Press, 1985), p. 19.

[142] Letty M. Russell, *Human Liberation in a Feminist Perspective: A Theology* (Philadelphia: Westminster Press, 1974), p. 138.

in Tennessee against Darwinism, they soon became weaker as attacks from the media made them unpopular.

In the 1970s, however, fundamentalism reemerged into the public arena, posing a strong cultural separation from the civil rights movement, the women's movement, gay rights, secular humanism, the banning of prayer in schools (based on a Supreme Court decision in 1963), abortion (legalized by the Supreme Court in 1973), and world communism. This new fundamentalism as an Abel-type school of theology was called "neo-fundamentalism," distinct from the historical fundamentalism of the early twentieth century.[143] Harvie M. Conn (1933–1999) observes that neo-fundamentalism was "more rigidly identified with dispensationalism," less Calvinistic, and had stronger tendencies toward "excessive emotionalism; social withdrawal; fear of cultural challenges to the gospel; neglect of ethical issues; theological pugnaciousness; pietistic individualism."[144] Neo-fundamentalists criticized evangelicals such as Billy Graham (1918–2018) for associating with liberals. Politically influential neo-fundamentalist groups included the Moral Majority founded in 1979 by Jerry Falwell (1933–2007), the American Coalition for Traditional Values founded in 1984 by Tim LaHaye (1926–2016), and the Christian Coalition of America founded in 1989 by Pat Robertson (1930–2023). James Dobson (1936–2025), who founded the Focus on the Family in 1977, was another influential neo-fundamentalist.

How about "neo-Pentecostalism," which emerged as an Abel-type movement in the 1960s? It also had a predecessor, the "Pentecostalism" of the early twentieth century. That Pentecostalism began from the Azusa Street Revival under William J. Seymour (1870–1922) from 1906 to 1909 in Los Angeles, California, which followed a smaller yet deeply spiritual movement at Bethel Biblical College in Topeka, Kansas in 1901. Participants received the baptism of the Holy Spirit and spoke in tongues. It gave rise to Pentecostal denominations such as the Pentecostal Holiness Church, the Assemblies of God, the International Church of the Foursquare Gospel, and the Church of God in Christ. Earlier Pentecostalism can be considered another part of the third reformation along with fundamentalism and Barthianism in the early twentieth century.

The beginning of neo-Pentecostalism is usually dated to April 1960, when the Episcopal priest Dennis J. Bennett (1917–1991) recounted his own

---

143 Paul Enns, *The Moody Handbook of Theology* (Chicago, IL: Moody Press, 1989), pp. 619-20.

144 Harvie M. Conn, *Contemporary World Theology: A Layman's Guidebook* (Phillipsburg, NJ: Presbyterian and Reformed Publishing Co., 1973), pp. 119-21.

personal experience of the baptism of the Holy Spirit, inspiring many of the congregants of his church in Van Nuys, California, to have the same experience. Neo-Pentecostalism differed from Pentecostalism in that it now involved virtually every mainline denomination, including even the Catholic Church and the Eastern Orthodox Church. Those people in all these various denominations who newly had Pentecostal experiences did not create new denominations, but remained in their own respective denominations to renew and revitalize them. Another difference was that while Pentecostals tended to stress the gift of speaking in tongues as the main evidence of receiving the baptism of the Spirit, neo-Pentecostals referred to a wider range of supernatural gifts as its evidence, with speaking in tongues as only one of them. Neo-Pentecostals are also called "charismatics." The Catholic Charismatic Renewal began in 1967 at Duquesne University in Pittsburg, Pennsylvania.

2. Foundation of Substance between Radical Theologies and Neo-fundamentalism (and Neo-Pentecostalism)

When the pre-1960s theology of synthesis disintegrated in the 1960s into Cain-type radical theologies such as death of God theology, black theology and feminist theology, on the one hand, and Abel-type theologies such as neo-fundamentalism and neo-Pentecostalism, on the other, tremendous theological and social chaos was brought forth in America in this "Decade of Tumult and Change." Now that the foundation of substance that had been laid in the third stage broke down, was Christianity finished?

Rev. Moon did not think so. He believed that Christianity could still be revitalized. That was the reason why he and his wife Hak Ja Han—who in 1960 had their holy wedding, what they believed to be the "marriage of the Lamb" (Rev. 19:7)—came to America at the end of 1971 to seriously start their ministry there. They began with three years of "Day of Hope" speaking tours from 1972 to 1974. Then, they launched many ecumenical projects, institutions and organizations such as the Unification Theological Seminary (UTS) in 1975, the New Ecumenical Research Association (New ERA) in 1980, the Inter-denominational Conference for Clergy (ICC) in 1985, and the American Clergy Leadership Conference (ACLC) in 2000, to which many Christians of all different theological persuasions were drawn. As head-wing thinkers, Rev. and Mrs. Moon's efforts to revitalize Christianity were geared toward restoring the unity of now-fragmented Christianity to establish the foundation of substance in a fourth stage for the return of the Lord of the Second Advent. In his 1973 speech, therefore, Moon stated:

> We must unite with the coming of the Lord. The end of the world signifies that the time of the arrival of the Lord of the Second Advent is near. He must have a basis somewhere, some foundation prepared upon which he can begin to fulfill his mission. America is meant to be that base, but America is deeply troubled.[145]

The head-wing thought of Rev. and Mrs. Moon is the Divine Principle, which teaches God's dynamic "dual characteristics" centering on his Heart of love. They contended that this makes possible genuine unity of God and the world, genuine unity of God and humans, genuine unity among humans, and genuine unity between humans and all things.[146] Rev. and Mrs. Moon also taught about the importance of love and reconciliation among enemies, following Jesus' tradition.

Within American Christianity itself, new attempts at theological reintegration to revitalize Christianity arose. These new attempts, in fact, were evangelicalism and reconstructive postmodernism.

Let us deal with evangelicalism first. The term "evangelical" originally stemmed from the New Testament word "gospel" and historically referenced the Reformation tradition in general because of its calling for a return to this gospel. But evangelicalism here refers to a particular movement which emerged out of fundamentalism in America around the middle of the twentieth century, and whose theological influence with its basic approach of reintegration was felt especially after the 1960s.

While joining fundamentalism in opposition to the liberal and secular tendency of mainline Protestantism, evangelicalism rejected fundamentalism's cultural separatism and anti-intellectualism in favor of greater dialogue with the culture of the world. Carl F. H. Henry (1913–2003) expressed this evangelical sentiment against fundamentalism in his *The Uneasy Conscience of Modern Fundamentalism* (1947). He called for a new effort for mediation, without compromising the centrality of the gospel from the Bible. Evangelicalism is often called "neo-evangelicalism," primarily in contrast to the evangelical aspect of fundamentalism, and secondarily in contrast to the historical evangelical tradition of the American Great Awakenings. Famous neo-evangelicals include Billy Graham and Carl F. H. Henry, and influential evangelical organizations include Fuller Theological Seminary, Wheaton College, the Billy Graham Evangelistic Association, InterVarsity Christian Fellowship, and William B. Eerdmans Publishing Company.

---

[145] Sun Myung Moon, *Christianity in Crisis: New Hope* (Washington, DC: HSA-UWC, 1974), p. 62.

[146] For a more detailed explanation of this aspect of the Divine Principle, see Chapter 4 in the present book.

While Carl Henry was still inclined to stay within his own more conservative version of evangelicalism, a growing number of evangelical theologians in America, such as Bernard Ramm (1916–1992) and Stanley J. Grenz (1950–2005), seriously wanted to reintegrate the theological left and right. Bernard Ramm was aware of the continuing menace of the Enlightenment. He therefore wanted to address it from the viewpoint of the biblical gospel by developing "a theological method that enables them [i.e., evangelicals] to be consistently evangelical in their theology and to be people of modern learning."[147] Interestingly, he found Karl Barth's mature theology to be promising in this regard.[148] Remember, the later Barth, too, was interested in mediating between the right and left. This was perhaps the reason why Ramm felt that Barth was appealing. Ramm was also interested in the unity of religion and science, given his initial scientific background. Stanley J. Grenz, another prolific evangelical writer, had a similar theological approach. He sought to integrate biblical truth and the cultural context in which the truth is expressed: "the process of contextualization requires a movement between two poles—the Bible as the source of truth and the culture as the source of the categories through which the theologian expresses biblical truth."[149]

It should be noted at this juncture that after mainline Protestant churches in America decided not to work with the Unification Church, as was evidenced in the 1977 release of a critique of its theology by the Commission on Faith and Order of the National Council of the Churches of Christ in the USA (NCC), Rev. and Mrs. Moon not only launched their own ecumenical projects such as the New ERA and the ICC for the revitalization of Christianity but also started to work with some evangelicals. In 1982 they founded *The Washington Times*, and it associated with the National Religious Broadcasters and the Religious Roundtable. This was how they were able to work, if indirectly, with evangelicals such as Billy Graham, Bill Bright (1921–2003) and Don Argue (1939–). Even as early as 1978, Unificationists engaged in theological dialogue with evangelicals.[150] Given the head-wing nature of Unificationism, it is very understandable that they were able to work with evangelicals. At the same time, the grave concern Rev. and Mrs. Moon had about secular humanism and world communism even led them to work with

---

[147] Bernard Ramm, *After Fundamentalism: The Future of Evangelical Theology* (New York: Harper & Row, Publishers, 1983), p. 27.

[148] Ibid., p. vii.

[149] Stanley J. Grenz, *Revisioning Evangelical Theology: A Fresh Agenda for the 21st Century* (Downers Grove, IL: InterVarsity Press, 1993), p. 90.

[150] Richard Quebedeaux and Rodney Sawatsky, eds., *Evangelical-Unification Dialogue* (New York: Rose of Sharon Press, 1979).

fundamentalists such as Jerry Falwell and Tim LaHaye through *The Washington Times*, the Coalition for Religious Freedom, etc.

Before discussing reconstructive postmodernism, let us deal with the impressive theologies of reintegration by two European theologians: Karl Rahner and Jürgen Moltmann. Their theologies became very influential in America and were definitely helpful for the establishment of the theological foundation of substance in the fourth stage.

Rahner, a German Jesuit theologian, inherited the tradition of the *nouvelle théologie* as a member of its "second generation."[151] He developed his theology even before the 1960s, based on Thomism, existentialism and Kantian transcendental philosophy. But it was after he served as a theological advisor to the Second Vatican Council (1962–1965) that his theology became well known and influential worldwide, making him "the most influential Roman Catholic theologian of the twentieth century."[152] He used special terms such as "supernatural existential," "obediential potency" and "unthematic" to talk about the presence of supernatural grace in human nature and the potential ability of every human being, whether Christian or not, to receive transcendental revelation. This was none other than a serious attempt to reintegrate God up there and humans down here.

Moltmann, a German Reformed theologian, had a different approach for reintegration. His *Theology of Hope* (1964 in German; 1967 in English) tried to mediate between the theological left and right by presenting a "forward looking and forward moving" eschatology, "revolutionizing and transforming the present."[153] Moltmann was involved with the Christian-Marxist dialogues of the late 1960s. His theology was not only eschatological but also practical, in that it encouraged the faithful to take up the cross for the underprivileged and marginalized, just like Christ did, for eventual social and political change. This change, according to Moltmann, is not simply man-made but rather from God's deep sacrificial love. He developed his theology based on a "social doctrine of the Trinity," which makes the reciprocal relationship between God and the world possible in the history of redemption headed for its eschaton.[154]

A surprising way of reintegration came from postmodernism. By postmodernism here, we mean a reaction to the long-standing "modernity" tradition that has held sway since the Enlightenment and not a reaction to the

---

[151] Simpson, *Modern Christian Theology*, p. 267.
[152] Grenz and Olson, *20th-Century Theology*, p. 239.
[153] Jürgen Moltmann, *Theology of Hope*, trans. James W. Leitch (London: SCM Press, 1967), p. 16.
[154] See, for example, Jürgen Moltmann, *The Trinity and the Kingdom: The Doctrine of God*, trans. Margaret Kohl (Minneapolis, MN: Fortress Press, 1993).

aesthetic "modernism" of the first half of the twentieth century in art, architecture and literature. Postmodernism in this sense was of two different types: 1) a "deconstructive" type, and 2) a "reconstructive" type. For our purpose, we are interested in the postmodernism of the reconstructive type.

But first, a word about the postmodernism of the deconstructive type. Deconstructive postmodernism was most famously presented by the French philosopher Jacques Derrida (1930–2004), who coined the term "deconstruction" (*déconstruction* in French) in the 1960s to show that we should unmask the problematic nature of all centers such as an Origin, a Truth, an Essence, a God and a Presence—problematic in the sense of being authoritarian, exclusivist, hierarchical and repressive—and subvert all these centers. Thus deconstructionism challenged all kinds of presumably dogmatic positions since the time of the Enlightenment, whether they were Cain-type or Abel-type, atheistic or theistic. Deconstructive postmodernism wanted to attack and undermine both sides of the "binary opposites" because it saw too much struggle and conflict between them due to their respective dogmatisms based on their own centers.

But destruction usually in the long run leads to a reconstruction. That was the case with Derrida's deconstruction. For although he was initially against any form of idolatry because he was not satisfied with anything at all, nevertheless it very likely meant that he was waiting for the Messiah, which he translated into the philosophical figure of the "to come" (*à venir*), of the future (*l'avenir*). His deconstruction, therefore, was not necessarily entirely nihilistic. Rather he had a passion for something yet to come, which is still incomprehensible and impossible, but which is "undeconstructible," and which is referred to as "justice."[155]

Thus the postmodernism of the reconstructive type in the 1980s and 1990s emerged, which went beyond deconstructive postmodernism. It tried, in the postmodern context in which Derrida's program of deconstruction was appreciated, to reintegrate and reconstruct both sides of the binary opposites at a higher level. Among the currents of this reconstructive postmodernism were "postmetaphysical theology," "postliberalism," and "postmodern Whiteheadianism." Postmetaphysical theology started from the French thinker Jean-Luc Marion (1946-), who was a student of Derrida but then went beyond him. In his influential work, *God Without Being* (1982 in French; 1991 in English), he maintained that God should be thought of purely as love with no reference

---

[155] John D. Caputo, *Deconstruction in a Nutshell: A Conversation with Jacques Derrida* (New York: Fordham University Press, 1997), p. 128.

to being. Postliberalism was created largely by the America Lutheran theologian George Lindbeck (1923–2018), who in his main work, *The Nature of Doctrine: Religion and Theology in a Postliberal Age* (1984), proposed experiential biblical narratives as a third way between the dogmatisms of both liberalism and the older orthodoxy. Postmodern Whiteheadianism came from scholars such as David Ray Griffin (1939–2022), who applied the philosophy of Alfred North Whitehead (1861–1947) to the postmodern situation. His edited volume, *Sacred Interconnections: Postmodern Spirituality, Political Economy, and Art* (1990), advocated interdependence beyond fragmentation and holism beyond the dichotomy of fact and value.

At the end of the present subsection, it needs to be noted that many of the head-wing thinkers were also interested in mediating between Christianity and other religions to help to lay the foundation of substance. Sun Myung Moon himself believed that all religions including Christianity were started by God to let humankind seek the God-centered "ideal of goodness" in various ways, and that they are all expected to be united eventually for the restoration of "one unified world."[156] With that in mind, he founded the International Religious Foundation in 1983 and the Inter-Religious Federation for World Peace in 1991. Karl Rahner, in his celebrated, if controversial, doctrine of "anonymous Christianity," linked Christianity to non-Christian religions by finding Christian elements in them.[157] Also, evangelicals such as Clark H. Pinnock (1937–2010) had an "inclusivist" approach to non-Christian religions.[158]

By the way, in the above-mentioned third stage of theological integration as well, Paul Tillich held that the unity of all religious faiths including Christianity is possible, as long as they all humbly remain "aware of the conditional and non-ultimate character" of their own traditional "symbols" or expressions of God who alone is ultimate.[159] In the second stage of theological integration as well, Friedrich Schleiermacher proposed that Christianity and other religions are connected with one another because they all have something in common, if to different degrees: our religious "feeling" of all created things

---

[156] EDP, p. 86.

[157] See, for example, Karl Rahner, *Karl Rahner in Dialogue: Conversations and Interviews 1965–1982*, ed. Paul Imhof and Hubert Biallowons, trans. Harvey D. Egan (New York: Crossroad Publishing Co., 1986), p. 207.

[158] Clark H. Pinnock, *A Wideness in God's Mercy: The Finality of Jesus Christ in a World of Religions* (Grand Rapids, MI: Zondervan Publishing House, 1992).

[159] Paul Tillich, *Dynamics of Faith* (New York: Harper & Row, Publishers, 1957), p. 125. See also his *Christianity and the Encounter of the World Religions* (New York: Columbia University Press, 1963).

"in and through the Infinite and Eternal."[160] Hegel mapped the religions of the world in an ascending teleological order with Christianity as its culmination, but at the same time appreciated non-Christian religions by saying: "In every religion there is a divine presence, a divine relation; and a philosophy of History has to seek out the spiritual element even in the most imperfect forms."[161]

3. The Fourth Adam

The Divine Principle calls Adam in the Garden of Eden the "first Adam,"[162] and it refers to Jesus Christ and Christ at the Second Advent as the "second Adam" and the "third Adam," respectively.[163] (Needless to say, besides Eve in the Garden of Eden, there must similarly be the second Eve and the third Eve as well, given the married messiahship of True Parents providentially.)

According to the Divine Principle, the fall of the first Adam resulted in Satan's invasion. Hence he had to be divided into Cain and Abel, his two sons representing Satan's side and God's, respectively, so that they might lay the foundation of substance between them in order to receive the Messiah, the second Adam. Unfortunately, Cain killed Abel, and the foundation of substance was not established, with the result that the Messiah could not come. Only much later, when the foundation of substance was accomplished at the national level, could Jesus finally come to Israel as the Messiah in the position of the second Adam.

But then Jesus was crucified, and his crucifixion occasioned the invasion of Satan again, although his unconditional love for his enemies, when he was crucified, resulted in his victorious resurrection, and this spiritual victory by him constituted the very foundation of Christianity.[164] Regardless of Christianity's successes based on that, however, Christ must return to consummate God's will as the third Adam. And, for him to return, the foundation of substance to receive him was needed within Christianity.

As was mentioned earlier, Christ at the Second Advent was initially supposed to come based on a foundation of substance laid between Charlemagne, in the position of Abel, and Pope Leo III who, in the position

---

[160] Schleiermacher, *On Religion*, p. 36.

[161] Georg W. F. Hegel, *Lectures on the Philosophy of History*, trans. J. Sibree (London: G. Bell and Sons, 1902), p. 204.

[162] EDP, pp. 178, 202.

[163] EDP, p. 202.

[164] Sun Myung Moon, "The Life of Jesus as Seen from God's Will, and God's Warning to the Present Age, the Period of the Last Days," speech delivered at the banquet held in honor of the 20th Anniversary of *The Washington Times*, May 21, 2002. http://www.unification.net/2002/20020521_2.html.

of Cain, crowned him Emperor of the Holy Roman Empire in 800. But the foundation of substance at the time was not really laid due to the lack of faith on the part of those who were involved. As a result, the medieval synthesis was defiled by Satan and had to be dismantled into the Cain-type Renaissance and the Abel-type Reformation, which would then have to be reintegrated to make a new foundation of substance. As has been seen throughout the present chapter, during the modern period of history since the end of the Middle Ages, there were three stages of division into Cain-type and Abel-type views of life, which were respectively followed by three stages of reintegration to lay the foundation of substance three times. As a result, the Second Advent became a reality by the end of World War II.

But mainline Protestantism, which was instrumental for the third stage of theological reintegration, afterward failed to fulfill its responsibility in its relationship to the Christ at the Second Advent. Hence that reintegration, which was meant to receive Christ at the Second Advent as the third Adam, broke down into Cain-type and Abel-type views of life in the 1960s, which unfortunately constituted a fourth stage of division.

Following the fourth stage of division in the 1960s, however, a fourth stage of reintegration between Cain-type and Abel-type views of life occurred in the 1970s through 1990s in order to lay the foundation of substance to receive the Messiah again, this time beyond the third Adam. This fourth stage of reintegration was made through Rev. Moon's own head-wing thought, after he came over to America in 1971 and worked to revitalize Christianity. It was also made through theologies of synthesis within Christianity such as evangelical theology and postmodern reconstructive theology, as well as the theologies of Rahner and Moltmann. All this made possible the coming of the Messiah as a fourth Adam. In 1997, therefore, Rev. Moon proclaimed the "era of the realm of the fourth Adam."[165]

According to Moon, this new era of the fourth Adam will be a time of joy, glory, liberation, fulfillment and settlement, without any indemnity or

---

165 Sung Bae Jin, ed., *가정연합시대 주요 의식과 선포식* III [Important Ceremonies and Proclamations in the Age of the Family Federation III] (Seoul, Korea: Sung Hwa Publishing Co., 1991), pp.165-75. Also in 1992, five years earlier than 1997, Rev. Moon publicly proclaimed for the first time that he and Hak Ja Han Moon are the "True Parents of all humankind"; see his "Becoming Leaders in Building a World of Peace," congratulatory banquet speech delivered at Little Angels Performing Arts Center, Seoul, Korea, August 24, 1992. http://www.tparents.org/moon-talks/sunmyungmoon92/SunMyungMoon-920824.pdf. The latter proclamation in 1992 was apparently made possible partly because Rev. and Mrs. Moon as head-wing thinkers laid a foundation of substance between the communist and democratic worlds, by meeting with President Mikhail Gorbachev of the Soviet Union in 1990 and with President Kim Il Sung of North Korea in 1991.

persecution, in contrast to the older eras of the first three Adams in which we saw fall, indemnity, persecution, sorrow and lamentation. To understand this point, it is worthwhile to quote his own words, although it may be lengthy:

> From today [September 11, 1997] the era of the realm of the fourth Adam starts. The first, second and third Adams needed indemnity. But in the realm of the era of the fourth Adam, no indemnity is needed. So, in order to enter the era of the realm of the fourth Adam, the realm of Sabbath and the realm of liberation are needed. We enter an era in which there is no persecution. We enter an era in which there is no sorrow and no lamentation.
>
> The first, second and third Adams came to this earth with the *han* [Korean term to denote lamentation over justice not done] of God. The fourth Adam is not supposed to carry such *han*. In the era of the realm of the fourth Adam, we have to go to an era of settlement. From the original family centering on the fourth Adam can start the Heavenly Kingdom. The era of the realm of the fourth Adam refers to the era in which Adam and Eve become perfect without a fall in such a way as to be able to establish an ideal family. Here, there are no such concepts as fall, indemnity and restoration. It refers to the original era in which the ideal of God is realized.
>
> The fourth Adam is an Adam who represents the first, second and third Adams. The first, second and third Adams received persecution, but from the era of the realm of the fourth Adam there is no persecution but glory, no sorrow but joy, and no indemnity but ideal and delight. In this era of the realm of the fourth Adam, a nation is sought, the world is sought, and the cosmos is sought. And in the cosmos, we have to attend God by preparing the realm of liberation and the realm of Sabbath. From the fourth Adam begins settlement for the first time. And from this family is the blessing connected to the cosmos in glory. From this time begins the Heavenly Kingdom on earth for the first time.[166]

From the above it can be understood that while the first three Adams experienced the invasion of Satan in one way or another, in the era of the realm of the fourth Adam, when the kingdom of God on earth is supposed to begin, there is no invasion of Satan. The fourth Adam is, therefore, *Christus Victor* ("Victorious Christ") in the sense that the Swedish Lutheran theologian Gustaf Aulén (1879–1977) used the term.[167] According to Aulén, Christ comes

---

[166] Ibid., pp. 165-66. English translation from the Korean by the present writer.

[167] Gustaf Aulén, *Christus Victor: An Historical Study of the Three Main Types of the Idea of the Atonement*, trans. A. G. Herbert (New York: Macmillan Publishing Co., 1978).

primarily to be victorious by defeating Satan and liberating the whole world from satanic sovereignty (the "classic" view) rather than just to propitiate God's offended honor or wrath on behalf of individual believers (the "objective" view) or to morally awaken them (the "subjective" view). As he put it, Christ's atonement "is not regarded as affecting men primarily as individuals, but is set forth as a drama of a world's salvation,"[168] i.e., as a drama of the reconciliation of the world to God through "a Divine conflict and victory" over the power of Satan.[169]

Moreover, the fourth Adam in this sense will surely be victorious because the number four, according to the Divine Principle, represents the "realm of God's direct dominion," which is the "fourth stage" after passing through the "three stages of the growing period."[170]

Another important feature of the era of the fourth Adam, according to Rev. Moon, is that we are all encouraged to be Christ-like, receiving the qualification of the fourth Adam and Eve to work responsibly toward the complete realization of the kingdom of God on earth: "Families who got blessed on earth are vertically related to True Parents and have the qualification of the fourth Adam [and Eve]."[171] We are, then, reminded of Jesus' words: "he who does not take his cross and follow me is not worthy of me" (Mt. 10:38). Indeed, we are all encouraged to be messianically responsible people in this new era, which is for each of us the "era of freedom and autonomy."[172]

---

[168] Ibid., p. 6.
[169] Ibid., p. 4.
[170] EDP, p. 296.
[171] Jin, *가정연합시대 주요 의식과 선포식* III, p. 166. English translation from the Korean by the present writer.
[172] *Cheon Seong Gyeong* (2006), p. 1616.

Chapter 12

Eschatology

Eschatology is the doctrine of "last things," dealing with the consummation of the history of salvation. It is customarily treated in the last chapter of systematic theology. But many believe that eschatology actually penetrates the entirety of systematic theology, for while it specifically deals with how God's will is going to be finally realized, God's will itself is the main theme of the entirety of systematic theology. Therefore Jürgen Moltmann (1926–2024) is right when he says: "Eschatology cannot really be only a part of Christian doctrine. Rather, the eschatological outlook is characteristic of all Christian proclamation."[1] Unification theology would agree with this on the importance of eschatology.

Eschatology usually covers two distinguishable yet interrelated topics: 1) the future destiny of each individual after physical death, and 2) the final consummation and eternal order of the world or cosmos. This corresponds to the distinction theologians usually make between "individual" eschatology and "cosmic," "general" or "universal" eschatology. The present chapter will follow this distinction, dealing with the two in Unification eschatology in two different sections.

The first section will treat individual eschatology in Unificationism on the final destiny of one's life after physical death. In doing so, it will primarily focus on addressing the difficult issue in Christianity as to whether or not one can grow spiritually after death in order to be able to advance to a higher realm in the other world.

---

[1] Jürgen Moltmann, *Theology of Hope: On the Ground and the Implications of a Christian Eschatology*, trans. James W. Leitch (New York: Harper & Row, Publishers, 1975), p. 16.

Individual eschatology in traditional Christianity holds, with the exception of the Roman Catholic doctrines of purgatory and the limbo of the Old Testament fathers (*limbus patrum*), that once one dies and goes to the other world, one cannot spiritually grow at all without one's body. So, once in hell, one will not be able to escape. But the Divine Principle uniquely argues that even after one's physical death one will be given a chance to spiritually grow. For one's spirit, immediately after shedding one's body at death, will *not* be completely "naked"[2] physically, as it has within itself an already built-in "spirit body"[3] that will at once begin to function as a body in the spirit world.

This Divine Principle notion of the spirit body can importantly be equated with St. Paul's notion of the resurrected "spiritual body" (1 Cor. 15:44). The only difference is that while the Divine Principle holds that the spirit body is already integral to the constitution of the spirit that consists of the dual characteristics of "spirit mind" (the *sungsang* part) and "spirit body" (the *hyungsang* part),[4] Paul believed that the spiritual body is acquired only through the resurrection of the dead (1 Cor. 15:52). But given this important equation between the two, the feasibility of the unique Unification idea of spiritual growth after physical death, involving the possibility of universal salvation, will be explored in the Christian context, so that it may be acceptable to Christians.

The second section will discuss general eschatology in Unificationism on the final consummation of the world. According to the Divine Principle, the consummation of the world in the last days means the complete realization of the "three great blessings" centered on God, which were originally granted to Adam and Eve in the Garden of Eden but which failed to be realized due to their fall centering on Satan.[5] They are: 1) individual perfection; 2) the multiplication of God's children in families, nations and the world; and 3) the human dominion of love over the rest of creation (Gen. 1:28).[6] The three great blessings are to be realized through the Lord of the Second Advent and his Bride in the last days on behalf of Adam and Eve. Hence the last days is the time "when the evil world under satanic sovereignty is transformed into the ideal world [of the three great blessings] under God's sovereignty. Hell on earth will be transformed into the Kingdom of Heaven on earth."[7]

---

[2] For the use of the word "naked" here, see St. Paul's description in 2 Corinthians 5:1-3 that we "may not be found naked" after physical death, as we will put on "a building from God" (spiritual body) upon shedding our "earthly tent" (physical body).

[3] *Exposition of the Divine Principle* (New York: H.S.A.-U.W.C., 1996), p. 48. Henceforth abbreviated as EDP.

[4] Ibid.

[5] EDP, pp. 88-89.

[6] EDP, pp. 33-36.

[7] EDP, p. 89.

This Unification view will be able to address the tension between the two opposing types of eschatology that exist in Christianity: 1) apocalyptic eschatology, and 2) non-apocalyptic utopian eschatology. "Apocalyptic" is the adjective of the word "apocalypse," which is from the Greek word *apokalypsis*, meaning the uncovering, disclosure or revelation of something hitherto hidden. Apocalyptic eschatology, whether it is premillennial, postmillennial or amillennial,[8] holds that the eternal state will be established in the other world, after the last judgment brings about the destruction of this world. By contrast, non-apocalyptic eschatology, which can be found in the optimistic German liberal thought of Albrecht Ritschl (1822–1889) and Adolf von Harnack (1851–1930), in the Social Gospel movement in America, in the various schools of liberation theology, and in the Jesus Seminar founded in America in 1985, holds that the eternal state should be a kind of earthly utopia to be realized in this world.

But the mediating position of Unificationism's general eschatology contends that the kingdom of God is both otherworldly and this-worldly, in that after it is firmly established on the earth, it will be established in the other world as well. Also, the kingdom of God both in the spirit world and in this world, says Unificationism, will continue for eternity.

Unification general eschatology also mediates between the two opposing types of Christian eschatology in another sense. Apocalyptic eschatology highlights God's initiative even to the neglect of human responsibility, whereas non-apocalyptic utopian eschatology emphasizes human responsibility for the building of the kingdom of God on earth. The Unification view harmonizes the two, holding that God's will is realized through the cooperation of God's responsibility and human responsibility.

§1. Life after Death

The present section on individual eschatology will primarily focus on addressing the difficult issue in Christianity as to whether or not one can still grow spiritually after death in order to be able to advance to a higher realm in the spirit world. To do that, we will begin by showing the Unification view of spiritual growth, given the constitution of the human person according to the Divine Principle.

---

[8] The meanings of premillennialism, postmillennialism and amillennialism will be explained later.

1. Role of the Physical Self for Spiritual Growth

This subsection is basically a summary of pages 47-50 ("The Reciprocal Relationship between the Physical Self and the Spirit Self") of *Exposition of the Divine Principle*, although the present writer's interpretation may also be contained.

According to the Divine Principle, each and every human being was created, in resemblance to God's dual characteristics of *Sungsang* (original internal nature) and *Hyungsang* (original external form), to assume the dual characteristics of *sungsang* (internal nature) and *hyungsang* (external form), thus consisting of "spirit self" (the *sungsang* part) and "physical self" (the *hyungsang* part).[9] The spirit self and the physical self, while respectively belonging to the spirit world and the physical world, are united together in the human person. But the spirit self sheds the physical self when the latter dies. The spirit self thereafter lives in the spirit world for eternity. This "dichotomism" of the spirit self and the physical self in the constitution of the human person is very familiar and accepted by the great majority of Christians, according to the American evangelical theologian Millard J. Erickson (1932–).[10] By dichotomism Erickson does not mean that the two are opposed to each other, unlike what the word "dichotomy" would normally mean. He simply means that they are distinguishable from each other in their unity.

The Divine Principle further holds, however, that the spirit self itself consists of the dual characteristics of "spirit mind" (the *sungsang* part) and "spirit body" (the *hyungsang* part), while the physical self itself similarly includes the dual characteristics of "physical mind" (the *sungsang* part) and "physical body" (the *hyungsang* part). It may appear complicated, but it all derives from the universal principle of dual characteristics. The Divine Principle, therefore, suggests "quadchotomism," so to speak, based on dichotomism. The spirit mind is "the center of the spirit self, and it is where God dwells"; while the physical mind is the center of the physical self, and it "directs the physical body to maintain the functions necessary for its survival, protection and reproduction."

---

[9] In this subsection, all the terms, phrases, clauses and sentences with quotation marks, except "dichotomism," "dichotomy," "quadchotomism" and the biblical quotations, are from EDP, pp. 47-50.

[10] Millard J. Erickson, *Introducing Christian Doctrine*, 3rd ed., ed. L. Arnold Hustad (Grand Rapids, MI: Baker Academic, 2015), p. 197. Erickson reports that regarding the constitution of the human person, there are two more options in Christianity besides dichotomism: trichotomism and monism (pp. 196-199). Trichotomism believes that the human person is composed of three parts: body, soul and spirit. But the terms "soul" and "spirit" are often used interchangeably, thus being virtually equivalent. Thus there is not as much difference between trichotomism and dichotomism. By contrast, monism is quite unique because under some influence of the Old Testament it insists that the human person is a unity, not being composed of separate parts.

Given this quadchotomous structure of the human person, the spirit mind of the spirit self receives "life elements" (the divine truth) directly from God and is engaged in give and take action with the spirit body within the spirit self to yield "living spirit elements." Living spirit elements are then communicated from the spirit self to the physical self, so that the physical self may be encouraged to do good deeds through God-centered give and take action between its two parts: physical mind and physical body. Good deeds by the physical self as "vitality elements" are then given as a response to the spirit self to be stored there in the unity of give and take action between the spirit mind and the spirit body for the spiritual growth of the spirit self.

Here we can see overall give and take action between the spirit self and the physical self for the growth of both as a whole human person. It is important to note that the physical self, for its physical growth, absorbs air, sunlight, food and water as well. The unity of give and take action between the spirit self with its dual characteristics of spirit mind (the *sungsang* part) and spirit body (the *hyungsang* part), on the one hand, and the physical self with its dual characteristics of physical mind (the *sungsang* part) and physical body (the *hyungsang* part), on the other, may, by analogy, be like the unity of resonance between two different tuning forks, which each have two oscillating prongs that symbolize the dual characteristics of *sungsang* and *hyungsang*.

The spiritual and physical growth of the human person based on the give and take action between the spirit self and the physical self goes through three different stages: "formation," "growth" and "perfection" stages. As for the spiritual growth of the spirit self, the spirit self in the formation stage is called "form spirit"; in the growth stage, "life spirit"; and in the perfection stage, "divine spirit." The spirit self will become a divine spirit that fully perceives God when the "four position foundation" of 1) God, 2) the spirit self, 3) the physical self, and 4) their unity in the human person, is completely realized. Those earthly people with divine spirits live in the kingdom of God on earth, and after they pass away, shedding their physical selves, they go to heaven, i.e., the kingdom of God in heaven in the spirit world, to live there for eternity.

What deserves our special attention here, however, is that the physical self in the fallen world often does evil deeds, sending evil vitality elements to the spirit self. If this happens, the spirit self grows evil, ending up going to a low place in the spirit world, say hell, after physical death. Thus "good or evil in the conduct of the physical self is the main determinant of whether the spirit self becomes good or evil." Consequently, "it is not God who decides whether a person's spirit [self] enters heaven or hell upon his death; it is decided by the spirit [self] itself" whose spiritual growth depends on the conduct of the physical self in the physical world. Hence the role of the physical self for the spiritual growth of the spirit self is extremely important. This point is quite well understood in Christianity, as the Bible talks about the importance of one's earthly life: "whatever you bind on earth shall be bound in heaven, and whatever you loose on earth shall be loosed in heaven" (Mt. 18:18); and "each one may receive good or evil [before the judgment seat of Christ], according to what he has done in the body" (2 Cor. 5:10).

2. Returning Resurrection

As seen above, the Divine Principle holds that if one does not live a moral life doing good deeds through one's physical self, one cannot provide good vitality elements for one's spirit self. In this case, upon physical death one will end up going to a low level of the spirit world. But the Divine Principle uniquely teaches that it is not the end of the story. For from a low place in the spirit world, one as a spirit self with no physical self can still spiritually "return" to an earthly person in the physical world, most likely one's bereaved spouse or descendant, for one's needed spiritual growth, which the Divine Principle calls "resurrection." One can have the benefit of "returning resurrection,"[11] in which one receives the merit of vitality elements from good deeds done by the physical self of one's earthly counterpart to whom one spiritually returns.

Resurrection, according to the Divine Principle, refers to the spiritual growth process of being restored from a spiritually *dead* state of fallenness under Satan to a realm in which one is spiritually *alive* under God's direct dominion, whether still on the earth or already in the spirit world.[12] It may be similar to the Christian notion of "sanctification," prominent especially in the Methodist tradition. If on the earth, one has the spiritual benefit of resurrection directly from good deeds done by one's own physical self in accordance with God's will. But if in the spirit world, one receives the benefit of resurrection from good deeds by the physical self of one's earthly counterpart to whom one spiritually returns.

Needless to say, this Divine Principle notion of resurrection as spiritual growth is very different in its meaning from the biblical and Christian idea of "physical resurrection," "bodily resurrection" or "resurrection of the body," which means that after one passes away and sheds one's body, one comes back to some kind of physical life by regaining a body. These two should not be confused here.

---

[11] EDP, pp. 144-48.

[12] "Resurrection may be defined as the process of being restored from the death caused by the Fall to life, from the realm of Satan's dominion to the realm of God's direct dominion, through the providence of restoration. Accordingly, whenever we repent of our sins and rise to a higher state of goodness, we are resurrected to that degree" (EDP, p. 136).

What is noteworthy in the Divine Principle notion of returning resurrection is that even if one passes away as a person of failure on the earth and happens to go to a low level of the spirit world, say hell, one will be given a second chance to spiritually grow there, by spiritually returning to one's earthly counterpart for one's resurrection. That way, one may be able to move to a higher level in the spirit world, even getting out of hell to reach heaven eventually, no matter how enormously slow and difficult a process it may be. This would amount to a doctrine of universal salvation, which actually has much biblical support (Mt. 18:12; Rom. 5:18; 1 Cor. 15:22; Phil. 2:10-11; 1 Tim. 2:4, 6; etc.), although it has never been popular in the Christian tradition.[13]

It is to be noted also that while one in the spirit world thus receives merit from one's earthly counterpart's good deeds, one, in turn, contributes something to that earthly person, by cooperatively assisting or at least expecting the earthly person to do good deeds in accordance with God's will.[14]

At this juncture, the way one in the spirit world receives merit from one's earthly counterpart needs to be explained further. As was mentioned in the preceding subsection, during physical lifetime one has one's spirit self and physical self, which have the relationship of the dual characteristics of *sungsang* and *hyungsang*. On passing away and shedding one's physical self, one will remain only as a spirit self in the spirit world. But in the spirit world one is *not* purely spiritual, since one's spirit self is created from the beginning to contain both spirit mind and spirit body, which have the relationship of the dual characteristics of *sungsang* and *hyungsang*. Upon physical death, therefore, one's spirit body starts to function as a kind of physical body in the spirit world.

Thus, when one as a spirit self in the spirit world faces one's earthly counterpart, whose physical self consists of physical mind (the *sungsang* part) and physical body (the *hyungsang* part), one does so with one's spirit self's dual characteristics of spirit mind (the *sungsang* part) and spirit body (the *hyungsang* part) that are related to them. There is something in common between one as a spirit self and one's earthly counterpart's physical self: the dual characteristics of *sungsang* and *hyungsang*.

Therefore, when good deeds are done by the physical self of one's earthly counterpart, they as good vitality elements affect one in such a way as to be received and absorbed into one's spirit self. This is how one receives merit from one's earthly counterpart. Again, what is striking here is the existence of the spirit body within the spirit self, so that one as a spirit self in the spirit world

---

[13] The reason why the doctrine of universal salvation has never been popular in Christianity is that there are also quite a few biblical passages against it such as Mt. 25:46; Mk. 9:48; Jn. 3:36; 1 Cor. 1:18; and Phil. 3:19.

[14] EDP, pp. 144-45.

will have the dual characteristics of *sungsang* and *hyungsang* to be able to relate to one's earthly counterpart who also has the same kind of dual characteristics.

Returning resurrection is not reincarnation,[15] as one who has passed away and one's earthly counterpart to whom one spiritually returns are two different individual persons and not one and the same person.

3. Its Acceptability in Christianity

But the question is: Is this returning resurrection in the Divine Principle acceptable to Christianity? The answer may initially be in the negative because Christianity usually does not accept spiritual growth for salvation in the spirit world. Christianity rather believes that the wicked, for example, upon physical death, will go to hell for eternal damnation (while the righteous will go to heaven for eternal blessing) without being able to spiritually return to their earthly counterparts, i.e., without being able to be given a second chance to grow spiritually through them for eventual salvation. They must stay in hell for eternity. Even after their physical resurrection, they will not be given a second chance. Their curse will be even more intensified with their physical resurrection.

Because of this, critics of Christianity usually say that the God of Christianity is very merciless and cruel toward people in hell. The famous British atheist philosopher Bertrand Russell (1872–1970) states: "I think all this doctrine, that hell-fire is a punishment for sin [everlastingly], is a doctrine of cruelty."[16] In an attempt to justify the love of God, therefore, some Christians have accepted reincarnation, which teaches that the soul can continuously grow through repeated life on the earth. For example, the Scottish American theologian Geddes MacGregor (1909–1998) has done so in his book *Reincarnation in Christianity: A New Vision of the Role of Rebirth in Christian Thought* (1978).[17] Strictly speaking, however, Christianity has no room for reincarnation.

The present writer, however, believes that Christianity, while not being able to accept the theory of reincarnation, would be able to accept the Divine Principle idea of returning resurrection, if it could understand its traditional Christian notion of physical resurrection *in a proper way* which is still non-heretical. In that way Christianity would be able to let the deceased wicked return to their earthly counterparts to be able to receive a second chance, so

---

[15] EDP, pp. 149-50.

[16] Bertrand Russell, *Why I Am Not a Christian and Other Essays on Religion and Related Subjects*, ed. Paul Edwards (New York: Simon & Schuster, 1957), p. 18.

[17] Geddes MacGregor, *Reincarnation in Christianity: A New Vision of the Role of Rebirth in Christian Thought* (Wheaton, IL: Theosophical Publishing House, 1978).

that it may be able to address the criticism of those who complain that the God of Christianity is a merciless God.

What, then, would be Christianity's proper way of understanding physical resurrection, so that it may be able to embrace the Divine Principle idea of returning resurrection? It would be by *equating* the resurrected body of a deceased person in the Christian tradition with the integral spirit body of a deceased person as explained in the Divine Principle, so that the duality of the spiritual part (soul) and the physical part (resurrected body) of the deceased person in Christianity may be *equated* with the dual characteristics of *sungsang* (spirit mind) and *hyungsang* (spirit body) of the deceased person in the Divine Principle.

This equation must entail the following two important points regarding physical resurrection in Christianity. First, physical resurrection would not mean the reanimation or resuscitation of the same physical corpse that the deceased person used to have on the earth, but rather the gaining of what Paul calls a "spiritual body" (1 Cor. 15:44), which is "celestial" (15:40), "imperishable" (15:42), "in glory" (15:43) and "in power" (15:43). This means that the deceased person does not literally come back to the earth with exactly the same body as before, but continues to live with a spiritual body in the spirit world after physical resurrection. Here, what Paul calls a "spiritual body" coincides name-wise with what the Divine Principle terms a "spirit body."

Second, physical resurrection would have to take place immediately upon physical death and not in the last days. Regarding the time of physical resurrection, Paul apparently had two different understandings: 1) immediately upon physical death (2 Cor. 5:1-3); and 2) in the last days (1 Cor. 15:51-52; 1 Thess. 4:16-17). According to the Welsh-American New Testament theologian W. D. Davies (1911–2001), the first understanding was developed by Paul later than the second, thus being more advanced and more important than the second,[18] although historically in the Christian tradition the second has been far more popular than the first. Also, if physical resurrection takes place in the last days, something inconvenient would emerge. It is that the deceased person would have to wait until the last days to be physically resurrected, i.e., that he would have to go through the so-called "intermediate state" between the time of physical death and the last days of physical resurrection, during which he would have to stay naked without a resurrected body. During the intermediate state in the spirit world, theoretically he would have no sense of personal self-identity whatsoever as a human being. According to the Scottish theologian

---

[18] W. D. Davies, *Paul and Rabbinic Judaism: Some Rabbinic Elements in Pauline Theology* (London: SPCK, 1970), pp. 317-18.

John Macquarrie (1919–2007), it is "a doctrine with severe problems" because it cannot support "personal identity, which requires memory."[19]

By retaining the above two points which are still biblical and therefore non-heretical, Christianity would be able to assert that for further spiritual growth in the spirit world, the deceased person with the dual characteristics of *sungsang* (soul) and *hyungsang* (resurrected body) can really relate to the earthly counterpart whose physical self consists of the dual characteristics of physical mind (the *sungsang* part) and physical body (the *hyungsang* part).

John Hick (1922–2012), therefore, is correct, when he maintains that there still will be "a divine purpose of person-making [i.e., spiritual growth]" after physical death, and that this person-making takes place because of physical resurrection, although according to him it takes place when the deceased person with a resurrected body (a spiritual body) relates to fellow inhabitants with resurrected bodies in the spirit world.[20] According to the Divine Principle, by contrast, the deceased person must be able to relate to the earthly counterpart for real spiritual growth. In this regard, Jürgen Moltmann agrees with the Divine Principle, when he says that for their eventual salvation "the dead [who are physically resurrected] are enduringly with us who are the living [on the earth]."[21]

If the Divine Principle idea of returning resurrection is acceptable to Christianity in the way mentioned above, the Catholic notion of purgatory can be better understood. According to Catholic theology, if one commits only venial sins on the earth, one will not go to hell but to purgatory for purification, to be eventually allowed to go to heaven. For purification in purgatory, one's earthly counterpart can pray and buy indulgences. From the viewpoint of the Divine Principle, the earthly counterpart's good deeds of praying and buying indulgences constitute merit received through the dual characteristics of *sungsang* and *hyungsang*, which both the deceased and their earthly counterparts have in common.

The Catholic notion of the limbo of the Old Testament fathers (*limbus patrum*) also can be understood in the same way. The Catholic Church teaches that the limbo of the fathers is the place in the spirit world where the Old Testament saints such as Abraham, Jacob and Moses stayed until Christ's

---

[19] John Macquarrie, "Identity," in *The Westminster Dictionary of Christian Theology*, ed. Alan Richardson and John Bowden (Philadelphia: Westminster Press, 1983), pp. 278-79. In the same article, he further says, however, that if a resurrected body is added, "the idea of an identity 'beyond death' is conceivable, and by no means nonsense."

[20] John Hick, "Life after Death," in *The Westminster Dictionary of Christian Theology*, pp. 331-34.

[21] Jürgen Moltmann, *The Coming of God: Christian Eschatology*, trans. Margaret Kohl (Minneapolis, MN: Fortress Press, 1996), p. 107.

coming and redemption, which opened heaven to them. The Divine Principle explains it by asserting that when Christ came, the Old Testament fathers were able to have the benefit of returning resurrection by receiving merit from the good deeds of the earthly Christians they helped through the dynamics of the dual characteristics of *sungsang* and *hyungsang*.[22]

Finally, however, there is a point of caution we have to bear in mind. When the Divine Principle teaches that even the wicked in hell will be given a second chance, it does not mean to say that their liberation from hell is an easy process. It is because the communication between the spirit world and the physical world is not easy. In particular, an unfortunate person in hell would not have much ability to relate to the physical world to receive good merit. Thus, while on the earth, we are encouraged to refrain from thinking that we can commit sin now because we will be liberated from hell anyway.

§2. Final Consummation of the World

This section will begin by presenting two opposing types of general eschatology in Christianity regarding the final consummation of the world: apocalyptic eschatology and non-apocalyptic utopian eschatology. After that, the mediating Unification view of the end of the world will be shown as a solution to the problem of the tension between the two.

1. Apocalyptic Eschatology

We have to touch upon apocalyptic eschatology in Judaism before dealing with Christian apocalyptic eschatology, because the latter was developed in the milieu of the former, which had emerged since the Babylonian exile in the sixth century B.C.

a. Apocalyptic eschatology in Judaism

Originally the eschatology of the Old Testament was predominantly non-apocalyptic, coming from classical prophets such as Amos, Hosea, Isaiah and Micah before the Babylonian exile. It taught that if the Israelites repent of their transgressions, for which they were warned they would be punished by God (Amos 2:6; 3:2; Hos. 8:13; 9:7, 9; Isa. 10:5; 13:3, 11, 13), they will enjoy in this

---

[22] The Divine Principle describes this as follows: "The spirits of the faithful Jews descended to the earth from the form-spirit level of the spirit world where they had been living. They returned to help the believers on earth, who had the opportunity to benefit from the redemption by the cross, to believe in Jesus and become life spirits. In doing so, the returning spirits also became life spirits" (EDP, p. 146).

world the day of the LORD or Yahweh (Amos 9:11; Hos. 2:16; Isa. 12:1, 4; Mic. 4:6; 5:10), the coming of a Davidic Messiah (Amos 9:11; Isa. 7:14-16; 9:6-7; 11:1-5; Mic. 5:2-4), and the restoration of Zion or Jerusalem (Amos 9:11-15; Isa. 2:2-4; 12:6; 33; Mic. 4:1-13; 7:11-13). This earthly kingdom of Yahweh through a Davidic Messiah apparently meant the fulfillment of the promised land "flowing with milk and honey" (Ex. 3:8; Num. 14:8; Deut. 31:20). There was no specific interest in life after death.

But as they still continued to sin, the Israelites received God's devastating punishment: The northern kingdom of Israel was destroyed by the Assyrians in 722 B.C., and the southern kingdom of Judah was thrown into the Babylonian exile for about 70 years in the sixth century B.C. As a result, "the hope for the fulfillment of the Davidic promise" was "revised" in such a way as to give rise in Deutro-Isaiah (Second Isaiah) to the notion of the Suffering Servant as the deliverer of the Israelites.[23] God laid on this Suffering Servant "the inequity of us all" (Isa. 53:6). Deutro-Isaiah, which covers Isaiah chapters 40-55, is considered among scholars to have been written during the Babylonian exile by someone other than the eighth-century B.C. prophet Isaiah himself.

Jewish eschatology then went through considerable change. It became apocalyptic and otherworldly, as can even be seen in the so-called "Isaiah Apocalypse" (Isa. 24-27) that proclaimed the cataclysmic destruction of the earth (24:1, 3, 18-20), the resurrection of the dead (26:19) and the victory of Yahweh over all evil at the end (24:21-23; 27:1). The Isaiah Apocalypse was written most likely after the Babylonian exile.

This apocalyptic shift or change of Jewish eschatology, which occurred because of the Israelites' loss of hope on the earth in the midst of the Babylonian exile, is well described by the American Lutheran theologian Carl E. Braaten (1929–2023): "A process of transcending took place which shifted the focus of attention from this world to the next, a transition that would be mediated by an apocalyptic transformation of the present age into a spiritual realm beyond time and space."[24]

Jewish apocalyptic eschatology was apparently shaped also under the influence of the Persian religion of Zoroastrianism, to which the Israelites were exposed during the exile.[25] In its resemblance to Zoroastrian apocalypticism, the apocalyptic eschatology of Judaism had at least two basic features: 1) the

---

[23] Hans Schwartz, *Eschatology* (Grand Rapids, MI: Wm. B. Eerdmans Publishing Co., 2000), p. 51.

[24] Carl E. Braaten, "The Kingdom of God and Life Everlasting," in *Christian Theology: An Introduction to Its Traditions and Tasks*, rev. and enl. ed., ed. Peter C. Hodgson and Robert H. King (Philadelphia: Fortress Press, 1985), p. 331.

[25] Schwarz, *Eschatology*, pp. 55-60.

hope for an otherworldly transfiguration and renewal of the world, and 2) the hope for the resurrection of the dead.[26] Furthermore, according to the American biblical scholar Bart D. Ehrman (1955–), Jewish apocalypticists believed in the following four things: 1) the dualism of God and Satan, according to which those who side with God have to suffer in the present age but will eventually witness the victory of God that annihilates all forces of evil; 2) pessimism about the present age, in which God's people have to suffer from the unbearable forces of evil; 3) the final vindication of God's people through the divine intervention involving the resurrection of the dead and the judgment of all people; and 4) the imminence of the coming of this vindication.[27]

Jewish apocalypticism reached its pinnacle when it was experienced and lived by the Jews of the second century B.C. as they were harshly persecuted by King Antiochus IV Epiphanes of the Seleucid Empire (r. 175–164 B.C.) with his policy of Hellenizing them. The king sacked Jerusalem, slaughtered many Jews, prohibited the Jewish laws, and made the Temple a temple for Zeus, compelling them to sacrifice swine's flesh on the alter. The Maccabean revolt took place from 167 to 160 B.C. The Jews suffered a great deal and were afraid that they might get killed any moment. For their vindication, therefore, they hoped for the physical resurrection of the dead and the imminent coming of God's cataclysmic judgment of this evil world.

The Book of Daniel, a Jewish apocalypse in the Old Testament, is believed to have been written in the second century B.C. Its verses such as 8:9-12, 23-25; 10:20; and 11:21 apparently refer to King Antiochus IV Epiphanes. In the context of the suffering of the Jews under him, it refers to the apocalyptic coming of "an anointed one" (10:25), God's final judgment of the evil world (10:27; 11:45; 12:7), and the resurrection of the dead (12:2). Other Jewish apocalypses such as the first Book of Enock were also written. Jewish apocalypticism became so widespread that when Christianity emerged and developed, it was very much colored by it.

b. Apocalyptic eschatology in Christianity

The Synoptic Gospels describe the events surrounding Jesus in quite an apocalyptic manner, in resemblance to Jewish apocalypticism. They apparently compare the rule of Herod Antipas (r. 4 B.C.–39 A.D.) in Galilee and Perea with that of King Antiochus IV Epiphanes. Jesus' life was threatened by Herod, but his coming as the Messiah "with the throne of his father David" (Lk.1:32) was believed to apocalyptically change the social order: "He [God] has put

---

[26] Ibid., p. 55.

[27] Bart D. Ehrman, "The Apocalyptic Context for Jesus' View of the Messiah." https://ehrmanblog.org/the-apocalyptic-context-for-jesus-view-of-the-messiah/.

down the mighty from their thrones, and exalted those of low degree," in the words of Mary (Lk. 1:52).

But it is the so-called "Olivet Discourse" of Jesus in the Synoptics (Mt. 24-25; Mk. 13; Lk. 21) that is very explicitly apocalyptic, showing judgment-filled predictions of the destruction of the Temple, the tribulation of the Israelites, the chaos of the world, the catastrophic destruction of the cosmos, and the final coming of the "Son of man" in clouds with power and glory.

The chapters prior to the Olivet Discourse describe Jesus' earthly ministry, during which he received much opposition from Jewish leaders, and the chapters following the discourse cover his trial, death on the cross, and resurrection. From this, we can surmise that it was the Jewish leaders' sinful opposition to Jesus that led him to predict apocalyptic events such as the destruction of the Temple and also caused his death and resurrection in the end. This point is supported by the American New Testament theologian William L. Lane (1931–1999), for example, when he holds that "the relationship which exists between the judgment upon Jerusalem implied by the discourse and the death of Jesus" was occasioned by his "conflict" with the Jewish authorities.[28]

We can therefore see parallels between what happened during and after the Babylonian exile, on the one hand, and what transpired in relation to Jesus' predictions, on the other. Just as the sin of the Israelites in front of God caused the ordeals of the Babylonian captivity in the sixth century B.C. and the persecution by Antiochus IV Epiphanes in the second century B.C., the sinful opposition to Jesus on the part of the Jewish leaders caused the destruction of the Temple by Rome and the tribulation of the Jews. Just as the sin of the Israelites was laid on the Suffering Servant according to Deutro-Isaiah, the sin of opposition to Jesus was laid on him on the cross according to the Synoptic Gospels. Just as the coming of "an anointed one" was hoped for in Daniel, the coming of the "Son of man" was expected in the Synoptics. The apocalyptic destruction of the sinful world was also expected to happen in both cases.

But the actual end of the world did not come as predicted by the Olivet Discourse of Jesus. Thus Christians came to understand that the discourse was about their own tribulation under the evil dominion of Rome rather than the tribulation of the Jews, and that they will be delivered when the end time comes sometime very soon. In that Christian context, the Book of Revelation, a New Testament apocalypse, was written around the end of the first century A.D.

---

[28] William L. Lane, *The Gospel of Mark* (Grand Rapids, MI: Wm. B. Eerdmans Publishing Co., 1974), p. 444.

The Book of Revelation describes multiple apocalyptic signs and symbols resembling those in the Book of Daniel in the Old Testament.

But again, the end-time did not come as was predicted in Revelation. Thus the apocalyptic hope and discourse have continued within the Christian tradition until today. This is the reason why there are various interpretations of the Olivet Discourse and Revelation, ranging from asserting that both purely talk about the situations of the first century, to asserting that both are about what will happen whenever the end of the world comes in the future.

The Book of Revelation references a thousand-year period during which Christ will reign over the millennial kingdom of God, and after which the final judgment will occur for the eternal state (20:1-21:8). There are three different interpretations of the millennium: premillennialism, postmillennialism and amillennialism.

Premillennialism holds that Christ will gloriously return *prior to* the millennium to defeat Satan-dominated history and inaugurate the millennial kingdom of God on earth. At the Second Coming, both the resurrected righteous dead (1 Thess. 4:16; Rev. 20:4-6) and the righteous believers alive in the church (1 Thess. 4:17) will be "caught up… to meet the Lord in the air" (1 Thess. 4:17); and then they will come down together with Christ to reign over the millennial kingdom on earth. After the millennium, the unrighteous dead will be resurrected for the final judgment (Rev. 20:5, 12-13).

Premillennialism is subdivided into two different kinds: posttribulational (the Second Coming *after* the seven-year tribulation) and pretribulational (the Second Coming *prior to* the seven-year tribulation). Posttribulational premillennialism was historically widespread in the ante-Nicene period, and is widely accepted today among evangelicals. Pretribulational premillennialism emerged in the 1830s through the dispensationalism of the Anglo-Irish Bible teacher John Nelson Darby (1800–1882) and became popular especially in America, where it is still widely accepted among conservative evangelicals and fundamentalists today.

Postmillennialism, by contrast, is less apocalyptic than premillennialism, as it holds that Christ will return *after*, or even based on, the optimistic millennium kingdom (although its length may not have to be taken literally) which is brought forth on the earth through the expansion and influence of the church conducting religious revivals throughout the world (Mt. 24:14; Mk. 13:10). At the Second Coming, the general "resurrection of both the just and the unjust" (Acts 24:15) will occur for the final judgment. Postmillennialism was popular at least in the first three rounds of Great Awakening in the history of American Christianity.

As for amillennialism, its prefix "a" ("not") means that there is "no" millennium except a symbolic millennial kingdom, which is the church on the earth. It is faced with tribulation and suffering, and only imperfectly points to God's kingdom in heaven. The Second Coming will take place to put an end to this pessimistic situation, and the general resurrection of both the just and the unjust (Acts 24:15) will take place for the final judgment. This position was proposed by St. Augustine (354–430), and it is adhered to today by the Eastern Orthodox Church, the Roman Catholic Church and the majority of mainline Protestant denominations.

What is important is that the three schools of millennialism, in spite of their differences, all accept that after the millennium and the resurrection (whether it is only of the unjust or the general one), the final judgment will bring natural calamities to destroy this world (Mt. 24:7, 29, 35; Mk. 13:8, 24-25, 31; Lk. 21:11; 21:25-26, 33; 2 Pet. 3:10-12; Rev. 20:9) and eternally assign the righteous and the unrighteous to heaven and hell respectively (Mt. 25:31-46; Rev. 20:12-15). That assignment will form the eternal state in the other world. The eternal state will be inhabited by all resurrected people with their resurrected bodies, whether they are righteous or unrighteous people. They may look as if they were tangibly living in this physical world, but the eternal state is actually otherworldly, because their resurrected bodies are merely "spiritual bodies" (1 Cor. 15:44). The righteous people will experience their otherworldly eternal state as "a new heaven and a new earth; for the first heaven and the first earth had passed away" (Rev. 21:1). The unrighteous people, by contrast, will experience the eternal state of hell.

In the modern period, theological liberalism emerged and became widespread, proposing this-worldly, non-apocalyptic approaches in opposition to the apocalypticism of the Christian tradition. But the German New Testament scholar Johannes Weiss (1863–1914) strongly reemphasized apocalypticism in his 1892 book, *Jesus' Proclamation of the Kingdom of God*.[29] The German Lutheran theologian Albert Schweitzer (1875–1965) popularized Weiss' thesis at the beginning of the twentieth century.[30] Weiss and Schweitzer had quite a big impact on New Testament studies later on.

---

[29] Johannes Weiss, *Jesus' Proclamation of the Kingdom of God*, trans. and ed. Richard Hyde Hiers and David Larrimore Holland (Philadelphia: Fortress Press, 1971).

[30] Albert Schweitzer, *The Quest of the Historical Jesus: A Critical Study of its Progress from Reimarus to Wrede*, trans. W. Montgomery (New York: Macmillan Co., 1961). The original German edition was published in 1906.

2. *Non-apocalyptic Eschatology*

In the history of Christianity, the Enlightenment emerged in the late seventeenth century, affirming this-worldliness, naturalism, rationalism and humanism. Under its influence, apocalypticism started to languish. Immanuel Kant (1724–1804) integrated the Enlightenment with Pietism in his moral philosophy,[31] and because of this he still was under the influence of the Enlightenment. In his book, *Religion within the Limits of Reason Alone* (1793), he held that if we, with Jesus as our moral teacher, autonomously follow the moral law (the categorical imperative) that exists within ourselves, we will always act right, to be able to build an "ethical commonwealth," which is the kingdom of God on earth.[32]

In the nineteenth century, the German Protestant theologian Albrecht Ritschl inherited Kant's understanding of moral religion and maintained that the kingdom of God as God's community "forms… the ethical ideal for whose attainment the members of the community bind themselves to each other through a definite type of reciprocal action."[33] Ritschl had little interest in the traditional Christian notions of heaven and hell in the other world. The kingdom of God on earth itself will be the eternal state of human beings. The death of Jesus on the cross is not a substitutionary death on our behalf to propitiate God's wrath for the forgiveness of our sin, but rather a great example of love which we can imitate to be morally influenced by it for our salvation. This is the so-called "moral influence theory" of the atonement.

Just several years after Johannes Weiss' 1892 publication of *Jesus' Proclamation of the Kingdom of God*, which showed his apocalyptic view of Jesus, Adolf von Harnack, a well-known Ritchlian professor, gave a series of sixteen lectures on the topic "What Is Christianity?" to some six hundred students at the University of Berlin in the academic year of 1899–1900. These lectures presented his non-apocalyptic understanding of the kingdom of God, and they were published as a book in 1901.[34] It was widely circulated not only in Germany but also in England and America.

According to Harnack, although Jesus spoke about the coming of the kingdom of God in an apocalyptic language that reflected the spread of Jewish

---

[31] This point was already discussed in Chapter 11, section 2, subsection 2, subsubsection a ("Moral religion of Immanuel Kant") in the present book.

[32] Immanuel Kant, *Religion within the Limits of Reason Alone*, trans. Theodore M. Greene and Hoyt H. Hudson (New York: Harper & Row, Polishers, 1960).

[33] Albrecht Ritschl, "Instruction in the Christian Religion," in *Three Essays*, trans. Philip Hefner (Philadelphia: Fortress Press, 1972), p. 222.

[34] Adolf von Harnack, *What Is Christianity?* trans. Thomas Bailey Saunders (New York: Harper & Row, Publishers, 1957).

apocalypticism in his day, all his apocalyptic imagery was just the dispensable "husk" of a "kernel."[35] The indispensable kernel of Jesus' message was about the non-apocalyptic kingdom of God on earth: "The kingdom of God comes by coming to the individual, by entering into his soul and laying hold of it… it is the rule of the holy God in the hearts of individuals: *it is God himself in his power*."[36] Apocalypticism vanished here: "From this point of view everything that is dramatic in the external and historical sense has vanished," and "It is not a question of angels and devils, thrones and principalities, but of God and the soul, the soul and its God."[37]

In the early twentieth century, this liberal trend was bequeathed to the Social Gospel movement of Walter Rauschenbusch (1861–1918) in America. Although the liberal trend receded in Europe and America after World War I, it reemerged after World War II in liberation theology including black theology, feminist theology and womanist theology in America, and Latin American liberation theology. These schools of liberation theology were slightly different from the optimistic tradition of Kant, Ritschl, Harnack and Rauschenbusch, in that they were seriously interested in the fight to do away with the social injustices of racism, sexism and classism in this world. But because of this, they were this-worldly rather than otherworldly. According to the American black theologian James H. Cone (1938–2018), for example, hope must not be related to life after death in such a way as to encourage us, as white slave masters have done, to forget about present injustice. "Hope must be related to the present, and it must serve as a means of transforming an oppressed community into a liberated—and liberating—community."[38] Carl Braaten states, therefore, that liberation theology resembles the tradition of Kantianism, Ritschlianism and the Social Gospel.[39]

This liberal tradition was also inherited by many American New Testament scholars such as Robert W. Funk (1926–2005), Marcus Borg (1942–2015) and John Dominic Crossan (1934–). In 1985 Funk founded the Jesus Seminar, whose prominent members included Borg and Crossan. The Jesus Seminar was deemed a controversial group by conservatives. Borg, echoing Harnack concerning the kingdom of God in the proclamation of Jesus, says: "For Jesus, the language of the kingdom was a way of speaking of the power

---

35 Ibid., p. 55.
36 Ibid., p. 56. Italics original.
37 Ibid.
38 James H. Cone, *A Black Theology of Liberation*, 2nd ed. (Maryknoll, NY: Orbis Books, 1986), p. 140.
39 Braaten, "The Kingdom of God and Life Everlasting," p. 347.

of the Spirit and the new life which it created. The coming of the kingdom is the coming of the Spirit, both into individual lives and into history itself."[40]

These scholars realized that the Synoptic Gospels contain many non-apocalyptic "wisdom sayings" of Jesus such as the one that says: "You have heard that it was said, 'You shall love your neighbor and hate your enemy.' But I say to you, Love your enemies and pray for those who persecute you" (Mt. 5:43-44). They also believed that the wisdom sayings of Jesus in Matthew and Luke came from both Mark and a hypothetical independent collection of Jesus' sayings called the "Q source." Additionally, there is the Gospel of Thomas, an old collection of Jesus' wisdom sayings, which was fully discovered at Nag Hamadi, Egypt, in 1945. These scholars held that the Q source and the Gospel of Thomas were produced earlier than the Synoptic Gospels, sometime soon after the death of Jesus in the first century,[41] so that both showed a true picture of Jesus as a wisdom Teacher/Messiah rather than an apocalyptic Messiah.

3. The Unification View

The Unification view of the end of the world offers a solution to the problem of the tension between the two opposing types of Christian eschatology discussed above.

a. Restoring the three great blessings

The Divine Principle holds that God's original purpose of creation was to realize the "three great blessings": 1) individual perfection; 2) the multiplication of God's children in families, nations and the world; and 3) the human dominion of love over the rest of creation, as written in the Bible: "Be fruitful and multiply, and fill the earth and subdue it; and have dominion over the fish of the sea and over the birds of the air and over every living thing that moves upon the earth" (Gen. 1:28).

Adam and Eve were expected to realize each of these three blessings through the "four position foundation" centered on God: 1) the four position foundation of God, mind, body, and their unity for individual perfection; 2) the four position foundation of God, husband, wife, and their children for the multiplication of children; and 3) the four position foundation of God, human beings, all things, and their unity for the human dominion of love over the rest of creation.[42] In this way the kingdom of God *on earth* was supposed to be built,

---

[40] Marcus Borg, *Jesus: A New Vision* (San Francisco: Harper & Row, Publishers, 1987), p. 198.
[41] Helmut Koester and Stephen J. Patterson, for example, argue that the Gospel of Thomas was written as early as 30s or the 40s of the first century. See their "The Gospel of Thomas: Does It Contain Authentic Sayings of Jesus?" *Bible View* 6, no. 2 (April 1990): 37.
[42] EDP pp. 33-36.

and then the kingdom of God *in heaven* was to be established in the spirit world after the physical death of human beings.[43] For the realization of the three great blessings through the four position foundation as the purpose of creation, both God and human beings were to fulfill their respective portions of responsibility.[44] And after the realization of this purpose of creation, both God and human beings were to experience "joy."[45]

Unfortunately, however, Adam and Eve failed to accomplish their human portion of responsibility and fell sexually centered on Satan.[46] They thus lost the three great blessings of God in this world and instead realized them through a four position foundation under the sovereignty of Satan.[47] This brought forth "hell on earth" and then "hell in the spirit world" after the physical death of human beings.[48]

From the viewpoint of the Divine Principle, therefore, the Messiah is to come on behalf of Adam in the last days to restore the three great blessings centered on God, in order that he may transform this satanic world for the realization of the kingdom of God on earth: "the world under the sovereignty of Satan must… be transformed into the world… where the three great blessings are fulfilled centered on God. The Messiah comes at this time of transformation."[49] Therefore the last days is the time "when the evil world under satanic sovereignty is transformed into the ideal world under God's sovereignty. Hell on earth will be transformed into the Kingdom of Heaven on earth." [50] This kingdom of God on earth is the kingdom of "interdependence, mutual prosperity and universally shared values."[51]

Furthermore, once the kingdom of God on earth is established in this world, it will continue to exist for eternity beyond the last days: It is "everlasting and indestructible."[52] "God, the subject partner, is eternal; likewise, [the] earth, the object partner, should be eternal."[53]This world, therefore, will not be apocalyptically destroyed by the final judgment. The biblical passages about the apocalyptic destruction of the world, then, should not be taken literally. They

---

43 EDP, pp. 36, 81.
44 EDP, pp. 43-44,
45 EDP, pp. 33-35.
46 EDP, pp. 63-65.
47 EDP, p. 68.
48 EDP, p. 82.
49 EDP, pp. 88-89.
50 EDP, p. 89.
51 EDP, pp. 342-44.
52 EDP, p. 118.
53 EDP, p. 91.

symbolically mean that "the tyranny of Satan will be overthrown" for the restoration of *this* world to "God's sovereignty founded on Christ."[54]

According to the Divine Principle, the day of Jesus as the second Adam was the last days, when he was to build the kingdom of God on earth by restoring the three great blessings in this world.[55] But the people of Israel did not believe in him and killed him on the cross. So the kingdom of God on earth was not built at that time, and only spiritual salvation was brought forth by the resurrected Jesus and the Holy Spirit. This means that the fulfillment of God's original will was prolonged until the day of the Lord of the Second Advent as the third Adam, so that the day of the Lord of the Second Advent will be the last days.[56] He and his Bride will restore the three great blessings to build the kingdom of God on earth, bringing forth both spiritual and physical salvation.

The Divine Principle asserts that the last days are today, i.e., the time of the Second Advent, because in the world of the present age we can recognize various phenomena leaning toward the restoration of the three great blessings, such as an increased recognition of the "true human value" of each person for the restoration of the first blessing, a trend today toward "the formation of one global cultural sphere based on Christian ideals" for the restoration of the second blessing, and an increased development today of our ability to "govern the creation" though "heart" and "highly advanced science" for the restoration of the third blessing.[57]

b. Mediating between the two opposing types of eschatology

As was seen above, Unification eschatology concerning the final consummation of the world is very this-worldly in character, not being apocalyptic. Then, does this mean that it is the same as the non-apocalyptic eschatology of Kant, Ritschl, Harnack and many other liberals? The answer is in the negative, because Unification eschatology is also very much interested in the kingdom of God in heaven in the other world, whereas the non-apocalyptic eschatology of Christianity is hardly interested in it. According to the Divine Principle, "Once people have attained full maturity and enjoyed life in God's earthly Kingdom, then when they shed their physical bodies and pass into the spirit world, they will form the Kingdom of Heaven in heaven."[58]

---

[54] Ibid.

[55] EDP, pp. 89-90.

[56] EDP, p. 90.

[57] EDP, pp. 96-103.

[58] EDP, p. 81.

God actually wants all of us as his beloved children to happily live an eternal life of true love in the kingdom of God in heaven in the other world, although in order for that to happen the kingdom of God on earth must be built first. Regarding this eternal life of love in the spirit world, Dr. Hak Ja Han Moon says:

> We are created to live an eternal life. We are similarly created to practice true love. Furthermore, we are to practice true love here on the Earth. We engage ourselves with many things in this world. These things become the material that insures our eternal life. In other words, everything we do in this world is training for eternal life [in the spirit world].[59]

There is another reason why Unification eschatology is not the same as the non-apocalyptic eschatology of Kant, Ritschl, etc. It is that the former actually talks about the behind-the-scenes cosmic struggle between God and Satan that lasts until the last days, when the final realization of the God-centered three great blessings and the defeat of the Satan-centered three great blessings occur in this world. The latter, on the other hand, is rather disinterested in this struggle between God and Satan. Unification eschatology thus accepts what Braaten refers to as the "fundamental story line" of biblical apocalyptic, being "the cosmic struggle between the Lord and Creator Spirit of life and 'the prince of demons,' 'the ruler of this world' of death, darkness, and destructiveness."[60] Unification eschatology may therefore sound quite apocalyptic, although it denies the apocalyptic destruction of the world.

From the above, it can be understood that Unification eschatology is basically *neither* an apocalyptic eschatology *nor* a non-apocalyptic eschatology, negatively speaking. What, then, is it, when it affirms both the eternity of the this-worldly kingdom of God on earth and the eternity of the otherworldly kingdom of God in heaven at the same time, and also when it may even sound quite apocalyptic because of its acknowledgment of the cosmic battle between God and Satan behind the scenes? Positively speaking, Unification eschatology is perhaps *both* a non-apocalyptic eschatology *and* an apocalyptic eschatology at the same time. If so, it can mediate between the two opposing types of eschatology in Christianity, putting an end to their conflict.

There seems to be still another way in which it can be said that Unification eschatology is a mediating eschatology. According to the Divine Principle, in

---

[59] Hak Ja Han Moon, "Blessed Marriage and Eternal Life," address given on a 16-city North American speaking tour April 1-16, 1996. http://www.tparents.org/Moon-Books/Tfwp/Tfwp-3-2.htm.

[60] Carl E. Braaten, "The Recovery of Apocalyptic Imagination," in *The Last Things: Biblical and Theological Perspectives on Eschatology*, ed. Carl E. Braaten and Robert W. Jenson (Grand Rapids, MI: Wm. B. Eerdmans Publishing Co., 2002), p. 17.

order for the three great blessings to be realized, both God and human beings are to fulfill their respective portions of responsibility. For when the three great blessings are each realized through the four position foundation to be formed centering on God, its formation involves both God and human beings. On the part of God, he fulfills his portion of responsibility when he totally negates and dedicates himself for the sake of his beloved human beings, by having sacrificial give and take action of his dual characteristics of *Sungsang* and *Hyungsang* centering on Heart. On the part of human beings, they similarly fulfill their portion of responsibility when they totally negate and dedicate themselves for God's will to love the world, by having sacrificial give and take action between a subject partner and object partner centering on God, whether they are mind and body for the first blessing, husband and wife for the second blessing, or humans and the rest of creation for the third blessing. This is how God and human beings can come to completely resemble each other and unite with each other to form the seamless four position foundation;[61] hence the mutual involvement of both God's responsibility and the human responsibility. Once this mutual involvement of God and human beings is accomplished on the earth, it will automatically be carried to the kingdom of God in heaven in the spirit world where we experience it for eternity.

However, apocalyptic and non-apocalyptic eschatology in Christianity are both one-sided, in that the former emphasizes God's responsibility to bring about the apocalyptic judgment in front of powerless, sinful humans in order to launch the eternal state in the other world, while the latter stresses the human ability to build the kingdom of God on earth without any apocalyptic involvement of God. Here we can say that Unification eschatology can mediate between the two conflicting types of Christian eschatology with respect to the tension of God's responsibility and the human responsibility.

c. Other mediating eschatologies

Carl Braaten is aware of the tension or opposition between apocalyptic and non-apocalyptic eschatology in Christianity when he says:

> Christianity today stands at the crossroads between two diametrically opposed interpretations of eschatology. On one side are the "conservative evangelicals" in all Christian denominations who think of eschatology in the traditional sense of "last things" to occur in some near or distant future. On the other sided there are "post-

[61] See Chapter 4, section 1, subsection 2 ("Dual Characteristics") in the present book for how the four position foundation is formed, given God's dual characteristics of *Sungsang* and *Hyungsang* and the world's dual characteristics of *sungsang* and *hyungsang*.

Enlightenment" Christians who think of eschatology more concretely in relation to social-ethical objectives.[62]

In order to help to solve this problem of the tension between the two, Braaten proposes that we should start our eschatology with the original Old Testament eschatology of the classical prophets such as Amos, Hosea and Isaiah before the Babylonian exile, which was not apocalyptic yet: "it is necessary to retrace the steps of Israel, as it were, and start our eschatology like the prophets with the struggles of people in this life" to be able to "escalate human hope… to enfold the totality of reality in a cosmic eschatology."[63] This proposal by Braaten makes sense, because it is important to go back to the original preexilic eschatology of the Old Testament to "enfold the totality of reality." Although the classical prophets did not have a developed doctrine of afterlife other than the still ethereal, shadowy notion of "Sheol" (Gen. 42:38; Ps. 141:7; Amos 9:2; Hos. 13:14; Isa. 5:14; 14:9; etc.), nevertheless Unification eschatology, with its capacity of mediating between apocalyptic and non-apocalyptic eschatology, would welcome Braaten's proposal.

Let us now deal with the eschatology of Jürgen Moltmann. Here we can be reminded of his "practical theodicy" to actually eradicate evil from this world based on our practicing the love and sacrifice of Christ who died on the cross and was resurrected.[64] Moltmann was a German prisoner of war from 1945 to 1948 in Belgium, Scotland and England, and came to feel the need for God as a real source of future hope to tackle the problem of pain and sorrow within this world. Somewhat influenced by the Jewish Marxist philosopher Ernst Bloch's (1885–1977) three-volume *The Principle of Hope*, Moltmann well expressed that need in his celebrated book on eschatology, *Theology of Hope* (1965 in German; 1967 in English).

Moltmann's eschatology resembles Unification eschatology in that it is neither an apocalyptic eschatology nor a non-apocalyptic eschatology. First, it is not an apocalyptic eschatology. According to him, if it were an apocalyptic eschatology, "it would be better to turn one's back on it altogether; for 'the last things' spoil one's taste for the penultimate ones, and the… end of history robs us of our freedom among history's many possibilities, and our tolerance" for all the "unfinished and provisional" things in history.[65] True Christin hope arises when we take responsibility together with Christ to tackle many problems related to the penultimate in the world. Second, however, his eschatology is not a non-apocalyptic utopian eschatology, either: We have to

---

[62] Braaten, "The Kingdom of God and Life Everlasting," p. 347.
[63] Ibid., p. 348.
[64] See Chapter 8, section 3, subsection 2 ("Jürgen Moltmann") in the present book.
[65] Moltmann, *The Coming of God*, p. x.

"distinguish the spirit of eschatology from that of utopia."[66] This means that eschatology involves God's radical power as well as our human responsibility, in order to transform human history and the world. If Moltmann's eschatology is thus neither an apocalyptic eschatology nor a non-apocalyptic eschatology, it can be regarded as a mediating eschatology.

The eschatology of Moltmann is also interested in both the eternity of the eventually transformed world on the earth and the eternity of eventually transformed life after death. For all the living people on the earth and all the resurrected dead in the other world are both "in community with Christ" for their eventual salvation.[67] For him, the eternity of life after death does not mean the immortality of the soul as understood in the Greek tradition, but rather the resurrection of the dead and its eternity in the Bible. According to him, the resurrection of the dead takes place immediately upon physical death; so there is no time whatsoever during which their souls are disembodied.[68] They are thus able to relate to earthly people for their eventual liberation in the other world: "The dead [who are physically resurrected] are enduringly with us who are the living [on the earth]."[69] There is no eternal hell in the other world, therefore.

Moltmann's eschatology has a single focus, which is the indwelling of God in his creation in the last days:

> The different horizons of eternal life, the eternal kingdom and the eternal creation draw together to a single focus: *the cosmic Shekinah of God*. God desires to come to his 'dwelling' in his creation, the home of his identity in the world, and in it to his 'rest', his perfected, eternal joy.[70]

Note that God's joy is mentioned here. This echoes Unification eschatology's assertion that in the last days God is to be able to dwell in the whole of creation to his joy, as the three great blessings for the eternal kingdom of God are completely realized on earth and in heaven as well.

But there seem to be at least two points of difference between Moltmann's eschatology and Unification eschatology. First, the former, not accepting apocalyptic eschatology, does not believe in the existence of Satan from the beginning, whereas the latter knows that Satan exists until the sovereignty of God is established in the last days.

---

[66] Moltmann, *Theology of Hope*, p. 17.
[67] Moltmann, *The Coming of God*, p. 106.
[68] Ibid., pp. 102-4.
[69] Ibid., p. 107.
[70] Ibid., xiii. Italics original.

A second point of difference between them concerns Christ and his Second Coming. Moltmann's eschatology holds that the death and resurrection of Christ out of his sacrificial love combined with the Holy Spirit constitute the ultimate driving force for our responsible work for the transformation of the world, and that when Christ returns, he will finish any unfinished work with us by use of the same way of his death and resurrection: "The parousia of Christ is first and foremost the completion of the way of Jesus: 'the Christ on the way' arrives at his goal. His saving work is completed."[71] By contrast, Unification eschatology maintains that while the resurrected Christ and the Holy Spirit brought forth spiritual salvation, the three great blessings were not completely realized on the earth due to his death on the cross. On behalf of Christ and the Holy Spirit, therefore, the Christ of the Second Coming and his Bride will carry out their enormously hard work of love and sacrifice, rather than literally dying on the cross, to realize God's three great blessings on the earth. As they can be called our "True Parents," we will responsibly work together with them as their children in front of God.

§3. Issues and Proposals

After dealing with both individual and general eschatology in Christianity, and with both apocalyptic and non-apocalyptic eschatology within general eschatology in Christianity as a context in which to discuss Unification eschatology, we can find at least three important issues that need to be addressed.

1. Universal Salvation

We have learned that apocalyptic eschatology, with its emphasis on God's final judgment, does not accept universal salvation. It understands that the wicked, even after their physical resurrection, will be eternally judged in hell in the other world. Its individual eschatology, therefore, is a miserable one. Non-apocalyptic eschatology, by contrast, is basically disinterested in heaven and hell in the other world, focusing instead on building an ethical world of goodness on the earth for as many people as possible. This is an earthly version of universal salvation, but does not talk about eternal life beyond the earth.

With Unification eschatology's unity and mediation between apocalyptic and non-apocalyptic eschatology through its notion of God's three great

[71] Jürgen Moltmann, *The Way of Jesus Christ: Christology in Messianic Dimensions*, trans. Margaret Kohl (Minneapolis, MN: Fortress Press, 1993), p. 319.

blessings to be realized for everybody not only here on the earth but also in the spirit world, it undoubtedly stands for universal salvation.

Braaten observes that the doctrine of universal salvation has been a minority opinion in the Christian tradition, and that the majority of Christians in their adherence to apocalyptic eschatology have resisted that doctrine, thinking chiefly of their own salvation in the other world. In addition, he wonders if what they have done to resist it is Christian: "Christians have done what comes naturally—to hope chiefly for themselves, their own family and friends, and let the rest go to hell. This is most natural, but is it Christian?"[72] Unification eschatology addresses this question in favor of universal salvation, by bringing back Christ's teaching of love for all people. So does Moltmann's eschatology as another mediating eschatology.

2. The Death and Resurrection of Jesus

We have learned that the original eschatology of the classical prophets such as Amos, Hosea and Isaiah before the Babylonian exile was not apocalyptic yet, and that Jewish eschatology later became apocalyptic because the Israelites experienced the harsh Babylonian exile in the sixth century B.C. as God's punishment for their sins. As a result, the idea that God was to lay their sins on the Suffering Servant as the deliverer of the Israelites emerged in Deutro-Isaiah. This means that if the Israelites had not committed sins serious enough to invite God's punishment, then the Babylonian exile would not have occurred, and apocalyptic eschatology would not even have been born in Judaism. In addition, the notion of the Suffering Servant would not have come into existence. This is, of course, speculation, but it may not be a very strange speculation.

We have also learned above that the apocalyptic eschatology of Christianity emerged within the milieu of the apocalyptic eschatology of Judaism. The Synoptic Gospels show that Jewish leaders' sinful rejection of Jesus most likely led him to present the apocalyptic Olivet Discourse to predict things like the destruction of the Temple and the tribulation of the Israelites as God's punishment for their sinful rejection, and that in that apocalyptic condition which worked against him, he had to carry their sin upon his shoulders like the Suffering Servant by being killed on the cross and resurrected. Therefore the American Lutheran theologian David P. Scaer (1936–), in his article on "Death and Resurrection as Apocalyptic Event," states: "His own

---

[72] Braaten, "The Kingdom of God and Life Everlasting," p. 350.

death and resurrection will be an apocalyptic judgment against the generation that rejected him."[73]

The same bold yet not strange speculation can be proposed here: If the leaders of the day had not committed the sin of rejecting Jesus, then his Olivet Discourse would not have been needed, and Christian apocalypticism could not even have been born. Also, the death and resurrection of Jesus would not have occurred. Instead, Jesus and his potential Bride, on behalf of Adam and Eve, could have simply worked hard to realize the three great blessings based on God's initial plan, as Unification eschatology asserts, in order to establish the kingdom of God on earth neither apocalyptically nor non-apocalyptically.

But the sin of opposing and rejecting Jesus was actually committed. Apocalyptic eschatology, therefore, became an alternative in Christianity, and in that context the necessity of the death and resurrection of Jesus for our redemption became a standard Christian doctrine. As a natural reaction against apocalypticism, therefore, utopian non-apocalypticism emerged, saying that the death and resurrection of Jesus was not an apocalyptic event but merely an example of love we can morally imitate to build a world of goodness. Unification eschatology goes beyond the tension of these two types of eschatology to say that the original mission of Jesus was to realize the three great blessings both on the earth and in the spirit world, without necessarily dying on the literal cross to be resurrected but rather by living a life of sacrifice and love continuously on the earth to defeat the power of Satan.[74] On this point, Unification eschatology diverges from Montmann's eschatology which stays with the centrality of the death and resurrection of Jesus, although the latter still is an eschatology to mediate apocalyptic and non-apocalyptic eschatology.

3. The Relationship of Individual and General Eschatology

The first and second sections of the present chapter have dealt with individual and general eschatology. But what is their relationship?

Individual eschatology within apocalyptic eschatology talks about the so-called "intermediate state" of the soul in the other world between the time of physical death and the future last days of physical resurrection, during which the soul would have to stay without yet having a resurrected body. The disembodied soul will have no sense of personal self-identity, self-consciousness and memory whatsoever as a human being, and thus have no ability whatsoever to relate to people in the earthly world in order to grow

---

[73] David. P. Scaer, "Death and Resurrection as Apocalyptic Event," *Concordia Theological Quarterly* 64:4 (October 2000): 280.

[74] To know this further, see Chapter 10 in the present book.

spiritually. This means that the disembodied soul during the intermediate stage in the other world would not grow spiritually and is cut off from the earthly world as it goes through the process of time until the final judgment in the last days. In this scenario, there is no real connection between the individual eschatology of the soul and the general eschatology of the world. Both are very much disconnected from each other.

What of individual eschatology in non-apocalyptic eschatology? Unfortunately, individual eschatology is virtually absent within non-apocalyptic eschatology, which is decidedly disinterested in the other world.

So let us look at the individual eschatology of Unification eschatology that mediates between apocalyptic and non-apocalyptic eschatology. According to the Divine Principle, once one dies physically, the spirit body within one's spirit self will start to function like a physical body in the spirit world, so that there will be nothing like what is called the intermediate stage of the disembodied soul. The spirit self with its dual characteristics of spirit mind (the *sungsang* part) and spirit body (the *hyungsang* part) in the spirit world, then, will be able to have give and take action with an earthly person's physical self with its dual characteristics of physical mind (the *sungsang* part) and physical body (the *hyungsang* part) in the physical world, due to their common dual characteristics of *sungsang* and *hyungsang*. Through that give and take action, the spirit self in the spirit world will be able to continue to grow spiritually. This means that individual and general eschatology in Unification eschatology are deeply interconnected.

Moltmann's eschatology, although it may not have such a detailed explanation of the relationship of the spirit world and the physical world as does the Divine Principle, nevertheless resembles Unification eschatology in acknowledging the close connection between individual and general eschatology. It acknowledges this close connection by "overcome[ing] the unfruitful and paralysing confrontation between the personal and the cosmic hope, individual and universal eschatology" centered on "*God*, God's kingdom and God's glory."[75] In this sense, he appropriately calls his eschatology an "integrating eschatology."[76]

---

[75] Moltmann, *The Coming of God*, p. xv.

[76] Ibid., p. xiv. Italics original.

Works Cited

Ahlstrom, Sydney E. *A Religious History of the American People.* 2nd ed. New Haven, CT: Yale University Press, 2004.

Altizer, Thomas J. J. , and Hamilton, William. *Radical Theology and the Death of God.* Indianapolis: Bobbs-Merrill, 1966.

Ambrose. *Hexameron, Paradise, and Cain and Abel.* Translated by John J. Savage. Washington, DC: Catholic University of America Press, 1961.

Anselm of Canterbury. *Anselm of Canterbury: The Major Works.* Translated by Brian Davies and Gillian Evans. New York: Oxford University Press, 1998.

__________. "The Virgin Conception and Original Sin (Selections)." In *A Scholastic Miscellany: Anselm to Ockham*, pp. 184-200. Edited and translated by Eugene R. Fairweather. Philadelphia: Westminster Press, 1956.

__________. *Why God Became Man and The Virgin Conception of Original Sin.* Translated by Joseph M. Colleran. Albany, NY: Magic Books, 1969.

Aquinas, Thomas. *An Aquinas Reader: Selections from the Writings of Thomas Aquinas.* Edited by Mary T. Clark. Garden City, NY: Image Books, 1972.

__________. *The Pocket Aquinas.* Edited by Vernon J. Bourke. New York: Washington Square Press, 1960.

__________. *Questiones Disputatae de Veritate.* https://isidore.co/aquinas/english/QDdeVer.htm.

__________. *Summa Contra Gentiles.* https://isidore.co/aquinas/ContraGentiles.htm.

__________. *Summa Theologiae.* https://www.newadvent.org/summa/.

__________. *Summa Theologiae.* Vol. I, part 1. Edited by Thomas Gilby. Garden City, NY: Image Books, 1969.

"Articles of Religion." http://www.eskimo.com/~lhowell/bcp1662/articles/articles.html.

Athanasius. *On the Incarnation.* Translated by John Behr. Yonkers, NY: St. Vladimir's Seminary Press, 2011.

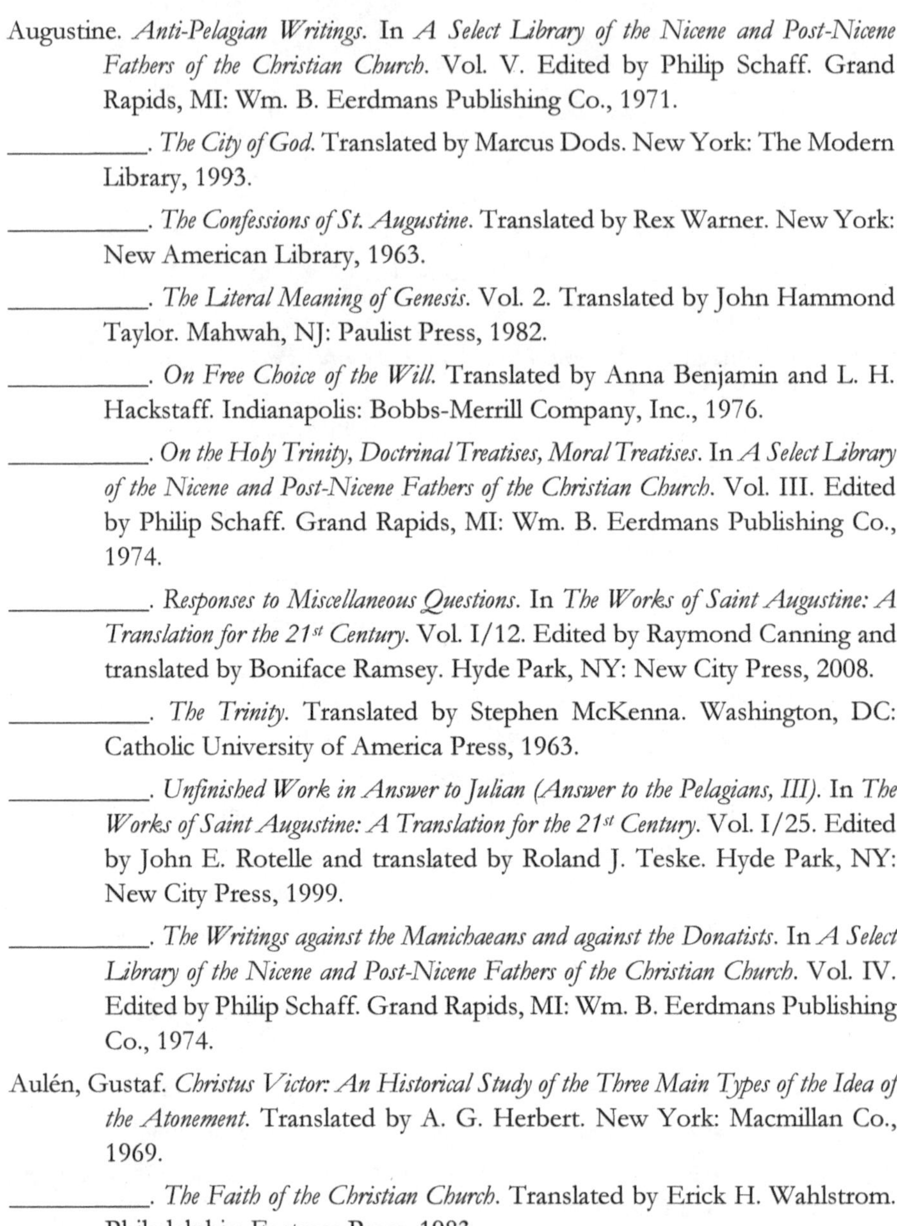

Augustine. *Anti-Pelagian Writings*. In *A Select Library of the Nicene and Post-Nicene Fathers of the Christian Church*. Vol. V. Edited by Philip Schaff. Grand Rapids, MI: Wm. B. Eerdmans Publishing Co., 1971.

__________. *The City of God*. Translated by Marcus Dods. New York: The Modern Library, 1993.

__________. *The Confessions of St. Augustine*. Translated by Rex Warner. New York: New American Library, 1963.

__________. *The Literal Meaning of Genesis*. Vol. 2. Translated by John Hammond Taylor. Mahwah, NJ: Paulist Press, 1982.

__________. *On Free Choice of the Will*. Translated by Anna Benjamin and L. H. Hackstaff. Indianapolis: Bobbs-Merrill Company, Inc., 1976.

__________. *On the Holy Trinity, Doctrinal Treatises, Moral Treatises*. In *A Select Library of the Nicene and Post-Nicene Fathers of the Christian Church*. Vol. III. Edited by Philip Schaff. Grand Rapids, MI: Wm. B. Eerdmans Publishing Co., 1974.

__________. *Responses to Miscellaneous Questions*. In *The Works of Saint Augustine: A Translation for the 21st Century*. Vol. I/12. Edited by Raymond Canning and translated by Boniface Ramsey. Hyde Park, NY: New City Press, 2008.

__________. *The Trinity*. Translated by Stephen McKenna. Washington, DC: Catholic University of America Press, 1963.

__________. *Unfinished Work in Answer to Julian (Answer to the Pelagians, III)*. In *The Works of Saint Augustine: A Translation for the 21st Century*. Vol. I/25. Edited by John E. Rotelle and translated by Roland J. Teske. Hyde Park, NY: New City Press, 1999.

__________. *The Writings against the Manichaeans and against the Donatists*. In *A Select Library of the Nicene and Post-Nicene Fathers of the Christian Church*. Vol. IV. Edited by Philip Schaff. Grand Rapids, MI: Wm. B. Eerdmans Publishing Co., 1974.

Aulén, Gustaf. *Christus Victor: An Historical Study of the Three Main Types of the Idea of the Atonement*. Translated by A. G. Herbert. New York: Macmillan Co., 1969.

__________. *The Faith of the Christian Church*. Translated by Erick H. Wahlstrom. Philadelphia: Fortress Press, 1983.

Ayer, Joseph Cullen, Jr. *A Source Book for Ancient Church History*. New York: AMS Press, 1970.

Barth, Karl. *Anselm: Fides Quaerens Intellectum: Anselm's Proof of the Existence of God in the Context of His Theological Scheme*. Translated by I. W. Robertson. London: SCM Press, 1960.

__________. *Christ and Adam: Man and Humanity in Romans 5*. Translated by T. A. Smail. New York: Collier Book, 1962.

__________. "The Church between East and West." In his *Against the Stream: Shorter Post-War Writings 1946-52*, pp. 125-46. Edited by Ronald Gregor Smith. New York: Philosophical Library, 1954.

__________. *Church Dogmatics*, 13 vols. Translated by Geoffrey W. Bromiley et al. London: T&T Clark, 1936-1969.

__________. *The Epistle to the Romans*. 6th ed. Translated by Edwyn C. Hoskyns. London: Oxford University Press, 1968.

__________. *Evangelical Theology: An Introduction*. Grand Rapids, MI: Wm. B. Eerdmans Publishing Co., 1979.

__________. *Fragments Grave and Gray*. Edited by Martin Rumscheidt and translated by Eric Mosbacher. London: HarperCollins, 1971.

__________. *The Humanity of God*. Translated by John Newton Thomas and Thomas Wieser. Atlanta, GA: John Knox Press, 1960.

__________. *Protestant Thought: From Rousseau to Ritschl*. Translated by Brian Cozens. New York: Simon and Schuster, 1959.

__________. *The Theology of Schleiermacher: Lectures at Göttingen, Winter Semester of 1923/24*. Edited by Dietrich Ritschl and translated by Geoffrey W. Bromiley. Grand Rapids, MI: Wm. B. Eerdmans Publishing Co., 1982.

Bartlett, Anthony W. *Cross Purposes: The Violent Grammar of Christian Atonement*. Harrisburg, PA: Trinity Press International, 2001.

Basil of Caesarea. "Letter 214." https://www.newadvent.org/fathers/3202214.htm.

Bayer, Oswald. *Martin Luther's Theology: A Contemporary Interpretation*. Translated by Thomas H. Trapp. Grand Rapids, MI: William B. Eerdmans Publishing Co., 2008.

Bebis, Vassilios. "The Unification Doctrine of the Fall and the Writings of Irenaeus of Lyon." *Journal of Unification Studies* 24 (2023):105-9.

Beegle, Dewey M. *Scripture, Tradition, and Infallibility*. Ann Arbor, MI: Pryor Pettengill, Publisher, 1979.

Berdyaev, Nikolai. *The Destiny of Man*. Translated by Natalie Duddington. London: The Century Press, 1937.

__________. *Freedom and the Spirit*. Translated by Oliver Fielding Clarke. New York: Charles Scribner's Sons, 1935.

__________. *The Meaning of History*. Translated by George Reavey. New York: Charles Scribner's Sons, 1936. p. 48.

__________. *The Meaning of the Creative Act*. Translated by Donald A. Lowrie. London: V. Gollancz, 1955.

__________. *Slavery and Freedom.* Translated by R. M. French. New York: Charles Scribner's Sons, 1944.

__________. "Studies Concerning Jacob Boehme: Etude I. The Teaching about the Ungrund and Freedom." Originally published in German in *Journal Put'* 20 (1930): 47-79. Translated by S. Janos. http://www.berdyaev.com/berdiaev/berd_lib/1930_349.html.

__________. "Studies Concerning Jacob Boehme: Etude II. The Teaching about Sophia and the Androgyne: J. Boehme and the Russian Sophiological Current." Originally published in German in *Journal Put'* 21 (1930): 34-62. Translated by S. Janos. http://www.berdyaev.com/berdiaev/berd_lib/1930_351.html.

Berkhof, Hendrikus. *Christian Faith: An Introduction to the Study of the Faith.* Rev. ed. Translated by Sierd Woudstra. Grand Rapids, MI: Wm. B. Eerdmans Publishing Co., 1986.

Berkouwer, G. C. *Holy Scripture.* Translated by Jack B. Rogers. Grand Rapids, MI: William B. Eerdmans Publishing Co., 1975.

Berlin, Isaiah. *The Roots of Romanticism.* Edited by Henry Hardy. Princeton, NJ: Princeton University Press, 1999.

Bettenson, Henry, ed. *Documents of the Christian Church.* 2nd ed. London: Oxford University Press, 1963.

Bloesch, Donald G. *Essentials of Evangelical Theology.* Vol. 1: *God, Authority, and Salvation.* San Francisco: Harper & Row, Publishers, 1978.

__________. *Holy Scripture: Revelation, Inspiration and Interpretation.* Downers Grove, IL: InterVarsity Press, 1994.

Boff, Leonardo. *Trinity and Society.* Translated by Paul Burns. Eugene, OR: Wipf & Stock Publishers, 1988.

Böhme, Jakob. "*Mysterium Pansophicum*, or A Fundamental Statement Concerning Earthly and Heavenly Mystery." http://www.mystic.tlchrist.info/mysterium.html.

Bonhoeffer, Dietrich. *Letters and Papers from Prison.* Enl. ed. Edited by Eberhard Bethge. New York: Macmillan Co., 1971.

Borg, Marcus. *Jesus: A New Vision.* San Francisco: Harper & Row, Publishers, 1987.

Braaten, Carl E. "The Kingdom of God and Life Everlasting." In *Christian Theology: An Introduction to Its Traditions and Tasks*, pp. 328-52. Rev. and enl. ed. Edited by Peter C. Hodgson and Robert H. King. Philadelphia: Fortress Press, 1985.

__________, and Jenson, Robert W., eds. *The Last Things: Biblical and Theological Perspectives on Eschatology*. Grand Rapids, MI: Wm. B. Eerdmans Publishing Co., 2002.

Bracken, Joseph A. *The Triune Symbol: Persons, Process, and Community*. New York: University Press of America, 1985.

Breen, Michael. *Sun Myung Moon: The Early Years 1920-53*. Hurstpierpoint, U.K.: Refuge Books, 1997.

Brierley, Michael W. "Introducing the Early British Passibilists." *Journal for the History of Modern Theology* 8 (2001): 218-33.

__________. "Naming a Quiet Revolution: The Panentheistic Turn in Modern Theology." *In Whom We Live and Move and Have Our Being: Panentheistic Reflections on God's Presence in a Scientific World*, pp. 1-15. Edited by Philip Clayton and Arthur Peacocke. Grand Rapids, MI: Wm. B. Eerdmans Publishing Co., 2004.

Brightman, Edgar Sheffield. *A Philosophy of Religion*. New York: Prentice-Hall, 1940.

Brown, Dan. *The Da Vinci Code*. New York: Doubleday, 2003.

Brown, Joanne Carlson, and Parker, Rebecca. "For God So Loved the World?" In *Christianity, Patriarchy and Abuse: A Feminist Critique*, pp. 1-30. Edited by Joanne Carlson Brown and Carole R. Bohn. New York: Pilgrim Press, 1989.

Bryant, Darrol, ed. *Proceedings of the Virgin Islands' Seminar on Unification Theology*. New York: Rose of Sharon Press, 1980.

__________, and Foster, Durwood, eds. *Hermeneutics and Unification Theology*. New York: Rose of Sharon Press, 1980.

__________, and Hodges, Susan, eds. *Exploring Unification Theology*. New York: Rose of Sharon Press, 1978.

__________, and Richardson, Herbert W., eds. *A Time for Consideration: A Scholarly Appraisal of the Unification Church*. New York: Edwin Mellen Press, 1978.

Bryce, James. "The Coronation as a Revival of the Roman Empire in the West." In *The Coronation of Charlemagne: What Did It Signify?*, pp. 41-49. Edited by Richard E. Sullivan. Boston: D. C. Heath and Co., 1959.

Burton, Douglas, and Kim, Lymha. "Hak Ja Han: Address God as 'Heavenly Parent'." http://www.tparents.org/Moon-Talks/HakJaHanMoon-13/HakJaHan-130108.pdf.

Calvin, John. *Commentaries on the Epistle of Paul the Apostle to the Hebrews*. Translated by John Owen. Grand Rapids, MI: Wm. B. Eerdmans Publishing Co., 1948.

__________. *Institutes of the Christian Religion*. Rev. ed. Translated by Henry Beveridge. Peabody, MA: Hendrickson Publishers, 2008.

Cameron, David W., and Groves, Colin P. *Bones, Stones and Molecules: "Out of Africa" and Human Origins*. Burlington, MA: Elsevier Academic Press, 2004.

Caputo, John D. *Deconstruction in a Nutshell: A Conversation with Jacques Derrida*. New York: Fordham University Press, 1997.

Case-Winters, Anna. *God's Power: Traditional Understandings and Contemporary Challenges*. Louisville, KY: Westminster/John Knox Press, 1990.

"Catechism of the Catholic Church." https://www.vatican.va/archive/ENG0015/_INDEX.HTM.

Centrella, Thomas J. "Is Theistic Evolution Truly Plausible?" http://kolbecenter.org/is-theistic-evolution-truly-plausible/.

Chalke, Steve, and Mann, Alan. *The Lost Message of Jesus*. Grand Rapids, MI: Zondervan, 2003.

Christian History Institute. "Christian History Sampler: Martin Luther on Marriage." https://christianhistoryinstitute.org/magazine/article/christian-history-sampler-martin-luther-on-marriage.

Chung, Su Wong. "Seung Do Kim, the Holy Lord Church and My Life as a 36 Couple." https://www.tparents.org/Library/Unification/Talks1/Chung/Chung-860400.htm.

Clark, Gordon H. *Religion, Reason and Revelation*. Nutley, NJ: Craig Press, 1961.

Cobb, John B., Jr., and Griffin, David Ray. *Process Theology: An Introductory Exposition*. Philadelphia: Westminster Press, 1976.

Collins, Francis S. *The Language of God: A Scientist Presents Evidence for Belief*. New York: Free Press, 2006.

Cone, James H. *A Black Theology of Liberation*. 2nd ed. Maryknoll, NY: Orbis Books, 1986.

Conn, Harvie M. *Contemporary World Theology: A Layman's Guidebook*. Phillipsburg, NJ: Presbyterian and Reformed Publishing Co., 1973.

Conradie, Ernst M. "John Haught on Original Sin: A Conversation." *HTS Theological Studies* 72, no. 4 (2016): 1-10.

Copleston, Frederick. *A History of Philosophy*. Vol. I, pt. I. Garden City, NY: Image Books, 1962.

Coppens, J. *La connaissance du bien et du mal et le péché du Paradis*. Gembloux: J. Duculot, 1948.

Couenhoven, Jesse. "St. Augustine's Doctrine of Original Sin." *Augustinian Studies* 36:2 (2005): 359-96.

"The Council of Trent, the Fifth Session: Decree Concerning Original Sin." https://history.hanover.edu/texts/trent/ct05.html.

Cox, Harvey. *The Secular City: Urbanization and Secularization in Theological Perspective*. New York: Macmillan Co., 1965.

Daly, Mary. *Beyond God the Father: Toward a Philosophy of Women's Liberation*. Boston: Beacon Press, 1985.

__________. *The Church and the Second Sex*. New York: Harper & Row, Publishers, 1975.

Davies, W. D. *Paul and Rabbinic Judaism: Some Rabbinic Elements in Pauline Theology*. London: SPCK, 1970.

Davis, Stephen T. *The Debate about the Bible: Inerrancy versus Infallibility*. Philadelphia: Westminster Press, 1977.

Davis, Ted. "Evolution and Original Sin: The Historical/Ideal View." https://biologos.org/articles/evolution-and-original-sin-the-historical-ideal-view.

__________. "Theistic Evolution: History and Beliefs." https://biologos.org/articles/theistic-evolution-history-and-beliefs.

Day, John. "The Serpent in the Garden of Eden and its Background." https://bibleinterp.arizona.edu/articles/2015/04/day398028.

De Spinoza, Benedict. *The Ethics*. Translated by R. H. M. Elwes. London: George Bell & Sons, 1891.

Dillenberger, John, and Welch, Claude. *Protestant Christianity: Interpreted through Its Development*. New York: Charles Scribner's Sons, 1954.

Divine Principle. New York: HSA-UWC, 1973.

Dostoevsky, Fyodor. *The Brothers Karamazov*. http://www.planetpublish.com/wp-content/uploads/2011/11/The_ Brothers_Karamazov_NT.pdf.

Duffy, Stephen J. "Genes, Original Sin and the Human Proclivity to Evil." *Horizons* 32, no. 2 (2005): 210-34.

__________. "Our Hearts of Darkness: Original Sin Revisited." *Theological Studies* 49 (1988): 597-622.

Eddy, Mary Baker. *Science and Health with Key to the Scriptures*. Authorized ed. Boston, MA: Christian Science Board of Directors, 2011.

Ehrman, Bart D. "The Apocalyptic Context for Jesus' View of the Messiah." https://ehrmanblog.org/the-apocalyptic-context-for-jesus-view-of-the-messiah/.

Enns, Paul. *The Moody Handbook of Theology*. Chicago, IL: Moody Press, 1989.

Enns, Peter. *The Evolution of Adam: What the Bible Does and Doesn't Say about Human Origins*. Grand Rapids, MI: Brozos Press, 2012.

__________. *Inspiration and Incarnation: Evangelicals and the Problem of the Old Testament*. Grand Rapids, MI: Baker Academic, 2005.

Epperly, Bruce G. *Process Theology: A Guide for the Perplexed.* New York: T&T Clark International, 2011.

Erickson, Millard J. *Christian Theology.* 3 vols. Grand Rapids, MI: Baker Book House, 1983-1985.

__________. *Introducing Christian Doctrine.* 3rd ed. Edited by L. Arnold Hustad. Grand Rapids, MI: Baker Academic, 2015.

Exposition of the Divine Principle. New York: H.S.A.-U.W.C., 1996.

Faculty of Concordia Seminary. *Faithful to Our Calling, Faithful to Our Lord.* Part 1: *A Witness to Our Faith: A Joint Statement and Discussion of Issues.* St. Louis, MO: Faculty of Concordia Seminary, 1973.

Ferré, Nels F. S. "Know Your Faith." https://www.religion-online.org/book-chapter/chapter-2-the-son-of-his-love/.

Feuerbach, Ludwig. *The Essence of Christianity.* Translated by George Eliot. New York: Harper Torchbooks, 1957.

Fiddes, Paul S. *The Creative Suffering of God.* New York: Oxford University Press, 1988.

Flew, Antony. "Divine Omnipotence and Human Freedom." In *New Essays in Philosophical Theology*, pp. 144-69. Edited by Anthony Flew and Alasdair MacIntyre. New York: Macmillan Co., 1955.

Ford, Lewis S. *The Lure of God: A Biblical Background for Process Theism.* Philadelphia: Fortress Press, 1978.

Fretheim, Terence E. *The Suffering of God: An Old Testament Perspective.* Philadelphia: Fortress Press, 1984.

Fuller, Daniel. "The Nature of Biblical Inerrancy." *Journal of the American Scientific Affiliation* 24 (June 1972): 47-51.

Gadamer, Hans-Georg. *Truth and Method.* 2nd rev. ed. Translated by Joel Weinsheimer and Donald G. Marshall. New York: Crossroad Publishing Corporation, 1991.

Gaffin, Richard B., Jr. "Redemption and Resurrection." http://l1nk.org/part-i-background-biblical-theology.

Gilkey, Langdon. "Tillich: The Master of Mediation." In *The Theology of Paul Tillich*, pp. 26-58. Edited by Charles W. Kegley. New York: The Pilgrim Press, 1982.

Girard, René. *I See Satan Fall Like Lightning.* Translated by James W. Williams. Maryknoll, NY: Orbis Books, 2001.

__________. *Things Hidden Since the Foundation of the World.* Translated by Stephen Bann and Michael Metteer. Stanford, CA: Stanford University Press, 1987.

Goetz, Ronald. "The Suffering God: The Rise of a New Orthodoxy." *The Christian Century* 103 (1986): 385-89.

Gordis, Robert. *The Word and the Book: Studies in Biblical Language and Literature*. New York: Ktav Publishing House, 1976.

Gragg, Larry. "A Mere Civil Friendship: Benjamin Franklin and George Whitefield." *History Today* 28 (1978): 574-79.

Gratsch, Edward J. *Principles of Catholic Theology: A Synthesis of Dogma and Morals*. New York: Alba House, 1981.

Grenz, Stanley J. *Revisioning Evangelical Theology: A Fresh Agenda for the 21st Century*. Downers Grove, IL: InterVarsity Press, 1993.

__________, and Olson, Roger E. *20th-Century Theology: God and the World in a Transitional Age*. Downers Grove, IL: InterVarsity Press, 1992.

Griffin, David R. *God, Power, and Evil: A Process Theodicy*. Philadelphia: Westminster Press, 1976.

__________. *A Process Christology*. Philadelphia: Westminster Press, 1973.

Guardini, Romano. *The Lord*. Translated by Elinor Castendyk Briefs. Washington, DC: Gateway Editions, 1982.

Guerra, Anthony J., ed. *Unification Theology in Comparative Perspectives*. Barrytown, NY: Unification Theological Seminary, 1988.

Gunton, Colin E. *The Promise of Trinitarian Theology*. Edinburgh: T&T Clark, 1991.

Haag, Herbert; Soelle, Dorothee; Elliger, Katharina; Grohmann, Marianne; Schüngel-Straumann, Helen; and Wetzel, Christoph. *Great Couples of the Bible*. Translated by Brian McNeil. Minneapolis, MN: Fortress Press, 2006.

Hamerton-Kelly, Robert G. *Sacred Violence: Paul's Hermeneutic of the Cross*. Minneapolis, MN: Fortress Press, 1992.

Harrison, Everett F. "The Phenomena of Scripture." In *Revelation and the Bible: Contemporary Evangelical Thought*, pp. 237-50. Edited by Carl F. H. Henry. Grand Rapids, MI: Baker Book House, 1958.

Hartshorne, Charles. *Omnipotence and Other Theological Mistakes*. Albany, NY: State University of New York Press, 1984.

Haught, John F. *God after Darwin: A Theology of Evolution*. 2nd ed. Boulder, CO: Westview Press, 2000.

Hegel, Georg W. F. *Lectures on the Philosophy of History*. Translated by J. Sibree. London: G. Bell and Sons, 1902.

__________. *Lectures on the Philosophy of Religion*. Vol. 3. Edited by E. B. Speirs and J. Burdon Sanderson. New York: Humanities Press, 1974.

Heschel, Abraham J. *The Prophets*. New York: Harper & Row, Publishers, 1962.

Hick, John. *Evil and the God of Love.* Rev. ed. San Francisco: Harper & Row, Publishers, 1978.

__________, ed. *The Myth of God Incarnate.* Philadelphia: Westminster Press, 1977.

Hill, William J. *The Three-Personed God.* Washington, DC: Catholic University of America Press, 1982.

Houdmann, S. Michael, ed. *Questions about God: The 100 Most Frequently Asked Questions about God.* Bloomington, IN: WestBow Press, 2014.

Hubbard, David. "The Irrelevancy of Inerrancy." In *Biblical Authority*, pp. 151-81. Edited by Jack Rogers. Waco, TX: Word Books, 1977.

Hulsbosch, Ansfried. *God in Creation and Evolution.* Translated by Martin Versfeld. New York: Sheed and Ward, 1965.

Hutchison, John A. *Faith, Reason, and Existence: An Introduction to Contemporary Philosophy of Religion.* New York: Oxford University Press, 1956.

Irenaeus. "Against Heresies." In *The Ante-Nicene Fathers: The Writing of the Fathers Down to A.D. 325.* American ed. Vol. I: *The Apostolic Fathers with Justin Martyr and Irenaeus*, pp. 309-568. Edited by Alexander Roberts, James Donaldson, and A. Cleveland Coxe. Grand Rapids, MI: Wm. B. Eerdmans Publishing Co., 1981.

Jerome, "Letter to Pammachius against John of Jerusalem." http://www.catholic-forum.com/saints/stj06001.htm.

Jin, Sung Bae, ed. *가정연합시대 주요 의식과 선포식* III [Important Ceremonies and Proclamations in the Age of the Family Federation III]. Seoul, Korea: Sung Hwa Publishing Co., 1991.

Joad, C. E. M. *God and Evil.* London: Farber & Farber, 1943.

Jones, David Albert. *The Soul of the Embryo: An Enquiry into the Status of the Human Embryo in the Christian Tradition.* London: Continuum, 2004.

Kan, Enkichi. "Keiji to Risei [Revelation and Reason]." In *Kyokai Kyogigaku Koza* [Course on Church Dogmatics]. Vol. 2, pp. 6-12. Edited by Toshio Sato and Toshikazu Takao. Tokyo: Nihon Kirisuto Kyodan Publications, 1972.

Kant, Immanuel. *Critique of Pure Reason.* Translated by Norman Kemp Smith. New York: St. Martin's Press, 1965.

__________. *Religion within the Limits of Reason Alone.* Translated by Theodore M. Greene and Hoyt H. Hudson. New York: Harper & Row, Polishers, 1960.

Kärkkäinen, Veli-Matti. *The Doctrine of God: A Global Introduction.* Grand Rapids, MI: Baker Academic, 2004.

Kasper, Walter. *Jesus the Christ.* Translated by V. Green. New York: Paulist Press, 1977.

Kelly, J. N. D. *Early Christian Doctrines*. Rev. ed. New York: Harper & Row, Publishers, 1978.

Kemp, Kenneth W. "Science, Theology, and Monogenesis." *American Catholic Philosophical Quarterly*, vol. 85, no. 2 (2011): 217-36.

Kennedy, Daniel. "St. Thomas Aquinas." https://www.newadvent.org/cathen/14663b.htm.

Kierkegaard, Søren. *Concluding Unscientific Postscript*. Translated by David F. Swenson and Walter Lowrie. Princeton: Princeton University Press, 1968.

__________. *The Sickness unto Death: A Christian Psychological Exposition for Upbuilding and Awakening*. Edited and translated by Howard V. Hong and Edna H. Hong. Princeton: Princeton University Press, 1983.

Kim, Young Oon. *Divine Principle and Its Application*. 7th ed. Washington, DC: The Holy Spirit Association for the Unification of World Christianity, 1969.

__________. *Unification Theology*. New York: The Holy Spirit Association for the Unification of World Christianity, 1980. Rev. ed., 1987.

__________. *Unification Theology and Christian Thought*. New York: Golden Gate Publishing, 1975. Rev. ed., 1976.

Koester, Helmut, and Patterson, Stephen J. "The Gospel of Thomas: Does It Contain Authentic Sayings of Jesus?" *Bible View* 6, no. 2 (April 1990): 28-39.

Korsmeyer, Jerry D. *Evolution and Eden: Balancing Original Sin and Contemporary Science*. New York: Paulist Press, 1998.

Kreeft, Peter, and Tacelli, Ronald K. *Handbook of Christian Apologetics*. Downers Grove, IL: InterVarsity Press, 1994.

Küng, Hans. *Theology for the Third Millennium: An Ecumenical View*. Translated by Peter Heinegg. New York: Doubleday, 1988.

LaCugna, Catherine Mowry. *God for Us: The Trinity and Christian Life*. New York: Harper Collins Publishers, 1991.

Ladd, George Eldon. *The New Testament and Criticism*. Grand Rapids, MI: Wm. B. Eerdmans Publishing Co., 1967.

Lamoureux, Denis O. *Evolutionary Creation: A Christian Approach to Evolution*. Eugene, OR: Wipf & Stock, 2008.

Lampe, G. W. H. "Christian Theology in the Patristic Period." In *A History of Christian Doctrine*, pp. 21-180. Edited by Hubert Cunliffe-Jones. Philadelphia: Fortress Press, 1981.

Lane, William L. *The Gospel of Mark*. Grand Rapids, MI: Wm. B. Eerdmans Publishing Co., 1974.

Leibniz, G. W. *Theodicy: Essays on the Goodness of God, the Freedom of Man and the Origin of Evil.* Translated by E. M. Huggard. London: Routledge & Kegan Paul, 1952.

Lenin, Vladimir. "The Criticism of Kantianism from the Left and from the Right." Chap. 4, sec. 1 of his *Materialism and Empirio-criticism.* https://www.marxists.org/archive/lenin/works/1908/mec/four1.htm.

Lewis, C. S. *God in the Dock: Essays on Theology and Ethics*. Grand Rapids, MI: Wm. B. Eerdmans Publishing Co., 1971.

Livingston, James C. *Modern Christian Thought.* Vol. 1: *The Enlightenment and the Nineteenth Century.* 2nd ed. Upper Saddle River, NJ: Prentice Hall, 1988.

Lorenzen, Lynne Faber. *The College Student's Introduction to the Trinity.* Collegeville, MN: Liturgical Press, 1999.

Luther, Martin. *Heidelberg Disputation.* https://bookofconcord.org/sources-and-context/heidelberg-disputation/.

__________. *Luther: Early Theological Works.* Translated and edited by James Atkinson. Philadelphia: Westminster Press, 1962.

__________. *Luther's Works.* Vol. 25: *Lectures on Romans.* Edited by Hilton C. Oswald. St. Louis, MO: Concordia Publishing House, 1972.

__________. *Luther's Works.* Vol. 29: *Lectures on Titus, Philemon & Hebrews.* Edited by Jaroslav Pelikan. St. Louis, MO: Concordia Publishing House, 1968.

__________. *Luther's Works.* Vol. 32: *Career of the Reformer II.* Edited by George W. Forell. Philadelphia: Muhlenberg Press, 1958.

__________. *Luther's Works.* Vol. 37: *Word and Sacrament III.* Edited by Robert H. Fischer. Philadelphia: Muhlenberg Press, 1961.

__________. *Martin Luther: Selections from His Writings.* Edited by John Dillenberger. Garden City, NY: Doubleday & Company, 1961.

__________. *Martin Luthers Werke: Kritische Gesamtausgabe.* Weimar: Herman Boehlaus Nachfolger, 1914.

MacGregor, Geddes. *He Who Lets Us Be: A New Theology of Love.* New York: Seabury Press, 1975.

__________. *Reincarnation in Christianity: A New Vision of the Role of Rebirth in Christian Thought.* Wheaton, IL: Theosophical Publishing House, 1978.

Mackie, J. L. "Evil and Omnipotence." *Mind* 64, no. 254 (April 1955): 200-12.

Macquarrie, John. *Principles of Christian Theology.* 2nd ed. New York: Charles Scribner's Sons, 1977.

Mahoney, Jack. *Christianity in Evolution: An Exploration.* Washington, DC: Georgetown University Press, 2011.

Marx, Karl. *Critique of Hegel's 'Philosophy of Right.'* Edited and translated by Joseph O'Malley. Cambridge: Cambridge University Press, 1977.

Marxsen, Willi. "The Resurrection of Jesus as a Historical and Theological Problem." In *The Significance of the Message of the Resurrection for Faith in Jesus Christ*, pp. 15-50. Edited by C. F. D. Moule and translated by Dorothea M. Barton and R. A. Wilson. London: SCM Press, 1968.

Matczak, Sebastian A. *Unificationism: A New Philosophy and Worldview*. Jamaica, NY: Learned Publications, 1982.

Mayor, F. E. *The Religious Bodies of America*. St. Louis, MO: Concordia Publishing House, 1961.

McConnachie, J. "The Teaching of Karl Barth." *Hibbert Journal* 25 (1926–1927): 385-400.

McDonald, H. D. *The Atonement of the Death of Christ: In Faith, Revelation, and History*. Grand Rapids, MI: Baker Book House, 1985.

McDougall, Ian; Brown, Francis H.; and Fleagle, John G. "Stratigraphic Placement and Age of Modern Humans from Kibish, Ethiopia." *Nature* 433 (2005): 733-36.

McGiffert, Arthur Cushman. *Protestant Thought before Kant*. London: Duckworth & Co., 1911.

McIntyre, John. *The Shape of Soteriology: Studies in the Doctrine of the Death of Christ*. Edinburgh: T&T Clark, 1992.

McWilliams, Warren. *The Passion of God: Divine Suffering in Contemporary Protestant Theology*. Macon, GA: Mercer University Press, 1985.

Mettepenningen, Jürgen. *Nouvelle Théologie – New Theology: Inheritor of Modernism, Precursor of Vatican II*. New York: T&T Clark International, 2010.

Meyendorff, John. *Byzantine Theology: Historical Trends and Doctrinal Themes*. New York: Fordham University Press, 1974.

Miller, Ed. L. *God and Reason: A Historical Approach to Philosophical Theology*. New York: Macmillan Publishing Co., 1972.

Moltmann, Jürgen. *The Coming of God: Christian Eschatology*. Translated by Margaret Kohl. Minneapolis, MN: Fortress Press, 1996.

__________. *The Crucified God: The Cross of Christ as the Foundation and Criticism of Christian Theology*. Translated by R. A. Wilson and John Bowden. New York: Harper & Row, Publishers, 1974.

__________. "God's Kenosis in the Creation and Consummation of the World." In *The Work of Love: Creation as Kenosis*, pp. 137-51. Edited by John Polkinghorne. Grand Rapids, MI: Wm. B. Eerdmans Publishing Co., 2001.

__________. "Justice for Victims and Perpetrators." *Reformed World* 44 (March 1994): 2-12.

__________. *The Spirit of Life: A Universal Affirmation*. Translated by Margaret Kohl. Minneapolis, MN: Fortress Press, 1993.

__________. *Theology of Hope: On the Ground and the Implications of a Christian Eschatology*. Translated by James W. Leitch. New York: Harper & Row, Publishers, 1975.

__________. *The Trinity and the Kingdom: The Doctrine of God*. Translated by Margaret Kohl. Minneapolis, MN: Fortress Press, 1993.

__________. *The Way of Jesus Christ: Christology in Messianic Dimensions*. Translated by Margaret Kohl. Minneapolis, MN: Fortress Press, 1993.

Montgomery, John Warwick. *Crisis in Lutheran Theology: The Validity and Relevance of Historic Lutheranism vs. Its Contemporary Rivals*. Vol. I. Grand Rapids, MI: Baker Book House, 1967.

__________. *In Defense of Martin Luther*. Milwaukee, WI: Northwestern Publishing House, 1970.

Moon, Hak Ja Han. "Blessed Marriage and Eternal Life." Address given on a 16-day North America speaking tour April 1-16, 1996. http://www.tparents.org/Moon-Books/tfwp/tfwp-3-2.htm.

__________. *Mother of Peace: A Memoir by Hak Ja Han Moon*. Washington, DC: Washington Times Global Media Group, 2020.

__________. *True Mother Hak Ja Han Moon: An Anthology*. Seoul, Korea: Sung Hwa Publishing, Inc., 2018.

__________, and Moon, Sun Myung. *The Holy Scripture of Cheon Il Guk: Cheon Seong Gyeong*. Seoul, Korea: Seonghwa Publications, 2014.

Moon, Sun Myung. *As a Peace-Loving Global Citizen*. Washington, DC: Washington Times Foundation, 2010.

__________. *Blessing and Ideal Family*. Part 2. Washington, DC: Family Federation for World Peace and Unification, 1998.

__________. *Bun Senmei Sensei no Mikotoba ni Manabu Touitsu Genri* [Learning the Divine Principle from the Words of Rev. Sun Myung Moon]. Part 1. Tokyo: Kogensha, 2012.

__________. *Cheon Seong Gyeong: Selections from the Speeches of True Parents*. Seoul, Korea: Sunghwa Publishing Co., 2006.

__________. *Christianity in Crisis: New Hope*. Washington, DC: HSA-UWC, 1974.

__________. "God's Day 1984." Sermon delivered at World Mission Center, New York, NY, January 1, 1984. http://www.unification.net/1984/840101a.html.

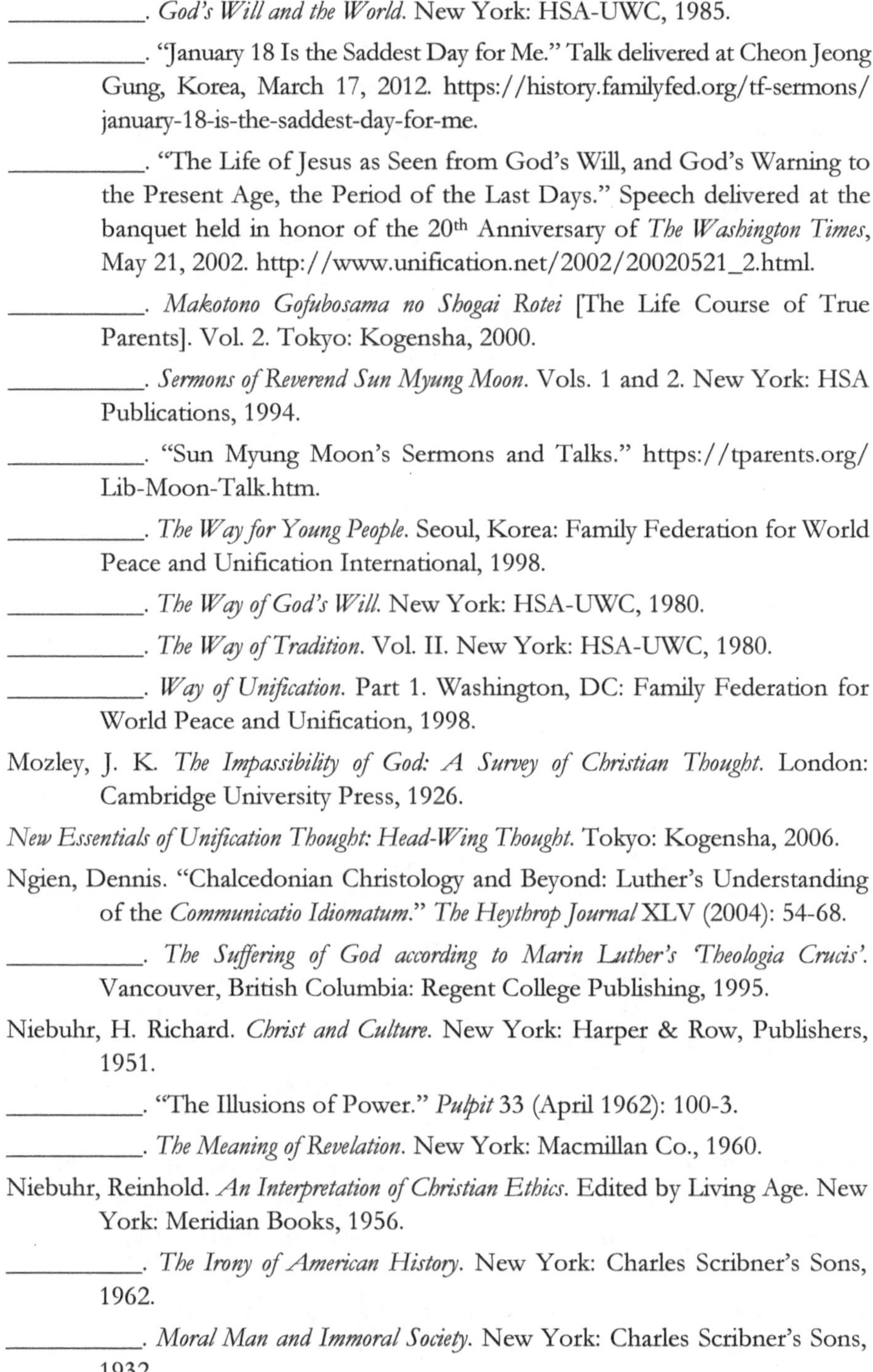

__________. *God's Will and the World.* New York: HSA-UWC, 1985.

__________. "January 18 Is the Saddest Day for Me." Talk delivered at Cheon Jeong Gung, Korea, March 17, 2012. https://history.familyfed.org/tf-sermons/january-18-is-the-saddest-day-for-me.

__________. "The Life of Jesus as Seen from God's Will, and God's Warning to the Present Age, the Period of the Last Days." Speech delivered at the banquet held in honor of the 20th Anniversary of *The Washington Times*, May 21, 2002. http://www.unification.net/2002/20020521_2.html.

__________. *Makotono Gofubosama no Shogai Rotei* [The Life Course of True Parents]. Vol. 2. Tokyo: Kogensha, 2000.

__________. *Sermons of Reverend Sun Myung Moon.* Vols. 1 and 2. New York: HSA Publications, 1994.

__________. "Sun Myung Moon's Sermons and Talks." https://tparents.org/Lib-Moon-Talk.htm.

__________. *The Way for Young People.* Seoul, Korea: Family Federation for World Peace and Unification International, 1998.

__________. *The Way of God's Will.* New York: HSA-UWC, 1980.

__________. *The Way of Tradition.* Vol. II. New York: HSA-UWC, 1980.

__________. *Way of Unification.* Part 1. Washington, DC: Family Federation for World Peace and Unification, 1998.

Mozley, J. K. *The Impassibility of God: A Survey of Christian Thought.* London: Cambridge University Press, 1926.

New Essentials of Unification Thought: Head-Wing Thought. Tokyo: Kogensha, 2006.

Ngien, Dennis. "Chalcedonian Christology and Beyond: Luther's Understanding of the *Communicatio Idiomatum.*" *The Heythrop Journal* XLV (2004): 54-68.

__________. *The Suffering of God according to Marin Luther's 'Theologia Crucis'.* Vancouver, British Columbia: Regent College Publishing, 1995.

Niebuhr, H. Richard. *Christ and Culture.* New York: Harper & Row, Publishers, 1951.

__________. "The Illusions of Power." *Pulpit* 33 (April 1962): 100-3.

__________. *The Meaning of Revelation.* New York: Macmillan Co., 1960.

Niebuhr, Reinhold. *An Interpretation of Christian Ethics.* Edited by Living Age. New York: Meridian Books, 1956.

__________. *The Irony of American History.* New York: Charles Scribner's Sons, 1962.

__________. *Moral Man and Immoral Society.* New York: Charles Scribner's Sons, 1932.

__________. *The Nature and Destiny of Man: A Christian Interpretation.* 2 vols. New York: Charles Scribner's Sons, 1964.

Novatian. *On the Trinity.* https://www.newadvent.org/fathers/0511.htm.

Nygren, Anders. *Agape and Eros.* Translated by Philip S. Watson. London: SPCK, 1953.

Olson, Roger E. "What Is 'Liberal Theology'?" http://www.patheos.com/blogs/rogereolson/2013/10/what-is-liberal-theology/.

Oord, Thomas Jay. *The Nature of Love: A Theology.* St. Louis, MO: Chalice Press, 2010.

Origen. *Contra Celsum.* Translated by Henry Chadwick. Cambridge: Cambridge University Press, 1980.

__________. "De Pricipiis." In *The Ante-Nicene Fathers: The Writings of the Fathers Down to A.D. 325.* American ed. Vol. IV: *Fathers of the Third Century*, pp. 239-384. Edited by Alexander Roberts, James Donaldson, and A. Cleveland Coxe. Grand Rapids, MI: Wm. B. Eerdmans Publishing Co., 1951.

__________. *First Principles.* Translated by G. W. Butterworth. London: S.P.C.K., 1936.

Ott, Ludwig. *Fundamentals of Catholic Dogma.* Edited by James Canon Bastible and translated by Patrick Lynch. Rockford, IL: Tan Books and Publishers, 1974.

Oulton, John Ernest Leonard, and Chadwick, Henry, eds. *Alexandrian Christianity: Selected Translations of Clement and Origen.* London: SCM Press, 1954.

Packer, J. I. *'Fundamentalism' and the Word of God: Some Evangelical Principles.* Grand Rapids, MI: Wm. B. Eerdmans Publishing Co., 1958.

Palmer, G. E. H.; Sherrard, Philip; and Ware, Kallistos, eds. *The Philokalia.* Vol. II. London: Farber and Faber, 1981.

Paul VI, Pope. *Credo of the People of God* (1968). http://w2.vatican.va/content/paul-vi/en/motu_proprio/documents/hf_p-vi_motu-proprio_19680630_credo.html.

__________. "Dogmatic Constitution on Divine Revelation *Dei Verbum*" (1965). http://www.cin.org/v2revel.html.

Peacocke, Arthur. *Theology for a Scientific Age.* Enl. ed. Minneapolis, MN: Fortress Press, 1993.

Peters, Ted, ed. *Science and Theology: The New Consonance.* Boulder, CO: Westview Press, 1998.

Phipps, William E. *Was Jesus Married?: The Distortion of Sexuality in the Christian Tradition.* New York: Harper & Row, Publishers, 1970.

Pinnock, Clark H. *A Wideness in God's Mercy: The Finality of Jesus Christ in a World of Religions*. Grand Rapids, MI: Zondervan Publishing House, 1992.

Pius XII, Pope. *Humani Generis* (1950). http://www.papalencyclicals.net/pius12/p12human.htm.

Plantinga, Alvin. *Does God Have a Nature?* Milwaukee: Marquette University Press, 1980.

__________. *God, Freedom, and Evil*. Grand Rapids, MI: Wm. B. Eerdmans Publishing Co., 1977.

__________. "Supralapsarianism, or '*O Felix Culpa*'." In *Christian Faith and the Problem of Evil*, pp. 1-25. Edited by Peter van Inwagen. Grand Rapids, MI: Wm. B. Eerdmans Publishing Co., 2004.

Polkinghorne, John. *Faith of a Physicist*. Princeton: Princeton University Press, 1994.

Poole, W. Scott. *Satan in America: The Devil We Know*. New York: Rowman & Littlefield Publishers, 2009.

Quasten, Johannes. *Patrology*. Vol. II: *The Ante-Nicene Literature after Irenaeus*. Westminster, MD: Christian Classics, Inc., 1986.

Quebedeaux, Richard, and Sawatsky, Rodney, eds. *Evangelical-Unification Dialogue*. New York: Rose of Sharon Press, 1979.

Rahner, Karl. "Evolution and Original Sin." In *The Evolving World and Theology*, pp. 61-73. Edited by Johannes Metz. New York: Paulist Press, 1967.

__________. *Foundations of Christian Faith: An Introduction to the Idea of Christianity*. Translated by William V. Dyck. New York: Seabury Press, 1978.

__________. *Hominisation: The Evolutionary Origin of Man as a Theological Problem*. Translated by W. J. O'Hara. Freiburg: Herder, 1958; London: Burns & Oates, 1965.

__________. *Karl Rahner in Dialogue: Conversations and Interviews 1965–1982*. Edited by Paul Imhof and Hubert Biallowons and translated by Harvey D. Egan. New York: Crossroad Publishing Co., 1986.

__________. *Theological Investigations*. Vol. I. Translated by Cornelius Ernst. Baltimore, MD: Helicon Press, 1965.

__________. *Theological Investigations*. Vol. IV. Translated by Kevin Smith. New York: Crossroad, 1982.

__________. *The Trinity*. Translated by Joseph Donceel. New York: Seabury Press, 1974.

__________, and Vorgrimler, Herbert. *Theological Dictionary*. Edited by Cornelius Ernst and translated by Richard Strachan. New York: Herder and Herder, 1965.

Ramm, Bernard. *After Fundamentalism: The Future of Evangelical Theology*. New York: Harper & Row, Publishers, 1983.

Rashdall, Hastings. *The Idea of Atonement in Christian Theology*. Charleston, SC; BiblioBazaar, 2009.

Reese, William L. *Philosophers Speak of God*. Chicago: The University of Chicago Press, 1953.

Reeves, Michael, and Madueme, Hans. "Threads in a Seamless Garment: Original Sin in Systematic Theology." In *Adam, the Fall, and Original Sin*, pp. 209-24. Edited by Hans Madueme and Michael Reeves. Grand Rapids, MI: Baker Academic, 2014.

Richardson, Alan, and Bowden, John. eds. *The Westminster Dictionary of Christian Theology*. Philadelphia: Westminster Press, 1983.

Richardson, Herbert W. "A Lecture to Students at the Unification Theological Seminary in Barrytown, New York." In *A Time for Consideration: A Scholarly Appraisal of the Unification Church*, pp. 290-317. Edited by M. Darrol Bryant and Herbert W. Richardson. New York: Edwin Mellen Press, 1978.

__________, ed. *Ten Theologians Respond to the Unification Church*. New York: Rose of Sharon Press, 1981.

Ricoeur, Paul. *The Conflict of Interpretations: Essays in Hermeneutics*. Edited by Don Ihde. Evanston, IL: Northwestern University Press, 1974.

Ritschl, Albrecht. *Three Essays*. Translated by Philip Hefner. Philadelphia: Fortress Press, 1972.

Rogers, Jack B., and McKim, Donald K. *The Authority and Interpretation of the Bible: An Historical Approach*. New York: Harper & Row, Publishers, 1979.

Runia, Klaas. *The Present-day Christological Debate*. Leicester, England: Inter-Varsity Press, 1984.

Russell, Bertrand. *Why I Am Not a Christian and Other Essays on Religion and Related Subjects*. Edited by Paul Edwards. New York: Simon & Schuster, 1957.

Russell, Letty M. *Human Liberation in a Feminist Perspective: A Theology*. Philadelphia: Westminster Press, 1974.

Scaer, David. P. "Death and Resurrection as Apocalyptic Event." *Concordia Theological Quarterly* 64:4 (October 2000): 279-94.

Schaff, Philip. *The Principle of Protestantism as Related to the Present State of the Church*. Translated by John W. Nevin. Chambersburg, PA: Publication Office of the German Reformed Church, 1845.

Schleiermacher, Friedrich. *The Christian Faith*. English trans. of 2nd German ed. Edited by H. R. Mackintosh and J. S. Stewart. Philadelphia: Fortress Press, 1976.

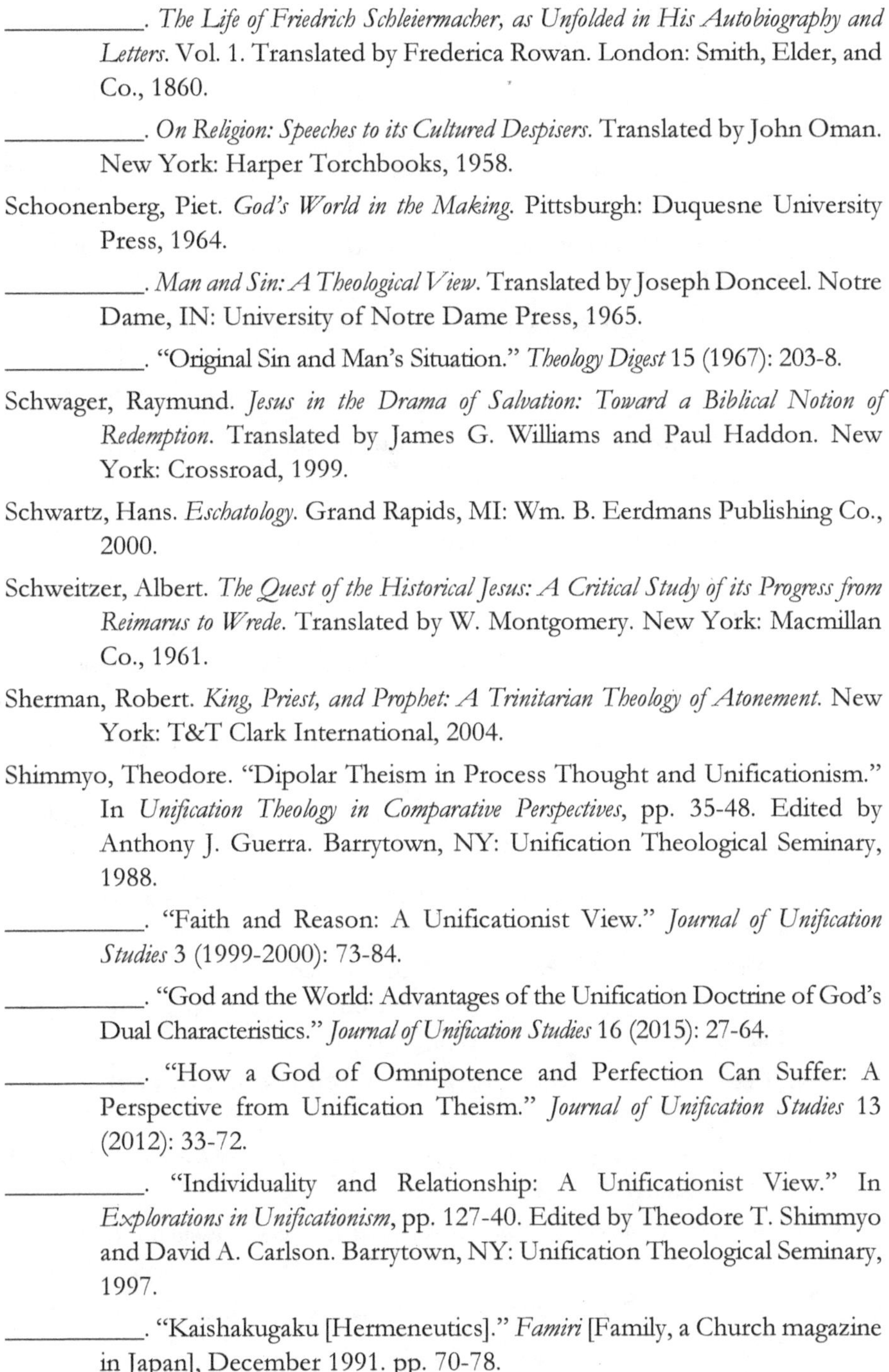

__________. *The Life of Friedrich Schleiermacher, as Unfolded in His Autobiography and Letters*. Vol. 1. Translated by Frederica Rowan. London: Smith, Elder, and Co., 1860.

__________. *On Religion: Speeches to its Cultured Despisers*. Translated by John Oman. New York: Harper Torchbooks, 1958.

Schoonenberg, Piet. *God's World in the Making*. Pittsburgh: Duquesne University Press, 1964.

__________. *Man and Sin: A Theological View*. Translated by Joseph Donceel. Notre Dame, IN: University of Notre Dame Press, 1965.

__________. "Original Sin and Man's Situation." *Theology Digest* 15 (1967): 203-8.

Schwager, Raymund. *Jesus in the Drama of Salvation: Toward a Biblical Notion of Redemption*. Translated by James G. Williams and Paul Haddon. New York: Crossroad, 1999.

Schwartz, Hans. *Eschatology*. Grand Rapids, MI: Wm. B. Eerdmans Publishing Co., 2000.

Schweitzer, Albert. *The Quest of the Historical Jesus: A Critical Study of its Progress from Reimarus to Wrede*. Translated by W. Montgomery. New York: Macmillan Co., 1961.

Sherman, Robert. *King, Priest, and Prophet: A Trinitarian Theology of Atonement*. New York: T&T Clark International, 2004.

Shimmyo, Theodore. "Dipolar Theism in Process Thought and Unificationism." In *Unification Theology in Comparative Perspectives*, pp. 35-48. Edited by Anthony J. Guerra. Barrytown, NY: Unification Theological Seminary, 1988.

__________. "Faith and Reason: A Unificationist View." *Journal of Unification Studies* 3 (1999-2000): 73-84.

__________. "God and the World: Advantages of the Unification Doctrine of God's Dual Characteristics." *Journal of Unification Studies* 16 (2015): 27-64.

__________. "How a God of Omnipotence and Perfection Can Suffer: A Perspective from Unification Theism." *Journal of Unification Studies* 13 (2012): 33-72.

__________. "Individuality and Relationship: A Unificationist View." In *Explorations in Unificationism*, pp. 127-40. Edited by Theodore T. Shimmyo and David A. Carlson. Barrytown, NY: Unification Theological Seminary, 1997.

__________. "Kaishakugaku [Hermeneutics]." *Famiri* [Family, a Church magazine in Japan], December 1991. pp. 70-78.

__________. "The Problem of Evil: Unification Theodicy." *Journal of Unification Studies*17 (2016)" 33-70.

__________. "Providential History of Modern Thought: A Unification Perspective." *Journal of Unification Studies*18 (2017): 1-54.

__________. "A Rejoinder to Dr. Bebis," *Journal of Unification Studies* 24 (2023):111-15.

__________. "Sun Myung Moon's Approach to the Bible." *Journal of Unification Studies* 14 (2013): 1-22.

__________. "Two Aspects of Love in God's Heart in Unification Theism: Biblical Evidence." *Journal of Unification Studies* 15 (2014): 101-13.

__________. "Unification Christology." *Journal of Unification Studies* 21 (2020): 51-75.

__________. "Unification Christology: A Fulfillment of Niceno-Chalcedonian Orthodoxy." In *Explorations in Unificationism*, pp. 17-36. Edited by Theodore T. Shimmyo and David A. Carlson. Barrytown, NY: Unification Theological Seminary, 1997.

__________. "The Unification Doctrine of the Atonement." *Journal of Unification Studies* 11 (2011): 11-40.

__________. "The Unification Doctrine of the Fall." *Journal of Unification Studies* 20 (2019): 57-112.

__________. "The Unification Doctrine of the Trinity." *Journal of Unification Studies* 2 (1998): 1-17.

__________. "Unification Eschatology as Compared with Christian Eschatology." *Journal of Unification Studies* 22 (2021): 87-115.

__________, and Carlson, David A., eds. *Explorations in Unificationism.* New York: HSA-UWC, 1997.

Shiner, Whitney T. "A Unificationist View of Scripture." In *Explorations in Unificationism*, pp. 3-16. Edited by Theodore T. Shimmyo and David A. Carlson. New York: HSA-UWC, 1997.

Simpson, Christopher Ben. *Modern Christian Theology*. London: Bloomsbury T&T Clark, 2016.

Snaith, Norman H. "Loving-Kindness." In *A Theological Word Book of the Bible*, pp. 136-37. Edited by Alan Richardson. New York: Macmillan Co., 1951.

Soelle, Dorothee. *Suffering*. Translated by Everett R. Kalin. Philadelphia: Fortress Press, 1975.

Soggin, J. Alberto. *Old Testament and Oriental Studies*. Rome: Biblical Institute Press, 1975.

Spong, John Shelby. *Resurrection: Myth or Reality?: A Bishop's Search for the Origins of Christianity*. San Francisco: Harper San Francisco, 1994.

Stevens, George Barker. *The Christian Doctrine of Salvation*. Edinburgh: T&T Clark, 1905.

Stone, Ronald H. "An Interview with Reinhold Niebuhr." *Christianity and Crisis*, March 17, 1969, pp. 48-52.

Suchocki, Marjorie. *God, Christ, Church: A Practical Guide to Process Theology*. New York: Crossroad, 1982.

__________. "Original Sin Revisited." http://www.religion-online.org/showarticle.asp?title=2817.

Surin, Kenneth. *Theology and the Problem of Evil*. New York: Basil Blackwell, 1986.

Szabados, Ádám. "Hellenistic Tendencies in John's Agape?: Andrew Nygren's Shipwreck on the Rocks of 1 John." http://szabadosadam.hu/divinity/wp-content/uploads/2010/09/HELLENISTIC-TENDENCIES-IN-JOHNS-AGAPE.pdf.

Teilhard de Chardin, Pierre. *Christianity and Evolution: Reflections on Science and Religion*. Translated by René Hague. New York: A Harvest Book, 1969.

Tennant, F. R. *The Origin and Propagation of Sin*. 2nd ed. Cambridge: Cambridge University Press, 1906.

__________. *The Sources of the Doctrines of the Fall and Original Sin*. New York: Schocken Books, 1968.

Tertullian. *Latic Christianity: Its Founder, Tertullian*. In *The Ante-Nicene Fathers: The Writings of the Fathers Down to A.D. 325*. American ed. Vol. III. Edited by Alexander Roberts, James Donaldson, and A. Cleveland Coxe. Grand Rapids, MI: Wm. B. Eerdmans Publishing Co., 1973.

Thiselton, Anthony T. *The Two Horizons: New Testament Hermeneutics and Philosophical Description*. Grand Rapids, MI: William B. Eerdmans Publishing Co., 1980.

Thompson, Henry O., ed. *Unity In Diversity: Essays in Religion by Members of the Faculty of the Unification Theological Seminary*. New York: Rose of Sharon Press, 1984.

Tidball, Derek; Hilborn, David; and Thacker, Justin, eds. *The Atonement Debate: Papers from the London Symposium on the Theology of Atonement*. Grand Rapids, MI: Zondervan, 2008.

Tillich, Paul. *Christianity and the Encounter of the World Religions*. New York: Columbia University Press, 1963.

__________. *Dynamics of Faith*. New York: Harper & Row, Publishers, 1957.

__________. *A History of Christian Thought: From Its Judaic and Hellenistic Origins to Existentialism*. New York: Simon and Schuster, 1968.

__________. *On the Boundary: An Autobiographical Sketch*. New York: Charles Scribner's Sons, 1966.

__________. *Political Expectation.* Edited by James Luther Adams. New York: Harper & Row, Publishers, 1971.

__________. *The Socialist Decision.* Translated by Franklin Sherman. New York: Harper & Row, Publishers, 1977.

__________. *Systematic Theology: Three Volumes in One.* Chicago: The University of Chicago Press, 1967.

Tixeront, J. *History of Dogmas.* Vol. I: *The Antenicene Theology.* Translated by H. L. B. St. Louis, MO: B. Herder, 1910.

Tracy, David. "Theological Method." In *Christian Theology: An Introduction to Its Traditions and Tasks*, pp. 35-60. Rev. and enl. ed. Edited by Peter C. Hodgson and Robert H. King. Philadelphia: Fortress Press, 1985.

Tradition. Book 1. New York: Rose of Sharon Press, 1985.

Troeltsch, Ernst. *Der Historismus und seine Probleme.* Tübingen: J. C. B. Mohr, 1922.

Trueman, Carl R. "Original Sin and Modern Theology." In *Adam, the Fall, and Original Sin*, pp. 167-86. Edited by Hans Madueme and Michael Reeves. Grand Rapids, MI: Baker Academic, 2014.

Tsirpanlis, Constantine N., ed. *Orthodox-Unification Dialogue.* New York: Rose of Sharon Press, 1981.

Venema, Dennis, and Falk, Darrel. "Does Genetics Point to a Single Primal Couple?" https://biologos.org/articles/does-genetics-point-to-a-single-primal-couple.

Von Balthasar, Hans Urs. *The Theology of Karl Barth: Exposition and Interpretation.* Translated by Edward T. Oakes. San Francisco: Ignatius Press, 1992.

Von Harnack, Adolf. *History of Dogma.* Vol. I. Translated by Neil Buchanan. New York: Dover, 1961.

__________. *What Is Christianity?* Translated by Thomas Bailey Saunders. New York: Harper & Row, Publishers, 1957.

Von Rad, Gerhard. *Genesis: A Commentary.* Rev. ed. Translated by John H. Marks. Philadelphia: Westminster Press, 1972.

Walker, Williston. *A History of the Christian Church.* New York: Charles Scribner's Sons, 1970.

Weaver, J. Denny. *The Nonviolent Atonement.* Grand Rapids, MI: Wm. B. Eerdmans Publishing Co., 2001.

Weinandy, Thomas G. *Does God Suffer?* Notre Dame, IN: University of Notre Dame Press, 2000.

__________. *Jesus the Christ.* Huntington, IN: Our Sunday Visitor, 2003.

Weiss, Johannes. *Jesus' Proclamation of the Kingdom of God*. Translated and edited by Richard Hyde Hiers and David Larrimore Holland. Philadelphia: Fortress Press, 1971.

Wells, Jonathan. "Evolution and Unification Thought." *Journal of Unification Studies* 12 (2011): 115-42.

__________. "God's Creation of Adam and Eve." December 11, 2013. https://www.tparents.org/Library/Unification/Talks/Wells/Wells-131211.pdf.

Wesley, John. *A Compend of Wesley's Theology*. Edited by Robert W. Burtner and Robert E. Chiles. Nashville: Abingdon Press, 1954.

"The Westminster Confession of Faith A.D. 1647." http://www.ccel.org/ccel/schaff/creeds3.iv.xvii.ii.html.

Whitehead, Alfred North. *Adventures of Ideas*. New York: Macmillan Co., 1933.

__________. *Process and Reality: An Essay in Cosmology*. New York: Macmillan Co., 1929. Corrected ed. Edited by David Ray Griffin and Donald W. Sherburne. New York: Free Press, 1978.

Wiley, Tatha. *Original Sin: Origins, Developments, Contemporary Meanings*. New York: Paulist Press, 2002.

Williams, Daniel Day. *God's Grace and Man's Hope*. New York: Harper & Brothers Publishers, 1949.

__________. *The Spirit and the Forms of Love*. New York: Harper & Row, Publishers, 1968.

Williams, Delores S. *Sisters in the Wilderness: The Challenge of Womanist God-Talk*. Maryknoll, NY: Orbis Books, 1993.

Wilson, Andrew. "Heavenly Mother." *Journal of Unification Studies* X (2009): 73-104.

__________. "The Sexual Interpretation of the Human Fall." In *Unification Theology in Comparative Perspectives*, pp. 51-70. Edited by Anthony J. Guerra. Barrytown, NY: Unification Theological Seminary, 1988.

__________, ed. *World Scripture and the Teachings of Sun Myung Moon*. Tarrytown, NY: Universal Peace Federation, 2007.

Wingren, Gustaf. *Theology in Conflict: Nygren, Barth, Bultmann*. Translated by Eric. H. Wahlstrom. Philadelphia: Muhlenberg Press, 1958.

Woodbridge, John D. *Biblical Authority: A Critique of the Rogers/McKim Proposal*. Grand Rapids, MI: Zondervan Publishing Co., 1982.

Zimmerman, Paul A., ed. *A Seminary in Crisis: The Inside Story of the Preus Fact Finding Committee*. St. Louis, MO: Concordia Publishing House, 2007.

Index of Names

A

B

C

D

E

F

G

H

I

J

K

L

M

N

O

P

Q

R

S

T

V

W

Z

Index of Subjects

D

E

F

G

H

S

T

U

V

W

Z

www.ingramcontent.com/pod-product-compliance
Lightning Source LLC
LaVergne TN
LVHW041054080826
845145LV00007B/1567

* 9 7 8 1 9 6 8 6 9 2 0 0 1 *